BATTLE
for the BEETLE

The untold story of the post-war battle for Adolf Hitler's giant Volkswagen factory and the Porsche-designed car that became an icon for generations around the globe.

Karl Ludvigsen
Foreword by Ivan Hirst

**BENTLEY
PUBLISHERS**

BATTLE for the BEETLE

Ferdinand Porsche opened an auto design office in 1930 in Stuttgart. Page 3

In 1940 the KdF works received contracts to manufacture bombs. Page 44

The elegant structural design of the factory featured high and well-lit production halls. Page 86

The factory was heavily damaged by wartime airstrikes. Page 99

The first car the VW factory produced after the war featured a Beetle body on a Kübel chassis. Page 110

Henry and Edsel Ford each responded to the challenge of the VW. Page 254

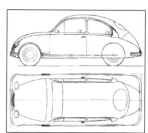

Roy Fedden's admiration for the VW car and factory was reflected in the designs for his own cars. Page 311

VW introduced its Export model in mid-1949. Page 361

BENTLEY PUBLISHERS | AUTOMOTIVE BOOKS & MANUALS

Information that makes
the difference.®

www.bentleypublishers.com

1734 Massachusetts Avenue
Cambridge, MA 02138 USA
800-423-4595 / 617-547-4170

Copies of this book may be purchased from selected booksellers, or directly from the publisher by mail. The publisher encourages comments from the reader of this book. Please write to Bentley Publishers at the address listed at the top of this page.

Library of Congress Cataloging-in-Publication Data

Ludvigsen, Karl, 1934–
    Battle for the Beetle: The untold story of the post-war battle for Adolf Hitler's giant Volkswagen factory and the Porsche-designed car that became an icon for generations around the globe / Karl Ludvigsen.
        p.cm
    Includes bibliographical references and index.
    ISBN 0-8376-0071-5 (alk. paper)
    1. Volkswagen Beetle automobile — History. 2. Automobile industry and trade — History. 3. Automobile industry and trade — Germany — Foreign ownership. 4. World War, 1939–1945 — Influence. I. Title.

    TL215.V6 L86 2000
    629.222'2—dc21

                                                            99-058859

ISBN 0-8376-0071-5
Bentley Stock No. GVBB

03 02 01 00 10 9 8 7 6 5 4 3 2 1

The paper used in this publication is acid free and meets the requirements of the National Standard for Information Sciences-Permanence of Paper for Printed Library Materials. ∞

Battle for the Beetle: The untold story of the post-war battle for Adolf Hitler's giant Volkswagen factory and the Porsche-designed car that became an icon for generations around the globe, by Karl Ludvigsen.
©2000 Karl Ludvigsen

Manufactured in the United States of America

Cover Photo courtesy of Karl Ludvigsen

To my mother,
Virginia Smith Ludvigsen,
who unerringly appreciated
and sought the best for her life,
her family, and her world

Foreword

This book examines what might have happened, as well as what did happen, to the Volkswagen factory and car after World War II and gives a detailed account of the Nazi party's Strength through Joy car project from its inception.

Battle for the Beetle covers the planning of the huge factory built on a greenfield site, its inevitable involvement in war work, and its partial destruction by Allied bombing, through to the start-up of Beetle production under the British military government and the emergence of the present-day Volkswagen AG.

I spent four years at the VW factory while it was the responsibility of the Military Government, first as hands-on manager and then in the back seat until the new German management had proved itself. I had already visited German factories as a young student, and after ten years on the industry side of the Military Government I moved to the Organization for Economic Cooperation and Development in Paris. Accordingly, I feel in some measure qualified to commend Karl Ludvigsen's book.

The author is an acknowledged authority on the automotive industry. As well, he has skillfully rendered a highly factual account based on extensive and thorough research into a very readable book.

Much of the material presented here has not previously been published. Ludvigsen's work will no doubt be of interest to political, economic, and social historians as well as people connected with the industry. The car enthusiast and the Beetle fraternity, too, will find it fascinating reading.

Battle for the Beetle is an outstanding, wide-ranging, and accurate account. Karl's research has filled in many gaps in my own knowledge, and he has certainly caught the spirit of those days.

— Ivan Hirst

Introduction

The time for decision had come. The Allies had vanquished the Nazi war machine that had menaced and destroyed much of Europe and Russia. In the last months of the war the advanced secret technologies of which Joseph Goebbels boasted had wrought their terrors when the V-1s and V-2s crashed down on London, Brussels, and Antwerp. German science and engineering, always respected, had been resourceful in extremis. All Germany's sea, land, and air technologies now lay open for exploitation for peace and war by the victorious Allies.

Among those technologies was Adolf Hitler's famous people's car, the Volkswagen. In civilian form it promised motoring for the masses on an unprecedented scale. Its boxy, crude-looking military version carried Germans to war on all their fronts. Publicized and promoted with all the power and skill of the Nazi regime, the VW was the showpiece of its achievements.

It began benignly enough. The Volkswagen had been conceived by the Nazis as a simple, cheap car for the masses that would be in the vanguard of Germany's drive to put its people on wheels. Made cooperatively by German car producers, which would share parts production and assembly, the cars were to be made to a single design originated by the engineering bureau newly established in Stuttgart by Professor Ferdinand Porsche, an Austrian who was one of Germany's most renowned motor designers. The anticipated mass production would compensate the German automakers for their losses of sales and production in the Great Depression.

Instead the VW metamorphosed with relentless energy and stunning speed into an independent project promoted and ultimately financed by the institutions of the Reich. Overnight it became a menace, not an ally, to Germany's automakers. So compelling and all-pervasive did the Volkswagen project become that it grew, for better and for worse, to symbolize not only the perverse dynamism of the Third Reich but also the flawed *Weltanschauung* of its fatally misguided leader, Adolf Hitler.

What was to be the postwar fate of this peculiar and still-unproven car and the mile-long factory built to produce it? The Allies and their automotive experts had to judge at first hand the properties and the potential of the Volkswagen.

Before the outbreak of war both car and factory had struck fear into the hearts of the German auto industry and all who owned and managed her. Its low price and high production volume threatened to dwarf their feeble efforts. European automakers were shocked by the VW's potential to swamp them in markets both at home and abroad.

Was it time to put this menace peacefully to rest? To dismantle and disperse its machinery to the winds? Or should it be exploited to the full by the victors? If so, which among them should benefit from the largest auto plant yet built outside America? The battle for the Beetle promised to be memorable.

1

Birth of a Menace

Passing the time of night of 24 January 1942 with some of his confidants Adolf Hitler remarked, "In former times I used to read regularly the publications devoted to the motorcar, but I no longer have the time." He assured them that he nevertheless continued to keep up with new developments in the automotive field.

Hitler was forty-four years old in the spring of 1933 when he put in motion the rumbling wheels of the benighted regime that would bring disaster to Germany — and bring the Volkswagen to life. Born virtually with the automobile, Hitler was infatuated with it, and with other forms of technology that he associated with his youth, throughout his life.

One easily pictures the leader of the National Socialists leafing through the *Allgemeine Automobil-Zeitung, Motor und Sport*, and even *Motor Kritik*, whose enthusiastic and knowledgeable engineer-editor Josef Ganz argued at length toward the end of the 1920s in favor of a small, affordable, and economic *Volksauto* — a car for the people. For the Hungarian-born Ganz the cars that came closest to his ideal were the air-cooled Czech Tatras with their backbone frames and independent rear suspension.

Hitler too was a fan of the Tatras and their designer Hans Ledwinka. He would meet Ledwinka, a fellow Austrian, early in the 1930s and be personally and privately briefed by him about the latest Tatra models at the Berlin Auto Shows. But in the early 1920s it was all Hitler could do to become mobile. When he couldn't be located, his aides quickly realized, he "would be discovered somewhere looking at second-hand motor-cars."

"Cars were an obsession with him," said his foreign press attaché Ernst "Putzi" Hanfstaengl. Hitler wanted to give his embryonic storm troopers the capacity to dodge and outwit the police who were trying to break up their brown-shirted demonstrations.

Although Adolf Hitler often rode in Mercedes-Benz cars, as here at the opening of a new section of Autobahn, he was enthusiastic about cars in general and particularly liked the advanced autos made by Tatra.

But first he needed a car for himself to get round to meetings more quickly. He picked up one vehicle which looked like a dismantled horse-cab without a top, but soon exchanged this for a Selve car, with funds he had drummed up in a mysterious way from someone. It was a rattling monster and each end looked as if it was going different ways, but he seemed to think it conferred additional dignity on him and from that time on I do not think I ever saw him take a tram or bus again.

By the time Hitler made his first abortive grab for power, the "beer hall putsch" of November 1923, he was riding in a bright-red Benz. *Riding* is the operative word. In the more than million and a half miles Hitler was said to have covered on the road as politician and dictator he was driven by his chauffeur Emil Maurice, who was succeeded by Julius Schreck and then Erich Kempka. In April 1945, Kempka would bring to the Chancellery garden the forty gallons of gasoline that hastened the incineration of the corpses of Hitler and his wife.

ADOLF HITLER WAS PERSUADED that enhanced motorization should be a major goal of the administration that began with his appointment as Germany's chancellor on Monday, 30 January 1933. Only a few days later in his speech at the opening of the Berlin Auto Show on Saturday, 11 February, "he set out the guidelines of a mass mobilization of Germany: tax abatements for car buyers, the building of the Autobahns, repeal of obligatory driving school, and encouragement of motorsport."

With considerable experience after working on many types of vehicles for Lohner, Austro-Daimler, Daimler, and Daimler-Benz, Ferdinand Porsche was well qualified to open an independent auto design office at the end of 1930 in Stuttgart.

The idea of a people's car was hotly discussed in the press at the time of the 1933 Berlin Show and Hitler was not one to overlook the potential of a people-pleasing idea. Discussions on the way such a car might be built began at once between the Reich Ministry of Transport, headed by its minister-director Dr. Ing. e. h. Brandenburg, and the association of German automakers, the *Reichsverband der deutschen Automobilindustrie* (RDA), and its president Robert Allmers.

The RDA's initial notions were either to stage a prize competition for the design of a new small car or to engage an "outstanding designer" to evaluate their existing models to see whether production costs could be reduced. No particular designer was mentioned, but one name came to everyone's mind.

Only one independent automotive engineer of real standing had his own design studio in Germany in 1933. Ferdinand Porsche, born in Bohemia, had joined Daimler Motor Company in 1923 as its engineering director. The company merged with Benz & Cie in 1926 and three years later Porsche, at age fifty-three, left Daimler-Benz, Germany's flagship producer, following disagreements with the new management over confused planning and decision-making.

A prototype of Porsche's Type 12, a small car designed for Zündapp in 1931 pow-ered by a radial five-cylinder engine in the rear, is pictured in front of the Porsche villa in Stuttgart-Feuerbach.

Although their differences were publicly smoothed over in the emollient German style, Porsche's exit from the Stuttgart-Untertürkheim design offices of Daimler-Benz was anything but amiable. Daimler-Benz had decided not to renew his contract after problems cropped up with some of the small cars and commercial vehicles that had come from his team's drafting boards. Porsche had celebrated his arrival in Stuttgart by building a handsome villa in the city's Feuerbach hills with a generous four-car garage and adjoining workshop/storeroom. Now, with his son-in-law Anton Piëch, he sued Daimler-Benz over his contract; the case was settled out of court in 1930.

Porsche did not contract again to design vehicles for a single producer. The new Auto Union AG, maker of DKW, Audi, Wanderer, and Horch cars, would have been delighted to have him; it became his first and one of his best customers. Porsche explained to his son Ferry, "It makes no sense for me to keep going from one company after another." The always practical Ferry put it differently. "My father found that when he signed a contract with a firm, they could live another ten years on his designs, but he couldn't!"

FROM THE MOMENT FERDINAND PORSCHE and his team of eleven men and women opened their doors at the end of 1930 they were immersed in small-car design projects. In 1931 and '32 three prototypes — Porsche always built them in threes — of a rear-engined small car were designed and built under contract to Zündapp of Nürnberg, a motorcycle firm which insisted on the use of a 1,200 cc five-cylinder radial engine. Numbered Type 12 in the Porsche project list, it never went into production.

Porsche's small-car prototype for NSU, the Type 32 designed in 1933, foreshadowed the main features of the Volkswagen with its torsion-bar springs and air-cooled flat-four engine. Its body shape would become familiar as well.

Neither did Porsche's next small car, the Type 32 designed for the NSU Works in Neckarsulm, another motorcycle maker with big ideas. But its three prototypes, also rear-engined, showed design features that were destined to become familiar. Porsche's new torsion-bar springs were used, with parallel trailing arms in front and swing axles in the rear. The engine was an air-cooled flat-four of 1,470 cc developing its twenty-six horsepower at the unusually low engine speed of 2,600 rpm.

Under construction in 1933 for NSU, the Type 32 prototypes were completed and tested in 1934. But when Fiat reminded the German firm that the two companies had mutual accords in the four-wheeled field, NSU had to abandon the project. For the second time in as many years, Porsche had trimmed his development contracts to the bone to solicit much-needed business, only to come up empty. No royalties would be generated by cars that didn't enter production. These were trying times for Germany's newest auto engineering company, which now had twenty-three people on staff.

To tap another possible source of revenue Porsche and his business partner Adolf Rosenberg began thinking about the design of a racing car. In October 1932 the authorities announced the new limits for cars eligible to take part in Grand Prix racing in 1934–36, setting a maximum car weight of 1,654 pounds (750 kilograms). Rosenberg, who had raced Benz two-liter cars of the 1920s with the engine behind the driver, encouraged the design of a similarly configured racer. Drawings were made and planning undertaken for Type 22 in the Porsche project list, a revolutionary supercharged sixteen-cylinder 4.4-liter racing car.

The firm approached wealthy drivers and other potential sponsors but it was soon obvious that developing the Type 22 would consume more money than they could provide. It was widely rumored at the end of 1932 that Mercedes-Benz would build a car to suit this new formula for Grand Prix racing, the world's premier category for car competition. Before gaining power Hitler had disclosed his intent to back racing-car construction in private meetings with Jakob Werlin, the Daimler-Benz representative in Munich, and well-connected Mercedes driver Manfred von Brauchitsch. He also spoke separately with the famous and popular racer Hans Stuck. He told them, in essence, "You'll get the money as soon as I'm in charge."

This was reason enough for the cash-strapped Porsche engineers to agree to draft and send to Hitler a telegram signed by Porsche complimenting the new chancellor on his encouragement of motorsports in his Berlin Show speech: "As the creator of many renowned designs in the realm of the German and Austrian motor and aviation field and as a co-combatant toward the present success for more than thirty years, I congratulate Your Excellency on the profound opening speech for the 'German Automobile Exhibition.'"

IN 1931 FOUR DEPRESSION-HIT car companies — Wanderer, Horch, DKW, and Audi — had sought protection by pooling their assets in a single organization, the Auto Union AG. One of its guiding lights was Baron Klaus Detlof von Oertzen, in charge of external relations at Wanderer. A keen motor sportsman and a fan of advanced design who had already initiated new projects with Porsche and Rosenberg at Wanderer, von Oertzen became a deputy management board member of the new Auto Union.

Here was an opportunity for Porsche's racing car. A new automotive combine needed powerful publicity. Its major market rival, especially for the Horch and Wanderer brands, would be Mercedes-Benz, and Mercedes-Benz was going racing. Auto Union could do the same, Rosenberg and von Oertzen agreed, with Porsche's new Type 22. But the new company's top executives, Richard Bruhn and William Werner, viewed this as a frivolous diversion from the tough job of making and selling cars in a depression. To win them over, von Oertzen would have to get some of the money Hitler was preparing to hand out — to Mercedes.

Von Oertzen's motorsports credentials were impeccable. In 1933 he personally led the company's team of open Wanderer roadsters, a Porsche design, in the long open-road rallies throughout Germany organized by the Nazi's Ve-

Having raced and hill-climbed successfully for Austro-Daimler, Hans Stuck is shown with one of that company's touring cars. Stuck was a catalyst in the first substantive meeting between Ferdinand Porsche and Adolf Hitler on 1 March 1933.

hicle Drivers Corps. As well, he was a committed National Socialist. His patrician background was not a handicap. But von Oertzen — a youthful figure with an amiable countenance in a nation that respected maturity — was not a heavy hitter at Auto Union, not a full management board member.

The baron was shrewd enough to realize that he would need all the help he could get. "I remembered that when Hitler had been released from his imprisonment at Landsberg a Mercedes had picked him up. Never forgetting that, he remained loyal to Mercedes and never drove any other car." Von Oertzen prepared his arguments well — but no one would let him in to see Hitler, who was immensely busy with the tasks of the first weeks of his administration.

"Then I went to see his deputy, Rudolf Hess," von Oertzen related. "He and I were pilots of yore; we knew each other from the Great War. I asked Hess to get us an appointment with Hitler. Hess then arranged it for the beginning of March." The Baron laid his plans carefully. The appointment was set for Wednesday, 1 March 1933. At a meeting on the preceding Monday, Porsche and Auto Union reached agreement in principle on the outlines of the racing-car project.

Von Oertzen: "To this meeting [with Hitler] I took Dr. Porsche and the racing driver Hans Stuck, who unlike myself was personally acquainted with Hitler." Porsche and Stuck compared notes the previous evening in the latter's flat in Berlin-Charlottenburg. "Under his arm he had a thick portfolio of drawings," Stuck recalled of Porsche. "He didn't yet know Hitler and asked 'what sort of fellow' he would be."

At the old Chancellery in Berlin, shaped like a horseshoe with its open court facing the Wilhelmstrasse, the trio were given a sombre reception by the Führer. Only his secretary accompanied him. As if they needed reminding, lowering down at them was an oil portrait of Germany's new leader — at the wheel of a Mercedes-Benz.

Hitler gave no hint of acquiescence to von Oertzen's opening overtures. The Baron persisted, saying he owed it to Auto Union's ten thousand employees to press his case for support. Turning sharply away from the emissary, Hitler addressed Porsche, who opened his portfolio on the glossy surface of the massive conference table. To the engineer's complete surprise, Hitler reminded Porsche that they had met at the German Grand Prix on Berlin's AVUS track on 11 July 1926, when Porsche was attending to his team of straight-eight Mercedes racers (young Rudy Caracciola won) and Hitler was in his political wilderness years.

The chancellor asked Porsche what sort of car he would build. One can imagine the impact of the first view of the drawings and plans of the ultra-radical Type 22 racing car with its torsion-bar springing, central fuel tank, stubby nose, and elongated tail covering sixteen supercharged cylinders. It looked like the fuselage of an advanced fighter plane. For almost half an hour, interrupted only by knowledgeable questions from Hitler, Porsche swiftly and in his broad accent explained his car and his ideas.

Sufficiently briefed, Hitler ended the meeting without commitment but with a remark that admitted some hope: "You will hear from me." Three days later von Oertzen was informed that the Auto Union project would receive government support. The executive had no illusions about the reason why. "Hitler supported the construction of our racing cars. But he did that not for liking me, but rather for liking Porsche."

BY THE AUTUMN OF 1933 THE PORSCHE design office in central Stuttgart was enjoying solvency for the first time. Its business affairs were now being managed by Baron Hans von Veyder-Malberg, a wealthy enthusiast and one-time Austro-Daimler racer who acquired the shareholding of Adolf Rosenberger. Sensing that winds would blow ill for the Jews in the new Germany, Rosenberger decamped to France where he represented Porsche's patent rights and later to California, where he became well-known in auto circles as Alan Roberts. He never had the chance to experience the magnificent Auto Union racing cars he had helped inspire.

Projects at their main offices on the Kronenstrasse, and in other Stuttgart spaces begged and borrowed by the Porsche engineers, included the P-Wagen racer for Auto Union, urgently needed for the 1934 season, the Type 32 small car for NSU, and various torsion-bar suspension designs for new-

In 1921 the Austrian engineer Edmund Rumpler, working in Germany, introduced the world's first aerodynamic rear-engined production car. The Rumpler Tropfen-Auto inspired rear-engined production cars at Benz and later Mercedes-Benz.

found licensees. So when Daimler-Benz's Jakob Werlin called ahead in the autumn to say that he was in Stuttgart to visit his own headquarters and would like to pay a courtesy call, Ferdinand Porsche had to sweep quite a few drawings and papers off the desk in his small office.

Why was Werlin visiting? Porsche had a personal affection for the suave salesman; Werlin had defended his designs and ideas in some of the heated Daimler-Benz boardroom battles. But relations between that company and Porsche were now so frosty that any contact between Daimler-Benz employees — even between their wives — and Porsche's people was grounds for peremptory dismissal. And Porsche was building the racing car that would be competing with the new Mercedes-Benz in 1934. Was Werlin hoping to pick up a speed secret or two?

Guiding the conversation away from racing cars, except for some morsels that had already been reported in the newspapers, Porsche felt himself on safe ground in discussing his new torsion-bar patents and his small-car projects for Zündapp and NSU.

But this ground may have been less safe than Porsche thought. Although it is hard to imagine the Daimler-Benz directors losing sleep over the ambitions of pipsqueak NSU, the proud Stuttgart company was in fact about to launch a new rear-engined small car of its own.

Rumpler's advanced conception of an automobile combined a W-6 engine with a transaxle and swing-axle rear suspension. Its deep-sided chassis was as aerodynamic as the body atop it.

Rear-engined Mercedes-Benz cars traced their lineage to the work of a remarkable Austrian innovator, Edmund Rumpler. The first Rumpler automobile was called "the star of the Berlin Show" when that exhibition opened at the end of September 1921 after a ten-year hiatus. On Edmund Rumpler's stand was a chassis, an open model, and a closed version of the car he called the *Tropfen-Auto* or teardrop auto after its uncompromisingly streamlined shape. "Here for the first time in more than ten years," one report glowed, "are shown fundamental transformations in the design of the automobile." Another noted, "These cars attracted immense attention and generally favorable comment, despite their unusual appearance."

The forty-nine-year-old Rumpler had married his background as an automotive engineer with the Adler motor company in Germany and his experience as an aviation pioneer with the Taube of Austrian Igo Etrich, Germany's first volume planemaker, to build a precedent-defying auto. It combined a central passenger compartment with a low-drag teardrop form in plan view, an engine between the passengers and the rear axle, and independent rear suspension by swing axles.

An experienced inventor who licensed many of his ideas to other manufacturers, Berlin-based Rumpler had been applying for patents since 1915 on various features of his car. At the 1921 Berlin Show his innovative design caught the fancy of Benz engineers Hans Nibel and Max Wagner. Here, they decided, was a promising foundation for the future of the Benz cars made in Mannheim. On 21 January 1922 the management of Benz advised its board

While still at Daimler-Benz Ferdinand Porsche initiated several small-car projects, including a rear-engined prototype powered by this air-cooled flat-four of 1.2 liters.

of directors that the company was negotiating a general license allowing un-limited sales of cars based on Rumpler's designs.

Accompanied by a preliminary agreement and a chest of technical draw-ings, a long-chassis open-topped Tropfen-Auto tourer arrived in Mannheim for experimental work. Its original Rumpler six-cylinder engine was replaced by a Benz side-valve unit. With this test vehicle Max Wagner's chassis men roamed the roads around Mannheim, searching out the car's strengths and weaknesses. Engineer Willy Walb was assigned the task of testing the Tropfen-Auto and conducting its initial assessment and development.

Walb reported to engineers Wagner, Nibel, and Fritz Nallinger that the Rumpler was not ready for volume production. The chassis had important and fundamental problems, especially with the guidance of its swing axles. Thus Edmund Rumpler had to be satisfied with the income from his prelim-inary agreement with Benz, which decided not to seek a full license after all.

In the meantime Benz had begun preparing to market such a car. Its con-servative management board, facing the economic chaos that was postwar Germany, bowed to arguments that it would be good propaganda to anticipate a future rear-engined production model with a racing car of similar layout. Benz engineers commenced work on the design of a rear-engined car to suit the 1922 Grand Prix formula for cars with engine displacements of two liters.

The Benz racer was ready in 1923 — a marvellously slim, perfect ma-chine, an engineer's idea of what a racing car should look like. Its teardrop form was realized in three dimensions, as sleek as a dirigible. This and its Rumpler ancestry won for it the *Tropfen-Wagen* nickname, although it was officially known as the Benz RH series (for *Rennwagen Heckmotor* or rear-engined racing car). Its engine was in fact mid-mounted, driving through a three-speed gearbox to the rear axle.

Competing only once in an international event outside Germany, in the five-hundred-mile Grand Prix of Europe at Monza, Italy, on 9 September 1923, three six-cylinder Benz racers performed creditably. Willy Walb was forced out early with engine trouble. The remaining two Benzes were outdistanced by two Fiats (one scoring the first Grand Prix victory for a supercharged car) and the third-place American Miller racer in this long and demanding event.

Fernando Minoia's Benz was fourth, four laps back at 84.8 mph. Franz Hörner, in the third Benz, was fifth at 79.9 mph, nine laps in arrears. For its entry of the most outstanding new car in the race, Benz received a gold medallion from the Monza organizers. Accepted by Max Wagner, it was an apposite honor for a man and a company trying to cope with the galloping inflation of late-1923 Germany.

Germany's struggling economy contributed to the merger, finalized in 1926, between Benz of Mannheim and Daimler of Stuttgart, makers of Mercedes cars. Three men from Mannheim — Fritz Nallinger, Hans Nibel, and Max Wagner — rose to top engineering positions at Daimler-Benz. These men rather than Daimler engineers would fill the vacuum left in the wake Ferdinand Porsche's departure.

Among Porsche's last projects at Daimler-Benz had been studies for cars much smaller than those the proud company normally produced. One, dubbed the 5/25, was powered by an overhead-valve six of 1,392 cc; in 1927 a test series of thirty cars was built for company executives to evaluate. In 1928 Porsche's attention turned to a 1.2-liter four-cylinder prototype of conventional layout and a more radical concept as well: a rear-engined car with independent suspension and a semi-monocoque body powered by an air-cooled flat-opposed four-cylinder engine of 1,201 cc.

Post-Porsche, Daimler-Benz took an even stronger interest in creating a good new small car that could compete with Opel, recently acquired by General Motors. "The times in which we only sold big luxury cars finally seemed to be over," recalled engineer Josef Müller. "A new era of popular motorization was announcing itself. This was reason enough to think anew about the overall design of the car, especially its space utilization. The four passengers should be given the best-sprung area between the axles." This, they agreed, was best achieved with a rear-mounted engine.

Nallinger, Nibel, and Wagner rejected the air-cooled flat-opposed four. Noisy and shaky in prototype form, it convinced them "that the engine-gearbox unit must not be attached directly to a backbone type of frame," Müller said. "For reasons of noise, it should be flexibly mounted in a fork-shaped frame and be water-cooled if possible. Unfortunately, we gave in to the temptation to use the longer, although simpler, in-line four-cylinder engine instead of the shorter boxer engine."

The Type 130 Mercedes-Benz cradled its 1.3-liter engine and transaxle in a fork at the rear of its backbone frame. An excess of weight on its rear wheels, combined with the swing-axle suspension, made the 130 a wayward handler.

THUS DAIMLER-BENZ REJECTED Porsche's ideas in favor of their own experience with the Tropfen-Wagen to create the 130, a smaller Mercedes-Benz model for Germany's straitened car market. Its water-cooled side-valve engine extended out behind the rear wheels, complete with radiator, a positioning that Josef Ganz wrote in *Motor Kritik* was not a pure rear engine but rather an "outboard-motor." This, he said, brought "undesirable tail-heaviness," with the car's rear-wheel weight amounting to 62–65 percent of the total.

By the time the Daimler-Benz engineers realized that they had erred it was too late to make major changes to the 130's layout:

> The first test drives were not at all satisfactory. The congenital defect of the swing axle, in combination with the car being very tail-heavy, had a stronger effect than expected. Nevertheless, by carefully adjusting the softness of tires and springs between the front and rear axles, and by solving the noise problem with tedious adjustments of the four rubber mountings, it was possible to turn an initially rather obstinate vehicle into a reasonably useable one.

The similarity in size and characteristics between the Mercedes-Benz 130 and Porsche's contemporary NSU prototype is discernible from a comparison:

Characteristic	Mercedes-Benz Type 130	NSU-Porsche Type 32
Wheelbase	2,500 mm	2,600 mm
Track	1,270 mm	1,200 mm
Weight	970 kg	750 kg
Engine size	1,308 cc	1,470 cc
Power output	26 bhp @ 3,400 rpm	26 bhp @ 2,600 rpm
Tires	5.00 x 17	5.25/5.75 x 16

Responding to a perceived need to offer a smaller and lower-cost auto in the difficult Depression years, Daimler-Benz launched its 130 model at the end of 1933. It clothed radical engineering in conservative bodywork.

In spite of its longer wheelbase the air-cooled Porsche construction was lighter in its prototype form; a production version might well have been heavier. The Beetle-shaped Porsche design was far more aerodynamic than the Mercedes, which kept a narrow body, running boards, and freestanding headlights. The 130 was priced ambitiously by Mercedes-Benz at RM 3,375; NSU's entry would have had to be cheaper. Nevertheless the two cars would have been close marketplace competitors.

At the end of 1933 the first Type 130 Mercedes-Benz models were launched; this was an important new model for which Daimler-Benz had high hopes. As the company's representative in a major market, Jakob Werlin certainly would have seen the 130s in their final preparation for the market during his Stuttgart stopover prior to his first meeting with Porsche. Small cars were not so alien to his agenda as Porsche might have supposed.

CAREFULLY COMPARTMENTALIZING his two strong loyalties, one to Daimler-Benz and one to Hitler, Jakob Werlin had in mind a conversation with the latter when he called Porsche, about a week after their Stuttgart meeting, and insisted that he come to Berlin for an urgent meeting the following afternoon at the Hotel Kaiserhof. Pressed though he was with tasks on all sides, Porsche acquiesced. Chauffeured the three hundred miles to Berlin by his faithful Joseph Goldinger, he presented himself in Werlin's suite at 4:00 P.M.

When Werlin came to the point after opening pleasantries Porsche knew at once that the Daimler-Benz man was a confidant of Hitler, for he, Hans Stuck, and Baron von Oertzen had kept entirely secret their March meeting with the chancellor:

> You see, Dr. Porsche, since Herr Hitler met you in connection with the Auto Union racing-car project, he has gained an even higher opinion of your professional capacity as a designer. Let me come straight to the point. Hitler is very interested in the possibility of small cars, he will be here any minute now and perhaps you can enlighten him on the subject. You told me that you have been working on problems associated with small cars for some time.

Acting as Hitler's unofficial but influential automotive advisor, Jakob Werlin (left) played a key role in introducing Ferdinand Porsche to the Volkswagen project. Officially he was the Mercedes-Benz representative in Munich.

Before Porsche had time to react to this revelation, a door to the suite swung open and Hitler entered. After tea was served and amenities observed, the dictator took the floor. Adolf Hitler held forth at length and in detail about the kind of car he had in mind, something to suit the German family with three children, a proper car but not too fancy, economic to run and repair, a real *Volkswagen* — a car that would suit his people.

Hitler, the auto designer manqué, did not hesitate to detail his thoughts. This was to be no crude three-wheeler or cyclecar but a genuine car for the German workingman. It should be four-wheel-drive, Hitler suggested, with a three-cylinder air-cooled diesel engine, preferably front-mounted. Hitler had indeed been reading his car magazines; nor had he overlooked the vehicle's military potential.

This was familiar territory to Porsche but Hitler's answer to the designer's question about the desired selling price was not. "At any price, Herr Dr. Porsche — at any price below 1,000 Marks!" The engineer was staggered. The small cars he was working on for Zündapp and NSU would have cost much more than that just to produce and would have retailed for around 2,200 marks. Porsche never claimed to be a production expert; he had not worked with high-volume car projects. But this seemed a chimerical goal.

After a last glance at his wristwatch Hitler left the suite's sitting room. Jakob Werlin was prepared for the next step. He asked Porsche to consider the matter and to put on paper his thoughts about such a car. The rule of three would apply here as well: one copy to Hitler, one to Werlin, and one to Minister Brandenburg at Transport.

THESE OFF-THE-RECORD ENCOUNTERS must have taken place in late August or early September of 1933, for the first internal Porsche discussion of the Volkswagen problem was held in the last week of September. Porsche's colleagues Karl Rabe (chassis) and Josef Kales (engine) agreed that the best way to approach the problem was to use the NSU Type 32 project as a basis from which such a car could be developed.

Draft after draft resulted in a final "Exposé" dated 17 January 1934 that was crafted with care and elegance. Its core was four long paragraphs, followed by a technical appendix, with sketches, and a table comparing the draft specifications with a dozen other German small cars. It was complete but easy to digest, revelatory to the expert but not so esoteric as to daunt the uninitiated.

Among the small cars listed in the table were several that Porsche did not intend to emulate, as he made clear with a certain wry wit. "As a 'Volkswagen' I comprehend no small car that carries forward the tradition of the pantograph in this sector by the artificial reduction of its dimensions, its power, its weight and so forth." With this he dismissed the heavy and costly small cars made by Opel, Ford, and Adler. He could also have dismissed the Mercedes-Benz 130, but although recently launched it did not appear on his comparison table.

Neither did Porsche and his team intend to build a cyclecar, which is the only appropriate description for some of the more quixotic German market offerings of the time. Josef Ganz had done more than talk about advanced and efficient small cars; he had designed and built them too. As with Porsche, his patrons had been motorcycle makers with ambitious ideas. Zündapp considered Ganz's ideas and Ardie built a Ganz-designed prototype. Best of all, in 1932 Standard introduced its Superior small car to Ganz's designs.

Advertised as the "deutschen Volkswagen," the Standard had a Tatra-like backbone frame with transverse leaf springs for independent springing at front and rear. There was no "outboard motor" here; Ganz practiced what he preached by putting his transverse air-cooled half-liter twin forward of the rear-wheel centerline.

Offering two-plus-two seating at best, the Standard had a wheelbase of only 79 inches and a small price as well: RM 1,590 in 1932 rising to RM 1,720 in 1934. This kept it below the RM 1,800 of the cheapest "proper" car, an Opel. But its sales were modest: 195 in 1933, 185 in 1934, and only handfuls in subsequent years.

Strikingly similar in appearance to the Standard with its coal-bucket nose, freestanding headlights, and two forward-opening doors, another cyclecar was introduced just before Porsche completed his report. This was the Bremen-built Hansa 400 launched by Carl Borgward. Its springing was like the Standard's but its proprietary Ilo air-cooled two-stroke engine was placed longitudinally behind the rear axle. It sought to accommodate four with its 94-inch wheelbase, yet it underpriced the Standard at RM 1,700 thanks to its body of plywood protected by leatherette.

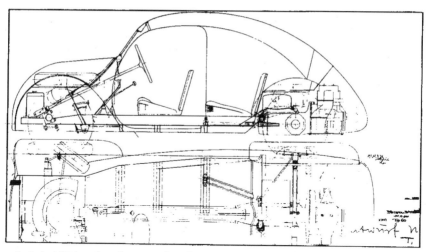

In July 1934, only a few months after Porsche submitted his January 1934 "Exposé" concerning the design criteria of a future Volkswagen, his staff was already generating sketches and layouts of just such a car — here with a two-stroke air-cooled engine.

Such crude small-car design strategies were tacitly rejected by Porsche in his "Exposé." A proper Volkswagen, he wrote, had to be a car of normal dimensions "but of relatively low weight, which is to be achieved through fundamentally new techniques." These methods were to include "equipment as foolproof as possible" to keep servicing simple and cheap. Porsche added that the car should not be designed for a narrow and limited market. "Rather through a simple change of its bodywork it should be adaptable to all reasonable circumstances, thus it should be suitable not only as a passenger car but also as a delivery vehicle and for certain designated military purposes." In making the latter statement Porsche showed the attention he had given to the briefing he had received from Hitler.

An accompanying sketch of the car's layout showed an NSU-like flat-four engine; in the specifications the alternative of a three-cylinder radial air-cooled two-stroke was presented. This clearly responded to Hitler's 1933 request although it did not specify whether the engine's ignition was by spark plug or high Diesel compression.

As to his car's selling price, Porsche was on the spot. He believed a thousand marks to be out of the question — yet this was what Hitler wanted. Clearly the car had to be priced lower than anything on the German market. After much cogitation Porsche opted for the figure of RM 1,550 in his "Exposé."

The implications of the pricing were subtly set out in the specification table that accompanied the report. It listed the cost per kilogram of the cars, which was typically in the range of three to four marks. Only GM-owned

Opel achieved lower figures, RM 2.7/kg for one model and RM 2.4/kg for another. The latter was a bewhiskered product, dating in concept from a decade earlier when Opel had introduced series production in Germany. At RM 1,550, Porsche's proposed cars would be in the specific cost bracket of RM 2.4–2.5/kg, similar to the best Opel performance.

To reach Hitler's desired price target, an unprecedented level of RM 1.6 per kilogram would have to be achieved. With high enough production volume this could be seen as possible; the total production of all types of Opel in 1933 had been a scant 39,000 units (Opel's output would jump to 72,000 in 1934).

The target of RM 1.6/kg could be reached, Porsche maintained in confidence to his associates, based on the production efficiency achieved in America not by mass-producer Ford, which was exceptional, but by mid-range producer Buick, part of the General Motors family. Buicks, said Porsche, sold for the equivalent of only RM 1.5/kg. All Germany had to do was produce as rationally, he argued, sometimes to the irritation of his listeners.

Clearly, however, to contemplate a selling price of RM 1,000 an order-of-magnitude production volume increase from traditional German levels would be needed. Such a leap in Germany's car output suddenly seemed possible on Saturday, 3 March 1934, when Hitler opened the Berlin Auto Show with an elaborately staged address in a swastika-bedecked hall. Porsche was in the audience for the highly politicized speech that began in the dying fanfare of an army band. Hitler, in military uniform, issued a clear call for action.

> Germany has only one automobile for every one hundred inhabitants. France has one for each twenty-eight and the United States one for each six. That disparity must be changed. I would like to see a German car mass-produced so it can be bought by anyone who can afford a motorcycle. Simple, reliable, economical transportation is needed. We must have a real car for the German people — a Volkswagen!

Hitler urged Germany's auto industry "more and more to design the cars that will compellingly attract new buyers by the millions."

IN 1933 GERMANY HAD ONLY 522,000 cars in circulation, less than half the size of the fleets of Britain or France. Its total vehicle production in 1934 was 147,000 units (127,000 of them cars) against Britain's 257,000 vehicles. Thus when in 1934 the first discussions of production rates of a putative people's car proposed 200,000 per year or, including exports, 300,000 at most, this was viewed as a colossal expansion of domestic car output.

The expansion plan was sugar-coated for the delicate digestion of the existing carmakers. It was presented as a means of creating a new cooperatively produced sedan that could absorb some of the excess capacity of the

German auto industry, still suffering from years of economic depression. But the industry was already increasing its output more than a year after Hitler had first promoted motorization; instead of being a new source of business for existing producers the Volkswagen was seen as a deadly rival.

In their conclaves at the RDA, Germany's automakers agreed among themselves that Hitler's thousand-mark price target was ludicrously low and that the high running costs of a car would prevent his intended motorization. Their natural instinct, in any case, was to curb the socialistic notions of this radical new government, which had been proclaimed the Third Reich with Roman symmetry on the ides of March 1933.

Based on a calculation by Opel, the RDA estimated that a price in the range of RM 1,200 to RM 1,500 might be possible. Asked to think in terms of a car that would cost about as much as a medium-sized motorcycle with sidecar, the RDA experts fastened on a three-wheeled configuration as desirable, with the engine and a single wheel at the rear. In this they received encouragement for a time from the Transport Ministry. Obviously, a three-wheeled car would offer minimum competition to their own more elaborate four-wheeled designs.

Through his Minister of Transport, Hitler expressly requested the carmakers' involvement. They had an obligation, their brief specified, of "furthering car ownership among the German people, on the basis of shared responsibility, by employing the leading forces in the automotive world, with all the means serving the good of the German people." In response, a small commission was set up within the RDA in 1934 to study the matter.

As Germany's leading producers, Adler, Auto Union, Daimler-Benz, and Opel were represented in the commission. Ford would have qualified for inclusion but it was omitted because, after all, the aim of the project was to "out-Ford Ford." In fact U.S.-owned Opel's participation would turn out to be short-lived.

The commission's éminence grise was a reticent executive, Franz Josef Popp, head of Munich's BMW, a maker of motorcycles and airplane engines that had become a carmaker in 1929 by taking over the bankrupt Dixi works. Also a member of the Daimler-Benz supervisory board, Popp was friendly with that company's chief Wilhelm Kissel, who would frequently compare notes with his colleague on the Volkswagen problem.

NO HOTTER POTATO HAD EVER BEEN dropped in the laps of the RDA, its political chief Robert Allmers, and its general secretary Wilhelm Scholz. Like most trade associations, the RDA functioned at the speed and wit of its lowest common denominator. It took the society much of April and the early part of May 1934 to get a ruling on a point it was debating with the Transport Ministry, one that had been decided long before by the Reich chief automobile designer, Adolf Hitler: namely that a three-wheeled vehicle would not after all be acceptable. Neither was the idea, mooted earlier, that three or four big carmakers should pool resources in a combine to produce the car.

The fourth and last paragraph of Ferdinand Porsche's January 1934 "Exposé" recommended that his company be commissioned by the government to design, build, and test a Volkswagen prototype. About a year would be needed, it stated, to prepare such a prototype in a form suitable for testing and evaluation by an independent commission. "In the event of a satisfactory outcome of the tests," Porsche wrote, "the government may decide to recommend to the industry the series production of this model as the German Volkswagen." Porsche asked that his development costs be reimbursed and that he be paid royalties on any of his patents that were used in the vehicle.

Listening to Hitler's speech at the opening of the auto show in Berlin, Porsche realized that his "Exposé" had been read by the Führer himself. After the show this was confirmed by Transport Minister Brandenburg, who added the obvious point that Porsche's proposed selling price was much higher than the figure specified by Hitler and thus would require further study by the engineer. The meeting gave Porsche cause for some confidence; he checked with Brandenburg's office in early May but was told there was still no news.

Unofficial, but no less effective for that, the Werlin channel opened again in the last week of May. In another "non-visit" to Porsche's office, Jakob Werlin ignored the exploits of the Porsche-designed Auto Union racing car, which was setting new speed records while its Mercedes-Benz rival was still in the garage. He turned instead to the matter of the people's car. "You will shortly receive an official order to proceed with the development of the Volkswagen. This order will come not from the Ministry of Transport but from the Society of German Automobile Manufacturers."

Werlin explained that this decision had been reached at the level of the chancellor in order to ensure a commitment by the car producers to the project. If they were paying for the development, Hitler had reasoned, they would be more likely to exploit its fruits. The RDA's special commission reached a decision to this effect on 8 May; the full RDA board endorsed it on 28 May.

Official notification to Porsche from the RDA's Robert Allmers followed in early June, after which a contract was hammered out. This was no easy matter.

> The Ministry of Transport after receiving Porsche's memorandum certainly treated it with bureaucratic thoroughness, in the way only ministry officials are capable. A few sheets of type-written matter and five drawings within not quite five months had become three hefty files, and within those last few weeks some of Herr Allmers' equally bureaucratic staff showed their capabilities not only by preparing a lengthy and very involved contract, but also an endless number of notes on points which had to be discussed at those meetings.

Ultimately the actual contract, signed on 22 June, was relatively brief. So was the time for its realization. It gave Porsche only six months to design the Volkswagen and four months to build it; when it entered production he would be entitled to a royalty of one mark per car.

Although the contract called for payments to Porsche's companies of twenty thousand marks monthly, adjustments were made in the course of the project. On 7 December 1934 the number of prototypes was increased from one to Porsche's traditional three. Work started at the agreed monthly fee, said the RDA's Wilhelm Vorwig, "then increased to 30,000 and 40,000 before hitting 50,000 marks [monthly] for a short period. The contract lasted about thirty months, instead of the agreed-upon ten, and payments came to a total of more than one million marks."

The Porsche people had no workshop of their own, so a drill press, milling machine, and two lathes were installed in the fortuitously large Porsche family garage in Stuttgart's Feuerbach. There the cars were assembled from components made by many subcontractors under the supervision of Porsche's son Ferry, for whom the premises had previously been a home workshop. By 1935 the Porsche staff consisted of thirty-three engineers and a workshop crew of five, which would grow to twelve the following year.

By the latter part of 1935 they had built two vehicles, a V1 sedan and V2 open model, to test various components and engines, the latter proving to be the toughest nut to crack. That the final engine used was designated the E-Motor indicates how many attempts had preceded it.

When he opened the Berlin Auto Show in February 1935, the chancellor could ignore the project's delays. In fact he identified Porsche publicly as the designer for the first time and hailed the fact that the plans for the revolutionary car were "completed." During 1935 Hitler was preoccupied with other tasks, such as the reoccupation of the Saarland, establishment of the swastika banner as the German national flag, elimination of the rights of the Jews, and coping with Germany's censure by the League of Nations.

The first car in the final VW3 trio of prototypes was ready in February 1936. Built with the help of Daimler-Benz, two of the three had wood-framed bodies and one an all-steel body of the proposed design. At the Berghof, his villa on the Obersalzberg in the Bavarian Alps, Hitler was shown two of the VW3 prototypes on the morning of 11 July 1936. One was presented to him again at teatime minus its body, demonstrating the easy adaptability of its chassis to military requirements.

Finally on Monday, 12 October 1936, after a weekend that must have been grueling, not three but five — including the first two test cars equipped with the final flat-four engine — ur-VWs were officially handed over to the RDA for testing. Wilhelm Vorwig directed the tests, which were conducted by drivers from the Porsche staff partnered with RDA observers, covering

Ferdinand Porsche inspects one of the VW3 prototypes in early 1937. A fleet of thirty of these cars, produced by Daimler-Benz, was subjected to extensive tests by teams of SS drivers.

both country roads and Autobahns at a rate of some 500 miles a day every day but Sunday. Problems were rife, but the little cars were convincing.

After 31,000 miles of tests, completed by three cars just before Christmas, Vorwig's conclusions were guardedly positive. "A number of shortcomings were discovered in the 50,000 kilometer drive. They are all, however, not of a basic nature and the expectation is that they can be overcome technically without great difficulty. Performance and handling characteristics are good. The car has shown qualities which would appear to recommend further development."

FURTHER DEVELOPMENT WAS ALREADY under way. The Porsche office prepared a revised design in 1936 which was built in a series of thirty by Daimler-Benz, to Porsche's drawings, at the end of 1936 and early in 1937. These cars became available at Eastertime for another round of tests, this time to be conducted by teams of drivers supplied by the SS, the elite Nazi police force. By now "the RDA really didn't matter any more, although nobody had bothered to tell them."

A car of manifest strengths and weaknesses, the VW was originated in its entirety by Ferdinand Porsche and his team.

A key Porsche engineering aide was Franz Xaver Reimspiess, left, with whom Ferdinand Porsche is discussing a cooling fan. Reimspiess is credited with the design of the distinctive VW circular emblem.

Free of any sort of tradition and without respect to the production methods that were customary in Germany or in any German auto factory at all, development could now take place purely from the standpoint of function, whereby Porsche, with his confident technical instinct, always took care that they designed with simplicity and lightness, *but not crudely.*

One of Opel's senior managers had ample opportunity to see Porsche and his men at work. Dubious though he was about their assignment, he respected the way they attacked it.

Porsche and his team really went to work. They meant business, not lip service. This outstanding man was engineer and designer not by profession, but at heart. Short-tempered and energetic, he easily got in trouble with his employers before long. He was not regarded as being successful in the normal sense of the word, but he was a fanatic and an unusually gifted engineer. He had his own very clear-cut ideas about a small car, and he gripped with all ten fingers this singular opportunity to materialize his dreams. He had the rare gift of surrounding himself with a team of devoted followers who loved him and were dedicated to his ideas. Among them there was a unity and a determination to accomplish the outstanding and an unbound willingness to follow their leader and idol. His was one of the truly great minds of engineering history.

The Porsche design team was led by Karl Rabe and included Josef Kales, Erwin Komenda, Karl Fröhlich, Josef Mickl, Josef Zahradnik, Franz Xaver Reimspiess, and Porsche's son Ferry. Other engineers would contribute to the VW as well, including those at Daimler-Benz who built the prototype

Checking a drawing of the final Type 60 KdF-Wagen with Ferdinand Porsche in 1938 is, left, Karl Rabe, Porsche's chief engineer. Rabe guided Porsche's visions along practical lines.

series and a cadre of German-Americans who had been recruited from the Detroit auto firms to help make the new car manufacturable.

The RDA's Wilhelm Vorwig was well aware of the special role of Karl Rabe. "It was Rabe's extraordinary ability that made the bold Porsche concept come into reality. Yet he was always in the background, never getting credit for his work. Without Rabe, there would be no Volkswagen."

Vorwig's RDA report was critical of the performance of the cars' cable-operated brakes. Ferry Porsche acknowledged that the mechanical brakes were an out-and-out economy measure. Not only were they cheaper to make, they also avoided royalty payments to Lockheed, which held the key patents on hydraulic brakes. The brakes, admitted Ferry, "were, in fact, a feature about which my father had always had misgivings."

While testing and development continued, a solution was still needed to the knotty problem of producing the people's car. The idea of sharing production among the domestic manufacturers was rapidly overtaken by their own increasing output in response to Hitler's twin-pronged promotion of both domestic motorization and export sales. German car and truck exports were soaring from 13,250 units in 1934 to 36,500 in 1936 and 68,500 in 1937. From May 1937 the pressure to export was further increased by a new system of steel allocation that rewarded auto companies for higher exports by granting them a larger share of the limited steel supply.

Franz Reimspiess originated the concept of the air-cooled flat-four engine that saved the VW project after a number of other alternatives had been explored. This is an early prototype of what an Opel executive called an "airplane engine."

Most aggravating for the Third Reich was the news that American-owned Adam Opel AG was accounting for almost half the nation's vehicle exports and was selling one-quarter of its output abroad. The company, one of the oldest in the industry, was benefiting from the production expertise of its General Motors parent. Opel was a member of the RDA, but that group soon became paranoid about showing Opel any of the VW project drawings in case the Americans were to steal their precious secrets.

The RDA had good reason to be wary of Opel. Backed by James Mooney, president of GM's Export Corporation, Opel's honorary head and RDA life member Wilhelm von Opel had gained an audience with Hitler to present his company's credentials to build its version of the Volkswagen but not, of course, at so low a price as one thousand marks — or RM 990 as it was now being interpreted. Hitler was polite but showed von Opel the door.

Pointedly, when the RDA called for a high-level discussion on the VW project at Coblenz at the time of the German Grand Prix on 27 July 1936, Opel was not invited. The RDA was taking literally Hitler's decree that the Volkswagen was to be a "purely national matter."

It didn't help that the Opel executive who spoke most often on his company's behalf at the RDA was consistently critical of the project. When he saw the flat-four air-cooled engine designed by Franz Xaver Reimspiess, the E-Motor that saved the project, he exclaimed, "This is an airplane engine! You can't afford to put an airplane engine in a car selling for a thousand marks."

Airplane engines of another kind were beginning to absorb both financial resources and precious raw materials in a Germany that was rich in neither. Rearmament and the Reich's ambitious goals for its motor industry were on a collision course. Carmakers complained that they couldn't achieve their production targets for lack of materials; what would be the added impact of a huge Volkswagen project? The RDA expressed its willingness to fund further action to produce a Volkswagen, but its exclusion of Ford and Opel made this a hollow promise that it lacked the resources to fulfill.

By the spring of 1936 the progress on the VW prototypes, slow though it was, was quicker than the resolution of the problem of manufacturing them. The solution was discovered not by the government but by the car industry, specifically by the fertile brain of BMW's Franz Josef Popp. A wealthy new institution established under the umbrella of the Third Reich was to provide the key.

THE NEW GOVERNMENT MOVED quickly on 2 May 1933 to abolish all of Germany's 169 trade unions. Only four days were needed to expropriate their funds and facilities and eradicate their existence. Sequestering their money was easy; the unions had established a central bank, the Bank of German Labor (BdA), which was simply seized. The BdA was soon relaunched as a Nazi full-service bank that ultimately boasted thirty-five branches.

The destruction of the unions and the creation in January 1934 of a new entity to replace them, the German Workers Front (DAF), were chiefly the work of Dr. Robert Ley, whom his biographer described as Hitler's "paladin."

> Ley was an important prototype of a certain Nazi — one whose fanaticism, idealism and commitment to Hitler and the movement made him an ideal "old fighter" but whose inadequacies in the management of power, whose inability to gauge means to ends, would cripple the effectiveness of the regime and eventually lead to its destruction. . . . He was rough and tough, uninhibited, given to emotional outbursts, venal and corrupt, and astonishingly lacking in good judgment. He was also a notorious womanizer who drank too much. At the same time, he was an intelligent man who had real organizational ability and a knack for choosing talented subordinates, at least in the upper echelons of his agencies, to run things for him during his frequent inspection tours across Germany. He was also exceedingly ambitious with a need to be "somebody."

Ley's role in the birth and adolescence of the Third Reich was no less important because labor was the societal group in Germany that had been least responsive to the appeal of the National Socialists. Under Ley's new Law for the Organization of National Labor it mattered not how workers felt; they were part of the DAF anyway. Strikes, needless to say, were outlawed.

The result, wrote Stephen Roberts in 1938, "is that today the Labour Front has 26,000,000 members as compared with the 5,000,000 members the unions had when they were taken over. When it is remembered that the population of Germany is only 66,000,000 and that women are discouraged from entering the employment market, it will be obvious that practically all working Germans belong to this new super-union."

Regular contributions to the DAF were made by both workers and employers in relation to the sizes of their pay envelopes and turnover respectively.

The funds were banked by the BdA. Money also flowed in from workers' subscriptions to the holiday layaway plans of the immensely successful *Kraft durch Freude* (KdF) or Strength through Joy movement, an idea copied by the German fascists from their Italian counterparts. In Italy the service was known as *dopo lavoro* (after work), which was literally translated into *Nach der Arbeit* when the Nazis set up a similar organization on 29 November 1933. Soon afterward *Kraft durch Freude* became the name of the scheme set up by Robert Ley to order the free time of his German workforce.

The KdF organized domestic and foreign travel and health-oriented holidays for workers at bargain prices. The cost of a complete two-week holiday in the Alps, everything included, was the equivalent of only sixteen dollars; a week by the North Sea was six dollars and a trip to Italy — a dream holiday for working-class Germans — thirty-nine dollars. Two ships were specially built and ten more chartered to float vacationing workers to Madeira or the Norwegian fjords.

Starting at two million KdF-organized holidays in 1934, the number boomed to five times that by 1938 — one German worker in three was enjoying a KdF-supported break. *Kultur* was also catered for by the KdF. It organized tickets at special rates for the theater, opera, and concerts, and even had its own ninety-member symphony orchestra bringing the acceptable classics to all parts of the nation.

The German Workers Front and the KdF movement became such money-spinners "that by mid-1934 the Reichsbank President, Hjalmar Schacht, was moved to complain to Hitler about it. While total deposits at the Deutsche Bank had scarcely increased at all during the first half of the year, BdA deposits had gone up by 100 million marks, in part, hinted Schacht, owing to its relations with party organizations. By 1938 the BdA had over 20 million marks in cash reserves, current deposits of over 512 million and a turnover of over 15 billion marks."

IN 1936 FRANZ POPP WAS pondering the dilemma that the VW project posed for the domestic motor industry. He foresaw numerous pitfalls. He rejected a role for U.S.-owned Opel, which he saw as gaining an unfair advantage from such participation. He was worried about the potential impact of the VW project on the industry's suppliers, who would try to gouge the other car producers to make up for the losses they would suffer on their enforced distress-priced sale of parts and materials to Hitler's pet car company.

Like his colleagues, Popp feared incursions by the Beetle into their traditional segments of the small German auto market. But one way to prevent this, he mulled in the summer of 1936, would be to restrict sales of the new car to members of the DAF — the self-defined working class of Germany, the people for whom the new car was really intended. And the DAF, he thought, could use its vast resources in some way to subsidize the cost of the car so that Hitler's price commitment could be met.

This was the seed of the idea that grew into a big beanstalk. In discussions with Daimler's Kissel, Popp developed it further. What would happen if the government didn't tax VW production? His experts told him "that twenty-five to thirty percent of a car's production costs at that time in Germany were made up of taxes." Around 20 percent of the sales price consisted of distribution costs. "From these thoughts," he wrote, "Kissel and I formulated the following solution:"

1. The Labour Front [DAF] would become the sponsor of the Volkswagen Works, because it was a union of all those for whom Hitler wanted to create the Volkswagen.

2. The Labour Front possessed enough capital to set up the Works so that neither the existing car industry nor the banks would be called upon financially.

3. To maintain tax exemption, the Volkswagen Works would have to be set up as a public utility, meaning that it would be non-profit-making.

4. To make savings on the majority of the distribution costs, the Labour Front would undertake every aspect of marketing through its many branches.

This made sense for the auto industry, but how was it to be transformed into an idea that Robert Ley would welcome? Franz Josef Popp decided to discuss the question with the Reich trustee for labor in BMW's home state of Bavaria, Kurt Frey, whom he thought to be a man with considerable influence in the court of Hitler's paladin. Frey encouraged Popp to write down and send him his ideas, which he did on 24 and 25 June 1936. After the RDA meeting in Coblenz in July Popp gave copies to Werlin as well.

Not long afterward Frey reported back that Ley had received the idea with "approbation." This was not on its face surprising, for Ley was the master of exploiting his beloved DAF, a worker's organization, in the world of capital enterprise. The Volkswagen was already widely discussed as following the example of Ley's *Volksempfänger* (people's radio), a standard design of which fifty thousand were installed in factories at 295 marks apiece to trumpet the latest wisdom of the Führer. Also in the DAF pipeline were the people's refrigerator (*Volkskühlschrank*) and the people's dwelling (*Volkswohnung*).

But Robert Ley was no babe in the dark forest that was the Third Reich. He protected his flanks by asking the DAF's Institute of Labor Science (AWI) to assess the merit of Popp's idea. This body, whose main mission was to propagate the teachings of the DAF, rendered its conclusion at the end of October. The AWI was entirely against the idea.

The institute judged that taking the project away from the existing industry would only encourage a "flight from management responsibility" of a kind that was already evident in Germany. Too many industrialists seemed ready to let the Nazis take the initiative in running their businesses; the AWI recognized that this placed entrepreneurship at risk. The VW project would also expose the DAF to potential perils of unknown dimensions of liability, not to mention hazards to its prestige and reputation among the very people it was intended to serve.

Independently and in parallel, another approach to the wealthy BdA bank was being made around the same time. Wilhelm Vorwig called upon the bank to help provide the funding that the RDA needed to carry out the tests of the just-delivered trio (plus two) of VW3 prototypes. Joining him in the request was Otto Schirz, who had close links to none other than the influential Jakob Werlin. Here was another substantive contact between the DAF and the VW project.

In the meantime, however, unbeknownst to Popp and his colleagues, Robert Ley continued to regard the DAF-VW link as commendable. The shrewd ally of Hitler solved the problem of the negative AWI finding with insouciant ease: he commissioned another study. Happily, this overturned the earlier conclusion and judged involvement with the Volkswagen to be an excellent idea for the DAF. By the end of 1936 the DAF and Ley had decided to take on the responsibility for building and selling Hitler's dream car.

Although Hitler hadn't yet blessed the alliance, Ley felt confident enough about his new role to discuss it with Reich Propaganda Minister Joseph Goebbels in January 1937. In his diary for 15 January Goebbels wrote, "There we carry out something big that will give the Führer pleasure." Hitler was indeed visibly relieved when, just prior to the 1937 Berlin Auto Show, Ley asked for and received his formal blessing to take charge of a task which was not only gargantuan but potentially, in economic terms, impossible.

On 20 February 1937, a Saturday as usual, Adolf Hitler opened the Berlin Show with a speech in which he made clear his determination to achieve the production of a car for the people. That evening the dictator invited four hundred car-industry workers to dine at the Kaiserhof Hotel in Berlin. There, in the presence of Italian labor leader Tulio Cianetti, Hitler announced his assignment of the VW project to Robert Ley and the DAF. Ley in turn named his deputy, Bodo Lafferentz, as his representative on the board of the Volkswagen project.

This momentous decision was not made public at the time. Popp and his colleagues were unaware that their solution to the problem of producing the people's car had been adopted. This news blackout prevailed for more than a year, indeed until just before the VW factory's cornerstone was laid in the spring of 1938. Ley couldn't resist mentioning his new task in a speech in mid-June at a congress in Hamburg, but only one journal ignored the "harmonizing" practices of the Reich press office and published his proud proclamation; it attracted little notice.

The DAF's reason for keeping the swaddling on its new baby was simple enough: it didn't want to arouse excessive public expectations in advance of the launch of the project, expectations that were already high enough and which, as the AWI report stated, could rebound against the DAF if the hopes of would-be Beetle owners were dashed. As well, many aspects of the actual financing of the project still remained to be resolved.

ONE DECISION THAT COULDN'T WAIT too long was the choice of a place to put the factory that would build the cars. In fact the need for a speedy decision was the principal reason for the selection of a large site on marshy ground north of the Mittelland Canal on the Lüneberg Heath near the village of Fallersleben, and south of the canal in Lower Saxony. Hitherto Fallersleben's claim to fame had been as the birthplace (in 1798) of author and poet August Heinrich Hoffmann, best known for his *Tales of Hoffmann* and his authorship of the words of Germany's national anthem.

Spotted from the air by Bodo Lafferentz, making a reconnaissance of the region west of Berlin in the summer of 1937 in a Junkers Ju 88, the site had one great advantage — most of its area was owned by only two noble families: the von der Schulenbergs and the von der Wenses. They did not give up the land readily, but give it up they ultimately did — the Schulenbergs 7,600 acres, the Wenses 2,500 acres, and twenty-eight other parties the balance of the 15,000-acre site that was needed for both factory and city, on both sides of the canal.

Isolated though it was, the site met Hitler's criteria, expressed on 11 July 1936, that it should be in central Germany for strategic reasons and have good transport connections. Rail links were close; the Autobahn was nearly finished and the Mittelland Canal joined the region to Prague, Berlin, and the Oder River in the east and the ports at Bremen and Hamburg in the west and north.

But the site was remote from its suppliers of parts and materials. It also required the building of a town on the south side of the canal to house its workforce. For these reasons the choice was openly and cheekily criticized by young Ferry Porsche. Ironically, however, its out-of-the-way location would contribute not only to the plant's ability to recover and resume operations after the war but also to its survival as a car-producing complex.

The DAF commissioned architects in the late summer of 1937. Planning of the new town (but not the factory) was the responsibility of an architect named Peter Koller, who trained under Professor Heinrich Tessenow and his assistant Albert Speer. Like some other students, wrote Speer's biographer, "Koller, a fresh recruit to Nazism, changed the subject in tutorials from architecture to politics."

Naming the new town was a particular challenge. Names favored by Robert Ley were *Neu-Fallersleben* and *Porschestadt*. Porsche's son-in-law, Austrian solicitor Anton Piëch, mooted *Volkswagenstadt*. Hitler made the

Watched by Porsche at left, Adolf Hitler examines the Beetle scale model he received on his birthday on 20 April 1938. Between Porsche and Hitler is Robert Ley, whose DAF would build the factory and sell the car. Behind Hitler is Jakob Werlin and at right Ley's deputy Bodo Lafferentz.

final decision. The town would be named *Stadt des KdF-Wagens* after the Strength through Joy movement, he decreed, at least until the end of the war. Then they could make a longer-term decision. *KdF-Stadt* was a suitable abbreviation.

Adolf Hitler received a preview of the definitive form of the Beetle-to-be when a one-tenth-scale model of the car was presented to him on his forty-ninth birthday, 20 April 1938. Porsche pointed out its features to a visibly delighted Führer as the tall, genial Bodo Lafferentz and other beaming aides looked on. Three final prototypes of Porsche's design, at last showing the Beetle as we know it, were revealed for the first time on 26 May 1938 when the cornerstone of their factory was laid by Hitler before six hundred honored guests and seventy thousand spectators.

The ceremony, on the north side of the canal, was adorned with swastikas in the spectacular and familiar panoply of Nazi pomp. Robert Ley, proudly introducing his leader, seized the day.

> What has been started here — this factory and everything which will come of it — is basically and singularly your work, my Führer. This Volkswagen factory is one of your own favourite creations. We know how you thought of giving the German people a good but inexpensive motor vehicle even before you came to power and how you have even since imbued with new strength all the designers and others who laboured on this car!

A handsome KdF-Wagen cabriolet was built for ceremonial purposes before the war. No serious consideration was given at that time to the manufacture of such a model — that would have to wait until after the war.

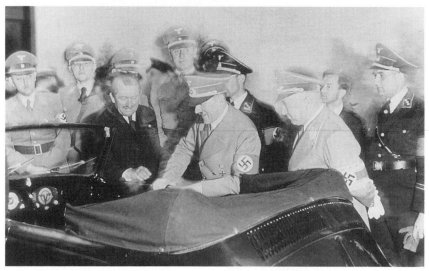

Standing between Porsche, left, and Robert Ley, Adolf Hitler inspects the only KdF Type 60 cabriolet built before the war. He was driven in it from the cornerstone-laying ceremony by young Ferry Porsche, just visible behind Ley.

Adolf Hitler amply repaid Ley in his remarks: "This car shall carry the name of the organisation which works hardest to provide the broadest masses of our people with joy and, therefore, strength. It shall be called the KdF-Wagen!" This decision was not news to project insiders; Lafferentz had told them at the end of 1937 that Hitler had decided on this name. The Porsches senior and junior were shocked, however. They privately declared themselves as unhappy about a name that was at best meaningless in the crucial export markets.

THE STRENGTH THROUGH JOY movement was anything but meaningless at home, especially to the people the DAF wanted to sign up as buyers. In 1938, ten million Germans would take part in one or another holiday trip or outing organized by the KdF. Hitler wanted them all to be on wheels, as he explained to the Fallersleben masses and the millions listening to his speech on the radio:

Standing next to Adolf Hitler, Ferdinand Porsche wears a trench coat at the cornerstone-laying ceremony on 26 May 1938 at Fallersleben. The robust figure of DAF leader Robert Ley is at right.

When I came to power in 1933 I saw one problem that had to be tackled at once — the problem of motorization. In this sphere Germany was behind everyone else. The output of private cars in Germany had reached the laughable figure of 46,000 a year. And the first step toward putting an end to this was to do away with the idea that a motorcar is a luxury. What I want is not a car for 200,000 or 300,000 persons who can afford it, but a car which six million or seven million persons can afford.

But could a German with 990 marks in his pocket consider splurging on a KdF-Wagen (RM 1,050 for the version with a sliding canvas roof) as soon as the production lines rolled, as they were expected to in 1939? At the cornerstone ceremony Bodo Lafferentz explained that it would not be as simple as that. Delivering a state-of-the-project review, he announced that a special savings plan for car purchasers would be launched. It was his brainchild. A car had been created that was radical by the standards of its day. The means chosen to finance the project to build it could hardly have been more radical. The factory itself was radical by European standards as Chapter 3 will reveal. Appropriately, the purchasing arrangements were to be radical as well.

They were seen as not so bizarre by the members of the DAF, accustomed as they were to paying the KdF in advance for their holidays. Now they would do the same for their new car. And there would be no way around it; this was the only way a KdF-Wagen could be purchased.

Dr. Robert Ley explained the system in detail for the first time at a workers' rally in Cologne on 1 August 1938. "It is the Führer's will that within a few years no less than six million Volkswagens will be on German roads," Ley declared. "In ten years' time there will be no working person in Germany who does not own a Volkswagen." Its factory, said Ley, would be "the materialization in stone and iron of the idea of classless education, settlement work, national health and the beauty of work."

Initiated that August by Ley, Lafferentz's layaway savings scheme was viewed by the DAF as an important means of securing the viability of its new factory, which soon would be birthing Beetles by the hundreds of thousands. They wanted to have purchasers signed up and standing by in an orderly manner to take delivery of their dark blue autos. By committing them to a savings scheme well in advance, meticulously organized and documented in the bureaucratic style of the Third Reich, the DAF aimed to achieve that goal.

The procedures were spelled out in detail. For twenty pfennigs someone who wanted to drive rather than walk could buy a handsome, richly illustrated brochure edited by Dr. Eberhard Moos; printed in Stuttgart in press runs of half a million, the brochure informed readers about the KdF-Wagen in excruciating detail and at laudatory length. An application form was stapled at its center which, completed and submitted with one mark, gave the buyer his first savings book and committed him to carry on saving until he had laid the purchase price away.

Savers were committed to buy, stick in their book, and self-cancel at least one red or green five-mark KdF-Wagen stamp each week; in special cases this could be relaxed to monthly. Savers could buy more stamps if they wanted to. Extra spaces were provided in each book to save for the convertible model or for the delivery charges to their home district if they didn't want to pick up their car from the KdF-Stadt.

When the saver turned in his third book, representing a total saved of at least 750 marks, he was sent a postcard which assigned to him a specific numbered place in the delivery queue for the cars that would be allocated to his district or *Gau*. Allocations would be in proportion to the number of signed-up savers in each *Gau*. When he completed the last books in the series he could expect to receive his brand-new Beetle. Withdrawal from the scheme was only permitted in special cases and then with an "administrative" deduction of 20 percent of the amount saved.

Participation in the scheme was not forced, as has sometimes been suggested, but was actively promoted and encouraged. The DAF presses rolled with promotional brochures and flyers, including a handsome booklet with transparent overlays that allowed the reader to "dismantle" a KdF-Wagen and view its components from above and below.

Details of the car were released to the press for the 1939 Berlin Auto Show, where two cars and a chassis were on display. Publicity photos showed

Promotional materials for marketing the KdF-Wagen were produced to a high stan-
dard. This was the cover of the brochure produced for the 1939 Berlin Auto Show.

components of the car and the plant under construction. They were provided to the press on the condition that they send copies of their articles to the VW offices at Taubertstrasse 4 in Berlin-Grunewald.

Linked with the opening of the show in Berlin was the release of a new set of postage stamps. The original Benz and Daimler cars were on the six pfennig stamp, the Auto Union and Mercedes-Benz racing cars on the seventeen pfennig, and the KdF-Wagen, whooshing along an Autobahn, on the twenty-five-pfennig stamp. Germany's automotive credentials were proudly displayed.

Aggressive advertising promoted the savings scheme. Employers were encouraged to credit their workers with stamps or books according to their length of service. A first savings book, it was suggested, would be just the thing to give as a present for Christmas. To encourage this a special KdF-Wagen display was organized for the Christmas fair in Berlin.

Entrepreneurs were quick to seize the KdF-Wagen opportunity. One created a board game that took the players through the pleasures of acquiring and running a KdF-Wagen. Surrounded by illustrations of the factory, Porsche's development center, and the KdF-Stadt were the many stages of life with the VW. The factory-authorized game progressed from the decision to buy through a frenzy of stamp-saving to passing the driving test, collecting the car from the factory, and many miles of joyful motoring that ended, tired but happy, at home.

Outside the doors of the 1939 Berlin Show the preproduction proto-types were ready for press demonstrations. Afterward these precious cars were kept constantly on the move to be admired by the public and cinema-goers in the company of the Nazi great and near-great. Their busy schedule in the spring of 1939 included appearances at the Eifelrennen on the Nür-burgring (three cars), the Breslau Fair (one car), the *Gau* and Culture Con-ference in Stettin (one car), and the Ufa film studios in Berlin (two cars in May, two in June, and then ten cars for a big film project in July).

The campaign's initial impact was gratifying. By the end of 1938, 170,000 savers had signed up. Rates continued to climb; by the end of 1939 the num-ber of savers in the KdF car-buying plan was 275,000. They had already put 110 million marks into the special kitty that would fund their purchases.

Promote though they might, however — and the DAF continued to push the benefit of saving right through the war — the rate of new signings fell sharply in 1940 and the subsequent years. It crept gradually to a peak of 336,668 savers in 1944; by 1945 savers had invested 275 million marks in the scheme. Yet this was far short of the number of Beetle buyers needed to sup-port the huge volumes of production expected for the plant. Optimists at the KdF headquarters prophesied that signing-on rates would soar as soon as the big works began spewing out its dark blue cars.

Analysis of the savers showed that the noble laborers so beloved of Ley and Hitler were dramatically underrepresented in the scheme: only 5 per-cent could be so described. Whereas their gross weekly income was in the range of seventeen to twenty-six marks, in which five marks made quite a dent, most savers were middle-class Germans earning eighty to ninety marks weekly. And one-third of them already owned a car! Worrisomely, only one in four of the workers in the VW plant itself had signed up to save for the car he hoped to build. Here was justification for the concerns of the German automakers that the KdF-Wagen would make inroads into their markets. The savers' composition also justified the original suggestion by Franz Josef Popp that only members of the DAF should be eligible to buy the cars, a recommendation that was meant to limit the damage to Germa-ny's other car producers. Simple economics indicated, however, that the number of those enrolled would have been far lower if this restriction had been imposed.

Following the lines advanced by Popp there were no dealers as such; the *Gau* offices of the DAF would handle sales in order to remove the dealer's overhead from the cost of distribution. Parts would be sold through existing independent retail outlets. By 1940, 223 contract workshops or service cen-ters were signed up across the country; an additional 1,000 affiliated work-shops were anticipated. Also, an agreement in principle had been obtained by Bodo Lafferentz from at least one carmaker, Daimler-Benz, to welcome KdF-Wagen owners to its dealers for service.

The KdF planners hoped to minimize workshop visits and encourage the do-it-yourself approach to maintenance by designing and printing a magnificently detailed and illustrated owner's manual. In its center pages a series of callout lines from the parts shown in a cutaway drawing of the Beetle led to thumb cuts around all three sides of both pages that guided the owner directly to the section of the manual he needed.

ON 6 SEPTEMBER 1938 THE organization that had been creating the Volkswagen car and factory, known since May 1937 as GEZUVOR (*Gesellschaft zur Vorbereitung des Volkswagens mbH*), was transformed into the Volkswagenwerk GmbH with its headquarters in Berlin. This was a logical but less evocative name than GEZUVOR, which in German implied "go ahead!"

Hans Kern, Porsche's new business manager, moved the company into spacious custom-built premises in Zuffenhausen, a suburb north of Stuttgart. Porsche's office had expanded dramatically to meet its new responsibilities. In 1938 Porsche had a turnover of RM 1.6 million and employed 72 engineers and 104 skilled workers; by 1940 those figures would increase to 117 and 174 respectively.

In September 1938, at a meeting of the East Prussian *Gau* in Königsberg, Robert Ley announced that production of the first series of 20,000 cars would start in a year's time. Then in 1940, 100,000 would be produced, twice as many in 1941, and then up to 450,000 per year during the first stage of the plant's development, with a workforce of 17,500 on two shifts. Before the year was out a plan was also on the table to gear up to produce 450,000 Beetles per year as early as 1940.

That was to be only the beginning. The huge, modern plant extending four-fifths of a mile along the Mittelland Canal was designed to be expanded in stages so that ultimately 30,000 workers could build 800,000 to one million cars yearly. Thus the KdF-Stadt was planned to expand to accommodate those workers and their families, 90,000 souls in all. As soon as the savers received their cars, more than half the Beetles produced would be exported to bring valuable currencies into the New Germany.

These were awesome volumes by the standards of the day. In the mid-1930s Ford was the world's leading auto manufacturer, producing 1.3 million cars per year. Chevrolet was next in output with one million, followed by Plymouth with 500,000, Dodge with 300,000, and Oldsmobile with 200,000 cars per year. GM's Opel was by a wide margin Germany's volume leader with its output of 140,580 vehicles in 1938, 82,000 of them private cars. The mammoth project at Fallersleben would dwarf these digits.

ON 7 JULY 1939 A MERCEDES-BENZ cortege motored west from Berlin and drew up at the gates of the plant-to-be at Fallersleben. Adolf Hitler and

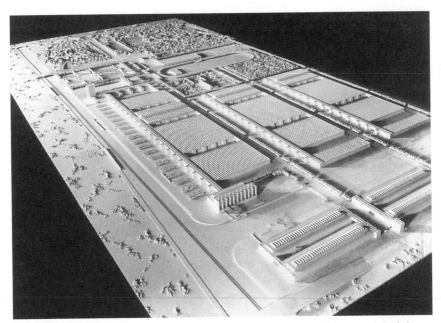

A major exhibit at the 1938 Berlin Auto Show was a magnificent model of the Volkswagen factory of the future. The model showed the works after the two expansions that would increase its capacity to 1.5 million cars per year.

his retinue were en route to the Berghof for the summer, but on his way the Führer wanted to view progress at the site which, according to Ferry Porsche, "resembled nothing so much as the world's biggest ant heap" with its earthworks and teeming Italian labor force.

> The four huge halls were completed. Machinery was being installed in the tool-and-die shop and the huge presses were in place. The Führer was driven through the vast buildings in his open-topped Mercedes. In each hall, Porsche and his staff would gather around the swastika-flagged Mercedes to explain what production process would take place there. After a tour of the nearly completed power plant, the parade of cars drove up to [a hillside] and looked down on the sprawling factory below.

Little more than a month later, on 16 August, the huge plant came to life for the first time when Ferdinand Porsche personally turned a valve the size of a massive steering wheel to initiate power and heat generation by one of the big coal-fed Borsig turbines. Job One, in modern parlance, was expected to be built in October and the goal was production of ten thousand cars by year's end. But a number of specialized machines ordered from America were not yet in place; mid-1940 looked more likely for Job One.

Ferdinand Porsche checks the gauges as he turns the big handwheel that brings the first power-generating Borsig turbine into operation at Fallersleben. The factory is almost ready. But when would it produce automobiles?

It could have happened that way. Hitler wanted the plant and its car to fulfill his promises. But he had conflicting priorities. Above all he wanted more land to the east for his people. In March 1938 he had annexed Austria; this was celebrated on the cornerstone he had laid at Fallersleben. The Sudeten region of Czechoslovakia had followed in September; March 1939 saw the rest of the Czech nation absorbed into Greater Germany.

In May 1939 Hitler's Germany allied in a Pact of Steel with Mussolini's Italy. Hitler challenged the world with his brazen march into Poland on the first of September of 1939; the world responded two days later with a declaration of a state of war by Britain, followed by France. KdF-Wagen production would have to wait while Adolf Hitler and his troops dealt with these inconveniences.

2

Beetles in Warpaint

Since 1938 the Porsche design team had a bolt-hole in the countryside southeast of Fallersleben. Little more than a hunting cottage among gardens and fruit trees, the brown-painted *Hütte* (hut), as it was dubbed, was expanded to serve as a base for Porsche and his aides. Ideally positioned on a hill, it commanded a view of the growing factory by the canal. Circling it were fields of tulips from ten thousand bulbs sent as a gift from Holland by Ben Pon, a Dutch entrepreneur who was bent on being among the first to market VWs abroad.

The Fallersleben plant was so important to his business enterprises that Professor Porsche arranged for his son-in-law Anton Piëch to be recalled from the Luftwaffe to take care of its commercial aspects. Piëch, a Viennese lawyer by training, managed the works for Porsche and made the hut his home during the war. There he and his colleagues would settle into antique chairs near the tiled stove in the big sitting room to discuss the issues of the day.

There was much to discuss. In April 1939 an advance guard of the Porsche design office moved into offices in the new mechanical workshops at Fallersleben. As of 31 May 1939, the KdF authorities had proudly proclaimed, the plant's intended production through 1940 was already fully committed, both to participants in the savings plan and to government offices, which were all-owed to pay cash for the cars. The audacious project was tantalizingly close to realization.

Completion of the plant and its workers' city would continue unabated in spite of the outbreak of war. Italian laborers borrowed from Mussolini were hard at work; they wouldn't be called up by Germany. But a meeting on 6 September, less than a week after hostilities were formally declared, revealed shortages of both the gasoline and oil needed by the construction machinery.

41

Anton Piëch, seen with an early Porsche Type 356 after the war, married Ferdinand Porsche's daughter Louise. In wartime attorney Piëch played a key role in the business management of the KdF factory.

To help fill the gap Otto Dyckhoff, technical director at the plant, released a thousand liters of his precious gasoline supply.

But larger priorities intruded. Construction was accelerating on Germany's West Wall, on Hitler's transformation of the city of Berlin into a capital city for the new Greater Germany, and on facilities dedicated to war materiel. The allocation of raw materials came under the control of the General Construction Inspectorate (GBI) headed by Albert Speer, the Reich's fast-rising technocrat. Although close to Hitler, Speer did not possess the easy intimacy with the dictator that Ferdinand Porsche enjoyed.

Only thirty-five years old in 1940, Speer sought to propagate a youth culture into which the elder Porsche would fit poorly, if at all. But the great engineer was untouchable. "At most, a half dozen men in all of Germany dared to speak their minds openly before Hitler, and my father was one of them," wrote Ferry Porsche. "The situation, in fact, was in some respects as though my father were also Hitler's father." Albert Speer could not stop the work of Hitler's favorite vehicle designer — but he could slow it down.

A bitter tug of wills followed. Speer gave little encouragement in a meeting at KdF-Stadt at the end of March 1940. Instead of the requested three thousand tons of steel for the works and twelve hundred tons for the city, a colleague told the Porsche men, only three hundred and four hundred tons respectively would be provided. Not even the new city's pressing need for a water supply could be granted a priority.

The plant's priority would soar, however, if it were a war production site. Opinions differed sharply over the merits of enlisting the plant in the war effort. Some in the government's Economics Ministry thought that such a huge factory could hardly be overlooked in time of war. Others, with an eye toward military ordnance, saw Fallersleben as a plant dedicated and equipped for civilian production — a plant that was and would remain unsuitable for wartime use.

Anticipating that the latter view would pose a risk to the short-term future of their factory, Porsche and his colleagues had suggested as early as November 1938 that parts of it — preferably parts yet to be built — should be used to produce aircraft engines, propellers, and vehicle engines of two to three hundred horsepower. In this they were supported by the Luftwaffe's technical procurement office, which was headed by Ernst Udet, a World War I ace and a personal ally of Porsche. Udet was already cooperating with Porsche by approving his use of the advanced and ultrasecret twelve-cylinder Mercedes DB603 airplane engine in a World Land Speed Record car that Porsche was designing for Daimler-Benz.

This initiative, cynically calculated to move the plant up the priority pecking order to help speed its completion, wasn't approved. But with the country at war in 1939, the factory's value to the aviation industry was recognized and exploited by the Junkers Flugzeug- und Motorenwerke AG based in Dessau, at the southern point of a triangle whose northern tips are Berlin and Fallersleben.

Ferdinand Porsche, facing the camera, discusses the progress of the KdF works in the single-story "hut" situated on a rise south of the Mittelland Canal.

The efforts of Porsche, Piëch, and Lafferentz to make the KdF works available for war production began to be rewarded in 1940 with contracts for the manufacture of bombs (shown) and "swimmer" kits for tanks.

At first Junkers' chief Heinrich Koppenberg made an outright grab for the Volkswagen factory-in-embryo. Hitler asked him for a monthly production of three hundred twin-engined Ju 88 fighter-bombers; Koppenberg would seize production capacity where he could find it. But with a little help from their friends, including Ernst Udet, the Porsches managed to ward off this thrust. Instead they inveigled successfully to be identified as a valid supplier to the aviation industry, a much more advantageous business position that preserved the economic integrity of the factory.

By the end of March 1940 Porsche and Lafferentz were complaining to Speer that almost half a year had passed since they had made their factory "comprehensively available" to the Luftwaffe which, frustratingly, had failed to place any major orders with them. This was a practical problem for the plant's managers. Robert Ley's DAF and its BdA bank were cheerfully carrying the cost of building and maintaining the works, but the Volkswagenwerk needed to start generating compensating cash flow by booking production orders.

As well, in the summer of 1940 the general sense in Germany was that the war would soon be over. Somehow, surely, the British and French would see the logic of reaching an accommodation with Hitler, who had already signed a nonaggression pact with the Soviet Union. The Volkswagen partners wanted to take every step possible to ensure that the plant would be completed so that car production could begin as soon as peace was declared.

Instead, as 1940 progressed production for war intensified. Some of that business was awarded to Porsche's plant. By February output was under way of wooden eighty-gallon wing tanks for aircraft. In March Fallersleben started making 550-pound bombs. A burst of business came in the autumn from the production of "swimmer" kits for tanks that allowed them to float and power themselves across rivers. These also loomed large in the program for 1941. Engine parts began to be machined for Junkers in Dessau.

In mid-1940 Junkers finally placed some bigger orders with Fallersleben. The factory became a key site for the repair of damaged Junkers Ju 88 aircraft; throughout the war this remained its largest single task. A special workshop was opened in a hangar at the Braunschweig Airport, where the plant's auto production experts set up a dismantling/assembly line to speed the Ju 88 refurbishment.

Phased in as well was the manufacture of new wings, tail assemblies, and stabilizers for the Ju 88 and most of the components for the new Junkers Ju 188, whose fuselage was made by Opel. This would be a substantial and ongoing contract to mid-1944, when the plant began producing the major parts of the Ju 388 as well.

Other KdF-Werke products were torpedo hulls and portable furnaces (of these one and a half million) to warm the German troops in the Russian winter. Land mines were produced in high volume in Hall 1, which had originally been set up as the KdF tool and die shop.

THE MOST EXOTIC PRODUCT to grace the Fallersleben factory during the war was the Fieseler Fi 103 pilotless aircraft, otherwise known as the V-1, buzz bomb, or doodlebug. This bug was no benign Beetle — the V-1 was a pulse-jet-powered small mid-wing airplane capable of carrying a one-ton explosive charge 150 miles, putting London in range of many of its launch sites on the European mainland. Achieving speeds of 430 mph, it would be very hard to shoot down.

The Fi 103 was developed by the Georg Fieseler Werke under the direction of Robert Lusser. Fieseler hoped to manufacture it, or at least much of it, but the sponsoring Luftwaffe had other ideas. They envisioned the mass production of these "vengeance weapons" by none other than the Volkswagen factory, for the V-1 was designed to be simply made of sheet steel. The idea was welcomed by the Porsche personnel, whose goal was to bring the high-value production of complete aircraft to Fallersleben. This was a small but promising start.

Getting the V-1 into production was another matter altogether. The Porsche and Fieseler engineers went back and forth over problems and their solutions;

The huge press shop in Hall 2 was fully equipped when the conflict began. Instead of making panels for Beetles it was retooled to stamp out parts for a variety of products, including the lethal V-1 flying bomb.

spot-welding that worked for cars didn't always keep a V-1's fuselage intact under the stress of launch and flight. Yet the Nazis craved urgent mass production of this underdeveloped forerunner of the cruise missile. Its accuracy was so poor, thought one Luftwaffe officer, that thirty thousand per month would need to be launched to cow the British into abandoning the war.

The struggle continued throughout 1943 to reach production-readiness for this radical new weapon. By September, 1,453 workers — mostly Germans, for security reasons — were dedicated to V-1 production at Fallersleben. In March 1944 series manufacture began and in mid-June of that year, just after the Allied landing at Normandy, V-1s began to be launched against England.

The KdF works was the prime contractor for V-1 production. The tail assemblies were made in the Vorwerk, the hulls and engine nacelles on two parallel assembly lines in its main plant. The wings, pulse-jet engines, and guidance systems were outsourced. As dictated by the war situation the works decentralized manufacturing for many components. Much of the final assembly took place near each missile's firing point.

THE V-1 CONTRACT BROUGHT THE Volkswagenwerk substantial business volume. Of some 31,000 V-1s made during the war, Volkswagen was responsible for 19,500, the lion's share. The V-1 brought something much less desirable as well: the attention of the Allied forces' target selectors. A failed attempt in late 1943 to involve the Peugeot works in Montbe-

A portion of a wing in the right foreground suggests that this was some of the dam-age wreaked on Hall 1 in April 1944 when a disabled British Lancaster crashed with a full bomb load aboard.

liard, France, in producing components for the 1114, as the VW people code-named the Fi 103, allowed some of its secrets to leak to the Allied side, including the key role of Fallersleben in its production.

This disclosure contributed to the previously obscure factory's designation as an important bombing target by the Allies. Earlier raids had been desultory. In mid-1940 Hall 1 was hit by a few small bombs that caused little damage and another raid that November did more damage to the nearby forest. Some bombs fell near the foundry in the summer of 1943 but caused no damage.

In 1944 the scale and accuracy of attack escalated. On 8 April, KdF-Stadt and its factory were visited by 56 aircraft from the U.S. Eighth Air Force, which dropped 146 tons of bombs from twenty thousand feet, damaging the roofs of Halls 2, 3, and 4 and hitting the railway lines and a transformer. A supply of timber went up in flames. Casualties included 13 killed and 40 wounded.

Missed by this raid, Hall 1, the tool and die shop making mines, took a bizarre random hit on 29 April when a disabled British Lancaster bomber crashed through its roof complete with its bomb load. Hall 1 was comprehensively defenestrated by the resulting explosions and its floor was penetrated in two places. The plane's RAF crew, who had bailed out, were rounded up by members of the plant's antiaircraft unit.

Left:

A *high-altitude view of the KdF works shows the Mittelland Canal running east–west and, south of it, the beginnings of KdF-Stadt. Open countryside surrounds the plant with the village of Fallersleben at the edge of the photo to the west.*

Below:

Fallersleben's production of flying bombs attracted the attention of the Allied target selectors, who produced this detailed view of the works in April 1944. Their identification of factory operations was impressively accurate.

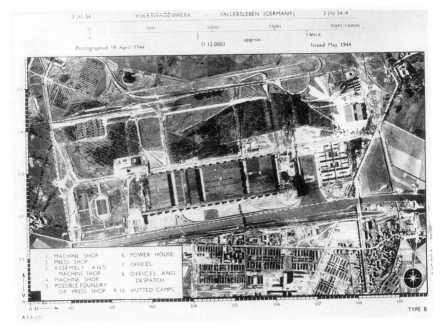

An air reconnaissance photo taken the following day showed the final appearance of the KdF works after the Allied bomb attack on 5 August 1944. The works looks badly damaged — but it will rise to fight again another day.

More air attacks came on 20 and 29 June and 5 August, delivering in all 675 tons of explosives. The first of these was the largest, with 137 B-17s dropping 130 one-ton high-explosive bombs over Fallersleben in four waves. The second June raid, richly equipped with incendiaries, caused a temporary power cut by disabling one generator turbine. The June raids killed 35 and wounded 107. Nevertheless the V-1 attack on Britain was already well launched; the two-thousandth firing took place on the day of the second June raid.

The final attack on 5 August was flown by 85 American B-24s. This was scheduled after "one plant, Fallersleben, had been firmly associated with the assembly of flying bomb fuselages. [Air Intelligence] recommended that this alone should be accorded the highest priority and that seventeen other plants believed to be associated with other stages of V-1 production should be treated as low priority targets."

The August attack was precautionary — after the June raids the Allies knew that "the damage inflicted led the Germans to transfer [Fallersleben's] flying bomb assembly plant to safer quarters." Production of powered fuselages for V-1s continued at the works in June and July; in August the tooling for the main components was transported sixty miles due south to the multipurpose Central Works near Nordhausen, a mammoth underground factory bored deep beneath the rock of the Kohnstein mountain range.

The move to Nordhausen was the result of a direct appeal from Ferdinand Porsche to SS leader Heinrich Himmler for a more protected site for production of the V-1, which still enjoyed Hitler's personal backing. When one deals with the Devil, however, one must accept the consequences. The shift meant a reduction in the authority of the Porsche/Lafferentz/Piëch troika and their on-site engineer, Josef Aengeneydt, in favor of the SS and Albert Speer's designated czar for V-weapon production, Gerhard Degenkolb.

By the beginning of November the Volkswagen team had reestablished V-1 production at the Nordhausen Central Works, now the nexus of a supply network of sixteen widely dispersed subcontractors. One was the plant at Fallersleben, which in spite of the damage it suffered could still account for 35.4 percent of V-1 fuselage production in 1945.

Compared to the elaborate V-2, the pulse-jet-powered V-1 was a weapon of moderate cost; the selling price to the Luftwaffe was five thousand marks apiece. This was very valuable trade for the Volkswagen works. Its total business turnover in 1944 was RM 290 million, of which the V-1 accounted for fully RM 100 million. Conditions worsened in 1945, when subcontractor Fallersleben began complaining to main contractor Central Works about its slow and partial renderings of payments due.

Low cost was one criterion for an assignment that the Luftwaffe gave the Porsche office for an improvement to the V-1: the design of a small jet engine to increase its speed and range. Speed was necessary because the Allied fighters, especially the Hawker Typhoon and later the jet-engined Meteor, were getting fast enough to keep pace with it in level flight. Range was needed because the invading Allies were steadily pushing back the V-1's firing bases and increasing the distance to prime-target London.

For this prestigious assignment the Porsche men reached well ahead of their current project numbers to award the magic Type 300. Success would be critical to keep the V-1 generating income. Competition was growing from the steadily improving V-2 and its long-range derivatives being promoted by the Wernher von Braun design team.

The jet-engine design itself "presented very little difficulty," Ferry Porsche recalled, "but there was a condition attached which turned the whole project into a nightmare. Our design had to be of such low cost that the loss or destruction of the bomb after only one flight would not add much to the war budget."

With a nine-stage axial compressor, the little jet was to propel the flying bomb at a 500-mph clip and extend the V-1's range to 310 miles. Air-cooled steel blades were specified for its turbine. Some laboratory tests were conducted but no Type 300 jet engine was completed before the invading Americans captured the drawings and pieces.

Production lost to Nordhausen was made up by Fallersleben in the last months of the war by adding the fabrication of subassemblies for the Focke-Wulf Ta 154 warplane and rushed mass production of the highly effective handheld *Panzerfaust* antitank weapon, a copy of America's bazooka. Three and a half million were made in the 1944–45 winter. Plans to make parts for

To help beat the drum for the continued sale of savings coupons, the first Beetles produced in the Fallersleben factory were photographed and promoted with suitable fanfare. They are pictured inside the still-pristine works.

other aircraft, including the new Messerschmitt Me 262 twin-jet fighter, ended with the general internal collapse of Germany in 1945.

ALMOST AS AN AFTERTHOUGHT, the Fallersleben plant also made Volkswagens. Before the war began in earnest only fifty-one Volkswagens of the final design had been built. All were hand-tooled and fabricated by Porsche and Daimler-Benz at a cost per copy said to be "about as much as a Rolls-Royce." They were used as development, press, show, and display vehicles and as toys for the Nazi elite. One, a rare cabriolet, was the factory's gift to Adolf Hitler. Ley and Göring were also presented with cabriolets, the model best suited to glorious public display.

Now it was Fallersleben's turn. One 1940 plan had called for it to ramp up to monthly production of 7,000 cars at the end of the first year. Three years after the end of the war, the planners forecast, output could reach 24,000 KdF-Wagens monthly. With the war on, this was not achievable. But any sign of automotive life at the factory would be psychologically important to a management and workforce that were doing all they could to convince the Nazi leadership that the Fallersleben plant deserved continued investment so that it could meet its commitments to the loyal DAF savers as soon as possible.

By combining the capabilities of a branch plant in Brunswick with those at Fallersleben, it finally became possible to produce Beetles in 1941 in spite

By August 1941 the Fallersleben factory had labored to bring forth 6 Type 60 Volkswagens — the first to be produced there. The factory would produce 630 such cars during the war years.

of the failure of some of the specialized American machine tools to arrive. The first KdF-Wagen made at Fallersleben left the production line on 11 July 1941; five more were completed in August. These first half-dozen cars were proudly grouped, with appropriately celebratory signs and banners, for the Reich's propaganda photographers.

KdF-Wagens produced during the war were sold not for their widely mooted price of RM 990 but for eight times as much: RM 8,000 apiece for the 41 cars made in 1941. The price fell to RM 4,614 in 1942, when 157 were made, plus four chassis for conversion to cabriolets. By 1944 the price was down to a nominal three thousand marks.

In all, 630 civilian VWs were made to Porsche's KdF-Wagen design at Fallersleben between the beginning of slow series production in 1941 and its termination on 17 August 1944, less than two weeks after the fourth and final bombing of the plant. These rare and much-admired Beetles served as wartime transport for Nazi party functionaries, allocated to the *Gau* leaders and others in the hierarchy. Many were used for development purposes by key members of the Porsche office. Prototypes and early production cars alike were driven by German-Americans without whose expertise the factory could not have been set up: Fritz Kuntze, Joe Werner, and Hans Mayr.

The man who had catalyzed the relationship between Hitler and Porsche, Jakob Werlin, was not forgotten. Neither were such key Nazis as Robert Ley and Albert Speer. A car from 1942 production was allocated to Emperor Hirohito as a gift from German foreign minister Joachim von Ribbentrop. Some of the early Beetles also served to cement business relations. When Ferdinand Porsche gave one to Willy Messerschmitt in November of 1943 it was to remind the great aircraft designer of Fallersleben's production capabilities.

CONTRARY TO MANY accounts that suggest that Fallersleben segued smoothly into wartime vehicle production, a surprisingly long time lapsed before attention turned to a military version of the Beetle. Such a vehicle had been in the mind of many since 1935, when Hitler introduced conscription and scrapped the name *Reichswehr* for his armed forces in favor of *Wehrmacht* (defense force), of which the *Heer* or army became a constituent. Within the army decisions about new vehicles were made by the *Heereswaffenamt* (HWA) or Army Weapons Office.

Motorization was a priority for the new Wehrmacht, its leaders proclaimed, and the HWA had already made up its mind about the kinds of vehicles it required. It looked favorably on rear-wheel drive, four-wheel drive, and rugged solid axles. For general troop-carrying and field service its vehicles were open-topped with bucket or *Kübel* seats that let fully equipped troops jump easily in and out. Such a vehicle was a "bucket-seat car" or *Kübelsitzwagen*, referred to simply as a *Kübelwagen*, whatever its make or size.

In the last years of peacetime the Reich had sought to persuade Germany's carmakers to simplify their model ranges. As well as improving production economies, such streamlining would create more robust and reliable vehicles for use by the military. "In 1936, therefore, the Reich Ministry of Economics repeatedly demanded of the Vehicle Industry Economic Group that it implement comprehensive and thorough measures to rationalize its ranges of types. The auto industry's readiness to do this was substantially influenced by its awareness that the needs of the military were strong enough for it to impose incisive measures against the wishes of the industry."

Thus quasi-voluntarily the industry set about this task, led by the chairman of the RDA's economic group, Ernst Hagemeier of the Adler motor company. From the forty-six model ranges being produced by the ten German automakers, not including Volkswagen, Hagemeier proposed a cutback to thirty-four. This sparked lively internal debate in the industry, especially from Daimler-Benz, which felt that the smaller makers had been allowed to keep too many models and that it had been docked too many by the hapless Hagemeier.

However, the industry was reminded by Carl Hahn of Auto Union that it should make every effort to agree on its own: "If the industry doesn't put forward adequate proposals, it will then ensue compulsorily that from the top down mandatory measures will be adopted that will have a much more uncomfortable outcome than if we take care of them ourselves. A development in parallel, as resulted in the question of the Volkswagen, should be avoided in any case." Hahn was reminding his colleagues that they had paid a heavy price — the creation of a strong new state-backed rival — for their earlier failure to agree in the RDA on a people's car plan.

Nevertheless, they could not so agree. Their competitive spirit was too great to allow them to give up models that they thought secured important market segments. As well, the increasing military procurement had brought a bloom to the cheeks of some of the smaller auto firms that had seemed on their last legs. Thus when Hermann Göring implemented his latest four-year plan in 1938 he named an army officer as the General Plenipotentiary for Motor Vehicles and gave him the power to sort out the automakers.

Col. Adolf von Schell was no novice in the field. In 1937 he had visited Detroit to study America's industry; when empowered by Göring he was already the HWA's chief of weaponry for armored vehicles, the cavalry, and army motorization. On taking office near the end of 1938 von Schell immediately barred any new vehicle development work and any new launch of a product range that his department had not approved. Also, sensibly enough, he turned to the auto industry again to ask them to agree on a program for slashing the numbers of their existing models.

Now the carmakers had to set seriously to work. They managed to get acceptance for a plan that gave them twenty-seven models, not including those made in the eastern occupied territories. Most blessed were Auto Union with seven models, Daimler-Benz with six, and Opel with four. But before the cuts could be implemented the even more draconian needs of the war economy intervened. In wartime, Germany's car ranges were officially cut to five: two for Auto Union and one each for Daimler-Benz, Ford, and Stoewer. The KdF-Werke wasn't mentioned.

THE STOEWER WORKS IN STETTIN was one of a number of smaller companies that had been kept alive by Germany's need to rearm. Stoewer designed and produced a vehicle for the army's lightest four-wheeled category, a channel-framed vehicle with both steering and drive to all four wheels. It was proudly displayed at the 1936 Berlin Auto Show.

This was supposed to be Uniform Chassis I for light passenger vehicles under the army's own internal vehicle rationalization program, but Stoewer's limited production capability meant that BMW and Hanomag had to tool up to make similar vehicles from 1936 to 1940. These naturally used many of their own engine and chassis parts so the notion of uniformity, meant to reduce production cost and ease service in the field, was honored more in the breach than in the observance.

Light vehicles were in use by the German army which in fact had proved their value in service in World War I: motorcycles with and without sidecars. "As a result when the Reichswehr was reorganized as of 1927, [the motorcycle's] range of use in reconnaissance, communication, and supply units and in tactical service was expanded considerably. Cycles with armed soldiers were soon organized into their own cycle companies as very-fast-moving attack units. When the Wehrmacht was organized in 1935, the motorcycle riflemen became a service arm of their own."

In this environment Porsche's Volkswagen was viewed askance by Hitler's armed services in the late 1930s. The rear engine was not regarded as an advantage; a *Kübelsitzwagen* version of the rear-engined Mercedes-Benz 130 had been hugely disappointing in the many off-road sporting events organized by the Nazis' National Socialist Motoring Corps (NSKK). The VW's lack of generous ground clearance was another fundamental drawback.

In the meantime, in 1937, the thirty Beetles in the first prototype series were racking up the miles on road tests in Germany. Under the supervision of Ferry Porsche the cars were test-driven by members of the SS. The SS men couldn't help falling under the spell of this newfangled automobile.

Encouraged by these beguiled SS motorists, the Porsche/GEZUVOR test workshop under Rudolf Ringel modified a test Beetle to improve its off-road mobility. Special tires were fitted and the ramp angles at both front and rear were increased by shifting the spare wheel and muffler upward. Tests from December 1937 showed that this made the little car quite agile across country.

The modified Bug was seen in action by an HWA officer, who approved the effort to extract "as much as possible for military application from the existing vehicle." But in January 1938 he wasn't able to make much more of a commitment than that to Porsche, simply pointing out that a military version would need much lighter bodywork if it were to be capable of carrying four troops plus all their equipment — a desirable objective.

Considerably more enthusiasm was generated at the higher levels of the SS that same January when the leader of the test cadre at Porsche, Hauptsturmführer Albert Liese, proselytized on behalf of the Beetle's military utility to Obergruppenführer Josef "Sepp" Dietrich. An intimate of Hitler's, the influential Dietrich could see the merits of the low profile of the VW, its light weight and, particularly, its potential for low cost which would facilitate a rapid conversion of Germany's military to more modern vehicles when the war started.

"Even if Dietrich led the negotiations with the Volkswagen works primarily to ventilate his resentments over the conservatism of the HWA, he supported the Porsche concept particularly on the grounds of technical modernization and thereby contributed substantially to the development of a long-term cooperation among the SS, the Volkswagen Works, and Porsche." Thus did Dietrich and his SS intervene in the fortunes of a military version of the budding Beetle.

A dollop of fertilizer for this flowering relationship was spread by Ferry Porsche in his stewardship of the prototype testing. At first, he said, he looked on the thirty SS drivers sent to him as snoops and spies:

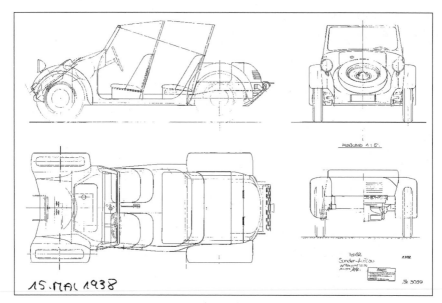

On 15 May 1938 the Porsche office completed a design for a sketchy military body on the VW38 chassis; it was commissioned two days later from Reutter. Although promising in tests, it lacked ground clearance and was called too "civilian" by the army.

Every little detail, each day, had to be recorded, and at first this was intolerable and struck me as quite absurd. It was often difficult for me to contain my anger. But after a while I discovered that few of those SS men were stupid thugs. Some could be approached and spoken to. Some would listen and a few even approved of our own suggestions about testing and performance evaluation.

His forbearance at a crucial juncture was to be richly repaid. In addition to the rest of his work on the VW project, Ferry became closely involved with the development and testing of the military versions of the Type 60.

A NOD FROM DIETRICH WAS enough to launch a project to design a warlike Beetle. On 1 February 1938 the HWA asked the Porsche office to design a military-body version of the Type 60; Porsche allocated it project Type 62. That it had a different type number indicated that it was to be a different vehicle; simple body variants on the standard chassis had K numbers for *Karosserie* (bodywork), such as the Type 60 K10 for the streamlined sports versions of the VW built for the aborted 1940 race over Axis roads from Berlin to Rome.

Before receiving the official go-ahead, the SS troops and the GEZUVOR workshop at Zuffenhausen — also the site of Porsche's research and development facility — built a crude Kübelwagen that consisted of little more than a VW platform frame with angled-sheet fenders, three bucket seats on

A cobbled-up prototype built on a redundant prototype platform, this pseudomilitary vehicle was nicknamed the Stuka after the famous dive-bomber. It showed the enthusiasm that many felt for the potential of the VW for military use.

the floor, and a mount for a massive machine gun. This resembled more a breadboard feasibility study than a serious proposal.

The actual Porsche design proposal, pictured in a Karl Rabe layout drawing of 15 May 1938, presented a distinctly civilian aspect with its rounded fenders and engine cover and luxurious pleated-leather bench seats. No Kübelwagen here! A clue to the reason for this may be that project Type 62 dated from 1936, according to the official Porsche project list. This suggests that the number was assigned quite early to what the project list calls an "off-road vehicle."

In 1936 the Porsche people were considering a version of their new small car that would be suitable for the off-road trials promoted by the NSKK. These popular and well-publicized events would have helped spread the word about the capabilities of the VW-to-be. The car they actually built as the Type 62 looked ideally suited to that application, its body details modified to suit the final chassis design.

An alternative body was built in 1938–39 to suit the same chassis. This was a low, aggressive-looking, and exiguous vehicle whose side-mounted spare wheels fooled some commentators into calling it a six-wheeled prototype. Nicknamed the *Stuka* after the dive bomber famous for its pugnacious looks, its appearance was as militaristic as Porsche's

Type 62 was civilian. The Stuka took part in comparison tests with the Type 62 and other vehicles.

The body of the official Type 62 was commissioned on 17 May 1938 from Porsche's traditional coachworks, Reutter of Stuttgart. The spare wheel was inset into the hood and the car's sides were completely open; a few straps were deployed to keep its occupants from spilling out. This prototype was ready for presentation to the HWA on 3 November 1938. Its kinship with the Beetle was apparent in the shape of its windshield and its rounded lines.

The army put the Type 62 to the test at its Münsingen Troop Training Grounds that same November, pitting it against one of the Class I military 4x4 vehicles. The Porsche people brought along a Beetle prototype for comparison. The open-topped Beetle fared well enough, although the army assessors thought it looked too "civilian" and asked for more "military elements" in its design.

While further tests were conducted on the first Type 62, the Porsche engineers produced a more militarized version. This Type 62 K1 kept the rounded fenders and recessed spare tire but had a more angular main body made of flat sheet steel ribbed for stiffness. One version resembled the first in having open sides with canvas doors; another had proper doors with side screens. The car with open sides was commandeered by the DAF's Robert Ley in October 1939 for a tour of Poland.

Tests of this new type, in comparison to two of the standard army vehicles at St. Johann in the Tyrol in March 1939, showed it to be promising but still lacking the ample ground clearance needed for military duty. Eighteen-inch wheels were fitted to increase the clearance but succeeded only in creating another problem — they raised the car's overall gear ratio when what was actually wanted was lower gearing.

A different ring gear and pinion were tried in the Type 62 to give a lower axle ratio, but with a pinion that was too small this was a major and risky departure from the standard VW design. Ferry Porsche explained the problem:

> You had to be able to go at about the walking speed of a soldier carrying his full backpack, so that he could keep pace with the vehicle. This was about 4 km/h (2.5 mph). Thus there was one serious drawback to overcome. Low gear in the regular transmission produced about 8 km/h (5 mph). This was adequate for civilian use but too high a speed for cross-country military purposes.

Porsche's solution was typically ingenious. A pair of reduction gears was installed at each rear-wheel hub, thereby raising the vehicle by five centimeters and reducing the gear ratio to give more pulling power at a lower road speed. The hub reduction gears had a ratio of 1.40:1, which combined with the standard final-drive ratio of 4.43:1 gave an overall ratio of 6.20:1. The front axles were modified to raise the ground clearance there as well.

Now the Porsche engineers were on their way toward a completely new vehicle design and accordingly awarded the VW-derived Kübel project a new

The first prototype series of the definitive Type 82 Kübelwagen was produced at Porsche's handsome new R&D center at Zuffenhausen in northern Stuttgart. It still serves as the Porsche headquarters.

number in 1939: Type 82. Another year was destined to pass after the presentation of the Type 62 before the first two samples of the Type 82 were formally accepted by the Army High Command in December 1939.

This new version reverted to sixteen-inch wheels for which tires were more readily available. Now the engine was idling at 780 rpm at the required walking pace of 2.5 mph, so Ferry's goal was successfully achieved. At 3,300 rpm in top gear the Type 82's maximum speed was 80 km/h or 50 mph.

There was no doubt about the new vehicle's military bearing. It had square-rigged, corrugated, high-sided coachwork built by Ambi-Budd in Berlin to Porsche's designs. Its spare wheel rested on top of a sloped hood, simplifying the body. A serviceable top and good side screens were provided. A version of the standard Type 60 speedometer was placed centrally, surrounded by warning lights.

A key decision was to fit the vehicle with doors. With doors keeping the soldiers inside, tight-fitting bucket seats were no longer needed. Flat front seats and a wide bench rear seat could be used instead, offering more flexible carrying capacity. It also rendered the Kübel nickname completely inappropriate — but it stuck.

THE PORSCHE MEN DEPLOYED several secret weapons in the design of the Type 82 that contributed to its military success. One was lightness. The original Type 60 Beetle of 1938 had a design weight of 1,510 pounds; ready for the road it weighed 1,544 pounds unfueled. Compar ed with the small passenger cars offered by Adler (1,808 pounds), DKW (1,720 pounds), and Opel (1,698 pounds), its lightness helped the civilian VW gain a power-to-weight advantage over these rivals.

The same philosophy helped the Type 82 shine compared to the heavy Class I military vehicles. Rigorously controlling weight in every aspect of the military Beetle, the Porsche engineers brought this version in at the same design weight as its sedan counterpart, 1,510 pounds. At 1,600 pounds, with all its skid plates and other battle fittings, it weighed only 3.6 percent more than the road-ready civilian car. This was an astounding accomplishment, even given the Type 82's open bodywork.

Another secret weapon in the car's design was its limited-slip differential developed by the ZF company. This unique device used a central cage to drive a ring of sliding pawls which engaged wavy-cam surfaces that drove each of the rear-wheel axle shafts. When one drive wheel started to slip and spin, friction in the unit rapidly built up and began transmitting driving traction to the wheel that wasn't spinning — the one that had a better grip on the ground.

The Porsche office exploited its early access to this ZF invention, first in a passenger car it was designing and then, in 1936, on the Auto Union racing cars. In these they gained an advantage on rival Mercedes-Benz until the Stuttgart firm caught on to what they were doing. It was only natural that Porsche would use the ZF limited-slip differential to help compensate for their Type 82's lack of four-wheel drive.

As a form of protection for the future of the project, four-wheel drive was also explored. This was done under Porsche's Type 87 designation, work on which continued into 1941. A driveshaft was taken forward from the front end of the secondary or output shaft of the gearbox to axle gears between the front wheels.

The front-axle gearing was given a drive ratio of 6.20:1 in order to match the gearing at the front to the double-reduction ratio at the rear wheels. In a clever design tweak, Porsche used hypoid gearing for its ring and pinion. This allowed the pinion to be offset upward from the center of the ring gear, helping to improve ground clearance at the front. Some Type 87 versions had self-locking front differentials.

Also added to the Type 87 was an extra-low gear for off-road use, controlled by a supplementary lever. Pushing the lever one notch forward engaged front-wheel drive, allowing four-wheel drive in all four normal forward speeds. Pushing the lever forward to the second notch engaged the extra-low gear as well. Thus extra-low was only available when the Type 87 was operating in 4 x 4 mode.

In wartime Fallersleben produced 667 vehicles with the Type 60 body atop a four-wheel-drive chassis. They resembled the vehicle shown, which was assembled after the war under the British occupation of the works.

Two Type 87s were tested by the army in February 1940 along with a wide range of other vehicles including trucks. They were driven south from the Berlin Kummersdorf test ground to the winter test site in the Tyrolean Alps at St. Johann, the town reputed to be the coldest in the region. "The two Type 86 [sic] vehicles attracted much interest from all the factory and Army drivers present on account of their speed, manoeuvrability and good road-holding on the icy superhighways and country roads," according to one account. A report by Porsche of 5 April 1940 on the Tyrolean trials elaborated:

> The Wünsdorf Test Centre is in general very enthusiastic about our vehicles. In the prevailing slippery ground conditions in the mountains, for example, our four-wheel-drive Types 86 and 87 cars without snow chains were vastly superior to the Army Uniform Personnel Car. For example, our Type 87 climbed the approximately 25-degree slope of the Hungerberg without trouble, while the wheels of the Uniform Car began to skid after a stretch of about 30 metres. Even our Type 82 with snow chains was better than the Uniform Car without chains, since the Uniform Car, with its inherent weight of 1,700 kg, reached its wheel limits too quickly despite its off-road gears.

THE REMARKABLE CAPABILITY OF THE two-wheel-driven Type 82 had been confirmed back in January of 1940 by army winter tests in Eisenach involving both versions of the military Beetle. The traditional Class I Uniform Chassis was a tough competitor, however. The first wartime production plan for vehicles, intended to take effect on New Year's Day of 1940, provided for very limited production from Fallersleben: a paltry two hundred Kübels a month.

Germany's entire motor industry was desperate in 1940. The army seemed uncertain about its vehicle needs in both qualitative and quantitative terms, not surprisingly in view of Hitler's fast-changing priorities for

After many false starts, production of the Type 82 for the German army began at Fallersleben in the spring of 1940. At last the huge factory was undertaking a task resembling that for which it had been built.

fronts on which to fight. Meanwhile, the carmakers' workforces were being gnawed away by conscription.

One of the most frustrated carmakers, in view of the proven performance excellence of his light and low-cost military vehicle, was Ferry Porsche. Tests had shown the clear advantage of the Type 82 over the heavy Class I Uniform Chassis, but no decisions were being made on the basis of this unambiguous evidence, wrote the younger Porsche:

> Weeks went by in this way, and I finally became so annoyed that I openly proposed we take a VW Kübelwagen and run it hard for several more weeks, under all conditions, against the "Jeep" designed by the Military Supply Office [HWA]. The offer was accepted, and far from weakening our case, the test decisively broke the deadlock in our favor. The Kübelwagen under many conditions came off better than the military version. But still the military held back giving us clearance to manufacture . . .

The Type 82 in its final form was featured, with the sedan and a display chassis, at the 1940 Vienna Spring Exhibition. The HWA was thawing, albeit slowly. Pilot production was cautiously launched at Porsche's Stuttgart plant with twenty-five units in April and thereafter with one hundred built in May at Fallersleben. In June, when two hundred were made, deliveries commenced to the army, which paid RM 2,945 for each of its Type 82s.

So slow was Kübel production at first that the thousandth was not completed until December 1940. Production was stepped up after reports of the vehicle's success in the field.

This early production "involved mostly an assembly job, the line occupying a small portion of the huge factory. Joe Werner's shop was producing the engine-transmission, but the rest of the vehicle was shipped in from suppliers. The foundry was still not finished so castings came from a supplier in the nearby Harz Mountains."

Joseph Werner was one of a handful of German-American engineers whom Porsche had recruited in Detroit in the 1930s to help mass-produce the KdF-Wagen. Werner had worked at Ford and he knew the art and science of volume production, especially for engines. So his instructions on the Kübelwagen job were especially frustrating: "I was ordered to build no special tools and not to make the mistake of having any tooling left over for use in building KdF-Wagens when we finished the 'jeep' order."

There was as yet no demand for hordes of Kübels; the thousandth car was not built until 20 December 1940. Of course, Germany still expected the war to be over soon. The cover of the KdF magazine in May 1941 showed a Type 82 in front of Sicilian temple ruins with an inset view of a peacetime KdF-Wagen, the headline "He too drives against England," and a caption:

> Mr. Churchill would certainly never have dreamed that so soon he would again meet the KdF-Wagen, which his radio broadcasts long ago consigned to the

In spite of its lack of four-wheel drive, the Kübel proved to be amazingly agile under the difficult conditions of Germany's eastern front with Russia. Its lightness and toughness were in its favor.

graveyard. With unshakeable confidence in "their KdF-Wagen" hundreds of thousands of citizens continue saving, hoping to receive them soon after the war ends victoriously.

Military interest in the little vehicle began to grow after the Germans invaded Russia in mid-1941. The original Uniform Chassis I for light army vehicles had been replaced by a new design in 1940, now made exclusively by Stoewer. Under the challenging conditions of the Russian Front, the Stoewer vehicle exhibited "severe defects in the frame, wheel suspension, clutch, driveshaft, steering, etc."

In contrast, VW Kübels, just becoming available in Russia, performed much better. As a result on 1 November 1941 an army report stated: "All special designs of the Wehrmacht in the realm of wheeled motor vehicles were weeded out . . . and, specifically, special designs for the Light Uniform Passenger Vehicle were replaced by the VW (two- and four-wheel drive)."

Before this decision could be reached the army set one more test for the military Beetle, one they were confident it would fail. They sent two samples to the North African desert, where the HWA and the Uniform Chassis builders were certain the Bugs would simply sink into the sand and never be seen again.

"If they proved right," Ferry Porsche reflected, "this ordeal would do us serious damage and cause Hitler's men to lose confidence in our capabilities. Our detractors were to be deeply disappointed, however. The military ver-

Completed Kübels began queuing up on the main drive south of the works as war production accelerated. Yet their production was still a minority activity for the huge Fallersleben factory.

sion of the Volkswagen performed without giving the least trouble, despite the desert heat, the sand and the brutally rough strains imposed on them. They seemed, on the contrary, to thrive on this kind of treatment!"

The final triumph of the Type 82 was affirmed on 19 March 1942 by a Hitler decree that gave Volkswagen a monopoly on the production of light military vehicles. In his table conversation among friends on 9 April Hitler elaborated on his thinking.

> For military reasons, a limitation of the German auto production to ten or twelve types after the war would be appropriate, in order to direct the genius of our inventors toward a far-reaching simplification of engines . . . The most important factor, though, would be the creation of a uniform engine that could be installed in field kitchens as well as ambulances, and also in reconnaissance vehicles, tractors, and towing vehicles for heavy infantry guns. The 28 horsepower motor of the Volkswagen would be quite sufficient for these military purposes. The uniform engine to be striven for . . . would have to be easily changeable, since — as this war is teaching us — the supplying of spare parts causes more trouble than taking an intact engine out of a vehicle with a damaged chassis.

Production now shifted up a gear; in 1942 the delivery of the five thousandth Kübel was celebrated. At that time its price to the army was RM 3,457. Production had been flat through most of 1941; it began to rise late in the year and kept climbing well into 1944. Tropical battle zones opened up to the versatile Kübel after proving trials were conducted successfully in occupied Afghanistan and Greece.

PORSCHE'S CONSUMMATE ADAPTATION of the Type 60 to wartime use was his amphibian version, the *Schwimmwagen* (swimming car). Its first iteration bore Type number 128. This was built in response to an army

Ferry Porsche is at the wheel while his colleagues discuss the maritime capability of the first prototype of the Type 128, being tested at the end of September 1940 in Stuttgart's Max Eyth Reservoir.

order issued on 1 July 1940, following up on an initial request prepared on 18 June. Issued by the HWA, the order made RM 200,000 available for this project. The amphibian was to be able to achieve 10 km/h (6 mph) in the water and its transition from water to land was to be achieved without the occupants having to leave the vehicle.

With remarkable speed Ferry Porsche's team adapted the 4x4 Type 87 platform to this new application. Its sides were high and there were, of course, no doors. The HWA had already made this generous concession. Porsche fitted watertight seals to the axles and speedometer-cable aperture and added an engine-driven propeller at the rear. Simply enough, the front wheels would act as rudders when turned, foreseen by the HWA in its guidance to Porsche. Watertight material covered the cables of the mechanical brakes.

Shortly after its completion on 21 September 1940, the first Type 128 plunged into Stuttgart's Max Eyth Reservoir in a bend of the Neckar River east of Zuffenhausen with Ferry Porsche at the wheel and four colleagues checking for leaks. It worked well enough, but it needed a healthy push from those colleagues and more to get it up the muddy bank and out of the reservoir.

The army's HWA lost no time in putting these first 128s to the test after it received them in early November. For six weeks they were driven on Autobahns, across country, on minor roads, and in the water in comparison with a front-engined amphibian that had been under development for six years by Hanns Trippel (most recently at the former Bugatti factory at Molsheim) and, incredibly, one of the Light Uniform Chassis vehicles swathed in a watertight linen covering.

"During this testing the vehicles covered between 3,207 and 3,496 km, 1,400 km on the Autobahn, 1,270 on roads, 180 km in rough country, 200 km in very rough country and 300 km on very rough mountain roads. Every vehicle spent 18 hours in the water." These figures did not apply to the linen-covered Uniform Chassis amphibian, which "was constantly defective and dropped out as unusable in the first water and off-road tests."

While waterborne the fuel economy of the Type 128 was an astonishing three times better than that of the Trippel; landborne it was twice as economical. They were similar in terms of road speed and the VW derivative was faster in the water at six versus five miles per hour. Even better, the air-cooled VW could maintain its peak water velocity for an hour while the water-cooled Opel Kapitän engine of the Trippel merely boiled over.

After this successful test debut the HWA approved the building of a pre-series of thirty Type 128s in 1941 for further tests and evaluation. But the speed with which this could be achieved would depend on the priority level granted to the project. Ferdinand Porsche seized the opportunity to ask for a higher priority when he presented the Type 128 to Hitler and General Field Marshal and Army Chief of Staff Wilhelm Keitel at the Berlin Chancellery.

"The Führer thought that this was do-able in view of the small quantities involved," wrote Porsche afterward in an aide mémoire, "and with respect to this he turned to General Field Marshal Keitel, who gave the assurance that he would make the 'special level' [of priority] available to the Schwimmwagen." Porsche reminded Keitel that in ordering materials for the Type 128 he was already operating at priority "special level" SS; the Nazis escalated priorities by adding new and more urgent levels at the top of the range as and when needed.

The priorities were secured and the 128s were built. The army's Wünsdorf proving grounds was the site for more trials in May and June. In August three of the pre-series cars traipsed 1,600 miles through the Alps. The testers said that this trip "demonstrated to us as never before the Type 128's extraordinary off-road capability when driven sensibly. We drove on paths that had never before seen a motor vehicle, and the total weight always amounted to almost half a ton."

ONE COULD REGARD 1941 EITHER as a year of essential trials or as a year of lost opportunity for the amphibian Volkswagen. But in the spring the project was given a sharp shove forward by the SS, aided by the quick thinking of Ferry Porsche. Thanks to his timely suggestion during a meeting in Stuttgart, Himmler's elite military staff seized on the versatile amphibian as a replacement for the motorcycles with sidecars used by its mobile guard units.

Motorcycles were proving unequal to the demands of modern warfare in difficult terrain. The utility of BMW, NSU, and Zündapp motorcycles in

As finally released for military service in May 1942, the Type 166 Schwimmwagen was one of the most versatile and capable light vehicles produced during the war. It was inspired by the need of the SS for a replacement for the motorcycle and sidecar.

the easy conditions of Hitler's first campaigns in West Europe was undisputed. But in Poland and Africa, where roads were poor or nonexistent, they fared poorly. To cap the argument against them, the motorcycles cost more than their VW-based counterpart, at least in Type 82 form.

From Africa a German repair facility reported to headquarters as follows: "In the light of recent experience, motorcycles are most unsuitable for the desert and are the type of wheeled vehicle that appears most commonly in the workshops. There is extraordinarily high wear on pistons and cylinders. Clutches, carburettors and Bowden [cable] equipment full of sand were the order of the day."

Built on the long 2.4-meter wheelbase of the Types 60 and 82/87, the Type 128 wasn't as gainly as it needed to be to replace motorcycles. Thus a new short-wheelbase (two-meter) version was developed by Porsche as its Type 166. "We began work on the drawing board in April 1941," wrote Ferry Porsche. "By August of that year the first prototype was ready for testing." The younger Porsche was just thirty-two in the autumn of that year. "I was asked to bring this car to Hitler's headquarters for a demonstration," he said, "and he appeared to be pleased." The headquarters in question was the famous Wolf's Lair in Rastenburg, East Prussia, and the request to bring the first Type 166 there was certainly made by Heinrich Himmler, whose SS had commissioned it.

The nearby Mittelland Canal made a convenient demonstration venue for the Type 166. With their propeller drive units still tucked up behind, three Schwimmwagen prepare to take the plunge during the war.

Looking even more obsequious than usual in the presence of his Führer, nervously crushing his gloves as he sought Hitler's approval, the odious Himmler was the man on the spot at the forest presentation of Porsche's spruce amphibian with its SS license plates. Mufti-garbed Ferry showed the features of the unique car to a platoon of uniformed military leaders including Jodl of the army and Wolff of the SS.

Many features of this first Type 166 differed from the final design. A design outline was confirmed in the late autumn of 1941 and within five months the first production prototypes were ready. The Max Eyth Reservoir was again the basin for the formal baptism of the new type in March 1942.

Although more compact than the 128, the ingeniously designed 166 was fitted with a larger fuel tank and could still carry four fully equipped soldiers. In this form the *Schwimmwagen* was accepted by the HWA on 29 May 1942. Like the Type 82's, its one-piece welded body-hull was produced in Berlin by Ambi-Budd and fitted at Fallersleben. Assembly there was given the green light and by 6 June the first hundred had been completed.

Inherently buoyant, the Type 166 combined manually selected four-wheel drive with a swing-down propeller at the rear driven directly by a dog clutch and roller chain from the engine's crankshaft. Its short wheelbase, extra-low gear, and four-wheel-drive made it an even more effective off-roader than the Type 82. The German army paid RM 4,200 for each of its water Beetles.

The price paid bore little relation to the real cost of the Type 166, a car so complex that it heavily burdened the largely Italian work force that assembled it. For this reason its production was halted on 26 August 1944 in the wake of the final bombing of the factory — 14,276 had been produced, far short of the 20,900 orders that the factory had booked for this remarkable vehicle.

BECAUSE OF, YET IN SPITE OF, the exigencies of the war years the Porsche designers created a bewildering array of variants based on the Type 60 and 82 designs. Dubbed the Type 82E was a high-ground-clearance Kübel chassis carrying a KdF-Wagen body. Two were built in 1941; from 1942 to 1944, 564 of the Type 82E sedan plus two cabriolets were built. They were chiefly used by SS units to fly the flag of the Third Reich in occupied lands.

Among the most confusing of Fallersleben's wartime automobile products — and at the same time among the most interesting — were those with Beetle bodies on four-wheel-drive chassis. Dubbed the *Kommandeurwagen* or Command Car, this Beetle look-alike had the full 4x4 drivetrain under its floorboards. This brought its dry weight to 1,740 pounds, making it one of the heaviest VW derivatives of the period. Only the much more elaborate Type 166 Schwimmwagen was heavier at 2,005 pounds empty.)

The Porsche records offer a plethora of type numbers that could refer to the Command Car. Type 86 is an "all-wheel-drive VW." This doesn't sound very military and the customer was the VW factory. Type 98 is a "Type 128 chassis with KdF bodywork." That seems more like it, but again the customer was the Volkswagen Works, not the army. Then there's the Type 287, which is the "*Komandowagen* based on the Type 87" — but once more the army wasn't Porsche's customer; the VW factory was.

Yet the Type 287 sounds most like the 667 Command Cars that were produced at Fallersleben during the war. The "commander" was seated behind the driver with free space to his right; an adjutant occupied the front passenger seat with a map and writing desk that folded out into position. Rifle racks, a machine-pistol holster, and first-aid kits were built in. Floors were covered with wooden slats for service in the mud of Russia.

Output of this highly specialized Beetle was 134 units in 1942, 382 the following year, and 151 in 1944. The car looked just like the famous peacetime KdF-Wagen yet was fully equipped to cope with wartime conditions — a heady combination that granted exceptional status to any officer fortunate enough to be assigned one of these rare military Beetles.

Ordinary rear-drive Kübels had their own terrain to conquer; one attempt to improve traction on the Type 82 was to mount twin tires at the rear. Porsche went even farther with half-track-like treads driven from the rear axles in several configurations. Officially the Type 155, this was the *Schneeraupe* (snow-caterpillar) intended to cope with conditions on the Russian front. High cost and complexity blocked its production.

In 1943 another version of the wartime VW (Type 157) was given flanged steel wheels to allow it to be driven on railways. In the Type 230 project, a VW was powered by generator gas from a wood-burning plant installed under its distended nose. The only surviving sedan from the prewar production, now in the VW Museum, was once so-equipped.

In 1943 the wartime Beetle's engine was enlarged from its original 985 cc to 1,130 cc. Its cylinder bore was expanded from 70 to 75 mm while its piston stroke remained at 65 mm. Horsepower rose only from 23 1/2 to 25, but torque or pulling power was usefully improved. The larger engine was better suited to the more demanding service imposed by heavier VW variants such as the Type 166.

Such improvements ultimately benefited the Beetles built after the war. Indeed, this was the motivation, admitted Ferry Porsche, behind many of the developments he and his colleagues carried out during the conflict. "It was vital that the Volkswagen be constantly reviewed, improved and kept up to date to meet changing conditions. So, since we were not allowed to design a synchromesh transmission or a hydraulic brake system for private use, we designed them for 'military use' instead — as 'improvements' to the people's car."

Several automatic transmissions were built and tested under this cover. One was the Kreis transmission; another was the infinitely variable gearbox conceived by Dr. Josef Beier using intermeshed discs. Under Porsche Project 89, commissioned by Fallersleben, Brown Boveri in Mannheim prepared three layouts of possible Beier-type VW automatic transmissions. One variant was built and successfully tested over 16,000 miles.

Among the many other studies carried out during the war were the design of an exhaust-driven turbocharger for the VW engine; a version of the engine using the disc-type valves developed by Felix Wankel, later famous for his rotary engine; a VW Beetle with a true integral body structure; a six-wheeled off-road vehicle powered by two VW engines; a five-speed gearbox; the use of fuel injection, and versions of the VW powered by wood-generator gas, acetylene, and electricity.

Tests with alternative materials were important as well in the straitened circumstances of the German wartime economy. Trials were conducted with cast iron instead of aluminum for the VW engine crankcase and gearbox casing, but this was found to be counterproductive. The added weight at the rear overstressed other components and disastrously impaired the vehicle's handling. It marked a retrogression to the "outboard motor" weight distribution deplored by Josef Ganz and Ferdinand Porsche alike.

THE PORSCHE ORGANIZATION WAS NOT conducting all this design work out of affection for the Third Reich. Through 1941, an accounting showed that Porsche's expenditure on the design and development of the KdF-Wagen amounted to RM 8.4 million ($2.8 million), paid from various sources. On average, through the subsequent war years, Porsche was billing Volkswagen 300,000 marks monthly for engineering work or some RM 3.6 million each year, equal to $1.2 million.

In 1944 the turnover of the Porsche office reached RM 5,825,000, of which Volkswagen-related engineering accounted for more than half. Working hard for the Reich, Porsche was also rewarded well. Its staffing in 1944, by then scattered throughout Greater Germany in Gmünd, St. Valentin, and Zell am See in Austria, in Stuttgart and at Fallersleben, amounted to 588 people — 299 technical staff and a workshop force of 289.

Included in its responsibilities was Porsche's work on the successful adaptation of the VW engine to many other tasks. The engine, compact, air-cooled, and self-contained, was a hugely versatile and useful prime mover. Fallersleben made many more engines than vehicles, both as field replacements in Kübels and for stationary power applications.

With magneto ignition and a speed-control governor, the flat-four was a portable power package for generators, compressors, barrage-balloon winches, and landing-craft power. With a Roots supercharger it powered a portable cable lift for mountain transport. A flat-twin engine based on half of a VW four produced twelve horsepower for use as an auxiliary power unit for armored vehicles and as a tank-engine starter.

Tuned to thirty-two horsepower, the KdF-Wagen engine took to the air on 25 January 1944. This was the first flight of the Horten H IIIe flying wing, essentially a powered glider. Very much in its element, the Type 247 air-cooled VW engine drove the Horten's folding pusher propeller through five V-belts. One of the most beautiful of the Horten brothers' tailless creations, the H IIIe had a wingspan of 67.3 feet. It was capable of 87 miles per hour and cruised at 74. The VW engine also served Hitler's Third Reich on the water, not only in the Schwimmwagen but also in light attack boats.

PARTS FOR THE ENGINES AND VEHICLES built at Fallersleben were sourced throughout Greater Germany. Castings and forgings came from Czechoslovakia. The Peugeot plant at Sochaux, which became a subsidiary of the Volkswagen Works in June 1943, supplied twenty thousand connecting rods, three thousand flywheels, and five thousand raw forgings for crankshafts — the last a rush order. Type 82 body panels were made in the press works of Ambi-Budd in Berlin and shipped west to the plant for assembly.

The plant's total output of the Type 82 bucket-cars was 50,435. Included in this total were such specialized versions as radio cars (3,326), intelligence cars (7,545), and repair vehicles (2,324). It was Germany's most abundant

The VW's versatile engine served many purposes during the war, including its role as the power unit for the elegant H IIIe flying wing built by the Horten brothers in 1944. The Horten could reach 87 mph on its 32 bhp.

light military vehicle, well ahead of the wartime version of the Mercedes-Benz 170V, of which 19,000 were built.

Substantial though they were by German standards, these Beetle numbers were an order of magnitude smaller than America's production of 650,000 Jeeps for use in World War II. Design and development of both vehicles had taken place at about the same time, but the American military was quick to see the value of its Jeep, which had been pioneered by its Quartermaster Corps and carmaker American Bantam, and both Willys and Ford shifted into high-gear production of the tough and versatile Jeep.

Kübel production slumped in the last year of the war when conditions worsened. Supply of vital components was fitful. Raids on Berlin kept Ambi-Budd from supplying bodies regularly. Literally in the last weeks of the war the Volkswagen works succeeded in bringing the Type 82 body dies to Fallersleben, where they stamped their own panels for the last 665 bodies made.

After the air raids, assembly of the engines and vehicles was moved to the sub-story of the plant, originally intended only for services and piping. The workforce was composed largely of Italians, Russians, Poles, and Frenchmen held there against their will. As early as 1943 only one worker in eight in the plant was German, and those were assembling the precious V-1s.

EQUIPPED WITH LARGE-SECTION (200 x 12) balloon tires on special Kronprinz wheels that let them take full advantage of the vehicle's light weight, the Type 82s proved their merit by skimming over the desert sands of North Africa. And if one did get stuck in a ditch it was easy enough for a few soldiers to heave its light chassis out and send it buzzing onward.

Ferry Porsche's testimony notwithstanding, it would be an exaggeration to say that the Kübels in North Africa were trouble-free. Said one German service report from the front, "At first this vehicle gave very good performance, but after 5,000 to 6,000 kilometres every possible type of trouble appeared." One weak spot was the rear hub reduction gears, a design feature which was unique and, as a result, tended to escape the routine maintenance so essential to its reliability.

Engineers from Porsche were quickly on the scene to diagnose such problems. They suggested field expedients and recommended changes to the production cars. The Porsche people considered it vital to build a cooperative relationship with the army vehicle service personnel; generally they succeeded. They realized that it was essential that the military version of the KdF-Wagen gain an excellent reputation among the soldiers and their families they were counting on to keep saving to buy the civilian edition. To this same end the technical manuals produced for the Type 82 carried the civilian KdF-Wagen service emblem on their covers. This, soldiers were to understand, was the wartime version of the same car they'd be driving after their victory.

Field-Marshal Erwin Rommel first made use of a handful of the fast-moving Kübels in the invasion of France. Later, saying that they could follow wherever a camel could go, the bold and brilliant Rommel exploited their capabilities to the full in leading his African campaigns. "With its black, white and red command flag on its fender," Rommel's "own Volkswagen Kübel car was clearly visible. From it, he set the angle and tempo of the attack. If his car was shot up or ran over a mine, he simply commandeered another."

"You saved my life," Rommel told an astonished Ferdinand Porsche when they met during the war. "I was using one of your Kübelwagens," the field marshal explained, "which went through a mine field without setting it off. The big Horch that was following me, with all our luggage, went sky-high!"

"It was a great car," Rommel's technical advisor John Eschenlohr would recall. "Everybody drove them, officers and men. You could trust it because you knew you would get back if you went in a Kübelwagen." If cars arrived without the oversized tires that coped easily with the sand dunes, troops installed their own from aircraft supplies.

Erwin Rommel mounted mock tanklike structures on some of his Kübels and motored them about among real tanks to mislead the British about the size of his resources. In Germany some Type 82s were equipped with turrets for use in training tank crews.

In the field the Kübels were ubiquitous in all German theaters. They were personnel carriers, munition carriers, fuel carriers, ambulances, siren cars, cannon tractors, engineer vehicles, and communications cars. Able though they were, however, the Type 82s could do little without fuel. Lack of fuel, especially in the more extended and remote fronts, meant that many serviceable vehicles of all kinds, including Kübels, were abandoned in the field.

There was enough fuel for one Kübel to make a long journey in March of 1945. The army's commander-in-chief decided to leave his Berlin headquarters and travel east in an inconspicuous Type 82 to a castle near the Oder River where his Ninth Army commanders were based. There the C in C urged them to do all they could to resist the Russian army's powerful attack on Germany and Berlin. Then Adolf Hitler returned to Berlin, chauffeured as usual by Erich Kempka. "Hitler sat silently," during the trip back, "deep in thought."

Thought was all that remained to resist the increasingly powerful Allies. In North Africa Kübels were left behind with only vapor in their fuel tanks when the rest of Rommel's army withdrew after the successful British counterattack late in 1942. A decade later, 350 wartime Volkswagens were still being driven happily by the local population in Libya and other Northern African nations.

The situation was no better on the Russian front.

> Since the German troops in the east were more and more involved in losing battles, at least since 1943, there was scarcely time for vehicle maintenance. In the front-line repair shops, only makeshift repairs were made, or damaged vehicles were cannibalized, in order to keep their time out of action short. As a rule, the life span of a vehicle lasted only three weeks. The German military vehicles of 1944–1945 thus made a miserable impression: bashed and bent body panels, missing parts, wrong wheels and tires, etc. Many a Volkswagen was simply left by the roadside as the German troops retreated.

Many examples, captured intact, were commandeered for use by the Allied forces, who valued their mobility. In the Sahara, the saying was that one Kübel was worth two Jeeps. And several were liberated for study back home. The Allies were deeply curious about the design of these agile German vehicles, based as they were on Hitler's famous yet mysterious, and indeed notorious, people's car. At long last that curiosity could be satisfied.

3

The Factory and its Survival

The historic development of volume production progresses naturally from small-series through large-series to mass production," wrote Otto Dyckhoff, technical director of the Volkswagen factory. "Most factories have followed this path, including Ford's classic single-model production. This road is long and penalizes with many modifications, most of which can't be carried out properly but end instead with compromises, especially with respect to the physical plant."

The Volkswagen makers would not, could not, follow this lengthy road to the creation of their factory. The moment the decision was taken to make the project free-standing, independent of Germany's indigenous auto industry, it was deprived of a base of expertise from which its production could be developed. Even if such a base had been available, that of Opel for example, it would only have been Dyckhoff's "large-series" manufacture, not true mass production as it was practiced in America.

The Volkswagen planners faced a daunting challenge. Their volume and cost targets could only be reached by authentic mass-production methods on a scale that was unknown outside America. They were also under intense time pressure. Simultaneously, of course, they were offered a unique opportunity. By building and equipping the right sort of factory from scratch they would give their new car an exceptional and lasting manufacturing-cost advantage.

Even in America mass-production methods were being refined and developed in the 1930s. During that decade, ex-Opel engineer Otto Dyckhoff told fellow members of the German Engineering Society in 1942, for the first time "the Americans began to enlarge their factories without reference to the layout of their original facilities, and set up large works halls that open broad perspectives in which alterations of any kind can be made easily." This path, which VW would follow, became the key to the adaptability of the Fall-ersleben works to the needs of wartime.

Dyckhoff and his colleagues enumerated the differences among the various types of car production. Small-series output came from a battery of versatile machine tools that were not set up specifically to make certain parts. To achieve large-series production, he said, more specialized machines and tools were set up with a one-minute cycle time that would allow 600 cars to be made in a 10-hour day or 150,000 cars in a 250-day working year. This was the highest state of the art then extant in Europe.

"*Mass* production," said the Volkswagen engineer, "is based almost entirely on automatic and pure single-purpose machines which give the best output in the least space and tolerate few changes in the design of the workpiece." Dyckhoff concluded that a car designed to be built in true mass production should ideally be stable in its overall design. When made, improvements should come in the form of complete new assemblies that would have decade-long design lifetimes.

This would be encouraged, he felt, by the limitations on model variety imposed in Germany in the late 1930s by Colonel von Schell. He judged that von Schell's standardization would help overcome what Otto Dyckhoff called the "nervousness" of the German market that had stood in the way of mass production. In Germany, he said, "the car buyer must demonstrate somewhat more self-confidence and not always believe that the introduction of a new competitor will be unqualifiedly better than his own model."

Following these guidelines, Dyckhoff explained, and using suitable machinery that gave fast cycling times, a single car model could be mass-produced at rates no less than 1,200 per day and potentially as high as 3,600 per day or 900,000 per year — a level more in line with the aims of the VW creators. But where was the expertise that would make this possible? Only in America.

FERDINAND PORSCHE AND HIS PEOPLE began grappling with these issues during the building of the first prototypes for the RDA over the 1935–36 winter. Hitler himself, according to Ferry Porsche, said "it would be a good idea for my father to take a quick trip to America and study the mass-production methods and equipment in use at that time by the Detroit industry."

Porsche needed little prompting. When he told Robert Allmers in 1936 that he needed to travel to the United States to look into racing-car developments and design trends, the RDA chief readily gave his approval. He saw such a trip as likely to put the fantastical Porsche people's-car project even more out of joint. Anything that would keep the preternaturally active Porsche out of the German industry's hair for a few weeks would be welcome.

What Herr Allmers did not know about Porsche's visit to the U.S.A. was that he spent only a few days on matters connected with the racing-car project and almost four weeks in visiting such industrial plants as General Motors, Ford, Packard, and the Cincinnati Milling Machine Corporation. Porsche stood, day in, day out, on mass-production lines with a stop watch in his hand, studying production methods and examining the latest types of machine tools. There was plenty for him to see.

Porsche had good cover for this trip in the autumn of 1936, thanks to his work on the Auto Union racing cars and his patents for torsion-bar suspension systems, which he also discussed with his American contacts. The Volkswagen project was then all but unheard of in the United States, apart from the sketchy and biased information on its natal stages sent back by the German affiliates of GM and Ford.

The advanced manufacturing techniques that Porsche saw in America did not dishearten the engineer — quite the opposite. "This trip certainly proved worthwhile in context with the plans we had for building the Volkswagen," recalled Ferry Porsche, "and my father returned in a mood that was both optimistic and confident."

Ferry said that his father told Adolf Hitler, "I am now convinced that given the same machinery and tooling facilities the Americans have, we can build and sell the Volkswagen for [RM 1,000] without hurting the economy." After this trip Porsche was able to wield against doubters his yardstick for the VW's production potential: all they had to do was be as efficient as GM's Buick in building cars. Ford's even higher efficiency wasn't necessary.

Some aspects of the Ford factory in Detroit, however, made a deep impression. It could hardly fail to do so. On virgin farmland where the little River Rouge wound its way to the St. Clair River, south of Detroit and its suburb of Dearborn, Ford had built a titanic motorworks. On twelve hundred acres it was the size of a small town in its own right. Its buildings had 9,650,000 square feet under cover and were served by a hundred-mile railroad network — *inside the factory grounds.*

The factory buildings at the Rouge were immense by European standards. The so-called B building for body and car assembly covered 1.4 million square feet. A separate 250,000-square-foot building prepared finished cars for shipment. Engines were produced in a building of 846,500 square feet and axles in one about half that size. A press shop of 1.3 million feet was added in 1938. Ford's foundry was the world's largest, covering 1.2 million square feet.

That Ford had its own foundry impressed Ferdinand Porsche, and likewise his colleagues who joined him on another U.S. tour in June 1937. Europeans usually bought their castings and forgings from outside suppliers; Ford not only had its own forge shop, but its own steel-making furnaces and rolling mills. It produced its own safety glass and tires on the Rouge site. The plant had its own powerhouse, the largest in private hands, and factories making paper and concrete using byproducts of other manufacturing processes.

Accompanied by Jakob Werlin, Bodo Lafferentz, Otto Dyckhoff, and his son Ferry, Porsche visited Detroit and the Rouge again during their four-week stay in 1937, leading up to the Vanderbilt Cup race (won by Rosemeyer's Auto Union) in New York on 5 July. This more intense survey of the American industry convinced the planners, formalized since May as the GEZUVOR, that they would have to implement a similar level of vertical integration if they were to achieve their ambitious volume goals.

They had little choice. Germany's component industry lacked the capacity to supply VW's volumes. Its companies were already expanding just to meet the needs of the existing vehicle producers, whose volumes were improving from the nadir of the early Depression years. Glass could be supplied. Continental would enlarge its Hannover plant to meet the tire demand. But the VW factory would need its own powerhouse, forge shop, foundry, and steel mill.

The 1937 trip to America was crucial in establishing the foundation of both skills and equipment for the new state-owned enterprise. Visits were facilitated by Dyckhoff's brother, a highly placed member of Germany's U.S. embassy staff. After their arrival in Detroit the GEZUVOR men interviewed Germans with U.S. industry experience whom they wished to hire to help them set up the new plant. Next they traveled to Chicago to order specialized machine tools from the big factories there.

For some carmaking tasks, the Germans found, only the Americans made suitable production machines. "A conspicuous characteristic of almost all American machines," said Otto Dyckhoff, "is their generous dimensioning of the source of power and their solid construction, without regard to weight." This contributed, he added, to their ability to maintain consistent dimensions and a precise surface finish. Some of the machines they needed cost upward of two million dollars. "Money," Ferdinand Porsche told one of the German-Americans they wanted to hire, "is not a problem."

After their machine-buying trip to Chicago the team returned to Detroit to quiz the German experts again; fifteen to twenty men accepted their offer on this trip and others joined the new venture later. They would render yeoman service to both the car and the factory, not only during but also after the war years.

"As for the Ford factory," recalled Ferry Porsche, "everything was thrown wide open to us. If we wanted to know anything at all, we only had to ask a question." As well, a highlight for the visitors was a meeting with Henry Ford. At the age of seventy-three Ford was still the master of all he surveyed in his fiefdoms in Dearborn and on the Rouge River. Ford provided an interpreter who coped easily with "a quick-flowing, sparkling conversation" between Ford and the twelve-years-younger Porsche.

According to one account, "Ford was interested in the Volkswagen project, and when Porsche asked him if he were not concerned about the idea his reply was: 'If someone else can build better and cheaper cars than I can, it serves me right.' Like Ford, all the executives of the American automobile industry whom Porsche met did not show the slightest concern about the Volkswagen project."

The Porsche team had come prepared to discuss with Ford the idea of future cooperation. Perhaps Ford would produce a version of their car under license in America. They nudged the discussion in that direction during a visit to the Ford Research Center but were dismayed to be rebuffed by Ford himself, who said that "Things are much too unsettled at this time. The whole world is in a mess and not getting any better. Even a war is not out of the question." That Ford held this view was incomprehensible to the Germans, whose ambitious plans would only be devastated by war.

The delegation nevertheless paid Ford the compliment of buying one of his current V-8 sedans, which they drove back to New York from Detroit with several stops to order more machine tools. "The design concept of the V-8 was totally different from what we had in mind for the new Volkswagen," Ferry Porsche explained, "but we were nonetheless filled with admiration for the ingenuity of the Ford Motor Company and the shrewdness of its Costing Department in working so well with the engineers."

BACK IN GERMANY IN JULY, THE GEZUVOR executives faced the practical challenge of designing a factory to build the car whose prototypes were then being flogged through a round of durability tests by SS drivers under Ferry's supervision. The site at Fallersleben was quickly identified by Lafferentz after his return, complete with canal and rail access, as specified by Hitler. But what would the factory look like? How, especially, would it be configured to allow future expansion so that production volume could be stepped up in stages?

The men they needed to help them were Charles Sorensen and Harry Hanson. With Hanson's help, Sorensen had planned the establishment and expansion of Ford's River Rouge plant and the building of Ford's completely new factory at Dagenham, England, in 1930. The Ford operations set the pattern that the Germans wanted to emulate; in their flow of work and high integration the Ford factories became GEZUVOR's model. Sorensen and Hanson, however, were still needed by Ford.

Instead of Sorensen and Hanson, the Porsche team had Hartley Barclay. They may not have had the personal services of the editor of *Mill and Factory*, but they had detailed articles about the Ford factories written for that magazine, serialized over many months and combined in a large-format book of more than two hundred pages, *Ford Production Methods* (New York : Harper & Brothers, 1936).

"The author has had the unusual privilege of making available, for the first time for public use, a vast body of information regarding production methods, as well as processing, engineering and technological procedure of the mammoth Ford Motor Company," wrote Barclay in the book's introduction. Literally every operation in every building of every plant of Ford, including its European facilities, was described and diagrammed. If there was a specific routine for cleaning the windows or details of the Rouge's mile-and-a-half-long service tunnel with its two twelve-inch steam lines, Barclay described it.

Ford Production Methods was a gold mine for the GEZUVOR. Among the German experts it recruited were Ford factory engineers as well, men who could help interpret Barclay's drawings and data. One was Fritz Kuntze, who had been an engineer in the Rouge powerplant with its eight electricity-generating turbines and matching smokestacks. Its expansion to use high-pressure steam in the mid-1930s cost more than five million dollars and was thought to be one of the largest capital investments made by industry for power in the midst of the Depression.

The Ford Rouge plant could be a model in principle, but not in fact. Hectically adapted to meet the needs of expanding production, it was not built to a master plan. New buildings had been added where there was room for them, not where they would suit an efficient flow of materials. A flow chart of the movement of parts and assemblies in and among the scattered buildings of the mammoth site looked like the meandering web of a drunken spider. The Rouge's hundred miles of internal railway were there because they were needed, not because they were wanted.

Organized chaos of a similar ilk was on display at the Ford plant in Cologne, Germany, which lacked its own body shop and stamping plant and spread its operations over two floors — a characteristic of many European plants on cramped city sites. The Ford factory on the Thames at Dagenham in England, however, had all the elements that the GEZUVOR needed: high integration combined with all its operations on a single level with direct water access.

Under Charles Sorensen's supervision Dagenham had been designed as a unified and integrated plant in 1929 to take full advantage of Ford's production know-how. It had its own iron ore smelting and foundry operation, its own forge shop, its own powerplant, and all required manufacturing and assembly operations except body framing, which was performed by the Briggs Manufacturing Company on an adjoining site.

Initially 610,000 square feet in area under a single roof, the Dagenham plant was being doubled in size to 1,220,000 square feet by the time the GEZUVOR planners were seriously at work in 1937. North of its river site and flanking the Thames, neatly and efficiently served by rail spurs curving into the plant, highly integrated and offering complete flexibility of machinery

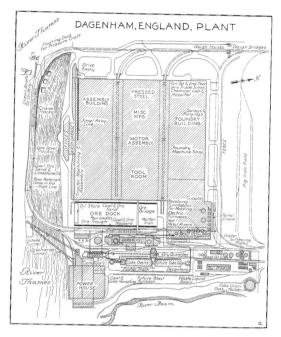

DAGENHAM, ENGLAND, PLANT

In contrast to the Ford plant at the Rouge south of Detroit, which sprawled over its vast site in a helter-skelter pattern, the new Ford factory at Dagenham was planned as an integrated production facility by Ford's experts in 1929. More than any other factory in the world it served as the model for the new production facility at Fallersleben.

placement on its single floor, Ford Dagenham was the only car factory in the world capable of serving as a model for VW Fallersleben.

IF ANYTHING, THE GEZUVOR EXPERTS improved on the general layouts used by Ford. Their first sketch on the back of a page of notepaper from Berlin's Hotel Bristol showed a series of seven factory buildings marching along the bank of the Mittelland Canal. Stretching for almost a mile, it placed the press shop and body shop on the east and the forge shop, foundry, and powerplant on the west. At the center was the machine shop and the final assembly. The total projected floor area was some 2.3 million square feet.

The locations of the operations were reversed around the central machine shop and final assembly buildings in a rough plan drawn up in August 1937 by Fritz Kuntze. Now the press and body shops were on the west and the powerplant and hot-metal-forming operations on the east. The plant was now 1.1 miles long. The machine shop's large size indicated that in Kuntze's layout, like the earlier one, the final assembly would take place under its roof. For the first time Kuntze sketched the way in which the six main buildings could be doubled and then tripled in size to achieve the desired future increments of added production.

Bodo Lafferentz commissioned a team of architects to bring these ideas rapidly to reality. A key role was played by Rudolf Mewes, whose experience included work for Ford at Cologne that would also have exposed him to the

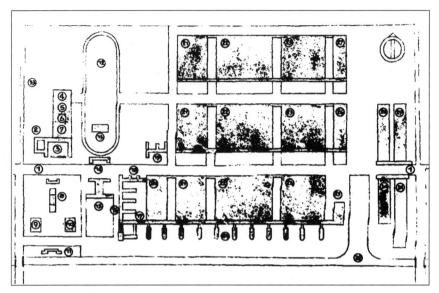

An early plan for the VW factory as a whole shows it after the completion of two stages of expansion, also shown in the model pictured in Chapter 1. Only the tool-making facilities were not to be duplicated in each expansion of the plant.

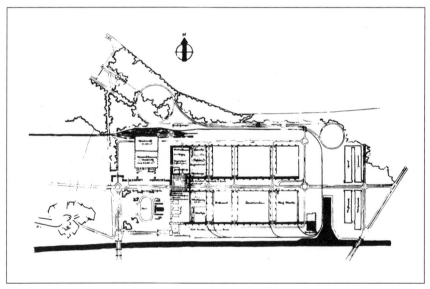

Plans for the VW factory were also sketched that provided for the initial creation of two of the three manufacturing modules. When the factory was built, space was left for the second module south of the dumbbell-shaped factory test track.

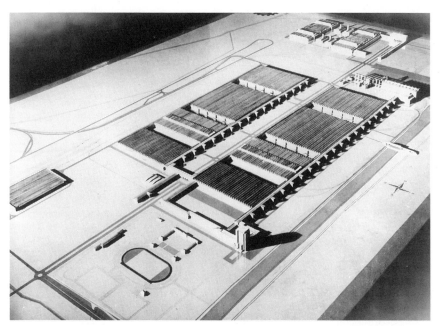

Had the VW factory been expanded to the first additional module shown in this model, its floor area would have approximated four million square feet. It could have approached the production of one million Beetles per year.

arrangements at Dagenham. His overall layout as completed in December 1937 showed the final factory plan, including the two expansion stages. Others employed in the design of the buildings included Karl Kohlbecker and the architectural firm of Schupp & Kremer. GEZUVOR engineers rushed back and forth from Stuttgart to Fallersleben to coordinate the work.

The initial site consisted of four main buildings, three of which were designated for duplication and later triplication to gain more capacity. The exception was Hall 1, at the western end, the tool and die shop of 420,000 square feet; its capacity was expected to be adequate for future increases in production. East of it was Hall 2, the press shop of 447,000 square feet with a ventilating cupola running north-south in the center of its roof.

Largest was Hall 3 — 775,000 square feet, where body framing, painting, and final assembly were to take place. This was more closely related to Ford's practice than the earlier plans requiring final assembly to share space with machining. Now the oil and grit of the latter were separated from the rest of the works inside Hall 4, the easternmost building of 527,000 square feet. There parts would be machined and mechanical subassemblies completed.

The floor area of the three production halls was some 1,750,000 square feet, not counting the separate foundry, forge, glass, and steel plants. These would occupy a site east of a harbor that would be dredged from the canal and adjacent to

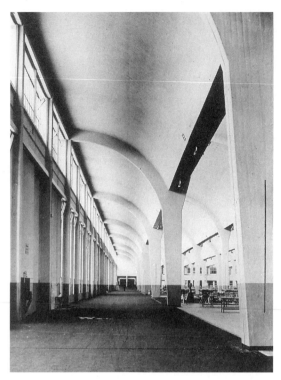

Commenting on the elegant structural design of the KdF works halls, a 1946 British report said that "it is not known whether this method of building is cheaper or quicker than the angular girder construction used in [Britain], but it certainly looks better." The production halls were high and well-lit.

the powerhouse, a refinement that only appeared in the final plans. In total the first stage of the plant would have some 2.2 million square feet of productive area.

The people's car factory was shown fully expanded in both the final plans and in the magnificent model of the completed plant that was presented to Hitler by Ferdinand Porsche early in 1938 and displayed at the Berlin Auto Show. The *Allgemeine Automobil-Zeitung* ran a full-page photo of the model as seen from the northwest, giving prominence to its spacious sports ground and social facilities. "In the new Volkswagen factory," the magazine commented, "technical requirements and social models meet to form an example that occupies a unique position, not only in Germany's but also in the world's automobile industry, in both its construction and its conditions for labor."

In fully expanded form the Volkswagen factory would have had not less than six million square feet available to build automobiles — no match for Ford, with almost ten million at the Rouge but, rationally arranged as it would have been, and making a smaller and simpler car, it would have come close to the same daily rate of production on a single site.

Otto Dyckhoff put the potential of the factory and its equipment in perspective for the readers of ATZ in 1942. From data in his files, he said, in 1920 a one-and-one-half-ton commercial vehicle required 2,447 production hours, and an electric transport vehicle required 555. But by 1930, Dyckhoff reported, a thirty-horsepower passenger car required only 234 production hours, not including the components sourced for it from outside suppliers.

These examples, wrote Dyckhoff, came from small-series production, which he defined as the output of versatile nonspecialized machine tools. "For large-series production in Germany before the war a passenger car of about 1.5-liter displacement needed about 160 hours; some 60 hours of this were required by the bodywork. If we now draw in the production time of the Volkswagen, projecting Germany's first mass production, an enormous advance can be clearly envisioned. In the preliminary calculation the production hours of the Volkswagen amount to almost exactly half the previously calculated number" — or about 80 hours.

This advance, according to Otto Dyckhoff, was made possible only by the closest cooperation between the car designers and the production engineers. In creating the KdF-Wagen plant he and his colleagues were plotting a unique way forward for Germany's Third Reich.

> We are not allowed to pay with our souls for mechanization. Two nations have already done this and have become soulless: the United States of America and Russia. Both have pursued the mechanization of life, one from the search for profit in the name of Mammon, the other from a fallacious ideology, an Asiatic lust for power. Both have become slaves of the machine. In Germany we want to find a synthesis between the intellectual Germany and the Germany that is the master and the user of the powers of nature and machinery. We must never allow ourselves to become slaves of the machine.

IN THE LIGHT OF LATER EVENTS, both the design and the construction methods chosen by Dyckhoff and his colleagues were significant. The individual factory halls were fully open-plan, their floor area obstructed by remarkably few rows of supporting pillars spaced at 26 1/4-foot intervals. This gave the production planners full flexibility of work-flow layout — and facilitated the wartime reallocation of space within the plant to the many tasks it ultimately performed.

Like so much construction in both Germany and the occupied countries at the end of the 1930s, the KdF works was built chiefly of reinforced concrete. Massive wooden forms made on the site were moved from section to section to receive the poured concrete; the plant's modular design facilitated this. Gigantic curved forms were used for the roof clerestories, which ran east-west across the buildings and had near-vertical glass windows facing the north light. The roof was 2.5 inches thick.

The height of the clear space of the body and assembly hall work areas above the reinforced-concrete floor was a little more than twenty-six feet. The height was twenty-three feet in the machine shop and forty-nine feet in Hall 2, the press shop. To support the rails carrying its traversing overhead crane, the press shop was steel-framed. The floor's robust supporting pillars held it thirteen feet above a sub-story in which all the plant's services were piped, wired, and ducted.

To create the north-facing skylights and arched roofs of the factory buildings, Italian workmen created giant wooden forms which were shifted from place to place to facilitate the pouring of steel-reinforced concrete. This is a view looking west.

The sub-story of the works, with ceilings thirteen feet high, was provided to give easy access to the plant for all the piping of services such as compressed air, heat, electricity, and cooling. It would prove to be crucial to the survivability of the VW factory.

North-south tunnel sections in the sub-story were allocated to all the service pipes for heat, cooling and drinking water, acetylene, oxygen, and compressed air. Like the building's open plan, this under-floor servicing was an asset to its adaptability. It was also destined to contribute to its survival as a production site.

The powerhouse, like the press shop, was also steel-framed. With six vertical stacks fronting its facade it challenged the east like an imperial ziggurat looming 150 feet high. Coal was delivered to it from the artificial harbor dredged from the canal, 1,310 feet long and 395 feet wide. To the east of the harbor the GEZUVOR planners hoped to build a rolling mill for steel for auto bodies that could supply not only the VW works but also the rest of Germany's vehicle industry. This, like the integrated glass and rubber production, was a dream that would be interrupted by war.

A view northwest from the powerplant gives a sense of the size and pace of work on the huge KdF works site near Fallersleben. The main halls are in place and the offices along the south face of the works are beginning to be erected.

Earth was first moved on the site on 24 February 1938, a scant six months after the architects had been commissioned by Bodo Lafferentz. Erection of the new factory went ahead with a will, helped — indeed made possible — by Mussolini's loan of some 3,000 Italian construction workers. Wrote historians Mommsen and Grieger, "Seldom has a heavy industrial building project been planned and initiated as quickly as was the case with the Volkswagen works."

Robert Ley's DAF, which was responsible for the project, faced competition for funds, material, and workforce from the massive Hermann Göring steelworks being built at Braunschweig, the nearest large town twenty miles to the southwest. The total labor force on the Fallersleben site reached a peak of 3,708 in August 1939, only 35 percent of whom were German.

The scale of the work was mind-boggling by European and even American standards. The DAF poured eighty thousand tons of concrete and twelve million bricks into the site in the first year alone. In April 1939 the factory's topping-out ceremony was held, symbolized by a KdF-Wagen-shaped evergreen poised high in the air above the powerplant's steelwork.

Estimates of the total cost of the factory, including its machinery, had been in the two-hundred-million-mark range. The actual cost of the work in 1939 alone was seventy-eight million marks, financed from the groaning cof-

Left:
The topping-out of the steelwork at the powerplant, the tallest structure at the factory, was celebrated not with the usual fir tree but rather with a Beetle crafted of evergreenery in April 1939.

Below:
Although the great works looked completed by the end of 1939, some halls were still unheated and the protruding stairwells were not all glazed. Nevertheless, the new factory, seen from the roof of the powerhouse, was an impressive sight.

fers of the BdA. In 1941 the capitalization of the plant was raised by the DAF from fifty million to one hundred million Reichsmarks.

A smaller associated project was under way at Braunschweig. There construction began in 1938 on a so-called *Vorwerk* (outpost) for Fallersleben, a two-story building with its own dormitories that would train apprentices for the main factory. The first 250 apprentices started their training elsewhere and moved into the Vorwerk in September 1938. By the spring of 1939 workforce training in its well-equipped machine parks was in full swing.

BY EARLY 1940 THE PRESSING demands on Germany's infrastructure applied the brakes to work on the plant and its adjoining town. The KdF-Stadt, far from becoming a model city for the New Germany, remained more a Wild West village than a model town. In December 1941, when all construction there was halted, 2,358 dwellings had been completed, only 10 percent of the intended number.

Matters were little better at the factory. Production sections in the main plant, such as the press shop, machining hall, and toolroom, were almost fully equipped, although there were critical gaps: some of the special machine tools had been delayed in their delivery from America, their shipment blockaded by the state of war. These, including half of the Gleason gear-cutting machines that VW had ordered, would never arrive. A still-neutral America could do no more to help the Allies.

Intensified demands of war production and the air attacks of the Allies made 1944 a turbulent year for the VW works and its machinery. The substory, designed to carry plant services, became a production site. Its thirteen-foot height was adequate for machine tools and engine- and vehicle-assembly lines sheltered by the factory's heavy reinforced-concrete floor. What couldn't be moved was protected. Sandbag walls surrounded the three vital turbines in the powerhouse. Heavy mortar-laid masonry walls were erected from floor to ceiling as protective baffles around the big presses that had to remain upstairs.

ON THE STEADILY SHRINKING TERRITORY of Greater Germany the trucks and trains struggled to keep rolling, under the sights of Allied bombers, to help the VW works meet the 1944 war production commitments that kept it viable as a business. Some brought inbound machinery. While the Allied land attack hesitated in France, in a fateful period of ten weeks between early September and mid-November, all but one-tenth of the industrial potential of the Peugeot plant at Montbeliard, near the Swiss border, was "brought to safety."

Some of Peugeot's machine tools went to Daimler-Benz. The bulk of them were delivered to an underground manufacturing site in an asphalt mine at Eschershausen, south of Hannover, where the KdF plant managers were struggling to maintain V-1 and aircraft-part production. Eschershausen replaced another underground factory at Tiercelet near the French border which had not been able to come on stream before the Allies approached.

Even as late as the end of 1944 the VW managers were able to get clearance to order 402 new machine tools and 22 grinding machines to equip the Eschershausen plant. Both there and at Fallersleben the wartime policy of the VW works favored ordering new machines, under the pressure of production demands, rather than trying to repair faulty ones — a tribute to the capacity for survival of Germany's machine-tool industry.

All the big presses at the works, including this massive press capable of stamping out a complete Beetle roof panel, had to remain in place during the war. Tall masonry baffles were built around them to protect them from bomb blasts.

Hundreds of the VW factory's machine tools were dispersed to cottage-industry sites that were close enough to Fallersleben to allow their parts to be delivered to its production lines; "[Joe] Werner and 5,000 workers (many of them POWs) removed about 600 machines, including the precious Bullards from America. Taking over scores of barns and sheds, they used farm tractors to drag the machines on sheet-metal sleds to nearby villages where they were set up and kept in production."

By 1945 components for the Kübelwagen were being made at Ahmstorff, Almke, Brackstedt, Gifhorn, Hehlingen, Lüneburg, Neindorf, Soltau, and Tülau. Only Soltau and Lüneburg were farther than twelve and a half miles from the plant. Four hundred machines were evacuated to the latter, and at the former 266 machine tools were making VW oil pans, cylinder heads, crankshafts, and gearbox casings.

The United States Strategic Bombing Survey determined that the VW works itself had 2,476 machine tools at the time the US Air Force commenced its 1944 raids. This was a 38-percent increase in the machine park from the 1,800 installed in 1939–40 — credible in light of the many machines added during the war for armament production. The Americans judged that their bombing had wrecked 10 percent and damaged 20 percent of these machines.

TEAMS OF EXPERTS RECRUITED by Britain's Society of Motor Manufacturers and Traders (SMMT) were authorized by the Ministry of Supply to visit Germany between July and September 1945 to see what the former enemy had wrought before and during the period of hostilities. The mission was under the overall direction of Capt. J. S. "Jack" Irving, as nearly an engineering icon as the British industry could muster.

Sunbeam racing cars built and perfected in Irving's experimental workshop had won the French and Spanish Grand Prix races in 1923 and 1924 respectively. Active in aeronautical work at Farnborough in World War I, Irving took naturally to speed on land. He built the twin-engined Sunbeam that was the first car to exceed two hundred miles per hour (203.79 mph at Daytona on 29 March 1927) and the Napier-powered Golden Arrow that Sir Henry de Hane Segrave drove at 231.45 mph on 11 March 1929 to better his own record set in the Sunbeam. Said Segrave, "Captain Irving is an unassuming but brilliant engineer who has never sought for, or been awarded, the praise that is due to him."

Both Segrave and Irving had left Sunbeam before starting the latter project, which resulted in one of the handsomest cars ever to set a Land Speed Record. The Golden Arrow was built in the well-equipped KLG-owned Robin Hood Engineering Works in London's Putney Vale. Irving went on to work for an engineering firm, Humfrey-Sandberg, where Segrave was a director, and later for Bendix and Girling.

For the SMMT mission, Irving's own headquarters team made the trip to Fallersleben. Acknowledged as the master of the "dry retort," Captain Irving was well able to ensure that they saw all that they required. Two of the other six teams visited the Beetle works, one led by a Rootes engineer and the other by a Vauxhall engineer. This SMMT sortie to Germany resulted in an extensive illustrated report.

The teams found the colossal plant in severe disarray. "Due to bomb damage and general dislocation," they reported, "all present manufacturing is confined to the basement floor which is fairly well equipped with the necessary tools."

So comprehensively was the sub-story being employed for production that the mission gained the impression that this was part of the original KdF-Werke plan, as a result of which they attributed to the factory a floor area of 400,000 square meters or 4.3 million square feet, fully double the actual area of the main production floors. A 1946 British report offered a more accurate floor area of 227,500 square meters, including the Vorwerk in Braunschweig.

Still in place, the British teams found, was "a full size Bonderising Plant to provide anti-corrosive treatment for all steel parts." They also commented on what they saw as the "novel" construction of the buildings. "The roof supports were all reinforced concrete, including the roof principals. It is not known whether this method of building is cheaper or quicker than the angular girder construction used in [Britain], but it certainly looks better."

Speculating on the apparent lack of advanced body engineering methods on the part of VW's car-building rivals, the report suggested that the latter were probably taking a wait and see attitude to the economic threat posed to their operations by this new DAF-funded rival. The account was highly positive about the merits of the vehicle and its factory:

> Without detracting in any way from the quality and standing of the other motor cars produced, it can be said that the Volkswagen is the most advanced and the most interesting for quantity production. It embodies most of the major requirements considered necessary for speedy and economical production, eliminating hand work to an unusual degree in the processes of cleaning, painting and finishing.
>
> Both the car and the factory in which it is produced are wonderful achievements in their respective spheres and should be given a great deal more detailed study than was possible during the short visit by the writer.

Any lingering notion that the KdF-Wagen project was a Nazi flimflam scheme was dispelled by the SMMT's visit to the huge factory by the Mittelland Canal. They concluded that "this proposition was really intended to fructify, and there is no doubt that but for the war, the People's Car would have created some disturbance in the world's markets."

This comment related to another aspect of the SMMT team's assignment, which was to study not only the industry but also the commercial arrangements of the German automakers. Moreover, "The [British] Government wanted advice on what steps it should take to prevent Germany from transferring her physical assets or technical experience to other countries, such as India or Spain, in an attempt to break away from Allied control and reestablish the German automobile industry elsewhere." The prewar menace posed by the German carmakers was still fresh in their memory.

Giving details of the layout of the plant, the SMMT report recommended "that a very close examination be made of the design of this vehicle as it would appear to offer, with perhaps a few modifications, a possible solution of the cheap utility vehicle that would be acceptable in [the United Kingdom] and in the overseas markets." To encourage such an examination the teams took away a number of KdF drawings and recommended the evacuation to Britain of three complete cars, three engines, a complete set of drawings, and a set of factory operation layout schedules.

Vauxhall and Rootes engineers in another SMMT team visited Fallersleben on 28 September 1945 and found the VW works "considerably damaged by bombing, particularly the body shop. On the other hand, only approximately 3% of the machine tools had been lost owing to dispersal. A number of machines are now being returned to the factory, but only a few components are at present machined there." They called the visit "disappointing, in view of the disorganisation of the production lines and of the comparatively small number of components actually machined at the Works."

THE FINDINGS OF THE SMMT TEAMS and other British technical and scientific research units visiting postwar Germany were reported to and through the British Intelligence Objectives Sub-Committee or BIOS. To study the skills of the vanquished Germans the BIOS drew upon various U.K. government ministries, all of which were represented on a subcommittee chaired by the Board of Trade.

This decentralized structure was no hindrance to the vast scope of the research conducted under the auspices of the BIOS, whose aim was to make available to British industry the finest fruits of the German wartime research and development effort. Their studies, conducted by knowledgeable British experts, resulted in more than two thousand reports covering the whole of German science and industry.

One of the BIOS study teams, including the famous Norton engineer Joe Craig, stopped over at Fallersleben on their first day in Germany, 1 October 1945. Their brief was to study Germany's prostrate motorcycle industry but they were persuaded by the source of their transport, a lively and knowledgeable colonel from the Royal Electrical and Mechanical Engineers named Michael McEvoy, that the VW plant was worth a visit; he showed them around personally.

The motorcycle men gave a detailed description of the engine and transmission of the Beetle. Although they saw no machining in process, they noted that "the machines were all of the latest type, and the design of the tooling was the best we saw during the whole of our tour."

Motorcycles were also the main interest of a BIOS-sanctioned trip to Germany by R. B. Douglas in September and October of 1946. He found little to admire or emulate in Germany's motorcycle manufacturing methods. At the VW works Douglas described the engine assembly on an eighteen-station circular table, saying that "the whole [engine] assembly set-up was not unlike practice in the very light aircraft engine industry in the United States." He added that "due to the extremely battered condition of the plant many improvisations were necessary."

After further rehabilitation of the VW works, an internal census of its machine tools was completed by the end of June 1946. It enumerated, by types, 1,888 machine tools on site and 265 presses for a total of 2,153 production machines. The census stated that "Major machine tools and presses in 1939/40 totalled 3,351," a figure that must actually reflect the maximum number of machines wielded by the VW plant and its satellites during the war. "Losses by air raids and dispersal sites in Russian Zone etc. totalled

1,298" machines and presses, the internal census stated, "leaving balance of 2,063 in 1946."

British visitors in February and March 1946 assessed the types of equipment that were being used to make VW vehicles. Ford's British production engineers found that "the factory and production methods are outstanding in the German automobile world and are comparable with the best British concerns."

This assessment, reached in spite of the confused and devastated condition of the VW plant less than a year after the end of the war, may be taken as an affirmation of the soundness and thoroughness of the work done by the GEZUVOR planners and experts. The assessment's value was all the greater in view of the men who made it: British experts intimately familiar with one of Europe's leading auto factories, the one the Germans had judged to be most worth emulating — Ford at Dagenham.

The postwar machine-tool complement of the VW works was found to be remarkably comprehensive and of a standard equal to Europe's best auto factories. In his overall report on the German motor industry for the BIOS, GM engineer Maurice Olley summed up the findings of the Ford team and those of other visitors to Fallersleben: "Observers agree that the manufacturing methods employed in this plant have been excellent. They mention the wealth of modern machine tools, the ample provision of power wrenches on assembly lines, fully conveyorized assembly, etc. They mention the bonderizing plant, said to be of modern type, the liberal use of Vomag fine boring machines, the special crankshaft machines and the good gear-cutting."

WHAT OF THE STATE OF THE FACTORY ITSELF? In 1945 it was a sorry mess of jumbled girders, collapsed roofs, and shattered pillars sprouting tangles of reinforcing rods. The huge Hall 3 had much more open space than roof and Hall 4, the machine shop, had been badly hit. That no effort had been made during the war to repair these halls was consistent with German practice: damage was left visible and even exaggerated for the benefit of British photo reconnaissance, so that the bombers would not be sent back to finish the job.

The powerplant was intact and operating, supplying electricity and heating to the factory and town. The main footbridge over the canal to KdF-Stadt was under instead of above the water. Water was also a feature of much of the still-functioning sub-story, pouring in from the spring rains through bomb-damaged floors. The visual evidence strongly supported the view — for many an integral part of the legend of the Beetle — that the factory's "destruction was in effect, total," as several sources have quoted Heinz Nordhoff, VW's later leader.

A Beetle sits forlornly amidst the wreckage of the bombed factory. Upper levels were left unrepaired during the war to provide convincing evidence of destruction while production continued in the sub-story.

"Closer examination," said historians Mommsen and Grieger, "shows that the initial position of the factory at the end of the war was in no wise un-favorable. To be sure the bomb damage was substantial but it did not notably affect the capacity of the works," thanks to the machine dispersal and the protection measures taken. "Destruction of the four assembly halls was in one instance [Hall 3] by sixty-eight percent and overall by twenty percent. Ninety-three percent of the machine park remained usable."

No favors were done to the plant by the forced laborers who realized in April 1945 that the war was over for them. Many detainees ran amok. In their vengeance they smashed and wrecked indiscriminately. Reported *Time* mag-azine with its usual apocalyptic hyperbole, "Every telephone had been torn from the walls, every typewriter had been sledgehammered to junk, every file and record had been scattered and burned." In an attempt to contain the workers' anger the plant's managers opened the doors of freight cars and gave them access to foodstuffs and clothing. French detainees helped Fritz Kuntze defend the vital powerplant.

By the time the British Ford study team arrived at the plant in early 1946 they were able to file the following impressions of the much-abused manufac-tory: "The factory was attacked from the air on several occasions, the Body

Shop being heavily damaged, and the body bonderising plant completely destroyed. 46 These attacks caused dispersal of the plant and removal of much of it to underground cellars. Some attempt is now being made to re-layout the plant — but much remains to be done."

Battered though it was, the great plant still manifested its virtues to the British visitors. "Compared with other automobile factories in Germany, and visualising the originally intended factory layout, the Volkswagen effort is outstanding and is the nearest approach to production as we know it." They also reported that "the condition of the plant and equipment is good, and could operate satisfactorily for many years."

This did not imply that the Ford men thought that the factory wrought by the GEZUVOR and DAF was in advance of the techniques that they were familiar with from America. "Despite the Volkswagen effort being outstanding in the German Automobile Industry," they found, "it contained no features of a revolutionary nature, nor any practice not known to the mass producers of Britain and the U.S.A."

More immediately relevant to the inhabitants of Fallersleben had been the arrival of American forces from the west on 10 April 1945 who, by the following morning, had taken control of the KdF works and town with two hundred troops and their Sherman tanks. By 15 April they had formally occupied the KdF-Stadt and its controversial factory.

On 20 April, while muted celebrants wished Adolf Hitler a happy fifty-sixth birthday in his bunker deep below the bomb-battered Chancellery in Berlin, readers of the New York Times learned about the capture of the "German 'Willow Run'," the Associated Press reporter likening it to the factory that Ford had built to produce the B-24 bombers that had done much of the damage to the VW works.

The Times stated that the works had "an assembly line identical to that in any small Ford assembly plant . . . A sadly beaten Herr Mayer [German-American Hans Mayr] stood today amid the rusting ruins of the plant he said was copied from the Ford plants in Michigan. He said he came here 'for my health' from Detroit in 1937. The plant, according to Mayer, had hit a production peak in May 1944 of 1,800 German-type jeeps, 1,000 amphibious jeeps, 1,200 V-1 bombs, 100,000 mines and the repair of thirty Junkers-88s a month."

Thanks to the contacts and persistence of Porsche, Piëch, and Lafferentz, the huge factory at Fallersleben — which could easily have been neglected during the war, a white elephant of epic proportions — had in fact been a valuable contributor to Germany's wartime production. Its total output was valued at 762,332,818 Reichsmarks. Of this turnover, vehicles accounted for 33.8 percent, aircraft parts and repairs 35.1 percent, and the rest (31.1 percent) other armaments contracts.

The U.S. forces that now occupied the factory were still fighting a war against a broken but not yet beaten Germany. To win that war they had to

Military and civilians alike seek to make some sense of the works after its wartime attacks from the air. Such damage led to shifting more production to the sub-story.

bridge more rivers, including the Elbe, during their drive east. Any steel that would help build those bridges was useful; they stripped the bomb-damaged plant of some of its internal steelworks. But the reinforced-concrete construction of all but Hall 2 and the powerhouse meant that much of the structure was safe, able to survive to face a still-uncertain future.

THAT FUTURE WOULD BE AFFECTED by the official policy of the four powers occupying Germany. After their conference at Potsdam from 17 July to 2 August 1945 the Allies imposed draconian controls on German industry. Production of war materiel of any kind was forbidden. All raw materials, chemicals, and machinery were placed under strict controls. Manufacture of goods and provision of services were only to be maintained to the level needed by the occupying powers, by displaced persons, and by the provision of a moderate standard of living to the German people. Any and all capacity in excess of these requirements was to be dismantled and/ or destroyed in accordance with a war reparations plan.

The factory at Fallersleben, which had overwhelmingly produced war materiel and had never enjoyed a civilian manufacturing role of any kind, was now in jeopardy. In accord with the Potsdam rulings, the occupation authorities listed the desolate, inert works as a candidate for destruction. They concluded that it served no useful purpose apart from the short-term repair of vehicles, a task that the remaining staff on the site immediately commenced in return for a modest midday meal.

"During the Christmas of 1945," recalled an RAF wing commander on occupation duty, "a complete list was being made by the Allied Control Commission of all war-potential factories still capable of producing war materials. I well remember, together with other staff at Hannover, getting out all the files of the big German factories, and writing alphabetical squares on a large floor space. Volkswagenwerk was listed under 'V' and was marked, provisionally, for demolition."

Such annihilation of assets was only to be expected, most Germans thought. Well within living memory, just twenty-five years before, another Allied Control Commission had mandated the reduction to rubble of much of Germany's industrial base. At steelmaker and armorer Krupp alone, for example, "about 9,300 machines weighing over 60,000 tons were demolished; 801,520 gauges, molds and other tools with a total weight of almost 1,000 tons, along with 379 installations such as hardening ovens, cranes, oil and water tanks and cooling plants were smashed." Why should things be different after this war?

There was a loophole, though not a very big one, in the ruling that decreed death for the huge factory on the Mittelland Canal. Instead of destruction, it could face constructive dismantlement.

The [British] Control Commission accepted that the Volkswagen factory had been genuinely built to produce civilian cars, despite its subsequent war work. Nevertheless, there was a policy called the "Level of Industry Plan for Germany." This policy intended to set a ceiling on the capacity of postwar German industry. It was deemed that any factory not in operation in 1938 would count as part of the war preparations effort. So Volkswagen was not designated a war plant to be abolished but, instead, was listed as surplus to the postwar level of industry and, as such, available for reparations.

This did not mean that the VW works, still chock full of machinery to make Panzerfausts and V-1 fuselages, would escape scot-free. In accord with the postwar occupation policy, any and all equipment in the plant that was intended for armaments production had to go. "The offending articles were disposed of in a variety of ways: large machines were cut in half and delivered to separate scrap metal dealers, smaller machinery and raw material was extensively vandalised whilst aircraft engines were earmarked for the RAF. All in all an estimated 1,300 tonnes of war material were removed from the Volkswagenwerk in this manner."

After this clearout, which was completed in the autumn of 1946, all production tools and equipment dedicated to the VW vehicles could and did remain. With the help of a skeleton staff, including some of the German-Americans who had helped create the car and factory, machine tools were retrieved from their dispersal sites and repatriated to the war-ravaged factory.

Critical machine parts and tools, which loyal Germans had removed, boxed, and hidden from the advancing Allies in the sub-story's service tunnels, were restored to operation.

Leading a fight against the razing of the VW factory was its most senior remaining manager, engineer Rudolf Brörmann. Brörmann, then fifty-four, had been in charge of manufacturing quality control in the KdF-Stadt era. Previously a chief of quality inspection at Adam Opel, he had joined the nascent VW operation in 1938. During the war Brörmann worked on the plant's production of V-1s, both at Fallersleben and at the Luftwaffe's site at the Peenemünde development center.

The factory was well-suited to civilian production, Brörmann argued, showing the Americans how it could still be used to manufacture useful vehicles. In May 1945, with a pick-up labor force, 110 Kübels were assembled from on-site parts for use by the American 9th Army under the supervision of a Captain Lee. His unit reported up the line: "Beginning production for US Army with 200 employees, will expand to 1,000. Stocks on hand for 200 vehicles, material for additional 800 can be procured." Early that same month, on the eighth of May, the war in Europe was declared officially ended.

So feisty and tenacious that one British official called him "a crazy man with no sense of judgment who antagonized everybody," Rudolf Brörmann succeeded in winning a stay of immediate execution for the huge plant. In fact the Americans placed him in charge of the factory, a post he took up on 28 May. With the Americans Brörmann mapped out an ambitious program to increase the production rate to five hundred vehicles per month. Despite an abundance of Jeeps, the American forces could make good use of some hundreds of Type 82s, especially because they received them free of charge as war reparations.

To prime the plant's financial pump the American occupiers authorized the Reichsbank in Braunschweig to loan RM 1,350,000 to the VW works' account in the Fallersleben BdA, against security that had been organized in Berlin before the war's end. Half this amount was used to catch up on salary payments to VW staff and pay various pending bills.

On 25 May the town council renamed KdF-Stadt "Wolfsburg," after the name of the von der Schulenberg's nearby castle and its grounds. As Hitler had intended, the town's original name did indeed last through the war — but not the war and its aftermath as he had envisioned it.

RUDOLF BRÖRMANN'S APPOINTMENT overlapped with the handover of responsibility for Wolfsburg to the British forces — the factory and town had been deemed to be in the agreed zone of German occupation of the British 21st Army Group. The transfer of control began on 26 May, with the arrival of units of the 52nd Division, and was completed formally on 3 June 1945.

The clash of German, American, British, and even Russian cultures in this isolated district, teeming with some thirty thousand persons displaced from all points of the compass, produced more than a few sparks. A British officer arriving at the plant in mid-May found that the Kübels it was producing "were still painted in Afrika Korps sand yellow. Asking why this colour was still in use despite the fact that the German Army had not been in North Africa for some time, he was informed that nobody had told them to stop!"

Administratively, Wolfsburg was in the Gifhorn District with headquarters at the small town of that name to the northwest. There the British 111 Military Government Detachment had responsibility for the district, initially including the VW works. While the army was responsible for the security of the British zone, its management and government were assigned to the British Element of the Control Commission for Germany, or CCG.

At their posts the CCG staff were known generically as Military Government or Mil Gov. The CCG had both military and civilian officers for whom wearing an Allied uniform was essential for unhampered travel in Germany in 1945. As well, Germans respect uniforms. Thus the civilian CCG staff wore a military-style uniform with touches of gold on the shoulders that resembled the war correspondents' uniform.

When the British occupied Wolfsburg, their Royal Electrical and Mechanical Engineers (REME) took over the workshop that the Americans had been using for vehicle repair. Designated the Number 2 Auxiliary Workshop, it was housed in one of the more habitable areas of the works and reported to Workshop Control Unit No. 30 at Hannover, which in turn was responsible to a colonel at the headquarters of the British Army of the Rhine (BAOR) at its Bad Oeynhausen headquarters: Michael A. McEvoy.

Michael McEvoy was an authentically knowledgeable and keen automotive engineer and entrepreneur with secure links to the German motor industry. Forty-two years old in 1945, his rank showed that he had distinguished himself during his war service with the 8th Armoured Corps, having risen from a modest lieutenancy with the British Territorial Army in 1939.

In wartime McEvoy had used what he called "motor-racing methods" to good effect to keep armored vehicles moving. "Michael came to prominence chiefly when he kept US-built tanks (Shermans and their predecessors) in operation for training purposes around 1942–43," a colleague recalled. "Ignoring 'channels,' he went direct to Hardy-Spicer, who made parts to replace defective items." Used to the speed of repair and revision needed in racing, McEvoy was not one to be deterred by the army's elaborate procurement procedures.

After an Eton education, McEvoy had served an apprenticeship at Rolls-Royce's Derby factory. From his father, a successful portrait painter in the Victorian era, he inherited a flair for design that stood him in good stead. The estate amassed by an Irish grandfather who had profited from the ex-

Michael McEvoy is seated on one of the powerful Big Twin motorcycles he produced during the 1920s. In the 1930s McEvoy began tuning and supercharging standard cars.

pansion of America's railroads allowed McEvoy to indulge his passion for racing motorcycles at the fast Brooklands track. From 1924 to 1929 he produced and sold his own McEvoy Big Twin motorcycles. They were mean machines, the Vincents of their day. One McEvoy held the record for the standing-start mile at an average of 91.02 mph in 1926.

First in 1929 at Derby and from 1933 in London's Notting Hill, Michael ran M. A. McEvoy Ltd. to add performance and exotic bodies to Morris, Wolseley, and MG models. One of McEvoy's customers for a supertuned Morris was young John Dugdale, car enthusiast, racer, artist, and journalist for *The Autocar.* "He was quite a figure in the car world then," Dugdale recalled. "We met on the beach at Dunkirk in May of 1940. There he was, almost enjoying it! To become a full colonel as early as he did was quite some going."

Early in the 1930s Laurence Pomeroy, Jr., whose engineer father had excelled at Vauxhall and other British ports of call, joined a firm that had acquired the U.K. rights to the vane-type supercharger developed in Germany and France by Swiss-born engineer Arnold Theodor Zoller. Efficient but costly, the Zoller blower needed capital for its exploitation, which led "Pom" to McEvoy and his business manager, Henry Laird. From 1933 Pomeroy was a director of McEvoy's firm, which applied Zollers to the successful British ERA racing cars as well as a number of road cars, and developed special twin-cam cylinder heads for racing MGs.

After Arnold Zoller's untimely death in December 1934, M. A. McEvoy Ltd. became the principal proponent of his patents and designs. A link with a German entrepreneur, Herr Fandi, led McEvoy to sell his British company in 1936 and move to Frankfurt to fit the highly strung Zoller supercharger to a series of 170V Mercedes-Benzes. McEvoy consulted directly with Mercedes-Benz in 1938 on the adaptation of a Zoller-type compressor to its three-liter V-12 racing engine. Although that effort was fruitless, Mercedes-Benz and McEvoy continued testing the Zoller with an eye on the 1940 racing season — which was aborted by the onset of war.

Laurence Pomeroy was often in Germany for these projects, which benefited from McEvoy's command of German. It also led to both men being present in Berlin for the demonstrations of the KdF-Wagen prototypes that were offered to invited press early in 1939.

Here, then, was an impressive Briton who was savvy not only about the German motor industry but also about the Volkswagen as originally designed — a concept that was not easily grasped from postwar experience of the rough and noisy Kübels that were bounding over the cratered and puddled German roads. McEvoy "was fascinated to see that Fallersleben, and the factory, were in the British Zone."

Visiting Wolfsburg from the BAOR headquarters, McEvoy saw no reason to interrupt the fitful production of Type 82s initiated by the Germans under American supervision — quite the contrary. McEvoy's assignment from the CCG was to kick-start the German garage trade; anything that abetted this aim was to be encouraged. He also supported the use of what they dubbed the Wolfsburg Motor Works as a workshop for truck repairs. Production lines for the overhaul of Jeep and Humber engines were established in the sub-story.

In England, in the early years of the war, the gregarious McEvoy had met a fellow former-territorial officer, a Yorkshireman named Ivan Hirst who had grown up in a family of clock manufacturers. The Hirst Brothers firm employed several hundred people in clock design and production. Trained in optical engineering, Ivan Hirst was assigned wartime responsibilities that initially saw him serving in the infantry in the Battle of France, in which he reached the rank of major.

In 1942 Major Hirst was transferred to the REME, in which he could make better use of his technical knowledge. After a stint running a factory for military instruments at London's Mill Hill, Hirst followed the invasion forces onto the continent. He became the manager of a repair shop for British tanks on the outskirts of Brussels that was capable of fixing some fifty tanks at a time.

His service in the 8th Armoured Corps meant that McEvoy was destined to meet his friend Hirst again at the Brussels workshop, where Hirst was successfully marshaling the tank-repair skills of several hundred British and Bel-

Michael McEvoy was a colonel in the Royal Electrical and Mechanical Engineers (REME) when he took the initiative not only to continue but also to expand the production of vehicles by the VW works. He knew well the capabilities of the cars it could produce.

Ivan Hirst's engineering background equipped him ideally to fulfill his assignment to take charge of a factory site near Hannover that turned out to be the VW works. He was then a major in the REME and had managed the repair of tanks and trucks during the war.

gian workmen. At war's end Ivan Hirst asked to be seconded to the CCG, a request that was granted when he returned to the continent from leave in August 1945. His assignment? "To take charge of" a factory site near Hannover. It turned out to be none other than the VW works at Wolfsburg, of which he became the Mil Gov's senior resident officer.

Ivan Hirst was aware of the factory and its products. "Before the war [Hirst] had read in The *Autocar* about Hitler's KdF Wagen and, whilst in Normandy, his unit had examined a captured Kubelwagen. He was impressed by it, especially by the light alloy engine and the all-independent suspension." It sounded as if McEvoy — who Hirst assumed had recommended him for this post — had spotted the right man for the job.

Initially Ivan Hirst was attached to the Military Government's Provincial Headquarters in nearby Hannover, as was a retired RAF wing commander, Richard Berryman. In response to a request from Hirst, Berryman arrived at Wolfsburg in February 1946 to bring some motor-industry expertise to the sprawling works. He began as an assistant to Hirst, who asked him to take charge of production operations.

Berryman had been demobilized from the RAF at the age of fifty in 1945 before he signed up again for German duty with the CCG in a grade below his

Responsible for light engineering industry in the British occupation zone, Col. Charles Radclyffe fortunately took a close interest in the VW works.

preretirement rank. After serving in the First World War, Berryman had been a production engineer at the General Motors assembly plant in Oshawa, Canada, and a service manager for the distributors of GM cars in Canada.

Berryman had just the freewheeling resourcefulness needed to break down the many barriers to car production at Wolfsburg. "He was a maverick, but pointed in the right direction, by God he was good," Hirst recalled. "I made him production chaser, which he did excellently."

Fortuitously, it must be said, automotive expertise was also available at the echelon above the CCG staff deputed to Wolfsburg. Charles R. Radclyffe was a fifty-eight-year-old colonel who had served as a tank engineer and expert in both world wars, and had won the confidence of fellow Harrovian Winston Churchill. In peacetime Radclyffe had represented America's White Truck Company in the Far East and India and, returning to Britain, had become a sales executive for Alvis.

After a stint in Berlin at the end of the war, Colonel Radclyffe was assigned to the Mechanical Engineering Branch of the CCG's Industry Division, headquartered in Minden, and made responsible for light engineering industry in the British zone of occupation. This included vehicle production, which Radclyffe saw firsthand at Wolfsburg in a snap inspection late in 1945. Radclyffe was destined to play a key role in the drama of the survival and disposition of the Volkswagen factory.

Dr. Hermann Münch, a Berlin lawyer, was named the official German custodian of the VW factory. More necessity than asset, Münch was not from the automotive world.

"Major Hirst recalls him as a wise, kindly and greatly respected man with a wide experience," wrote one historian. "The managers at Volkswagen felt that, in him, they had somebody to back them up at headquarters. He gave sound advice and his support on supply matters would prove very valuable in the months to come." Charles Radclyffe tightened his ties with the VW works by arranging for Ivan Hirst to report directly to him at Minden.

These men were charged with the control of operational matters affecting the factory and its German staff and workforce. They were not responsible for its assets, however. Under occupation rules the legal authority for the Wolfsburg property, both the factory and its housing, was lodged with a German custodian, Dr. Hermann Münch, after February 1946. Münch, a Berlin lawyer, had survived denazification procedures, which Rudolf Brörmann had not. Actual authority under the occupation, however, remained with the Property Control Branch of the CCG's Finance Division. A civilian, Leslie E. D. Barber, became the responsible official.

Barber, an economist, had been in the British Economic Warfare Ministry during the war. "His interest was in the *ownership* of the Volkswagen company and its subsidiaries," Ivan Hirst recalled. That ownership, of course, was still lodged with the German Workers Front or DAF created by Robert Ley.

"He was a quiet, deep-thinking man," Hirst said of Barber. "But when the authorities heard he was knowledgeable about 'labor' they put him in the 'manpower' section. I got him transferred from the DAF section of the Manpower Division to the Property Control Branch. The structure was changed so that Property Control had a DAF Division." Not only did the raffish Leslie Barber eschew uniform, he also favored a casual style of mufti. But he brought precise and profound ideas to the management of the Wolfsburg properties.

Together Hirst and Barber set about establishing a Board of Control that would bring together the senior occupation officials responsible for Wolfsburg. "He was almost teetotal," said Hirst. "We stayed up almost all night drinking tea to draft the plan for the Board of Control." Under the plant's British stewardship the board would meet thirty-nine times from 1945 to 1949.

Other British officers and officials were assigned to the VW works, which the REME saw as a good training ground for its technical personnel. At Hirst's request the Berlin-based Barber recruited an accountant, Capt. Alasdair McInnes, to be seconded to the factory to manage its finances and administration. Plant personnel on the army side included Capt. Charles Bryce, who took charge of quality control, and Capt. Ted Weeks who supervised engine and vehicle overhauls. Maj. H. A. Goff of the CCG represented Property Control at the plant on many occasions. At the end of 1946 Mr. F. T. Neal succeeded Alasdair McInnes as the resident officer for Property Control.

Although wracked by successive waves of denazification procedures, the works was able to assemble a German management team of some merit. Karl Huland was in charge of production and Hans Hiemenz of finance. Porsche engineer Josef Kales was still on site with a small drawing office. Hans Goransch became responsible for personnel, a critical post due to high absenteeism and workforce turnover. A council representing the workforce was formed and Karl Heber became its chairman.

Of course these Germans were grateful for any kind of work in the dire months of occupation. But why particularly at Volkswagen? Was it the car that attracted them? Its links to the DAF? A remnant of Hitler's Third Reich? No, they testified, the force that drew them was the reputation and the reality of the work of Ferdinand Porsche. They saw themselves as Porsche's acolytes, whose mission it was to help realize his dream of a great works building a car for the people.

THESE APPOINTMENTS IMPLY THAT the VW works was being gainfully employed. This was, in fact, the case. The factory's first major customer was the very body that controlled it, the CCG. The British found themselves with a lot of real estate to monitor. Their highly industrialized occupation zone included Hamburg, Hannover, Essen, Düsseldorf, Dortmund, and Cologne, and extended from Schleswig-Holstein on the Danish border in the north to the borders with Holland and Belgium in the west and south.

The CCG was much in need of vehicles to govern its zone of a divided Germany. Local organizations on which it depended for assistance, such as the post office, the police, and the Red Cross, were also strapped for transport. Anything that could move under its own power had long ago been requisitioned for the defense of the homeland. As a January 1945 British report put it, "So far as non-military vehicles are concerned it has been Germany's policy to live on capital — her own and that of the occupied countries. After five years of war there is not a great deal of it left." The railways, battered by Allied bombing and their rolling stock deteriorated, offered little help.

Light vehicles were also needed by the BAOR. It had 200,000 troops stationed in Germany and another 60,000 in its Austrian zone of occupation. In addition some two hundred aircraft and 20,000 RAF personnel were on the ground in the occupation zones, all requiring servicing and transport.

To what extent could the British vehicle fleet come to the rescue? The few available big Humbers in both standard and four-wheel-drive versions were suitable as military staff cars but they burned far too much scarce gasoline to be practical for day-to-day missions. Smaller types were also available: the Two-Seater and the Light Utility. British counterparts to the Volkswagen, they were the vehicles that, in principle, the CCG should have been using for its zonal monitoring missions.

The British military Two-Seater was a prewar Austin 900-cc car with an open touring body, fold-down windshield, and sporty cut-down doors — it was distinguished from its civilian counterpart only by a pair of louvers on each side at the rear of the hood. Power output was almost identical to the VW's at 23 1/2 horsepower.

British Light Utilities were slightly larger. They came in several varieties, usually with engines of ten taxable horsepower and pickup-style rear bodywork covered by a canvas hutch. A spare wheel was carried on the top of the two-seater cab. Engines were 1.1 to 1.2 liters in displacement and developed around thirty horsepower. Hillman supplied one, based on its pre-war Minx model. Morris and Standard both made Light Utilities, the latter a twelve-taxable-horsepower version. Austin built a Light Utility for the War Office on its civilian "ten" chassis, close kin to its "eight" Two-Seater. Its channel frame was strengthened by a steel pressing welded underneath it and the tunnel for the propeller shaft added rigidity.

The army's prospects of obtaining more vehicles of this ilk from the British carmakers were poor. Britain was bankrupted by the war. In an August 1945 strategy paper Lord Keynes, advising the treasury, set out three conditions under which he felt Britain might remain technically solvent: "(a) an intense concentration on the expansion of exports, (b) drastic and immediate economies in our overseas expenditures, and (c) substantial aid from the United States on terms which we can accept."

Just struggling back into production, the British auto producers were under severe pressure from their government to earn the steel allocations that they needed by aggressively exporting cars to dollar-earning markets to fulfill Keynes's first condition. The domestic market came a distant second to this requirement and the needs of the CCG and BAOR were so far behind in third place as to be imperceptible.

Keynes's second condition ruled against Britain spending any more on the occupation of Germany than was absolutely essential. The government's

The first type of car that the VW factory could produce after the war was modeled on the high-legged wartime Type 82E, with a Beetle body on a Kübel chassis. Ivan Hirst is second in this row of British officials with the cars they called the Type 51.

need to keep overseas spending down meant that the needs of the British forces abroad had to be met by local means wherever possible. The VW works, and its potential to provide transport to the British occupiers at no cost as a form of war reparations and even, eventually, to generate export trade, could be a godsend — if its products were deemed worthy and if it could make them.

Someone had to make a connection between the Wolfsburg plant's capability and the transport needs of the army and the German economy. That someone turned out to be Michael McEvoy. "He had the inspiration that if we could get VWs built it would be a good idea." Even better, McEvoy took positive steps to make that connection click in the minds of his superiors.

In the autumn of 1945 a beetle-shaped two-door car, powered by a strangely spluttering engine at the rear and painted in the characteristic British khaki green, drove up to the doors of the headquarters of the BAOR at Bad Oeynhausen. Behind its wheel was a driver from Wolfsburg where, under the direction of Ivan Hirst, the three-year-old VW, found in the factory, was put in order and decorated in British warpaint.

The Type 60 was personally presented to the officers of the BAOR by Michael McEvoy, who had no lack of experience selling motorcars. He would never seek a more important sale. The enthusiastic McEvoy explained and demonstrated the VW's merits to his army and CCG colleagues. The immediate need was that of the CCG, but the BAOR was the channel for its equipment requirements and ultimately had to approve it.

Here was an elegant solution indeed. Technically, Ford in Cologne was the designated vehicle producer in the British zone. The Level of Industry Plan for Germany agreed by the Allies allowed Ford to make up to twenty

Production started using existing subassemblies in the factory, such as these front axles for the Type 51 chassis. Soon, however, the works began to source such components both inside and outside the awakening plant.

thousand cars a year, but the American-owned company was many months away from resuming car production, although it was beginning to meet the British need for trucks. The road was open, for the time being, for Volkswagen to supply cars.

A further aim of the British was to energize the economy in their zone of Germany; getting Wolfsburg on line could speed that process. Given the BAOR's approval, after McEvoy's persuasive presentation, the CCG placed an initial order with the works for five thousand Volkswagens. Quite soon it raised that commitment to twenty thousand.

An important question remained: What kind of car could Wolfsburg actually build? Using up Type 82 chassis found at the plant and adapting the KdF-Wagen sedan body to them after the fashion of the wartime Type 82E, the plant produced a vehicle that it designated the Type 51. This was its first standard product. Its high ground clearance and low gearing were advantageous, if anything, in the prevailing conditions.

"The big presses were found to be repairable," said Ivan Hirst. "New body assembly jigs and welding equipment had to be made. VW had to start its own production of carburetors, fuel pumps, clutches and dampers — all items normally bought out. It was also necessary to open a foundry for the crankcases and transmission housings. The outside supplier had been suddenly shut down, since it had mainly supplied the aircraft industry which was being eliminated." After suitable chassis parts were sourced Wolfsburg could also build the Type 11, as it dubbed the standard Beetle.

Cars with sedan bodies had to predominate because the supply of Kübelwagen bodies ended after the Soviets dismantled the Ambi-Budd press and body plant in Berlin that had made them and transported it back to Russia. In fact the British successfully negotiated with the Soviets for some Kübel body dies but these ultimately proved unusable.

In 1945 Wolfsburg was able to build 539 Kübels by using up available bodies, many found abandoned on a train that had between Berlin and the factory. They called this the postwar Type 21 model. The plant's total 1945 output was 1,785 units, about as many as were being made monthly in late 1944 to early 1945. Six thousand people considered themselves fortunate to be working in the factory.

WHILE THE VW WORKS BUSIED itself by filling the CCG order, the BAOR and mandarins back in London agonized at length over the issue of whether Britain could in fact justify taking cars from Wolfsburg to meet her zonal transport needs. To merit doing so, Whitehall needed to satisfy itself that the British equivalents were unsuitable. Only if its conscience were clear on this point could the British army defend itself from any accusations that it was favoring the dreaded Huns at the expense of Britain's fine motor manufacturers.

Policy guidance on this point was sought from Sir George Turner of the Ministry of Supply by Maj. Gen. D. R. D. Fisher of the War Office on 18 March 1946. Wrote Fisher, "It is alleged that the two seater light utility is so unsuitable for German roads that it creates a very heavy load on the REME repair organisation in BAOR. It has, therefore, been proposed that BAOR should gradually re-equip themselves with Volkswagen from local production. But we obviously could not agree to this project without your concurrence on policy grounds."

Supply's civil servants sought various views on this issue. Internally, one put the following alternatives on 21 March:

> Looking at the proposal from the standpoint of general policy, we have to ask ourselves whether it is in the national interest that vehicles to meet BAOR's requirements should be provided from German, instead of British sources of production.
>
> Arguments in favour of this view are that the supply of these vehicles by Germany, provided the vehicles are not taken out of Germany, imposes no foreign exchange liability; it adds to our stock of commodities of which the supply is deficient at the present time; it leaves British production fully available to meet export and home requirements; and finally, it is in effect a form of reparations from Germany.
>
> As against this it can be argued that the effect of the proposal would be to encourage the development of a German industry which has a considerable war potential; it would create a continuous demand for spares and replacement; it

The body drop in the early months of post-war production was a leisurely affair. The important thing was that the factory was serious about producing automobiles at long last and was providing gainful employment to workers who desperately needed it.

might set up a prejudice in military circles in favour of a German as opposed to a British type of vehicle for military use; it would be a bad advertisement from the point of view of the British motor industry.

On 23 March another Supply assessment pointed out that "there has been no official statement that the two seater light utility is in fact mechanically unsuitable for road work on the Continent," and recommended that the War Office make an official confirmation to this effect that would rule out the use in Germany of "two-seater Austin cars, which they have already declared surplus, and which could be repaired for return to the Army.

"Clearly the vehicle which BAOR requires is a jeep," the assessment continued, "and the British jeep will not be in production for at least a year. Even if an ordinary light 2-seater car from British production were acceptable I should have great difficulty in getting the order accepted by a manufacturer, and it would undoubtedly mean a corresponding reduction on the numbers of these cars made available to the public."

Sir George Turner's reply of the 28 March to General Fisher's inquiry left matters up in the air. He brought up the issue raised by his briefers that "there has been no official intimation to us that the two-seater light utility is in fact mechanically unsuitable for road work on the Continent. It is a little difficult to have this said with particular reference to the roads in Germany as for other purposes we are told that the German roads are superior to ours here. Moreover, if the use of [German vehicles] is defended by saying that our cars will not stand up to German roads, I am afraid the Motor Industry will have something to say."

On 5 April the parties met at the Ministry of Supply to discuss the pros and cons. This led to a letter to the relevant ministers on 28 April from Secretary of State for War Lawson, who said "I am prepared to approve the BAOR proposals and defend the use of a German vehicle by the British army if necessary." In so doing he stated that "It has been found that the British 2-seater Light Utility car cannot stand up to the strain of constant use on the inferior German roads and no suitable British substitute is at present available, though it is hoped that one may be in due course."

Secretary Lawson pointed out, in support of his approval, that U.K. production of military vehicles had been cut back by three thousand units and that the demobilization of troops had reduced the ability of an already heavily burdened REME to repair vehicles in Germany. If he was misleading in any respect, it was in his statement that "the orders proposed [1,331 cars] would meet all BAOR needs up to 31st March 1947, and we should not propose to have any further recourse to Volkswagen if it can be avoided . . .." BAOR supplies from Wolfsburg would ultimately number well into five figures.

NO MATTER HOW IT WAS INTERPRETED — and it was interpreted in several different ways — this finding secured the immediate future of the VW works. By mid-1946, during the debate in Whitehall, the plant had completed and delivered the first five thousand cars ordered by the CCG. On 15 July the decision was taken that over the following two years the British zone of occupation would need a total of eighty thousand new cars for all purposes. In effect this meant that the complete Level of Industry quota for occupied Germany — forty thousand cars a year — would be met from the British zone, where Wolfsburg was home to the only factory making cars. Initially this requirement took the form of a "firm" contract for forty thousand cars for the BAOR, the VW Board of Control was told at its seventh meeting on 12 August 1946. This was more than enough to be getting on with. Almost a year earlier, on 17 September 1945, at Gifhorn, Maj. R. Bisset had dictated a memo that instructed the Bank of Braunschweig to provide the works with a "credit loan" of twenty million marks to support its production. "It is confirmed," he wrote, "that Volks-wagen GmbH have been ordered by Military Government to produce more than 20,000 Volkswagen vehicles." The cars were ultimately paid for by German entities, which in turn gave the completed VWs to the British CCG as a form of war reparations.

In 1946 the plant's production was 10,020 vehicles, a remarkable achievement in the difficult postwar environment. From October 1945 it built the first postwar Type 11 models, proper Volkswagens after the original Type 60 design. The British and American occupation zones were fused in September 1946 to form the Bizone, in which American GIs could buy Beetles through their Post Exchange stores for a heady $645. In 1947 individual British officers were allowed to buy VWs at a price of £160.

At the Hannover Trade Fair in 1947 the car was launched on the German market and offered for export as well. Those few Germans who could get a rare

A key breakthrough in the revival of the VW works was its assignment to build twenty thousand Beetles for the occupying forces of Britain and other nations. This secured its future, and prevented dismantling, at least for the short term.

and treasured priority voucher could buy a Type 11 for a price-controlled RM 3,600. So desperate was the transport situation then that a new Beetle sold on the black market for thirty thousand marks. According to Steven Tolliday, "In July 1947 one VW car could be exchanged for 100 to 150 tons of cement or 200,000 bricks!" The official price increased on 1 April 1947 to RM 5,000 and became DM 5,400 after the currency reform in 1948.

By 1948 VW had forty dealers in Germany and a sales organization headed by the energetic Dr. Karl Feuereissen, who had been the Auto Union racing team's manager in the 1930s. VW, which was by a clear margin the first German company to resume car manufacture, had not dissipated its advantage. Adler's failure to resume production after the war meant that many of that respected marque's dealers were available to sell Volkswagens. The new VW marque was slowly and steadily insinuating itself into the civilian sector in Germany.

During December 1947 the plant produced its twenty-thousandth car, a milestone auto that was set aside for display in the works. As of 31 December total production had reached 20,673 units. In July of that year the British Property Control authorities stated that "The vehicles produced at the Volkswagenwerke have become a fundamental part of the transport position of all the occupying powers and therefore the production is mandatory in every respect."

By December 1947 the VW works had produced more than twenty thousand cars. But it was a cold winter, and the wounded plant was not yet fully covered in. Its long-term future would depend on the Allied assessment of its condition and potential.

VISITORS TO THE PLANT TWO YEARS after the war were struck by the evidence that still remained of the bombings that once silenced the huge motor works. The mission of the British controllers was to build cars and keep order in that quarter of the Gifhorn District, not to invest in the fixed assets of the factory. Operations were more orderly, but many repairs were provisional, not permanent.

New roofing for the press shop now replaced the tarpaulins once spread over fir trees felled and stripped from the nearby forests. Floors were repaired and the main works floor was again in service. But as late as November 1947 "covering in" of parts of the plant was continuing. Not until that was completed, the Board of Control was told, would the works be "sufficiently weather-proofed for the winter."

Still wounded, still struggling to find the supplies it needed to build cars, still listed as available for dismantlement for war reparations — the great works was an object of both pride and pity a decade after its architects had been commissioned. What would ultimately become of it? Much would depend on the assessment by the victorious Allies of the vehicles it could build. First to have that opportunity, for obvious reasons, were the British.

4

Britain Meets the Beetle

L ike their counterparts in Germany, carmakers in Britain were losing
  sleep at the end of the 1930s over the immense potential for harm
  they faced from the ambitious, indeed megalomaniacal, KdF-Wagen
project. "Besides satisfying her workers and the demands of her national
economy," the *New York Times Magazine* reported in October 1938, "Germany also hopes to capture the export market with this car, and British
automobile interests are already highly apprehensive."

Their apprehension was in no way diminished when they read the detailed coverage given to the budding Volkswagen project by Britain's quality
automotive press. *The Motor* and *The Autocar*, competitive weeklies, were
gentlemanly but energetic rivals to be first with the news about the auto
business. Europe in the 1930s offered them no bigger story than Nazi Germany's plans for a true people's car.

Those plans were already well known outside Germany. Opening the
Berlin Auto Show in February of 1935, Adolf Hitler had announced that "the
skill of a brilliant designer and the co-operation of his staff, have already produced the preliminary plans." Knowing full well the identity of the "brilliant
designer," *The Motor* kept an eye on new patent applications from Ferdinand
Porsche's offices. It hit pay dirt.

In its New Year's Eve issue of 1935 *The Motor* showed a sketch of a frame
and suspension, a dead ringer for the final VW design, that had been described in a new patent granted to Porsche. The torsion-bar springs and suspensions were exactly as later used; the frame ultimately became a full steel
platform instead of the patent's steel-backbone-with-plywood-flooring. The
engine shown in the patent wasn't of the final type, simply because Porsche
hadn't designed it yet.

"It is a fair deduction," opined *The Motor*, "that this may well be the basis of the national car, which Herr Hitler had in mind, to sell at the price of a medium-sized motorcycle. The whole scheme has been most carefully thought out, and the chassis appears suitable for carrying light two-seater and four-seater styles of coachwork."

The Motor consolidated its pole position in reporting on the VW project with a lead article by "an expert Continental Commentator" in April 1937. He characterized the paucity of hard news about so important a project:

> The disciplined German press, probably acting on a hint "from above," publishes very little information and so tends to create the impression that something is wrong with the project, despite the insistence of the "Führer" that it should be carried through. The truth is that Germany's engineers are working hard to fulfil the wishes of Herr Hitler and the lack of published information is due to the sensible attitude taken by all concerned. It must be remembered that this "Volkswagen" is going to be produced not in thousands, or hundred thousands, but in millions. The preparatory work must therefore, of necessity, be prolonged and everyone acquainted with the problems knew, from the outset, that a period of years would be required.

The anonymous author was "expert" enough to be able to report that Daimler-Benz had built thirty prototypes to the latest design; in fact this task was just being completed at the time he was writing. He was accurate about their use of a flat-four-cylinder four-stroke engine but wrong about water cooling and a fully synchronized gearbox.

If visitors to the Berlin Auto Show in February 1938 expected to see the VW they were disappointed but, *The Autocar* reported, "The factory for the manufacture of the car is being erected and a fine scale model revealed that the factory is to be on the most modern and ambitious lines, with its own testing track." It quoted the German chancellor as saying "that Dr. Porsche's design is being still further tested, and that efforts are being made to achieve the lowest production costs."

Revelation of the definitive form and specification of the KdF-Wagen was saved for the cornerstone-laying ceremonies at Fallersleben at the end of May 1938, which was reported on by the British weeklies. *The Autocar* told its readers that "Germany is in high glee as a result of the Führer's promises of a small car at 990 marks — that is, £80 at normal exchange. English journals have quoted £50 and £60 as the price of the car, but that is an exaggeration. Herr Hitler's task of producing a complete runabout in three types at £80 is sufficiently great in itself."

At the end of 1938 *The Motor* again gained the advantage on its rival with a report from Rolf Binder that showed the huge plant under construction and said that 150,000 orders had already been booked for the car that it would build. In fact this was an unusual understatement by the KdF promoters; at the close of 1938 the number of signed-up savers was 169,741.

Two Volkswagens flanked Adolf Hitler when he gave the opening address for the 1939 Berlin Show. A press campaign promoting the car kicked into high gear with the first detailed revelations of the car's radical engineering.

Engineers and executives in Britain read extensive descriptions of the new KdF-Wagen in early 1939 issues of *The Automobile Engineer*. It reported on the new cars at the 1939 Berlin Show, which was opened by Adolf Hitler from a rostrum positioned between two of the strangely shaped cars.

NEITHER BRITISH JOURNAL HAD an advantage in advance of the show opening on 17 February 1939, when full technical details of the KdF-Wagen were first publicly confirmed. Coverage in *The Autocar* was detailed but dry. Its correspondent had more to tell readers about the German wondercar after taking part in a mass demonstration for foreign journalists conducted during the show.

Drivers were recruited from the SS to pilot the press in prototype VWs at the time of the Berlin Show in February 1939. Here some of the cars are being marshaled near Berlin's Brandenburg Gate.

The test run, he said, was "over a course of over 200 miles, from Berlin to Dessau and Magdeburg. Eleven samples of the Volkswagen left the centre of Berlin accompanied by a convoy of a dozen other cars and buses, most of which carried film units and press photographers, who must have exposed miles of film on the whole run. Each car was driven by an S.S. trooper with three others in the car." Many photos were taken when the caravan paused under the bridge that spanned the special wide section of Autobahn near Dessau that was built expressly to suit the Porsche-designed Mercedes-Benz Land Speed Record contender.

During the demonstration the writer was "struck by several features which make this car strange to the average British taste." He found the rear-seat leg room ungenerous, the suspension "somewhat harsh at low speeds," the engine air intake and the intermediate gears noisy, and the heating system ineffectual. He considered the braking "harsh though powerful," adding that "this impression may have been helped by the German method of driving, which is never to stop till you are forced to, and then to do so as abruptly as possible."

In summary, "Its greatest assets are its ability to keep up a steady 50 mph for very long periods, its simplicity of layout and upkeep, its really good head room (you can wear a hat in the rear seats) and, of course, its very low price." With a calibration of its speedometer (10 percent fast) he estimated its maximum speed at 60–62 miles per hour.

Gordon Wilkins was also among the journalists invited to experience Porsche's new creation. Recalled Wilkins, "The feature that impressed me most was the VW's ability to cruise flat out at the maximum speed of 62 mph [100 km/h] without the risk of breaking the engine. This was something unique in small-car design when the new Autobahnen were littered with the smoking bits of engines that had failed during sustained fast driving."

A Herr Deine was at the wheel of a demonstration Beetle in which "Monoposto," a correspondent of The Light Car, cadged a ride around the Nürburgring in the summer of 1939. His account, amusing after the fact, suggested that there were moments when he wondered if he hadn't been a bit rash. Deine, he found, "combines the skill of the test pilot with the abandon of a Paris taxi driver."

In achieving the astonishing feat of lapping the 'Ring with four people aboard in less than twenty minutes, an average speed of 42.8 mph, the redoubtable Deine conducted "what novelists are prone to describe as a 'nightmare drive.' " The first shock came in the south curve after the pit straight:

> Experience of the smaller type of British car on roundabouts prompted us to commend ourselves to Providence as Deine slung the car into the corner at about 40 mph. The tail slid slightly, Deine worked at the wheel with his customary expression of fierce determination, and we were round. We could scarcely

Members of the press were driven in the prototype VWs to a hillside south of the factory where they could see the remarkable progress of its construction. British journalists had their first personal exposure to the ambitious project at this time.

have had more convincing proof of the efficiency of the suspension. We left Herr Deine with a profound respect for both his driving and his car.

British engineers as well had direct personal experience of the qualities of the first Beetles. In July 1942 members of the Institution of Automobile Engineers debated a paper on the subject of an inexpensive car for the postwar world. "Incidentally," intervened Gordon Mackenzie Junner, "nobody has mentioned the German Volkswagen, as it is called." Junner, assistant editor of *The Commercial Motor*, was personally acquainted with one of the prewar first-series cars:

> I do not know if anybody has been out in it, but I had an hour's run in this car and it struck me as being a very useful and interesting vehicle. It had four independently-sprung wheels, with torsion-bar springs, a four-cylindered horizontally-opposed engine at the back, ample room for four adults and a child, interior space for several large suitcases, also it got over one of the common wind-screen troubles, for the hot air from the engine was carried right through the car and up the inside of the wind screen to prevent internal fogging. There was a fixed wind screen and one wind screen wiper.

The Scotsman's perceptive remarks were not followed up in the discussion at the institution.

Some of the more hysterical assertions about the KdF project in the British daily press were addressed by *The Motor's* technical editor Laurence Pomeroy, Jr., in his report on the new car. He rejected the two extremes of opinion that were widely expressed: one, that it was a Nazi "stunt" and "myth" and the other, that such a state-backed mass-produced car was certain to usurp traditional British export markets and invade the U.K. domestic market as well with a subsidized low price that would make a mockery of Britain's tariff wall, which imposed an additional duty of one-third of the imported price of an automobile.

By 1939 Britain's carmakers were already alarmed about Germany's car export campaign, which was geared to earn the hard currency that the Nazis needed to pay for vital imports. John Bullock of Rootes Motors recalled that U.K. auto producers were "very concerned" about "the way in which Hitler was subsidizing the country's motor industry. The German Government was paying a subsidy of up to 43 per cent on the cars being imported into Britain and as much as 60 per cent in countries like Holland."

As a result, Bullock explained, "at £135 the [Opel 11.3 h.p.] Cadet was £50 cheaper than the Austin 10 h.p. and the Morris 10 h.p., £34 cheaper than the Hillman Minx and £22 less even than the Ford 10 h.p. Within four years, imports of German cars had risen from just over three cars a month to 1,000 cars a month. In countries like Norway, Sweden, Denmark and Belgium, sales of German cars had risen by as much as 500 per cent in only three years." And now there was a new threat:

> Production of the Volkswagen at the new factory at Fallersleben was looking even more menacing, because the company had been given the powers to purchase its raw materials and other supplies from the producers at cost price, based on the cost of labour, materials and floating overheads, but without any allowance for fixed overheads. The cost of each Volkswagen would accordingly be far lower than any of the models being produced in even the most efficient American plant.

In 1939 *The Motor* estimated that the likely export price of the KdF-Wagen in England would be "fixed at slightly under or over £110 . . . not so very much lower than the cheapest 8 h.p. car at present on the British market. The appearance," Pomeroy informed his readers, "is, to British eyes, entirely unconventional, which is not a feature which has been found to help sales in this country, and the interior finish and equipment are, by our standards, crude."

Such remarks about the VW's appearance echoed the views of most managers in Britain's motor industry. The car's only saving grace, the British car magnates assured each other, was that it was "not only unconventional but ugly in the extreme." With no radiator grille like a proper motor car, its engine where the trunk should be and cooled by air, of all things, they considered that even at its ridiculously low price the car might not catch on.

Laurence Pomeroy took their side where the U.K. domestic market was concerned. In that respect, he concluded, "our manufacturers may, I think, to use a Fisherism, 'sleep quietly in their beds.' " Abroad, he warned, they should be more alert. He considered that "the vehicle has been designed with particular brilliance by Dr. Porsche to fit the German market and German roads. In the export markets the car may be a tougher customer, for it is a very practical job viewed on a strictly engineering basis."

Later in 1939 the erudite Pomeroy treated his readers to a think piece on the merits and demerits of a change of engine location. In an article seemingly intended further to calm the slumbers of British motor executives, he addressed "predictions on both sides of the Atlantic that the power unit will gradually be driven off the front end of the car and will, so to speak, complete a circle and reappear on the back end."

Pomeroy pointed to problems in cooling the rear engine and in providing enough luggage room, especially between the front wheels with their need to turn for steering. "There is also," he said, "the introduction of nasty problems in weight distribution," assuming that equality of weight on all four wheels is a desirable goal. Even with the best efforts of designers to shift weight forward, Pomeroy felt, "the weight on the back tends to promote skidding and the lightness at the front tends to loss of adhesion on the front wheels and that most dangerous of all motoring phenomena, front-wheel skids."

The engineer-author granted that "the extra weight at the back does, of course, give improved grip to the rear wheels, which is valuable when surmounting difficult country and in colonial use." Here again was an argument favoring the suitability of the KdF-Wagen to export markets. "But apart from this," Laurence Pomeroy concluded, the rear engine "seems to offer few real advantages and to present a number of awkward snags. It would be a bold man who would say that any problem is insoluble, but I, for one, doubt greatly whether rear-engined cars will ever attain real success."

Pomeroy addressed business rather than technical issues in a 1941 article in which he aimed to tell "the truth behind the KdF." He dismissed speculation that the huge Fallersleben plant had actually been intended all along to make battle tanks. He advanced economic arguments supporting the launching of such a huge project. He stressed the strenuous efforts that had been made by the Porsche team to keep down the car's operating costs:

> It is quite certainly a car that would have been suitable for all German motoring conditions and also to export to world markets where car value is measured, not by eye appeal as it so often is in this country, but by sheer utilitarian considerations. Finally, it is well to remember that the enormous works may be turned back to the production of cars with the cessation of war and that the design is sufficiently advanced not to have become out of date during the period of hostilities. The KdF may well, therefore, become a competitor for export business in the post-war period.

The export business was not inconsequential. Focused, to be sure, on the Empire members who had preferential tariff privileges, Britain's car exports were worth a hefty twenty-one million pounds Sterling in 1937. Australia took the most with a 38-percent share, ahead of New Zealand, Ireland, South Africa, Denmark, India, Malaya, Sweden, and Ceylon. Britain's big indigenous producers, Austin and Morris above all, would need those markets and more in the future to gain manufacturing economies of scale.

As for the British market, Pomeroy and some others agreed, the Beetle seemed to be a nonstarter. All it was likely to have in its favor was low price.

Its large cylinder bore would attract a hefty RAC-formula tax. High-geared, it required frequent shifting that the British driver was spared by his home models' low gear ratios. Good aerodynamics were of no value in a nation that had yet to build its first real highways. Its rear engine seemed an aberration, and it looked like no other car on earth — certainly no British car.

LABORING IN A BENIGHTED ALLIANCE, the British carmakers and their domestic customers resolutely resisted change. Only Alvis and BSA briefly essayed the front-wheel-drive solutions that were being introduced in Germany, France, and even America. Independent suspensions and backbone or platform frames were all but unknown. Aerodynamics were anathema. "By the end of [the 1930s]," wrote historian Jonathan Wood, "the industry was manufacturing the most technologically backward cars in Europe." He could have said "the world."

To understand why this was so, one would have to appreciate the contrast between Britain, where a technical education and engineering were likened to blacksmithery, and the Continental nations, above all Germany, in which engineers were not only respected for their contributions but were also able to earn prized doctorates for their advanced studies and research.

"The university mind is a hindrance rather than a help" in the motor industry, held Sir Herbert Austin, founder of the auto company that bore his name. This was typical of the conservative line taken by the leaders of Britain's principal carmakers in the 1930s — Austin, Morris, and Ford. Both Herbert Austin and William Morris "were farmers' sons and essentially self-taught men, in the spirit of the mechanics and tinkerers who had created so much of British industry in the first half of the nineteenth century. Cast in the Victorian mould, they might have stepped straight out of the pages of Samuel Smiles's Self Help, having triumphed by drive, intuition and sheer hard work but possessing little more than a superficial technical knowledge," wrote Jonathan Wood, who gave specific examples of their reluctance to hack out new paths in their industry:

> It is no accident that the two most popular Morris engines of the inter-war years, those of the "Bullnose" and the 8 h.p. car, were cribbed from American designs. Significantly, the Morris Minor, one of the most outstanding British cars of the post-1945 years, was developed during the war without Lord Nuffield's knowledge, and when he eventually saw it he expressed his extreme displeasure.

Britain's only progressive producer in the 1930s was GM-owned Vauxhall, which introduced integral steel body-frame construction and modern independent front suspension to the British car. Both initiatives had originated in GM's engineering labs in America.

BOTH "UNIVERSITY MINDS" AND "tinkerers" in the British tradition had tried their hands at more advanced motor cars in the pre-Beetle years

With its boat-shaped body and exposed wheels the North-Lucas of 1922 had certain affinities with the work of Edmund Rumpler. Nevertheless, it was a completely independent British project.

only to be disappointed by an unreceptive industry and public. Rumpler's inspiration could be seen in one of their best efforts, the North-Lucas prototype completed in only eight months in 1922. Its chassis was made in the Robin Hood Engineering Works in London's Putney Vale where Captain Irving would later build the record-breaking Golden Arrow.

The shockingly advanced North-Lucas was inspired and financed by Ralph Lucas, a Greenwich barge owner and motoring enthusiast. Lucas had been making and marketing cars in his own name since 1901, most with two-stroke engines. The car's designer was engineer Oliver D. North, who had been with Straker-Squire and Scammell. A North-designed drive line was still being used by Scammell more than thirty years after its creation.

Among the many radical features of the North-Lucas were an integral body-frame of riveted aircraft aluminum, a single cyclops headlight, all-independent suspension with inboard rear brakes, and a rear-mounted air-cooled five-cylinder radial engine of 1,460 cc placed pancake-fashion above the rear axle. Seating four in a closed two-door body with a translucent airplane-fabric roof and weighing only 1,710 pounds, the North-Lucas was a superbly engineered car that departed decisively from the accepted norm.

Features of the North-Lucas included a five-cylinder air-cooled radial engine mounted pancake-fashion, inboard rear brakes, and fully independent suspension at all four wheels. It had distinctly maritime detailing.

The one and only North-Lucas proto-type of 1922 was hailed by the British press for its sophisticated ride and handling. Regrettably, it failed to find a patron in Britain's motor industry.

Driving it, *The Automobile Engineer* found that "the engine, naturally quiet, is practically indiscernible as far as the occupants of the vehicle are concerned. In addition to the comfort of the suspension, there is a noticeable absence of bouncing, the car holding the road with remarkable tenacity, even on extremely bad surfaces." The technical magazine added a comment that would later be echoed by many drivers new to rear-engined cars: "To the driver, the vehicle offers an entirely fresh set of sensations." He found it "a most attractive vehicle to handle" and remarked on the "sweet and light" controls of the North-Lucas.

"It is certainly a car over which one becomes utterly enthusiastic," *The Light Car and Cyclecar* told its readers, "and one in which all those who are concerned in the progress of automobilism should take the closest interest, for in it are embodied a very large number of thoroughly practical ideas and ideals."

The Motor sent a raw cub reporter, twenty-five-year-old Miles Thomas, to see, drive, and describe the radical prototype. Calling it "a storybook car in reality," Thomas wrote of the one and only North-Lucas:

> Perhaps the outstanding impressions left by a run in this car on the road are its lightness and airiness. This impression is both physical and mental. When driving the car one finds that the steering is beautifully light, the controls are positive and direct, its response to the accelerator is very good. In fact, the North-Lucas is not merely an unconventional design, but it attains in performance the ideals that were aimed at in its original conception. It is lively, silent, fast, and absolutely vibrationless. The quality of the springing is excellent, and it seems very economical in operation.

Uncannily, these comments and many other reactions to the North-Lucas prefigured those that would be made about another rear-engined air-cooled car some twenty years later. This was particularly true of a finding by *The Autocar*: "As the engine and all the mechanism are at the back, there is little or no chance of wheel slip even in exceptional circumstances — for example, when the little car was driven up a long hill several inches deep with fallen leaves and thick with mud."

With subtle courtesy *The Motor's* Miles Thomas said that "it certainly appears that it possesses definite commercial possibilities which its constructors would probably be prepared to discuss with persons interested." Its builders and promoters covered ninety thousand miles in the North-Lucas over sixteen years of searching for "persons interested," but in vain. No British car producer was willing to give houseroom to such an unorthodox vehicle.

IN 1922 LEYLAND, A COMMERCIAL-VEHICLE maker, began producing the Trojan auto, an unorthodox and rustic vehicle that could be considered the Citroën 2CV of its era. It was known for its "notably lethargic performance and somewhat uncouth appearance," in the words of Anthony Bird. A throwback to the natal years of the automobile, the Trojan had an under-floor two-stroke engine, exposed planetary transmission, and solid-rubber tires.

Trojan may have done more than any other automaker to blacken the reputation of the rear-engined car in Britain. Its guiding genius, Leslie Hounsfield, was said to have had reservations about the major redesign of his brainchild that was launched at the 1929 Olympia Motor Show by a Trojan that was now independent of Leyland. The two-stroke engine was now behind the rear axle and placed vertically in a boxed trunk or boot at the tail of a wholly conventional-looking car.

Capable of little more than forty-five miles per hour, judged to need brakes on the rear wheels only, the new rear-engined RE Trojan was infested with bugs when it took to the road in 1930. Boiling off its coolant on hills was just one of its party tricks. Its more conventional appearance was belied by the peculiarities of its two-stroke engine, the starting of which — including necessary priming through Trojan's unique carburetor — was the subject of two pages in the owner's manual.

The press managed to curb its enthusiasm. "As unorthodoxy is the one sin the British motor world will not tolerate," wrote Anthony Bird, "the Trojan was praised with the faintest of damns in the motor journals." Nevertheless *The Motor* noted that one of its advantages was that "the fact that all the noise-generating machinery is at the back makes the car purr along very quietly on the road."

Although only two hundred or so of the rear-engined RE Trojan were sold, the Croydon-based company remained faithful to the concept. Indeed at Olympia in 1935 it unveiled two still-incomplete examples of its most ambitious car yet, the Mastra.

Anyone seeking an example of rudimentary blacksmithery in the guise of automotive engineering as practiced in 1930s Britain needed to look no farther than the drivetrain of the Mastra. Its engine drove through a three-speed gearbox to a chain drive and thence to a driveshaft forward to a worm gear atop an offset live axle on leaf springs. No greater contrast could be imagined than

With its two-stroke engine located under the floor boards, the 1925 Trojan was a rustic creation much beloved of country folk. It led to a new generation of rear-engined Trojans.

between its crude layout and the elegance of the engineering of the North-Lucas or the contemporary work of Hans Ledwinka at Tatra in Czechoslovakia and John Tjaarda at Briggs in America, not to mention FerdinandPorsche.

THAT THE MASTRA REMAINED a prototype and Trojan gave up the manufacture of cars altogether seemed another strike against the rear-engined car in Britain after the lack of interest shown by the industry in the North-Lucas. Another blow was the failure of a prototype that was remarkably well engineered to reach production, a prototype in some respects better than the Beetle: the Rover Scarab.

Established in 1904, the Rover Motor Company was best known in the early 1930s for its sedate cars in the medium-price category. Thus its British dealers were bemused when, on 1 September 1931, they "received a brochure, on the back of which was the shadowy silhouette of the new car with the background of the Egyptian pyramids." The British discovery of the tomb of the young Pharaoh Tutankhamen was less than a decade in the past; Egyptian themes were still à la mode.

Introduced in 1929, the new RE Trojan placed its two-stroke engine vertically in a box at the rear of the chassis. It kept a planetary transmission but abandoned solid tires in favor of pneumatic ones.

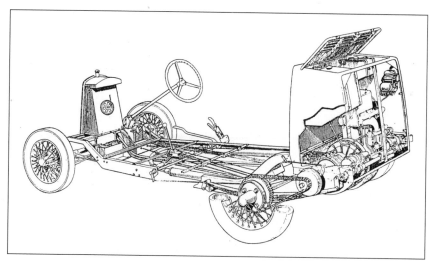

Above:
Chassis details of the Trojan
RE show the chain drive to
its solid rear axle and the
remote location of the rad-
iator at the front of the car,
a cooling arrangement
which proved inadequate.

Right:
Fortunately, in view of its
extreme crudity — charac-
teristic of much British
engineering of the era —
Trojan's 1935 Mastra pro-
totype was not inflicted on
the motoring public.

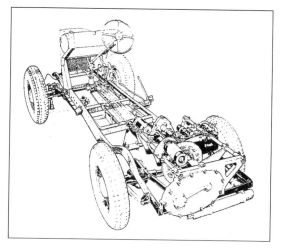

The description in the sumptuous suede-green gold-blocked brochure announcing the 1932 Rovers said only that the new car would be called the Scarab and would sell for eighty-five pounds — a price that would make it a lively competitor not only for volume-produced small cars but also for motorcycles with sidecars in a country where affordable transport was still at a premium. The price was still low when it was finally fixed in October: eighty-nine pounds.

That Rover was a company that abjured the hiring of qualified engineers became evident when the specification of the Scarab was revealed at the 1931 Olympia Show. In looks it was orthodox, a disc-wheeled open two/four-seater on an 84-inch wheelbase with a curved and louvered beetle-back and

Starting in 1930, Rover spent £10,000 on the design and construction of six prototypes of a new small car, the Scarab, that looked conventional but, in fact, was radical. The Scarab was to cost £89 and was exhibited at the 1931 Olympia Show, but it never entered production. The car in the middle picture is fitted with test instrumentation. Powered by a rear-mounted air-cooled vee-twin of 839 cc, the Scarab had a sophisticated rear suspension design and was tested by both Hans Nibel of Daimler-Benz and Ferdinand Porsche.

helmet-shaped front fenders. Its hood and radiator grille were deceptive, for its engine was in the rear.

Its power package consisted of a differential with inboard drum brakes and behind it an extremely compact motorcycle-type three-speed gearbox, an oil-filled clutch, and a sixty-degree vee-twin engine of 839 cc with push-rod-operated overhead valves and finned iron cylinders cooled by an un-cowled fan. Its output was enough to get the little Scarab up to fifty or fifty-five miles per hour.

As if this were not iconoclastic enough, the Scarab's designers gave it in-dependent suspension by coil springs at all four wheels. At the front the wheels slid up and down on the same pillar around which they steered, some-what like contemporary Lancias and Morgans; springing was by two coils in tension at each side.

Rear suspension was by a wide-based A-shaped arm at each side, its lon-gitudinal pivot axis passing through the inboard universal joint for the drive half-shaft. A damping effect was provided by friction elements inside the A-arms' pivots. Above the arms were large coil springs which abutted against a transverse steel beam attached to the top of the differential housing.

The astonishing feature of the Scarab's advanced design was that the transverse beam was pivoted to the housing, not fixed rigidly to it. In roll, consequently, the beam would simply pivot at its center and the coil springs would exert no resistance to rolling or leaning in corners. All the resistance to rolling would be provided by the front wheels and tires, which thus would ap-proach their limit of grip sooner and give the car's handling a stabilizing ef-fect instead of the tail-happy behavior that would normally have been induced by the mass of its overhung rear engine.

This steadying rear suspension was aided and abetted by the positioning of the Scarab's front coil springs so that they exerted a self-centering effect on the steering. Taken overall, these represented advanced concepts for 1931, concepts of suspension tailoring to weight distribution that would only be widely used years later. "In fact," wrote Michael Frostick, "the car handled particularly well by the standards of its day, having fairly pro-nounced understeer."

The chief Daimler-Benz chassis engineer Hans Nibel came to Britain to assess one of the Scarab prototypes. Although Nibel died in 1934 the con-cept may have lingered at Stuttgart; later in the decade a form of roll decou-pling of the rear swing axles of some Mercedes-Benz cars was introduced. Not until the launch of the 1500 model in 1966 would VW's Beetle enjoy similar sophistication.

Only a year or so after founding his own consulting engineering busi-ness in the early thirties, Ferdinand Porsche also tried a Scarab prototype at Rover's Coventry works. At that time he was already working on his Type 12 project, a small rear-engined car design which he eventually sold to motor-

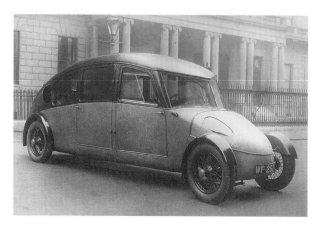

In the early 1930s airship designer Sir Charles Dennistoun Burney designed and built a series of rear-engined cars. This was his first (relatively small) prototype.

cycle-maker Zündapp. Links existed between Zündapp and Rover; in 1925 the German firm had considered producing Rovers under license. But the Scarab ideas did not influence the Type 12, which had transverse leaf springs, and Porsche's future small-car designs would use his space-saving torsion-bar springs.

Since 1930, at a secret experimental workshop at the home of the Rover chairman, engineers Robert Boyle and Maurice Wilks had been working on the Scarab. They built six in all, including a van version, spending ten thousand pounds on the project and allocating five thousand pounds to initial tooling. But to make economic sense the Scarab would have had to be produced at 30,000 units per year, with tooling costs of fifty thousand pounds, at a time when Rover was making no more than 3,500 cars annually and barely avoiding liquidation. With the arrival of new management, including the brother of Maurice Wilks, the Scarab was jettisoned — another strike against the rear-engined car in Britain.

AT THE OPPOSITE END OF THE PRICE scale from the Scarab was a £1,500 British rear-engined car of 1930–31 that gained more column-inches than customers. Its appearance and design gave the popular press a

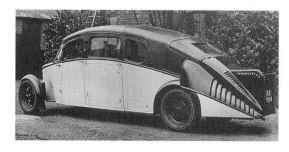

Burney actively promoted his larger prototype to engineers and companies throughout the world, including a visit to America in 1932. Rolls-Royce found the Burney's road behavior to be "sufficiently good to be very disturbing."

Burney hung the engines of his cars (in this car a twin-cam straight-eight Beverley-Barnes) out behind the rear wheels. Twin radiators were mounted athwart the engine.

field day in Britain. The motoring editor of the *Daily Express* said that it saved on tires because they scarcely touched the road at speed; if it could reach 180 miles per hour the new Burney Streamline would lift right off the ground!

A hint of nicknames to come was the description by the newspapers of this spectacular new car as "an enormous 'lady bug'." Photos of it circulating in London in 1930 were highly newsworthy — when *The Motor* first described the Burney in five pages in September 1930 it hailed it as "everything that the artists and writers of the past have termed 'the car of the future'." Its writer waxed eloquent:

> Sitting in the utmost luxury, one gazes out upon the countryside through large, clear, glass windows. There is no bonnet ahead of one, there are no visible wheels or wings. There is no noise, no smell, no heat from the engine. All that one hears is a faint swish as the wind races past the beautifully streamlined contours of the vehicle. One might be in the forward gondola of an absolutely noiseless airship. One feels that one has gone to sleep and awakened, like Rip Van Winkle, 100 years hence. It is an entirely fresh motoring sensation.

The "airship" reference was not by chance. The car was the creation of Comdr. Sir Charles Dennistoun Burney, an inventor-engineer-promoter whose R-100 airship was at that time the world's largest and fastest lighter-than-air craft. However, by 1931 Britain's government had withdrawn all support for airship development and Burney's entirely serviceable and successful R-100 was steamrollered into scrap aluminum.

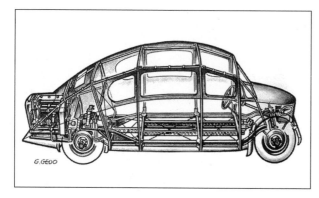

The Burney cars had conventional steel chassis and wood-framed bodies. Suspension was independent at both front and rear by transverse leaf springs.

Burney then applied his considerable energies to his rear-engined auto and the company he formed to develop it, Streamline Cars. The huge (149-inch wheelbase) rear-engined car had its seven-hundred-pound straight-eight engine behind the worm final drive, with a center-pinion drive going forward to a four-speed gearbox ahead of the axle. Weight distribution was sharply rearward, as much as 70 percent on some Burneys.

The seven-passenger 4,260-pound Burney Streamline lacked the ingenuity of the Rover Scarab's suspension system. Nevertheless testers considered that "the springing is as near perfect as it can be." Flat-sided and with a profile like the section of a thick airplane wing, the Burney was thought to be spectacularly streamlined by the standards of 1931 and a potential trendsetter in this respect, according to *The Motor*:

> Now that the public have become accustomed to the idea of properly stream-lined forms through familiarity with airships and submarines, the unconventional appearance of the car under review is not likely to prove any deterrent to those who want real comfort at half the cost of the average car with equivalent passenger accommodation.

One who felt such a need was H.R.H. Edward, Prince of Wales, who took delivery of a royal blue Burney. His was one of a dozen or so such cars that left the Maidenhead workshops.

"The actual running of this car, its general performance and comfort, is sufficiently good to be very disturbing," reported Rolls-Royce engineer Ernest Hives to Sir Henry Royce after a Burney test drive from London to Maidenhead. Here was an impressively quiet and efficient big car. Should Rolls-Royce consider a car on Burney lines? "We admit it is irritating to have to think of an entirely new motor car," noted Hives, "but, as it has several sound fundamental advantages, I should not like the responsibility of turning it down."

Rolls-Royce cars nevertheless remained resolutely orthodox, but it was a sign of the merit of Burney's ideas that the august firm took them so seriously. Indeed they paid him the compliment, as a potential rival, of refusing to

Manchester-based Crossley was licensed by Burney to produce a car to his designs. Introduced in 1933, the rear-engined Crossley sold little better by virtue of its lower price and more conventional front-end styling.

make components for Burney and declaring the Rolls factory at Derby off limits to him.

Mooted links with Lagonda, Standard, and Riley failed to make progress. Burney finally found a customer in Crossley Motors of Gorton, Manchester. Crossley had been producing cars since 1904, as well as making commercial vehicles, but was in fact on its last legs as an automaker when it took a license to make a car on Burney principles.

Announced at Olympia in October 1933, the rear-engined Crossley was still expensive at £795 and carried over the unfortunate but patented Burney notion that the best place for the spare wheel was inside one of the rear passenger doors. Half the price of the original Burney, the Crossley version achieved double the sales volume: some two dozen were made through 1934. That was the end of experiments with radical cars for Sir Dennis, who died in Bermuda in 1968 at the age of seventy-nine.

Burney had overlooked one of the secrets of success of the rear-engined car with its engine behind the axle: use a short engine. With a rear engine, *The Autocar* understood well enough in 1933, "it is understood, of course, that the normal 'in line' six- or eight-cylinder engine has to be discarded in favour of a compact vee or horizontal engine. With this the designer has the whole of the space ahead of the rear axle free for passenger carrying and has sufficient length on which to design a body offering the lowest head resistance."

Unlike his counterparts in the United States in the 1930s (see chapter 5), the persuasive Burney did at least succeed in having his ideas implemented by a carmaker. That Crossley flopped with its rear-engined model, however, and stopped making cars altogether after 1937, did nothing to convince William Morris and Herbert Austin that they were on the wrong track with their traditional motorcars. Britain had seen heterodoxy from Trojan, Rover, and Burney, among others, and had found it unsettling.

FRUSTRATED FAR MORE THAN they dared mention in print by the stultifying banality of their domestic products, Britain's auto journalists continued to bang the drum in favor of progressive change. They could and did point to Tatra and Mercedes-Benz — although the abortive rear-engined efforts of the latter did not always give them strong ammunition in their fight for novel engineering.

The ride quality of the Mercedes-Benz 130 was "remarkable," said *The Autocar* in its 1934 test of this four-cylinder car with its "outboard" water-cooled rear engine (see chapter 1). It remarked on "the soft and extremely comfortable springing given by the independent suspension for all four wheels." Stability was another matter, however.

> There is a curious impression, less noticeable as one becomes used to the car, of a slight swaying motion, so that the car does not appear to be following an absolutely straight course on a good main road; this is linked up perhaps with the suppleness of the springing, is more apparent than real, in all probability, and to some extent is accounted for by the unusually direct, quick-acting steering, which, however, is very light.

The reference to the 130's steering hinted at the strong oversteer that could easily be provoked in this tail-heavy car with its swing-axle suspension. If during his visit to Coventry Hans Nibel had taken note of the rear-suspension roll decoupling used on the Rover Scarab, and its beneficial effect, he had overlooked the value of its application to the 130 and its successors the 170 and 160. The 130 "was a vicious tail-wagger," wrote Ronald Barker, commenting on a reprint of this road test, "and German owners used to think twice before taking one out on wet or gusty days."

Thanks to their lighter air-cooled engines with many aluminum parts, Tatras were less vulnerable to — although not immune from — this criticism. In Czechoslovakia since the early 1930s Tatra had been producing air-cooled rear-engined independently sprung aerodynamic cars engineered by Hans Ledwinka. Rare outside their home country, they were exceptionally scarce in Britain, where a V-8 Tatra Type 77 was priced at a princely £990 in 1935.

The Autocar acquainted its readers with the advanced specification of the ninety-miles-per-hour Type 77 Tatra in February 1935. It explained that the big (seventeen-foot-long) car was "a complete breakaway from orthodox practices" which was "built for use in conditions on the Continent which, as regards road surfaces and distances to be covered, are markedly different from those obtaining here." Among its road impressions:

> The riding was most comfortable, and a demonstration at speed down a hill abounding in potholes and such obstructions as manholes standing high above the ground was, to say the least, astounding. None of the party of four in the car would have dared to have taken any normal car over the surface in question at half the speed. Yet inside the car very little shock was felt, and there [were] none of those disconcerting shocks which suggest that machinery is being ill-treated.
>
> From English standards the engine and gears are noisy, but this is not apparent to the driver and his passengers.

A year later the same journal published an article by Roy Fedden, chief engineer for airplane engines at Bristol, in which he put forward the merits of a rear-engined car powered by an air-cooled radial engine using sleeve valves like those in the Bristol aviation engines. This brought unexpected consequences, Fedden later recalled.

> Two or three weeks afterwards an eight-cylinder Tatra arrived one morning at my office, the driver of which bore a letter from my friend, Oliver Boden, then managing director of Morris Motors, Ltd., stating that my article met with the approval of the chief engineer of Tatra, who had telephoned Boden asking him to send over to Bristol the eight-cylinder Tatra which was undergoing extended trials at Oxford, and to allow me to keep the car a few days and let him have a report on it.

Fedden and his engineers took full advantage of this gesture by Hans Ledwinka. "There were several most interesting features about the Tatra," he wrote, "the most outstanding of which were its eight-cylinder air-cooled rear engine, road-holding capacity and ability to maintain high average speed." Although the maximum speed of this Type 77 was measured by Fedden at a modest seventy-eight miles per hour, over his personal fifty-five-mile test route he found it to be second in average speed only to "a four-seater Alfa Romeo spare Mille Miglia car."

Firmly committed to air cooling for his airplane engines, Fedden flew in the face of British convention by espousing it for automobiles: "I am a believer in this type of engine for the future, not necessarily as a solution for the mass-produced cheap car, but also for the power plant of a good, sound all-round type, provided always that the layout of the engine and the type of valve mechanism are suited for air-cooling." Writing this in 1942, Roy Fedden had already progressed farther than he cared to reveal in the application of a sleeve-valve air-cooled radial to a rear-engined car of his own design.

What had this radical Czech car been doing in Oxford? The answer was disclosed by an article less than a month later in *The Autocar* by Miles Thomas, former head of Wolseley who had been named vice-chairman and managing director of Nuffield in 1940 to replace the deceased Oliver Boden. Thomas's memory had been triggered by Roy Fedden's letter. "That Tatra in many respects was a most interesting car," the executive wrote, "which is why we bought it to add to our experimental fleet" at Morris, part of the Nuffield Group.

Thomas recalled that "as a piece of unusual automobile engineering the Tatra commanded great respect. It was probably built to fulfil certain specific desiderata, and it probably fulfilled them brilliantly. But it did not enthuse me with the idea of rear-engined cars as a whole." He and the Morris engineers were unhappy about the poor cabin heating, lack of rear vision, and "very critical and very vicious" breakaway of the rear tires at the cornering limit of this first series-built rear-engined Tatra.

Miles Thomas had yet another complaint. "As in the North-Lucas, which I 'tested' as a cub-journalist in 1922 or '23 [1922 for *The Motor*], I noticed when driving the Tatra that one was bothered by the shortness of the bonnet and the forward driving position. The effect is not induced by a feeling that one is sitting too close to the accident, as it were, but because one can see the ground whizzing under one's feet, so fast and so close."

On the positive side the Nuffield executive cited the Tatra's ability to achieve high average speeds over varied roads and surfaces, by virtue of "the extraordinary suspension, the good road-holding, and the perfect geometry of the steering. Thanks to the chassis stiffness, independent springing and good steering layout, one could wheel round corners with amazing verve. But there was a catch in it" — sudden rear-wheel breakaway when traction was lost.

In the polite style of the day the editor of *The Autocar* remarked that "This article reveals the genuine interest in the nicer points of design of such great concerns as the Nuffield Organisation in their endeavor to study development and the motoring public's taste." On their face, however, the Nuffield vice-chairman's comments on the Tatra also served to demonstrate the inability of the British motor industry to discern the good in a new concept when the less good was also present. They seized eagerly on the latter to the disadvantage of the former.

This is not to tar Miles Thomas (later Sir Miles) with the brush of blind obstruction of progressive change. When he wrote to *The Autocar* Thomas was already encouraging "a shy, reserved young man named Alec Issigonis" to think about a new low-priced four-passenger sedan for the postwar market. "He had some very fundamental new ideas about motor car construction," Thomas recalled, "and the first thing we decided in the make-up of this small saloon was that we would throw away the conventional chassis, make the body take the reaction stresses from the axles, and employ independent suspension at the front and if possible at the rear."

This new Morris car, code-named Mosquito, was designed in the mid-1940s by Issigonis with the encouragement of Thomas and Morris chief engineer Vic Oak. It evolved into the Morris Minor, one of the outstanding small-car designs of the postwar era and one of the few European models which, had it been given enough development, support, and manufacturing investment, might have rivaled the Beetle's success in global markets.

WHILE BRITAIN'S MOTOR TYCOONS were experimenting with (and in some instances learning from) advanced Continental cars, British magazine readers were learning about the use the Germans had been making of their newfangled rear-engined air-cooled car. From neutral sources, reported *The Motor* in September 1941, it learned that the KdF cars "have proved extremely useful in the Libyan campaign as well as in Russia. Many

One of the two Type 82 Volkswagens brought to John Dugdale's vehicle repair unit in the West African desert was photographed by him in front of his unit's four-wheel-drive Chevrolet truck.

company commanders use them and find that they corner well and run smoothly over rough roads." It added some convincing detail:

> The first severe tests were, it appears, imposed upon the cars around the town of Mikulnico some weeks ago, when some slippery grass meadows and half-ploughed fields had to be crossed. The KdF crossed these and later passed over water-filled ditches before successfully climbing a steep and slippery hill. As it has proved itself adaptable in many cases where the heavier cars have failed, KdF has gained the general admiration of the troops who have seen it perform and has been referred to as the "Wunderding" or "a little wonder."

Not mentioned in the article, however, was the important news that the wartime KdF-Wagen carried a different body to its civilian counterpart and indeed differed in important engineering details as well. Three weeks before *The Motor's* article appeared, a correspondent for its weekly rival was driving, drawing, and photographing two samples of the authentic wartime Beetle in its native North African habitat.

Reporting on motoring matters was far from John Dugdale's mind in the early autumn of 1941. A successful correspondent for *The Autocar* before the war with several racing scoops and initiatives to his credit, Dugdale had joined the army in December 1939 after returning from America, where he covered John Cobb's successful attack on the World Land Speed Record in August.

Dugdale was sent to France in February 1940, then evacuated at Dunkirk. In March 1941 he was posted to Africa's western desert as a captain in the Royal Army Service Corps' Mechanical Transport arm. With a

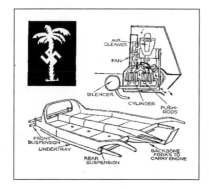

Based on his inspection of the African Type 82s, marked by the Afrika Corps emblem, John Dugdale sketched details of their engine and chassis.

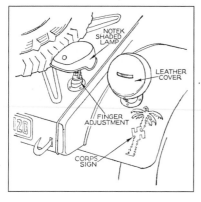

John Dugdale's detailed sketches of the captured Kübels were lightly retouched by The Autocar in London and published in its issue of 17 October 1941.

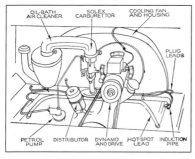

Experienced automotive journalist Dugdale, now a captain in the Royal Army Service Corps, was well qualified to make notes on the contents of the engine compartment of the Kübels he found in North Africa in 1941.

Chevrolet four-wheel-drive truck and a six-wheeled Leyland rolling workshop he was trusted with the care and maintenance of some four hundred military vehicles.

"Desert warfare was like being at sea," Dugdale said. "You saw a vehicle coming over the horizon and had no idea what it was." One day some unusual vehicles came over the horizon. "We were the workshop, so all kinds of vehicles were brought to us. These were captured in the summer of 1941 after the first siege of Tobruk," he recalled.

John Dugdale photographed the battered interior of one of two captured Kübels, showing the two fuse boxes at the sides of the central speedometer.

Seen in the summer of 1941, the two African Kübels were among the first to be closely examined by Allied units. The rugged design of their "jerricans" made a deep impression.

Two Type 82s fell into Dugdale's hands. One had the large-section balloon tires used in the desert and carried welding equipment while the other, built in 1940, wore conventional treaded tires and a rear-seat machine-gun mounting. These were among the first such vehicles that Allied troops had seen; they were certainly the first to be seen by someone who knew very well what he was looking at.

Captain Dugdale, an artist among his other skills, pencil-sketched exterior and interior details of the treaded-tire Kübelwagen on the first two days of September 1941. He made some educated guesses about its frame design and its engine's cooling system. His sketches, his photos of the Type 82, and a lengthy text describing it were sent off to London by the next courier.

This was a sensational scoop to which *The Autocar* gave four of its precious wartime pages on 17 October. Five of Dugdale's photos appeared and his six sketches were only lightly redrawn. He spotted the hub reduction gears, the oil-bath air cleaner for desert operation, and the similarity of the suspension to that of the Auto Union racing cars.

Pointing out the lightness of the Type 82's construction, which "has been achieved only at the expense of flimsiness," Dugdale judged it to be "an altogether too delicate piece of mechanism" by Allied standards as a result of its civilian origins. The journalist-officer reported further:

> As to performance, this is livelier than previous reports had indicated, the getaway being particularly snappy. Considering the distance from pedals to engine, the controls were positive, but this particular clutch was fierce. The gear lever was noticeably positive, and must have an excellent remote control. In spite of four-wheel independent suspension, the springing was not so outstanding as might have been expected, but then the desert, with its multitude of small rocks and hillocks, is the worst surface in the world.

John Dugdale was guarded in his praise of the KdF-based Kübelwagen as he found it; this was after all a creation of the detested Germans. But he drew special attention to the two four-gallon water cans slung in sockets above the rear wings. With their built-in handles, these were utterly unlike the flimsy square canisters used by the Allies. "To withstand rough usage and in order that they should be of the maximum possible strength, the cans are rounded on all corners and ribbed." This was an early sighting of the soon-to-be-ubiquitous "jerrican" named after the enemy, which the Allies copied and put into mass production.

ONE OF THESE DESERT TYPE 82S, its frame members still stuffed with one hundred pounds of Saharan sand, arrived in the British Midlands in the cold of January 1943. Built in 1941, the Kübel carried chassis number 1339 and Ambi-Budd body number 1777. It rolled on balloon tires and its bracketry suggested that it was the very car Dugdale had found that had carried a welding kit to repair its fellow warriors.

Here was a vehicle that the British Intelligence Objectives Sub-Committee investigators wanted studied so that its hidden secrets could be placed at the disposal of the Allied makers of military vehicles. Within the BIOS motor vehicles were the responsibility of the Ministry of Supply, which allocated the captured Kübelwagen to Humber Ltd. of Coventry for study.

In addition to being one of the marques of the Rootes Group, acquired by the Rootes family interests in 1931, Humber was also the unit that engineered and built all its vehicles. Hillmans and, later, Sunbeam-Talbots as well as Humbers were engineered and built by Humber under the technical direction of Bernard "B. B." Winter.

A dispatch rider in the Great War, Winter had served in India for Ford before joining Rootes in 1923. Rising through the Rootes organization from a service engineering post, he became head of service before moving to the technical side of the company in 1935. B. B. Winter — "a nice man," John Dugdale recalled — enjoyed the confidence of arch-salesman Billy Rootes and his administrator brother Reginald.

Winter was an advocate of the progressive development of the status quo; innovation was not an objective, as his car designs amply illustrated.

"He was not a born, nor an intuitive designer," wrote Graham Robson. "B. B. was a loyal Rootes man who always reflected what the family wanted rather than encouraged his engineers to stretch themselves. Perhaps this explains why several accomplished designers left Rootes before they were suffocated by the limited aspirations of the Winter regime."

Winter's team at Humber provided a meticulous and well-illustrated description and discussion of the Type 82 as they found it. A sixty-four-page version of the Rootes report was made available by the BIOS at the end of 1943. With the later addition of several reports by other motor companies on technical aspects of the wartime and early postwar Beetles, the full assessment was ultimately released in 1947 as BIOS Final Report No. 998.

Humber highlighted the Type 82's use of lightweight magnesium for the camshaft gear, blower rotor, oil pump housing, and engine crankcase (although the latter is described as "aluminum" in the text). It drew attention to the shrewd way the engine-cooling fan also drew cooling air through the dynamo.

The drivetrain received special coverage. Humber noted the neat ring of pins that slid fore and aft to engage the third and fourth gears of the four-speed gearbox. It described in detail the patented ZF cam-type differential that gave the Type 82 its grip in slippery terrain in spite of having only two-wheel drive. It showed how the reduction gearing at the rear hubs was ingeniously used both to raise ground clearance and to lower the final-drive ratio.

A simple idiot light warned of low oil pressure, Humber reported. The tubular suspension dampers at the front worked only on rebound, when they were compressed. The wheels were cheaply and neatly attached directly to the brake drums by five studs.

Lucas provided a detailed study of the electrical system. This included the lamp at the rear that allowed the following driver in a convoy to judge his distance at either fifty meters (165 feet) or one hundred and forty meters (460 feet) according to his perceived merging of illuminated windows.

Astonishingly, Humber was unwilling to grant that the VW design achieved any advantage in weight. It criticized the engine for not producing higher specific power. In doing so it chose to overlook the fact that Porsche had intentionally designed it as a *Drosselmotor*, deliberately throttled below its full power potential to improve its reliability and durability.

Most devastating to the British perception of the KdF-Wagen was the final paragraph of Humber's general observations:

> Looking at the general picture, we do not consider that the design represents any special brilliance, apart from certain of the detail points, and it is suggested that it is not to be regarded as an example of first class modern design to be copied by the British industry.

To be sure, Humber said that these remarks "should be treated purely as their views." But both at the time and later this oft-quoted verdict on the

Type 82 by the Bernard Winter team tended to obscure the many merits of the VW design. Once again, British engineers had allowed the negatives to overwhelm the positives of a new vehicle concept.

This report was excerpted in *The Autocar* of 3 December 1943, which repeated its damning conclusion verbatim, and in *The Motor* of the fifteenth of the same month. Much of the text, with many illustrations, was published over eleven pages of the July 1944 issue of *Automobile Engineer*.

MEANWHILE, BRITONS WERE GAINING firsthand experience of the KdF-Wagen in its Kübelwagen form amongst the hedgerows of Normandy. *The Autocar's* correspondent, H. E. Ellis, cadged a drive in one courtesy of the U.S. Army in the autumn of 1944. He expressed surprise at its "flimsy" construction and the resultant brisk performance, and also at the fact that it handled "remarkably well."

Remarked Ellis about the mud-splattered Bug of war:

> The engine is quite flexible and the suspension and seating seemed, from my short experience of the car, to make for comfortable riding. The rear engine practically eliminates noise and heat in the driving compartment and the gear box is reasonably good.
>
> If one took this badly knocked about example of the Volkswagen as a criterion I would say that, if one is prepared to put up with a car that rattles like fury and has absolutely no refinements, then the Volkswagen is not at all a bad car. But it is definitely not my idea of what I want for my wife and family après la guerre.

The Motor fought back a year later when Laurence Pomeroy made a lightning visit to American-occupied Germany. He told his readers in November of 1945 that "the U.S. Army uses the jeep almost invariably for personal travel, but it cannot be considered a very suitable vehicle for this job. The few German Army editions of the K.d.F. which have been taken over by the occupying forces are regarded with considerable envy."

Pomeroy remarked on wartime experiments with improved cylinder heads and an axial cooling fan which improved the Beetle engine. He was not able to visit the works — travel in Germany at the time was fearfully difficult — but he reported that "even after visitation by the R.A.F., the factory is capable of making over 150 cars a day, and a considerable production programme has been authorised for next year." In fact not until much later, in mid-1949, could the plant claim to be making 150 cars daily.

The captured KdF-Wagens referred to were largely in the hands of forces that were American, not British. The U.S. Eighth Army took a liberal view of the adoption of German vehicles where appropriate but the responsible British inspectorate hewed to a tougher line. They were, reflected Ivan Hirst, "perhaps a little over-zealous in Normandy and beyond:"

> I believe that their initial purpose was to ensure that every unit had the equipment it needed, but the man in charge had a "bee in his bonnet" where captured

enemy vehicles were concerned. His view was that a unit's authorised scale of vehicles, etc. was correct and that ex-German vehicles in excess of that were an encumbrance and an unnecessary waste of fuel and road space.

In practice, said one U.K. observer, "a liberal mixture of Eighth Army personnel with those of us who came direct from England considerably altered one's evaluation of Army Law." The technical illegality of possessing a Kübelwagen was increasingly overlooked.

THE RESUMPTION OF PRODUCTION at Wolfsburg allowed the British intelligence analysts to get their hands on newly built sedan-style Beetles. "The first VWs exported from Wolfsburg were two cars which were sent to London for expert examination and evaluation," wrote Maj. Charles Bryce, the REME officer sent to the VW works to oversee quality control. "They were produced at the end of the summer of 1946 under very strict inspection control, and were as perfect in detail as possible under the prevailing circumstances." These were the first of the Type 11 models, series production of which began in October 1946.

Thus we have to question the provenance of the Beetle that was evaluated in part 2 of the 1947 version of the BIOS report. This consisted of a performance comparison by Humber between a Hillman Minx and a civilian version of the VW which was received by Humber on 18 February 1946 — months before the two Type 11 sample cars were passed as fit for export by Major Bryce and his chief inspector, Herr Half, and chief of testing, Herr Steltgis. We can only surmise that Humber's test car was a rare wartime Beetle that had made its way to Britain.

Humber's comparison Minx was not the prewar Mark II but a prototype of Hillman's postwar Mark III model. A dimensional and performance check gives support to the assumption that this did not yet have the envelope body of the final Mark III Minx, introduced in September 1948, but was already equipped with that model's independent front suspension.

Humber reported that the subject VW, which it called Type 11 using the postwar British designation, was down a good 25 percent in compression pressure in one cylinder and 8 percent in another cylinder, both on the right-hand bank, "but no action was taken to dismantle the engine to find the cause." Low cylinder compression was a sign of faulty valves that would greatly degrade the engine's power. Certainly no such fault would have crippled either of the two cars specially prepared by the works.

Perversely, Humber took the view that the VW should be penalized for its lighter weight by being loaded more heavily than the Minx for the tests. Described as "definitely poor" by Humber, the VW's braking performance was in fact dismal. Eighty pounds of pressure on the pedal (quite a lot) generated only half the deceleration of the Minx when both cars were fully laden.

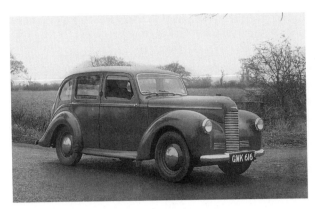

When Humber Ltd. evaluated a Type 60 Volkswagen in 1946 it compared its performance to a Hillman Minx Mark II (like the car shown), albeit equipped with the independent front suspension that would be used on the envelope-bodied Mark III Minx.

When the cars were carrying equal loads, a driver plus a passenger, the VW at 1,861 pounds yielded much better fuel consumption than the 2,324-pound Minx prototype. At average speeds of 37.6 and 36.0 mph respectively the VW and Minx returned 43.0 and 34.6 miles per Imperial gallon, in that order. Even when burdened with five passengers and 160 pounds of "luggage" the plucky VW managed 40.0 mpg at 36.3 mph. Humber admitted that no more than four people could squeeze into the Minx prototype with its prewar-style body.

In part 3 of the final BIOS report the Pressed Steel Co. Ltd., assessed the body design and structure of a Type 11 VW sedan. It produced an excellent set of drawings of details of the body as it was built by the VW plant under its British controllers. The assessors gave it as their "considered opinion that from the Body Engineering point of view the design of this vehicle is exceptionally good, and shows a great advance on previous constructional methods."

Points of particular interest on the body included the built-in heating and demisting system, with its ducts integral with the body structure, and the facia panel designed to suit both right-hand- and left-hand-drive versions. Pressed Steel found that the design sought to reduce welding as much as possible by stamping "large complete panels, often of a complex type," and joining panels by wrapping their edges over instead of welding them.

The report drew attention to the light yet stiff design of the hood and trunk lids. Features that came to be taken for granted much later, such as pull-out door handles and an automatic self-latching stay for the hood, were part of the design. Such details as the stamped parts of the door latches and window regulators attracted positive comment from Pressed Steel on the construction of what was called "an exceptionally rigid and semi-unitary vehicle."

Parts 4 and 5 of the report were peculiar contributions to the VW's assessment by Singer Motors and A.C. Cars respectively. Both drove what was evidently one of the few Kübelwagens of postwar construction, which they called a Type 21 although the designation used by the British was Type 51 for this model.

That quality control was not yet up to VW's later standards was clear from the faults enumerated by Singer, which included a "collapsed" wheel bearing and inoperative wipers, horn, and speedometer. Singer found the engine, gearbox, and ZF differential "extremely noisy" but the roadholding "extremely good" with positive steering and little pitch and roll. The clutch and gear shifting were praised.

Faults that transformed themselves into virtues after a few miles of driving the Type 21 Beetle were featured in the brief assessment by A.C. Cars. The instant response of the close-coupled power train, initially disconcerting, soon won admirers. So too did the unfamiliar closeness of the driver to the front of the car. "Soon overcome with a little practice," A.C. said, "the excellent forward visibility is then appreciated."

The A.C. assessor seemed to pay the Porsche designers a compliment by concluding "that this vehicle is a useful education for those who think there is a future for the rear engined car," well reflecting the debate in Britain during the 1920s and 1930s over the projects of North-Lucas, Rover, Trojan, Burney, and Crossley. Added A.C., "The case for all round independent suspension is clearly demonstrated to be a valuable feature." Ironically A.C. itself, in the event, was one of the last British carmakers to cease putting solid axles under the noses of its cars.

A 1,131 cc engine from this Kübelwagen was transported to Dagenham in Essex. There Ford extracted its secrets on one of its dynamometers and recorded them on 8 February 1946 for publication in part 6 of the final BIOS report. At a measured 5.63:1 the compression ratio was lower than the specified 5.80:1, but the engine's peak output of 24.3 horsepower at 3,250 rpm was about what the VW's designers would have expected. Ford placed the torque peak at 2,000 rpm, also in accord with VW's tests.

Ford considered that the flat-four had an excessive thirst for fuel and tried different carburetor jettings to reduce the richness of the mixture. This brought a 16-percent reduction in specific fuel consumption. Stating that "the carburetion could be improved to give a more economic fuel consumption," Ford concluded its report by saying, "The performance is not outstanding and the general noise in operation is excessive, the engine could not be recommended *in its present form* [emphasis added]."

ALTHOUGH THE FINAL BIOS REPORT concluded with Ford's dusty view of the engine, *en masse* the British assessors found much to admire and indeed to emulate in the VW's radical and ruthlessly simplified design. The sedan's body construction was rife with advanced and clever simplifications and cost reductions. The VW was substantially lighter than its nearest British counterpart and yielded much better fuel consumption.

It shifted easily, handled well, and gave a good ride. How, then, to make sense of the general observations volunteered by Humber Engineering, observations that have often been quoted as sounding the last post for any acceptance of the VW vehicle and its factory among the victorious powers?

For an industry obsessed by refined running, viewing the Rolls-Royce as the best car in the world, the rough and raucous wartime Volkswagens must have come as a rude shock. Even the first postwar cars presented their virtues in a crude, coarse, and — in the case of the Type 82 dismantled by Humber — worn-out form. Bouncing along in a bellowing bucket-car, without sound damping of any kind, some British engineers were unimpressed.

We can excuse the Humber technicians to the extent that they were rushed to complete their assessment during the war. Neither did they have the benefit of the later analyses, especially the positive findings of Pressed Steel about the KdF sedan body, that were included in the final BIOS report.

Industry minnow A.C. seemed to grasp the essence of the situation: "From the general construction one gets the impression that the designer has given just enough but no more, therefore as a war vehicle this is no doubt acceptable, but as a civilian vehicle considerable modification would be required to conform to the standard expected." Bearing in mind that A.C. was assessing the open military version of the VW, this was incontrovertible.

In a major BIOS report published in 1949 that summarized and reviewed all the British and American intelligence reports on the German vehicle industry, British-born General Motors engineer Maurice Olley made clear his view that some of the assessors of the KdF-Wagen had missed the point:

> Although a number of the reports give space to the Volkswagen, and one report is devoted exclusively to it, one doubts whether they convey a true idea of the possibilities of this car. They refer chiefly to captured military equipment, or to staff cars hastily "run up" from pre-war stocks for the military government, and subjected to military usage. We have yet to see what the makers, left to themselves, can make of this car in the way of a vehicle suitable for normal civilian use. Perhaps the critics of the vehicle forget that large areas of the world are still looking for cheap transportation, and that the Model T Ford, which started world motorization, also had technical faults.

On balance, then, the contemporary assessments of the VW vehicle and its factory by British experts under BIOS auspices were favorable. Anyone weighing seriously the potential of the product would have found much in the postwar governmental reporting that stressed its strengths and merits, especially its suitability for export. Although Maurice Olley's wise words were heard too late to influence the fate of the factory, they reflected the tenor of thinking in the English engineering community about the controversial KdF-Wagen. That that thinking was overwhelmingly negative is myth, not fact.

At the end of 1943, just after his company's report on the Kübelwagen was published, Bernard Winter offered his thoughts to readers of *The Motor*

Drivers adept at piloting the Type 166 Schwimmwagen used the Mittelland Canal for demonstrations to visiting dignitaries. The dies to make its elegantly engineered hull had to be let go, said Ivan Hirst, because the British government said "no money was available for that sort of thing."

on the future of cars and the motor industry. Smaller cars were part of his plan to appeal to a global postwar market:

> Let us design and make small cars which will meet world requirements. I suggest that after this war the markets of the world will definitely require the smaller as well as the larger types of cars . . . I would take this opportunity of expressing the hope that we shall not see again a large crop of "mushroom" automobile manufacturers springing up. Our industry is a highly complicated and specialized one, and it will be a national misfortune if numerous war factories are turned over to produce new makes of car, with inexperienced engineers to see them through. By all means let some of the great war plants be turned over to our industry, but let the people who understand this job handle it.

Improvisationally equipped though it was, the greatest of all those war plants in Europe rested five hundred miles east of Coventry on so nearly the same latitude that there was little in it.

ANOTHER IMPORTANT POSTWAR assessment of the VW factory's products was made by a British general who had been responsible during the war for the "peculiar" vehicles in the Tank Corps: flamethrowers, mine-destroying flails, and the like. Through Gifhorn he set up a visit to Wolfsburg, especially to see and assess the Type 166 Schwimmwagen.

Although the works could not then produce its four-wheel-drive system for lack of certain forgings, it still had the complex and costly dies for the steel pressings that made up its sophisticated hull. Ivan Hirst took care to set these aside for possible future use.

"The general arrived in a Jeep," Hirst recalled, "and we had a contest with the Schwimmwagen. It easily went where the Jeep couldn't. As a result of these trials he tried to get the British government interested in the Schwimmwagen, but he was told that no money was available for that sort of thing. So I had to let the dies go." A vehicle that could justly be termed one of the masterworks of the Porsche office could no longer be made.

Early in 1946 a visiting British Ford production engineering team found much of interest in the car that the plant was struggling to produce. "The car is a highly interesting product," they reported. "The design is of outstanding merit, combining desirable technical features with the utmost economy of production cost. Various minor refinements could be made to increase the quality of the vehicle and provide a more comfortable ride. For an extremely cheap car, however, the Volkswagen is exceptionally good and extremely popular with military personnel on the continent."

The conception of its power unit won praise from the Ford manufacturing engineers. "The engine is of practical design for mass production and economical operation, all items being broken down into their simplest forms. Thus machining is a simple matter when compared with orthodox engines of similar capacity." This was the very same type of engine that their colleagues in Dagenham had dismissed after tests, only a few weeks earlier, as one that "could not be recommended in its present form."

The Ford experts interviewed one of Porsche's senior engineers, Josef Kales, about features of the VW's design. Kales was still on site running a small engineering office. Ivan Hirst told *Automobile Quarterly*:

> He was one of the original Porsche team, but it was not a car-design department. And the Experimental Department was also a very small affair. I would not say that Porsche was the first cousin of God and therefore his work must not be changed, but that is what the VW people thought in 1946–47.

Why, the Britons asked Kales, did the VW have a platform frame with attached body instead of fully integral construction? "Karlos [sic] said that the original intention had been to build the vehicle with frame and body as an integral unit, but direct orders had come from Hitler that provision should be made for the adoption of an alternative body design and it was imperative, therefore, to have a separate frame."

Why, Kales was quizzed, was rear-engine mounting adopted? He named three points in his response: the rear is less vulnerable than the front; the construction is cheaper; the engine, rear drive, and gearbox are in one unit and easily detachable. In his summary of the reports on the German industry Maurice Olley could not resist a wry comment on the first reason: "It would appear that the less vulnerable position of the engine implies a more vulnerable position for the passengers."

As for the future of the VW design, Kales told the Ford men, "The intentions of Porsche had been to keep the vehicle substantially in its present form and concentrate on the improvement of individual items." Kales mentioned, as an example, the development work that had been done during the war on the Beier infinitely variable automatic transmission. Its inventor, Dr. Josef Beier, "worked with Dr. Porsche of KdF and claims Dr. Porsche intended to adopt it on KdF cars," according to an American army intelligence report.

Pressed about possible refinements to the VW's design, Joseph Kales "pointed out that the Volkswagen was not meant to contain all the essential features of technical perfection, but was to be a compromise which would give the best results with minimum cost."

THANKS TO THE CAR'S SIMPLICITY of design the plant was able to turn out Type 11 Volkswagens which, with their military counterparts, were reaching Britain by one means or another. Some were brought officially by the Ministry of Supply to display their attributes to British industrialists. One such occasion was an exhibition at the Chobham, Surrey proving grounds in late July 1946, where both landlocked and amphibian KdF variants were displayed and demonstrated. This was the first stop in Britain for the two cars that Major Bryce's workmen had so carefully prepared.

After his visit to Chobham the motoring correspondent of the *News Chronicle*, Charles Fothergill, wrote to the effect that the highly touted Volkswagen was not up to much after all, and that a major British motormaker had declined to produce it because a sample car had failed its "drive it to the death" test. Fothergill's reward for this was an avalanche of mail from members of the British Army of the Rhine, who vociferously defended the VW's toughness and reliability.

Fothergill's mailbox, he admitted in September 1946, bulged with "an immediate outcry from the BAOR. British Service men who have driven the car almost continuously during the war and since, and found it a most reliable utility vehicle, expressed complete astonishment at the result of the test." The soldiers, he added, were telling him, in effect, "This is the type of cheap car I want in civvy life."

Scenting a fresh story, the editor of *News Chronicle* asked Fothergill to see if he could borrow a car to drive and test. "This was given," wrote Charles A. Dunphie of the Ministry of Supply, "as is the normal policy for all engineering representatives of the Press." As a result Fothergill wrote what amounted to an outright retraction headlined "£100 people's car comes well out of new, severe trial" above a photo of a civilian Beetle.

"I have just completed a most intensive test of the civilian type," Fothergill said, calling the VW "a car without frills, essentially practical." Finding the early Beetle "fast, easy to drive and comfortable," Fothergill said that as a result of his findings he "would strongly suggest to the British motor industry that it should inquire closely into the possibility of producing a similarly cheap, austere family model for sale in this country."

That Fothergill's recommendation was not being vigorously pursued by Britain's tradition-bound industry was suggested by a sight that chanced to meet the eyes of Maj. Charles Bryce:

> It seems that the experts in London could not have had a very good opinion of the VW, for when I was on leave in London a few months [after preparing the cars] I saw the same two export cars parked, in an appalling condition, in the centre of London! They were actually outside a doorway in Oxford Street leading to an exhibition showing what was being done in Germany by CCG, UNRRA, etc.
>
> The two formerly immaculate Beetles were dirty, and looked neglected and forlorn, and I remembered thinking that the sight of these two extremely shoddy cars would make anyone who saw them in London decide firmly that he would never buy a Volkswagen!

Another drab-looking postwar VW, this one built on the Kübel platform, was beetling around Britain in the spring of 1946 in the hands of journalist/racer/stylist Gordon Wilkins. Wilkins wrote about the car in *The Motor*, saying that "it has the civilian saloon body on the military chassis with the higher ground clearance, and it looks rather like a beetle on stilts."

Wilkins found it "a really lively car" with "very respectable acceleration and a top-gear pick-up that dominates most traffic situations," noting that the engine displacement had been increased over that of the KdF-Wagen in which he was driven by an SS man in 1939. Wilkins commented further on its merits and demerits:

> The finish is primitive; even Sir Cripps [sic] could not ask for anything more austere — and the noise is tremendous. Amid the general pandemonium one can discern the howl from the reduction gears in the military hubs, and the scream from the cooling fan, while on sharp corners a fearful rending noise arises from the special limited-slip cam and roller differential.
>
> Yet one can forgive it all these things for its general pep and good handling. Here is a rear-engined car which can be crammed into fast open bends without a thought of whether the engine is at the front, the rear, or amidships. The suspension is very hard, to cope with heavy overloads of troops and ammo., and doubtless this and the special diff. contribute to the spectacular cornering capacity.

Newspaper reports quoted by Wilkins were premature in suggesting that "the defeated Germans are to be able to buy the car at £87 10s." However, in 1947 the Fallersleben works was selling them to British servicemen for £160. When a member of the RAF on home leave brought his Beetle across the Channel, he kindly placed it at the disposal of *The Motor* for a full road test, during which it was driven "some hundreds of miles."

Here was a chance to see whether the magazine's technical editor had been right in 1941 when he opined that the KdF-Wagen's design was "sufficiently advanced not to have become out of date during the period of hostilities." Six years later *The Motor's* tester found that "it has the appearance of an orthodox modern small car in everything but details. A stranger coming freshly to the car would in actual fact find little indication of the unorthodoxy of the design."

Some trepidation at the absence of synchromesh was quickly overcome when "the gearbox quickly proved altogether delightful to handle." This was advantageous, because the high top gear that gave comfortable cruising also demanded downshifting on grades to a third gear in which fifty miles per hour could be reached, only seven miles per hour less than the timed top speed. The testers found "no feeling of tail heaviness due to the rear engine position."

This was no ordinary automobile, warned *The Motor*: "It is difficult to think of any car in the popular priced class which is in more striking contrast to current British models." It wasn't very refined, with its noisy engine and lower gears, but "on the open road, the overdrive top gear provides immensely effortless cruising." *The Motor* summed up its opportunistic road test in the following manner:

> Lacking some of the refinement which British cars show, the German "people's car" that was to have been, strikes the driver as a sound job which should give long years of service with the minimum of professional attention. It is sturdily built, mechanically simple, and the main components seem readily accessible. It will carry four people anywhere in adequate comfort, and, given a driver prepared to use the gears in the manner intended, it can complete any journey in a creditably short time.

Another in Britain with firsthand Beetle experience was Mr. A. F. Carlisle, who bought his VW from the works early in 1947 and in two years had driven it some twenty thousand miles, as he told the readers of *Motor Sport* in April 1949. "The car was on sale to the Forces for a short time," he said, "and quite a few have been brought over to this country."

Mr. Carlisle had a perceptive grasp of the merits and demerits of his radical automobile:

> The Volkswagen is a strange mixture of very advanced and unorthodox design and utilitarianism. At best it is a modern saloon, with independent suspension of all four wheels, an air-cooled o.h.v. flat-four engine mounted at the rear, built-in heating and possessed of a high cruising speed. At worst, it is a light-gauge tin box, in the construction of which self-cutting screws, cardboard and rubber solution feature.

Carlisle found the springing "firm and completely unbreakable," the braking "disappointing," the electrics "first-class," and the engine "perfectly smooth at speed" with cooling that was "most satisfactory under all conditions." He was also among the first to experience a phenomenon that became a trademark idiosyncrasy of the VW Beetle: "The interior is austere and typically Continental, with cloth upholstery, but it is completely rain and draught-proof, to the extent that the doors cannot easily be shut unless a window is opened to permit air to escape."

HERE WERE RINGING REMINDERS to Britain's government and its carmakers that a factory under their control and scheduled to be dealt with as war reparations was producing exactly the kind of car that their future customers, now soldiers in Germany, were extremely enthusiastic about and that their own engineers were saying would be in great demand in export markets in the years to come. The government was listening, as we shall see, but its carmakers still seemed inclined to view the VW as a menace to be throttled in the cradle rather than as an asset to be seized.

Britain seemed to have pole position in any race to exploit the Wolfsburg factory, which was in the British occupation zone. But the credentials of the other Allies also require inspection. They too could join a battle for the Beetle. Of these the most powerful by far was America. American technical teams had ruthlessly stripped Germany of its best rocket scientists, research laboratories, and aircraft prototypes. Were the world's most advanced light car and its factory of any interest?

America's carmakers were the acknowledged world leaders, stronger than ever after gearing up for prodigious production feats during World War II. They were regrouping after the war to assess their opportunities in Europe. Much would depend on what the American government and its largest car companies made of this controversial rear-engined car and its sprawling Nazi-built factory. It would be the matter of a moment for one of them to take responsibility for both.

5

Assessment by the Americans

Hitler looked to his auto industry as an engine to drive his nation and his people out of the Great Depression. More than any other country in Europe, with the exception of neighbors (and later vassals) Austria and Czechoslovakia, Hitler's technocratic Germany had been open to the idea that new kinds of cars and new ways to make them could provide a fresh impulse to a struggling economy.

The same motivation powered advances in car design in America during the 1930s. Automakers cut costs and merged operations to effect savings. Marginal car producers went out of business. At the same time, however, auto designers and engineers were given new freedom to search out innovations and breakthroughs that would seduce buyers back to the sagging new-car market. This in turn was intended to spark the renaissance not only of the car business but of producers of all goods and materials in America's lethargic industrial complex.

Some such responses were valiant but in vain. Chrysler survived the depression years in spite of customer rejection of its technologically advanced but aesthetically challenged Airflow models, which attracted few customers. The same must be said of the radical front-drive Cord 810 of 1936. Advanced and handsome though it was, the Cord was too costly and insufficiently mature at its launch to save an already failing Auburn Automobile Company, let alone an entire industry.

At General Motors, stylist Harley Earl was making cars longer, lower, and sleeker to catch the public's attention. Starting with his low-cost V-8 engine in 1932, Henry Ford's cars advanced impressively in styling during the 1930s thanks to the eye for line of his son Edsel Ford. Ford's relationship with body-maker Briggs Manufacturing led to the adoption by its Lincoln subsidiary of John Tjaarda's beautiful new integral body for the V-12 Lincoln Zephyr, although without the rear-mounted engine that Tjaarda so tirelessly advocated.

WHAT ABOUT PUTTING THE ENGINE in the rear of an American car? Would Americans be interested in owning and driving a car like the one Porsche had created? This would be an important criterion for the possible interest of the American auto industry in the asset that Wolfsburg represented.

The rear-engined idea was being debated in the nation's automotive technical press early in the 1930s. In April and May 1931 one of the industry's most influential organs, *Automotive Industries*, carried a three-part survey of the prospects for rear-engine adoption, headed by a dramatic rendering of an advanced new car, headlights blazing, rushing down an elevated highway in a spectacular city of the future.

Introducing his magazine's major survey by respected technical author Peter M. Heldt, the editor pointed out that engines in the rear were not a novelty, but quite the contrary:

> Thirty years ago the rear-engined-car was dealt what seemed a death-blow. Now its ghost walks, and it is to all appearances a very live ghost. It stalked boldly through some of the sessions of the last S.A.E. Annual Meeting. It flits fugitively through the experimental laboratories, a lurking shadow in the background. What is going to be done about it? Shall the industry remain haunted?

Indeed in America the rear-mounted engine, with which the automobile had been born, had been totally superseded by the end of the 1920s by front-engined designs. The long hood with the powerful in-line eight-cylinder engine was the industry's ideal. Heldt, however, pointed out that rear-engined cars "are actually in production in a small scale in England and France, and new models involving the feature have been announced by inventors or promoters at decreasing intervals."

Heldt credited Rumpler in Germany with arousing interest in the rear-engined chassis and its suitability for streamlining, with the engine tucked inside a tapered tail. He cited the English examples of the North-Lucas, the Trojan, and the Burney, the French cars of Emile Claveau, the convincing although still unbuilt designs of Dutch engineer John Tjaarda.

One example oddly overlooked was built in Syracuse, New York, by Julian Brown. The Julian was an American prototype that strikingly echoed the North-Lucas in its mechanical layout and was contemporaneous with it. Although clothed in a conventional-looking aluminum coupé body by Fleetwood, the 1925 Julian had a radial engine placed pancake-style above the rear wheels. Independent swing axles were used at the rear and a solid axle in front, both sprung by transverse leaf springs.

"At its June 1925 announcement," wrote historian Michael Lamm, "the Julian was due to go into production 'soon' at a retail price of $2,500, or roughly what a six-cylinder Packard cost that year. Yet the 1925 Julian proto-

A peek under the lid at the rear of the 1925 Julian prototype reveals its air-cooled radial six-cylinder engine placed pancake-style above the rear axle.

type reportedly cost $60,000 to build." This elegant and well-engineered rear-engined car was stillborn, even to the extent of being forgotten by contemporary observers of the industry.

Inadequate engine cooling and poor high-speed stability were highlighted by Peter Heldt as potential faults of the streamlined rear-engined car. Saying that "this type will confront designers with many knotty problems," Heldt added, "But the solution of difficult technical problems is the very object of existence of the engineering profession. Many of the difficulties and disadvantages of the rear-engined design may seem much less formidable after the automobile engineering profession has devoted several years to their elimination."

Members of that very profession in the summer 1931 meeting of the Society of Automotive Engineers (SAE) gave a warm reception to a presentation on the streamlined rear-engined car by Walter T. Fishleigh, formerly with Ford. Car body design had stagnated between 1913 and 1931, he said, illustrating his points with lantern slides. Instead, said Fishleigh, a "teardrop form" was needed to bring the automobile up to the high aerodynamic standard of the airplane and dirigible.

Modeling a low, clean-lined car in one-quarter scale, albeit still with attached front and rear fenders, Fishleigh had conducted a market survey of its acceptability compared to a standard design of the day during his Ford employment. Of the thirty-eight people he questioned, including industry experts as

James Martin's envelope-bodied rear-engined prototype of 1932 displayed in the metal a possible vision of the car of the future. Its greenhouse showed a striking similarity to the designs of Edmund Rumpler a decade earlier.

well as motorists, "all except four expressed approval," Herbert Chase reported on the SAE meeting, "ranking from simple statements that they 'thought such a design would be successful' to enthusiastic endorsements that 'the design is absolutely right and the public would fall for it immediately.' "

One dissenter was vocal, Fishleigh said, quoting his remark that "if you drove that thing down [Detroit's] Woodward Avenue, people would run for fright." But the reaction of his fellow engineers was positive that summer, judging by the many questions and comments that made the meeting run an hour overtime and the sincere congratulations that Fishleigh accepted at its conclusion. A debate that would echo through the next two decades had been well and truly launched.

AT NEW YORK'S AUTO SHOW at the beginning of 1932 Herbert Chase had more to talk about than quarter-scale models of rear-engined cars. On display were two streamlined rear-engined prototypes built by the Martin Aeroplane Company of Garden City on New York's Long Island. Not to be confused with Glenn L. Martin's famous aircraft firm, this was headed by James V. Martin, whose aviation work focused on landing gear.

James Martin built his envelope-bodied cars on 86-inch wheelbases, one four-wheeled and one three-wheeled. "From an engineering standpoint the cars are noteworthy," wrote Chase, "not only because they involve placing

In 1928 visionary engineer John Tjaarda was seeking financial support for the production of his Sterkenburg C3. Although conventional in appearance, its engine was to be mounted ahead of the rear axle.

the engine in the rear, but because they combine in a road vehicle many features characteristic of airplane design."

Meanwhile one of America's major auto producers had been testing the rear-engine concept. In the late 1920s Carl Breer and his engineering colleagues at Chrysler discovered the value of low air resistance in improving car performance. Tests in the wind tunnel, they found, showed that the angular autos of the day had less aerodynamic drag going backward than forward!

Working to perfect the configuration of a radical new Chrysler, the engineers concluded that they should put the engine in the rear of a much more streamlined shape. They followed the example of the British Burney, with its long straight-eight engine projecting rearward from the car's rear axle. With the heavy water-cooled cast-iron engines available to them, however, their rear-engined prototype was too tail-heavy and needed a costly independent rear suspension.

Instead, the Breer team chose a front location for the engines of their all-new low-drag Chryslers and DeSotos, introduced in January 1934 as the Airflow models. Even more radical in their appearance than in their engineering, the Airflows were poor marketplace performers; this placed a damper on innovation in Detroit, a city with a long memory for failures.

AUTOMOTIVE INDUSTRIES KEPT THE rear-engined debate alive with a submission by one of the industry's advanced thinkers, engineer Bela Barenyi. He filed an article from Vienna that was worthy of four pages in an April 1934 issue. His theme was the integration of streamlining with the rear engine, independent suspension, and the tubular backbone frame. Said the inventor:

> Many objections have been raised against the rear-engined car, and it is interesting as well as instructive to investigate these. The change in weight distribution, of course, deserves consideration. Rumpler tried to find the solution of the problem from the design point of view, but Burney fifteen years later made extensive scientific researches and experiments on the effects of changes in weight distribution and in the location of the center of gravity. Since then a number of rear-engine cars, all of them streamlined, have been built, and some even placed in regular production.

Barenyi referred to the aerodynamic studies of Jaray and to rear-engined cars built by Ganz, Martin, Porsche, and Tjaarda. This is likely to have been one of the first references in the American engineering literature to Ferdinand Porsche and his coming rear-engined road and racing car designs.

Barenyi also referred to John Tjaarda. No one came closer than this inventive, entrepreneurial, and persistent immigrant from the Netherlands to introducing the rear-engined car into the American mainstream during the turbulent 1930s. His adventurous automotive ideas mandated new concepts in manufacturing and appearance and forced the automakers to consider embracing radical change — not always an appealing prospect.

In common with many others who tried to revolutionize the automobile in the 1930s, John Tjaarda's background included aircraft training and experience. Born and raised in Holland, Tjaarda attended college in England and studied there under Dr. Alexander Klemin, a pioneer aerodynamicist and a specialist in rotary-wing aircraft. By 1926 he was in Rochester, New York, at the coachbuilding firm of Locke and Company, designing custom bodies for Stutz, Chrysler, Pierce Arrow, Packard, and Hispano-Suiza chassis and for the great Duesenberg Model J.

"Sterkenburg," part of the Tjaarda family name, was the equally exotic marque that the engineer used for his personal automotive design explorations. The first phase of Tjaarda's Sterkenburg studies was completed in 1926, when he sought financial backing to build prototypes of a Sterkenburg Type C3. He saw the C3 as a small, simple four-door sedan, powered by a four- or six-cylinder engine placed at the rear, mounted forward of the rear axle.

Unlike Ledwinka and Porsche, John Tjaarda "never made one design with the engine behind the rear axle." In this he was in full agreement with Josef Ganz's rejection of the "outboard motor" school of design. Said Tjaarda, "It is, with the present type of engine, the wrong place. It offers no advantage; it multiplies the gimmicks required to make the car behave."

John Tjaarda moved to Detroit in 1930 as a recruit to Harley Earl's new General Motors Art and Color Section; he continued designing and promoting Sterkenburgs on the side. His uninhibited ideas entitled Tjaarda to considerable coverage in the automotive press of the early 1930s when the debate over radical car designs warmed up. Unbuilt though they were, the Sterkenburgs received detailed coverage in the 28 March 1931 issue of *Automobile Topics*. This may well have drawn Tjaarda's skills to the attention of his next employer, Mr. Walter O. Briggs.

FOR MANY YEARS DETROIT'S Briggs Manufacturing Company made bodies for the Ford Motor Company, for both Fords and Lincolns. On the Ford side of the relationship a key executive was Henry's son Edsel Ford, who as the firm's president was granted leave by his tyrannical father to take an interest in advanced planning, styling, sales, and advertising. To

By 1931 John Tjaarda had developed his Sterkenburg ideas further, including an integral body-frame structure, all-independent suspension, and a V-8 engine mounted ahead of the rear wheels.

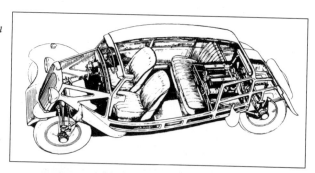

As an alternative to conventional body styles for his proposed Sterkenburg automobiles, Tjaarda modeled some attractively advanced shapes for his rear-engined proposals in 1931.

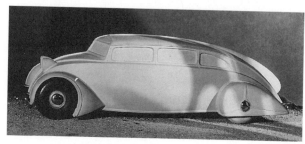

improve relations with Ford in general and with Edsel in particular, Walter Briggs hired several new creative people. Among them was John Tjaarda, who began work in 1932 on advanced designs for a new Ford product in a secluded fifth-floor office-laboratory.

In 1935 Tjaarda began work on a small car with a transverse-engine layout, using an air-cooled aluminum four-cylinder engine. The design featured a platform frame and all-independent suspension by torsion bars at the rear and rubber springing of trailing arms at the front. Such a car, Walter Briggs felt, could have potential for production and sales in Europe, where his plant at Dagenham was supplying Ford. Briggs saw England's Daimler as a potential business partner for the production of Tjaarda's design in Britain. Briggs itself would build the car in America, limning the first outlines of a potential world-car project.

Other plausible partners began to climb aboard, attracted by the maturity and sophistication of Tjaarda's design. Swedish industrialist Axel Wenner-Gren would see to its manufacture in Scandinavia. Wenner-Gren had business ties as well with a French industrialist who was unbundling his troubled ties with Ford and looking for a new product for his plant in Strasbourg: Emil Ernst Carl Mathis.

Fifty-six years old in 1936, Emil Mathis had enjoyed a colorful pan-European career since the turn of the century as an automotive distributor, dealer, and manufacturer. A maker of dour, worthy cars in contrast to the brilliance of the sleek steeds crafted by Ettore Bugatti, his neighbor in France's Alsace region, Mathis was France's fourth-largest auto producer in the mid-1930s. He and Wenner-Gren were intrigued by the Briggs world-car scheme.

The German auto company that Briggs hoped to entice into its new combine was ambitious and expansionist Auto Union, one of the customers of Ferdinand Porsche. During his 1936 trip to America Porsche was shown the advanced vehicle work that Tjaarda was doing at Briggs. Porsche had one eye on the needs and interests of Auto Union and the other on the prospects of a brilliant Danish engineer-entrepreneur who had been a prime mover in the formation of the Auto Union company but was now on the outside of the combine looking in: Jörgen Skafte Rasmussen.

The shrewd and adventurous Rasmussen was the founder of small-car producer DKW, which contributed more than half the turnover of Auto Union and the lion's share of its profits. After Auto Union was formed he expected the founding banks to step aside and cede the company's leadership to him; the bankers had other ideas. Two days after Christmas of 1934 they formally dismissed Rasmussen from the management board of Auto Union.

The Dane fought back, bringing the dispute into the public arena — an uncomfortable and unpleasant eventuality for any German company and especially for newborn Auto Union, a major employer in the state of Saxony. Getting wind of the undignified goings-on, Adolf Hitler unleashed an adjutant in the direction of Auto Union equipped with firm instructions to reach a generous settlement with Rasmussen. The engineer was satisfied with a golden handshake of $640,000.

Related his son, "After his dismissal from Auto Union my father still wanted to build cars again. He was not to be dissuaded; he wanted to show them in Chemnitz" — the home of Auto Union. In 1936 Jörgen Rasmussen, as creative as ever at age fifty-eight, was in America with Porsche looking over the work of John Tjaarda. The designer related that the two visiting European engineers "were actually shown the car at Briggs and were given permission to use any information they felt was of value as part of a program of organizing an international car project."

This revelation of the small Briggs prototype with its four-cylinder air-cooled engine, Tjaarda's son recalled, was strenuously objected to by the senior Tjaarda, who was well informed about European developments in general and Porsche's activities in particular. Not unreasonably he feared his concepts would be leaked without due compensation. But he was obliged to bow to the wishes of Edsel Ford, with whom Briggs was eager to curry favor.

Later, Porsche was informed even more fully about the advanced Briggs design, Tjaarda's widow said. "Dr. Porsche actually obtained the drawings of the rear engine car from Mr. Tjaarda when he visited him at Briggs in the company of Messrs. Mathis and Wenner-Gren. Dr. Porsche felt this design the finest aerodynamically he had ever seen and he asked for a complete set of drawings and Mr. Tjaarda gave them to him."

Relatively small though it was by American standards, the Tjaarda design was larger than the VW-in-the-making. The drawings may well have been passed on to the interested European partners in the Briggs project; Porsche's project list shows no entry that even hints that his design team contributed in any way to the ultimately unrealized world-car dreams of Rasmussen, Briggs, Mathis, Wenner-Gren, et al. But in the vigorous cross-pollination of ideas that ultimately led to the VW, John Tjaarda was one of the busier bees.

BIZARRELY, A MID-1930S AMERICAN connection to the work of both John Tjaarda in America and Ferdinand Porsche in Germany was sparked by the automotive innovations of lone-wolf entrepreneur and engineer Paul M. Lewis of Denver, Colorado. In 1934 Lewis began planning a light, teardrop-shaped three-wheeled five-passenger car that he hoped his Lewis American Airways would build and sell for as little as three hundred dollars.

Lewis wanted his car's two front wheels to be driven, steered, and braked ahead of a single wheel simply trailing at the rear to create a near-perfect aerodynamic form. For the first sketches and designs incorporating his ideas Lewis turned to Briggs and John Tjaarda. For Lewis the Dutch engineer created drawings, models, and mockups of a radically streamlined car.

In mid-1936 Paul Lewis contracted with Carl Doman and Ed Marks to design a running prototype incorporating his ideas. Engineered by Fred Henderson and built by their Doman-Marks Engine Company of Syracuse, New York, the car was delivered to Paul Lewis in April 1937. Cost estimates made in parallel with the development forecast a retail price of five hundred dollars. The Airomobile, as Lewis dubbed it, had cost him about twenty-five thousand dollars. It was demonstrated and promoted throughout the United States by its creator but failed to gain the backing needed to put it into production.

Syracuse had been the home of the Franklin company, famous for its air-cooled cars until production ended in 1934. Carl Doman and Ed Marks had been Franklin engineers, so the engine they designed for the Airomobile was an air-cooled flat-opposed four developing fifty-seven horsepower at 3,700 rpm. It had a single camshaft operating overhead valves through pushrods, a single central carburetor, and a sirocco-type cooling fan driven by the nose of the crankshaft.

This Volkswagen-like engine was under development at Syracuse when one of Porsche's engineers, Josef Kales, paid a visit to that mecca of automotive air-cooled engineering. Kales stopped over for ten days, during which he studied the art and science of air cooling at Doman-Marks. Although costing much more than Porsche could afford for his people's car, with its integral-head aluminum cylinders on an iron crankcase, the Airomobile's engine may well have had some influence on the design of the VW's flat four.

Doman and Marks "objected strenuously" to the peculiar three-wheeled layout of the Airomobile. They urged Lewis to give it up in favor of a four-wheeled design with the engine in the rear. Carl Doman: "We did make many design studies with the engine located in the rear, using four wheels, but we just couldn't sell Mr. Lewis. While Mr. Lewis felt that the streamline design would have been harmed with two rear wheels, I personally felt that the appearance of the car would have been improved." Had the engineers been more persuasive or Lewis more receptive, an American counterpart to the Volkswagen might have been born in the 1930s.

When he spoke to members of the Society of Automotive Engineers in New York in November of 1943, Doman urged them to consider the merits of rear mounting an air-cooled engine for their future products. Providing a drawing of a sedan with a hundred-horsepower air-cooled flat-six engine mounted ahead of its rear wheels, Doman stressed the advances in technology that had suppressed the noisiness that was associated with earlier air-cooled engines.

A Philadelphia financier, Philip Pearson, provided the funds for another American three-wheeled-car project. This one was launched in 1933 by one of the world's most original thinkers about technology in the service of mankind, R. Buckminster Fuller. With Pearson's backing and an inheritance from his mother, Fuller built three Dymaxion cars in 1933 and 1934.

Sleek as dirigibles, the Dymaxions were shaped to sail through the air by yacht designer Starling Burgess. Steered by their single tail wheel and driven through their two front wheels by a Ford V-8 engine in the rear, the Dymaxion cars had the most radical architecture of any land vehicles of their time.

Radical in this case did not mean advanced or even particularly good, for their steering and structural arrangements failed to suit the Dymaxions to any roads that existed at that time. Nevertheless Chrysler and Packard were among the American carmakers who expressed guarded interest in developing Fuller's Dymaxion further. Another was Studebaker, which took over Pierce Arrow but did not require its Buffalo factory — where plans were made but never realized by Curtiss Wright — to produce smaller, lighter, and sportier Dymaxions.

PHILIP PEARSON HAD BEEN WARNED that Fuller's automotive ideas would prove too radical by another great American innovator of the depression years, William Bushnell Stout. As much at home in the air as on the ground, Stout had worked with Scripps-Booth and Packard before establishing the Stout Metal Plane Company in the 1920s. Acquired by Ford in 1924, this was the nest from which the famous Ford Tri-Motor transport flew.

Stout was a prolific proselytizer of advanced design ideas for all forms of transportation. Hailed as an "imagineer," he urged his engineering col-

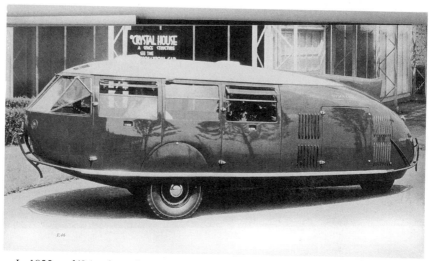

In 1933 and '34 polymath engineer R. Buckminster Fuller built three cars to his Dymaxion design. Although some American carmakers expressed interest in Fuller's concept, no more Dymaxions were made.

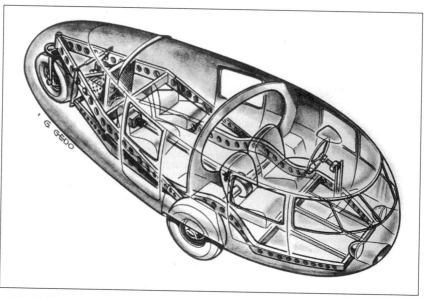

The Fuller Dymaxion car had a rear-mounted engine that drove the two forward wheels while the single rear wheel was used for steering. The suspension design showed little awareness of the risks of excessive unsprung weight.

Rear-mounted engines and aerodynamic bodies for cars were embodied in the mid-1930s by William Bushnell Stout in his Scarab automobiles. Stout was one of the most active and respected advocates of the rear-engined auto in America.

leagues to "simplicate and add more lightness." Said a visitor of Bill Stout, "His dark brown eyes twinkle behind thick, owlish glasses, with curiosity suggestive of a fox terrier's. His face has a look of perpetual astonishment." Radical though Stout's ideas were, he was much more in the mainstream of the motor industry than was Fuller, to the extent that Stout was elected president of the Society of Automotive Engineers in 1935 when he was fifty-five. Two years earlier, contemporaneously with Fuller, Stout had built a rear-engined car of his own. It was the first of his justly famous Stout Scarabs. Unlike Rover's Scarab in Britain, Bill Stout actually gave his cars something of the scaly look of the Egyptian dung beetle.

Not until 1935 did Stout go public with his new automobile concept. In March 1935 *Scientific American* reported on it as follows:

> This new car has been under development by Mr. Stout for several years and preliminary models have been undergoing actual road tests for the past two years. According to the designer this new car marks the first real departure of the automobile from its classification as a development of the "horseless carriage" which initiated the present type of automobile design.

The roomy design of his Ford-V-8-powered Scarabs marked Stout as an early advocate of the versatile and spacious auto architecture that we know today as the one-box car or people carrier. "The engine in this car takes up the space of the usual trunk rack," he said. "Being housed away in the tail of the beetle shape, the usual hood space up front — up to a point corresponding to the radiator ornament of the ordinary type of car — is available for passenger room."

Although he might have found ways to mount his Ford V-8 engine lower in the chassis, Stout showed foresight with the all-metal structure and strut-type independent suspension of his Scarabs.

In his advertising for the Scarab, Stout called it "a friendly but direct challenge to the necessary conservatism of the big-production motor car manufacturers." But even in the innovation-receptive 1930s a change as radical as a rear engine was considered by the American auto industry as much too daring.

"The car was described in all the trade papers and many of the magazines of the day," Stout related, "and was discussed in most of the automotive-design conferences — but the word came back to us very definitely that the industry was not interested in that kind of car." The Stout Motor Car Corporation announced plans to make one hundred cars a year at the steep price of five thousand dollars but in fact is estimated to have built only nine Scarabs in all, plus a tenth after the war.

Bill Stout was an equally tireless advocate of air instead of liquid cooling for auto engines. Although he used water-cooled Ford and Mercury V-8 engines in his Scarabs, Stout argued persuasively, publicly, and at length that the air-cooled rear-mounted engine was the way of the future for the automobile.

"The rear-mounted engine will probably be the greatest single trend in the new motor car," Stout told the readers of the *New York Times* in 1943, looking forward to the exciting new autos that peacetime was expected to bring. He added his conviction that the rear engine "gives better traction and balance on turns and a more economical and comfortable arrangement of passengers."

The engine in the rear will be directly cooled by air like most aviation engines, Bill Stout had written in the same newspaper in the late 1930s: "Future motor car engines will be air-cooled — real cooling, real horsepowers and lower cost." "Being the pancake type — horizontal construction with the cylinders arranged on their sides instead of standing on end — the engine will fit low down in the back of the vehicle and leave plenty of room for luggage," Stout forecast fearlessly in 1942.

In the spacious and elegant interiors of his Scarabs William Stout accurately foreshadowed the flexible characteristics of the later minivan. The Stout Motor Car Corporation built and sold nine of the prewar Scarabs.

Bill Stout deserves credit for doing much in the 1930s and 1940s to pre-pare the way in America for acceptance of the air-cooled rear-engined car. He argued logically and at length for it. In 1944, while associated with carmaker Graham-Paige, he began work on a new rear-engined prototype, using many Scarab parts, that was the first vehicle ever made with a complete integral structure of glass-fiber-reinforced plastic.

THUS MANY INNOVATORS, Tjaarda and Stout in particular, did much to condition both the car industry and the car owner in America to the potential benefits of a more radical kind of automobile and especially one with an air-cooled engine in the rear. What arguments were being used against it? Early in 1937 GM's technical director, W. J. Davidson, told an industry gathering that in his view the rear-mounted engine "had draw-backs which he considered serious." He elaborated as follows:

> The engine in the rear would give better visibility, and might eliminate some en-gine noise if the car were properly sound-proofed. Floor boards could also be lowered without affecting appearance, but maneuverability and ease of control are vital factors of design in the interest of safety, and they can be attained only by approximately equal loading on all four wheels. To accomplish this in a rear-engine car would require a power plant of about one-half the present engine weight. This, of course, we would like to attain even for the front-engine car, but it is not immediately in sight.
>
> Also, in rear-engine design, the radiator would probably have to remain in front or [a] forced draft, using up a lot of horsepower, [would need to] be provided for cooling. The modern car must also have room for baggage, and obviously there must be plenty of room to cramp the front wheels for steering. These are definitely problems of the rear-engine design.

Mr. Davidson was not speaking without practical experience. During the 1930s GM was building and testing samples of a radical rear-engined car of its own, the Martia, using an X-pattern two-stroke engine developed under the direction of renowned innovator Charles Kettering (see chapter 8). Martias experienced just these problems, plus an unpleasant odor from the two-stroke engine's exhaust that GM was never able to eliminate. Porsche, of course, had rejected the two-stroke for the Beetle in favor of his light air-cooled flat four.

MEANWHILE AMERICANS WERE gradually learning more about the rear-engined, air-cooled KdF-Wagen and Adolf Hitler's vaunting ambitions for it. "Hitler Making Cheap Auto for Masses in Reich," headlined the *New York Herald Tribune* on the eve of the Berlin Auto Show on 19 February 1937. The dictator's dream, said the newspaper, was "a 'volkswagen,' a small, strongly built automobile so inexpensive that a large number of Germans and other Europeans who hitherto have not had enough money to own a car can afford to buy it."

The secrecy surrounding the details of the project was such that its designer was named as "Dr. Hans Prosche" and the engine was thought to be a vertical two-stroke twin of the type tried but abandoned by Porsche more than a year earlier. Accurate, however, was the article's assertion that the German car industry was "opposed to [Hitler's] project, and in fact is following a course of passive resistance (so far as that is possible under a dictatorship)."

American carmakers were more authoritatively informed by the veteran European correspondent of *Automotive Industries*, W. F. Bradley, in March of 1937. Bradley, who had known Ferdinand Porsche since the early 1920s, had the correct specifications, and mentioned the intended selling price of 995 marks, then about four hundred dollars at the official exchange rate, when the cheapest German car cost 1,450 marks, or just under six hundred dollars.

Meeting Porsche in his Stuttgart office, Bradley found that the famous engineer "maintained a reserved attitude, but appeared to be surprised at some of the statements which had been made in Germany regarding the date of appearance of the car and its selling price." He quoted Porsche as saying:

> We need production facilities, and although we have a good machine tool industry, it is not in a position to make immediate deliveries, and unfortunately it has not worked hand in hand with the automotive industry, as is the case in the United States. Our problem now is one of production.

The car, Porsche told Bradley, "is a full sized model, capable of carrying four big people. My reason for adopting an air cooled engine is to simplify garaging, for the car can be left in the open without danger of freezing."

After the May 1938 cornerstone-laying at Fallersleben and the display of definitive KdF-Wagen prototypes the reporting on the project in America accelerated. The *New York Times* shrewdly captured the VW concept in a major article in early July. Said the paper, presciently giving the new car an apt nickname,

> In a short time, Der Fuehrer is going to plaster his great sweeps of smooth motor highways with thousands and thousands of shiny little beetles, purring along from the Baltic to Switzerland and from Poland to France, with father, mother and up to three kids packed inside and seeing their Fatherland for the first time through their own windshield.

On 2 August 1938 the two New York papers reported on the previous day's announcement at a worker's rally in Cologne by Robert Ley that what the *Herald Tribune* called a "pay-before-you-get-it" installment plan would be used to sell the cars. Called a "Volksauto" by the *Times*, the new car was described as a four/five seater that would be available in sedan, cabrio-sedan, and open body styles. It was to be capable of reaching sixty-two miles per hour with its twenty-four-horsepower engine and traveling thirty-three miles on each U.S. gallon of fuel.

Reflecting the *gleichschaltung* or "harmonization" policies of the Reich press office, the tone of the American reporting was becoming less sarcastic and more respectful of the Hitler-Ley-Porsche idea, even as the idea itself was ballooning to a more and more outlandish scale. The declared aim of out-Fording Ford in a rearming German nation desperately short of the needed quantity and quality of raw materials was reported in a matter-of-fact manner.

ONLY A HANDFUL OF BEETLE prototypes to the final design had been completed at the time of the cornerstone-laying ceremony that led to an outburst of global publicity about the new KdF-Wagen and its dedicated factory-to-be. None was yet available for purchase, not even to the savers who began paying in their five marks weekly in August 1938. But that didn't keep one influential American buyer from trying to get a Beetle.

In 1938 the American film studios were masters of their cinematic universe and none more so than Metro-Goldwyn-Mayer. MGM had a film in the works in which it wanted to feature this different-looking German car of the future. It applied directly to the German government for one of the new cars, doubtless arguing that its appearance in a film would be wonderful publicity for the new KdF-Wagen.

"The Nazi German government would not cooperate," said an MGM military history consultant who saw the thick file on this transaction. On this occasion the all-powerful Louis B. Mayer met his match. But MGM did at least acquire extensive information about the new VW, including one of the rare Transart booklets that disclosed the interior and components of the car in a series of transparent overlays.

Automotive Industries reported accurately on the state of the KdF-Wagen project in September 1938, explaining to its American readers that "the initials K.d.F. are as familiar in Germany as W.P.A., C.C.C. and others in this country." Garaging the KdF-Wagen was not a necessity, it said, thanks to its air-cooled engine. Traffic that the cars would create was being catered for by building the Autobahns and improving highways throughout Germany.

"The German automobile industry stands by, probably with mingled emotions," said the magazine's well-informed correspondent, "but it is beginning to view the situation in a somewhat more comforting light. Hitherto Hitler's measures in every branch of government and business have proven so successful that gradually the impression is growing that the development of the Volkswagen after all may not sound the death knell of the established industry, but may even open new opportunities for the older manufacturers."

Adolf Hitler, *Automotive Industries* added, had "tried to allay the fears of the manufacturers by pointing out to them that Ford, with his large-scale production, instead of 'killing off' other manufacturers had actually drawn them along with him to an unprecedented success." Most of these manufacturers were increasingly busy with rearmament tasks by this time. For them the KdF-Wagen project was a growing rival for priorities in every sector of their sourcing of machines and materials.

Most American auto engineers had their first look at the technical details of the KdF-Wagen when Automotive Industries reported on the Berlin Auto Show of March 1939. Official photos released by the company's commercial office in Berlin showed the car's engine, platform frame, front and rear suspensions, and details of its torsion-bar springing. Full specifications of the radical new car were disclosed and described.

IN THE MEANTIME THE GERMAN offices of Ford and GM's Adam Opel were keeping their executives in Michigan informed of the threat that the KdF-Wagen project represented to their operations. Opel, a pioneer of mass-production operations in Europe, was the sales leader in Germany with growing production that first surpassed 100,000 units per year in 1935.

As early as May 1934 Adolf Hitler had used the term *Volkswagen* in a conversation with General Motors Export Company president James D. Mooney. Hitler stressed then that he wanted a real car, not a cyclecar, that would have many of the features of the small 1.2-liter Opel — at less than half its selling price. In 1935 Opel launched its response: the P-4, an updating of its still-primitive *Laubfrosch* (tree-toad) of the 1920s, selling for 1,450 Reichsmarks.

One of the five sons of founder Adam Opel, Wilhelm von Opel, remained president of the company from 1929 to 1931 after its purchase by General Motors; he was sixty in the latter year. Von Opel was also a life member of the RDA, in whose councils he had robustly resisted the original plan to harness Germany's existing car industry to the making of Porsche's people's car. He had an ally in William S. Knudsen, the Danish-born president of Gen-

eral Motors, a practical and plain-speaking executive with firsthand experience in mass production gained during years with Ford.

Knudsen received a personal introduction to the VW project during a
visit to Germany in 1936. He was shown a scale model of a version of the car
with a two-stroke engine. After his visit he briefed American army officers on
his findings:

> Hitler has an idea of what he calls the Volkswagen which he wants to have made
> cooperatively between the manufacturers over there. The Volkswagen is a small
> car with just a box body and a driver's seat. I presume he wanted to use them in
> connection with those marvellous roads he has built over there. The Automo-
> bile Chamber of Commerce in Germany has put an engineer on the job to de-
> sign this Volkswagen, which was going to be the motor car and was supposed to
> sell for 1,200 marks. I presume the design of that was scheduled to be used in
> connection with military movement.

Visiting Berlin, Bill Knudsen was struck by the city's orderliness and apparent prosperity, noting the absence of "streetwalkers, bums and beggars"
in the depths of a worldwide depression. He was given sharp Nazi salutes
during his visits to Opel's plants near Frankfurt and Berlin. There were no
strikes, he found: "The Brown Shirts are around just looking for somebody
to beat up."

"While Knudsen was in Germany," his biographer related, "Hitler announced that within four years Germany would be independent from the
world in rubber. Knudsen thought Hitler was whistling up the river. He considered lack of rubber the greatest of Germany's manufacturing problems."

Neither was Bill Knudsen convinced that Germany could compete in
volume production as it was practiced in America, as it would need to do if it
were to increase its car production by an order of magnitude. "From experience, he knew that German machinery was not as good as was American machinery. They had German machinery in the General Motors plants, and
from his viewpoint it was too light."

During his visit Knudsen met with Opel's production manager W. G.
Guthrie, an American. Guthrie echoed many of Knudsen's criticisms in the
downbeat briefing he gave to journalist W. F. Bradley in March 1937 on the
subject of Hitler's ambitious goals for the Volkswagen:

> Germany is handicapped by the shortage of raw materials. Production is constantly
> being held back because of lack of supplies: we may be held up for forgings, or if
> forgings are on hand, we are handicapped by lack of sheet steel. There is a general
> shortage of copper, brass, zinc, rubber, wool, which can only be paid for by exports
> — hence our efforts towards increased exports. We are having to find substitutes
> all along the line. Rubber has been produced synthetically, but costing 3 to 4 times
> the price of natural rubber it is not a commercial proposition.

Guthrie told Bradley that "Hitler's advisers appear to have overlooked
the fact that 60 to 70 per cent of the production costs of a car are beyond the
control of the automobile manufacturer." This traditional proportion in the

German industry did, of course, ultimately lead to the decision to make the VW factory more self-reliant or vertically integrated than any other in Europe save, perhaps, Ford's Dagenham plant in England. Buying sheet steel good enough to make auto bodies would remain a challenge. Noted Guthrie, "There is not a single continuous rolling mill in the whole of Germany."

Ford's Cologne operations were similarly knowledgeable about the day-to-day challenges of making cars in Germany. Thus by the end of the 1930s the two biggest American automakers were well informed in depth and detail in the prewar years about the KdF-Wagen project and the many hurdles that it would need to vault if it were to become a reality.

Of immediate concern to Ford and Opel were the restrictions being placed on their own operations by the Nazi government. Exports of their earnings had been prohibited since 1934. Under the control of Colonel (later General) von Schell, car model ranges were being pruned and pared. In 1940, Opel reported, more than 240 government departments were interested in its affairs. For a single exported car fifty-four forms and applications were required.

An apparent respite was enjoyed in 1939. On another visit to Europe in that year Bill Knudsen found workmen dismantling the antiaircraft cannon installations around Opel's plants. Perhaps there was to be no war after all. So it seemed — but Knudsen saw and heard evidence of Germany's militarization, especially in the air.

In a bizarre meeting with aviation minister Ernst Udet and Luftwaffe chief Hermann Göring at the latter's Karinhall estate the GM president was asked whether Opel would be able to manufacture a V-12 aero engine that he interpreted, from its drawings, as a fair copy of GM's own Allison V-12. Opel could, he said, but Knudsen was relieved not to be asked to do it. He would have had to refuse, and his refusal, he was sure, would have triggered Opel's confiscation by the Nazis.

As it happened, early in 1940 Opel was asked to shift some of its production to munitions needed by the German military. In June Opel rejected the invitation. Aware as it was of the trend of events in Germany, General Motors relinquished at the same time any and all responsibility for the activities of Adam Opel. "I have to report with some regret that Mr. Hitler is the boss of our Germany factory," Bill Knudsen told his GM colleagues.

HENCEFORTH, AMERICANS WOULD MEET the KdF-Wagen on the battlefield. First encounters with its battle-ready version were in the North African desert, where gas shortages left perfectly functional Kübelwagens abandoned in the sand. Later, Type 82s were captured in Europe and driven by American soldiers.

In mid-1942 a Kübelwagen captured in Libya by the British forces, complete with its *Afrika Korps* palm-tree stenciling, arrived at the U.S. Army's Proving Grounds in Aberdeen, Maryland. Unlike Humber's sample, which had big balloon tires fitted for desert use, the vehicle shipped to America had conventional treaded tires. Showing only 3,900 kilometers (2,425 miles) on its odometer, it bore the registration number WH-249624.

The American army found the Kübelwagen quite a different animal than their own Jeep, which was 650 pounds heavier and offered four-wheel drive. They reported that the Volkswagen, as they called it, was "a 'civilian chassis' equipped with an open body for military use." As "salient features" of its engineering they noted the following four points:

(1) Good design on all important chassis components.

(2) The use of the best materials where needed, with nonstrategic materials used on nonessential items.

(3) Fine steering balance and roadability obtained by having light unsprung weight and sensible distribution of weight.

(4) Throughout the vehicle it is noticeable that lightness and simplicity have been the keynote. Simplicity has, in itself, brought lightness.

As an unsolicited testimonial to the achievement of Porsche's design goals, this assessment would be hard to surpass.

Although they could not have been aware of the circumstances that had led to the creation of the Type 82's hub reduction gears, the Aberdeen engineers showed shrewd insight into one of their advantages: "By utilizing the . . . gear reductions at the wheels, it is possible to make all the transmission and differential parts small because they are not called upon to deliver as much torque as would be the case with a direct wheel drive. The unsprung weight of the rear wheels is thus raised, but this is a disadvantage only on very rough roads."

The American army assessors noted the small size of the car's carburetor, which they took as "indicating an attempt to save fuel." Air cooling was unusual by American standards, they noted. "Because of the high speed of the blower," they found, "a high whine is emitted by the engine at high speeds." They described the car's road behavior as follows:

On the road, the car handles well for its weight and power. Revolutions of the engine have to be kept up and the gear box used all the time to use the small engine properly. A speed of 45 miles per hour can be maintained easily and 60 miles per hour is possible if the car is given enough room. Steering is very light, due in most part to the lack of weight on the front wheels. Because of good balance, the car takes corners well at comparatively high speeds. Hydraulic shock absorbers are used on all wheels and do their job well.

The cable-operated brakes — an acknowledged weakness of the original KdF-Wagen design — were less impressive.

Comparative tests at Aberdeen showed the Jeep to have the greater load-carrying capacity, some twelve hundred pounds against a maximum of eight hundred pounds for the Type 82. "One point which was stressed," recalled an observer, "was that the Kübelwagen couldn't tow a trailer like our half-ton Jeep trailer and that it was too light to mount weapons like the calibre .30 and .50 machine guns commonly mounted on Jeeps."

With its four driven wheels the Jeep was judged to be superior at clawing through rough terrain. On mud and sand, however, the Type 82's lightness, flat underbelly, and ZF limited-slip differential gave it extra agility. And when the lighter German car did bog down, it was easier to heave free of an obstacle.

The "positive locking" differential, said the Aberdeen experts, is "a device seldom used in America. It is almost a substitute for 4-wheel drive, as both rear wheels can be made to drive at once. With this type of differential, it is possible to put one wheel on a slippery surface and the other on a good tractive surface and still pull away. This could not be done with a gear differential."

The liberated Libyan Volkswagen was completely dismantled at Aberdeen at the end of 1942 and its contents analyzed by other American authorities as well. Captured vehicles and components were received and investigated by the Automotive Industries Subcommittee of the Joint Intelligence Objectives Agency in Washington. Studies were also conducted by the auto makers, working through the Captured Enemy Equipment Committee of the SAE's War Engineering Board, and in Detroit by the Office of the Chief of Ordnance.

At the SAE's January 1945 meeting Col. J. H. Frye of the army's Ordnance Department presented a magnificently comprehensive paper on the materials situation in both Germany and Japan before and during the war and on the military applications of materials as assessed from captured vehicles. "The wide range of metals and metallurgy that enters into automotive materiel offers an excellent opportunity to expand our knowledge of the enemy through a metallurgical study of their vehicles," wrote the colonel, after crediting the Assyrians in 700 B.C. with the first extensive use of iron in their army's attack weapons.

Included in his survey was the analysis of a Type 82 which was assessed as having been made in late 1940 or early 1941. "This is the much advertised 'Peoples Car' which Hitler promised to place in every German family's garage," the officer explained. Overall, he reported, "the selection of steels and processing methods for the various components represent sound metallurgical practice." This was impressive and even surprising in view of the low priority given to the early production months of Porsche's military adaptation of the Beetle.

A macrograph of a cross-sectioned engine crankshaft showed a smooth pattern of grain flow achieved through first-class forging. Also sectioning and macrographing the magnesium transmission case, Colonel Frye commented on "the unusual soundness of this rather intricate casting. The use of magnesium for such purposes is uncommon in this country. The Germans apparently used it because of its ready availability and to contribute to the light weight of the vehicle."

Ingenious uses of materials in the Type 82 were identified by the analysts at Aberdeen. They found that its engine's ignition system was served by "exceptionally heavy" stranded copper wires but the harness for the lighting used less-critical stranded-iron wiring. "Practically all the German electrical fittings are smaller and more delicate than American fittings," they said. They highlighted another subtlety:

> One interesting point is a grease seal found between the transmission and the differential housing. This is of normal construction but is remarkable in that the rubber (synthetic) used for the seal is harder at the outside than where it bears on the shaft. This would indicate that the Germans are able to vary the consistency of rubber within a single piece.

When they were found abandoned, the Kübels were put to immediate use by the Americans in the field, first in Africa and later in Italy and then in France. They were useful as light personnel carriers and where terrain was not too daunting they scored over the Jeep with their much better fuel economy.

So useful were these captured vehicles that the U.S. War Department prepared a comprehensive 140-page technical manual for them, TM E9-803. It described in detail the functions, operations, and maintenance of the vehicle it called simply the "German Volkswagen."

Submitted for publication on 23 March 1944, the manual (curiously referred to in the transmittal sheet as "German Volkswagenwerk") was approved for release on 11 May and printed by the army's Raritan Arsenal in Metuchen, New Jersey, effective 6 June 1944. The first print run was 37,500 copies and the manuals were in the field by July, 27,650 of them going straight to the Port of New York for shipment to Europe.

The manual was illustrated by retouched photos of the KdF-Wagen that had been analyzed by Aberdeen in 1942; it looked to have been given a makeover for its starring role. Explained the manual, "The Volkswagen is a four-wheeled, rubber-tired, rear axle drive personnel carrier and reconnaissance car, comparable in purpose and size to the American "quarter-ton 4 x 4 truck" — namely, the Jeep. Both had been designed and built with precisely the same purpose in view: the replacement in the field of the motorcycle with sidecar.

The novel torsion bars were referred to by the manual's authors as "torque rods." Maximum speed was given as 49.7 mph and normal fuel consumption as approximately thirty miles per U.S. gallon. Full details were provided on engine and chassis adjustments and troubleshooting procedures. Suitable lubricants and service intervals were spelled out, although in the latter case the intervals were unhelpfully specified in miles for a vehicle whose odometer was calibrated in kilometers.

The need for proper tire pressures was highlighted; they were to be twenty pounds per square inch in front and twenty-six in the rear. We can assume that inattention here led to some crashed Kübels, because the difference between the front and rear pressures was vital to safe handling on paved roads. And if the oil gauge failed to register any pressure the instruction was explicit: "Stop engine and notify higher authority."

HIGHLY DETAILED INFORMATION on the KdF-Wagen and its engine was provided by the chief of ordnance in time for inclusion in a paper on air-cooled engines given at an SAE meeting in Detroit in January 1944. Illustrations showed the prewar brochure's transparent phantom views of the KdF-Wagen and its engine, the oiling system, and details of the cylinder head.

"One of the most interesting developments during the past 10 years," said the paper's author Chester Ricker, "has been the volkswagen [sic], which was turned into the Nazi 'Jeep' during the war period. Perhaps I will be forgiven for analyzing this enemy product first, for it represents the most thoroughly tested aircooled engine passenger vehicle today and illustrates almost every aircooling problem."

In an extensive and detailed analysis, Ricker came down as a firm advocate of air-cooled engines for postwar cars. Like Bill Stout, he noted that "the aircooled engine lends itself to rear-engine installations because it simplifies the installation due to the simplicity of the cooling system."

Chet Ricker, spared during the war from his duties as chief timer and scorer of the Indianapolis 500, described a new engine designed by Carl Doman, enlarged from the flat-four that was built for the Airomobile. An oil cooler like the VW's would be an added complication, Ricker admitted, but he thought that future high-performance liquid-cooled engines would need them as well.

Further details of the wartime Type 82 were revealed to Americans in April 1944 when *Automotive and Aviation Industries* published an illustrated article based on the British BIOS study piloted by Humber. This was presented without Humber's editorial comments on the design's lack of potential for civilian use. The Humber report on the Kübel had in fact been used by the SAE's War Engineering Board as the basis of its report on the same vehicle.

As in Britain, so too in America a certain dichotomy was evident between the generally positive findings of these technically based wartime analyses and the less impartial and more critical executive-summary appraisals that were made of the Type 82. A restricted U.S. Army review of the assets of the German war machine took a dusty view of the merits of much of its rolling stock:

In general, German military automotive equipment consists of adaptations of civilian types, and these in most cases do not reach the high standard of American or British vehicles either in reliability or performance. The German branches of Ford and General Motors appear to have been incapable of reproducing their prototypes with unimpaired efficiency. With half-tracked prime-movers and personnel-carriers, however, the Germans have excelled; in this class they have produced vehicles which have given excellent service and which are unrivalled for cross-country performance.

Light Army Car (Volkswagen). This four-seat vehicle was developed from the famous "People's Car," which in fact never came into the hands of the German people. The military version has a touring body with a folding top instead of the civilian sedan type body. The Volkswagen, the German equivalent of the American "Jeep," *is inferior in every way* except in the comfort of its seating accommodations [emphasis added].

Ubiquitous on the battlefield, produced in nearly ten times the volume of the military VWs, the Jeep was a magnificent workhorse. Its merits were and are beyond dispute. But had the Jeep become such an icon of the American army by 1945 that no hint could be given that an enemy vehicle could approach its merits in any important respect? Especially one based on the Volkswagen, derided by many as a blatant Hitler swindle? The latter point was touched on by a 1943 American army training manual:

Captured *Volkswagens* have been tested and they are nothing to brag about. They have a two-wheel drive and the jeep [sic] drive is four-wheel. Their top speed is thirty miles per hour and the jeep's is fifty. Their suspension and general construction doesn't permit the tough cross-country driving the jeep can take. What's true of these cars is pretty true of German and American trucks, personnel carriers and tractors. We make them better as well as faster.

For years Hitler has been promising the Germans a car in every garage, and has deducted vast sums from people's pay as advance payments on these cars. The German people never did get their cars — for the entire production was intended for the army from the very beginning.

Much of this was pure propaganda, intended to reassure the American fighting man that he was better equipped than his enemy. Information about the VW's speed was inaccurate and its many advantages, well understood at Aberdeen, were ignored. In addition for good measure the hated Germans were portrayed as liars and cheats.

Prejudice certainly colored such assessments, or at least the style in which the assessments were couched for public consumption in wartime. "It was inevitable that those of us in the US Army compared the Kübelwagen with the Jeep, our tactical equivalent," recalled ordnance aide Konrad F. Schreier, Jr. "The criticisms of the Kübelwagen I remember hearing repeatedly stressed its lack of four-wheel-drive and resulting lack of the cross-country mobility required for our tactical vehicles."

"As we know," Schreier added, "the Nazi Germans lacked the industrial capacity to equip many of their military vehicles with four-wheel-drive. The

USA had only developed that capability shortly prior to WW II." In fact the engineering requirement for the vehicle that was destined to become the Jeep was only laid down in mid-1940; no such small four-wheel-drive military vehicle had previously existed. By the time the Germans gave belated attention to the design of the bespoke military vehicles that their carmakers could produce, their priority had to be the production of existing models — even at the expense of much-needed spare parts — instead of new all-wheel-driven types.

ONE FOUR-WHEEL-DRIVEN VERSION of the Beetle was in fact engineered and built in significant quantity during the war: the Type 166 Schwimmwagen. It was of great interest to the Americans. A fully operational sample was shipped to Aberdeen and given an initial assessment in a memorandum report dated 30 October 1944. This included a translation of the technical specifications of the Type 166 and gave the first impressions of the U.S. Army ordnance experts on this Porsche creation.

They liked it. "The torsion bar suspension on this vehicle enabled it to perform extremely well over smooth and rough terrain," the Aberdeen experts found, and "the front and rear locking differentials were very effective for mud operation." Its engineering attracted admiration: "The simplicity in design of this vehicle lends itself well to mass production."

Its seaworthiness won plaudits too. "The all-around performance of this vehicle in water was exceptionally good," read the report. "Front wheel steering in water instead of using a conventional rudder was found to be very effective." Summing up the Aberdeen appraisal, Lt. Col. G. B. Jarrett found the Water Beetle worth emulating: "Because of the excellent performance of this vehicle during limited tests and because of the simplicity of the design, it is recommended that the vehicle be further investigated with a view toward having our automotive industry adopt some of its salient features."

With just such a technology transfer in mind another captured Type 166 was forwarded by Aberdeen to the General Motors Proving Ground at Milford, Michigan, where the auto industry could test it on a rich variety of surfaces and gradients, including GM's "Mud and Billy Goat Hill Test," and piloted into and across Sloan Lake. All the members of the Overall Vehicle Sub-Committee of the SAE's Captured Enemy Equipment Committee drove and rode in the little vehicle blazoned with its stenciled Aberdeen address.

They liked it too. Their well-illustrated report, issued in August 1945, could hardly have been more complimentary to the Type 166 and the engineers who conceived it. Their general observations were as follows:

> On the surfaced road the smoothness of the ride and the way the vehicle hugged the road and floated along were noteworthy.

The wartime Type 166 Schwimmwagen was intensively tested by the Americans after the war, both at their Aberdeen Proving Grounds and, as here, by American engineering executives at GM's proving ground.

> The vehicle covered the mud and hilly route with much greater ease and smoothness than the American Jeep, which followed it on each trip around the circuit.
>
> The vehicle was impressive for the manner in which it was maneuvered by its front wheels in the water, its steadiness in the water and the ease with which it entered and left the lake.
>
> The general overall performance was highly satisfactory for the purpose of reconnaissance for which it was designed.

The Porsche engineers, then sheltering in a sawmill in Austria, would have been gratified by this assessment of their work by the enemy industry whose mass-production skills they had sought to emulate. But clearly the Type 166 was a vehicle of a type that the Americans would not have thought of building. As the engineers remarked, "American vehicles because of their surplus power can always do more than they were designed for." They added:

> However, in the judgment of the committee this vehicle has sufficient power for its intended purpose, namely that of a reconnaissance vehicle in which it may be called on to cross ponds, small lakes and rivers, soft ground, etc. More power would mean the necessity of larger component parts, which would mean that the vehicle would lose many of its outstanding characteristics. If this vehicle had the power plant of an American Jeep it would probably mean that its weight would go up to that of the standard Jeep. The American Amphibious Jeep weighs approximately 3400 pounds compared to slightly more than 1700 pounds [1725] for the German amphibious Volkswagen.

When empty the two vehicles had similar ratios of power to weight, the SAE experts reported, although the Jeep weighed almost twice as much as its amphibious Beetle equivalent. "There are important lessons in the reduction and saving of weight in this vehicle, especially in the engine, and the hull construction," they added.

After a meticulous analysis of the structure and concept of the Schwimmwagen the American auto engineers gave it a rave review: "The

The Sloan Lake at the General Motors Proving Ground in Milford, Michigan, was used for waterborne tests of the captured Schwimmwagen. It was judged to be extremely competent both on land and at sea.

general architecture of the job offers an ideal combination of structural strength, maximum passenger space and low silhouette. Such items as the elimination of side-entrance openings, the relocation of exhaust system and the torsion bar method of suspension, while lending themselves to the nautical personality of the job, have definitely contributed to its light weight as well as to its performance and stability as a land vehicle."

A detailed breakdown of the welded-steel hull of the Type 166 was performed. "Efficient shaping of the body panels," said the report, "has resulted in a job having unusual roominess and a pleasing appearance. It has also contributed to light weight, structural stability and seaworthiness." Specifically, the SAE engineers concluded:

> In the judgment of the committee the body or hull of this vehicle creates the impression of a well engineered product. It is composed of a minimum number of stampings of substantial size, calling for an elaborate and expensive tooling program. The entire vehicle would be costly to build from our standard for small vehicles. However, cost in a military vehicle is secondary to the man hours required in manufacture.

In this judgment, of course, they had put their fingers on some of the considerations — complexity and the manufacturing manpower requirement — that had led to the VW works' decision to cease production of the Type 166 in August 1944 after the waves of Allied bombings.

Their experiences in and out of GM's Sloan Lake impressed the assessors with the shrewdness of the Schwimmwagen's hull contours. They praised the way the underside of its "bow" was configured to permit the front wheels to steer the craft so effectively. "Road and water tests have proven [that] a great deal of thought has been given to the actual contour of the hull," they found, adding, "It may well be advisable to make a more complete study of this hull by making a female plaster cast of same, which could be used as a basis for further experimentation and development." The careful evolution from the 128 to the 166 in the waters of the Max Eyth Reservoir had rewarded the Porsche team with enviable engineering success in the eyes of their peers.

The cream of the engineering talent of America's automakers turned out to be photographed with the Type 166 they had evaluated at Milford and judged to be "a well engineered product." The Porsche designers had done excellent work.

A dichotomy of the Type 166 design was noted in the report: "The general feeling of the engineers present was that they would not design an amphibious vehicle for an air cooled engine." With all that water around, they thought it should be exploited! The engineers hadn't been party to the German tests in which the Trippel amphibian's water-cooled Opel engine overheated. They assumed that "the definite trend of the German designers toward air cooled engines resulted from the problem they faced in winter fighting on the eastern Russian front."

A complaint common to all the early KdF-Wagen designs was expressed here as well. "Brakes are inferior. When the vehicle comes out of the water there are no brakes. They are not kept dry. It was explained that the brakes had not been good since the vehicle arrived from Germany."

Many of the American engineers — among them the technical directors of their respective firms — were having a first opportunity to experience Beetle-style handling. "There was a feeling that the vehicle steers too fast — over steers — on land," they reported. "It was pointed out that even though the steering is fast in [comparison] with American practice it probably is a national German desire to have fast steering. It will hold anywhere on a curve." The Aberdeen assessors had also noted "a tendency to over-steer."

AMERICANS, BOTH SOLDIERS AND CIVILIANS based in occupied Germany, were getting a firsthand chance to evaluate the VW in its many variants in the months that followed V-E Day. As early as 1946 the Wolfsburg factory was releasing newly built cars both to the U.S. military authorities for use in the American zone and to the Post Exchange system for private sale.

"Thus it came about," wrote Menno Duerksen, United Press correspondent in Germany, "that a few of those early post-war Volkswagens began to trickle into the hands of Americans, Army officers, civilians and non-coms. Several of my press colleagues made the trek to Wolfsburg and came back with their shiny new cars. Well, not so shiny, for the paint on those first cars resembled something like faded blue barn paint."

These early cars were rife with faults, Duerksen recalled, in addition to their crude finish and the mediocre performance given by their "sissy" one-liter engines:

> They were noisy. Hard to start in cold weather. The valves burned out. The torsion bar suspension sagged after a few months of hard use. This certainly was not the car on which Ferdinand Porsche had "worked out the bugs." But there was an explanation for all this. It wasn't the design that was lousy. It was the poor material available in Germany in those first post-war months. High quality steel for valves and torsion suspension just didn't exist at any price, barter or steal.

Soon enough some of these austere Type 11 VWs made their way back to the United States. What MGM could not achieve before the war was now possible for GM. Graeme Howard of the General Motors Overseas Operations Division in New York placed an order with the British authorities for one car. Relayed on an urgent basis through Brigadier General Draper of the American occupation, the order for "Graham" Howard was received by the British in mid-September 1946 and confirmed by them on 1 October. Not long thereafter Mr. Howard must have received his Type 11 VW.

Returning servicemen brought their "faded blue" Beetles back from Europe. At Maryland's Aberdeen Proving Grounds in 1947, staff members passing the parking lot at the officers' club saw one parked there at lunchtime. "The Beetle belonged to a US Army Major just transferred from Germany back to the USA," said Konrad Schreier. "A number of people who had never seen one were looking at it."

Among those onlookers, Schreier recalled, was Carl Breer. Active in the creation of the original Chrysler in the 1920s, Breer was then a leading figure in Chrysler's engineering department. "He, of course, designed the radical Chrysler Airflow," related Schreier, who knew Breer. "He had seen a Beetle and he had a low opinion of its entire design. He also opined that the American car buyer wouldn't have anything to do with such a tiny and austere car."

WHAT OF THE VOLKSWAGEN FACTORY ITSELF? How well were Americans informed about it in the critical months and years that led up to its postwar disposition? Members of the American Society of Body Engineers met in Detroit on 1 April 1947 to hear about it from Lloyd D. Worden, chief of the automotive and aeronautics unit of the Department of Commerce's Office of Technical Services.

Worden told the engineers that a visit to Fallersleben had established that "manufacturing plans were in an advanced stage just before the war broke out, with the plant scheduled to turn out one thousand cars a day." He described the VW's novel design, which he said "makes the car very sturdy for its weight." The U.S. official described some of the exceptional equipment thought to be at the plant:

> What is believed to be the world's largest forging press, of 30,000-ton capacity, put into operation by I. G. Farbenindustrie in 1943; Lindner jig-borer capable of tolerances of 1-400,000 inch; a precision grinder with which the operator can translate a drawing directly into metal, thus making hand work on templates unnecessary; a profile milling machine designed by Messerschmitt and used to produce the exact contours of a model in a block of hard wood or light metal.

Another U.S. government organization with an interest in the postwar condition of the VW factory was the U.S. Strategic Bombing Survey team. It carried out meticulous examinations of all of Germany's industrial installations to assess the amount of industrial disruption that bombing had caused in relation to the tons of munitions bestowed from the air.

Not until the middle war years, the bombing surveyors found, had Germany's vehicle makers been converted to purely military production. "The Volkswagen plant at Fallersleben was another example of non-utilization of motor vehicle facilities," it reported. The American surveyors continued:

> This plant, finished in 1939, was the largest factory of its type in Germany, had the largest press shop in Europe, and was capable of producing in excess of 150,000 cars per year. According to the management, however, the start of the war found the plant's management as well as the authorities in Berlin unprepared for utilization of the plant in the war effort. The German government expected a short war and accordingly decided to keep the plant intact for postwar production of automobiles. This is supported by the fact that the plant remained virtually idle, its 1941 production representing only 20–25 percent of the plant's capabilities. During the entire course of the war the plant never produced more than 50 percent of its capacity.

If this finding was not strictly correct in terms of the overall utilization of the Fallersleben plant, the report nevertheless did provide, and presented in graphical form, an accurate assessment of the vehicle production it achieved during the war years and contrasted that with the various plans intending to boost vehicle production to 4,000 units per month. In fact the best output level was reached consistently in 1943 at some 2,500 per month.

In September 1947 a member of the staff of the American consulate in Hamburg visited and reported on Fallersleben. Another such visit was the subject of a report of 17 June 1948, which called it "one of the most modern automobile plants in Europe" and said that "it is a huge structure; from the office building at one end to the power plant at the other end of the factory is a distance of two-thirds of a mile."

Recapping the VW's dramatic history, the consular official called the car "extremely well designed, compact, with the engine in the rear, has space for five people, and a luggage compartment both in the front and over the engine in the rear. The car has four speeds forward, a unique individual wheel springing and is surprisingly comfortable on rough roads in spite of its short wheel base and light weight."

Conditions at the plant were detailed in the report, which was circulated to the American automakers by their trade association, the Automobile Manufacturers Association. It mentioned problems with workforce stability, adequacy of housing, competence of the senior plant staff, and maintenance of the machine tools, many of which were so highly specialized that "in many cases production is held up while a vital machine tool is out of order and a substitute machine cannot be used."

Nevertheless, stated the Hamburg consular report, "Production now averages 1,200 units a month with plans to increase this figure to 1,500 by early fall, the goal being 2,400 cars per month by early 1949. The Volkswagen plant," the report concluded, "is an excellent example of that type of production which could be vastly increased if a few essential materials could be made available."

Over their Sunday coffee, orange juice, bacon, and scrambled eggs, Detroit's motor moguls could see and read about Beetles being assembled in the *Detroit Free Press* of 7 November 1948. "They sell for $800 each in bulk," said the article, which highlighted the plant's export success to Sweden, Denmark, Holland, Belgium, Luxembourg, and Switzerland. "There is a big drive on to increase the present monthly production of 2,100," the executives read. "The German prewar plan was to make 30,000 a month."

Another Sunday was spoiled for Detroiters in April 1949. In its pictorial section the *Detroit News* showed serried rows of Beetles representing "about two day's production" and workers at Wolfsburg bolting the "stubby, one-style jobs" together "on an American-style production line." Stating that "The chiefs at Wolfsburg say they can get rid of every Volkswagen their 8,000 workers produce," even at the price of DM 5,300 ($1,590), the *Detroit News* added that "a few have been imported [into the United States] for exhibition purposes and eventually more may follow into the U.S. market."

NINETEEN FORTY-EIGHT AND EARLY 1949 provided the last opportunities for the U.S.-based auto producers to take the Beetle and its factory seriously before the British four-year reservation of the facility expired. Behind the propaganda headlines, the American evaluations of both Volkswagen plant and product had been overwhelmingly positive. Both were acknowledged to be potential threats to the home and export markets of the autos made overseas by Ford and GM's Opel.

After the war Americans were ready for an advanced rear-engined car, as Preston Tucker found from the enthusiastic response given to his plans to build the Tucker '48. The Chicago factory that Tucker optioned to produce it had twice the floor area of the VW works.

Derived from a Franklin air-cooled airplane engine, the power unit of the Tucker was a flat-opposed six with pushrod-operated overhead valves. It was mounted "outboard" behind the rear wheels.

Decisions on such matters were still made in the United States, however. There, most auto industry executives could not bring themselves to take seriously the noisy, crude, and odd-looking Beetles emerging from the British-controlled factory. They had their hands full meeting the huge American postwar demand for new cars, cars that were bigger and thirstier than ever. The tiny and tinny VW seemed to be a step in the wrong direction.

Unlike their British counterparts, neither the car buyers nor the industry in America were antipathetic to the idea of an advanced, aerodynamic rear-engined car. In fact they had long been conditioned by Stout, Tjaarda, and other enthusiasts to expect just such an auto to be parked in the carports of their postwar split-level homes.

When Preston Tucker revealed his sleek Tucker '48 in 1947 with a flat-six engine mounted in the rear it was enthusiastically greeted by dealers and the public as the wonderful new car America had long been promised. To build

William Stout used suspension and power train features based on his prewar designs for the remarkably advanced prototype he built in 1946 with the backing of Graham-Paige. With the help of Owens Corning it had an integral fiberglass body-frame. Americans, many felt, were eager for something new.

it Tucker Motors took an option on a factory, erected in Chicago during the war to produce aircraft engines, that offered more than four million square feet of floor area under one roof — almost double the area of the VW works. But Tucker's tussles with America's Securities Exchange Commission brought his company to its knees after it had hand-built some fifty prototypes — about as many as the final Volkswagen test-car series.

Other Americans were thinking rear-engined too. The budding Keller company built some rear-engined prototype cars. Independent producer Studebaker introduced Loewy-styled short-nosed, long-tailed models that looked rear-engined even though they weren't. Bill Stout built his all-glass-fiber postwar Scarab derivative under the auspices of Graham-Paige, which was also encouraging the design by John Tjaarda of an advanced six-cylinder rear-engined car. At General Motors, engineer Edward N. Cole was beginning the rear-engined studies that would lead to the introduction of the air-cooled Corvair at the end of the 1950s.

But a small, economical rear-engined car? Was this on anyone's agenda in a prosperous America, powered out of the depression by a war economy and eager to sample the pleasures of peacetime? Some American automakers would take an interest in the Volkswagen's fate. They would seek answers to the question posed to readers of *Automotive News* in mid-1944 by a former German citizen working in the American auto industry: "What will the Allies do with the German automobile industry after victory?"

The anonymous analyst argued that "the German automobile industry is a menace to the world; it is . . . much too large for the German needs and a dangerous spoiler of the international markets." In particular, he asked, before describing the VW project in outline, "What are we going to do with the KdF plant?

"Something should be decided now," continued the lengthy article, "before we have the problem on our hands and might slip up on making the right and final decisions. This German industry certainly will cry out, 'Don't do anything against us; we are good people and produce only automobiles for the German people, and anybody who does not like us does this purely from a standpoint of competition.' Will they succeed and fool a war-weary world once more?"

This was an issue to which, in fact, consideration had already been given during the war by the Allies, especially those in Europe. Among those Allies the French had been closest to the KdF-Wagen export threat, closest to the vast plant at Fallersleben, closest to the menace of Adolf Hitler. Now France had to cope with the challenge of the huge works on the Mittelland Canal, healing with insouciant ease its scars from Allied air attacks to make its peculiar cars again. France would address the issue with imagination and vigor.

6

The French Nearly Prevail

Although it was invented in Germany, the motor car was industrially developed and actively promoted in France. France's major automakers had been launched as businesses before the turn of the century and by 1902 had broken through to five-figure annual volumes. French producers made more than 20,000 cars in 1905 and 45,000 in 1913 with Peugeot and Renault the leaders at some 5,000 cars apiece.

Their pioneers, among them Panhard et Levassor, de Dion, and Renault, made France the early leader in the production of motors and the promotion of motoring. Soon the French were building bigger and faster cars to compete in road races from city to city. They established the first club for motorists, led the founding of the first international association of motoring clubs, and organized the first Grand Prix race in 1906.

Technologically progressive, the French were the first to remove the engine from a hutch under the car's seats and place it at the front where it could be more easily cooled and virtually unlimited in size. They created the change-speed gearbox and the direct-drive top gear from engine to rear axle.

The first mechanized war was the 1914–18 conflict, for which neighboring Britain was unready. France was still the European leader in the motor industry in production volume, product design, and manufacturing methods. Thus France was the destination when the British army sent officers abroad before war broke out to learn lessons that could be applied at home. One such officer was the young Charles Radclyffe, later to be influential in the fate of the Beetle.

While the Britons were being persuaded only slowly down from their beloved horses, the French were parking cars in their stables and coach houses, cars which were ideally suited to traversing vast distances on the straight poplar-lined roads of this nation at the heart of Europe. And if they lost their

The first rear-engined prototype built by Emile Claveau in 1926 was an open car, starkly defiant of the conventions of the day. A front view shows the sliding-pillar suspension that also served as a steering axis.

industrial lead in the motor business to other nations, most of all America, they did not lose their appetite for technological innovation.

SEVENTEENTH-CENTURY PHILOSOPHER René Descartes was the source of life-long inspiration for one of France's most persistent advocates of advanced automobiles. Emile Claveau cited Descartes' *Discours de la Méthode* of 1637 as the origin of the guiding principles in his own work:

> I always had a strong desire to learn to distinguish the truth from the falsehood, to see clearly in my actions and to march with assurance along the chosen path.
> It is difficult, by only using the work of others, to achieve anything perfect.
> There is not as much perfection in work composed of several pieces made by different masters as that wrought by one alone.
> Buildings undertaken and completed by the same architect are likely to be more beautiful and better ordered than those where several have tried to accommodate outworn ideas which have been coined for other purposes.

Throughout his life Claveau was dedicated to improving the automobile. "No firm," wrote Claveau, "pursues a technically and commercially rational program in the choice and characteristics of cars, all of which proves that they have been *studied by everybody and conceived by nobody.*"

Claveau, like Descartes, believed in the synthesizing power of the lone creator. Like others of his era, Claveau was fully capable of conceiving all the elements of a complete automobile. He used this talent to propose advanced, integrated designs that retain their compelling rationality and appeal seventy years later.

Born before the turn of the century, Emile Claveau gained experience of technology in the aviation industry. After the Great War, like Edmund Rumpler and later John Tjaarda, he turned his attention to ground vehicles. The automobile, he felt, was much in need of the advances in engineering and aerody-

In the manner of Rumpler, Claveau did not seek to envelop the wheels in his 1927 rear-engined design. Its integral steel body-frame construction, however, allowed the Claveau to be much lighter and lower than other cars of its time.

namics that had moved the technology of the airplane forward so rapidly during and after the war.

In September 1923 Claveau settled himself at his drawing board and commenced conceiving a new kind of automobile that owed little to existing designs. Descartes sat at his elbow, guiding the Parisian's pencil into entirely new and logical patterns. By 1926, he and his workmen had created a first open prototype of the Claveau automobile in his small atelier in the shadow of *La Madeleine*, the great Greek-revival church between the Place de la Concorde and the Place de l'Opéra. It was shown at the Paris Salon that same year and joined on the Claveau stand in 1927 by a strikingly advanced closed version.

Apart from the roundness of their wheels and tires, no features of the Claveaus on display resembled any other models at the Salon. Their bodies were rectangular in cross-section and welded of steel to form a self-supporting structure that was innocent of any separate chassis. Described as "wing-section" in profile, the bodies tapered to a point in the rear, which was louvered for engine cooling. Wheels were exposed with close-fitting cycle-type fenders.

In Claveau's design the engine was mid-mounted — in the rear but forward of the rear axle. The gearbox was between the engine and the final-drive gears, like Rumpler's Tropfen-Auto and the Benz racing cars that it inspired. The engine was a compact flat-opposed four of 1.5 liters with two roller-type main bearings and two camshafts mounted in the crankcase and opening side valves. Liquid-cooled versions were sketched but the final design was air-cooled.

All four wheels were independently suspended. Vertical sliding pillars containing small coil springs carried each wheel, pillars that were proudly mounted out in the open. The front pillars also served as the steering kingpins in the Lancia manner. Each rear wheel slid on a pair of pillars, between which a universally jointed driveshaft powered each wheel.

The closed Claveau was a purposeful-looking car with a curved two-piece windshield and a sloping nose that foreshadowed France's handsome

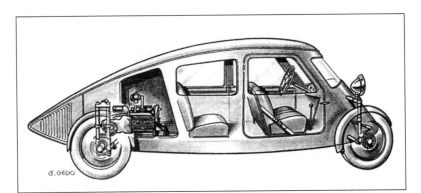

Sliding pillars suspended the rear wheels of the 1927 Claveau prototype, which had a flat-four air-cooled engine with aluminum cylinder heads mounted forward of the rear wheels. Claveau would later become a convert to front-wheel drive.

TGV trains. A large door on each side gave access to two rows of seats. Thanks to its revolutionary closed monocoque construction the Claveau sedan weighed only 2,135 pounds, one-third less than a conventional car of similar carrying capacity. Its advantages in reduced fuel consumption and improved riding comfort were sensational by 1920s standards.

Emile Claveau had rethought the concept of the medium-sized automobile with triumphant success. He did so, he told the members of the Société des Ingenieurs de l'Automobile (SIA), by keeping in mind the principles he saw as guiding the design of the car of the future:

1. It should be able to keep up a good average speed. Close attention should therefore be paid to the aerodynamics.

2. Independent suspension for all four wheels.

3. Interior space should be good.

4. Highest degree of comfort and practical layout inside.

5. All mechanical parts to be located as a single unit.

6. Primary safety must be high, to be gained with the help of a maximum of directional stability and a low centre of gravity which should not be unduly influenced by the number of passengers, and a monocoque construction.

7. Low price obtained by low weight and a small engine.

8. Easy manufacturing process, obtained with the help of a simple body and as great a use as possible of electric welding.

Journalists who experienced Claveau's cars were deeply impressed by their performance, economy, and ride quality. Many of their positive remarks echoed those made about the contemporary North-Lucas in Britain. Respected editor Charles Faroux praised the flexibility of its performance and said that corners he usually took at twenty-five miles per hour were negotiated at forty-five in the Claveau "without any dramatics."

Magazine editor P. Rawson Lamb declared that "no car, unless fitted with articulated or independent road wheels, could perform such feats as we witnessed during the demonstration run." In Lamb's view, "whilst perhaps contrary to accepted ideas, the Claveau is undoubtedly constructed on lines that will be more general in a year or two."

By contrast, Britons would have to wait until 1943 before *The Motor* reminded its readers that "in 1926 a Frenchman named Claveau produced a car which in all essentials anticipated the K.d.F.[-Wagen] by 12 years." When the Beetle was shown in 1938, it said, "it created enormous interest in the motoring world. It looked like something revolutionary, and so it was in so far as vehicles destined for large-scale production were concerned." A dozen years earlier, however, Claveau had combined all the VW's major features in a single vehicle.

The potential of the design was recognized at the time by the magazine *Omnia*: "Sponsored by a big industry, this could well be a people's car," it opined. Lacking big-industry backing, Automobiles Claveau of 22 Place de la Madeleine offered an attractive range of mid-engined cars in its handsome 1929 catalog, but few are known to have been built for sale. Burney and Stout had greater sales success than Emile Claveau.

Progressive though the French were and are in many respects, those among them who could afford to be motorists were reluctant to buck the conventional wisdom by being seen at the wheel of a Claveau. In the meantime, as well, Claveau had experienced a *volte-face* in his thinking about car design. He abandoned rear engines and became an advocate of front-wheel drive.

Most commentators have interpreted this turnabout as a whimsical decision by M. Claveau, lacking in the Cartesian logic he so actively espoused. In fact it was a difficult decision for him, not without a "moral cost" for an engineer who had advocated the rear-engine layout since 1923. But it was one that he had to face, he explained, because front-wheel drive "is the only arrangement which places the maximum area and volume at the disposition of a car's passengers."

This had been a minor issue between 1923 and 1929, Claveau said, "when long family journeys by road were unthinkable and thus did not pose the question of baggage, which is why the problem of a trunk did not exist." Addressing the need for his cars to have more luggage room so their owners (should there ever be any) could travel increasingly longer distances, Claveau changed his allegiance to front-wheel drive for his future prototypes — none of which reached production.

This doughty pioneer remained active through the 1960s in automotive engineering, patenting and promoting a new type of enclosed disc brake among other new ideas. Said a GM executive who met him in 1966, "He is a fascinating old gentleman who has been trying all his life and with only modest success to introduce rational, revolutionary design concepts into an industry which, outward appearances to the contrary, is often reluctant to accept real change." This is an adept summary of the career of an engineer whose automotive ideas were too radical even for a nation that was relatively accepting of new automotive concepts.

IN THE 1930S EMILE CLAVEAU was among the sixty-two members of the SIA who responded to that society's competition to design a two-passenger small car intended to be low in cost (less than eight thousand francs, or $525) and economical to run. The SIA's president Maurice Goudard also headed the French society of automotive vehicle and parts makers, the *Chambre Syndicale*; Goudard persuaded the organization to offer a prize fund of two hundred thousand francs to reward the successful competitors.

Dubbed the *Voiture SIA*, such a car was well understood by the SIA's members as being in a size category below the normal French four-passenger small car — and smaller than the coming KdF-Wagen. Yet it was judged by the engineers to be a size of car well worth encouraging for future development and exploitation in an industry and market still hobbled by the Great Depression.

The powers of creativity and indeed fantasy for which French automotive engineers are justly famed were displayed in spectacular fashion by the 102 submissions, many executed in convincing and beguiling detail.

Significantly, in the view of the judges, 55 percent of the proposals favored a rear-mounted engine. Only 36 percent chose to drive the front wheels, while the rest were of the classic layout with a front engine driving the rear wheels. Their preference for a rear-mounted engine prevailed among the French engineers in spite of the fact that their industry had not yet adopted this layout in production.

Most popular among the engine possibilities was an air-cooled flat-opposed twin (30 percent) with a cylinder capacity in the range of 700 cc to 800 cc. Four wheels were preferred by 89 percent of the studies. Indeed, an analysis of the three-wheeled minority showed that the weight advantage often claimed for this configuration was not actually realized.

Here, then, was a French engineering consensus that favored a small-car layout that strikingly paralleled the design that Porsche and his technicians had selected for the Beetle. If the views of the engineer members of the SIA had value, placing an air-cooled engine at the rear (a decade after Claveau) was an idea whose time was fast approaching.

ANOTHER VOITURE SIA DESIGNER, the eminent aerodynamicist Jean Andreau, created competition entries that emphasized low-drag shapes above all. His was the genius behind the shape of an extraordinary rear-engined prototype financed by André Dubonnet. Andreau created an auto-

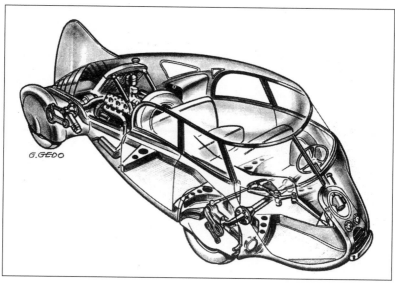

One of the most radical designs to be created in the ferment of the automotive revolution of the 1930s was the rear-engined Narval designed for André Dubonnet by aerodynamicist Jean Andreau. Its single central headlight was an echo of the design solution favored by the Rumpler Tropfen-Auto and the North-Lucas.

mobile so radical that its only recognizable component was the Ford V-8 engine mounted forward of the rear wheels.

So cab-forward was the architecture of Dubonnet's *Narval* (Dolphin), with its front seats between the wheels, that entry for the driver was through a door in front of the right front wheel. In this prototype Andreau had taken to the limit the concept of a teardrop-shaped body of low drag that was made possible by placing the engine in the tail of the chassis. Conventional side doors gave access to a roomy rear passenger compartment. The disadvantage of the rear engine perceived by Claveau was evident: the Dolphin had no dedicated luggage space.

By using a Ford engine, Dubonnet shrewdly fostered a direct comparison with the conventional Ford passenger car. They were similar in weight (3,050 pounds) and bench tests showed the Dolphin's engine to be 10 percent below the Ford's eighty horsepower. Nevertheless tests at the Montlhéry oval track near Paris showed a maximum speed for the Dolphin of 108 mph against 80 for the standard Ford. At similar constant speeds the French car consumed 29 percent less fuel. The economy advantage over the twisty Montlhéry road course was 22 percent.

These were convincing calling cards for André Dubonnet and his uncompromisingly aerodynamic Dolphin, with its single central headlamp,

The tiny rear-engined Erfiag, of which three dozen were built in Switzerland to a design by Josef Ganz, was being considered for production by France's Automobiles L. Rosengart before those plans were interrupted by the war.

when they were decanted on the American shore in April 1936 to begin a tour of the world's largest car manufacturers. But the cost-conscious American producers, still rocking from the public's rejection of a Chrysler Airflow that was far less radical than Dubonnet's Dolphin, saw the latter as intriguing but inappropriate for their market.

It was inappropriate for France as well. But at the other end of the size scale a small rear-engined car made a mini-breakthrough in France. It was the work of none other than the former pioneering editor of *Motor Kritik*, Josef Ganz. Ganz had succeeded in having his rear-engined small-car design produced by Standard in the early 1930s and, as a Jew, had had the good sense to leave Germany in 1934 to settle in Switzerland.

Still keen on small cars, Ganz continued to develop them in his Swiss surroundings. By 1938 he had completed the prototype of a new open two-seater — the Erfiag. He powered it with a 350 cc M.A.G. single-cylinder engine. But what was to become of it? Ganz made contact with Max Hoffman, an influential friend.

An entrepreneur, Austrian by birth, Hoffman too had decided that Germany was not the place to be in the 1930s. He had been representing the sales of many British, French, and Italian marques in Central Europe before he moved to Paris, for his health, in 1938. There he formed close contacts with Automobiles L. Rosengart, which specialized in manufacturing foreign designs under license in France, such as Austins and Adlers.

In its heyday under Ganz's editorship, Max Hoffman had always admired the outspoken and polemic *Motor Kritik* and had made it his business to get to know its editor. Now the former editor got in touch with Hoffman to explore the potential for his Erfiag. Max Hoffman, an excellent driver, demonstrator, and salesman, saw distinct possibilities:

> With associates, [Hoffman] made arrangements for the Erfiag prototype to be brought from Zurich to Paris to be demonstrated by Hoffman for Rosengart as a possible future production model. There he put it through its paces, which included a session on the tank-testing ground at Vincennes. Rosengart liked what it saw and bought, through Hoffman, a license to manufacture the Ganz design. But just two weeks later, there was no thought of building Rosengarts, or any other cars, for France and Germany were at war.

IN THE MEANTIME THE FRENCH were learning from their motoring press about the creation in Germany of a new car for the masses. The cornerstone-laying ceremony at Fallersleben attracted the attention of *La Pratique Automobile*, whose correspondent misunderstood the terms of the KdF-Wagen layaway plan, gathering that each prospective buyer would pay in five marks *monthly* rather than weekly. "This is the first time," it remarked with understandable amazement, "that a car will be sold with almost twenty years to pay for it."

The new car, according to *La Pratique*, was to be built in a "monster factory destined to manufacture a car which Hitler will make available to every 'Aryan' citizen." The car's shape, it said, "aerodynamic at both front and rear, somewhat resembles that of the Peugeot." The latter firm had been introducing new models in the 1930s which epitomized the decade's trend toward more aerodynamic forms. The French found nothing shocking in the Beetle's shape.

La Pratique told its readers about the plan to build a works employing twenty thousand and an adjoining town for seventy thousand inhabitants. "Will all this vast project be realizable?" it asked. "Where will they get the money?" As the magazine had noted earlier in the story, "It's true that after several years the Germans are getting the world used to their doing things that have never been done!"

Published in Liège, the *Englebert Magazine* acquainted the Francophone world with details of the KdF-Wagen and its associated factory at the beginning of 1939. In its engine placement and cooling, wrote engineer Alfred Nauck, the new car diverged from the norm: "Here we encounter a profound and fundamental modification of the disposition of the engine, very generally placed at the front. Moreover, the air cooling represents a realization which has never been adopted for large-volume production."

In glowing reportage which manifested the "harmonizing" efforts of the Germans' press monitoring, Nauck referred to the "extraordinary elan" which the KdF car project was imparting to the German auto market, "which could absorb six to seven million cars." He said that three body styles were planned for "this beautiful vehicle": a roadster, sedan, and cabriolet, and added that "the solution of the bodywork line is most fortuitous for the three models."

In its next issue *Englebert Magazine* featured the doings at the 1939 Berlin Auto Show where "the great attraction," Henri Petit reported, was the "Volkswagen." Petit reminded his readers of the requirements that contributed to its design — the need to carry four passengers, the lack of any need for garaging, minimizing the need for service, and the achievement of design solutions which are "sufficiently advanced and proven to be valid for five or even ten years without any important modification in the design being shown to be needed, an essential condition for a very large production series extending over several years."

Henri Petit provided a detailed technical description based on the material released at Berlin, including four photos of the engine and chassis. He devoted special attention to the material from which the body was to be made:

> The bodywork is entirely in steel; emphasizing this point, because last year we thought, following on the publicity given by the Germans to their synthetic products or nationalized products (such as compressed wood or synthetic resins), that materials of these types would be used. That's not the case, and the advertising emphasizes this fact with a publicity picture shown in the brochure for this people's car: it shows a potential customer who is tapping a finger on the bodywork and verifying with satisfaction that it is actually of steel.

Interestingly, Petit gained the impression that after the launch of the two-door model "later on, a cabriolet will be produced and possibly a four-door model." The latter would have been of great interest to the French market, which had a preference for four-door body styles.

All of this, wrote Petit, added up to a significant challenge to the existing industry: "If, as is hoped, they can sell four hundred of these cars daily in Germany from 1941 and if, following the original plan, the factory's production is increased to 1,500,000 in 1945, not only for Germany but also for the rest of the world this could result in a serious perturbation of the automobile market."

In a lead article in the same issue the doyen of French motoring editors, Charles Faroux, also emphasized that the KdF-Wagen threatened such existing makers of small cars as DKW and Opel "because its buyers will not only be those coming to the automobile for this first time." Faroux cited even higher population figures for the factory and city: 60,000 workers and 200,000 inhabitants, looking ahead to 1945.

Shrewdly, Faroux assessed the running cost of a KdF-Wagen as adding up to a substantial forty marks weekly. For this reason, he hazarded, at least at the beginning the new cars from Fallersleben would be bought by the German middle classes while "the working masses would have to wait." This was a savvy forecast of the actual composition of the signed-up members of the saving program.

THE "SERIOUS PERTURBATION" FORECAST for the auto markets of 1945 — flooding them with a million and a half cheap VWs — inspired industry reactions in France. Louis Renault was among those who reacted most strongly. Widely regarded as the Henry Ford of France, the founder of the nation's volume-production car industry, Renault was still the sole proprietor of the company that bore his name. Also like Ford, Renault was regarded as a difficult personality. Confident in his instincts, conservative in his actions, and renowned for his volcanic temper, Louis Renault did not respond readily to outside influences; indeed he took pride in defying them.

"Even though he was exceptionally successful," wrote engineer Jean-Albert Grégoire, "or perhaps because of it, Louis Renault was not liked in the motor-car world. His taciturn ways, his timidity, his power and pride doomed him to solitude." Like Ford, Renault mistrusted industry bodies and associations like the SIA and Chambre Syndicale. With age he also suffered from an intensifying speech defect that contributed to his reticence and constrained his range of contacts.

Louis Renault had contributed to France's armament in World War I but he had little appetite for a comparable commitment to the vacillating French military in the 1930s. His plan for a fast light two-man tank was ignored until it was too late to produce it. Quickly forgetting the mobility lessons of the Great War, the French produced only 110,000 military vehicles between 1934 and 1938, less than half the Germans' 264,000 in the same period.

His biographer Anthony Rhodes portrayed Renault's attitude as follows:

> Interested only in civilian vehicles, [Renault] believed that war production in the First World War had been the primary cause of the decay in the French car industry after 1918. If this was to be repeated in 1939, while America concentrated on civilian vehicles, the French motor-car industry would be forced out of the world's peacetime markets. He had seen the destruction of his country in the first war, and had fought the commercial battle after to rebuild and make her capable of competing in the world automobile market. Now, it appeared, the whole process was to be repeated.

With or without war, Renault could see that the Volkswagen project was a potential menace to his markets at home and abroad. "He certainly admired German industrial efficiency," said Rhodes, "and wanted to see the *Autobahnen*, which did not exist in France." For these and other business reasons the sixty-one-year-old Renault journeyed to Berlin for the February 1938 Auto show. Although the Beetle was not yet on public display, the model of its factory was and its general design features were an open secret in the industry.

Invited to the Berlin Show's opening ceremony, Renault and his colleagues took their reserved seats not far from the rostrum in a hall set apart from the exhibition areas by rich and imposing brown curtaining. Purplish

Louis Renault, as authentic a pioneer of the motor industry as Henry Ford, was also as dogged, stubborn, and pacifist as his American counterpart. His was the order that started Renault's engineers working on "a car like the Germans have" — a people's car for France.

lighting effects played about the hall as a symphony orchestra opened the proceedings with the overture from Carl Maria von Weber's *Oberon*. After speeches from the RDA president and Josef Goebbels, Hitler took the floor.

In a muted mood, the Führer delivered "a short and calm speech," an onlooker recalled. "Amongst other points, he spoke of the dangers of motoring and the toll of life it claimed every year, which he compared to the losses in the 1870 war." Not knowing German, Louis Renault turned to his neighbor, the engineer Grégoire, who interpreted some of the key points for him. The industrialist asked the engineer to accompany him to the Renault stand, where they joined some of Renault's colleagues and French diplomatic officials.

> A few minutes later Hitler came along to our group. Louis Renault, who did not hide his admiration for the illustrious visitor, asked him in a voice choking with emotion, "Don't you think, Excellency, that good relations between France and Germany are indispensable for the prosperity of our two countries and for the equilibrium of Europe?"
>
> Hitler, beside whom I was then standing, gave this reply, the impudence of which amazed me: "If one talks too much and too particularly about war, this is attributable to the French journalists who are always using the word in their columns!"

Unedifying though this was for Renault, he was able to learn enough about the Volkswagen and Hitler's plans for it to return to Paris persuaded that he should take the German challenge seriously. We can surmise with confidence that Louis Renault's aim was not solely to be able to offer an economical, industrially produced car to his fellow countrymen. Beyond that,

Expanding away from its site at Billancourt in southwest Paris, Louis Renault's vehicle factory had also occupied the Seguin Island in the Seine. Before the war, however, Renault produced too many car and truck models and too few of each.

he surely saw a good offense as the best defense against the export menace that the KdF-Wagen posed to his domestic market in France.

Time passed as Louis Renault brooded on the challenge while his factories generated the highest turnover of any French vehicle firm in the last twelve months before the outbreak of war. Citroën was first in private cars with 61,460 units, ahead of Peugeot (52,976), and Renault (45,388). In high-value truck output, however, Renault was ahead of Citroën (15,613 compared with 9,789) and Berliet occupied third place (4,305).

While Renault was in America in June 1940 on a mission for his government the Germans occupied France and on 22 June an armistice between France and Germany was signed by Marshal Pétain at Vichy — a spa city that would stand forever for France's ignominious subjugation by her neighbor. By 22 July Renault was back at his headquarters in Paris's Billancourt, where he had converted the Seguin Island in the midst of the River Seine into a production powerhouse. Renault shrugged off the German tank-repair problems brought to him by his aides. He was thinking about cars instead.

On a gloomy autumn day of 1940 the Renault chief gathered his technical team. Included was his long-time product design chief, Charles Edmond Serre, who had been to Berlin in 1939 to see the KdF-Wagen in the metal. Also present was Fernand Picard, Serre's second-in-command. Picard, formerly with Automobiles Delage, had joined Renault in 1935 at the age of twenty-nine at the suggestion of Jean-Auguste Riolfo, a former Delage colleague who had become chief of testing at Renault.

"After the war France will be poor," Renault said. His aides leaned forward to hear him clearly. "We must build a small car that sells at a low price and is cheap on petrol. You must make me a car like the one the Germans have," he told the startled engineers.

Working under Charles Edmond Serre, Fernand Picard (pictured) was a key member of the engineering team that clandestinely developed the 4CV at Renault during the war. Although he inclined toward front-wheel drive, he was persuaded by the high cost of the needed universal joints to make the little 4CV rear-engined like the VW.

In the months to come Louis Renault would waver in his personal resolve to commit his company to build such a car. He followed its development personally and encouraged it, but when decision time loomed with the approach of peace he preferred to stay with the products he knew.

"We'll build the Juvaquatre and Primaquatre. Nothing else," Renault said to Serre during a weekend at his home at Herqueville. Renault would die (on 24 October 1944 at the age of sixty-seven) before the final decision had to be made. In the meantime it was up to his engineers to keep faith with his small-car idea. Eventually it became as much theirs as his.

Their approach was enlightened by French logic — Cartesian in the sense meant by Emile Claveau. Like Renault, Serre and Picard envisioned one certainty after the coming peace:

> The poverty in our country following liberation would be widespread, of raw materials, gasoline, and the means of purchasing. How many French people would be in a position to purchase and maintain a car? This meant that our prewar-program vehicles, the Juvaquatre, Novaquatre, Primaquatre, Vivaquatre, and Vivasix, would not be suited to the new situation. This led us to believe that there was a need to consider a completely different vehicle, small in size so as to need very little steel, of economical construction so that it could be sold cheaply, and with reduced performance and light weight so as to keep gas consumption low. Not a cyclecar such as had been built after the First World War. A real vehicle. An improved Simca 5, not a Zèbre.

The latter reference was to a crude small car made in France in the first decade of the twentieth century.

The new car's length was fixed at 3.7 meters (just over twelve feet) or less by the size of garage that attracted the lowest rental rates at the time. Four French taxable horsepower seemed adequate, hence a displacement of 760 cc or less and a 4CV designation were indicated. Although in 1938 the offering of a two-door body on the Juvaquatre had not been a success, this

Strikingly Beetle-like, the first prototype of the 4CV-to-be had only two doors. Completed in 1942, it took to the road with wartime-shrouded headlights and Rosengart hubcaps — a modest enough disguise. Its light green paint was from the 1939 Renault range.

had been good enough for the Germans and would do as well for Renault's small car.

The engineers agreed that both the engine and drive had to be either at the front or the back, to ensure a flat floor, but which was best? Fernand Picard:

> Serre, who had seen the only examples in existence of Dr. Porsche's KdF-Wagen exhibited at the Berlin Motor Show in February 1939, inclined *a priori* toward the rear-engine solution. Of course, no documentation was available to enable reference to be made to it, because it had not yet been mass-produced. There were no journalists' judgments after making their tests. There were a few photographs in the magazines in 1939: *La Vie Automobile* dated 10 March and *Science et Vie* dated May, in which Charles Faroux and Henri Petit reported on the Berlin Motor Show.

Picard favored front-wheel drive, which had been technically (although not commercially) successful in the Citroïns of the 1930s. He had also heard unsettling reports about poor handling of the rear-engined Czech Tatras. He researched the alternatives in the technical papers of the previous decade while a colleague carried out comparative cost calculations, which showed that for a small, low-priced car the high cost of the constant-velocity universal joints needed for front-wheel drive would be the stumbling block. Renault's 4CV would be rear-engined.

With this background, and entered through only two doors, the first prototype of the 4CV Renault could not help looking strikingly like the VW. Its headlights were mounted in the nose panel instead of the fenders; it had a hint of a notchback in its profile and the "outboard" engine under its trunk was an in-line liquid-cooled four of 757 cc with pushrod-operated overhead valves. It was ready for testing on 23 December 1942.

The project bore no type number, because its discovery on a casting could only betray to the occupying Germans that Renault was expending energy on something other than the trucks it was supposed to be building for the Wehr-

The 1942 4CV prototype's four-cylinder engine with pushrod-operated overhead valves went into production almost unchanged. This first sample 4CV had a body made of aluminum for ease of fabrication; later ones were made of steel.

macht. The tiny engine parts were passed off as being "for a compressor." Prototype power units were assembled outside Renault by a trusted supplier.

On the morning of 17 May 1943 Fernand Picard was called in to explain reports of unauthorized car-development activities by the German "special delegate" responsible for the running of the plant, Prince von Urach. Wrote Picard of von Urach,

> Big, corpulent, with a pleasant but distant manner, he was just over forty and looked it. His face, with its flabby features, showed fatigue which accentuated the gloominess of his look. He spoke perfect French, almost without an accent. As heir to the crown of Wittenberg he had, since Hitler came to power, held public relations positions with the Daimler-Benz management in Stuttgart, which had automatically earmarked him in 1940 for being the controller of Renault.

For four years the lugubrious von Urach visited the Renault plant daily, maintaining contacts only at the top of the company. "Louis Renault had no liking for the Germans," his biographer wrote, "whom he referred to on all occasions contemptuously as 'Boches'; but he could not object to this tall and punctilious German who occasionally sat in on his business conferences."

It would not have been an everyday matter for someone at Picard's level to be called on the carpet, however politely, by Prince von Urach. To the German's face, however, Picard denied any inappropriate activity. The unflappable von Urach calmly took note of his response and said he would make Picard personally responsible for any infraction of the prohibition.

DEVELOPMENT OF THE ANONYMOUS new car continued. But would Renault now need to produce such a minuscule motorcar? This decision would be made by Pierre Lefaucheux, who from August 1944 was sent to Renault's Billancourt factory by the French government to take over its management when revolutionary riots broke out after the liberation. The government dropped the other shoe in January 1945 when, after the death of Louis Renault, it made his company a ward of France. Thus was founded the RÈgie Renault, in which the state, as well, would have a hand in decision-making.

One of the government's first decisions was hardly favorable to its new ward. In 1944 France's master planners were reaching decisions similar to those that had been imposed in Germany before the war and would be timidly jawboned by the government in Britain: that the auto industry needed to make fewer vehicle models in larger volumes, reducing costs to meet the looming postwar American competition.

Meanwhile the government had made its own assessments. An analysis of France's car-production performance in 1939 by Paul-Marie Pons of the Ministry of Industrial Production showed that each of its automakers was making 4.2 models on average, against 3.2 for the British and 2.3 for the Americans, even though the French car market was the smallest of the three. Explained Pons,

> Every manufacturer had to follow the disastrous custom of producing a new model for each annual salon. This meant that the tools and machinery, which had to be changed at the same time to produce the new model, were hastily adapted and indifferent. France had still not realised that her automobile industry must concentrate on a limited number of models, or perish. Instead of quantity, which was essential for war, she preferred peace-time variety.

This was one of the themes on which Pons and Bellier of the ministry lectured the Renault managers in Pierre Lefaucheux's office on 26 October 1944. They spoke of the economic situation and the postwar recovery program that they foresaw for the French motor industry. Their plan "was not lacking in boldness," Fernand Picard recalled. He wrote that the ministry directors had the following message:

> General de Gaulle had established as an objective the achievement, within five years, of annual production of 500,000 motor vehicles. To bring about this result, in a world in which customs barriers would, of necessity, be lowered, we needed to reduce our production costs to the lowest possible level, that is to the Americans' price level and, to do that, to manufacture in long production runs, as they did.

In place of their 121 prewar vehicle types, French makers were now to be harshly restricted to only 16 models. Citroën was to make the larger cars and Peugeot the medium-sized models. As for the small cars, they were to be built by Panhard.

How did Renault fare in the ministry's rationalization scheme? The company that had ranked second in private-car production in France before the war was now to make only trucks. It would share that market with Berliet. No more Renault cars would be produced. But an outfit that had not allowed the

Obviously influenced by prewar American designs, the 11CV Primaquatre (called Prima-Lègére in this version) was the candidate of Renault's management for postwar production. They saw it as just what they needed to take on Citroën.

In the war years Renault also came up with a possible successor to the prewar Juvaquatre, changing it from two doors to four and grafting on a Prima-style front end. Like the 11CV, this 6–8CV model was ultimately rejected as a candidate for postwar production in favor of all-out concentration on the 4CV.

German occupation to slow the development of its new small car would not yield so easily to mere ministers. Resolute, Lefaucheux fought hard with Bellier and his assistant Pons for Renault's right to carry on making automobiles.

The discussions continued into 1945. On 9 January Paul-Marie Pons presented his plan to the management of the new Régie Nationale des Usines Renault and was left in no doubt about their unanimous desire to carry on with cars as well as trucks. On 6 February Bellier and Pons were invited

Pierre Lefaucheux, the man who took on the decision to commit all of Renault's resources to the rear-engined 4CV, towers over an early model fitted with an accessory front bumper. Lefaucheux headed Renault under its new French state ownership.

to test the newest Renault prototypes. "After a few trials in the Meudon Forest," recalled Fernand Picard, "we stopped for lunch at Popote des Ailes, in Chaville, where in spite of the restrictions, which were still very harsh, it was possible to have a modest but decent meal at a reasonable price." The proprieties were scrupulously maintained.

The government representatives drove two types of test car: the 4CV, progressing in prototype form, still as a two-door model, and an 11CV proposal, a much larger four-door car reminiscent of a prewar Plymouth. The latter was the preferred choice of the Renault old guard, which in fact still made up the bulk of the company's management under its new leader. To help the chances of the 4CV Lefaucheux urged Serre and Picard to give it four doors, explaining that the French would never buy a two-door car. They complied, producing an attractive and shapely design.

On 9 November 1945 the decision was made. Of Lefaucheux's fellow board members, seven favored building the larger 11CV car and only two the little 4CV. Mulling the choice overnight, the Renault chief decided against the majority: "We'll build the 4CV," he said. As a sop to his disappointed and indeed hostile colleagues he agreed that an 11CV program would be kept in the wings in case the little 4CV was less than a resounding success.

"We'll put all our eggs in one basket," Pierre Lefaucheux said. "That means that we shall watch over the basket, but also that it will be larger. Our first objective will be to make three hundred cars a day." At its height before the war Renault had never made more than 250 a day of its six pas-

The change to four doors for the 4CV production model, to meet French tastes, was urged on the engineers by Lefaucheux in the final stages of the car's development. Robert Barthaud, in charge of bodywork, succeeded in giving the tiny four-seater a svelte Gallic style.

Relying on market studies that indicated a broad demand in France for an economical small car, Pierre Lefaucheux boldly committed the now nationalized Renault to volume production of the 4CV, aided by new and unique transfer-line machining methods developed during the war.

senger car ranges offered in twenty-four body styles — this was to be a colossal new challenge.

THE CHALLENGE WOULD HAVE BEEN even greater if another government minister had had his way. A leading member of the Parti Communiste Français (PCF), Marcel Paul, took over the French ministerial portfolio for industrial production near the end of 1945. Little did Lefaucheux and his colleagues know that when they were planning the future of Renault their own government had sent representatives to Germany who were doing all they could to bring a menacing rival to France.

Intellectually, the Beetle was a modern realization of the advanced and logical vehicle that Emile Claveau had offered to France a score of years earlier. In practical terms it was a tough and useful automobile to which the French army had taken quite a fancy. This was a clear enough sign to Marcel Paul that the VW could be a basis for a new popular vehicle for France.

The small experimental shop in the reviving VW factory, under skilled ex-Porsche veteran Rudolf Ringel, had built two examples of a four-wheel-drive version of the Beetle sedan using Schwimmwagen chassis components for their drivetrains. "We had the shop," said Ivan Hirst. "It was a matter of finding something for them to do."

These were postwar recreations of the wartime 4 x 4 Kommandeur-wagen. One of these was kept by the works; the other was tested thoroughly by the French military authorities, who liked it so much that they ordered one hundred of this Type 287, as the postwar car was known. The French told Ivan Hirst that the 4 x 4 Beetles would be used for forestry work. Like the other occupying Allies, the French were seizing their chance to chop down the German forests.

Welcome though this order was, Wolfsburg could not fulfill it. The Type 287's drivetrain components were made from forgings that came from a forge shop operated by VW in Silesia, which was now under the control of the Russians. No more forgings would come from that source, where the dies to stamp out the forgings also languished.

Ordinary Beetles were also of interest to the French, who were no better equipped than the British military with vehicles suited to the roads and conditions in their zone of occupation. Based in Baden-Baden, the French authorities were sometimes awkward in their relations with their British and American zonal neighbors because they "had not been invited to Potsdam and therefore felt in no way bound to the agreements reached there." Lacking any car production at all in their zone, they had to come knocking on the steel doors of the VW works.

In the early months of the occupation the various zonal occupiers made bilateral business deals to satisfy their immediate needs. One such deal between the French and British was a trade of steel for Volkswagens. Although the French zone of Germany had no indigenous steel production, the French were entitled to a share of the output of the steel works in the Ruhr under British control.

In mid-1946 an agreement was struck for the French to debit 2,800 tons of steel from their account and credit it to the CCG's vehicle industry section. This was to cover the production for France of two thousand Type 11 Beetles and spares to be delivered in the fourth quarter of 1946. Under a new coupon allocation system (*Eisenschein*) for steel introduced by the CCG, a further 1,735 tons of the French steel entitlement was to be exchanged early in 1947 for one thousand more Beetles and other vehicles from British-zone producers.

Production of VWs for the French forces began after the light-gray paint required by their military was sourced. This helped them blend in with the other vehicles in the French fleet but also made them instantly identifiable to the Germans through whose farms and towns the train taking them to Baden-Baden would pass. This had its consequences as production expediter Richard Berryman recalled:

> The first consignment for the French was loaded on flat trucks, and the train was ready to pull out that same afternoon, but in some strange way the steam engine ceased to function and the train did not leave until it was nearly dark. Then, when the train stopped at the end of the spur line to get on to the main line, it was invaded by local Germans who knocked off wheels and tyres and various other parts

of the consignment of VWs, and I understand that by the time the train reached Baden-Baden quite a lot of the cars' components were missing.

Not slow to learn, the French augmented the two soldiers that had been assigned to the first train with many more guards and gendarmes manning the next shipments. By the spring of 1947, however, the allocators of Wolfsburg's production were looking ahead to the completion of deliveries to the CCG and the BAOR and the commencement of the exports that would earn hard currencies, badly needed to buy food for the population in the British zone. The last shipment of Beetles for the French had not yet left the plant.

By May of 1947 R. H. King of the British Interzonal Trade Branch in Berlin was writing to the Priorities and Allocations Branch in the same city to warn that in the early months of the year Britain was falling behind in its agreed trade reciprocity with the French and that Volkswagens were an important part of that shortfall. The VW works had been shut down completely in the first two months of the year by shortages of raw materials and transport problems caused by an exceptionally harsh winter. Only by April was it back to the one-thousand-per-month production rate that it could maintain.

Suggestions that the French should pay dollars for the Beetles that were already promised to them under the steel swap scheme were rejected by King: "I think that the French, who have taken the demand for dollars with some bitterness, would charge us with bad faith if we proceeded to demand dollars for Volkswagens which had been the subject of a Trade Agreement." The temptation to ask for dollars for Volkswagens was great. At that time the export of one thousand VWs would earn half a million dollars for the economically hard-pressed British zone.

The matter was still outstanding on 26 June 1947 when King wrote again:

> As you know, we have a firm commitment with the French for 1,000 Volkswagen, for which we have accepted and used steel provided by the French out of their allocation. These Volkswagen should have been delivered a long time ago, and the late delivery is a matter about which the French have already made complaints. We have given undertakings to the French that they should receive some Volkswagen this month and the balance of their 1,000 in the third quarter. I understand in fact that if they receive any Volkswagen this month, they will be deducted from the 800 which you propose to deliver to them in the third quarter. If the French choose to make a fuss about this, I cannot see that we shall have any defense.
>
> I am not in a position to suggest any method of avoiding trouble by transferring from any other source, beyond saying I think it would be most unfortunate if you touched export. The figures are low enough as it is.

Others must have had to wait for their Volkswagens, for the allocators successfully cleared the commitment to the French by the end of the year. Of the first twenty thousand VWs made after the war at Wolfsburg the French received some three thousand. In the meantime, however, communist Industry Minister Marcel Paul was working on behalf of the French nation to give her an ample supply of Beetles of her very own

MARCEL PAUL DECIDED THAT the best way to approach a factory that was not in the French zone of occupation was through its creators. At the beginning of November, 1945 his delegation was received by Ferry Porsche at the Porsche family estate at Zell am See in Austria. In 1943 the Porsche engineering organization had been obliged to move to Austria to keep out of harm's way. Some of its members were in Zell and others worked near the little town of Gmünd in Austria's Carinthian region.

The French contact was not uninteresting to Ferry, whose university-trained engineers were keeping busy at Gmünd by repairing wartime Beetle derivatives for the Allies. Although his father was initially detained for questioning by the Allies at Kransberg Castle, he had not remained there long. "We soon discovered," Ferry Porsche related, "what Marcel Paul had in mind. It was nothing less than taking over the entire Volkswagen factory at Wolfsburg as a war reparations payment."

Although this factory in the British zone was not a likely reparations candidate for them, or perhaps *because* it was such an unlikely proposition, the French were especially determined. Neither were they much deterred by the initial two-year reservation of the plant for CCG vehicle production, which could always be waived at high levels. Ferry said that the French representative "pushed hard in the discussions that followed with the British and American authorities. In fact, he pushed so hard that they were on the brink of saying, 'Okay. You French can have the Volkswagen works for reparations.' "

Behind the scenes, supporting justification for the hard-line French tactic was being provided by the auto firms that had suffered under the German occupation, Peugeot the worst of all. Managed as it had been by the Volkswagenwerk, Peugeot held that company to blame for stripping its equipment and materials from Montbeliard. His company, said Jean-Pierre Peugeot, should have the "right to help ourselves from the German manufacturers in order to replace the materials taken during the pillages suffered." It was only a short step from this view to the complete relocation of the VW works to France.

The discussions continued after 16 November 1945 at the Hotel Mueller in the French zone's capital city, Baden-Baden, to which the Porsches, father and son, were invited. There they met a Colonel Trevoux who, as Ferry Porsche recalled, "wasted no time getting down to business. He at once told my father, as a *fait accompli*, that the French were to get one half of everything at Wolfsburg, including machinery and equipment. He also explained to our assembled group that the French wanted to start a nationalized automobile factory and that in due course proper use would be made of the equipment shipped from Germany."

Communist minister Marcel Paul desired nothing less than at least half of the Volkswagen factory and all of the services of the dynasty that had designed and developed it: Ferdinand Porsche and his son Ferry, who were to engineer a new French version of the Beetle. The French detained both men with this objective in view.

The French colonel added that he expected the Porsche organization to be "heavily involved in this affair." The Porsche people were expected by the French to oversee the transport of the factory to its new location (not yet decided) and to direct the launch of manufacturing there. They were also to restyle the car around the existing chassis, to reduce its resemblance to the dream car of the despised Hitler and give it "a typical French look." As Professor Porsche later remarked to his son, "It seems to me that the French are handling this thing on a pretty big scale."

The scale was so big, in fact, that it sent shivers through yet another established auto industry. Britain's carmakers were not the only ones who had felt on their necks the warm breath of the German car industry in general and the VW in particular in the late 1930s.

"As soon as the word got out about our visits to Baden-Baden," Ferry Porsche told his biographer John Bentley, "the French auto industry began thinking up ways of blocking the whole project. The serious competition which a French version of the Volkswagen would offer them on the home market bothered them a great deal. In fact, it is fair to say that the entire French automotive industrial complex was dead set against the project."

The French automakers did not have to look far to find a way to upset this applecart. They reverted to the records of the wartime relationship between Peugeot at Sochaux and the Volkswagen works. When they spoke to Allied investigators in December 1944 the Peugeot people volunteered no complaints about the way they had been treated by Professor Porsche and other representatives of VW, for whom they were making vehicle and V-1 parts. Neither, as suggested earlier, did they mention the removal of machine tools by the Germans, although those interviews would have provided an ideal opportunity to put such an issue on record.

In fact, as Ferry Porsche recalled later, Ferdinand Porsche the designer had worked amiably with Jean-Pierre Peugeot the industrialist. Born in 1896, Jean-Pierre had joined the family firm in 1922 and by 1941 had been named its president. Peugeot had visited Fallersleben during the war at his own request to review joint projects. There he had made it clear that he desired the best possible relations with the Porsches and Fallersleben because he hoped to benefit from steady orders for parts from his plants from Volkswagen after the war.

Now, however, the agile Jean-Pierre Peugeot had adapted himself to postwar realities. He became the French industry's point man for a fusillade of accusations of the most heinous behavior on the part of Professor Porsche. "No doubt to their intense satisfaction," his son related, "the French car manufacturers came up with 'evidence' that my father was really a 'war criminal.'"

Not only the Porsches but also Marcel Paul were unaware of these looming storm clouds when, on Sunday, 16 December, the minister fêted them at dinner in Baden-Baden. Always keen on racing, the Porsches were interested in hearing more about Paul's other pet project, the creation of a national racing car for France, the CTA-Arsenal. With the coffee lightning struck when the Porsches were arrested by the order of Justice Minister Pierre Henri Teitgen. Then seventy, the senior Porsche was bound over to be tried, along with Anton Piëch.

Ferdinand Porsche had to wait a year for his trial in a procedure which, wrote historian Hans Mommsen, was "not a glorious page in the annals of French justice." Testimony in his favor benefited from the role at the KdF-Werke of none other than Alfred Nauck, who had written so enthusiastically about the newborn Beetles in *Englebert Magazine* early in 1939. From a departmental job in Albert Speer's Ministry of Armaments, Nauck had been deputized to Fallersleben during the war expressly to maintain some control over the expensively hyperactive Porsche team, at the personal request of Speer.

In the troubled year of 1944, Alfred Nauck behaved so high-handedly at the works that Bodo Lafferentz accused him of acting "like a Russian commissar." Lafferentz and Porsche were certainly relieved when Nauck was reassigned to chase Arado bomber production in October 1944. Well into 1945, however, they were importuning the engineer to return the Kübelwagen he had been assigned as a duty car by Fallersleben.

Although his stay there had been brief, Nauck had been so highly visible that ample evidence existed that he had taken the lead in exploiting Peugeot and in uprooting its machine tools for expatriation to Germany. Not until 2047 will we know exactly what happened at Porsche's trial; the French have sealed the documents for one hundred years. But by August 1947 the charges against Ferdinand Porsche were dismissed and he and his son-in-law were freed against the payment of a costly bond organized by Ferry's sister Louise Piëch.

Incredibly, in the meantime other Frenchmen were pressuring Ferry to set about preparing the design of a French people's car. After his release in March 1945 he was put up at a hotel in Bad Rippoldsau in the Black Forest in the company of several French engineers and sundry gendarmes and minders. His assignment, which seemed as fantastic as any that Porsche had ever undertaken, was to create a completely new design that the French would build with their half-share of the transplanted Wolfsburg machine tools.

Ferry Porsche judged that his skills might be the bargaining chip that would free his father and brother-in-law, but the French denied any connection between their detention and his assigned task. "In that case," said Ferry, "we can discuss the weather or cars in general, but I'm not interested in the Volkswagenwerk or anything to do with that enterprise."

Gradually the French interest in taking over the VW plant seemed to wane. "I believe Marcel Paul was facing a progressively tougher problem in trying to put over his grandiose idea," Ferry Porsche surmised. And when Paul left the government soon thereafter, the impetus behind removing of all or part of the VW plant to France was lost. Thus did France's carmakers breathe easy again, spared the threat of a new volume competitor on their own home ground.

WHILE THESE TROUBLING DISCUSSIONS were under way, the Régie Renault decided to see for itself what all the fuss was about. During the bitter 1945–46 winter the VW works had a visitor from Paris: the courteous and diplomatic Jean Louis, former confidant and deputy to Louis Renault. Working closely with Lefaucheux, who had restructured the company in June 1945, the forty-seven-year-old Tunisian-born Louis now headed the technical and sales departments of the Règie. Apprised of the visit, Ivan Hirst conferred with Charles Radclyffe about Louis's itinerary. "We don't want Renault taking the plant over at this point, do we?" the officers agreed. "Let's show him the worst!"

M. Louis was given a tour of the plant, the icy wind whistling through its ruined halls, by the gruff, truculent Rudolf Brörmann. Production of proper Beetles was only fitfully commencing after the retooling from Kübel-making. The German piloted Louis quickly over the frozen, rutted grounds of the plant in an open Schwimmwagen. The French official must have thanked his lucky stars to have survived his visit to what was obviously an unsuitable place to make cars.

Jean Louis returned to Paris where, after all, a French national small car, government-owned and -supported, was destined to be produced, a car that in fact achieved the goal that Louis Renault had set in 1938: economically to build a popular small car "like the one the Germans have." However the 4CV would be French in steel and spirit.

That small car would have, in a fateful way, the blessing under duress of the creator of the Volkswagen. On 6 May 1946 the government authorities brought Professor Ferdinand Porsche and Anton Piëch to Paris and made them available to Renault to advise on the 4CV. Still under detention, the engineer and his son-in-law were housed in the servant's quarters of a villa called Galice House in the Meudon Hills, not far from the Renault factories.

"Clearly there was no spirit of cooperation on either side" of this forced marriage, Fernand Picard recalled. "Often the conversation turned into a dialogue of the deaf." But Porsche and Piëch remained in Paris and nominally at the beck and call of Renault and its engineers for more than nine months. Both sides were obliged to go through the motions of cooperation, however desultory. Said Picard,

> Porsche was, in fact, a sick man and his morale was telling both on his position and his state of health. He was then seventy-one, but gave the impression of being a very old man. His dark gray clothing, hanging from his wasted body, looked like a hospital uniform. He was badly shaved, his complexion was wan, his nose was red, his look gloomy, and he spent a large part of his days in bed.

Joined by two engineers from Renault — Henri Guettier and Ernst Metzmaïer, who acted as interpreter — Fernand Picard met with Porsche nine times between 17 September and 6 December 1946. "Nothing positive came out of these meetings," said Picard, "which were simply a long catalogue of complaints: requests by the Germans for the drawings and equipment to carry out research on a racing car and insistence on bringing over their families."

The French could hardly be surprised that the apolitical Porsche, detained with little rhyme or reason, complained about his situation. Said his son, "He tried to explain to his captors that if they really wanted him to design a new car and plan a new factory and after that proceed to the manufacturing stage, it would be absolutely essential for him to regain his freedom. The request fell on deaf ears."

By this time, of course, the engineering of the 4CV was well advanced. It was shown in its final four-door form at the Paris Salon in 1946 and volume production began on 12 August 1947. So there was little scope for any of Porsche's recommendations to be implemented in the short term. But the great engineer reviewed the plans for the car and the factory and tested the available prototypes.

"He apparently found a good many things wrong with the car," Ferry wrote later, "and in his report suggested changes to the suspension, weight distribution, tire dimensions and other features. He also did some planning for mass production at the Renault factory." This cannot surprise us; even at seventy-one and in ill health the elder Porsche was an engineer with whom to reckon. And what engineer, shown the plans of another, can fail to find fault?

In a report of 21 September 1946, the same month in which Renault acquired one of the new postwar Beetles, Porsche submitted views concerning the 4CV that included the following:

> We consider that the 4CV can be launched in full production within a year. We believe also that because of its low [fuel] consumption, this vehicle offers interesting sales possibilities in France and Europe. The advanced state of production tooling now makes it impossible to introduce any of the potential modifications which our manufacturing experience with the rear-engined vehicle placed us in a position to point out.

Porsche's specific technical recommendations for the 4CV may have addressed the swing axles of the Renault, which were pivoted from trunnions at the gearbox that took all the fore-and-aft drive and braking loads. This was a much less stable and wear-resistant layout than the VW's with its trailing arms bracing each wheel hub to the car's frame.

When both cars were jointly tested in America by *Motor Trend* in 1956 the shares of their weight that rested on their rear wheels were found to be 59 percent for the VW and a much higher 65 percent for the Renault. Porsche was comfortable with the former but would have seen the latter as very much too tail-heavy, as he had told engineer Maurice Olley before the war when they discussed the rear-engined Mercedes-Benz cars.

Both cars had fifteen-inch wheels, but to help cope with the rearward weight bias the Renault's tires were larger with a 5.60-inch section against the VW's 5.00. Although 16 percent lighter than the VW, the Renault had only 8 percent less weight on its rear tires. To reduce the 4CV's strong oversteer Renault spring-loaded its steering and fitted restraint straps to its rear swing axles to keep them from jacking up the rear of the car in corners.

His hopes dashed for a humming transplant of Wolfsburg to France, the PCF's Marcel Paul left the Ministry of Industrial Production on 28 November 1946. On 27 January 1947 Pierre Lefaucheux gained the regime's approval for the departure of Porsche and Piëch, who were removed on 17 February to face even worse: their detention in Dijon.

IN OCTOBER 1947 THE SMALL RENAULT on which Porsche had advised was shown at the Paris Salon in its final production form. Visitors to the Grand Palais could press to the front of the crowds to admire a cross-

After reviewing the virtually completed engineering of the Renault 4CV, Ferdinand Porsche provided his views on it in September 1946. He would have objected to the tail-heaviness caused by the "outboard" rear mounting of an in-line engine complete with radiator.

sectioned 4CV mounted proudly on a wood-faced plinth and guarded by stainless-steel railings in art deco style. Among the onlookers were two men in British military uniform: Charles Radclyffe and Ivan Hirst.

"We were just starting our VW exports," Hirst explained, "and this was our first chance to assess the prices of other cars so that we could fix a price for the Volkswagen in the international market." While in Paris the two Britons arranged to visit Renault. (By that time the thawed-out Jean Louis, uncomfortable in the nationalized company, had left the Régie to take the presidency of Babcock & Wilcox. He would join the Peugeot board in 1948.)

When touring the production facilities for the 4CV, the CCG officers were impressed by Renault's extensive use of transfer machines and multi-station machining operations. "During the war years they had developed and built universal building-block bases for various machining operations," Ivan Hirst learned. "Instead of heavy castings they used fabrications for their bases, welded of steel plate. This made them easy to set up quickly to start production after the war."

Late in 1947 another auto show brought two wartime colleagues together. "I ran into Prince von Urach at the London Motor Show in 1947," Fernand Picard recalled. "He had resumed his position at Daimler-Benz, where he was managing the car museum. We met in front of the 4CV vehicles on display at the Renault Limited stand." The former German special delegate to the Renault plant said to the Frenchman,

> When I sent for you, in May 1943, I was fully familiar with your research activities for this vehicle, and with all other matters, through a number of anonymous letters. I used to put them in the bin, like many others. I intervened on that day as I was instructed by higher authorities, who had also been informed.

On the foundation of the 4CV, Renault built its attractive and successful Dauphine, which entered production in 1956. Although pleasingly styled and equipped, the light and efficient Dauphine failed to receive the quality and logistics support it needed to rival the Volkswagen on world markets.

I was not taken in by your statements. I reported them to the [occupying authorities] without comment. I would have done the same thing in your position. And I wish every success and long life to this little car, with which I was also involved a little . . .

Picard had underestimated von Urach, and not solely his powers of observation. The Württemberg heir, thought by the French to be a public relations man, was in fact a trained engineer who had joined Daimler-Benz from Bugatti early in the 1930s in order to help build the company's new Grand Prix cars for the 1934 season. His colleague and successor Josef Müller thought highly of "Mister von Urach," as he was called, "not only for his human qualities but also for his irresistible inclination towards the engineering profession. He was a personality that found the greatest pleasure and satisfaction in practicing the profession he had chosen for himself."

When not at work on the Grand Prix Mercedes-Benz, von Urach had been deeply involved with another project: the design and development of the rear-engined Type 130 passenger car. As an engineer he must have looked with wry amusement and some compassion at Renault's efforts to design and build a new small car that he knew to have many of the faults with which he and Josef Müller had struggled a decade earlier.

With its faults less evident on the scale of a smaller vehicle, the 4CV enjoyed a much better run in the marketplace than the ill-fated Type 130. Appropriate enough to the needs of its home market, especially with its excellent fuel economy, the 4CV was produced at rates of up to six hundred a day. This was double the seemingly utopian level set as a challenge to his engineers by Pierre Lefaucheux. The total 4CV production through 1961, including forty-three pre-series cars, came to 1,131,693.

THE POWERFUL RENAULT PUBLICITY machine did all it could to stress to the public the benefits of the rear-mounted engine. In advertisements and brochures it pointed out the easy service of the accessible engine, the construction's lightness and roominess, and the excellent traction of the heavily loaded drive wheels.

In France, the nation that had first taken front-wheel drive to its heart, this was no small task for Renault. Wrote front-drive advocate Grégoire, "From 1934, Renault had been orchestrating Citroën's difficulties with the [front-drive] 7CV. During the launch and the production of the 4CV, the Régie Nationale lauded rear-wheel drives and attacked front-wheel drives in order to defend itself against worrying competitors like Panhard."

One might have expected Pierre Lefaucheux to take a positive view of the car that had inspired his 4CV, but in this he was guarded. In 1954 he said that he considered the Beetle to be "a miracle — not a technical miracle, but a commercial one." The burly Lefaucheux did not survive a crash on a slippery road in February 1955, only a year before the launch of production of the Dauphine, which would give the design a newfound popularity. Its successor in 1963 would be the Renault R8.

The Dauphine kept the rear-engined layout that was established by the 4CV, which in turn had been inspired, as we have seen, by the Volkswagen. Indeed, Renault was so committed to and convinced by the rear-engined layout that it was adopted for its Project 108, a larger 11CV car to renew Renault's challenge in a higher class. The old guard would have its bigger Renault after all.

Launched by Lefaucheux at the end of 1947, the 108 project produced prototypes by the spring of 1949; production was planned for the end of 1951. Looking like a cross between a Saab 92 and a Tatraplan, the 108 was smooth-lined except for the air scoops needed to cool its rear-mounted radiator. Its four-cylinder engine was mounted above the gearbox to keep the power package as short as possible. By November 1949, however, the technical challenges presented by the radical 108 were assessed as too great to overcome. A conventional car, the Frégate, was hurriedly designed instead. There would be no large rear-engined Renaults.

Conceptually the four-door Dauphine — light, efficient, and modern, lacking only the four-speed gearbox that Serre and Picard originally wanted for the 4CV — could have challenged the VW in world markets. But Renault failed to support it abroad with parts and service on a par with Volkswagen's exports.

Fernand Picard acknowledged that Renault had fallen short in backing its products abroad. He considered that the main reason for the VW's success, after its low price, "was its robustness and absence of problems. A car owner does not complain about a breakdown if, close to his home, he has a service station which is always prepared to repair his vehicle quickly and inexpensively."

We may be permitted a smile, however, when we read Picard's view of the reason why the VW was eventually so successful in establishing a beachhead in North America:

> Demobilized GIs, who had been occupying Germany, took one of these Beetles purchased under special conditions, and which they had used over there, back home as part of their baggage. For them it was a reminder of sentimental memories, walks with the Fräuleins, not menacing. They kept it, praised its virtues, and the market took off, first in the states where Germans predominated, such as Illinois and Wisconsin, before winning over the others.

7

Australia, Belgium, Russia and Other Contenders

B ritons and Americans had had their chances to inspect and assess the Volkswagen and its factory. They were yet to decide whether, when, and how to take advantage of this asset of the fallen Third Reich. The French had made a bold grab for both the factory and the car's creators, but their reach had exceeded their grasp. Others among the victorious nations had urgent needs for motorization, some with compelling claims on both the Beetle and its well-equipped works.

The Volkswagen, however, also had a profound impact on the auto industries of two other countries that were caught up in the turmoil of World War II: Czechoslovakia and Sweden.

CZECHOSLOVAKIA, A NATION THAT had strong business links with Germany, had been propelled into the German camp in March of 1939. The Czech Ringhoffer-Tatra-Werke AG and its chief designer Hans Ledwinka were leading advocates of the aerodynamic automobile with an air-cooled engine in the rear.

Apart from two sojourns with other firms, one to explore steam-powered vehicles (1902–05) and the other to create a new vehicle range for Steyr-Daimler-Puch AG (1916–21), the Austrian-born Ledwinka had worked with the company that became Tatra since September 1897. Like Ferdinand Porsche, Ledwinka displayed a knack for innovative yet practical engineering. Unlike Porsche, he had no interest in racing. Not speaking Czech, Ledwinka gathered around him a talented German-speaking team and used German in the company's technical documents.

At the end of the 1930s Tatra had 4,500 employees and the capacity to produce five thousand cars, five thousand trucks, and five hundred buses yearly. It was also under the direct control of the Germans. Its factory at Ko-

After the way he was treated by the Czechs following the war, Hans Ledwinka declined an invitation to return to an engineering post at Tatra. He is seen presenting his personal Type 87 Tatra to the Deutsches Museum.

Ledwinka used the engine housing as the front of the backbone frame of his innovative Tatra T11, introduced in 1923. Adolf Hitler was much impressed by its rugged and reliable air-cooled flat-twin engine.

privnice, formerly Nesseldorf, was just within the borders of the Sudetenland that Germany annexed in 1938. The Tatra works came under German administration on 10 October 1938.

Ledwinka had first displayed his ability to revolutionize auto design in 1923 with his Tatra T11. A small car of 1,056 cc, it had a flat-twin air-cooled engine with pushrod overhead valves. Mounted at the front, the engine and its gearbox were bolted to a central tube that ran to, and was joined to, the final-drive gear casing. The body sat astride the tube, which was sprung at the front by a solid axle and a transverse leaf spring. Rear suspension was independent by swing axles.

A new large Tatra stunned the motor engineering world when it was introduced to the press on 5 March 1934: the rear-engined Type 77. Tatra had built smaller rear-engined prototypes in 1931 and 1933, cars that were strikingly similar to the models Porsche was then developing for Zündapp and NSU. But this was a big car seating six, powered by an air-cooled V-8 overhung behind the rear axle. And it was spectacularly streamlined.

Engineer Erich Übelacker is credited by Tatra historians with the initiative that led to the company's commitment to advanced rear-engined

Hitler also took a fancy to the big rear-engined T77 sedan that Tatra introduced in 1934, powered by an air-cooled side-valve V-8. This was called the ideal "Autobahn car" for the New Germany.

From the Tatra T77 engineer Erich Übelacker developed the T87 of 1937. The fast, quiet, and efficient T87 remained in production throughout the years of the war.

cars. He worked under Ledwinka to create the astonishingly aerodynamic forms of the T77 and its successor the T87 (Übelacker had a penchant for sevens). Before he left to join Steyr in 1936, Übelacker had completed the upgrading of the first model to the T77a and the design and initial proving of its successor.

A smaller sister model was developed in parallel, the 1,749 cc Type 97. This had a flat-opposed air-cooled four-cylinder engine developing forty horsepower and sufficing for eighty miles per hour. It was a full five-passenger four-door car, shorter and lighter than the T87. Technically the T97 was similar to its bigger sister, with the result, wrote Gordon Wilkins, that "it will corner at speeds which produce pop-eyed awe in passengers whose standards of roadholding are based on experience with cheap small saloons."

Priced at RM 5,600 ($2,240), the T97 was anything but a people's car. By late-1930s Tatra standards it was an attempt to offer a more affordable version of the company's new direction in design. Nor would it ever have been produced in more than five-figure annual volumes. Nevertheless Tatraphiles are convinced that the T97's similarity to the forthcoming

Volkswagen led to its suppression by the German regime after the production of only 508 units.

It is beyond dispute that Third Reich officials dealt peremptorily with Tatra. At the 1939 Berlin Show they made Tatra remove its 6x6 truck with swing-axle suspension as well as a large back-lit transparency showing the typical Tatra chassis design — not wildly different from that of the new KdF-Wagen, although Tatra continued with leaf springs instead of Porsche's pet torsion bars.

The KdF-Werke's managers were under no illusion about the way in which the Ledwinka and Porsche engineering teams had worked in parallel during the 1930s. At Berlin in 1939 Fallersleben's Otto Dyckhoff found Hans Ledwinka and guided him to the first motor show display of the Beetles, saying, "Have you already seen the new Tatra that we're building after our own fashion?"

Neither was the new Tatra T97 allowed to be displayed at Berlin. This constraint must be viewed as well from the perspective of the von Schell plan to achieve a sharp reduction of the numbers of types of vehicles that were being produced in Greater Germany, of which Czechoslovakia was now a part.

In a September 1940 speech Colonel von Schell made clear that his rationalization program was to be extended to vehicle production in the newly annexed territories, not only in France but also in the eastern protectorates, where Tatra was seen as a valuable producer of heavy trucks and advanced air-cooled diesel engines. Its cars were marginal to Germany's effort to slim and strengthen its domestic industry to help rearm for war.

An exception was made, however, for Tatra's T87, a car that was enthusiastically welcomed by the German high command. This big, fast, comfortable courier seemed tailor-made for the four-lane Autobahns that Fritz Todt's engineers were building throughout the Greater Reich. Todt himself owned and was driven in one. As a result the T87 remained in production at Koprivnice throughout the war years. That the Nazis granted a special dispensation for Ledwinka's masterpiece scarcely suggests that the Third Reich had its knives out for Tatra.

Shorter and lighter than the T77, the T87 was the first Tatra to combine air cooling with a single overhead camshaft for each cylinder bank, opening the V-inclined valves through rocker arms. Built like a light-aircraft engine, it looked like one when the oversized trunk lid was unlocked and lifted. From its three liters it developed seventy-four horsepower. Modest though this seems today, its V-8 engine was capable of speeding the T87 to 100 mph. This was because the T87 not only looked aerodynamic, it *was* aerodynamic.

TATRA'S OPERATIONS WERE INTEGRATED into those of the Third Reich's wartime vehicle sector; the rugged and fast T87 was seen as a useful addition to its military capability. Among other applications the Luft-

The T87 Tatra had a vestigial backbone frame and a V-8 engine with a single overhead cam for each cylinder bank and twin cooling blowers. Suspension was fully independent.

waffe was assigned one as an experimental vehicle. A military police unit serving in Italy and Yugoslavia maintained a fleet of T87s. And when a T87 was found in good condition by the British CCG at Wolfsburg it was reconditioned and used by them as senior staff transport in the late 1940s.

The spiritual similarity between the Tatra and the Volkswagen intrigued Ivan Hirst and his colleagues at Wolfsburg. Both were "outboard" rear-engined air-cooled cars built on steel platform chassis. In their actual engineering, however, in suspension and drivetrain design as well as their appearance — the Tatras aimed much more for aerodynamic perfection — they differed dramatically. Indeed they had to, if Porsche's independent design office were to gain any royalties from the unique solutions it had patented for its KdF-Wagen design.

Ledwinka and his team had been keeping the patent offices busy as well. He and his design team were ultimately credited with more than one thousand patents. Ledwinka would have priority over Porsche in several areas, including engine position, the layout of the gearbox, and the ducted-fan cooling.

Ordinarily Tatra's patent priority would have worried Porsche and his business managers, first Baron Hans von Veyder-Malberg and later Hans Kern. In fact they had to be alert to possible infringements of the whole web of patents woven by the motor industry. At the time, however, the advice they were given by Berlin was that they shouldn't worry about patents, they should just press on with the KdF-Wagen and those details would all be sorted out later.

In fact they *were* sorted out later at the initiative of the heirs of the von Ringhoffer family that had owned Tatra before and during the war. They brought suit against the Volkswagen company, which in the meantime had regularized its relationship with the Porsche design office and its panoply of patents. Testimony in their favor was given by an Austrian garage proprietor who had been able to scrutinize a KdF prototype whose body panels were being changed in his workshop.

Before a trial verdict was reached the parties settled out of court. Ringhoffer-Tatra received three million marks in compensation for the use of its patents by Volkswagen. Meanwhile the engineer whose work was now duly acknowledged languished in captivity. The vindictive Soviets ensured that the Czechs accused Hans Ledwinka as a collaborator — his only crime had been to stay at his post while Tatra continued making military vehicles for the Greater Germany in which the company had found itself. Ledwinka would fare much worse than Porsche. Not until December 1951 would he be a free man again.

CZECHOSLOVAKIA AND THE PORSCHE PATENTS were a preoccupation of other parties in the weeks immediately after the end of the war. With Anton Piëch, the Porsches senior and junior were at the family properties at Zell am See in Austria, in the American zone of occupation. There the Americans had warded off an attempt by a police detachment from Gifhorn to collect the executives and take them back to Wolfsburg to face charges of having misappropriated VW factory property.

The Americans had their own interest in the Porsche personnel, as they demonstrated in seventeen interviews between 19 June and 12 July of 1945. From these and other sources they gained the impression that the Porsche engineers and executives, adrift as they were in the aftermath of war, were planning to negotiate a sale of their patent rights to the Czech authorities. With Ledwinka undergoing trial Tatra lacked an engineering leader; this was a vacuum into which the Porsches would have been neatly drawn.

With or (as it turned out) without Porsche the Czech motor industry was committed to the production of rear-engined passenger cars. Ledwinka's son Erich succeeded him at the works; the elder engineer refused an invitation to return to Koprivnice after his release from captivity. A smaller flat-four-cylinder model was reborn as the Tatraplan and big air-cooled Tatra V-8 automobiles continued in production into the 1990s.

In the early 1960s another Czechoslovakian company, Skoda, adopted rear engines, albeit water-cooled, for its smaller passenger cars. With car production facilities at Mlada Boleslav, north of Prague, Skoda's industrial complex was the inheritor of the proud patrimony of Czech motoring pioneer Laurin und Klement AG.

In the hothouse that was then Central European auto engineering, Skoda had flirted with rear-mounted engines as early as the first years of the 1930s. One 1932 prototype, looking like an elegant coach with a rounded hood and

Among Skoda's experiments with rear-engined cars in the 1930s was the 935 prototype. Powered by an "outboard"-mounted water-cooled engine, it was completed and tested in 1935.

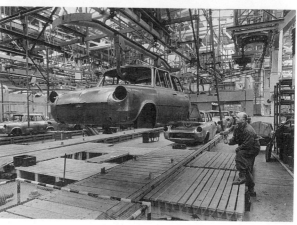

Starting in 1959, Skoda built a huge new factory to produce the 1000MB, the initials standing for its site at Mlada Boleslav. Its main workspace areas rivaled those of the original VW works.

trunk, had a flat-four engine that may have been a legacy from engineer Josef Kales, who had left Skoda in 1930 to join the Porsche office in Stuttgart.

Another 1932 rear-engined Skoda test car, also a two-door model, had a water-cooled engine and a more conventional hood and radiator. The fully aerodynamic Skoda 935 prototype of 1935 featured four doors, each pair hung from a central pillar, and was powered by a two-liter water-cooled rear engine placed "outboard," as in the other rear-engined experiments.

Although none of these researches led to volume production, Skoda gained some experience with rear-engined cars as a subcontractor to Tatra after the war. Starting in 1950, Skoda produced some two thousand Tatra-plans for its Czech sister company. Then in 1959 it began construction of a completely new plant at Mlada Boleslav to build a new rear-engined Skoda — the 1000MB.

The immense factory — the largest of its kind yet built in the Czech nation — bore striking similarities to the original Volkswagen factory. At 646,000 square feet its mechanical workshop was 23 percent larger than the VW works to provide space for toolmaking. Its body shop was 4 percent larger at 807,000 square feet — close enough to the area originally allocated to the same functions at Wolfsburg. Although planned output was 1,000 a

Skoda reckoned that it was going with the mainstream of European car design when it chose an "outboard" rear engine mounting for its new 1000MB model introduced in 1964. Extensive use of aluminum kept its engine from being too heavy.

day, some 250,000 each year, production never greatly exceeded 200,000 annual units.

The VW's popularity contributed to Skoda's decision to put the 1000MB's 988 cc engine in the r ear. Edward Eves was told by Skoda's chief engineer Frantisek Sajdl that Europe's acceptance of the rear engine was shown by the fact that it accounted for 50 percent of car production. Also in favor of the layout "was the low variation in axle weights which can be achieved with this layout under different conditions of loading, coupled with more efficient braking and good utilisation of available space."

Sajdl favored water cooling to give his 1000MB better cabin heating. But he lavished aluminum on the block of his four-cylinder engine to keep it light enough (225 pounds) not to overburden the rear axle. The front/rear distribution of weight was 40.4 percent and 59.6 percent respectively — similar to that of Beetles of the same era. With updates and restyling, this plucky Skoda lasted well into the 1990s, when it was the world's last rear-engined family car in volume production.

IN A NORTHERLY COUNTRY THAT had been neutral during the war an engineer considered engaging the design services of Ferdinand Porsche in 1945 but hesitated, fearing that this would be overly presumptuous — a typical sentiment for a modest Swede. "I thought of inviting Porsche to help in the design of the Saab," Gunnar Ljungström would recall, "but I lacked the

Skoda was understandably proud of the indigenous design of the 1964 1000MB, whose use of a rear-mounted engine was encouraged by the popularity of designs by VW, Renault, and Fiat.

confidence to make an approach. How I regret not having pressed forward. Saab and Porsche, that would have been a great alliance."

Nevertheless Ljungström, a member of a family famed for its inventive skills, had the courage to contradict Porsche's advocacy of a rear engine for small cars. He was in charge of a small team designing a car to be produced by Saab, the Swedish airplane maker that had decided that car production would be an exciting and interesting second line that would protect and even expand its business after the war.

As a neutral country, Sweden had no claim on the skills and assets of the conquered Germans. Nevertheless at least one Swede, Gunnar V. Philipson, was quick off the mark in getting permission to visit the vanquished nation in 1945. His Stockholm company, Philipsons Automobil AB, had been importing the Auto UnionAuto Union range of cars including DKW, which was Sweden's most popular small car before the war.

Philipson's overriding impression of Germany in 1945 was that it was not going to be exporting new cars to Sweden for some years yet. It was time, he decided, to put into action his plan to make a car of his own; with this in mind, he had bought an auto assembly plant in a Stockholm suburb before the war. Using a drivetrain and chassis ideas from the popular DKW, Philipson's engineers designed the Philipin, a two-door sedan. He would start by buying DKW engines from Germany and later would make his own in Sweden.

While the Philipin was taking shape the other Gunnar, Ljungström at Saab, was also inspired by DKW. The small DKW with its transverse two-cylinder two-stroke engine driving through the front wheels had proven its suitability for Sweden's long unpaved roads under both dry and wintry conditions. Ljungström was convinced in any case that the engine, transmission, and axle had to be in a single package, whether at the rear or front. He was urged toward the latter by Saab's talented consultant designer, Sixten Sason.

In retrospect, "It was a bold step for Ljungström, goaded by Sason, to contradict Porsche and Ledwinka on such fundamentals as tubular backbone frames, swing-axle suspension and air-cooled, rear-mounted opposed boxer-motors." The Saab engineers did consider air cooling to eliminate coolant-freezing problems in wintry weather, but gave it up on the grounds of the extra development funds that would be needed to design and test an air-cooled engine. This had never been a constraint for Porsche.

Thus the first Saab 92s produced in December 1949 were aerodynamic two-door cars of monocoque construction, a concept not at all alien to Porsche, but with their two-stroke engines driving the front wheels. When Gunnar Philipson heard about the Saab project in 1946 he gave up the Philipin in favor of a contract to distribute and sell Saabs. "Philipson knew a Saab-DKW concept would work in Sweden," recalled Saab engineer Rolf Mellde. "Germany could not yet deliver, and he saw the Saab as a DKW substitute."

It took longer to get the new Saab ready than Philipson had hoped, however, and in the meantime Germany was starting to build and deliver . . . Volks-wagens. As Sweden's successful prewar importer of Auto UnionAuto Union cars, Philipson was an obvious candidate to become the national agent for the new KdF-Wagen. Doubtless considering that his future with Auto UnionAuto Union was secure, he rejected the Swedish VW sales rights when they were offered to him.

With the new Saabs still more promise than reality, Swedish truck maker Scania-Vabis had taken on the VW importership. The first four sample cars were imported before the autumn of 1948. Approval to import more took some time (Gunnar Philipson was most likely doing all he could in Stockholm to delay them), but by August of 1949 Scania had imported 337 of the new Beetles. An air-cooled rear-engined car would turn out to be quite good for Sweden too.

AS EARLY AS MID-1946 the British officials who were caretaking the Wolfsburg factory and its production were being pressured to make decisions about exports. The economic desirability of exports from the zone of occupation was incontrovertible. This, however, was implacably opposed by Britain's carmakers. Their situation was aptly summarized in a report from Germany in the *New York Times* in July of 1946:

The conflict between the interests of Britain as an exporting country and the interests of Britain as the caretaker of the highly industrialized section of Germany is finding its first important expression in a difference of view between parts of the British Government in London and parts of the British administration in Germany over the desirability of exporting the Volkswagen. It is an open secret here that the export of Volkswagens is not being pushed because of the fear of competition with British cars in Scandinavia, South America and other markets. And yet the British are bewailing the fact that they have nothing to export from the zone to pay for imports of food. The zone needs exports, but so does Britain.

Their fear was grounded in the fact that at the exchange rates of the time the British authorities at Wolfsburg thought they could economically sell Volkswagens abroad at £110 Sterling when a broadly comparable Austin sold for £275. This could have been because the new car and its plant were so efficient by 1946 standards, but the artificiality of the prevailing exchange rates made it difficult to draw meaningful comparisons.

This argument played out to the advantage of the British treasury and the disadvantage of the British auto producers. The United Kingdom could not afford to meet the financial commitments to its zone of German occupation without the additional funding provided by exports from the zone to hard-currency countries — especially to the American zone with its desirable dollars.

The treasury ultimately overruled the objections of the Society of Motor Manufacturers and Traders and approved the export of Volkswagens from Wolfsburg. But commitments to the Control Commission for Germany, the British Army of the Rhine, and Britain's fellow occupiers took priority, as did the need to refresh the exhausted German civil fleet. In 1947 exports would commence in response to considerable interest from all points of the compass.

Eligibility to acquire exported Beetles — and ultimately to bid for the assets of the factory — was highest among the nations that had suffered under Hitler's Germany or had joined the Allies to fight the Germans to a standstill. The numbers of the latter grew startlingly in the last months of the war. No one could accuse Brazil, which had declared war on Germany in August 1942, of opportunism. Even Italy joined the Allies in October 1943. Bulgaria followed in September 1944 and Hungary in January 1945.

Nineteen forty-five saw latecomers scrambling to get aboard the victory bandwagon and share any benefits that it might bring. Newcomers to the Allied ranks in February were Chile, Ecuador, Egypt, Lebanon, Paraguay, Peru, Syria, Turkey, Uruguay, and Venezuela. The last to declare war on Germany in March were Finland, Saudi Arabia, and — cutting it fine on 27 March — Juan Peron's Argentina.

Brazil could justify her position among the nations that lodged requests for Volkswagens with the Commerce Branch of the Transport and Industry Division of the British CCG in Berlin. Initially that was the channel through which requests for Beetles were sorted and coordinated. From 1947 to 1948 the U.S./U.K. Joint Export/Import Agency (JEIA), took over this allocation task.

"In order of priority and having regard to the quantities involved," a member of the Commerce Branch wrote on 29 August 1946, "the needs of the Military Missions may be deemed to come first, charity and other organisations second, and supplies for American personnel for sale through Army Exchange Services possibly third. A suggested price for both sale to Missions and other organisations, as well as for British personnel, is £160, having regard to comparable world prices."

The CCG's Commerce Branch set out the requests it had received and commented on them as follows:

Applicant	Numbers	Remarks
Brazilian Military Mission	6	Payment offered in U.S. dollars. Suggest supply 2 as a start.
Luxembourg Military Mission	4	Suggest supply 1 very urgently required, but still subject to price negotiation.
Chinese Military Mission	2	Payment offered in U.S. dollars. Suggest supply both.
Greek Military Mission	2	Already supplied and payment in Sterling agreed in principle.
Polish Military Mission	6	Suggest supply 2, but question of payment will be subject to negotiation.
Swiss delegation for repatriation of Swiss Nationals (16)	2	Payment to be subject to negotiation.
OMGUS (U.S. Military Goverment)	500 a month up to possibly 5,000	For sale to Army Exchange for resale to American personnel.
UNRRA (United Nations Rescue and Relief)	1,200	Demand refused. May shortly be reopened.
International YMCA	35	Subject to negotiation.
Soviet Military Government	2	For test purposes with view to obtaining larger quantities.
France	450	Export
Holland	1,000	Export

Ben Pon, left, used the plausible cover story of a plan to set up a VW factory in Holland to reintroduce himself to the VW works after the war. He played a key role in the export of the products of Wolfsburg, as here to the United States.

That the first exports of Beetles for commercial sale were to Holland has entered into Volkswagen legend. Success went to the persistent and resourceful Ben Pon, who had first staked his claim with ten thousand tulips around the Porsche hut at Fallersleben. Pon, who had signed an export contract before the war, was the first to be named to sell Volkswagens outside Germany.

Said Pon, recalling a demonstration he was given in 1939 on the Berlin ring road by the senior Porsche, who was wearing brocaded carpet slippers, "The car was too noisy, but it was well made and I was sure we could sell it in Holland. I never did believe the 990-mark price, though. That was just propaganda."

Pon pressed his case with the British in the debris of the VW works after the war. Ivan Hirst recalled his arrival togged out in "a Dutch Army Medical Corps uniform — very ill-fitting." Wrote Arthur Railton, "Not sure of which side was in charge, British or German, Pon did not bring up his old contract or his interest in selling Volkswagens. He acted the part of a Dutch colonel investigating the possibility of setting up a similar factory in Holland.

"It was pure theatre all the way," Railton added, "a role Pon played with gusto." Later placing his cards on the table, the flamboyant Pon was first in line when postwar commercial export contracts were awarded. The Pon brothers became VW agents for Holland on 8 August 1947 and on 16 October received their first six cars.

Chimerical though it turned out to be, Ben Pon's idea of setting up a factory in Holland to make or assemble Volkswagens had not struck the British officers at Wolfsburg as being all that odd. In fact they had received a number of approaches from national and commercial enterprises pitching similar ideas. From the British side this had its attractions, as the Foreign Office's J. L. B. T itchener wrote to the CCG's Economic Sub-Commission (ECOSC) in Berlin on 5 November 1947:

The Volkswagen car is arousing considerable interest in other countries and I feel we ought to have your views as to the degree we can exploit it as an export.

As it will probably be a considerable time before we can hope to produce a guaranteed export quota of these vehicles (and spares) on anything like the scale necessary to meet the demands of even a small importing country, we ought to consider what would be gained by permitting partial, or even total, manufacture outside Germany under license.

A proposition of this kind was already on the table from the Danes, Titchener reported, although not very specific as yet. But interest from that latecomer to the conflict, Argentina, was strong because "the development of their motor-car industry forms an important part of their Government's Five Year Economic Plan." Argentine interest was welcome as well because its sunny prosperity at the peak of the Peron years contrasted with Europe's troubled economic state.

The Mayorga Hermanos firm, said Titchener, wanted to assemble Beetles in Argentina from imported components plus local manufacture of "the more simple and bulk parts." Royalties would be paid on the assembled cars in return for the rights and technical help in setting up production. The Foreign Office official explained the background to the request:

> The London end of the firm of Mayorga Hermanos is, in fact, already planning to part-assemble American cars in the Argentine and now wishes to examine the possibility of entering into a similar arrangement with us in respect of the Volkswagen which, with its cheapness and low petrol consumption would, they feel, appeal to a section of the Argentine public as yet untouched by the motor-car trade on account of the very high prices for imported cars, which now prevail in that country. The design is apparently highly suitable both for the Argentine roads and for the climate.

Here was a country that seemed eager and able to make a fist of local production of the Beetle. But providing the technical know-how that would have been needed to set up such an operation would have strained both the British and German capabilities at Wolfsburg; they had their hands full trying to sustain production of the built-up cars that could meet the dollar-earning demand already on their doorstep in Europe. Besides, they already had on their table an attractive proposition from neighboring Belgium, which was struggling to rebuild and sustain a viable motor industry.

FRENCH-SPEAKING BELGIANS HAD BEEN kept well informed of the KdF-Wagen's progress before the war by writers such as Henri Petit, Charles Faroux, and Alfred Nauck, among others. After the war some of the first Beetles built in Wolfsburg found their way to Belgium, among them cars bought by the Belgian army. In July 1946 the Belgian quartermaster general learned that his German occupying forces would receive forty VWs as war reparations; by September the vehicles were being allocated to field units.

A new Beetle — perhaps one of these military units — was driven in the autumn of 1946 by Pierre D'Ieteren, then the vice chairman of D'Ieteren Frères, importer and assembler of Studebaker cars and trucks. To a British colleague D'Ieteren wrote in October, "This car really shows a wonderful study and its size is a very reasonable one. I tested the car and was surprised to feel its road holding and its mechanical efficiency." D'Ieteren expressed interest in importing VWs as soon as they could be made available.

Exports of cars or parts from Wolfsburg on any substantial scale were still in the future in March of 1946 when Britain's Board of Trade at London's Millbank tower had a visit from Col. John Dufour, who was described as "a senior State servant reporting direct to the Belgian cabinet with authority to investigate and reorganise the Belgian automobile industry."

At the end of 1945 John Dufour had held the rank of captain-commander in the army and was president of the Defense Ministry's Supply Commission, which had asked him to research and report on the vehicle situation of the Belgian Military Liaison in Germany. Clearly his findings referenced both the poor state of Belgium's indigenous motor industry and his knowledge of the Volkswagen. In the wake of his report, Dufour was commissioned a colonel and given powers to negotiate an ambitious program with the British guardians of the VW works.

John Dufour, the Board of Trade's meeting minutes advised, was seeking "component parts to assist him in his plans for building a Belgian car in quantity." In particular, he was hoping to achieve this in cooperation with Volkswagen. Meeting with Ivan Hirst at Wolfsburg in mid-April, the ambitious Belgian colonel was accompanied by a civilian expert, James Van Luppen, who was soon to be placed in charge of Ford's Antwerp branch and who later headed the Belgian car industry association.

Colonel Dufour set out plans which he detailed in a letter a week later. These were described by the Industry Division of the CCG in Minden as exports of semi-knocked-down Volkswagens on the following lines:

> 500 Volkswagens to be delivered in Belgium, unassembled and unpainted, consisting of the chassis and body with front and rear bonnets as a shell in which will be packed the engine, gear box, axles etc. as separate assemblies; wheels, tyres, tubes, safety glass, batteries and upholstery will be supplied from Belgian sources and the whole will be assembled in Belgium.
>
> 5,000 Volkswagen to be delivered as above, excepting that in this case the chassis and body will be supplied as pressings to be assembled and welded together in Belgium.

As far as the Board of Trade was concerned such a Belgian adventure would not founder on the rocks of rivalry to Britain's exports of its own new postwar automobiles. One of its mandarins minuted that "Such a car will be on austerity standards to meet the domestic demands for a car below the price charged for imported vehicles. This policy does not appear to entail any considerable conflict with British car sales worth worrying about." Reassured another, "I gather that we need not be too seriously alarmed about possible future competition with British small car interests in the European market since even if the scheme comes off it is unlikely to be well under way before the present Volkswagen model is obsolete."

At Minden the relevant CCG office greeted the idea positively, saying that "we would view this deal with great favor as we have surplus press capacity at the present time and if the sheet steel was supplied by the Belgians we would be able to supply the necessary castings." The Belgian representatives assured the British that the steel would be made available in rolled sheet form, ready for pressing into body and frame parts.

After his meeting with Colonel Dufour, Ivan Hirst thought that the deal had every chance of going through. At Minden, though, he recalled, "Radclyffe was skeptical, probably more than I was. He said, 'Go down and have a look at the steel.' I went down to Charleroi where they were supposed to be making it. There they told me that their production was fully committed for three years forward to Britain, I think to Nuffield. The Belgians were embarrassed by that. They went away with their tails between their legs."

Exit Dufour but enter another Belgian party: before the end of 1946 a private Belgian group suggested forming an Anglo/Belgian company and proposed a range of Volkswagen importing and assembly actions up to and including "complete manufacture in Belgium from German drawings." This too was judged by the British authorities to be premature in light of the prior commitment of the plant to production for the British forces and for Europe's essential infrastructure.

ANOTHER ALLIED FORCE WITH a strong interest in the VW was Russia. The works filled the original Soviet military request for two test cars, which must have been satisfactory because it was followed up with an order for fifty more maroon-painted cars for the Russians. When these were ready for delivery a problem arose, as Dick Berryman recalled: "We had to teach the Russian contingent who came to pick up those first fifty export vehicles how to drive them. They just hadn't a clue technically."

Unlike the British and (later) the Americans, who were genuinely concerned to take actions that would allow the West German economy to commence functioning again, at least at subsistence level, the Soviets lost no sleep over such obligations. They saw their occupied sector of Germany as a prize of war to be exploited for the benefit of Mother Russia. These were, after all, the despised Germans who had killed millions in the Soviet Union and very nearly brought it to its knees.

That the Russians took this view was all the more understandable when one toured the territory over which they had battled the Germans. West of Moscow the landscape was devastated, the infrastructure obliterated. Such amenities and such industry as had once existed were annihilated. More than twenty million Russians had fallen in the Great Patriotic War. The Soviets felt, and in a sense were, justified in any recoupment they could obtain from prostrate Germany.

Each day the Germans, Poles, and others living and working at Wolfsburg awoke and gave thanks that they had narrowly escaped finding themselves in the Russian zone. Russia's army had penetrated well to the west, past the factory, reaching Hannover with its tanks and troops. Only the final definition of the zonal boundaries by the four Allied powers placed the dividing line five miles to the east of the factory.

This was too close for comfort, said Dick Berryman: "From time to time the political situation flared up with the Russians, and none of us wanted to be overrun and taken prisoner. So we always kept our staff cars fully gassed up and under floodlights outside the mess so that if any political trouble broke out during the night, we could get away fast."

A fast getaway was a luxury denied the locals, who were grateful that they lived west of the border. Berryman: "I think their relief at ending up in the British zone helped a great deal when it came to seeking their cooperation in getting the factory straightened out. They were thankful that their future rested in British hands even if they were more or less surrounded by Russian troops."

Britons and Germans alike were reminded of the lowering presence of the Russians by an extraordinary erection in Wolfsburg some five hundred yards from the British mess, which occupied the former KdF-Werke guest house. There, at their encampment, the Soviets built a thirty-foot tower bedecked with portraits of Marshal Joseph Stalin and his military leaders. Floodlighting made this hardboard ziggurat even more conspicuous, if possible, at nighttime.

Apart from propaganda, the task of this small unit — thirty men and three officers — was to act as an outpost aiding the repatriation of Soviet citizens. Its visibility also reminded those tasked with the fortunes of the VW works that they had to find ways to maintain its viability if it were not to be dismantled as war reparations — from which the Russians could also benefit.

Just such a demonstration of viability had miraculously spared another German car plant from the Russian wrecking ball. The BMW car factory at Eisenach in the Soviet zone of occupation had been making Munich-designed sporty luxury models that seemed irrelevant both to Russian needs and to an impoverished Germany. The plant was allowed to rev up its motorcycle production line but cars seemed to be nonstarters.

The saga of Eisenach was an eastern echo of Wolfsburg's experience. A workforce committee took a sedan from BMW's prewar production, a four-door Type 321, to Berlin to be inspected by Russia's senior occupier, Marshal Zhukov. "In a week," they told him, "we can make five more like it." Intrigued, Zhukov allowed them to try. The appearance in Berlin of five more 321s a week later gained them the right to make more. Eisenach received an order for three thousand 321s, an order that saved the factory from dismantlement. In a mild pastiche of their original name these cars were later marketed as EMWs after BMW protested.

Many other factories — and their workforces — exposed to the Russians were less fortunate. Wrote one VW historian,

> The last life blood of Germany's productive capacity was let at the direction of occupying governments; the heavy machinery, which might otherwise have led to an early recovery for Leipzig, Dresden, Chemnitz and other East German industrial areas, was immediately uprooted by the Russians from factory sites. Reports, documented with photographs, poured into Western Allied intelligence offices, telling of the machinery's sad fate. Numberless railroad sidings in East Germany, Poland and Russia were choked with idle railway cars, still packed with the machine tools that had once been the heart of Eastern Germany's industrial might.

This assessment of the value to Russia of the dismantled plants was an extreme one; "contrary to the prevailing view," wrote another researcher, the Soviets' "reparations procedure was both systematic and rewarding."

Some of the evidence in the motor-vehicle field supports the latter view. On one hand, we have no evidence that the Russians made good use of the machinery plundered from the Ambi-Budd factory in Berlin. On the other hand, Opel's new and first-class truck-producing facilities in Berlin's Brandenburg were uprooted — not forgetting the window frames and bathroom fittings — and set up again at a site near the Ural Mountains. There they produced trucks that Russia certainly needed.

In another instance, however, Russian perfidy took center stage. The Soviets approached the military authorities in the American zone, where the Opel factory was located at Rüsselsheim near Frankfurt. "Opel has a subsidiary in Leipzig in our territory," spun the plausible Russian line. "Let us have the tools and equipment to build the Kadett and we'll set them up to produce Opel cars in Leipzig." Opel's Kadett, introduced in December 1936, was a modern two-door unit-bodied car that had proved its merit with total sales of more than 100,000 units before the war. It was just the Opel that was needed for the postwar European market.

When the Russians came calling they were lucky on two counts. Opel's nominal owner, General Motors, was waffling on the issue of reasserting its authority over the factory. Also in the early months after the war the American occupiers, in an avenging frame of mind, were not inclined to raise objections to such a transplant to what was, after all, just another part of Germany.

In June 1946 the requested tools and machinery were delivered, as war reparations, to the Soviet authorities. But Leipzig was not on the freight train's itinerary. In 1947 Opel's Kadett appeared on the market as the Moskvitch 400, built at the Moscow factory in which the equipment was installed. By late

1950 these "Kremlin Kadetts" were being exported to Belgium; their sales materials stressed that spare parts could easily be sourced from Germany.

Here was an example of a successful reparations action by the Russians —and incidentally an extraction from West Germany of the tooling to make a car that could have been a serious rival, indeed the only possible rival, for the Beetle in its early years of production. The net effect for Germany, of course, was negative:

> Reparations activity caused German production potential to drop to an all-time low, as 744 key industrial installations were dismantled and removed from German soil, shipped off to the west and the east. The Western Allies' first break with the USSR in post-war Germany came over reparations policy as the Russians began to remove the facilities of production even from East Germany's deficit economy. As the U.S. and Great Britain poured food and supplies into their Zones, Russia withdrew huge quantities of raw materials and whatever finished products it could find from its Zone, all the while causing the people of the area to subsist on the remaining resources.

Small wonder that the Germans and others who had found work at Wolfsburg regarded the nearby border with the East with deep-seated dread.

The border, of course, was just a line on a map agreed to by the wartime Allies. This gave the Soviets an idea. Why not move the border? The VW plant at Wolfsburg was just too attractive a prize. And the British, it seemed in 1948, were ready to consider alternatives for its future. "The Russians one day proposed acquiring the factory as a reparation by simply moving the border about five miles west in order to append Wolfsburg to the Eastern zone in a sort of peninsula." The British authorities rejected this as far too greedy a grab.

Ivan Hirst recalled no official visit to the VW factory by Russian technicians assessing it for its war reparations value. After the exports of VWs had started, however, in the 1947–48 period, he received a request to arrange a visit to the plant by four Soviet journalists. Hirst checked with Charles Radclyffe on the ground rules for the tour and was told, "You can be entirely open with them, show them anything they want."

Accompanied by an East-West liaison officer the Russians duly dropped by the plant, where they expressed special interest in the trade mechanisms being used for exporting from Germany. Hirst and his colleagues helped all they could, even to the extent of providing them with fuel to drive to their next appointment. Their findings were suitably reported in *Pravda*, from which the *Manchester Guardian* published a translated extract that mentioned "Major Hirst, that typical lying mouthpiece of Western imperialismus." So much for the merits of candor.

Had the Russians been successful, with one ploy or another, they would have acquired an asset that they had tried to win by fairer means more than a decade earlier. In 1932, when the Porsche design office was still in its infancy, Ferdinand Porsche was approached by representatives of the Soviet Union.

They wanted no less than his complete capability, including his settlement in Russia as a state designer in charge of all engineering works.

They rolled out the most crimson of red carpets during a tour by train of Russia's engineering facilities. "Porsche went to Kiev, Kursk, Nijni-Novgorod and to Odessa," wrote one biographer. "They took him down to the Caucasus and as far as the Krim. He saw motor car works and foundries, turbines and tanks, tractors and aircraft, works and yet more engineering works. He was even taken as far as the secret industrial centres behind the Ural."

It was a fascinating prospect for an engineer like Porsche, a historic opportunity to mobilize millions to advance the technology of a complete economy. But it would mean severing Porsche's links to his homelands, to the Austria and Germany where he well knew both the challenges and the possibilities. In spite of the terrible depression in the economies of those countries and his consequent struggle to establish his new engineering business, Ferdinand Porsche decided to commit his future to them.

TROOPS FIGHTING ON THE SIDE of the Russians but in other theaters in World War II were getting their first exposure to Porsche's Type 82 at the same time. Australia's soldiers were as familiar with the wartime Kübelwagen as were the British military with whom they battled the Germans on the sand ocean of North Africa. Australia suffered 4,863 killed or wounded in the desert campaigns of 1940 to 1943, including the defense of Tobruk and the battle of El Alamein. Where available, they commandeered and drove serviceable Kübels.

One of the first Aussies to be Kübel-mounted was an army chaplain, Padre A. J. "Robbie" Robjohns of the 9th Division's 2/13th Battalion. "The vehicle had been discovered abandoned in 'no-man's-land' between our forward line and the enemy's," Robjohns recalled, "and our battalion night patrol dragged it back. The transport officer had it sent back to 9th Division Light Aid Detachment who did what they could with it, and it was returned, suitably decorated, for my use."

"Decorated" referred to red crosses on white roundels on both the rear doors and chaplain signage that in theory identified the vehicle as a noncombatant's that should not be fired upon. Padre Robjohns found the Germans to be better at observing this convention than the Italians in North Africa. The Kübel was "quite good to drive," he recalled after assuming ownership of it in the summer of 1942.

"This type of VW was issued to most German officers needing transport," Robjohns said. "It was virtually just a metal hull without any soft furnishings. In mine there were bullet holes in the muffler box, and it developed a high-pitched scream when accelerating. The lads of our unit christened me 'the low-flying Padre'." When his unit left the desert in December 1942, said the Padre, "there was no time for sentiment, we just knew it had to remain behind. I just had to slam the door."

For Robbie Robjohns the captured Kübel was vital transport, but not all his flock were fond of it. "I wouldn't have been seen dead in one of those," said a battalion staff sergeant. "It made more noise than a fleet of tanks. None of the boys would go near it!" Nevertheless at least one captured wartime Beetle made its way back to Australia, where it can be seen on display in Canberra's Australian War Memorial.

"There is some evidence also that two 1945-model VW Beetles were brought to Australia by the military shortly after the end of the war," wrote two Australian VW researchers.

> One was in near-new condition, the other having been put to an extensive road test by the Army. These two cars, together with a large quantity of VW spares, many other Army vehicles and other miscellaneous materiel, were auctioned off by the Commonwealth Disposals Commission in Tottenham, Victoria in February 1946. The components of one of these VWs, in derelict condition, survive today in the collection of Graham Lees, proprietor of Brookvale Spares at Brookvale in Sydney. He has checked particulars with Wolfsburg, who confirm the car was constructed in October 1945, in that first post-war batch of 1,785 cars.

Provisional and ad hoc though these ur-Beetles were, they must have demonstrated some adaptability to Australia's climatic conditions and long unpaved roads. By the beginning of 1947 the Canberra government had expressly asked its emissaries in Europe to assess the suitability of the car and its factory for transplantation to Australia as a complete vehicle-manufacturing facility. It was not the only company in which they were interested; inquiries were also made at Adler and DKW, but neither had much in the way of assets to offer.

The Australians made contact with the VW works, where production expediter Dick Berryman was asked to liaise with them. In January, Berryman recalled, he was "instructed to prepare a complete set of drawings and a written explanation of the special tools used," a task which he completed on the seventeenth. In an eleven-page typed report he set out the car's specifications with drawing references, the required machine tools, the manufacturing hours (172 hours per car), and the material r equirements.

On 31 January these documents were forwarded to Australia from Germany by J. T. O. Loorham, controller of the Australian Reparations Plant and Stores Team. Some working drawings were yet to be supplied; these were being prepared, with relevant tolerances, under Berryman's direction. In his transmittal Loorham adumbrated some features of the VW including its ease of repair: "A feature of the Volkswagen is the small number of parts and accessibility for replacement, as compared with the orthodox motor car. For instance, it was planned that a new engine could be obtained for £10 and the old engine could be taken out and the new engine assembled by people with just an ordinary knowledge of motor mechanics in 1–2 hours."

Loorham drew attention to the specialized machinery that had been installed at Wolfsburg to make the Beetle and that would be desired if the car were to be made in Australia: "Briefly, the special machines cover four machine tools used for the crank-case and gear box. On the crank-case about six operations are involved, including one of broaching. The special jigs in the main represent jig frames for spot welding the body in one unit and for welding the floor of the vehicle.

"If it is intended to take up manufacture of this car in Australia," Loorham added, "it is recommended that a production engineer should visit the factory and that Mr. Berryman's services be secured by Australia . . . It is also suggested for consideration that a few key German technicians now employed by the Volkswagen factory be brought to Australia in connection with production. For instance, the man-in-charge of the tool room, the press, the body assembly, engine manufacture and assembly, etc."

Loorham had not recommended Berryman without making some inquiries into his bona fides:

> Mr. Berryman is a mechanical engineer, was in the R.A.F. during the war, and for twenty years was on the production side of General Motors in Canada. I have checked up on his statements with senior officials in the mechanical engineering branch of the Control Commission for Germany at Minden and they confirm the statements made to me by Mr. Berryman. They also state that Berryman is a first-class man on production and has been responsible for the re-starting of Volkswagen manufacture and re-lay-out of some of the shops due to the attention they received from the R.A.F.

This was followed up on 11 February with additional information on the VW car sent by the Australian Scientific and Technical Mission (ASTM) from London. The ASTM had been established there in 1945 to help assess Australia's reparations opportunities in Germany.

Interest was intensifying in February, when Berryman "received instructions to meet two official representatives from Australia House, London and explain what I could about the production." That this was no casual invitation was verified by the status conferred upon Dick Berryman. With a colleague he was designated a member of the Australian Reparations Mission in the movement order that assigned them a Volkswagen and driver for a trip to Antwerp, Belgium on 20 February. There they met two Australians, members of its War Reparations Commission.

The Australians explained what they had in mind, Berryman recalled: "Apparently it was thought that a plant which had been used in Australia to make aircraft could be converted to produce the VW, which was really only a spot-welded job with an engine and a couple of axles. It was considered that to open up Australia commercially what was needed was a light and cheap car which could negotiate rough going without breaking up, and that the VW was it."

SERIOUS CAR PRODUCTION IN AUSTRALIA was just beginning at this time. During World War II establishing an indigenous automobile industry, proposed by various governments at least since 1927, was given a higher priority to improve Australia's industrial infrastructure, raise postwar employment prospects, and make the country less dependent upon others for military materiel. The last point was dramatized by the events of the war, which brought an awareness to Australians that they were more vulnerable than they had thought.

Although never invaded by the Japanese, Australia was surprised to come under attack from the Pacific marauders:

> The northern city of Darwin was bombed by the Japanese fifty-nine times between February 1942 and November 1943 and nine other Australian towns and cities were also bombed. The initial raid on Darwin cost two hundred and thirty-eight lives. Five merchant ships and three warships were sunk and thirteen other vessels damaged. Twenty-three aircraft were also destroyed. Small beer, perhaps, compared to the European experience but a shock to a nation that had always considered itself to be isolated from the main events.

Another positive factor favoring car-building down under was that Australians had gained confidence during the war in their ability to produce manufactured goods at high levels of both quantity and quality. An economy based on the export of wheat and wool began to weigh the value to it of establishing indigenous manufacturing industries. The motor industry, so valuable in developing production and servicing skills and encouraging other industries, was a prime candidate.

Government actions initiated in 1943 led to the issuance by Canberra late in 1944 of a letter of invitation to the nation's motor companies, soliciting proposals for the production of complete vehicles. Accompanying the carrot of this opportunity was a stick: if they didn't react, the socialist-minded government would set up its own car company.

Many firms responded; one company was chosen and by 1946–47 it was preparing for the production in Australia of a medium-sized car in moderate annual volumes. But this was just one producer. There seemed to be room in the Australian economy for another carmaker offering a smaller and less costly utility vehicle. Defeated Germany's auto infrastructure seemed able to provide just such an automobile. Enter the Australian representatives meeting in Antwerp with VW's Dick Berryman.

Following up on their meeting with and briefing by Berryman, the Australians assigned a team of engineers to visit Wolfsburg in March 1947 and form their own opinion of the factory and its products. "They sent four chaps," Ivan Hirst recalled. "They were good men, technicians. They spent two or three weeks there."

Their visit resulted in the shipment via Loorham to Australia of eight packages of drawings and data on all aspects of the car, the factory, and the equipment needed to produce the Beetle at a rate of four hundred cars a day. The team's J. W. Carter covered the shipment with a hand-written memo that detailed the marking and cutting of the car's upholstery with "a hand operated, electric driven circular knife" and described two modifications to the VW's engine — twin carburetors and "a straight manifold from the carburetors to the inlet valves" — to improve its performance.

"With regard to the toolroom," Carter reported, "there is nothing outstanding. Most of the large body dies are made by special firms outside the factory." Yet he found the level of precision achieved impressive: "I was struck by the small amount of gauging [inspection] on the different parts. In fact there was no gauging of the body, yet there was very little adjustment necessary on the assembly chain." The Australian interest was knowledgeable and clearly much more than casual.

Emphasis was added to that interest by a cable, originated by the British Foreign Office on 12 August 1947, and repeated to the CCG at Minden on 14 August as follows:

IMPORTANT

WE UNDERSTAND THAT MR. L.J. HARTNETT IS VISITING GERMANY BETWEEN AUGUST 20TH AND 26TH ON BEHALF OF THE AUSTRALIAN GOVERNMENT. VISIT IS BEING ARRANGED BY BIOS IN CONJUNCTION WITH AUSTRALIAN MISSION AT LOHNE.

MR. HARTNETT WOULD BE GLAD OF OPPORTUNITY TO VISIT THE VOLKSWAGEN FACTORY DURING HIS STAY. PLEASE MAKE APPROPRIATE ARRANGEMENTS IN CONJUNCTION WITH THE AUSTRALIAN MISSION AT LOHNE WHO ARE ARRANGING HARTNETT'S PROGRAMME.

Here was an alert of an impending visit by a man who had already achieved legendary albeit controversial standing in Australia's budding motor industry. Born in Britain in 1898, Laurence John "Larry" Hartnett was introduced to the engineering profession by Epsom College and trained as a military aviator in World War I, just too late to see active service.

Hartnett became active in car dealing and distribution and joined GM's Overseas Operations Division (GMOO). He held sales posts in the Near East, Sweden, and at GM's British car-producing company, Vauxhall, where he was named a board member in 1933. From there, in 1934, Hartnett was assigned by GMOO's general manager, Graeme Howard, as managing director to General Motors-Holden's in Australia.

On a mission to Europe on behalf of both himself and Australia, Laurence "Larry" Hartnett gave the Volkswagen product and works a thorough evaluation. He concluded that both had great merit but that the risk of bringing the plant to Australia would be too great.

The ambitious Hartnett became a key player in Australia's push for domestic car production. When he arrived, cars were being assembled from imported chassis parts and were being bodied locally to meet government-imposed local-content requirements. It would not be too great a step, he and others realized, to build cars from scratch in Australia.

During the war Hartnett was asked by Canberra to add the job of director of ordnance production to his post at Holden's. But when in 1944 the Labor government under prime minister Ben Chifley requested tenders from aspiring auto producers he spun into a whirlwind of activity. Hartnett obtained a commitment to the project from General Motors, selected an American-designed GM prototype to be developed into the Holden car, found local financing, and grappled with the myriad other problems attendant upon the creation of a full-fledged car company.

His efforts were crowned with success. In November 1948 the first Holden cars were released to the Australian market. For many years Holden would enjoy the distinction of being Australia's own car. But to his great personal regret, an exhausted Larry Hartnett was not in attendance. Two years earlier he and GMOO had fallen out. Rather than move to a New York desk job, Hartnett had resigned.

GM's Holden was a medium-sized car produced in relatively small volumes. Output started at seven a day and not until 1952 did it reach two hundred daily, fifty thousand a year. Its positioning in the market seemed to

Larry Hartnett to leave room for a smaller car that could be built in larger volumes to put more of the eight million Australians on wheels. As well the proud Hartnett, dubbed "a technological brigand" by his biographer, felt he had something to prove to the big auto company that had snubbed him just when he had put its Holden on the road.

With that objective in view Hartnett, now a free agent and with the assistance although not the formal blessing of Canberra, started contacting automakers abroad at the beginning of 1947. His aim was to find "a large group or major interest . . . who would like . . . to establish themselves or expand in Australia." In America he contacted Willys, one of the few makers of small cars there, but without success. In late April Hartnett and his family sailed to Europe, the homeland of the world's best makers of smaller autos, to see what they had wrought. They arrived in London on 16 May.

Europe had been alerted to Hartnett's imminent arrival. Clarification of his role was requested on 26 April by the head of the ASTM in London. On 2 May he was informed by Canberra that although Hartnett was traveling as a private businessman he was doing so for a nation that had certain expectations: "The Australian Government is fully aware of the purpose of Mr Hartnett's visit, and we would like him to secure facilities in the expectation that there would emerge a proposition of a nature which the Government believes is particularly desirable in Australia." This was strong support that gave Larry Hartnett the high-level access he felt he deserved.

On the European continent Hartnett assessed the new Renault 4CV and Fiat's small-car range. Both Renault and Fiat were keen to work with Hartnett, flattering the entrepreneur by meeting with him late into the evening, but insisted that their cars be built down under in their original form, with no design changes. Because, wrote Hartnett, "my self-imposed mission was to give Australia a self-contained national product unencumbered by overseas direction, influence or pressure," he judged this constraint to be unsatisfactory.

Larry Hartnett also concluded that "Britain at that stage had nothing to interest me" after contacting both Rootes and Jowett. His meetings with British officials gave him some encouragement, however. He was invited "to meet a select group of the War Office with a view of having perhaps incorporated in my car certain features applicable for Empire Defence." Slender though it was, this was a reed at which to grasp.

In the midst of his deliberations Hartnett was cabled from Geneva by the Australian minister for postwar reconstruction, John J. Dedman, who was in that city on one of his many diplomatic missions abroad. "Dedman's cable said the British and Americans had both been offered the Volkswagen plant as war reparations, and both had turned the offer down," Hartnett recalled. "Why shouldn't Australia pick it up and make the VW in Australia? If Australia wanted the plant, it seemed she could have it — and every little beetle car in it." Thereupon followed the message cabled to Minden to announce the impending arrival at Wolfsburg of Larry Hartnett.

DULY COMMISSIONED A BRIGADIER to ease his travel to and in Germany, Hartnett flew from London's Northolt military airport to Hannover and was driven to Wolfsburg. There he hit it off at once with Ivan Hirst, who found the affable and worldly-wise Hartnett a welcome change from the puffed-up self-important grandees who so often darkened his portals. "I liked Hartnett very much," said Hirst. "He was a man of very broad views, what I would call an 'American' outlook."

What began as a brief visit extended into three weeks. Inspecting the factory, Hartnett found it "beautifully designed." Ivan Hirst was struggling at the time to improve the German management of the plant; "It was always like pushing a bag of jelly to get anything changed on the German side," he recalled. Hartnett suggested that Hirst try extending the authority of the purchasing manager to jobs inside the plant as well. Hirst followed this advice, appointing a supply manager to gain better control of all the plant's processes.

Evaluating the real worth of the Volkswagen as a product was no easy task at the time, but Hartnett was as qualified as anyone to have a stab at it. He knew that the prices at which the VWs being produced (thirty per day then) were being sold bore little relation to their real cost: "Currency values in Europe hadn't begun to settle down," he wrote.

"To my mind," Hartnett reflected, "it was *not* low-priced in terms of its design and manufacture. It *could* be brought down in cost, but only with a pretty high volume of production — at least 250,000 units a year. I couldn't see Australians going for it in such numbers. There was no proof then that the VW would have public acceptance."

The knowledgeable Hartnett had grasped the essence of the VW concept: that it was designed to be built economically in high volumes. The idea that a huge share of that volume could be absorbed by export markets was alien to a postwar world that was subdivided by tariffs and trade zones — and to an Australia that, to this day, has not become a significant vehicle exporter.

Larry Hartnett elected not to recommend a bid by Australia to obtain the Volkswagen plant as a whole. "What did interest Hartnett, however, was the press shop which still contained the latest tools from the USA acquired prior to the outbreak of war six years earlier. On his return to London, Hartnett therefore reported his rejection of the Volkswagen itself, but his wish to obtain the press shop equipment. Typically, the Australian government was initially unsure and dithered, but later backed the request. In the end the Australians didn't even get a single spanner."

The Aussies' uncertainty was fueled by the status of the VW factory. Yes, it was technically available for dismantling as war reparations, but no, not quite yet, as Ivan Hirst pointed out to the Australian experts who visited the factory after their Antwerp meeting with Richard Berryman: "I told them that there was a reserve on the plant, and that they'd have to wait three years for it. After that they were withdrawn from Wolfsburg. They seemed to lose interest."

Australia did not quite lose interest altogether. Contemporaneously with Larry Hartnett's visit to Wolfsburg the ASTM bought some samples for inspection back home. "Two German cars (VOLKSWAGEN) have been purchased," stated a cabinet subcommittee agenda of 4 September 1947, "and are at present held by the Department of Munitions. A Mercedes-Benz car was also bought and has been shipped per SS Port Jackson. These have been obtained as being of great interest from the point of possible manufacture of an Australian 'People's Car.' Auto Union"

Well into 1948 these samples, successors to the military Volkswagens that had been auctioned off in 1946, were still being tested and evaluated. "One of these cars has been given a very long trial under Australian conditions," advised a government note of 4 February 1948, "and the other dismantled and displayed for inspection purposes. Publicity is now being given in order that interested manufacturers can inspect the car." Whether and when the VW works might be available as reparations seemed not to be an issue; making a version of the Beetle in Australia was still an opportunity as far as the government was concerned. It would happen, but not for six years and then only as the small-scale assembly of imported components.

Wolfsburg would not be reborn in Australia after all. The failure of this initiative to bear fruit was especially poignant for Dick Berryman, who had seen it as his next step forward in the industry. "I was particularly sorry," he told *Safer Motoring*, "as I had been promised the job of production manager if the Australian VW plan had come off." Berryman would continue to reach out on his own initiative to try to find someone who would take responsibility for the huge factory and recognize the valuable role that Berryman could continue to play in its management.

Another who looked back on these developments with some angst was Larry Hartnett: "Some people may think it is a very embarrassing blot on my escutcheon that I rejected the Volkswagen, including the plant and sole manufacturing rights, when it was virtually thrown at me. The subsequent rise of the VW to world popularity proved that I had made a pretty poor assessment of its potential. But before I turned it down, the British and American motor industries had looked it over and come to exactly the same conclusions as I had."

This was not quite correct. In 1947 the British were still in the driver's seat at Wolfsburg; the ultimate fate of the factory was by no means decided. If an initiative came from Britain it would enjoy priority. And the Americans had still to be heard from. They, after all, with their huge home market and well-developed export trade, were fully able to grasp the potential of a factory that was geared to manufacture cars in high volumes.

8

America Rides to the Rescue

A merica's automakers were well-informed about Hitler's wonder car for Germany's masses. General Motors had its own postwar Type 11 to assess, the car that their Overseas Operations Division's Graeme Howard had ordered through the American occupation authorities in September 1946. GM engineers took part in the various trials of wartime VWs conducted under the auspices of the Society of Automotive Engineers. And GM was kept advised by Opel about the KdF-Wagen in its natal years.

In part because it was influenced by the negative tone of the prewar news about the project it had received from Opel, General Motors was officially unimpressed. Senior GM and Vauxhall engineer Maurice Platt later admitted that he and his colleagues in the world's largest carmaker had shared in the general postwar perception that the VW was not only an ugly duckling but also a dead duck:

> Some examples of that unattractive machine had been made available, for assessment, to British and American car manufacturers soon after the war, and they had all dismissed it out of hand. My own view, at the time, was that it was noisy, uncomfortable and tricky to handle; a crash gearbox and mechanically operated four-wheel brakes (requiring a considerable pedal effort) added to the driver's difficulties. The appearance of the two-door saloon was dated and the integral body-cum-platform structure presented manufacturing problems. Of all the pre-war cars available for resurrection, this seemed to be one of the least promising.

General Motors was not inherently antagonistic to new vehicle concepts, even to rear-engined ones. Its engineers had been as responsive as others in the industry to the wave of experimentation with new shapes and structures that swept in with the 1930s. Since 1926 GM had been experimenting with two-stroke engines under the enthusiastic guidance of its inspirational research director, Charles Kettering.

In 1929 GM selected a configuration for two-stroke engines — which give a power stroke every revolution instead of every other revolution like the conventional four-stroke engine — which used two pistons sharing a common combustion chamber. A fresh charge entered in one cylinder and the burned gases were exhausted in the other. Experimental air-cooled engines of just this layout were designed and built by Josef Kales for Porsche in the first experimental phase of the Volkswagen project.

GM built what it called a workbench engine with four paired U cylinders of this type in a radial configuration in 1932. Kettering had this power unit in mind on 1 February 1934 when the parameters were set for a new GM car project. It was to be a light five-passenger car with good ride comfort, a high level of safety, and "such streamlining as is considered for style reasons to have maximum utility value."

Reflecting on the purpose of this small-car project, Charles Kettering wrote to GM chairman Alfred P. Sloan that "we started out to produce a car that would have a reduction in weight of one-third its counterpart of conventional design, and would give at least 40% better fuel economy over all driving conditions." The objective, Kettering said, was to build "an economy car which would sell for less than $500, without a corresponding sacrifice in comfort and utility."

Kettering's price target showed that Adolf Hitler was not the only leader who wanted to place less costly transport at the disposal of his people. In 1934, 500 dollars was equivalent to 100 pounds or 1,250 marks — a fair proportion more than the Beetle's 1,000-mark target for a car designed to seat five instead of four. This tough task was assigned by Kettering to a Swedish engineer, E. Olle Schjolin, who headed GM's new central Automotive Design Department.

Schjolin's team settled on an integral body/frame structure for the four-door light car, which they dubbed the Martia. Tests showed it to be almost four times stiffer in torsion than the contemporary Chevrolet. The Martia used independent suspension at all four wheels, which were vestigial rims bolted to the brake drums, akin to those later used on the Beetle. Steering was by rack and pinion.

A clean-sheet-of-paper approach was taken to the engine's location. "Both front and rear compartments were available," the engineers reported, "the latter being the larger. A survey of weight distributions, accessibility and space conditions indicated the rear location as the more suitable. This eliminated the need of a propeller shaft tunnel in the body and suggested the possibility of a unit engine-transmission-differential assembly."

The consistency of weight distribution afforded by a rear engine location was borne out by the Martia's front/rear weight proportion; over the range from empty to fully laden it differed only from 45/55 percent to 41/59 percent. Using magnesium for the engine, placed laterally above the rear ax-

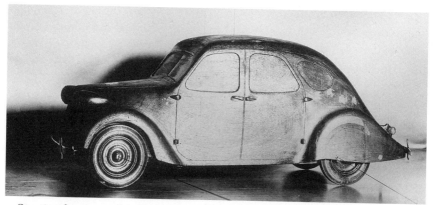

Starting from scratch in the 1930s with the design of a small, light, low-priced car, GM engineers under Charles Kettering decided that a rear-mounted engine would be best. Here a wind-tunnel test is being conducted on a model of the GM Martia.

les, helped keep the Martia's share of weight on its rear wheels below the critical 60-percent level.

Here, then, was a shockingly radical small car which GM developed in secret during the 1930s. Although its X-shaped Roots-blower-scavenged engine displaced only 1,650 cc it produced eighty horsepower that gave the light Martias lively performance. "Prototypes were built and run," recalled engineer Archie McDuffie, "and they did a pretty good job — up to 45 mpg and performance comparable to a four-cycle engine in a similar car. The two-cycle would get 15%–20% better fuel economy. We found that to be true throughout all our development."

Martia's cover was finally blown in April 1939 when *Automotive Industries* identified eight of Olle Schjolin's patents describing key features of the Martias — three of which were built. The article's author was well informed: "The writer understands that General Motors not only has worked out the designs for this car on paper and secured patent protection on its various novel features, but has actually built and tested the car."

Not only that; General Motors was also in the early stages of planning to produce Martias. Charles Kettering pointed out to his boss Alfred Sloan that such a radically new car would not fit easily within the existing GM system, which was geared more for "handling the work of manufacturing products which have been in production for some time and in which the details have been well worked out." Effective though they were for handling incremental change, in Kettering's view GM's methods weren't suited to the introduction of something wholly new.

This led Kettering to recommend that an entirely new factory be set up expressly to make a car of the Martia design. Kettering's biographer quoted the great engineer, creator of the self-starter and the electrical system for cars: " 'These procedures of mass-production are almost diametrically opposite to those which are essential in the development and early production of a new product.' Therefore he recommended an entirely new plant for the light car, headed by sympathetic research engineers, so that General Motors would 'not have to repeat the great waste of time, money and human effort in trying to overcome these fixed-mind conditions.' "

Thus at the end of the 1930s in America Charles Kettering was recommending a course of action that another innovative engineer, Ferdinand Porsche, was actively implementing, in order to build his own low-cost light car, at the same time. Alfred Sloan was not very receptive to the idea; he had not forgotten how Kettering had virtually bankrupted GM's Chevrolet Division with his "copper-cooled" engines in the early 1920s. Sloan would have to be satisfied that his production-savvy engineers were more than happy with any new Kettering brainstorm.

With the onset of war preparations GM's development of the Martia car was suspended. Larger versions of the two-stroke engine were built and tested during the war in both cars and aircraft. At war's end the Martia could well have been resurrected as a new small General Motors car for the postwar market. But as GM engineer Darl Caris recalled, the times were just not right:

> It is my impression that these rear-engined light cars were ahead of their time and also just happened to be caught in the unusual market following World War II. After the war, there was such a demand for automobiles that the obvious course was to resume where we left off. It wasn't the time to bring out a new car, especially a light, small car. There simply wasn't a market for such a car in the US at that time.

THE MARTIA COULD HAVE ENTERED the picture in 1947 when GM's largely autonomous Overseas Operations Division (GMOO) began thinking of building an austerity model abroad to meet developing-world requirements. The American market wanted cars longer, lower, wider, faster, and damn the fuel economy, and it soon became evident that cars for the domestic market were going to evolve in directions that would make them unsuitable for sale anywhere else on the globe.

Considering how best to tap the potential of the third-world markets, one of GMOO's young engineers, William Swallow, said that instead of adapting its own components GM should acquire the Volkswagen, which would be ideal for such conditions. Swallow had previously been a development engineer at the Pressed Steel Company, where the body structure and design of the Type 11 sedan were assessed in highly positive terms for one of the BIOS reports.

GM's Maurice Platt reflected on Swallow's initiative: "His report was studied by the engineering hierarchy in Detroit with the predictable result that his recommendation was dismissed. Detroit was as critical of the primitive Volkswagen as Luton or Coventry and was certain that it could not survive for more than a year or two, even in underdeveloped countries, in competition with the postwar American cars that would soon come into production. Bill nearly lost his job through having shown such poor judgement." Reprieved by GM, Bill Swallow later became the knighted chairman of Vauxhall.

The British military authorities never directly approached General Motors about the future of Volkswagen. They were aware of the astonishing fact that GM was wavering over whether it should resume control of Opel, which before the war had been by far Germany's largest automaker. Not until November 1948 did GM's board again agree to accept responsibility for Opel, and then only for a two-year probationary period. If GM was uncertain about its own Opel, the British assumed, and rightly, it would hardly be thrilled by the prospect of taking charge of Volkswagen.

EXECUTIVES OF OTHER AMERICAN AUTO FIRMS saw merit in the Beetle as a product for America. Studebaker's Richard Hutchinson, a twenty-nine-year veteran of the firm, took a postwar interest in the Volkswagen in his capacity as vice president in charge of exports. He contacted the British Mil Gov in Germany, first to get a sample car and then to negotiate for the American sales rights. In fact Hutchinson felt he had these in his grasp but was thwarted by Studebaker's president, Harold Vance. A production man at heart, Vance was uninterested in importing any autos, let alone Volkswagens.

At Ford in America it was the man with his name on the building himself, the legendary Henry, who took a special interest in the Beetle. Among the many controversies that swirled around the pioneering Henry Ford during his long lifetime the least seemly was his aversion to Jews. "I think everybody knows his feelings towards Jews was quite severe," recalled a close technical colleague, German-born Emil Zoerlein. "He told me once, 'You know, a Jew is an individual that kicks you down in the gutter, but you've got to have them. He keeps the white man going.' He was referring more to Wall Street financial capitalists than the racial type."

Continued Zoerlein, "Mr. Ford seemed to think Hitler's program against the Jews was good. He thought it was hitting in one of the trouble spots. He said, 'Maybe this fellow Hitler will do away with the trouble makers over there, but I feel that behind him the Jews are pushing him on.' I think he meant the Jews as a race rather than the capitalistic group in Germany that was backing him."

While it would be absurd to portray Ford as an admirer of Hitler, evidence is ample that he did not disapprove of the man and his actions. Only three days before war in Europe erupted in 1939 Ford told a New England

Seen during their prime in the 1930s examining a Ford V-8 engine, Henry Ford, right, and his son Edsel each responded in his own way to the challenge of the Volkswagen and the need to design more advanced automobiles.

The elegant full-size mock-up of an advanced auto that John Tjaarda created at Briggs so delighted Edsel Ford that he arranged for it to be part of Ford and Lincoln traveling exhibitions at the end of 1933 and in 1934.

newspaperman, "I don't know Hitler personally, but at least Germany keeps its people at work."

Ford was an admirer, moreover, of Germans in general. "Of all the people in the world," said Emil Zoerlein, "as a race, he had the highest respect for the Germans. He mentioned that. He said, 'The Germans are industrious. They are good and hard workers. They are precise in their work. A lot of them are honest. You can trust them.'"

The feelings were mutual. In mid-1938 the Grand Cross of the Supreme Order of the German Eagle was conferred upon Ford in his office by German Consuls Fritz Hailer and Karl Kapp on behalf of its creator and grantor, Adolf Hitler. The industrialist was photographed "wearing the wide sash of the order, standing at attention as Kapp attached a cross and star to the cloth." It was the highest decoration that Germany could then award to a foreigner, the fourth of its kind ever granted and the first presented to an American.

Although the photo of the presentation appeared in several newspapers, it might have remained a low-key expression of Hitler's admiration for Ford, which he had already mentioned in *Mein Kampf*. "Every year makes [the Jews] more and more the controlling masters of the producers in a nation of one hundred and twenty millions," Hitler wrote during his Landsberg imprisonment; "only a single great man, Ford, to their fury, still maintains full independence."

But the 1938 honor to Henry Ford from the man who had already annexed Austria and was menacing Czechoslovakia was widely publicized. "The citation accompanying the medal (offered 'in recognition of [Ford's] pioneering in making motor cars available for the masses') was read by Kapp at Ford's birthday dinner, attended by 1,500 prominent Detroiters. Hitler's personal congratulations were simultaneously extended to Ford."

This was not the first time that Germany's leader had made his feelings known to Ford personally. Said Hitler in 1933 to the second grandson of Kaiser Wilhelm II, Prince Louis Ferdinand, "You can tell Herr Ford that I am a great admirer of his." The prince was about to depart for the New World, where he spent two and a half years as a Ford employee, working in Argentina as a salesman and at the Rouge plant as a production trainee. After an earlier visit to Dearborn, the German prince had asked Ford for the opportunity to work for his motor company.

Some at Ford had nursed hopes that Louis Ferdinand's closeness to Ford might ultimately yield benefits to Ford's German company, which was languishing in sixth place in that nation's car production. In 1940 the motor magnate expressed his solidarity with the prince by agreeing to be the godfather of his second son.

These gestures had negative repercussions in America for Ford, who was rumored to have paid the hefty sum of $300,000 to Louis Ferdinand. "Ford officials admitted that the company had been solicited by the Nazis" — a reference to an approach made in 1924 — "but they emphatically denied that any contributions had been made. A company spokesman also declared that the use of Ford's name on Nazi propaganda was unauthorized and that Louis Ferdinand received only regular wages during his employment by the company."

THESE CONTROVERSIES, SHRUGGED OFF by the obdurate Ford, were a source of mortification to a man whose gentility, thoughtfulness, and elegance of thought and expression were legendary in the industry — Edsel Ford, the only son of Henry and Clara Ford and the president of the family firm. Just before car production was suspended in 1942, Edsel qui-

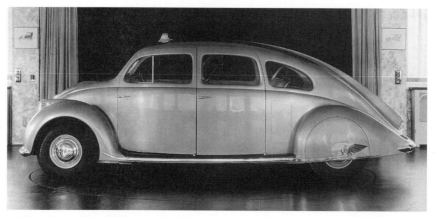

With hints of his earlier Sterkenburg creations, John Tjaarda's mock-up for Briggs was intended to have a rear-mounted V-8 engine. Visitors to Ford's exhibitions favored its style but were ambivalent about its rear-mounted engine.

etly approved a special marketing and advertising effort that was intended to counterbalance the antagonism to Ford products in the marketplace that his father's views were generating.

Edsel's interest in elegant car styling and advanced technology had found a kindred spirit in Dutch-born engineer and innovator John Tjaarda. Soon after joining the Briggs Manufacturing Company in 1932, Tjaarda was able to show Edsel Ford preliminary sketches and a structural model of a new integrally constructed car, one which was suitable for engine placement at either front or rear. There's no doubt which location was favored by John Tjaarda.

A full-size, fully detailed mockup of a rear-engined version of Tjaarda's Briggs design was produced. It so pleased Edsel that he persuaded his father to include it in a Ford Exhibition of Progress which opened in New York on 9 December 1933 after a preview in Dearborn. So popular was the elegant, sleek Tjaarda-designed dream car that it was added to the exhibits in Ford's rotunda at the June 1934 opening of the Chicago Century of Progress World's Fair.

Opinion sampling of visitors to these shows indicated that some 80 percent favored the Briggs car's high, wide tube-framed seats and streamlined shape, but only half favored an engine in the rear. Overall, interest in the car was strong enough to warrant the construction of a running rear-engined car to join the two front-engined prototypes Briggs had already built to try out Tjaarda's body engineering.

While the Briggs prototypes with engines at both front and back were undergoing tests — all generally successful — Ford's cost analysts were trying to figure where such a car might fit into the Dearborn line. It was too costly, they

Pictured at Briggs with his running rear-engined prototype, John Tjaarda had come close to interesting Ford in the production of the radically different type of car he so ardently espoused. Surprisingly, Henry Ford would follow his lead.

knew, to be a Ford, but it seemed to hold promise for the medium-price range, from seven hundred to fifteen hundred dollars, where Ford had no entries in 1933. There it could be a low-priced adjunct to Ford's costly and money-losing V-12 Lincolns. To sell at such prices, however, tooling up to produce a completely new rear-engine drivetrain was out of the question.

"Briggs thought the rear-engined job would go," recalled Eugene T. "Bob" Gregorie, in charge of Ford's styling at that time. "But Mr. Ford was very adamant about throwing that idea out the window. The tooling for the car was held up for some time" while debate raged over the Briggs car's engineering. Gregorie: "John had done a good front for a rear-engined car. But Mr. Ford had me go over to Briggs and change the front end from the windshield forward. He wanted something pointy that simulated something more conventional. I did that one morning at Briggs." With a soft pencil Bob Gregorie sketched the new nose, with its cooling grille, on the back of a blueprint.

That decisively ended the rear-engined dream at Ford — for the moment. The respect shown Tjaarda's design by Gregorie resulted in a good-looking albeit front-engined car, powered by a new side-valve V-12 engine, making use of many parts already being produced by Ford. It entered production in June 1935.

That November Ford sales manager William C. Cowling unveiled it as the Lincoln Zephyr, rightly hailing the launch of "a sensational, completely new motor car." The Zephyr was priced right, at $1,275 as a two-door and $1,320 with four doors, to compete with Packard's 120 and GM's LaSalle, Cadillac's cheaper cousin. Ford sold 17,715 in the 1936 model year and reached a prewar sales peak of 28,333 1937-model Zephyrs.

Mounted inboard at the rear of John Tjaarda's running Briggs prototype, in accord with his design principles, its engine was made substantially of aluminum. The transmission had semiautomatic operation.

A view inside the Briggs rear-engined prototype shows both the position of the V-8 engine and Tjaarda's elegant engineering of its unit body-frame that led to the very sucessful design of the 1936 Lincoln Zephyr.

SO NEAR . . . AND YET SO FAR for a rear-engined Ford. As Bob Gregorie recalled, "There was considerable conjecture on the part of the auto companies concerning rear-engined cars at that time. We bought some cars, Tatras for example. It was mostly individuals, some people at the Rouge plant, who took an interest in these ideas. As department heads we could keep our fingers in the water."

Wedded though he was by the physical demands of his Rouge factory to a rigid set of design formulae for the production cars that made his fortune, Henry Ford could not resist experimenting with new and exotic engineering solutions in the many fields that caught his interest. Ultimately he seemed to do so simply because he could, drawing on the skill and resourcefulness of a hand-picked team of engineers and designers whom he kept well out of the way of the accountants and production experts who disparaged what they saw as Henry's wanton dissipation of the Ford corporate resources.

Ford had a particular way of working on his advanced projects, as recalled by colleague Charles Sorensen, who began his auto industry career as a talented maker of wooden patterns for castings:

> It was apparent that Ford never quite understood what a design looked like until it was put into a three-dimensional pattern. I also discovered that he was not a draftsman and couldn't make a sketch that was any too clear. Now he found that when he explained to me what he wanted he could get some of his ideas developed and worked out in the plant. I began making sketches of his ideas and final drawings for some of their details. Then I went to the pattern shop to get some wooden form or model under way so that Mr. Ford could see what his idea would look like. Mr. Ford would give this a final look to determine whether there should be changes or corrections in the design.

From engines to transmissions and chassis, this method of working with skilled craftsmen to realize his ideas in wooden model form before committing them to metal characterized Ford's life-long exploration of new engineering ideas in many fields. The experience of one of Ford's engineers was not atypical. "The assignments which Mr. Ford gave me," recalled Albert Roberts, "were of a wide variety:"

> They included work on clocks, sawmills, steam engines, plate glass grinders, battery grid castings, tomato juice plant conveyors, Johansen gauge blocks, liquid air apparatus, rear engine cars, a V-8 engine, a six-cylinder engine of two-inch bore and six-inch stroke, tractor wheels, a number of planetary transmissions, etcetera. He had other men also doing engineering jobs directly for him, but we were entirely independent of each other. One of my projects was a solar motor constructed of bimetal. It turned but ever so slowly.

Cars were on the experimental agenda too and, as the engineer said, some of them were rear-engined. The world only found out about them when Henry filed in his own name to obtain patent coverage. And one of the first such patents to be disclosed was one of the most bizarre: a car with a rear-mounted engine that powered the front wheels! This 1934 disclosure also suggested steering by all four wheels to achieve a tight turning circle.

In a 1935 patent Henry Ford was credited with positioning a rear-mounted V-8 engine transversely in the chassis, in line with its transmission, placed "outboard" behind the rear-wheel centerline. A refinement of this layout was patented in Ford's name at the end of 1936, an event that inspired the headline "MOTOR MAY GO TO REAR" in the *New York Times* of Sunday, 3 January 1937. Whatever Henry Ford did, or seemed likely to do, could still inspire thirty column-inches of fraught speculation.

According to Ford's chief engineer Lawrence Sheldrick, there was metal behind these paper patents. He was involved with a prototype dubbed the 92-A, powered by a rear-mounted sixty-horsepower V-8 engine, intended to be a smaller Ford. Built around the end of 1937, the experiment, Sheldrick said, "didn't go very far and it certainly wasn't successful. I couldn't mention any one specific problem with it; it was just so full of radical experiments, it was similar to the Tucker car in some respects. It would have taken [Ford] years to work it out and make a successful commercial thing out of it."

Nevertheless, ideas for rear-engine cars were richly fermenting in Detroit during the 1930s. "At that time there was a lot of talk of rear-engine drives on both the competitive sides, and everybody was talking about it," Emil Zoerlein recalled. And now in the last years of the decade there was a new factor as well, one that everybody was indeed talking about, Zoerlein added: "It was started over in Germany on the Volkswagen. We were working on a chassis which would simulate this German car, the Volkswagen. The suspension we had was similar to that of the latter.

"Emery Nador was working on one rear-engine drive," Zoerlein said, "and Roberts was working on another. These were Henry Ford's private ideas." With his hand-picked engineers, Ford was reaching his own independent conclusions about the way the problems of the rear-engined car had been solved by the politically naïve German engineer who had visited him three years earlier. Ford hadn't warmed to the proposition that he become the North American assembler of Porsche's people's car. But now that Porsche's auto was in the public domain and forecast by many to do great things, even to "out-Ford Ford," Henry Ford was stimulated to take a closer look by creating a smaller car of his own.

Albert Roberts related the way one rear-engined project came about:

> In 1940 Mr. Ford took me to the Bagley Shop which had been moved into Green-field Village. He said, "You can make this your headquarters for awhile. This is where I made my first car and here I will make my last one. Make it little and simple. Put a little four-cylinder engine in the rear, use a planetary transmission and control it by pedals."
>
> With one young man, Stanley Groth, to help me, we built a chassis right in that little shop. We had the parts made in scattered shops so that no one could find out much about the car. It was unconventional from one end to the other. The rear axle was of the De Dion type, and the engine was bolted to the center portion. The engine stuck out back of the axle with no support on the rear end. It could be removed and replaced in a few minutes by removing six bolts. The throttle control was pneumatic.
>
> There were no frame side rails, these being replaced by a tubular backbone in the center. The steering gear was a simple screw and nut. The springs were transverse and mounted high so as to reduce body roll on curves. The planetary transmission was a part of the rear axle assembly. The spare wheel and tire were mounted in front to serve as a pneumatic bumper.

"We completed the chassis," said Roberts, "mounted a seat on it, and found that it operated quite well. Mr. Ford had me drive him around in it on the polished hardwood floor of the big Engineering Laboratory. From the gasoline economy standpoint, it was marvelous — 51 miles per gallon." Even with the addition of a body the Roberts prototype would have been a highly economical small auto, an America people's car that was just what the

One of several rear-engined prototypes built to satisfy Henry Ford's curiosity about the design direction taken by Porsche's Volkswagen, this one looks like a breadboard layout for the car built for Ford in 1940 by Albert Roberts.

doctor would have ordered for the gas rationing to come in the war years ahead for America.

Thoughts of producing such a car extended beyond Henry Ford's private projects, according to Lawrence Sheldrick. "He had been talking about smaller cars since 1935. However, they were always wrapped up in a package with these radical ideas that could never materialise." That was, of course, an engineer's view from the American perspective; Porsche's package had been every bit as radical but was able to be gift-wrapped in a Europe that was more accustomed to, and positively inclined toward, unorthodox engineering solutions.

Another and more daunting obstacle blocked the introduction of a smaller Ford, Sheldrick added: "We were always confronted with the same thing — that every time we would get up to the point of talking seriously about a small car, the matter of the used-car market would come up." Would such a car, available new at the price of a used Ford, divert customers away from the latter and thus slow the sales of larger new cars? The risk seemed too great to warrant such an experiment.

IN THE MEANTIME HENRY FORD'S gallant band of independent engineers had not been idle. Their experiments with light rear-engined cars in 1939 and 1940, inspired by the Volkswagen, were married in a stunningly

By the end of 1940 designers working under Henry Ford's direction had prepared this mock-up of a full-sized sedan to have a tubular steel frame, plastic body, and a transverse V-8 engine mounted low in the chassis and just ahead of the rear wheels. It was a revolutionary automotive concept.

innovative way with another new technology that Henry was developing: the plastic-bodied car. Robert Boyer led the creation at Ford of a plastic sheet made from agricultural products such as soybeans, wheat, hemp, flax, and ramie. The Boyer team fabricated panels from this plastic that were suitable for use as auto body skins.

"In 1940 Boyer installed a plastic trunk lid on one of Ford's personal cars," according to one account. "The industrialist delighted in walloping the lid with an ax for the benefit of sceptics who questioned its dent-resistance; then he would invite them to swing the ax on their own cars." At a dramatic demonstration to the press in November of 1940 Ford made the startling forecast that his company would be producing plastic-bodied cars within one to three years. Back at the research laboratory, in fact, Ford was preparing two prototypes with plastic bodies — one of them exotically rear-engined.

In April 1941 Ford revealed one of these prototypes, a front-engined model with a complete plastic body. Recalled one engineer a decade later:

> We designed a whole car which looked like the present-day cars with straight lines down the sides so we didn't have a lot of curves in it. They made molds and made the whole car. It had a welded, tubular [steel] frame because this type of frame is strong, but it cost too much to make. Nowadays, since they have [automatic] welders, it wouldn't cost so much. Then, it had to be all welded by hand.

Built to suit Henry Ford's radical rear-engined concept was a 4.2-liter engine composed of two adjoining V-4s, between which a semiautomatic transmission powered the differential and thence the rear wheels. The cooling radiator would have been rear-mounted.

This plastic-bodied car used conventional Ford power train and suspension parts which were carried by an internal structure of steel tubes that also supported the body panels. Its disclosure "occurred at a time when Americans were just becoming aware of plastics. The new car generated great publicity and stirred the imagination of editorial writers as had few other Ford-related events for some years. Henry Ford was heavily praised for his vision and achievement in building a 'plastic' car. The unveiling of the vehicle was one of the last occasions on which concerted praise would be heaped upon him by the nation's press."

Their praise would have been all the louder if they could have seen the car that Ford actually wanted to build using this new technology: a full-sized plastic-bodied auto powered by a radical rear-mounted V-8 engine.

By November 1940, when Henry was challenging reporters to clout his car's plastic trunk lid with an ax, the concept engineering and styling of the proposed new rear-engined Ford had been completed. In typical Henry Ford style its frame, chassis, and engine were mocked up in wood and steel for close study. It was planned as a full-sized automobile on a 113-inch wheelbase with a 56-inch track. At that time, for the 1941 model year, the standard Ford had just stretched its wheelbase from 112 to 114 inches.

The frame of Ford's proposed car was tubular steel, with two three-inch tubes as longerons running from front to rear and several similarly sized crossmembers. Welded above this was a cage of one-and-a-half-inch steel tubes rising up along the main body pillars and intersecting above the rear seat. Calculated to weigh 260.46 pounds in all, the structure added up to a tubular-steel space frame that would have been stiffened further by its steel floor panels.

Tucked behind the rear seat, yet forward of the rear axle shafts, was one of the most unusual V-8 engines ever made. Its ninety-degree vee and its side-mounted valves were ordinary enough by Ford standards. But its eight cylinders were split into two separate V-4s on a common crankshaft, leaving space at the middle for an extremely compact transaxle and its drive to the differential gears at the rear of the engine.

Displacing 4.2 liters, the eight was 12 percent larger than the engines then being used in Fords and could easily have developed around one hundred horsepower. For the ultimate in lightness its main housings were all cast in aluminum. A single central downdraft carburetor served both of the closely conjoined V-4s. The design left open the location of the coolant radiator; styling models showed grilles at the front that were more tokens for visual effect than for engine cooling.

Here was a rear-engine layout that was ideal for a big car. Instead of an outboard placing with its much-discussed weight-distribution disadvantages, the V-8 was forward of the wheels and remarkably low to the ground. Each rear wheel was suspended by a swing axle, with a single universal joint at the differential, and braced by a trailing arm pivoted near the center of the frame. Henry's favored transverse leaf provided the springing at the rear and also at the front, where a V-shaped tubular solid axle trailed from a central frame pivot.

For this radical chassis Bob Gregorie's designers readied a full-size clay model of a body that was equally unorthodox by 1940 standards. Fully flush-sided with enclosed rear wheels, its wide, low forms anticipated those of the "step-down" Hudson introduced in 1948. Large glass area was a feature of the plastic-skinned body. Foreshadowing shapes of a decade in the future, a smoothly rounded nose did away with the prow that was then de rigueur — although this reappeared hesitantly on a scale-model styling study of February 1941.

This was a completely new concept, radical in every respect. Lawrence Sheldrick's insight regarding the earlier 92-A would surely have applied here as well, that it would take Ford years to work out the design and production to make it commercially successful. It was, however, a quite astonishing achievement for a man of seventy-seven who had already suffered one stroke in 1938; he would have another in 1941. Ford simply lacked the years he needed.

"The outbreak of World War II and the suspension of automobile production forced Ford to abandon his efforts to mass produce plastic car bodies," not to mention creating a completely new kind of rear-engined Ford. "Until 1943, however, he maintained that he would build them as soon as the war was over." Coincidentally, that year saw the death in May of the man of taste and discretion who had granted such generous support to John Tjaarda's advanced design ideas, Edsel Ford, who succumbed to cancer.

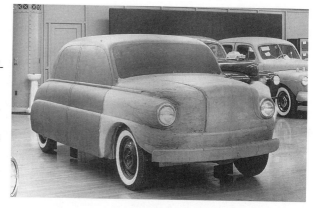

Strikingly clean lines were achieved on the full-size models developed in the Ford styling studios to suit Henry's rear-engined concept. Henry Ford had been encouraged by his son Edsel to pursue this radical new design direction.

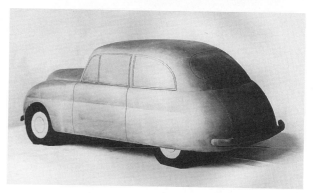

Thanks to its ingenious engine placement, the styling model produced in February 1941 did not make it obvious that this proposed plastic-bodied Ford had its engine in the rear. Not until 1949 would Ford introduce a car with a full enveloped body.

In fact, the outbreak of war did not deter Henry Ford from continuing to pursue this radical design. Dead set against the production of Jeeps, bombers, and aircraft engines that was commencing in his factories, Ford the pacifist saw this advanced car project as a way of distracting his executives from war work.

"Among his projects," recalled Charles Sorensen, was "a new lightweight car. He kept a crew doing special work for him. The basic idea was a tubular body and framework, light but strong where strength was needed. He showed it to me, hoping that he could divert me from the war program; and he hoped to divert Edsel the same way. So long as he was actively engaged on this project, it was a godsend to me, because it diverted Mr. Ford too." Instead of conflicting with the Ford Motor Company's dedication to war work, the radical car actually facilitated it.

THERE IS EVERY REASON TO SUPPOSE that before Henry Ford died in April of 1947 he finally had a look at the hardware, in the metal, of the Volkswagen whose introduction in 1939 had so stimulated his creativity and that of his small team of willing engineers. Before that, however, he

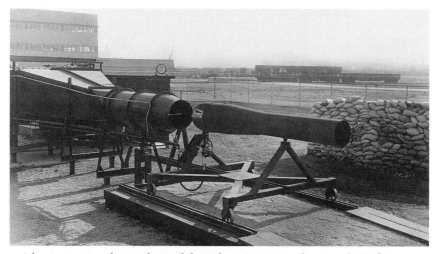

After inspecting the wreckage of the pulse-jet engines of captured V-1 flying bombs, Ford's engineers designed and produced this improved version. The noisy but effective jet is seen on static test in Dearborn.

certainly saw and handled the parts of an equally radical power unit that had been mounted to a quite different vehicle at the Fallersleben factory: the Argus pulse-jet engine that powered the V-1 robot bomb.

On 11 July 1944 word reached Col. D. J. Keirn of the U.S. Air Force at Wright-Patterson Field that a transport plane in Britain was being laden with parts of V-1s that had survived their crash-landings. Keirn, acting chief of the renowned air force research establishment at Dayton, Ohio, realized that the V-1 could be the basis of a weapon that America could use against its enemies in both theaters of war. The colonel "telephoned the Ford Motor Company, and asked if Ford would be interested in building robot bombs. Company officials replied they would not be interested in building the whole bomb but they would be interested in building a jet propulsion engine."

Ford engineers were already at Dayton on the evening of 13 July when the transport arrived from England with its cargo of V-1 components. They had been given the green light by Henry Ford II to work with the Air Force to replicate and indeed improve the V-1's crude but effective pulse-jet engine. From a document in the Ford archives:

> The German propulsion engine parts — all badly mutilated by their 400 mile an hour contact with the earth — were studied closely, their metals analyzed. Drawings were made on the spot and rushed to the Rouge plant in Dearborn. Strictest secrecy was observed. Trusted production men worked day and night, in widely scattered parts of the plant, to complete the hundreds of precision parts needed for the powerful, revolutionary propulsion unit. But the impossible was achieved; three weeks to the day after the initial telephone call from Colonel Keirn, the first Ford intermittent jet propulsion engine was successfully operated at the Rouge plant.

In 1946 Ford's design and proving ground engineers were able to test and evaluate a Type 82 Kübelwagen, the wartime version of the Beetle. Its design characteristics were carefully assessed and noted.

Asked initially to tool up to reach an eventual production rate of three thousand engines a month, Ford put its production experts to work on the engine's details. They cut manufacturing time by substituting die castings for forgings in the grid that held its 256 reed valves. Making the reeds of stainless instead of spring steel improved reliability and increased the jet's thrust by 12 percent. Better fuel nozzles enhanced high-altitude performance. Meanwhile the Republic Aviation Corporation on Long Island was busy with the engineering of the airframe; its production would later be subcontracted to Jeep maker Willys-Overland in an ironic echo of V-1 production by Kübel maker KdF-Werke.

Named the JB-2 by the Air Force, the Yankee doodlebug was first flight-tested on 12 October 1944. By June 1945 successful launches had been achieved in 78 percent of 164 attempts. Calling its version the "Loon," the navy launched several from surfaced submarines. Although controversy was rife over the value and nature of a possible field role for the Ford-powered JB-2, forward production orders exceeded ten thousand. But the end of the war ended the project as well in September 1945; by then some 1,385 of this predecessor of the cruise missile had been delivered to the War Department.

Not long thereafter Ford received its first sample of another product of the KdF-Werke at Fallersleben: Porsche's Type 82 Kübelwagen. With its treaded tires and simple camouflage paint this was a run-of-the-mill Kübel from the European theater. No one was interested in asking Ford to produce more like it; rather this was a chance for Ford's designers to see for themselves the workings of the car that was engineered to trounce them in peace rather than in war.

During an exhaustive process of dismantling and weighing the components of their Kübel, the Ford engineers exposed its rear hub reduction gears and determined that the weight of the chassis alone was 871 pounds. Every component of the car was dismantled and weighed.

Following their time-honored procedures the Ford technicians began a dissection and depiction of the Type 82 on 25 March 1946. As the vehicle was dismantled, photos were taken that showed its remaining weight at each stage of the process. Complete it scaled 1,578 pounds. Chassis alone was 871 pounds and the body shell weighed 337 pounds. Engine weight was 170 pounds dry and the platform frame scaled 176 pounds. Each rugged steel wheel was remarkably heavy: 71.6 pounds.

By early April of 1946 the engineers were well into the innards of Porsche's design. The components of the 55-pound transaxle were laid out for the flash camera, as were the brakes, steering gear, suspension components, and even the jack (6.4 pounds). In mid-May the disassembly of the engine was complete and its parts were laid out for photography. At 14 pounds, each cast-iron cylinder weighed almost as much as the 14.8-pound aluminum cylinder head.

Ford's next close look at Volkswagen entrails came in the winter of 1948, when the company made a detailed examination of a complete Beetle engine fresh from the British-controlled Wolfsburg factory. Through December and January it was photographed in detail by Ford's technical analysts. Such an engine could easily have arrived in Dearborn as a result of the friendly working relationship that the VW plant's British supervisors enjoyed with their counterparts at Ford's factory in Cologne, Germany.

YEARS EARLIER, THE PATTERN of Ford operations in Europe had been set when the Ford interests in Britain, largely locally owned, had been given responsibility for Ford's business activities in Europe. This would change, but in the years after the war the direct supervision of Ford's Cologne factory was from its company at Dagenham in Britain.

During the war, of course, Herr Hitler was in command at Cologne and also at the Ford plants in France, Belgium, and Holland. The latter trio of factories operated in triangular fashion to produce Ford trucks for the Wehrmacht during the war; trials and brief imprisonment for collaboration were the reward for managers at Antwerp and Amsterdam.

At Cologne in Germany, where a Ford plant had been operating with 40 percent British capital from 1931 until the war, production for the Wehrmacht concentrated on much-needed trucks. Chiefly three-ton trucks powered by various Ford V-8s, these were joined in 1942 by a half-track version for the muddy Russian front, the so-called *Maultier* or "mule." With a two-ton capacity, some fifteen thousand Maultiers were produced by Ford.

Considering the Wehrmacht's desperate need for wheeled transport on all fronts, Cologne's wartime truck production was surprisingly modest. Output averaged about fifteen thousand trucks each year of the conflict. But on 2 March 1945, softening up Cologne for their advance, the Allies sent some fourteen hundred bombers over the city. Four days later their troops marched in. Truck production was terminated. Although its ancillary facilities were badly damaged and its sources of supply cut off, the Ford factory itself in the Cologne suburb of Niehl was miraculously intact.

Two Ford emissaries, in the wake of the advancing armies, reached Cologne in April. They found that "everything was down and smoking" and concluded at first "that the plant was badly destroyed." Closer examination, however, showed that the plant itself was healthy but exposed to damage "being done by rain and weather, because nearly all of the windows in both roof and sides were shattered."

Arriving from Dagenham on 4 May with a small British Ford cadre, the resourceful Charles Thacker succeeded in restoring the plant's truck production an astonishing four days later. By the end of 1945 Niehl, the authorized truck producer in the British zone of occupation, had built 2,443 of the total German truck output of 5,512 units.

At year's end Thacker left to sort out Ford Belgium and was succeeded at Cologne by more emissaries from Dagenham: administrator John Lonsdale and manufacturing man George MacDonald. Although now based at Dagenham, these were executives who had begun their Ford careers at the company's previous assembly plant at Trafford Park, Manchester. They were members of a "Manchester mafia" which would strongly influence the company's policy in both Britain and Germany after the war.

Lonsdale was Ford's representative at the first meeting of the German vehicle manufacturers' association, the former RDA, reestablished by Charles Radclyffe as the VDA to help bring some order into the affairs of the industry and to set up self-regulating allocations of steel to the vehicle makers. Surrounded by Germans at the VDA gathering at the offices of Hanomag in Hannover, Lonsdale was pleased to find a fellow Brit among them:

Ivan Hirst, representing the VW works. They exchanged phone numbers and agreed to keep in touch.

"We spoke often on the phone after that," Hirst recalled. "We had an informal friendship, helping each other sort out supply problems." One such problem proved intractable, however. Hirst and an REME recovery unit, wielding a massive Ward-LaFrance truck, had successfully helped Hanomag retrieve the dies for its truck cabs from the tangled wreckage of the Russian-held Ambi-Budd plant in Berlin. Budd also held dies for the Ford car bodies. Could Hirst help with their release? Lonsdale asked.

Hirst agreed to try. The techniques that had been successful at Hanomag were applied a second time. Steel scrap was offered in exchange for the dies. Negotiations were generously lubricated with free-flowing schnapps. The REME team marshaled its rolling stock as before to haul out the dies — only to be confronted by armed guards. A Russian officer pointed angrily to the stenciled designation still visible on some of the rusty dies: "V-8." Here was another example of Western treachery: trying to reclaim under the guise of auto tools the parts of a highly advanced vengeance weapon! Hirst shook his head ruefully: "That was the end of any deals with the Russians."

THIS RECOVERY MISSION WAS IN PROGRESS but had not yet been aborted on New Year's Eve of 1946 when John Portas of the Mechanical Engineering Branch reported to Sir Cecil Weir, president of the CCG's Economic Sub-Commission, on the status of Ford's German plant. He said that through November Ford had produced 4,451 three-ton trucks in 1946. After wartime recapitalization, said Portas, shareholdings in the plant stood at Ford U.S. 52.0 percent, Ford U.K. 6.25 percent, chemical giant I.G. Farben 5.6 percent, and other German shareholders 36.15 percent.

Portas's note had been prompted by a query from Sir Cecil in Berlin that followed his receipt of a vague inquiry about the state of the German factory from the managing director of Ford in Britain, Sir Patrick Hennessy. Writing on 17 December, Sir Patrick reminded Weir of their wartime meetings on military production issues "during Lord Beaverbrook's hectic period of office" and his contacts with Weir's predecessor in Berlin, Sir Percy Mills.

Sir Patrick's letter had the fingerprints of an attempt, inspired by new Ford management in Dearborn, to get closer to those of his fellow Britons who would influence the future of Ford in Cologne and elsewhere in Germany. To Weir he expressed a desire "to meet you and discuss German industrial conditions — particularly as they may relate in the future to the Ford Factory in Cologne." Hennessy's hope that they might meet soon in Britain was disabused by Weir's 21 December reply: "There is so much to do here at the present time that my visits to Britain are few and far between."

Hennessy met instead early in 1947 with W. Leonard Tregoning, who had taken over as chief of the CCG's Industry Division at the first of the year. Tregoning, a Cornishman with industrial experience, won the accolade "good chap" from Ivan Hirst. "As regards the situation at the Ford Works at Köln," Tregoning wrote to Hennessy on 10 January, after being updated by Portas's report, "it seems that this plant will be fully utilised within the limits of supplies available. I expect to be in London in February and would be very pleased to meet you for a general talk."

The increasingly friendly relations between British Ford personnel and the CCG in Germany were further enhanced by a visit to Dagenham early in 1947 by Ivan Hirst. Word had reached Ford from Lonsdale and MacGregor in Cologne about the qualities of this CCG officer with whom they were having such productive contacts — in spite of the aborted recovery of the dies for the Ford V-8. Hirst was received at the highest level of the British Ford organization.

Ford suffered no shortage of ennobled and knighted senior officials in these years. Lord Perry, founder of the British company, was retiring and being replaced by Lord Airedale. Sir Rowland Smith was his deputy, anointed for future chairmanship. Sir Stanford Cooper was vice chairman, with special legal and financial responsibilities. All these ranked above managing director Sir Patrick Hennessy, the operating executive to whom Ford's American management looked as their main hope for the future of their British company.

Hirst met and talked with Cooper, whom he particularly liked. And his conversation with Sir Rowland Smith took a dramatic turn: Hirst was offered the post of assistant to managing director Hennessy. This was no minor position. Ford policy in Britain, set out in a report a year later, was to support Sir Patrick "by two or even possibly three executive assistants who have the potential qualifications for Assistant Managing Director, and ultimately Managing Director when Sir Patrick Hennessy moves up to the chief executive post of Board Chairman."

"I turned it down," Ivan Hirst related. "I wanted to see the Volkswagen job through." There were other factors as well, he acknowledged. The chemistry was "not very good" when engineer Hirst met accountant Hennessy on whom, Hirst felt, "I was being imposed by Cooper and Lonsdale." Also life in Germany promised to improve with the imminent arrival there of Marjorie, his wife since 1940.

Nevertheless Ivan Hirst's decision was impressive, and even more so in light of the situation at Wolfsburg in the first half of 1947, when the British were attempting to reduce their direct control and grant more autonomy to the German management. Technically Hirst was no longer based there then — "but I never packed up my kit," he recalled. The great works and its remarkable product continued to weave their compelling fascination.

WHILE AMERICA WAS STILL AT WAR the death of Henry's son Edsel had brought to the fore Edsel's eldest son. At the age of twenty-seven, just out of the navy, Henry Ford II became an executive vice president of the Ford Motor Company late in 1944. His grandfather's health declined in the spring of 1945 and on 20 September, backed by his mother Eleanor, Edsel's widow, young Henry was named president of Ford. He had been twenty-eight for just three days. A new generation was taking charge in Dearborn — and not a minute too soon.

Bold and brave dreams though they were, Henry Ford's plastic-bodied rear-engined cars were not ready to meet the demands of the postwar market. Ford was so badly managed that some departments estimated the value of their incoming invoices by weighing them. Its products were more in tune with the 1920s than the 1940s, its engineering cupboards were bare of viable new models, and the company was losing money and hemorrhaging cash at a fatal rate. Young Henry had his hands full.

In the last months of the war Henry II turned frequently for counsel to Ernest R. Breech, president of Bendix Aviation Corporation, a division of General Motors that was an important supplier of aircraft components. Breech was a GM high-flyer with an excellent track record who impressed young Henry with his no-nonsense approach to business. Breech recalled the beginning of their relationship:

> I was attracted to Ford Motor Company by Henry Ford II when he was an important Bendix customer. When he first invited me to join Ford, I turned him down as graciously as I could, but I did agree to give him advice and help him out as much as was possible. While doing this I became more and more involved. One day, I asked to see the company's books and, well, that did it. The company was really in a mess. Not only did it need help, it had to have help or the Big Three would surely become the Surviving Two.

By mid-1946 Breech was on board at Ford as an executive vice president.

Henry II raided General Motors for another key employee. He needed a man of experience abroad to head the new Ford International Division that he established as one of the first acts of his presidency. Graeme K. Howard qualified, and then some. His more than twenty years of service with GM, beginning in 1920, were all overseas or based in New York with global responsibilities. By 1939 Howard had risen to a General Motors vice-presidency.

During World War II Howard was on General Eisenhower's staff at Supreme Headquarters Allied Forces in Europe before he was named to the economic division of America's occupation authority. There he argued against the decimation of Germany's industrial base that some were urging: "I advocated the restoration of German industry. I believed such restoration was necessary for peaceful purposes not only on behalf of the German people but, more importantly, for the benefit of Europe and for the relief of the American taxpayer."

Howard returned to New York and GM's Overseas Operations Division in January 1945. In September 1946 he ordered a newly built Beetle for GM through the U.S. military occupation channels with which he was very well acquainted. A year later Graeme Howard was taking up the huge challenge of bringing order to Ford's chaotic overseas organization. He began as an advisor to Ford and on 15 April 1948 was named a vice president of the company and director of its International Division.

"Lincolnesque in stature, flamboyant in manner and aggressively self-assertive in presenting his ideas and opinions, he made a dynamic addition to the Dearborn family," wrote historians Nevins and Hill of Howard — "perhaps a bit too dynamic. He had brains, energy and fearlessness, with plenty of brashness thrown in. His wealth of information on the motor industry abroad made him probably the best guide the company could then have found."

IN THE MEANTIME ANOTHER key change of personnel was under way at another auto company much in need of experienced and capable management: the Volkswagenwerk GmbH at Germany's Wolfsburg. This first became an issue in the latter part of 1946 when the Mil Gov decided to set up a *Vorstand* (management committee) for the works on the German model. In August 1946 it named to the post of general manager Dr. Hermann Münch, who had been the legally designated German custodian of the factory since February.

A lawyer by training, Dr. Münch had been discovered in Berlin by a branch of the Mil Gov and assigned to the VW works. Interested though Münch was in assisting VW, his lack of understanding of the motor industry soon showed its limitations. One of the lawyer's several endowments to the plant was a badly designed punched-card system for inventory control that "imposed a stranglehold on the place," Hirst said. Control was one thing but rigor mortis imposed by an unsuitable outsider was quite another.

Works administration worsened in the Arctic winter of 1946–47 and in the early months of 1947 when the Mil Gov's Industry Division sought to withdraw from active supervision of the factory in accord with a blanket ruling that none of its officials should have offices in a German factory. Volkswagen was soon recognized as a special case and Ivan Hirst was not obliged to decamp from Wolfsburg.

As Hirst recalled, however, the ruling "was a warning shot that reminded us that we weren't there forever. It was time for the German management to stand on their own two feet, so to speak." Hirst and Charles Radclyffe resolved to find a qualified German who, while serving as a deputy to Münch, would effectively take charge of the day-to-day running of the factory.

*Management changes at Volks-
wagen in 1946 involved Dr. Hermann Münch, who was named general manager of the works in
August of that year. Subsequently
his proven incompetence set the
British looking for a more capable
German manager.*

For nominees the Britons turned to one of the true survivors of the German motor industry, Wilhelm Vorwig, an engineer with the RDA — the motormakers' association which would become the VDA after the war — who had directed the official tests of Porsche's first three VW3 Volkswagen prototypes. In the last months of the war, at the direction of Albert Speer, Vorwig had relocated the RDA from Berlin to the small town of Zorge in the Harz Mountains north of Nordhausen, where the KdF Werke was supervising V-1 production.

From Zorge in June and the first week of July 1945 Vorwig and a colleague made a grueling round trip to assess the condition of those German motor companies that they could reach. Back at Zorge Vorwig was quizzed by various American and British investigative teams; the British took away the RDA's files in seven wooden crates. By August Wilhelm Vorwig had made contact with Charles Radclyffe's industry group in Minden. He assisted in setting up on 27 August the Production Board of the Vehicle Industry, PADA in its German acronym, the predecessor of the postwar VDA.

"I never saw a man who looked more in need of food than Vorwig when he first came," said John MacGregor, one of Radclyffe's team. A good-looking man in peacetime, Vorwig was nearer a semblance of his normal self in 1947 when Charles Radclyffe asked him to suggest some executives who had survived denazification and might thus be considered for a senior post at the VW works. Among those whom Vorwig put forward was his companion on his June–July 1945 travels in Germany and fellow resident in the Harz Mountains, Heinrich "Heinz" Nordhoff.

A former Opel executive, Heinrich "Heinz" Nordhoff was talent-spotted to be Volkswagen's general manager. In 1948 he played a key role in discussions that could have led to a merger of Volkswagen with Ford's existing German operations.

When they made that journey, Nordhoff had every expectation that he would soon be back at Opel's plant in Rüsselsheim, gainfully employed. Before the war he had been sent to Berlin by Opel to assist the company's main dealer there, Eduard Winter, with the sales of Opel vehicles being ordered by the army. Winter, not unreasonably, insisted that if the Wehrmacht was buying all these trucks from its offices in Berlin, they would only do so through the official channel of Opel's resident agent, Opel Winter. Subsequently Nordhoff managed the Opel truck factory in Berlin's Brandenburg sector.

His industry connections came to Eduard Winter's rescue when the Nazis discovered that he had a Jewish grandmother. "You'll be all right," Winter was told, "if you have a manufacturing company." He found one in Hamburg, a firm producing fuel-injection pumps for airplane engines. There Winter was contacted after the war by Nordhoff, who had found that the Americans, strict anti-Nazi interpreters, were unhappy about Nordhoff's wartime title of *Wehrwirtschaftsführer*, defense economy leader. With Opel in the American zone, he would not be welcome there after all.

When the search went out for someone to help manage the sprawling VW works Heinz Nordhoff was managing nothing more prepossessing than the service department of Eduard Winter's Hamburg garage business. There he had been talent-spotted by a Mil Gov officer named Kerkhof, in parallel with his nomination by Vorwig, and was introduced to Hirst at Wolfsburg. Nordhoff, who had been a vigorous opponent of both the car and the concept of a Volkswagen before the war, had deep doubts about the merits of the post. But he was heartened when Ivan Hirst recommended him for full general managership rather than as a deputy to Münch.

At a meeting in Minden, Charles Radclyffe assured Nordhoff that he would have complete authority in the works, albeit reporting to the Board of Control in the role of the customary German supervisory board. Radclyffe set out the terms in a contractual letter of 7 November 1947 which read in part:

> (1) This CCG Board of Control for the Volkswagenwerk group of companies offers you the appointment of General Manager for Volkswagenwerk G.m.b.H.

> (2) Terms of reference governing this appointment are that you will be responsible to the Board of Control for new car production and Army overhaul contracts and all that this entails — namely: — All Works Departments, including Vorwerk Branch, Supply Department, Personnel Department, Commercial Departments, Sales and Service including Export, and ancillaries.

> (3) You will work in the closest cooperation with the Resident Executive Officer of this Board, to whom all your difficulties should be referred as soon as they become evident.

> (4) You will also be responsible for Volkswagenwerk's relations with German governmental and economic authorities, manufacturer's associations and Trades Unions.

The letter also referred to the pro forma custodial role of Dr. Münch, to remuneration at a rate to which they would mutually agree, and to Radclyffe's desire that Nordhoff "assume the duties as soon as possible" if the offer were agreeable.

On the day it was drafted this letter was read to the Board of Control, at its eighteenth meeting, and its terms agreed by the board. Nordhoff's remuneration, the board agreed, would not exceed 4,000 marks per month; it was later set at that amount. On 25 November Messrs. Hirst, Neal, and Nordhoff met with Dr. Münch and broke the news that he was being relieved of the title and responsibilities of general manager, but was to carry on as custodian. His pay was established as 2,500 marks in December.

Heinz Nordhoff assumed his post at Wolfsburg on New Year's Day, Friday, 1948 at the age of forty-eight. Gradually and reluctantly Dr. Münch gathered that his services were redundant and he was relieved of custodial duty after the first quarter of the year. The Mil Gov economized in making its offer of 1,500 marks per month to his successor, Dr. Hermann Knott, who assumed the custodial role on 1 May 1948. Although engaged for a three-month probationary period, Dr. Knott would last out the next year and a half of British stewardship.

Nordhoff, never a fan of the Volkswagen, nevertheless grew to comprehend its peculiar virtues. He later told Gordon Wilkins that "when I assumed the responsibility of putting this wrecked factory into high-volume production, the car itself was still full of 'bugs.' It really was what you call an ugly duckling." To others he said, "This car had as many faults as a dog has fleas. But you don't kill a dog to get rid of its fleas. Once the fleas were gone, we found we had a pedigreed dog."

THUS TWO AUTO COMPANIES, one a great American firm fallen on hard times and the other a potentially great German firm with an uncertain future, girded themselves with new managers in whom they dared place their hopes. The two men were soon to meet, for the Americans decided to visit the Old World to assess the value of their holdings there. One of Graeme Howard's first tasks at Ford was the organization of a tour of Europe in February and March of 1948 for himself and Mr. and Mrs. Henry Ford II.

Under the command of Comdr. C. G. Illingworth, the party sailed from New York on the Cunard line's Queen Mary on Thursday, 5 February 1948. The great ship cast off her restraining lines at 6:26 in the morning. Discomfort levels on board were high, with a rough sea and, on Sunday and Monday, a heavy and confused swell. The Queen made the quieter waters of Southampton on the morning of 10 February after a crossing of exactly four days and nineteen hours.

A meticulously planned itinerary awaited the Fords and Graeme Howard. Reported the latter,

> As a standard order of procedure, the visit to each country included the following events:
>
> A press conference.
>
> A dealer meeting.
>
> A formal dinner with distinguished guests at which a speech was made.
>
> A meeting of the Board of Directors.
>
> A visit to the plant — with emphasis on personal meetings with the workers.
>
> Individual conferences with government, industrial and financial leaders.

The Fords completed the ritual at Ford in Britain and were briefed for the next leg of the trip before flying to Paris in chartered Pan American DC-3 *Clipper Line Yankee*, arriving on 18 February. Ford and his wife were ensconced at the Plaza Athenee; the rest of the party stayed at the George V, where they were joined on the twenty-third by British Ford executives Sir Stanford Cooper and Sir Rowland Smith.

At the George V a gala dinner in Ford's honor was organized for the evening of Tuesday the twenty-fourth by the head of Ford of France, Maurice Dollfuss. Then tooling up to launch a new model that had originally been designed in Dearborn as a potential postwar small Ford, Dollfuss was described by Graeme Howard as "a fine asset, one of our ablest executives in Europe, who has made great accomplishments under most difficult conditions. He has unusual courage, a fine mind, is absolutely financially honest."

He was also capable of organizing a slap-up repast. His guests in the gilded salon of the rococo hotel enjoyed Curry Consommè, Lobster American Style, Poularde de Bresse Rotie, cheese, and Bombe Batavia accompanied by vintage 1928 Heidsieck Monopole champagne in magnums and one of Bordeaux's grandest offerings, Chateau Haut-Brion of 1938.

Seated around the oval table at dinner to pay respects to the young Ford scion and his wife Anne was a remarkable cast of characters. The doyen of the French auto industry association, Baron Petiet, was present, as was racing driver Jean-Pierre Wimille, who was readying the prototype of a radical Ford-powered mid-engined passenger car. Industry pioneer Paul Panhard joined them. So did Jean-Albert Grègoire, the peripatetic and persuasive engineer who had interpreted Hitler's remarks for Louis Renault at the 1938 Berlin Show and whose AFG prototype would fuel the automotive ambitions of Denis Kendall in Britain and Larry Hartnett in Australia.

Renault's Pierre Lefaucheux, who had completed the work inspired by Louis Renault on a rear-engined popular car for France in the Beetle mould, dined with Ford. Present at table also was Jean-Pierre Peugeot, the two-faced leader of his family firm who obsequiously buttered up Ferdinand Porsche during the war and afterward led the effort to have the engineer detained as a war criminal. The next day the opportunist Peugeot would meet with Graeme Howard to discuss a possible future association between his company and Ford in France.

The meetings in Paris were followed by trips to Antwerp and then to Amsterdam to review the Ford operations. They traveled by car, changing cars at the borders to cope with the rigorous customs barriers still in force. Charles Thacker, the manager of Ford in Belgium, met them at the French border with three Lincolns. Fog kept the party from flying on from Amsterdam to Cologne on March second so they drove instead. Wrote a Ford historian:

> Ironically when the Ford party eventually arrived at the Ford plant in Cologne-Niehl in the afternoon of Tuesday March 2, there was no sign of the fog that had caused them to come by road; a warm spring sun shone brilliantly out of a clear blue sky as the Lincoln drove in through the gate. The journalists who had been waiting anxiously for their arrival swarmed forward, flash [bulbs] popping, to get their news photos and ask their questions. The schedule had slipped irretrievably and the workers who had been waiting for Henry Ford to drive the 10,000th postwar Ford truck off the production line shrugged their shoulders, gave up and went home.

On the next morning, 3 March, young Henry was driven from the farm where he spent the night to the Niehl factory, its windows now replaced, to complete his symbolic truck-driving task. His next appointment was a press conference downtown at the Excelsior Hotel to which, surprising his entourage, he traveled some six miles with Graeme Howard and his chief engineer in Cologne, Richard Bussien, in the shabby grey Type 11 Volkswagen that Bussien was using as his company runabout.

Assisted by his German chief engineer Richard Bussien, Henry Ford II steps out of Bussien's Beetle after a test-drive in Cologne on 3 March 1948. Although Ford was not impressed by the car, he did not dissent from an ambitious scheme that would have given Ford both a part interest in VW's production and global rights to its sales.

With Howard in the back seat and the burly Ford next to him, Bussien drove the first mile or two over the rutted road to Cologne, shattered as it was by the tracks of countless armored vehicles. Then they stopped and Ford took the wheel. Over the engine's roar and thumping tires Bussien heard Ford say, "Well, it's a car." Arriving at the Excelsior, Henry Ford II stepped out and uttered just one word to Bussien about his experience: "No." He was more diplomatic when asked about the Beetle by a press man. "I was agreeably surprised by its comfort and efficiency," Ford said, "But it won't do for America. There we want rooms on wheels . . . ."

But it *would* do for Germany and Europe, the Americans realized, and much better than anything they were able to produce in Cologne. Drawing on his Mil Gov connections, Graeme Howard had been busy in advance of their trip. A meeting was set up at the Excelsior with Col. Charles Radclyffe, under whose aegis Ford was operating in the British zone. The senior British officer who represented the power of the Mil Gov in the province, Brigadier Barraclough, was also in Cologne for the discussions, as were (as needed) Lord Airedale, Sir Rowland Smith, and Sir Stanford Cooper.

Radclyffe was primed to bring up the question of the disposition of the VW factory. "Radclyffe felt that it might be better if an established company took the reins at Volkswagen," Ivan Hirst recalled. "That solution also seemed to address one of the difficulties we had, which was finding suitable managers for the factory." Prompted or not by Charles Radclyffe, the Ford men present expressed interest in a possible investment in the VW works.

This news eased its way by back channels into the Mil Gov network, in a report to the Finance Division chief, Sir Eric Coates, on 15 April: "I hear unofficially that Mr. Henry Ford has ideas about buying the Volkswagen factory, with a view to concentrating truck production at Cologne and car production at the Volkswagen works. This proposal is most interesting, and I believe would receive a certain amount of support on the German side. I personally would be in favor of it, as I think that it would do much to ensure the maximum use of the Volkswagen factory at the earliest possible date, and such an arrangement would also probably facilitate material supplies" — one of the main problems of the British custodians, who often found themselves in the middle of arguments over allocations.

Two weeks later, a follow-up was sent to the German Section of the Foreign Office in London, "No official proposal has as yet been received, but Colonel Radclyffe of the late Mechanical Engineering Branch, who has the responsibility for the general supervision of the Volkswagenwerk, was informed of this proposal, and has subsequently been approached by Sir Stanford Cooper in the matter." The Commerce and Industry Group chief still took a positive view: "[Flint] Cahan and I would be in favor of a suitable arrangement which would undoubtedly receive support on the American side."

A WARM REGARD AMONG THE BRITISH, then, and every promise, they thought, of a welcome for such a role for Ford among the American occupiers and the Germans themselves. Ford was dead keen as well. With Henry Ford II's concurrence Graeme Howard wrote a confidential forty-seven-page report on their European trip. He completed it on 5 April and the report was given limited distribution by Henry on the twelfth. One of its instructions to a key executive was "to study and recommend steps which could lead to our acquiring a controlling interest in the Volkswagon [sic] Werke A.G."

Howard set out at some length the nature of the Ford interest in the company and its product, concerning which he and Henry had been well informed:

> The Volkswagon Werke A.G. was conceived by the Nazi Government. It is modern in construction, machine tools and equipment. It possesses a press shop and a foundry. It has no forge shop.
> At the present time the Volkswagon, contrary to opinion, cannot accurately be described as having been socialized. Originally government constructed and

owned (going into operation just after the outbreak of the war, on the Volkswagon, the German counterpart of the Jeep), the Volkswagon Werke A.G. has been taken over by Allied Property Control. Therefore, technically, if the Potsdam Agreement stands, its future is for the disposition of the Control Council.

Our proposal calls for our purchase — one way or another — of control, say 51%, the balance being for suitable local capital. Arrangements for purchase, of course, must be through the British Zonal Authorities with approval of the United States Authorities.

The product — known as the Volkswagon — enjoys a universal acceptance on the European continent almost identical in its passenger car category to that enjoyed by the Jeep among the Allied armies. It has a definite appeal owing to its operating economy, low purchase cost, and its unique design and performance. There is ample room for improvement in its design, and particularly in the quality of its materials and fabrication. These weaknesses, however, are correctible and do not prevent an amazing future for this little car.

No greater single contribution of equivalent importance and influence could be made to the German automotive industry, or perhaps to German industry as a whole, than for Ford to take over the management and ownership responsibility for the Volkswagon; to integrate the Volkswagon and Ford Werke A.G. engineering, purchasing and fabricating facilities and programs; and to arrange for the distribution of the resulting product. We believe that this action would have a great effect on the entire German economy and the morale of the German people.

Such action would not only give tremendous faith, hope and courage to the two organizations, but by example would exert an important influence on reestablishing practical interest on the part of American private capital in Germany, so necessary to its revival. The immediate availability of our assembly plants and distribution facilities all over the world is a priceless asset to a product which has never been exported, and which has the stigma of German origin.

In summary our proposal provides the most important segment of the German automotive industry with sponsorship, management, technical staff, domestic and export distribution [VW needs that had been pointed out to Ford]; and beyond this, it recognizes the inherent ability of German labor and technique, symbolizes faith in the same and in its uses, and is a constructive practical force in winning the peace.

Here was as bold a manifesto as could have been contemplated in favor of a Ford commitment to the VW works. All that was needed now was a quick and concrete follow-up by the executive whom Ford and Howard had given the assignment of recommending the steps needed to implement the plan. They had picked a man with whom they were already acquainted, who was on the spot, who knew the industry well and who had agreed to join and run the future Ford of Germany: none other than Heinrich Nordhoff.

From their mutual General Motors years, Nordhoff and Howard were on first-name terms. After the briefing in Cologne by Radclyffe, Howard contacted the ex-GM executive and arranged a personal meeting with Henry Ford. It wasn't secret; it could hardly have been with Nordhoff's need to be absent from the factory for two days around the eighth and ninth of March when the still-touring Ford party was based at Stockholm's magnificent

Grand Hotel. Neither was the hurried trip low-key: Ford sent his chartered Pan Am DC-3 to fetch Nordhoff for the Stockholm meeting. This trip, in "the very epitome of luxury," Nordhoff recalled, was his first outside Germany since the war.

Among the Ford executives touring Europe with the party Sir Stanford Cooper certainly joined Ford and Howard in their Stockholm meeting with Nordhoff; Cooper was a director of the German Ford company. Nordhoff brought with him the documentary details of the VW factory and its product that enriched Howard's trip report and its voluminous attachments.

Not yet fully comfortable in his new assignment at Wolfsburg, where the prospects of the still war-torn works were dubious, Heinz Nordhoff was susceptible to this flattering interest from the only auto company in the world that could rival his former employer. To himself he thought, "Well, perhaps it would be for the best; the only hope for this company is to be taken under the wing of a powerful American manufacturer." He agreed in principle to join Ford. Howard explained the plan:

> The acquisition of Heinz Nordhoff, the outstanding executive, prewar and during the war of Adam Opel A.G., and currently General Manager of the Volkswagon Werke A.G. Nordhoff was offered the job as head of the Ford interests in Germany and has accepted.
> Nordhoff was asked to contact Carl Stiev and Hans Wagner, who up to the time of the American occupation served as Chief Engineer and Manufacturing Manager of Adam Opel A.G., and sign them up in similar capacities for Ford. He was further authorized to ask Stiev and Wagner to sign up their leading engineers and production men.
> Finally, Nordhoff was instructed to study and recommend steps which could lead to our acquiring a controlling interest in the Volkswagon Werke A.G., coordinating with Dr. [Carl W.] Hauss, Chairman of the Board of Ford Werke A.G., and with his English associate, Sir Stanford Cooper.

Here was an action plan for Europe that paralleled Ford's strategy in America: the recruitment of capable General Motors executives to bolster the ranks of Ford, depleted by decades of its founder's fondness for obsequious yes-men. Henry Ford II concurred with Howard's nomination of Nordhoff as his point man in Germany. The VW executive was keen as well, as he stated in a letter to Howard of 6 April which he followed up with a handwritten note on 2 May. Nordhoff expressed his willingness to serve as managing director of the Ford Werke: "If you think it possible and advisable I would be very glad to come to an agreement with you already now — I leave that to you."

The experienced and well-connected Howard thought it best to touch base at this point with the U.S. government offices that would affect his plans. In Washington, "Howard discussed the idea with Under-Secretary of State for War William Draper, the head of the Economics Division. Draper, who as a former partner in the investment bank Dillon Read had been closely involved in the extensive networks of U.S./German business interests in the 1920s, responded strongly to the idea" of a link between Ford and VW.

Graeme Howard responded to Nordhoff in a letter of 7 June sent directly to him at the Volkswagenwerk — another sign that these maneuvers were anything but clandestine. A full merger of the Ford and VW interests in Germany was envisioned, he explained, resulting in a company which "should have a distinctly German name and that the name should apply to its products. In other words, the name 'Ford' should be entirely eliminated." Possibly, although not certainly, its products would be sold throughout the world by the Ford network.

Considering the relative sizes of the assets involved, Howard was now comfortable with a merger in which Ford would be the minority shareholder. "Probably from a public relations standpoint," he explained, "this would be desirable so as to eliminate the inevitable unfavorable reaction to foreign acquisition and control of such an important and dramatic company as the Volkswagenwerk." Actual control, Howard assured Nordhoff, would "have to rest with the local Board of Directors. Experience has indicated the impracticability of operational control or management being exercised from a remote distance."

Graeme Howard avoided overconfidence on the prospect of achieving such an amalgamation:

> Whether such a proposed merger could be arranged and would meet with the approval of military government authorities is unknown. It is possible that it might be regarded as contrary to the policy of decartelization.
>
> In any event, it is believed that the matter could only be explored and arranged on the ground, and would properly be a matter for direct discussion and negotiation between Lieutenant General Lucius Clay [commander of the American occupation] and the writer or some other representative of the Ford Motor Company.

Suggesting a conference with Clay was no idle boast on Howard's part. He had served with Clay in Germany and knew him well enough to secure an audience with the general for Henry Ford II during their brief stopover in Berlin in early March. "General Clay," they reported to their Ford colleagues, "heretofore tense, dour and combative, was relaxed and in good spirits. His altered state of mind seemed to be drawn from two basic factors — the promise of approximately a billion dollars for financing essential raw material imports and the excellent crop outlook. Just as important is the knowledge that a policy has been substituted for the Morgenthau thesis which recognizes the absolute necessity for the economic recovery of Germany and its accomplishment as part and parcel of the European Recovery Program."

In making his proposals to Nordhoff, Howard also had the benefit of feedback from explorations made in Europe by Sir Stanford Cooper, who had kept in touch with the British occupation authorities. The latter, in the meantime, had been exchanging views about the merits and the feasibility of the Ford proposition.

THE MIL GOV INDUSTRY DIVISION'S Flint Cahan aired at length the subject of a Ford role at Wolfsburg to Sir Eric Coates on 27 April. He reiterated the view, common to so many of the British occupiers, that "it is a good vehicle and both the vehicle itself and the factory in which it is made embody principles of mechanics and engineering which are not found elsewhere. I do not know whether this vehicle is protected by patents which are of any value outside Germany today, but we are probably in any case protected by the fact that no one is likely to be prepared to make the capital investment required to produce these vehicles anywhere else."

Subtly yet clearly Cahan expressed his "strong suspicion that if [VW] were acquired by Henry Ford, he would not necessarily develop it in the best interests of the German economy. I believe that the vehicle would compete seriously in European countries with the small Fords which are made at Dagenham and we might, under Ford management, find that there was considerable reluctance to spoil the Dagenham market."

On the condition that Ford would provide assurances that it would not restrain the sales opportunities available to the VW works, "for an agreed period of time at least," Cahan "would not wish to oppose the transfer of ownership to the Ford Motor Company." The Briton expressed himself as "generally in favour of any investment of what the Americans used to call the 'direct' type by American business interests, particularly in enterprises in which they had an interest before the war."

And capital, Flint Cahan made clear, was a pressing requirement: "In favour of the scheme I would also add that because of bomb damage, new capital is required which it seems unlikely that we shall obtain in Germany in any reasonable period of time. If we could repair the damage we could considerably increase production of the factory and if there were no restrictions on exports, this would be a very paying business indeed." Conserved but not fully repaired under its British stewardship, the great works needed fresh investment to realize its potential. Thanks to the European Recovery Program, better known as the Marshall Plan, new capital was made available to Germany sooner than Cahan had expected.

The Mil Gov office that would have to deal with the disposition of the VW works, Property Control, was heard from at the end of April. Richard Parker discussed the position with Charles Radclyffe during a visit to the latter's Minden office on the twenty-eighth and responded to Leonard Tregoning on the twenty-ninth. "Cahan had a word with me on the 'phone just before I left Berlin," Parker said, "and I did not infer any very great enthusiasm for the Ford project if I correctly understood him." Flint Cahan may have been emphasizing his positive views less and his negative concerns more over the constraints that Ford might impose on VW's freedom to sell its products.

Parker recapped the administrative aspects of the plant's situation. "The position of the Volkswagen Werke," he wrote, "is that it was originally earmarked for reparations, and at that time, it might have been possible for Ford's [sic] to move a bid for the Works though the American delegate at IARA [the reparations authority]. It has now been removed from the reparations list, that opportunity has gone . . .

"What seems clear at present is that we are not in any position to discuss the sale of Volkswagen Werke to Ford or any one else," continued the Property Control chief. "I ought to add perhaps that the purchase, by Ford's, even if we had title to grant, would appear to go far beyond the present doctrine on investment in Germany; it is unlikely that we can obtain any wider agreement with the Americans until after the reform of the currency." Here was a reference to the earlier American view that Germany was to be kept on her knees by a dearth of investment, a policy just then in the process of being overturned by the Marshall Plan to rebuild Europe as a bulwark against communism.

A currency reform was not long in coming, as Parker doubtless knew. A new national bank was founded in March 1948 and on 18 June the currency was reformed with the introduction of the Deutschmark. An example of its impact was related by Ford's Ernest Breech: "In effect, our German company's cash was revalued from thirty million Reichsmarks to two million Deutschmarks, or about six cents for each dollar. When the currency reform took place, food and other supplies commenced to appear in markets almost immediately."

A flurry of Mil Gov activity in early May was triggered by an invitation from Sir Stanford Cooper. The Ford vice chairman asked Charles Radclyffe to meet him in London to discuss the scheme. A meeting was set for 7 May; Radclyffe was to travel to London on the fifth and visit the German Section of the Foreign Office for preliminary talks on the sixth. There he met with G. P. Hampshire, who "told him that the proposal was obviously beyond the ambit of the investment policy. Since the rigidity of that was due to the Americans, he advised application by Ford in Washington." Radclyffe conveyed these and other views to Cooper, who knew that "Washington" had already been covered by Graeme Howard.

On 11 May Hampshire and Richard Parker conducted a telephone postmortem on the London meetings. On the twelfth Parker summarized his views by letter to his Foreign Office colleague. "I cannot help thinking," he dictated in his conclusion, "that other considerations of a political, as well as of an economical, or commercial character would require to be taken into account before deciding to sell so important and so purely German an asset to a representative of one of the presently Occupying Powers."

It is noteworthy that the approach to VW delineated by Graeme Howard to Heinz Nordhoff on 7 June neatly sidestepped these hazards. By suggesting a merger of the Ford and VW interests in Germany, Howard rendered moot the issues of investment constraints and of the "selling" of the VW works by the British. Instead a new company would be formed in which Ford would be a minority shareholder based on the assets it already held in Germany. Giving it a German name, a German board, and a German managing director would address the political considerations highlighted by Richard Parker. Ford was approaching the matter both seriously and ingeniously.

Meanwhile, Charles Radclyffe's role in all this was attracting attention at Property Control, as Parker noted on 12 May: "His conduct seems at least ambiguous, [very] likely to involve himself in difficulties. He has a connection with the English motoring trade, as he told me, and lived for many years in [the] U.S.A. engaged in the motoring industry." In pursuing the Ford relationship was Radclyffe acting in the impartial manner expected of a Mil Gov official? Parker clearly had his doubts.

RADCLYFFE'S NEXT CHANCE TO PUT HIS CASE to senior Ford brass would come in the autumn. On Monday, 18 October a Pan Am airliner would bring to Cologne a Ford delegation including Howard, executive vice president Ernest Breech, and general counsel William T. Gossett. Graeme Howard issued an invitation to Heinz Nordhoff to join the meeting, saying "I would also like to see the Volkswagen plant, but doubt if the itinerary will permit."

By the summer of 1948, Heinz Nordhoff's view from the window of his small office on the fourth floor of the Wolfsburg headquarters was brighter by far. "The currency reform, Nordhoff said later, was the most important single act in Volkswagen's climb to success," wrote one historian. "Once it occurred, he could set a fair price for the car. More important, it took the British Occupation Forces out of the automobile business. No longer did a German buyer have to have a permit to purchase a new car. Anyone with the money could buy one. That freeing up of the market was all that Nordhoff needed to get the struggling company moving."

And Nordhoff had cars to sell to those with freshly minted Deutsche-marks — the plant's sub-story was filled with them. Until the reform, he said, "sales had been down, but we had continued to produce cars because that was our only choice at the time." He had ample inventory to meet the sudden surge in demand. Exports were also well under way. In May of 1948 the plant celebrated its twenty-five-thousandth car and for the year the VW works would produce 19,244 cars, more than twice the tally of the year before. It was beginning to look like an automobile business — and Heinz Nordhoff was its unchallenged boss.

The proud and independent Nordhoff could see that life with Ford would be different. Others would be tugging at his sleeve, including Erhard Vitger who, Howard wrote on 7 June, had been with Ford in Germany "for some twenty years and, if you are agreeable, it is believed, on account of his long experience and intimate knowledge of the company, his services should be retained in the capacity of Assistant General Manager."

Howard put Vitger forward again on 26 June, informing Nordhoff that "I told Mr. Vitger confidentially that I had discussed with you the possibilities of a merger with Volkswagen, believing it better that I should acquaint him with this fact than that he should learn the thing indirectly. As might be anticipated, he was enthusiastic with regard to the idea." Heinz Nordhoff's enthusiasm was orders of magnitude less. Having shrugged off the attempts of Mil Gov officials to keep him on a tight rein, Nordhoff had no intention of sharing his power with anyone. He eschewed a response to Howard's proddings about accepting the senior Ford post in Germany.

Doubtless calculating that he could deal with Vitger in his own good time, Heinz Nordhoff told Graeme Howard in July that he still favored a merger between Ford and VW in Germany. In this spirit he joined the meeting early in the week of 18 October which was led by Ford's Ernest Breech.

"It was all but a pleasant visit," Breech wrote in a personal letter to Henry Ford II, calling conditions in Cologne "a real nightmare, even to rats trying to gnaw through our wall in the reconstructed hotel floor which we occupied at night." Quieter in the daytime, the rats did not interrupt the hotel-room meeting among Breech, Gossett, Howard, Vitger, and Dr. Hauss on the Ford side and Messrs. Nordhoff and Radclyffe representing the VW works.

The Briton and Germans, reported Breech to Ford, "were quite anxious for a merger of Volkswagen and Ford, but the complications from the standpoint of who owns Volkswagen, how it would be financed, etc., appear at this moment almost insurmountable. However, we outlined a plan of study, which is under way, and this will be followed by Nordhof [sic] and Vitger, as well as by Mr. Bogdan and Mr. McKee. However, again let me say that I do not expect any tangible result."

This assessment by the experienced Breech proved correct. Further studies were desultory and barren. Charles Radclyffe came away from the final meetings convinced that the proximity of the VW works to the border with the Russian zone of Germany was a major concern for the Ford people, especially Henry Ford II. The Russian blockade of Berlin had begun on 24 June and some twelve hundred transport planes were forming the Luftbrücke — the Berlin airlift — to supply coal, food, and other necessities to the city's two million inhabitants. Not without reason, many Americans were apprehensive about the threat to peace posed by the belligerent Bolsheviks clanging down their iron curtains across Europe. Ford was no exception.

It's also possible to envision a less-than-positive stance on the part of the British Ford Motor Company, the entity that actually held many of Ford's ownership interests in Europe. The titan that a merger between Ford Werke and the Volkswagenwerk would create would far overshadow the proud Dagenham plant that had served as a model for Wolfsburg. This was not attractive to the men from Manchester who ran Ford in Britain. "I think that they were the ones who recommended the thumbs-down [on VW] to the British government," said Sir Terence Beckett, who joined Ford in the United Kingdom in 1950. Neither would they have been enthusiastic about a Ford acquisition of the huge plant.

They had second thoughts later, however, Terry Beckett recalled: "It was part of the folklore that I inherited when I joined Ford. In those days Volkswagen was already starting to do well. It was seen as an opportunity missed by Ford." But would VW, under Ford's control, have grown into the business that built the car that displaced Ford's Model T on 12 February 1972 as the most-produced auto in history? We are obliged to have our doubts.

FORD FAILED TO MERGE WITH VOLKSWAGEN and could not get Nordhoff. It was blithely unaware that it was also nearly offered the chance to hire the man whose organization had built the plant and marketed the car. In the cell in Germany's Nuremberg Prison at which he awaited trial in 1945, Dr. Robert Ley was writing a letter. He addressed it to "Sir Henry Ford, Detroit, USA". He was "reminding [Ford] of his connections with the Volkswagen factory and applying for a job with Ford Motor Company on the basis of his 'extensive automotive experience.'"

This was not a random selection of an addressee by Ley. Like other Nazis, he was aware of Ford's record of anti-Semitism. The German stressed in his letter that, like Ford, all he had done was "written essays and books against the Jews." He denied any criminality and placed himself at the service of Ford. But Ley did not post the letter, written in August 1945. On the night of 25 October the builder of the Volkswagen factory hanged himself rather than face trial.

9

Britain Chances Her Hand

D rawing lessons from the events and aftermath of World War I, A. C. Armstrong, managing editor of *The Motor*, put forward his thoughts on a brighter future for the British motorist and his motor industry in February of 1941, when some were saying the end of the war could be only months away. "Even the most fervent opponent of the expansion of motor transport would, I think, agree that, properly developed, it would produce for this country a substantial basis for building up national prosperity in the years succeeding the war," he wrote.

Of all the industries that offer a promise of future prosperity, none holds out such prospects as that of the manufacture of motor vehicles of all kinds. The motor industry could replace and multiply in volume the products of the great iron and steel engineering age of the 19th century. In the years immediately preceding this war the motor industry had become the third largest in the country, despite the fact that it was, and still is, under the spell of many malign influences.

Look at it from the point of view of car ownership. If all or most of the workers had cars, the great home industry created would, as in America, be in a position to dominate the export markets of the world.

All should have the right to own and use a motorcar, instead of it being kept deliberately as the prerogative of the comparative few. Some laugh at the German "people's car" and regard it as a Machiavellian scheme for extracting contributions by the German exchequer, but it was a genuine movement to motorize the German nation. Hitler himself is motor-minded; therefore, he saw clearly the importance, with a war in view, of making the nation also motor-minded.

Here, as early as 1941, the KdF-Wagen project was being held up as a positive example, less for specific emulation than as an indication of how far some of Britain's rivals among nations were willing to go to encourage both motoring and a car industry. Under three photos of the Type 60 a caption asked, "The German People's Car was an inspiration; why should not Britain have its cars for the masses?"

Summed up Armstrong, "Is there a politician with vision who could plan for Britain an era of industrial greatness which the production of an article such as the motor vehicle, obviously required in increasing numbers in every part of the world, would ensure?" Armstrong had accurately foreseen the role that the automobile would have in the second half of the twentieth century as an economic and technological motivator with the power to lift economies. However, apart from Hitler — a role model not all that appealing in Britain — no politician anywhere in the world had yet both envisioned and implemented such a policy.

TO THE SURPRISE OF MANY and the joy of many as well, the ministers coping with the postwar political issues were Labour. This feisty young party led by Clement Attlee, all but strangled at birth, was no more than an adolescent in the 1940s but, like many adolescents, it was sure it knew what was wrong with the world and how those wrongs should be righted. Labour was in a coalition with the Tories and Liberals during the war, but after the May 1945 surrender of Germany the coalition was seen as redundant. In their 5 July election Britons gave Labour a chance to put its socialist principles into action with the launching of bold and costly programs to provide medical care and housing for all.

With the Lend Lease tap turned off and its bridging loan from the Americans falling short of expectations, Great Britain was facing a "financial Dunkirk," warned treasury adviser Lord Keynes, unless the country acted with "a combination of the greatest enterprise, ruthlessness and tact" — the first to expand exports, the second to cut spending overseas in the tattered remnants of the British Empire, and the third to gain aid and succor from the power that had kept England solvent during the war, the United States.

The man in the street would not have known that his government failed to be draconian enough in cutting spending overseas but he was well aware of the privations he was suffering at home so that Labour could afford its nationalized New Jerusalem. "The government was obliged to institute a dual policy: Spartan self-denial at home and a relentless drive to sell abroad," wrote one historian. "It was a time of clothing coupons and bread units, shop queues and coal shortages, . . . dried eggs and watery beer, prefabs and spivs, the black market and red petrol (so coloured to prevent its illicit sale and use, though straining it through a gas mask removed the dye)."

Was anyone in Whitehall considering the benefit to Britain's economy that a strong motor industry could generate? Surprisingly, perhaps, they were. Some in the government were aware of the postwar opportunity that awaited a switched-on car industry, although any encouragement of that industry would go against the grain of decades of its suppression by governments that had refused to regard the car as anything but a frivolous luxury.

A Whitehall working party convened to consider the fate of the German motor industry concluded in January 1945 that at war's end "there will be a world shortage of motor vehicles of all kinds which is not likely to be overtaken in much less than four years from the end of the German war unless production is temporarily undertaken on a scale far in excess of the ultimate absorptive capacity of world markets. The shortage will be most acutely felt in continental Europe where wastage has been on a far greater scale than elsewhere." Although the report dealt with the issue of Germany's industry, its implications for Britain's were obvious.

Not only was there an opportunity; there was also a need, as suggested by papers prepared for the government's Reconstruction Committee: "The motor car industry was rapidly expanding before the war and can be regarded as one of the most prosperous and successful of our industries." Britain desperately needed carmakers who were able to continue the prewar momentum after an armistice. But did Whitehall expect them to seize the postwar opportunity of their own volition? In the spring of 1945 the Reconstruction Committee weighed the situation as follows:

> The [U.K.] motor industry has developed under conditions tending to give it a monopoly in the home market which has been mainly on low-powered cars of a wide variety of different models. Manufacturers at present show little sign that they intend after the war to produce one or two models on a large scale, in the expectation that demand will materialize great enough to absorb them. Nor does it seem that they propose to treat the export market as more than an accessory to the home market.

In this the motor industry differed little from its British contemporaries. In June 1944 the Board of Trade reported on a survey of the postwar export perspective as perceived by fifty-two of the nation's industries. "Only two, cosmetics and sewage-disposal plant, expressed optimism. Almost all pleaded for government protection; almost all feared American competition and a revival of German and Japanese competition; many referred to the growth of new industries making their products in the Commonwealth; many even doubted their ability to hold on to their own home markets." Small wonder that the Board of Trade's president called the outlook "pretty bleak."

ONE WELL-PLACED MINISTER in the new Labour government, a man acquainted at first hand with the ways of industry, saw the potential of the car to help a nation that desperately needed to generate dollar-earning exports. He tried to persuade Britain's automakers to produce robust, practical, world-exportable cars. He did so in that hotbed of car-industry activity, the Society of Motor Manufacturers and Traders, at its traditional dinner in November 1945. The speaker was Sir Stafford Cripps, president of the Board of Trade in the Attlee government.

An eminently successful and wealthy solicitor, Cripps read chemistry with distinction in his youth. In both wars he managed armaments production, at the Queen's Ferry munitions plant in the first and as minister for aircraft production in the second, during which, uninhibited by false modesty, Cripps liked to say he held sway over fifteen thousand companies.

Sir Stafford placed, and would continue to place, heavy emphasis on Britain's need for car exports. Carmakers were already aware that they would only be allocated steel under Labour's rigorous controls if they were producing for export. Stafford Cripps knew just what sort of car would be needed to do the job, and he did not shrink from describing it. To the auto company leaders attending the SMMT dinner Cripps went public with his government's internal views on the shortcomings of its car industry:

> We must provide a cheap, tough, good-looking car of decent size — not the sort of car we have hitherto produced for the smooth roads and short journeys of this country. And we must produce them in sufficient quantities to get the benefits of mass production. That is what we had to do with aircraft engines, and so we concentrated on two or three types only and mass produced them — not a dozen different ones in penny numbers. My own belief is that we cannot succeed in getting the volume of export we must have if we disperse our efforts over numberless types and makes.

This was pie-in-the sky stuff for the carmakers, who would not have been surprised to hear how Cripps had been described by a colleague: "He was an individualist; he would think of some scheme, often a good one, would judge it to be very good indeed, and would then launch it without giving himself time to reflect, and with the very minimum of consultation with either his friends or other people or organisations." In this instance Cripps was on to a very good scheme indeed. But with his usual impetuousness he had not laid the ground sufficiently for his audience.

When he stated that car exports should account for fully half of production, Sir Stafford was shouted down with calls of "No, no!" and "Tripe!" Calling the speech a "string of platitudes, an ideology utterly divorced from reality," *The Motor* said that the Cripps text "was greeted with ironical cheers and angrier derision as he went on to display a complete misunderstanding of the problems of production when not backed, regardless of cost, by extravagant Government control."

Cripps and his colleagues were inclined to use the stick much more than the carrot to motivate this balky donkey of an industry. They were short of carrots in any case, having vastly overcommitted Britain's meager resources. However the stick turned out to be so effective that within five years British carmakers would be exporting not 50 percent of their production, not 70 percent, but fully 80 percent. Sir Stafford's goal was met, and then some — although without the supporting services abroad and the product quality that could have maintained that initial momentum.

Reluctance to cooperate with Labour was rooted in the car industry's fear that its demands were only the thin end of a socialist wedge. Soon after coming to power Labour commenced the nationalization of banking, aviation, telephones, coal, electricity, gas, railways, coach services and, as it said, "certain appropriate ancillary activities."

Would that include the carmakers? No one could be sure it wouldn't. "There is growing surmise in the motor industry," commented *The Motor*, "that the anti-motoring attitude of the Government is part of a policy to simplify [the industry's] eventual acquisition." This was not an atmosphere in which a spirit of cooperation could or would flourish.

WHITEHALL WAS WELL AWARE that the largest auto plant in Europe was struggling back into production under the administration of the British Military Government — indeed the largest industrial plant in Germany was listed as available as war reparations. And any lack of awareness was overcome by the frequent memos and messages from the continent advising about developments at Wolfsburg and asking for guidance on many difficult issues.

Sheer size was an issue to the British Intelligence Objectives Sub-Committee, which went beyond its initial intelligence brief to take an interest in the facilities and technologies it had investigated and reported upon. The chairman of its Group V informed the Board of Trade in November of 1945 that it was having difficulty responding to questions from the motor industry about the availability of equipment as war reparations because so much about the plant machinery and its value was uncertain. As for Volkswagen, well, that was the big enchilada:

> In the case of the Motor Industry which is handled by this Group, there is probably no single firm in England that could bid for a complete plant such as the Volkswagen plant. In actual fact, it would probably be beyond the capacity of the Industry as a whole. The Volkswagen plant has a main floor space of approximately 3 1/2 million square feet and as the biggest shadow factory in England is, I understand, something just over 1 million square feet, it seems improbably [sic] that any single firm would want to take on such a huge concern.

Although in principle the proposition was improbable, the BIOS continued, "It is, however, desirable that a plant such as the Volkswagen Plant should have a bid made for it if only to prevent the removal of the plant to some continental power as this particular plant could be a crippling factor in the export trade of the Motor Industry." Here was a paradox indeed: a car factory that was so big it could disrupt Britain's exports but too big for Britain herself to handle. Was a certain leap of imagination lacking?

The Board of Trade's civil servants weren't bothered. It wasn't their problem. They responded to the BIOS that they were "bringing to the notice of the Board of Trade, who are co-ordinating all these claims, the point you make about the difficulty of any single firm in the U.K. or even the motor industry as a whole, making a bid for a complete plant such as the Volkswagen plant. I think that all that is needed now is for industry to state their case for our putting in a claim for such a plant."

Britain was manifestly the nation with the best opportunity to acquire and exploit Volkswagen. As a working hypothesis in the first months after the war, the Ministry of Supply postulated that when the VW factory could be made available for reparations, Britain should reach agreement to divide its equipment with the French. France's representatives had expressed strong, indeed intense, interest in all or part of the facility. This conclusion carried the clear implication that British ministers had little desire to see the VW plant survive as a complete entity, in the hands of the Germans or anyone else — especially not the French!

In the February–March period of 1946 stock was taken of the status of claims on the Volkswagen plant. The French claim on the plant was logged. An entity called AFV listed the VW works on its list of requirements. The Board of Trade had lodged a notification that the plant was under consideration for reparations but had added a caveat that it was "with reservation — Release only in 18 months to 2 years." This should not inspire inaction, G. S. Knight of the Ministry of Supply pointed out, because the plant could be allocated for reparations by the Inter-Allied Reparations Agency (IARA) in Brussels in advance of its release. Anyone interested, in other words, should not be slow to step forward.

In view of VW's magnitude, and following the line already laid down by Supply, Knight speculated on whether "a proper solution would be to split it up between the nations interested, so that they each obtain a section with a full range of plant for the manufacture of cars." He admitted that this "may be technically impossible," as indeed it was. Nevertheless Knight suggested that the British IARA representative discuss a possible "share out" with the French and added, "It would not seem impossible that Russia — despite the size of the plant — would make a bid for the whole." Indeed, as we know there was active interest from the Soviet side.

Within the Ministry of Supply, G. S. Knight identified Policy Branch E.5(b) as the office best placed to judge whether Britain herself should bid for the VW plant in opposition to what appeared to be a strong challenge from the French. In a memorandum Knight allowed that "it is of course up to you to weigh up the advantages and disadvantages of taking on this enormous concern, and how far its allocation to another nation might jeopardise our export markets, but I should like to draw attention to the need to consult not only with the motor industry but [also] with the other Government Departments concerned, to ensure that if we make a firm bid the necessary building work could be carried out in time to accommodate the plant and manpower could be made available for running it."

Circumscribed by caveats though it was, warning of the need to consult with the motor industry, here nevertheless was a bold suggestion that Britain should at least consider planning for the possible reestablishment on its soil of the machinery and equipment of the VW works. One of the key benefits of this — neutralizing a serious potential threat to British car exports — was subtly yet strongly delineated.

Knight addressed related issues in these passages of his memorandum:

> . . . if, as I suppose, the absorption of this vast concern will be likely to prove too big a mouthful for our industry we should consider how best to render its competition from abroad relatively innocuous. This might be achieved by pressing at the Inter-Allied Reparations Agency for the sub-division of the plant among such nations as may be interested, assuming that the plant does not get allocated to Russia as a whole. It would be important to try to assess how much of the plant is removable outside the actual machine tools. It might be found that after allowing for the proportion of the plant which is incapable of removal and possibly the destruction of the jigs and tools for making the actual Volkswagen model (assuming that we should not want to make the precise German model), the residue would comprise little more than a vast assortment of common purpose machine tools . . . It might also be that your technical advisers could give some idea of the effect of up-rooting the movable part of the plant and re-erecting it elsewhere.

In making the latter suggestion, Knight was hinting broadly that it would be useful to know how great a menace the plant would pose if it were transported to Russia, say, or France. "It is possible," he continued, "that the competition we should expect from the plant after such a forceable move would be considerably less than might be supposed at first sight, and we could resign ourselves to it. Quite frankly, it seems to me that if the U.K. finds difficulty in absorbing the plant there can be few other European countries who would be better able to do it."

So wide-ranging were these proposals that Knight's colleagues in E.5(b) were stymied for some weeks. In the meantime Lt. Col. R. H. Bright of the BIOS Group V kept stirring the pot on behalf of his unit. BIOS was dependent on British ministries for its services; Bright was affiliated with Supply. On 14 June 1946, Bright joined "a meeting held with SMMT which was attended by the heads of most of the major Motor Vehicle Manufacturers."

The manufacturers were briefed on German war reparations procedures and available auto plants by Brigadier Galpin, who had flown over for the meeting.

> The industry, which up to then had not shown very much interest in getting plants from Germany, despite Col. Bright's having kept them well informed of the position, showed some considerable eagerness to acquire plants but more in the nature of quantities of machine tools rather than complete plants.
>
> In view of the Motor Industry's proposal to adopt a "plum picking" policy some action should be taken to explain the difficulty of implementing this policy as compared with bidding for complete plants.

Colonel Bright provided a note that listed the plants of BMW (Munich) and Borgward (torpedo production section only) as being available for reparations and those of Büssing, Hanomag, Vidal und Sohn, and Volkswagen as "probable availability. Not yet cleared for bidding purposes." In Volkswagen's case there was still a reservation "for 18 months to 2 years." Bright was to produce inventories of tools and equipment so the carmakers could commence their plum picking.

To the extent that the British automakers were working together, they were doing so to disable and dismember a potential rival. If they couldn't keep Wolfsburg from exporting, perhaps they could stop it making cars altogether. That this was their objective was clear in the recollection of another attendee, Lt. Col. C. P. "Guy" Boas of the Control Commission for Germany: "It was recommended that H. M. [Government] be asked to bid for all factories in order that certain selected machine tools be acquired, and the balance junked. The meeting was definitely of the opinion that no factories were to be acquired for setting up in this country."

However, in the three weeks between 21 June and 15 July the Volkswagen plant moved further out of reach of the plum pickers. In a note on a meeting on the latter date, G. S. Knight wrote, "I explained that the latest news was that the Volkswagen plant would not be available until after May 1949 and it might be many months from that date before it could be in England. By that time it would be three years older."

This extension of the reservation on the huge but still struggling works by the Mittelland Canal discouraged many who might otherwise have sought to claim it. It helped significantly to preserve the factory as a producing entity. But it didn't discourage those who felt that Britain, at the level of its national government, should not relinquish its grip on the promising people's car and the plant that was making it.

THE CARMAKERS HAD BEEN ACTING in their own self-interest in evaluating the VW opportunity. Big though the Wolfsburg plant was, if it offered an advantage to any British firm, each wanted to be the one to exploit it. In doing so, however, they had to take into account the circumstances that they encountered at home, which were unusual, to say the least.

For a start, pent-up demand for cars was immense. The frustration of the U.K. motorist, denied the new cars being introduced under his nose, was further exacerbated by the government's pressure to emphasize dollar-earning exports at the expense of the home motorist. As a result, wrote Sir Miles Thomas of the Nuffield Organisation, "As soon as [cars] began to be available at all, with delivery dates stretching for years ahead being quoted by agents and salesmen, those of us who were in executive control of factories suddenly found that we had an enormous number of very close friends —

most of whom we had never heard of before — to whom we apparently had tremendous obligations."

Far from encouraging Britain's carmakers to invest in new plant and technology, here was an engraved invitation to them to produce greater numbers of more or less the same products with machinery which was on average twenty years old. Even when they had an attractive new car in front of their noses they were reluctant to acknowledge the desirability of releasing it. Miles Thomas's departure from Nuffield (maker of Morris cars) was triggered in no small part by Lord Nuffield's desire to carry on making the Morris Eight instead of the brilliant new small car designed by Alec Issigonis, the Morris Minor. Fortunately, for the motorist at least, the Minor won out in the end.

Britain's automakers were facing another problem: what, if anything, to do with the shadow factories that had been built before and during the war so that they could put their shoulders to the wheel of the war effort. The shadow factories originated a decade earlier when Britain's airmen were working out ways to accelerate the production of warplanes and their engines to meet the goal of numerical parity with the Luftwaffe. The technique they developed was called "shadowing because its aim is to create a second image of the original," said Air Marshal Sir Hugh Dowding.

After some initial skirmishing the shadow plants went up quickly. The big modern aircraft and engine plants, ranging in area up to a maximum of one million square feet, were in most cases close to each firm's existing factories. Most shadow-scheme participants ultimately managed two. Daimler's were at Radford and Brown's Lane, Allesley, both on the Coventry outskirts. Rootes shadows were at Stoke and Ryton-on-Dunsmore. Rover added a second shadow plant at Solihull to its first at Acocks Green, Birmingham. Austin had a single shadow and Standard managed two in the Coventry area, one at Canley and the other, the largest of the lot, at Banner Lane.

These place names will be familiar to followers of Britain's motor industry, for after the war (and for Rover and Standard before the end of the war) almost all these plants were leased by the carmakers who had managed them. Some did so to compensate for bombing damage to older works (Rover) and others saw the plants as heaven-sent to give them room to expand to meet the postwar demand for cars. All in all, then, Britain's automakers had some eight million square feet of nearly new space to move into, almost four times the floor area of the VW factory at Wolfsburg.

Governmental doubts about the feasibility of transporting the VW factory to Britain hinged in part on a supposed lack of suitable factory space. These doubts were fueled by the inaccurate reports that some BIOS teams had filed on the German plant's size. Counting the sub-story that had been pressed into emergency wartime service, one rated it at a staggering 4.3 million square feet. Another government document reported that the factory's floor area was 3.5 million square feet. In fact the production area, not including the oversized tool shop, was 1,750,000 square feet.

Any one of the four British motor companies who had access to two shadow factories would have had, on two sites, easily enough floor space to absorb Volkswagen's productive machinery. Most of the shadow plants were built on greenfield sites; allocating one of them to accommodate VW would not have been unduly taxing. Although restraints on further factory building had been imposed in the Birmingham and Oxford areas, these could have been waived for such a project.

Physically, at least, any assessment that the VW works was beyond the capacity of Britain to absorb looks less valid in view of the ready availability of the shadow factories in peacetime Britain. At the same time, however, the shadow plants on or near their doorsteps were an affirmation to those carmakers who had them that they would not be denied the space they needed to expand their indigenous production to meet the postwar demand.

AFTER AN INITIAL CONTRETEMPS in his dealings with the Air Ministry, Lord Nuffield kept his companies (Morris, Riley, Wolseley, MG) out of the shadow scheme. However his firm did serve the war effort in premises erected for it by the government. One was a plant at Eaglescliffe, near Stockton-on-Tees in the northeast, put up to reclaim valuable metals from crashed aircraft, both Allied and Axis. This requirement was being phased out with the end of the war.

In June, 1946 Sir Miles Thomas, vice-chairman and managing director of Nuffield, paid a call on G. W. Turner, second secretary at the Ministry of Supply, to propose a future for Eaglescliffe. Sir Miles explained that his firm had successfully developed a small farm tractor using a wartime twenty-five-horsepower engine in a tractor designed by Dr. H. E. Merritt, who had authored a report on Fallersleben's productive machinery and whom Thomas had lured from a rival firm. Nuffield had also been asked to develop a Jeep substitute for the British Army.

Added to these projects, said Sir Miles in an aide-mémoire, Nuffield was experiencing "very heavy demand for current cars and trucks and spare parts for old models." He continued as follows:

> It seems, therefore, a logical solution to several problems for there to be located at Eaglescliffe a productive unit for the purpose of manufacturing Jeeps, Armoured Carriers, and heavy Tank equipment, with which it is at present proposed to entrust the Nuffield Organisation as part of the post-war Army re-equipment programme.
>
> Equally it seems wise for the manufacture of the Nuffield Agricultural Tractor, which is of the same class of engineering, to be located in this area.
>
> The necessary machine tools for this purpose have a value of approximately £1,750,000. Most of these are already in the hands of the Nuffield Organisation

and the proposal is that they should continue to be rented from [Ministry of Supply] and that the buildings should also be rented to house them.

The project would be financed by the Nuffield Organisation on an agreed rental basis, and if it is found that the German Volkswagen plant is suitable for the manufacture of the Jeep, or could assist in any of the other projects, this also would be acquired on an approved rental basis.

After his meeting with Thomas, Turner clarified the last paragraph: "If the German Volkswagen plant is allocated to this country and subject to other claims upon it, the Nuffield Organisation would propose to use any suitable portions of this plant to reinforce the equipment at Eaglescliffe with particular reference to the development work on the British Jeep."

This proposal must be seen in the context of the effort that Britain's motor industry was making in 1946 to achieve the destructive dismantlement of the VW works. Nuffield "was especially active in the SMMT campaign to break up VW." What better way to remove VW as a threat in the postwar marketplace than to have its machine tools making Jeeps and tractors in the British northeast? Ploy or not, this initiative foundered on the news, given to Thomas at his next meeting with Turner, that the Mil Gov's reservation on the Wolfsburg plant had just been lengthened to well into 1949.

Miles Thomas had turned to the creation of a tractor of his own after his boss, Lord Nuffield, had lost patience with a prolix presentation by Harry Ferguson, the ingenious and (usually) persuasive Ulsterman who had enjoyed a tempestuous relationship with Henry Ford over their effort to build tractors to Ferguson's designs in North America.

Held in Ferguson's elegant suite in Claridges Hotel, the presentation was interrupted by a telephone call which the inventor took in an adjoining room. It was from Sir John Black, head of Standard Motors. Ferguson, it seemed, could have the key to the Banner Lane shadow factory that Standard had agreed to lease. He no longer needed Nuffield.

Black fell famously and fortuitously on his feet in this instance. He was helped by preparatory work that Ferguson had done in the summer of 1945 with the new Board of Trade president, Sir Stafford Cripps. Steel was his critical requirement. "Ferguson promised Cripps that his equipment would be a big dollar earner, pointing out too that more home-produced food would cut down on costly imports. Thus it was in the nation's interest to sanction steel supplies for the production of tractors and implements. The appeal was one that had immediate impact, but Cripps could not commit himself at once."

A demonstration of the Ferguson System tractor and its patented implement attachments was arranged west of London; the imperious John Black could see its merits for himself. And he had a factory waiting to build it at Banner Lane. All he needed now was a steel allocation and enough dollars to launch the project. As his biographer related, Ferguson paid another visit to the austere yet surprisingly impressionable Cripps:

Standard's Sir John Black, pictured with the Standard Eight introduced in 1953, enjoyed financial support from the Labour government to produce Harry Ferguson's new tractor at Banner Lane, a former wartime shadow factory.

"I need steel for two hundred tractors a day," Ferguson told Cripps bluntly.

"I think you would be wiser to ask for steel for a hundred a day," Sir Stafford counselled him. "Then there'll be less risk of your being cut back."

The gleam of battle fever lit in those blue eyes behind their rimless glasses.

"If you are going to cut me back, then I'm going to ask for material for four hundred tractors a day," Ferguson retorted. "The country and the world could use them, in any case, and more besides."

Before such an assertion, Cripps backed smoothly down. Ferguson applied for material for 200 tractors a day and Cripps granted the request; in fact, not only did he grant it but he also instructed the Standard Motor Company to take on the production.

In no sense was this an unwelcome instruction, but there was still the matter of dollars to be settled. Black and Ferguson asked for, and received from the treasury, half a million dollars for special machine tools, five million dollars to buy American Continental engines until they had their own tooled up, and three million dollars for related purposes. The treasury cautioned the entrepreneurs that in "any public statement on this new project there must be no reference to the amount of preliminary dollar expenditure without prior reference to us." If British businessmen knew dollars were flying about, they would all want some.

This episode is edifying not only in relation to the shadow factories and their use but also because it demonstrates that Cripps and his treasury colleagues were willing to back new British automotive projects with steel and hard cash in the years just after the war if they held promise of an export benefit. Where were the Porsche projects in all this? The merits of both the Volkswagen and the Volkspflug tractor had been put forward; they were readily available — although there was little hard tooling for the tractor with its horizontal two-cylinder engine.

When Standard Motors swept aside all other models from its range and concentrated production on the Vanguard, introduced in 1947, it seemed to be following the controversial 1945 advice of Sir Stafford Cripps. Undertested and underdeveloped, however, the Vanguard was not the car the world was waiting for.

The tractor of course was low-profile compared to a car project and the volumes were relatively low as well. Nevertheless the popular Fergie tractor became as great a success as the partners had promised. Production started in the last weeks of 1946 and "within a very short time, Standard were making more tractors at the Banner Lane plant than cars at Canley, and because there were no selling or support services to provide, the tractor business was profitable and clean of all unwanted wrinkles. The tractor was to dominate Standard-Triumph activities for the next fourteen years, and ultimately was to contribute to the company's takeover by Leyland in 1960/61."

SIR STAFFORD AND SIR JOHN were to find themselves on common ground in 1947 when, at a London luncheon in July, John Black announced that Standard would scrap its separate car lines rated at eight, twelve, and fourteen taxable horsepower and concentrate all its carmaking resources on one single model: the new 2.1-liter Vanguard saloon. This was a radical step for a British company, so much so that Standard bragged that its launch "may well write in the history of motoring a chapter as memorable as the introduction of the gearbox by Levasseur or the launching by Henry Ford of the immortal 'Model T'."

Modern in appearance with its flush-sided bodywork and smooth fast-back, the Vanguard was compact in overall size yet with its bench seating "accommodates four people with abnormal elbow room and six in reasonable comfort," according to *The Motor*. In all its attributes the handsome and well-equipped Vanguard seemed to be the car Stafford Cripps was asking for in his November 1945 speech to the SMMT.

It was surely no coincidence that "the one-model policy was conceived in its entirety in 1945 and the decision was made then," wrote John Dugdale, now back with *The Autocar* after his military service. "The aim behind all this was to concentrate on an economy car of the widest appeal, up to British standards of refinement. Here indeed seemed to be a car for the world." Its first prototypes took to the road in the summer of 1946.

Needless to say, the British motoring press could not mention the name Cripps in association with the Vanguard, after having so reviled Sir Stafford's suggestion that the industry prune its multibranched model tree and concentrate on fewer models with more export potential. Dugdale quoted Black on the merits of the decision: "I do not think that any objectors can appreciate, until they see them, the benefits of rationalization." That the Vanguard had appeal abroad was shown by the eleven overseas assembly plants that were quickly established for it.

Unfortunately, Sir John let Sir Stafford down. Too eager to get the car into production, he failed to insist on sufficiently strenuous testing for it. Instead of Woomera, White Sands, or Winnipeg, nearby Wales was the "overseas" test site for prototype Vanguards. The production cars soon established a reputation for poor durability — not at all what was needed to fill the thousand-units-per-day engine plant that Standard had laid down for both car and tractor or the five-hundred-car-per-day capacity planned for the Vanguard, even with the addition of estate, van, and pickup versions.

Among the volume British manufacturers Standard had been one of those least exposed to the Volkswagen car and factory. However, Sir John Black had a close-up look at a VW chassis in the heart of London. A complete powered Beetle chassis was brought back from Germany in a DC-3 Dakota by former Bristol engineer Sir Roy Fedden, who set it up in his office suite and showed it to invited motor company leaders. Black was among those who attended.

ANOTHER FEDDEN VISITOR WAS William Edward "Billy" Rootes, the chief of Rootes Motors. Having a look at the chassis was a moment's work for Rootes, whose offices in Devonshire House were on the floor above Fedden's suite. "Rootes came down and stomped around the chassis," recalled Sir Roy's aide Peter Ware. "It's actually got some ingenious features," Rootes pronounced, "Indeed I'm grateful to you, Roy, for bringing it over. But of course it's all a waste of time. Even if the Germans try to go on making it, it'll never sell, Roy. Never sell."

As the leader of the group that bore his family name, Rootes was on a roll. "The 1930s were, to a great extent, Billy Rootes's decade," wrote one automotive historian. During those years he and his brother Reggie added Sunbeam and Clement Talbot to their core marques of Hillman and Humber, merging them to create Sunbeam-Talbot. Rootes has been characterized as "after all, not an engineer but 'a supersalesman *par excellence* . . . with that gift of persuading anyone he met that that was the person he had been waiting to see all day'."

Highly visible in the industry though the Rootes brothers and their company were, they were paired with Standard as the little two of Britain's big six carmakers. The total production capacity before the war of the Humber plants, which produced all the Rootes marques, was a scant 50,000 units per annum, a distinctly minor role in an industry that made 341,000 cars in 1938.

This must be weighed as the background for Humber's summing-up of its infamous wartime report on the military version of the KdF-Wagen. It gave the view that "little or no special advantage has been obtained in production cost," in spite of ample evidence to the contrary, even without the benefit of the positive views given later by Pressed Steel on the Beetle's body design.

It is reasonable to assess Humber as having been incompetent to comment on the economics of car production on the massive six-figure scale foreseen for the Fallersleben factory. Its conservative engineers were unable to project their thinking to volumes that would be a full order of magnitude higher than those to which they were accustomed.

Nevertheless Rootes Motors was the first non-German auto company to have intimate familiarity with the VW design as the result of its BIOS assignment and would have been best placed to lodge a claim for part or all of the plant as war reparations, either to run in situ or to transplant to the United Kingdom. However, Billy Rootes not only declined to seek the plant but also openly and cordially ridiculed its product.

This is not to suggest that Rootes would have been the first choice for an involvement with the VW works in the minds of the Britons overseeing its operations. "We had no love for Rootes," recalled Ivan Hirst, "because they were making such a mess of building cars. In the Midlands you could see their bodies-in-white going every which way on lorries, criss-crossing each other."

Neither did Billy Rootes endear himself to Hirst and his colleagues when he paid a personal visit to the Wolfsburg plant while it was still in spectacular disarray. His guide was Sir Percy Mills, who headed the Economic Division of the CCG. "Mills had a vague general interest and knowledge of Volkswagen," said Hirst. "He brought Rootes, who was a very blunt character. 'What I've come for is a Keller,' Rootes said in his blunt way.

"At first I wasn't sure what he meant," Hirst added. "I very nearly said there's a cellar under all the buildings [*Keller* being cellar in German]. I called in Höhne, our production man. He said, 'Yes, we had two Kellers. One was in the forge plant in Silesia; that's in the hands of the Russians. The other was here in the die shop; it was hit by a bomb.'"

A Keller was well worth looking for. It was a sophisticated and valuable machine that traced wooden die models or forging patterns to cut precisely matching metal dies that could be used for pressing or forging auto parts. Wolfsburg would have been hard pressed to justify keeping a Keller at a time when new model development was far beyond its capabilities. Accordingly, Rootes pounced.

"Let's go and see it," he said. They trudged through the plant's debris to Hall 1, the tool and die shop, where Höhne led them to a large bed plate of which about a third was missing. "They had mounted a slotting machine on it," said Hirst. "Freshly painted, it was slotting some parts." Burst out Rootes, "There you are! Bunch of liars . . ." The magnate noted down the identifying numbers of the slotting machine — most assuredly not a Keller — and departed.

"In due course he sent a request for the machine," Hirst recalled. "I wrote back and said that there must be some mistake. I sent a photo of the slotting machine, which probably dated from 1925. I said, it's not the Keller you want at all. When Charles Radclyffe heard about it he laughed and said, 'You should have sent him the machine!'"

Hirst vividly recalled the last remark that Billy Rootes addressed to him as he was leaving the plant. When they were walking down the stairs from the offices Rootes said, "If you think you're going to get motor cars made here you're a bloody fool, young man."

A maker of conventional cars with conventional appeal, Rootes the super-salesman could not grasp the sales appeal of the Beetle in its crude postwar form. "For a whole generation," wrote one motor-car historian, "Rootes tended to make conservatively engineered cars with good looks, which confirmed the way that Billy in particular wanted to see them. To him the style of a car was much more important than what was under the attractive skin."

The Beetle was just the opposite: a radically engineered car with looks that were controversial at best — not a Rootes sort of car at all. "We took a good look at it," Billy Rootes told John Dugdale, "but . . . we'd rather do it ourselves." They did do it themselves in the form of the Hillman Minx Mark III, handsomely styled by Raymond Loewy — not a bad car but no Beetle.

Wrote his biographer, "Billy and the Rootes engineers may have been influenced by the military version of the Volkswagen which had been captured in the Western Desert and sent to them during the war for extensive testing and the production of a detailed report on its capabilities. The version they tested was very basic in design compared with similar British models." Although available, as near to hand as Roy Fedden's suite on the floor below, later information on the car and factory failed to register at the Rootes offices in Devonshire House.

Billy Rootes, knighted in 1942, was given at least one more chance to change his mind about the value of Volkswagen. Early in 1947 he received a call from Dick Berryman, on home leave from his production-expediting role at Wolfsburg. Reminded of Berryman's role as an aide in the Ministry of Supply early in the war, where Rootes was Lord Beaverbrook's deputy, Sir William granted him an appointment.

This was a private venture by Berryman. Thinking of his own future, he had high hopes for the Australian initiative that was simmering away at the same time. Any interest that Rootes might display could also result in a job for Berryman. The former airman was welcomed to Sir William's sparsely furnished office with its view overlooking Green Park. Facing Rootes across the barren table that served as a desk, Berryman made his pitch:

> I went over to see him and his brother Reginald. I told them all about the VW's construction, and the production problems that had been overcome.
>
> I said that I had tried to break up the VW on numerous occasions in "destruction tests" over the most atrocious roads, and that I had failed to destroy the car, and had proved to my own satisfaction that it was exceptionally durable and practical.
>
> I told the Rootes brothers that I thought Volkswagenwerk was a gold mine waiting to be exploited, and I suggested that the whole place could be bought for reparations at a comparatively low figure — a few million pounds maybe.

Billy Rootes reminded the officer that his company had tested one of the wartime Volkswagens and had judged that it fell well short of acceptable standards. Such a crude vehicle, he told the former RAF man, would not have much of a future beyond the few austere years of the immediate post-war period.

Recalled Berryman, "Rootes said they did not like the over-square engine [bore larger than stroke] and in any case they had more orders than they could fill for years to come, both for the domestic and export markets. He thanked me for coming to see him, and called in his Advertising Manager to see some of the printed VW specifications I had brought with me." Thus Rootes shut the door on the Beetle.

THE ACTIONS AND REACTIONS OF BRITAIN'S existing auto producers with respect to the opportunity and challenge represented by the VW Beetle reflected "sufficient examples of the ineptitude, complacency, lack of vision and venality of British industry." But if the existing industry was so short of imagination and enterprise, didn't this leave opportunities

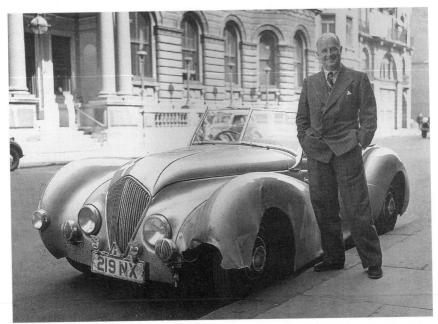

Donald Healey, who had experimented during the war with VW front suspension on his Sunbeam-Talbot, adopted a similar trailing-link design for his own Healey sports car. This one has just finished ninth in the 1948 Mille Miglia.

for newcomers? They would not be duty-bound to belittle the potential of the Volkswagen.

At least one car man at Humbers had taken advantage of his company's early exposure to a Kübelwagen by noting some of the positive attributes of Porsche's design. Arch-enthusiast and engineer Donald Healey had been technical director of Triumph cars from 1934 to 1939, when the faltering little car company was liquidated. Its factories were bought by the Air Ministry and the spare parts and trading name were acquired by Sir John Black of Standard.

After a brief wartime spell at the old Triumph works, managing the production of carburetors for Claudel-Hobson airplane engines, Healey looked for something more automotive to help the war effort and found it at Humber, working on armored cars. There, in the experimental garage, Donald Healey was among the first engineers on the Allied side to have a close look at the entrails of a Type 82.

Healey did more than just gaze at what Porsche had wrought. He was intrigued by the VW's ingenious independent front suspension, with its neat combination of parallel trailing arms with torsion bars made of leaf-spring bundles. When the Kübel had been dismantled and minutely examined, drawn, and described by Humber's engineers, the latter lost interest in its bits and pieces. But not Healey. In his spare time he whipped off the solid front axle and leaf springs of his personal Sunbeam-Talbot and fitted the VW suspension in its place.

Healey had cause to rue this adventurous transplant. On V-E Day, he said, "I tried to drive my Sunbeam-Talbot up the steps of the Officer's Mess, losing the two front wings on the way. It was unwise of me, in retrospect, to treat the car in such a manner. Interesting though it was, it was not a great success, as I had overlooked the fact that a whippy chassis-frame could never allow the [independent front suspension] to do its job properly."

While at Humber, Healey began thinking of building a car of his own after war's end. His allies in this venture were Ben Bowden, a Humber body designer, and A. C. "Sammy" Sampietro, a versatile Italian engineer then working on Humber chassis. James Watt joined the team on the commercial side. Ultimately the Riley company provided engines and drivetrain parts for what became the Healey cars. James Watt described the design gestation:

> While Ben was busy with his sketches, Sammy was experimenting with various suspension ideas. Hitler's Volkswagen, designed by Porsche, had made quite an impression on the motor industry, particularly the trailing link front suspension. We thought about various ideas of making i f s, remembering the troubles that Alvis had had as the first British touring car to have this form of suspension. Standards also had not been all that successful when they applied it to an inexpensive production car. We all felt that if we were going to have i f s, then trailing links would be the best.

Using coil springs instead of torsion bars, Sampietro engineered an elaborate and expensive but effective trailing-arm suspension that served the Riley-, Alvis- and Nash-powered Healeys very well. Porsche's trailing arms had also been seen in action before the war on Auto Union, Alfa Romeo, and ERA racing cars; their evident success led to their use after the war by Aston Martin and Britain's great Grand Prix hope, the V-16 BRM.

WHAT OF OTHER NEWCOMERS to carmaking in Britain? Two more are discussed in a letter that Lieutenant Colonel Bright of the Ministry of Supply wrote to Derek Wood at the Ministry of Trade in September 1946, covering the controversial topic of the technical transfer to Britain of Porsche's design ideas and patents. He mentioned, "for your information only, and not for publication," outright grants of Volkswagen samples to two budding automakers.

> Kendall of Grantham, and Sir Roy Feddon [sic] at Cheltenham, are both designing and appear to intend to go into production with a vehicle much similar in design and estimated performance to Volkswagen. Both have received indirect assistance from the Ministry in that Kendall has been allocated a Volkswagen Engine for investigation and subsequent test to destruction if necessary, and Sir Roy Feddon a complete Volkswagen. Neither Kendall nor Sir Roy Feddon have used the good offices of the Society of Motor Manufacturers and

Traders to request our assistance, but this engine and vehicle were both allocated directly by this Section in accordance with our policy of assisting the Industry whether or not any particular manufacturer may be a Member of the relevant Trade Association.

Roy Fedden was an admirer of the Tatra car and an advocate of the rear-mounted air-cooled engine. While chief engineer at the Bristol Aeroplane Company, Fedden had done his best, in the columns of the motoring weeklies, to bring attention to the merits of more radical engineering of the automobile in a nation that seemed deaf to such iconoclastic notions.

What Fedden didn't mention at that time was that in the course of his work with aviation engines he had thoroughly toured the counterpart industry in Germany in 1937 and again in 1938, when the Germans were doing all they could to persuade Britain that it would be pointless to engage their growing military strength in armed combat. During the October 1938 visit Air Marshal Milch departed from their aviation itinerary to make a side trip to the small town where a big auto plant was being built: Fallersleben. Thus Fedden was among the first outsiders to see the VW legend in the making.

Roy Fedden was a man of automobiles as well as aviation. Born in 1885, Fedden had designed the Straker-Squire cars produced before World War I. During that war his Bristol-based firm, Brazil Straker, built military vehicles and airplane engines, including an air-cooled engine of its own design, the nine-cylinder Jupiter.

At the war's end Fedden's engineering team built and showed a prototype of a small car powered by a front-mounted one-liter three-cylinder air-cooled radial engine driving the rear wheels. They styled themselves the Cosmos Engineering Company and called their vehicle the C.A.R. Although capable of forty-five miles per hour with good fuel economy, Fedden's C.A.R. failed to reach production.

In 1920 Bristol Aeroplane was pressed by the government to acquire the assets of Cosmos Engineering, somewhat against its better judgment. Thus did Roy Fedden commence a rewarding career as the architect of the Bristol air-cooled radial airplane engines. These were known from the 1930s for their use of sleeve valves, which surrounded the piston and opened and closed inlet and exhaust ports in the cylinder wall.

Fedden was a hard-driving hands-on executive, a big man, built like a rugby player, and a difficult colleague. "He had an unhappy knack of framing his utterances in a way carefully designed to be polite — much more polite than was common in industry — yet which had the effect of being intensely irritating. Though brash clumsiness was something he abhorred, he had such a monumental lack of tact that he achieved even worse results with his painstaking care."

Ultimately Fedden exhausted the patience of the Bristol board on which they felt he had been foisted two decades earlier. No little jealousy was also attendant upon the knighthood that Fedden had been awarded. Bristol handed him his walking papers in October 1942 — just at the height of Britain's desperate need for more and better airplane engines.

In his life after Bristol, Roy Fedden was taking to cars again. He was said to be developing a Volkswagen-like car which he appeared "to intend to put into production." How on earth did he consider this possible? The existing British automakers resented any attempt to tread on their turf with materials in short supply and were quick to make their resentment known.

As Miles Thomas testified from his personal experience, demand for cars after the war was fierce. Charles Dunphie and his colleagues at Supply were under huge pressure from the established firms to allocate steel and other scarce materials; no wonder Colonel Bright warned Derek Wood not to say too much about the help being given to Fedden and Kendall, nugatory though it was. The dollar backing given to Standard to build tractors was also kept quiet at the time.

How did Fedden expect to swim against this current? Sir Roy was not easily swayed from a course of action and, more usefully, he had friends in high places. One was Sir Stafford Cripps, whom Fedden met and worked with on airplane engine production in the early war years. Another was Ernest Bevin, staunch Labourite in the key post of the Labour Ministry in wartime. Both saw Fedden as a man of action, capable of implementing some of Labour's ambitious plans.

Cripps immediately snaffled up the engineer when he left Bristol and named him special technical advisor to the minister (STAM). Fedden charged into chairing massive projects: heading a special navy committee to decide on a new engine for motor torpedo boats, investigating the feeder airline market and its engine needs, masterminding the establishment of the Cranfield College of Aeronautical Engineering, and leading a 1944 mission to Italy to see whether its liberated manufacturers around Rome could help Britain produce materiel for the long war still expected against the Japanese. (The answer: no chance.)

In his spare time in 1943 Sir Roy founded a company in his own image: Roy Fedden Ltd. "His dream was of a company where everyone was imbued with his intense motivation, his wish to make fast progress, and his complete dedication . . . Fedden believed his company could be a place where superb engineering could flourish, and where saleable products could emerge as a natural product of the central process of leading the field in design and development."

Fedden's company had three strings to its ambitious bow. One was a range of small flat-opposed light aircraft engines, financed by a potential customer. Another was a 1,300-horsepower gas turbine for turbo-prop applications, for which he wangled a contract from the Ministry of Supply. The third string was Fedden's car project. This was funded by Sir Roy himself

During the war a team of young engineers and designers dreamed of the car of the future on behalf of innovative engineer Sir Roy Fedden, who had been fired by Bristol in 1942. This was the appealing design they created for a new Fedden automobile.

with help from a long-time friend, financier Leo d'Erlanger, and Hugo Cunliffe-Owen. Overall backing came from the Government Finance Corporation for Industry.

What sort of car would Fedden build? As long ago as 1936 in the pages of *The Autocar* he had advocated the merits of a rear-engined car with an air-cooled sleeve-valved radial engine. He reiterated this publicly as a desirable goal in 1942. Now in 1943 he set about realizing it. Early that year he rendezvoused in Bristol with journalist and stylist Gordon Wilkins, who had been at the KdF-Wagen launch in 1939. They met in the flat of Alex Moulton, a Cambridge-trained engineer who had assisted Fedden with sleeve-valve engine development at Bristol.

Their conversations centered on the type of car that would be needed most by Britain after the war. They had in mind a small car with an engine of about 1,100 cc; what had been near enough right for Germany could also be near enough right for Britain. The VW was not the model for the project, yet in a sense it was. "Fedden was anxious to produce what was in effect a British Volkswagen, though he might have been offended to hear it called that. He

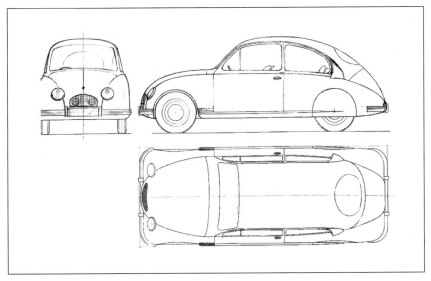

Roy Fedden had admired both the Volkswagen car and factory; the designs created for his own car reflected that admiration. Gordon Wilkins was responsible for the clean lines of the proposed Fedden car.

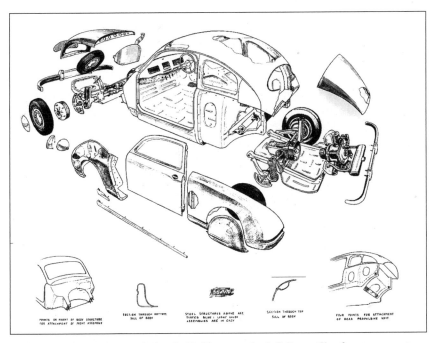

The 1943 design proposals for the Fedden attached sliding-pillar front suspension, rack and pinion steering, and rear swing axles to a monocoque body-frame. Light-alloy exterior body panels were specified.

wanted a better people's car, and his knowledge of the innate conservatism of the British car industry merely spurred him all the harder along the path of radical innovation."

Fedden's team was also spurred to innovate by the perception, widespread at the time and not without good reason, that carmakers were using the war years to prepare much more advanced autos to spring on an eager public after they had satisfied the initial replacement demand. This point was made in the first Fedden car brochure: "American manufacturers are already planning to produce smaller and more economical cars, following the trend indicated by the Studebaker Champion and Willys American and utilising war experience with such vehicles as the Jeep. In approximately three years from the end of the war, the true post-war cars will appear and these are already being planned to render all existing cars obsolete."

Fired up by the inspirational Fedden, the young conspirators began work in Alex Moulton's flat in 1943 and by midyear had completed the outline specification, engine layout drawings, concept engineering, and styling of the planned Fedden car. As depicted in Wilkins's superb drawings and Moulton's performance calculations, it was a knockout.

Stressing that "much is to be learned from such designs as the Citroen, Tatra, Lancia Aprilia and the state-produced K.D.F., cars of exceptional technical merit produced under the stimulus of extreme road conditions" on the Continent, the team proposed a car about the size of the Aprilia. By European standards this made it a medium-sized car on a 102-inch wheelbase weighing 1,790 pounds. Yet it had wide seating intended to equal that of the typical prewar American car.

With flush sides, enclosed rear wheels, and delicate air scoops behind its rear windows the planned Fedden had Tatra-like overtones, but in place of the Czech car's fins and harsh architectonic lines the Fedden had a subtle and curvaceous delicacy of form that was highly promising — and a decent-sized rear window. A small mesh grille in its nose allowed the horns to sound and admitted interior ventilation air. Wilkins drew versions with two and four doors, both charming.

The vertical-pillar front suspension with rack-and-pinion steering was inspired by Lancia; the rear suspension used semi-trailing swing axles. A feature of the design was its "axes of link pivots inclined to pass through universal joint centres to give Porsche toe-in effect." Thanks or not to the BIOS, some technical transfer was occurring.

Fedden's men decided on a welded-steel monocoque for the car's main structure with aluminum panels for the attached front and rear sections and the doors, hood, and trunk lid, taking advantage of the wartime advances made in forming aluminum. VW-style wheels were specified — exiguous rims bolted to the brake drums. The Lancia-type front suspension left room

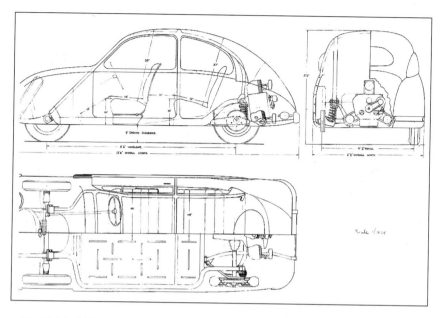

The Fedden's three-cylinder sleeve-valve radial engine was tucked compactly just behind the rear wheels of the 1943 design proposal. Aiming as they were at an English equivalent of the design elegance of Lancia cars, the team seemed to have succeeded.

for a spacious baggage compartment in the Fedden's nose; stowage space was also available behind the rear seats. Sound familiar?

Its three cylinders positioned like the rays of the Mercedes star, the air-cooled engine was mounted just behind the rear wheels and drove forward through a hydraulic coupling and clutch to a four-speed gearbox forward of the final drive gears. The assembly had to be tilted up slightly, about fifteen degrees, to give enough clearance below the two bottom cylinders and the ground.

The car's layout was neat and logical with rational echoes of Porsche's five-cylinder radial prototype for Zündapp. The Fedden team commented knowledgeably about its choice in the brochure:

> A number of rear-engined cars have been built, notably the Burney, Crossley, Mercedes Benz 170 H, Tatra and most recently the K.D.F. With the exception of the K.D.F., all these cars employed a lengthy rear engine of relatively poor power-to-weight ratio. Consequently they all suffered from excessive overhung weight at the rear; and in every case, handling was affected to a greater or lesser degree. Luggage accommodation was restricted and on the Tatra the inherent advantage of quietness was thrown away by the use of an excessively noisy engine.
>
> Dr. Porsche offered a sound solution in the K.D.F. design, using a flat four air cooled engine of low weight, giving the satisfactory weight distribution of

46% front and 54% rear. This was, however, a low powered vehicle, and in a different class from the type of car under discussion.

[In the Fedden] the radial engine in its sound-proofed compartment projects even less than the K.D.F. unit; and in fact there is less overhung structure than on many front-engined cars, which frequently have spare wheel, fuel tank, luggage trunk and toolbox projecting behind the rear axle.

Although the brochure did not specify the expected front/rear weight distribution of the Fedden, its layout did indeed promise to avoid the "outboard motor" effect so detested by Josef Ganz and Ferdinand Porsche alike.

The citation gives further evidence of the Porsche/KdF influence on the Fedden project. "We followed the Volkswagen theme in the design of the Fedden," Alex Moulton recalled, "but I don't think that we were bewitched by it." Confirmed Gordon Wilkins, "The VW certainly did inspire Fedden."

The designers summed up their mid-1943 expectations for the Fedden:

The FEDDEN car has been planned to provide the passenger accommodation and performance of a pre-war American car, with the overall dimensions of a pre-war British "Twelve" and the running costs of a British "Ten." The design has been kept as simple as possible, so that if produced in similar quantities to pre-war British cars, the FEDDEN could be sold at the same price or less. If it is necessary to begin with a smaller production, it is anticipated that the unique advantages of the car can still be made available at a thoroughly competitive price.

Had the latter been the case, the Fedden would have been a British home-market counterpart to the sophisticated and efficient Lancias its designers rightly admired — not at all an uncomfortable positioning.

THEN IT ALL WENT WRONG. Suspicion must attach to Ian Duncan's appointment as the project's chief engineer. Formerly chief technical assistant to Fedden at Bristol, Duncan initially concentrated on the design of the five-port three-cylinder sleeve-valve engine for the Fedden. In 1944, with Duncan in charge, the team moved to Benton House in The Park, Cheltenham, a converted private house with shed outbuildings leased from Fedden's friend George Dowty of Dowty airplane landing gear fame.

From the admirably straightforward although advanced original concept arrived at in 1943, the Fedden car became a festival of engineering exotica in the 1945–46 period. Its radial engine was tipped up to sit flat on top of the axle, like that of the North-Lucas, and under it was an experimental torque-converter transmission and a solenoid-operated epicyclic reverse gear. The whole assembly "was quite a tower block," said Peter Ware, a Fedden engineer at both Bristol and the STAM office, who arrived at Benton House in time to design the engine's cylinders, pistons, and rods.

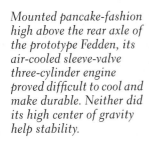

Mounted pancake-fashion high above the rear axle of the prototype Fedden, its air-cooled sleeve-valve three-cylinder engine proved difficult to cool and make durable. Neither did its high center of gravity help stability.

Lockheed oil-pneumatic struts replaced the simple coil springs. Also tried were struts devised of compressed rubber doughnuts by Alex Moulton, whose family were pioneers in Britain in rubber processing and use. By 1945 Moulton had joined that business, although he still supported the Fedden efforts when he was needed.

Worst of all, the car got bigger while the engine did not — by much. Although it developed its target output, sixty-eight horsepower, it suffered from a wide range of cooling, vibration, and durability problems. In an April 1947 progress report Peter Ware was obliged to say that even with new die-cast cylinder heads "the power plant was still terribly hot, and when the bonnet was opened, presented itself as a rather frightening, hot and smoky mass of machinery."

Larger and heavier in the form in which it was built as a single prototype, the Fedden first ran on 14 November 1945, with mediocre performance. The handsome lines sketched by Gordon Wilkins were suggested but not shown by the actual car. "We had the chassis built and we needed to put a body on it to demonstrate it," said Wilkins, "so we got some panel beaters in. They did their best but the result only hinted at the design I had in mind."

That the Fedden cast off its slim youthfulness and matured to bulky overweight we can impute to the influence of one of Roy Fedden's teachers in Whitehall, Sir Stafford Cripps. Cripps specifically commissioned Fedden to prepare a design for a car that could give Britain a strong performance in the world's auto markets. Cripps was said to have done so after despairing of convincing the carmakers to adopt one of their own types as a volume-production proposition that would meet his world-beating criteria: production in volume and size and performance to match the Americans.

To be sure, this line was echoed by Sir Roy's description of his project as "a serious attempt to make a vehicle which has a ready sale at home and yet will, with a new formula, have a large export sale and be truly, in fact rather

Growing in size, in part to meet the desire of Stafford Cripps for a car that would sell well in world markets, the Fedden prototype of 1945 was both bigger and uglier than the smaller cars styled by Gordon Wilkins.

than in theory, a competitive counterpart of the modern American car." This was little more than a paraphrase of the marching orders that Cripps had given to the car industry in 1945.

Fedden's reference to "the modern American car" was significant. Before the war the American auto producers, driven by their high manufacturing efficiency and attractive, high-value products, were by far the most successful car exporters. Popular everywhere in the world, American cars were expected to resume their ravaging of world auto markets in the postwar years. Indeed, this was one of the excuses often given for a lack of interest in the Volkswagen: many thought that it was bound to be overwhelmed as an export competitor by the resurgent products of Detroit.

Although there is no evidence that the Fedden car project was directly commissioned by Cripps or the British government, it is certain that Fedden desired to do right, and to be seen to be doing right, by his friends in Whitehall on whom so many future development contracts would depend. As an independent entrepreneur, it was vital for him to be on the best of terms with the excellent high-level contacts he had made over many years. Sir Roy said as much to Peter Ware: "We must get this right, because if it isn't right the minister will catch me a crack."

Whitehall was definitely assisting Fedden, if only to relieve the pressures that the automakers tried to apply to discourage a potential rival. This was mentioned by Ernest Bevin when he met with Board of Trade president Hugh Dalton on 14 April 1944. Recorded Dalton, "[Bevin] wants to do a wangle with me to help work on postwar models. He is particularly keen that Roy Fedden should be allowed to go on making his postwar car. He met Miles Thomas of Nuffields the other day and told him that the other manufacturers were a lot of bloody fools and that, if they went on threatening Parliamentary questions about Fedden and a few others who were getting any facilities, it would mean that he would denounce them." That kind of support deserved a best effort in return.

Sadly this was not to be forthcoming from the car project. Ian Duncan left the venture around the time the engine first ran. Peter Ware recalled that Fedden's relationship with Duncan suffered as a result of problems with the project and that he was becoming disillusioned with the car's concept. Fedden shed no tears when the jacking effect of the rear swing axles and the high engine center of gravity contributed to a crash that wrote off the sole prototype during a test of its stability.

THESE EVENTS, INCLUDING THE CLOSING of Roy Fedden Ltd. after the light-aircraft engine customer went belly-up, were still in the future in the summer of 1945 when Fedden carried out a special task for Stafford Cripps: a major investigation of the state of the aircraft industry and its technology in defeated Germany. He did this Fedden-fashion: with a brace of Dakota transport planes, each carrying a Jeep and ramps on which it was manhandled on and off.

After a first sortie to Germany Fedden made a second, between 17 and 25 July 1945, to follow up on some points, taking Peter Ware with him. "The main party went to Brunswick," recalled Ware. "Fedden and I sort of snuck off and saw the Volkswagen works. When we went there they were making the post office vans. It was the first time I'd ever seen anything like that; it was an amazing facility. My understanding then was that if the British were interested, they could have the whole thing."

This unofficial visit, not mentioned in Fedden's trip report, made an impact on the Mil Gov staff at Wolfsburg too. "One of the knowledgeable fellows who visited us was Roy Fedden," Ivan Hirst said. "He knew what he was looking at. In fact he floored me with a question. He asked, 'Is it a stressed-skin structure?' I wasn't sure!"

It wasn't, of course, although the sedan body did add strength to the platform chassis — a sample of which Fedden took back to Northolt in Britain in his Dakota, later to have it gazed upon by Messrs. Black and Rootes. Other industry experts, including those from Ford, saw it at Devonshire House as well and were described as scathing in their rejection of its design. Fedden was having a similar experience with his displays of advanced aeronautical technology. The general reaction from the British military was, "Why waste time looking at these German things? Haven't we won the war?"

Half in jest, reflecting on the Fedden car adventure, Peter Ware said, "He might have done better with the Volkswagen!" The dynamism of Roy Fedden combined with the VW factory's assets would indeed have been a powerful alliance for Britain. But like Porsche, Fedden was a creative and adventurous engineer. That was his obsession above all. Unlike Porsche, however, Fedden and his team had not been steeped for decades in the latest advances in automobile technology. Nor is there any evidence that his designers were aware, as Porsche was, of the manufacturing methods that the Americans used so successfully to keep down the cost of their cars.

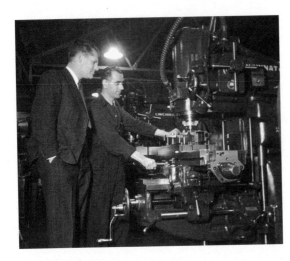

As chief executive during the war of the British Manufacture and Research Company at Grantham, Denis Kendall (left) oversaw the production of airborne and antiaircraft cannon during the war in his well-equipped plants. Meanwhile he dreamed of creating a popular car.

Fedden's team explored new alternatives on paper. Their next project, designated the 2 EX, would have had an in-line water-cooled sleeve-valve four-cylinder engine driving the rear wheels. Its suspension would have used Alex Moulton's rubber springs in torsion. A handsome four-door body would have foreshadowed Howard Darrin's 1951 Kaiser. But instead the Fedden team dispersed.

ROY FEDDEN WAS ONE OF THE ASPIRING auto producers who was provided, in some confidence, by the Ministry of Supply with Volkswagen hardware samples for evaluation. The other was "Kendall of Grantham," who Colonel Bright said had been given a complete VW engine. This was appropriate, for Kendall had declared outright his bold plan to launch production of a new hundred-pound-Sterling people's car for Britain. This was well under half the basic price of any car then available in the United Kingdom. If Kendall were successful, the VW would be roundly upstaged and Britain's carmakers would find out for themselves how their counterparts in Germany were feeling about the threat of the thousand-mark Beetle before the war.

Much like the early assessment of the KdF-Wagen, the launch of the astonishing Kendall project in November 1944 divided Britain's two motoring weeklies. This time *The Motor* was the more muted in its response to the sensational announcement "of an unconventional post-war car to be sold at an estimated price of £100 by a large gun-manufacturing concern. Needless to say, when the car is in a more advanced stage, this proposition will be examined closely by *The Motor* and will be dealt with thoroughly on its merits."

In contrast *The Autocar* gave two and a half pages to a detailed description of the two-door four-passenger car to be built by Grantham Productions

In 1945 Denis Kendall unveiled the first prototype of the car his Grantham Productions would build and sell for only £100. Britain seemed to have her own people's car. Did it need the Volkswagen as well?

Ltd. and to be styled the Kendall-Beaumont car. At that time only the engine was complete; by the summer of 1945 the car itself was up and running. It immediately seized the headlines in the popular press, to whom the headline "The £100 Car" was manna from Grantham.

Among the many startling aspects of this bold venture in carmaking was the broad resemblance, certainly coincidental, between the Kendall-Beaumont and the Fedden. Both had rear-mounted air-cooled engines with three radial cylinders, configured like the Mercedes star. The Kendall's short-stroke engine (66 x 58 mm) was compact enough for its crankshaft to be mounted horizontally. And like some versions of Fedden's car the Kendall had rubber springing, the "new idea" espoused by so many postwar car developers.

Rolled out in the metal for the first time in the summer of 1945, with its coachbuilt body by Arthur Mulliner of Northampton, the Kendall was a two-door car on a ninety-inch wheelbase intended to carry four passengers on Citroën-2CV-style hammock-like seats. While the Fedden enjoyed contemporary styling, the Kendall seemed to have been designed by someone who was inspired (or frightened) by the 1937 Cord, with its bold prow, hood side strakes, and lushly rounded fenders. A single headlight was centrally mounted on the hood, which had space for luggage.

So far there was no sign of the Volkswagen engine that had been sent for testing to destruction, if necessary, by Denis Kendall. Instead the engineering of the car was the work of a certain Horace C. M. Beaumont. His back-

A 597 cc overhead-valve three-cylinder radial rear engine powered the original Kendall prototype. It, and the car as a whole, were the work of little-known engineer Horace C. M. Beaumont.

ground included the production of a motorcycle with a three-cylinder engine after World War I and, according to *The Motor*, by "coupling two power units [he] was responsible for the Redrup Radial." With its pushrod-operated overhead valves and lubrication by oil in the gasoline the Kendall's engine smacked very much of motorcycle practice.

As for the prime mover of the project, Denis Kendall, his credentials as a potential motor magnate left little to be desired. Born in Yorkshire in 1903, Kendall attended Halifax Technical College. After a spell at sea he left his last berth in New York and sought a future in the New World. Starting in the motor industry as a General Motors test driver, Kendall then moved to the Budd Company in Philadelphia, the world pioneer in the construction of steel auto bodies and the American parent of Berlin's Ambi-Budd pressworks.

France's auto pioneer André Citroën had close ties with Budd, perceiving as he did that he had to use the latest American technology if he hoped to produce his cars efficiently. Various Citroën car bodies, including that of the famous *Traction Avant*, were actually prototype-built at Budd. No shrinking violet, Kendall came to the fore in the Citroën project, with the result that the Yorkshireman with an American accent visited Paris in 1929 and again in 1933 to supervise the installation of new Budd tooling at Citroën's Quai de Javel factory. There he remained, taking charge of body production. In spite of his cordial relationship with André Citroën, Kendall was kept on when the faltering company fell into the hands of its tire supplier, Michelin.

Kendall's return to Britain was triggered by the granting of a license by Hispano-Suiza of Switzerland to the British Manufacture and Research Company (BMARCO) of Grantham in Lincolnshire to produce its Type 404 twenty-millimeter cannon, the weapon used so successfully by Spitfires and Hurricanes in the Battle of Britain. A director of Hispano, Prince Stanislas Poniatowski, picked Kendall to run the plant. He took up his post in 1938.

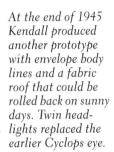

At the end of 1945 Kendall produced another prototype with envelope body lines and a fabric roof that could be rolled back on sunny days. Twin head- lights replaced the earlier Cyclops eye.

To help produce more of these vital weapons the government erected additional factory buildings for BMARCO, which also started producing Oerlikon antiaircraft cannon. Zurich's Oerlikon ultimately acquired BMAR- CO. A charismatic individual, Kendall flew high in Grantham on the wings of these responsibilities. He ran as an Independent candidate for Parliament against the ruling wartime coalition in a 1942 by-election and won, an out- come which the *Manchester Guardian* described as being about as likely as "the suspension of the law of gravitation."

Badly infected by the automobile bacillus, Kendall unburdened himself to his BMARCO colleagues at a January 1944 social gathering:

> There is just one plan in my own line of business which is well worthy of exami- nation and I am very hopeful that something may come of it. I refer to the build- ing of a popular car for the people which shall be truly economical in price, running and upkeep. I am sure there is scope for the production of such a car outside the large manufacturing organisations which have practically monopo- lised the light car business in the past.

Indeed, he had already started the process of commissioning Beaumont with the results that were announced so sensationally the following November. Kendall set up a new company of his own, Grantham Productions, to imple- ment his ambitious plan.

THE PROTOTYPE KENDALL-BEAUMONT continued to attract press attention through 1945. *Picture Post* informed its readers in October about this amazing new car. "Naturally the car is not as quiet running as is the watercooled type," the report read. "Nor do three cylinders give the smoothness of six, or even four. When under way you are well aware of the engine, but that is not to say that it is excessively noisy or rough.

"A man of unusual push, Kendall is not going to let his project fall through if he can help it. The Kendall car is now going into production at

The new side-valve three-cylinder engine of his second prototype was no more reliable than the earlier version, so Member of Parliament Kendall powered this car with the VW engine he had been given by the Ministry of Supply. That at least assured him of a trouble-free drive to Westminster.

Grantham after long negotiations with the Government for factory space. Kendall says that in 18 weeks he can be turning out cars." Those "negotiations" had included, in August, threats "to ask questions in Parliament as to why the Government has not given him factory facilities for producing the car."

Rather more than Fedden, Kendall had a love-hate relationship with Whitehall. He was successful in his campaign, being granted use of the new factories the government had built for BMARCO during the war, even though they had been provisionally allocated to Aveling Barford, a supplier to the car industry. But after an unsuccessful attempt to drive his first prototype to the House of Commons Kendall fired Beaumont and commenced the design of a new Kendall.

A brand-new Kendall was on show at the end of 1945. It looked vaguely Teutonic with an envelope body, forward-opening doors, a fabric roof, and a long downsloping hood. Twin headlights were now a feature. Front suspension reverted to a leaf-sprung solid axle. A radial air-cooled triple at the rear still powered the car, but now with side valves for 700 cc (66 x 68 mm).

Here was a much more handsome proposition for Denis Kendall to drive to Westminster to impress his fellow MPs. There was only one snag: it

By 1946 Denis Kendall had changed tack and was planning to base his car on a prototype developed by Jean-Albert Grégoire. Its high aluminum content was attractive to U.K. foundries which no longer had big aviation-engine markets.

was no more reliable than its predecessor. Kendall had a solution for this: the VW engine provided by the Ministry of Supply. He had it installed under the louvered rear deck of his new prototype, which was kept firmly shut on all ceremonial occasions.

Still overseeing cannon production in Grantham, Prince Poniatowski of Hispano-Suiza kept up with the progress of Kendall's car project. "Poniatowski frowned disapprovingly when he saw this DIY effort in 1944," wrote Jean-Albert Grégoire. "Kendall, obstinate as ever, clung to his project all the more firmly, especially having attracted the interest of a wealthy Indian Maharajah. This landowner opened up unlimited credit for Kendall to develop his vehicle."

Grégoire had attended the 1938 Berlin Show and served as interpreter for Louis Renault. In cooperation with Aluminium Français he was now developing a small front-drive car powered by a flat-twin engine. Both engine and chassis of his AFG prototype made extensive use of aluminum. Grégoire explained the evolution of events:

> At the end of 1944, one of my best friends, Walter Sleator, director of Rolls-Royce in France, came to me with Prince Stanislas Poniatowski, director of Hispano-Suiza. The obvious solution leapt at him — abandon Kendall's hopeless project and take out an exclusive licence for our car in Britain.
>
> The AFG found an influential supporter in Colonel Devereux, director of the Rolls-Royce foundry in Glasgow (Renfrew Foundry). The principle of cast bodywork struck a chord with him, and he shared his opinion with Lord Hives, head of Rolls-Royce.
>
> In a quickly signed contract, [Kendall] accepted all our conditions without discussion — a significant cash injection of £25,000 and large royalties. After the conclusion of this agreement, I realised I could have asked him for twice as much.
>
> Original, stubborn, very likeable, Kendall was a real nobleman. His generosity knew no bounds, as if he had all the treasure of Golconda behind him. For a while, money was pouring in. In a country devastated by the war, I was received as a prince. However, I still worried that my new friend was not throwing himself seriously enough into the creation of his production tools.

When Grantham Productions crashed in November 1946 Kendall had built only a few of these Grégoire-designed prototypes. These, and such tooling as existed, were acquired by Larry Hartnett who wished to produce a car under his own name in Australia. By 1956 he too had given up.

Grégoire was right. Actual production did not seem to be a priority for Kendall. The supply shortages of the 1940s also had a part to play. Grégoire: "Grantham Productions began to encounter supply problems. If there were no problems with cast pieces from the foundry and most of the mechanical parts, there were bottlenecks due to electrical equipment. Their manufacturers found themselves controlled by the nation's automobile manufacturers, who took a very dim view of the appearance of a new model in which the public seemed to take far too much interest."

The latter comment, coming naturally to a conspiratorially minded Frenchman, echoes strikingly the rumors that swirled around another car project during the same period: the American Tucker, with which the Kendall has certain unavoidable parallels. In both cases, however, the entrepreneurs seem to have been fully capable of creating enough obstacles for themselves.

The Kendall car dream crashed on 15 November 1946, just two years after its launching, with a deficiency on its books of £445,379 14s 9d. The Indian backers had departed, but some tools, equipment, and car components did remain. In the meantime Jean-Albert Grégoire had met a Briton who was touring Europe to find a car that he could produce in Australia — none other than Larry Hartnett. Driving the AFG prototype that was in England, Hartnett "fell in love with it immediately." But Hartnett had to wait to see how Kendall, who had priority rights to the design, would develop it.

Hartnett could see that unlike the Volkswagen, Grégoire's cast-aluminum AFG design could be tooled to be economically produced in the smaller volumes that he thought Australia could absorb. So when Kendall collapsed, Hartnett bought the British Empire production rights from Grégoire (ten thousand pounds this time) and acquired the assets of the company, valued at sixty-eight thousand pounds, for twenty-five thousand.

Hartnett is so appealing a personality in this saga that it would be warming to relate that he was successful in exploiting a British version of a French design in Australia. But after making parts for 120 or so AFG-based Hartnetts and completing some 70, he too was forced to throw in the towel. The Hartnett Motor Company was struck off the register of companies in 1956.

DENIS KENDALL RETURNED TO AMERICA to do very well for himself. Two additional aspects of his story are worth noting here. One is that Kendall was a big fish in the small pond of Grantham, its Member of Parliament until 1950, and its most prominent industrialist and employer. Thus his crash was hugely disillusioning for that small city, in which a shopkeeper's daughter, Margaret Roberts, was growing up.

At the age of nineteen Miss Roberts, a newly minted Conservative, assisted in the 1945 election campaign against the Independent Denis Kendall, who nevertheless prevailed to hold his Grantham seat. In 1945, as well, her father was elected mayor of Grantham. He was deeply involved in the issues swirling about Kendall. Who can say that as Margaret Roberts Thatcher her hostile attitude toward another automotive entrepreneur, John De Lorean, was not rooted in the firsthand recollections of herself and her family during the Denis Kendall boom and bust years in Grantham?

The other item of note is that Kendall was quick to thumb his nose at the established motor industry in Britain and in particular at the traditional network of dealers and agents. Instead, he said, "I shall distribute my car through the Co-operative Wholesale Society." Better known as the CWS or the Co-op, this was and is a nonprofit society dealing in household goods and foodstuffs through its many storefronts blanketing Britain.

"Recoiling from the shock of this outrageously unconventional proposal," wrote one historian, "the British motoring and financial establishments closed ranks against him immediately. The banks refused to assist with funding and supplies of raw materials and component parts from the motor trade were suddenly withdrawn." Whether or not the reaction was in fact that severe, the idea of bypassing the traditional dealer network was certainly as hackle-raising in the 1940s as Daewoo's direct sales network was in the Britain of the 1990s.

DURING THE BOOM AND BUST of the Fedden and Kendall projects the British government continued to monitor progress at the German car factory for which it was responsible. At the beginning of August 1946 Chancellor Hugh Dalton received a letter from George Gibson of the National Savings Committee recommending that production be stepped up at Wolfsburg so more cars could be exported to continental and Scandinavian markets. Gibson enclosed a two-page aide-mémoire on the characteristics of the factory and an argument that increased exports of Beetles would keep the Americans from gaining ground in Europe, would earn seven million pounds for Britain, and, most controversially, would fill a gap left by British carmakers, by whom Gibson said it was "unlikely that special production for continental markets can be undertaken for say at least two years."

Not until after the summer holidays did the Treasury commence addressing the questions raised by Gibson. In the meantime several other missiles, not unlike the V-1s once built at Fallersleben, came crashing down in Whitehall. One was a friendly "Dear Bill" letter to William Ritchie of the Occupation Control Office in London from Richard Parker of Property Control in Berlin. "Everyone seems interested in Volkswagen except the U.K.," Parker wrote. "Two of Lord Nuffield's men did visit our factory near Hannover and took away a few drawings. I can't but feel that if Brazil, France and the U.S.A. are interested, our Motor Industry ought to be."

Richard Parker followed up his letter with another semiguided missile, a report dated 15 August 1946 compiled by the VW works Board of Control and transmitted by Parker to the Control Office for Germany & Austria in London. This was a very live round. Over two single-spaced pages and seventeen paragraphs it set out what was known of the relationships between the Porsche executives and businesses and the VW works. It also raised for the first time in depth the issue of the People's Tractor, a pet project of Robert Ley's which reached prototype form during the war.

The thrust of the Parker document was that the Porsche people were busily exploiting their patents and product ideas for the benefit of almost everybody but the British. It made clear that Porsche had never signed the fully drafted contract that would have given the VW works the rights to the Porsche designs used in its products. It sought to make the case that the Porsche ventures were under British control with both Zell am See and Gmünd in the British sector of Austria, even though the old Stuttgart Porsche office was in the American zone of Germany. It was occupied by the American army.

Setting out in an attachment the details of the funds received by Ferdinand Porsche and his family members before and during the war from various organs of the Third Reich, the Parker document added that "Porsche himself was given the honourary rank of Standartenführer in the S.S., was deeply implicated in Nazi industry, and received large sums of money from it. He therefore qualifies for arrest." The latter point was reiterated in paragraph seventeen, which was action-orientated:

ACTION

17. Since various countries consider Porsche's inventions worth their active support, it is recommended that:

(1) It should be considered whether, in the light of the above, an immediate investigation into the possibilities of exploiting the Porsche inventions for the benefit of British industry should be undertaken.

(2) The personal position of Dr. Porsche should be considered so as

(a) to ensure that his knowledge and equipment be fully exploited in the interests of British industry,

(b) to secure his arrest if his past activities merit this.

The French were well ahead in this stakes race. At the time this document was written the senior Porsche and Anton Piëch were detained in Paris and about to commence their meetings with the Renault engineers over the nascent 4CV while Ferry Porsche, in Germany, was being urged to redesign the Beetle to suit French tastes. Two paragraphs of the document did refer to this without indicating any awareness that Porsche had in fact already been "arrested":

10. We are informed that Renault Motors are setting up an experimental works for Porsche products in Paris, and that they are going to start up production in their zone of Germany or Austria.

14. Porsche is working with and for the French authorities. He resides in the French Zone of Germany and has recently visited Paris. It is understood that the French (rightly) take the view that all German patents are available for exploitation by the Allies and are accordingly exploiting the Porsche patents.

In addition to illustrating the difficulty of obtaining accurate intelligence in peace as well as in war, the content and style of these assertions show no reluctance to flaunt the French flag in front of John Bull — a gesture then as now effective in getting his attention. That someone at Norfolk House understood the Porsches' situation was suggested by the omission of the "arrest" item from the action paragraph — although not from the text — of the retyped document, which was given wide circulation in Whitehall.

In sending a copy of the report to Derek Wood at the Board of Trade, D. A. Johnston of the Control Office was so confused by it that he wrote, "Frankly, this report on the People's Car Company and the Porsche Company covers so wide a field that I do not know what to do with it. I shall be very pleased to hear from you and from the other recipients of this letter what are your reactions and theirs to it." Wood knew just what to do with the report. On his copy of the letter he wrote, "We can leave this one to Supply."

SOMEONE AT THE CONTROL OFFICE'S Norfolk House headquarters on London's leafy St. James's Square must have been shouting "Incoming!" during August. Another V-1 landed in the square in the form of a letter from Guy Boas, now retired but not retiring. The former Control Commission lieutenant-colonel had put his case personally to the chancellor that Britain should acquire the VW factory. As a result, wrote a member of the Control Office, "The Chancellor is very interested in any possible developments which would make constructive use of the plant, or any part of it, at the Volkswagen factory."

Just how had Guy Boas so successfully marshaled his argument? On 22 August he wrote from Manchester to A. M. Skeffington of the Control Office, with whom he had already discussed the topic of the VW works. The salient paragraphs of Boas's letter deserve quoting at length:

> Among the surplus [German] plants is the Volkswagen Works (at present making the 14hp. Volkswagen Saloon). At the end of June over 5,000 had been built for Military Government needs. I have an intimate knowledge of this car and the factory and came to the conclusion that it was a first class car and a novel piece of engineering. The acquisition of this plant would be a splendid investment for this country, especially for overseas markets. Its simple design lends itself to mass production and a small number of machine operations. The pre-war plan for the saloon car was 130 man/hours, including pressing out, machining, and assembling. This figure has never been approached by any English car manufacturer.
>
> During the war over 70,000 L.A.D. type V.W.82 were produced and successfully operated by the Wehrmacht in the African Campaign and elsewhere. This chassis is identical with the present saloon car, only the body differing.
>
> In the light of my personal experience in making and testing this car I consider that the acquisition of the complete plant for this country would not only satisfy a low price demand of the domestic motor user but [also] be an extremely attractive proposition for overseas markets.
>
> Lastly it would form the nucleus of a national or semi-national motor industry in England. However, while the decision and or advice rest with established interests it cannot be expected that any disinterested point of view will be tendered to H.M.G. [His Majesty's Government].

Boas's last paragraph raised hackles of various sizes in various places. Although entirely in tune with the ideas of the socialist Labour government, the idea of a "national or semi-national motor industry" was as much anathema to Britain's carmakers in the 1940s as it had been to their German counterparts in the 1930s. Yet the core of the Boas argument was that it would be better to have a nationalized car company of huge capability in Britain to exploit the VW windfall than none at all, which seemed to Boas to be the way things were going.

Umbrage was also taken to the last paragraph by Derek Wood at the Board of Trade. He referred in a note to its "subtle and objectionable insinuation" that the auto companies were running the government. However Wood said, in his official reply, "I understand that the Advisory Committee of the British Motor Manufacturers has been considering whether to take this plant into the U.K. to make the people's tractor or the car or whether to bid for it with the idea of dispersing the machines throughout British Industry as a preemptive measure against foreign competition." This scarcely sounded like a robust rebuttal of Boas's assertion.

Some peculiar ideas about the Volkswagen were circulating in Whitehall during these deliberations. An example was a hand-written note from John Selwyn to Derek Wood referring to an unidentified third party:

I've talked to Binny & I've racked my brains about this one but there is really nothing we, as the [Board of Trade], can say.

You see the car is only suitable for town use & not exports. We have a large capacity for town cars in the U.K. & Binny wishes the mfgrs. to make something for exports. The ideal arrangement would be to take the plant to make a car for the home market, thus releasing capacity for an export car. But home mfgrs. are chary of getting yet one more home model!

It would have been news to Ferdinand Porsche that his Type 60, so assiduously designed and developed to be durable at its maximum speed over long distances on the world's only superhighway network, was thought in Britain to be a town car. Although many in the United Kingdom were remarkably well informed about the VW, such knowledge did not appear to have penetrated to some levels of the government.

On behalf of the Ministry of Supply, Colonel Bright responded to these challenges in a letter to Derek Wood in the beginning of September. Anyone interested in the Porsche inventions, he counseled, had only to refer to the many widely circulated reports from BIOS among others. Sample VWs had been provided for both government and industry evaluation, he pointed out. "It is presumed, therefore," Bright wrote, "that all manufacturers interested will profit as regards any revolutionary developments in design which are incorporated."

Continued Bright, "It is difficult to see what further advantage as regards technical exploitation can be reaped unless some manufacturers, or the British Government, are prepared to go in for the manufacture of Volkswagen, or light tractor, in toto. As regards plant, a firm requirement has been put in to the relevant Department for the Volkswagen Works to be included in the plant and equipment for which bids will be made as a part of German Reparations to be allocated to this country."

Bright was well aware of the divide and conquer philosophy of the British carmakers toward the VW factory and its tools and equipment: "At present, it would appear that the Motor Industry in this country do not wish to obtain the Volkswagen Plant complete in order to manufacture Volkswagen cars, but merely in order to break it up and utilise the machine tools. Whether they will be permitted to do this, I do not at present know."

Colonel Bright left little doubt that he found the breaking up of the great VW factory an unappealing prospect. In this he had an ally in Maj. Gen. Charles Dunphie in the Ministry of Supply. Just three days after Bright's letter was written Dunphie dictated a cover memo for Dr. Merritt's report on the German motor factories and their machine tool complements. All the plants visited would be bid for at the IARA, he wrote. Breaking up a plant might be an option for Hanomag or Büssing, but not for Volkswagen:

It is suggested that consideration should be given to the question of whether the best National Interest would be served by breaking down the Volkswagen works. This Works was designed for the mass production of a cheap car which it is pos-

sible to manufacture with a smaller expenditure of man-hours and at a smaller
cost than any small car can at present be produced in this country.

The anxiety of the British Motor Manufacturers that it should not be allocated to any other Nation who might compete in foreign markets is fully justified, but it is questionable at the present time whether the best National
Interest would be served by the virtual destruction of a production unit of this
nature, considering the shortage of vehicles of all types in Europe, and the high
cost of a small car in this country.

Here was a valuable perspective from a sensible civil servant who won
praise from Sir Miles Thomas of Nuffield as "one man who kept his head in
the Ministry of Supply. He had the unenviable task of sorting the wheat from
the chaff" of the postwar scramble for raw material permits. Dunphie
showed similar perspicacity in summing up the situation of the VW works.

LATER IN 1946 WHITEHALL still favored a British bid for the Beetle
factory. During the discussions over the possible assembly of VWs in Belgium, thwarted by the failure of the Belgians to come up with their steel in
exchange, P. B. Hunt declared on 4 December that the VW factory "is
being retained temporarily to manufacture cars for the occupation forces.
Should it eventually be offered for reparations, Great Britain will certainly
offer a strong bid for the plant to be allocated to us."

Governmental authorities continued to receive reminders from Wolfsburg about the merits of the plant and its product — not all of them favoring
continued Beetle production. Some British Military Government officials at
Wolfsburg had mixed feelings about their role in helping build up the capabilities of this Brobdingnagian motor works.

"We British at Wolfsburg might well have had divided loyalties," said
Ivan Hirst, "when it became clear that the VW could one day become a serious competitor for UK manufacturers." Hirst tried to look on the bright side:
"Privately, we felt that in building up the VW company we must eventually
but inevitably prompt firms at home to review their designs and to improve
their marketing and servicing organisations."

One of the Mil Gov officers who was well aware of the VW menace decided
to do something about it. Maj. Alasdair McInnes, finance and property control
officer in 1945–46, "very quickly realised the threat the car would represent to
the British car industry in the future. Right from the start I realised it was a jolly
good car. Anyone with any foresight at all, I would have thought, was bound to
realise — knowing as much about the quality of the vehicle as I did, and after
driving the car — that it had a big future."

After only a month or so at Wolfsburg his awareness of this peril led
McInnes to prepare a back-channel memo of recommendations to the Ministry of Supply: "I briefly suggested that Volkswagenwerk should be converted into an industrial estate. The factory then was admirably suited for
conversion to a series of light engineering works, and every section, although

often damaged by bombing, was self-contained. If we had been able to utilise the factory as an industrial estate we would still have required the same
number of workers, possibly more, in fact, and there would have been a wider
variety of work."

Although McInnes discussed his misgivings with some of his colleagues,
his memo was a solo initiative that he did not tell them about. It didn't take
long for him to get a reaction: "A report of this nature no doubt went through
the Ministry of Supply like a buzz bomb. Within a week or two weeks [Leslie]
Barber came down from Berlin to see me and told me, 'The factory must carry
on as a car-production factory.' And that was that."

Another Mil Gov officer in Germany was granted an opportunity to advance his views when in June 1947 a pioneer motorist, Lord Brabazon of
Tara, put pen to paper to write a letter to the *Times*. Brabazon was not convinced by the trend, exemplified in part by the Standard Vanguard, to try to
move British cars into more direct combat with the Americans in world markets. This was unwise, he said in his letter published on 2 July, because poorer
economic conditions in the rest of the world meant that many people could
not afford to buy or run the big Yank cars or their mooted British counterparts. Thus Brabazon judged that a great albeit different opportunity awaited Britain:

> It seems to me remarkable that anyone should deliberately want to fight America
> in a big car duel when the whole world is hungry for a light, tiny car. As big a revo-
> lution is upon us as was brought about by the introduction of the original Ford,
> yet apparently we are to leave this world market to be fulfilled by the Italians and
> French while we try to shadow copy America.
>
> Here is a world export market surpassing anything that has ever been
> dreamt of, waiting to be satisfied. It will be a national calamity if we do not seize
> the opportunity with both hands to pioneer and produce this new type of cheap
> transportation, for which the whole world outside America is waiting.

At his office in Minden, Col. Charles Radclyffe had to wait a week or so to
receive his *Times*. Reading Brabazon's letter, he lit up a fresh cigar. Here was
an opportunity. He had been at Harrow with Brabazon. The man was addressing a theme close to Radclyffe's heart. Overseeing all light engineering in the
British zone, he had seen what the Volkswagen plant could achieve and he
was anxious that his nation not lose its chance to exploit fully this great asset.

On 15 July, on a visit to London, Radclyffe dictated and sent a two-page
letter to Lord Brabazon at his Pall Mall address. Reminding him of their
school acquaintance, he seconded the futility of trying to compete with the
Americans on their own ground. Radclyffe mentioned his role in revving up
the VW factory, which at the time of writing had built 15,000 cars, he said.
With adequate material supply, he told Brabazon, they could make 2,500
cars per month even though the plant had, he added, suffered 40 percent
bomb damage.

Frustrated by the unwillingness of his nation's carmakers to take an interest in the VW works, apart from seeking its destruction, Col. Charles Radclyffe addressed a heartfelt appeal to Lord Brabazon of Tara in July 1947, urging that action be taken at the British national level to exploit the asset that VW represented, either in Germany or in transplanted form in the United Kingdom. His initiative was dealt with and dismissed at the top of the Ministry of Supply.

"The manufacturing costs are ridiculously low, and the whole car has been designed to be produced at the lowest possible man hours per car," the colonel told the peer. He added the following:

> The whole question of this factory has been flogged out at high level discussions, and the only interest taken by the British Motor Trade was a desire to dismantle the factory for the sake of a few odd machine tools which were to be distributed throughout the trade. Luckily the necessity of a light cheap motor car for use out here has been able to defeat this vandalism. Nobody, however, has thought of manufacturing the car in Germany on British account for the export market, or dismantling the plant and taking it on reparations, and re-erecting it in England.
>
> The design of the car is a good five years ahead of anything being produced in England to-day, having torsion bar suspension all round, air cooled engine, and a simple sliding constant mesh gearbox. In fact in every way, here is a ready made car which has been tried and proved itself satisfactory on German roads, and for the most part in the hands of very inefficient German drivers.
>
> Why shouldn't the British Government take a leaf out of the Russian Government's book, and operate this Company for export in the same way that Russia are doing with the BMW?

Radclyffe closed by suggesting that if Brabazon were in Germany he would be happy to show him the VW works, "so that you could see for yourself what a valuable asset we have here, which I am afraid is going to be dismantled and lost." Here was a *cri de coeur* from a man who cared deeply about both the Beetle and Britain. Like many others, he hoped there was a way they could get together for good after their postwar romance.

The colonel had chosen a valid channel. On the very next day Brabazon sent a brief letter to Sir Archibald Rowlands at the Ministry of Supply. He told him that it "came to me from a cove who was at school with me and whom, curiously enough, I have never seen since." He added, "This is a new point of view and a new possibility which might indeed be hunted up for the general welfare of our economic position." He suggested a review by "whomever deals with motorcars in your ministry" before signing "Brab."

The peer's letter included (twice) a seemingly innocuous but in fact dangerous word: *new*. The postwar Whitehall wagon was rolling along well-laid tracks, with all the nation's slender resources committed to Labour's programs of nationalization and social welfare. Britain was destined to receive more American Marshall Plan aid than any other nation, and was destined to spend it on housekeeping instead of investing it in the country's run-down infrastructure. Anything new inspired only suspicion.

Sir Archibald responded on 28 July in a letter to Brabazon that admirably summed up the British attitude to the Volkswagen, deftly avoiding the contemplation of any ideas that might be considered new. He recapitulated the efforts that were being made to provide VW designs and samples to the industry for their edification. He added that "That, however, is not to say that the industry, or our own Ministry of Supply technicians, would accept the view of your correspondent that the design of the car is a good five years ahead of anything being produced in England to-day." He continued:

> We were, of course, also aware that the Volkswagen plant was laid out with machines, jigs, tools and dies for mass production on a considerable scale and we did consider with industry, through the Motor Advisory Council, the possibility of adopting the Volkswagen for manufacture in this country if this plant could be obtained as reparation and re-erected here. This, however, was too big an "if." The plant would first have to be declared as surplus capacity available for reparation and then this country would have to be successful, against other countries, in its bid for the plant with the International Allied Reparations Agency of Brussels. It was clearly impossible for the industry or any firm in the industry to base large scale plans for motorcar manufacture on the highly hypothetical availability of plant at some indeterminate and obviously not very early date in the future.

Sir Archibald closed his discussion-dampening letter by saying that "I don't know what manufacturing on British account for the export market means in the circumstances of Germany to-day . . ." Fortunately the VW works was just about to be cleared to do exactly that.

Some of the facts of the minister's response to Charles Radclyffe's initiative are, of course, open to debate. The plant had been declared available in principle for reparations. There was nothing "indeterminate" about the reservation placed on the plant for production for the Allies; nor was the reservation irrevocable. At the very highest governmental level it could have been waived. As to whether the VW's design was five years ahead of Britain's cars at that time, this can be said to be debatable. What the Beetle's advocates endeavored in vain to communicate to the British authorities was that *it was a very good car.* This would soon become all too obvious.

MINISTER OF SUPPLY SIR ARCHIBALD ROWLANDS and his colleagues had in fact been dutifully endeavoring to interest their industry in a joint approach to the production of a more attractive exportable car for Britain. Back in 1945 the U.K.'s Reconstruction Committee had concluded that government intervention would be needed if the motor industry were to be obliged to be more export-driven through the economic production of fewer types of cars in larger volumes. Ideally such an effort would focus on one car that was ideal for export.

Such an initiative had been discussed in the body referred to by Sir Archibald, the National Advisory Council on the U.K. Motor Manufacturing Industry, set up in April, 1946 by the Ministry of Supply "to provide a means of regular consultation between the Government and the motor manufacturers on such matters as the location of industry, exports, imports, research, design and technical development, production methods and the general progress of the industry." Chaired by Sir George Turner of Supply, the council was clearly intended by the government to help it come to grips with one of its most obdurate industries.

A summary of the council's deliberations through September 1947 averred to the idea of cooperative schemes among the British motormakers to produce autos that could conquer world markets. Had they implemented such a scheme, it would have been very like the German effort backed by the RDA that gave birth to the Volkswagen a decade earlier — before it became a stand-alone *Reich* project.

THE EXPORT CAR

The suggestion that manufacturers should combine to mass produce a common large car model for the export market was not favoured because of the difficulties of building up a large new organisation; selection of the model would be speculative and all types will probably be required; and the stimulus of competition other than foreign competition would be lost.

THE PEOPLE'S CAR

The suggestion that a cheap small car for the people be produced on a co-operative basis or by the State was subject to the same difficulties. The industry had already developed mass production with large price reductions. Adoption of a German model such as the Volkswagen would be out of line with continuous evolutionary development; it would have to be brought up to date; and, in any case, the industry has applied lessons learnt from the latest German models.

With just such insouciant ease the British motor industry could shrug off these suggestions from its government, complacently describing itself as "vigorous and efficient" and an aggressive pursuer of economies of scale through standardization of components.

By mid-1947, however, little practical prospect remained of an actual physical transplantation of the Volkswagen factory's tools and machines as a result of direct action by Britain. In a discussion of the plant's future in London on 17 June, Leslie Barber of Property Control pointed out that "the town of Wolfsburg (17,000 pop) depends entirely on the works, and as it is situated in an agricultural area, and no other employment opportunities exist, in the present housing shortage in the British Zone it would be quite indefensible to try and disperse the population and waste the accommodation."

Elsewhere in London six days earlier at the Ministry of Supply Mr. E. J. J. Bailiss responded to an inquiry from Toronto about the possibility that the VW might be manufactured in Britain. "I understand this is most unlikely," he wrote, adding:

> As you are aware this car was designed for production on an extremely large scale and its introduction into any country for manufacturing purposes would be a very costly business.
>
> Extensive mass production would be necessary in order to produce this car at a price approaching the original planned cost and apart from the quantities of raw materials involved, and which are not available, there is also the problem of the large labour force which would be needed.
>
> I think therefore, whilst the present circumstances obtain, there is no likelihood of the "Peoples Car" being manufactured in the United Kingdom.

THIS SEEMED THE FINAL WORD, in a minor key, on the possibility that the VW works could be acquired as a physical asset, to be transported to Britain as a nationalized carmaker obtained from Germany as war reparations. But it did not mean that the Labour government had given up on its efforts to find a way to circumvent its obstinate motor industry in order to establish an important domestic vehicle producer.

The Co-operative Wholesale Society that Denis Kendall had conjured up as the diabolical distribution channel for his Kendall cars had formed an automotive division to consider such opportunities. The Co-op was serious about getting into the automobile business — and it had the strong and personal support of none other than Stafford Cripps.

"As an avowed nationaliser," wrote Sir Miles Thomas, "he saw no reason why a nationalised, or at least a socialised, industry should not enter the motor trade. He asked me to discuss with the Co-operative Wholesale Society the possibility of their building cars, vans and lorries."

Sir Miles was a first-class candidate for the assignment, having just left the Nuffield Organisation after fourteen years in the motor industry. As Cripps expected, he was not daunted by the magnitude of the task:

> There was in point of fact nothing far-fetched or wholly impracticable about the idea, providing the necessary capital was forthcoming. When all is said and done, the percentage of the motor car that is actually made by the manufacturers who give it a name is still comparatively small. Components like chassis frames, body panels, wheels, tyres, electrical equipment, radiators and in several cases engines and gear-boxes are all bought out from specialists. All that is needed is an assembly factory, a sales organisation and provision for giving service to the customers. The CWS had a ready-made sales organisation with an almost captive market.

Miles Thomas set to work in 1948, preparing schemes that would establish the Co-op in the motor industry. Shrewdly, he counseled that it might be best to start with light delivery vans. This would arouse the least initial hostility and suspicion, because the Co-op naturally needed such vans. Then, using the same components in those halcyon years of the simple vehicle, passenger cars could be derived and marketed later.

"In the event," wrote Thomas, "the CWS board did not seem disposed to put up the many millions of pounds needed to finance the project, and between us we dissuaded Sir Stafford from pressing the idea forward." Here, intriguingly, was a British project that had strong overtones of the original KdF undertaking — a factory built by a socialized trade union, in that instance, with its cars to be sold through its many offices throughout Germany to keep retail overheads low.

Here, moreover, was irrefutable evidence, if more were needed, of the frustration of Cripps and his colleagues in the Attlee government with their backward, divided, irresolute, navel-gazing motor industry. Given this, were he and other ministers themselves not able to think and act laterally enough to embrace the potential value, in some form, to Britain of the Volkswagen car and factory? Regrettably, for the long-term welfare of their nation, they were not.

10

The Making of a Non-Decision

Some people wanted me to fly a British flag over the plant! I said, 'No, it's not "captured property." It's not war booty. It doesn't *belong* to the British.'" Ivan Hirst remembered early debates about the status of the VW works. "If anything it would have 'belonged' to the Americans; they were the first to occupy the area. But unlike some other things they couldn't very well have hidden the plant in a knapsack or a six-by-six."

To whom, then, did or would the VW works belong? The peacetime had come in which the factory had always been expected to hit its stride, turning out Beetles to satisfy 336,668 faithful German savers — and that was to be just the beginning. Now, from the beginning of the British administration of the sprawling factory and town of Wolfsburg the topic of its eventual fate was ever-present. It affected every decision, colored every assessment of the future. Yet time could not be obliged to stand still. In this isolated industrial island floating west of Berlin, decisions had to be made.

DECISIONS WOULD BE MADE in the context of the authority of the victorious Allied powers. On 5 June 1945, in the Declaration of Berlin, they assumed "supreme authority with respect to Germany, including all the powers possessed by the German Government, the High Command, and any state, municipality or local government authority." Comprehensive though this was, it left open the question of what would ultimately become of the nation, its people, and its businesses.

Guidance in the case of the Volkswagen works was provided by Law 52, Blocking and Control of Property, promulgated early in 1945 by the Supreme Headquarters Allied Forces in Europe (SHAEF) for action by all Military Government in Germany. It set out a wide category of institutions, entities, businesses, offices, and governmental bodies which were to be seized, man-

aged, supervised, or otherwise taken into the control of the Mil Gov. This included "The NSDAP [Nazi Party], all offices, departments, agencies and
organizations forming part of, attached to, or controlled by it."

Any and all parties who had custodial responsibilities for property were
instructed to act in accord with Article III of Law 52: "To hold the same subject to the directions of the Military Government and, pending such direction, not to transfer, deliver or otherwise dispose of the same; to preserve,
maintain and safeguard, and not to cause or permit any action which will im-
pair the value or utility of such property; to maintain accurate records and
accounts with respect thereto and the income thereof." Business enterprises
held under the law could engage in all their normal activities "within occupied Germany" so long as no transaction "directly or indirectly substantially
diminishes or imperils the assets of such enterprise or otherwise prejudicially
affects its financial position."

Thus Law 52 circumscribed the range of options available to Mil Gov.
"Preserve, maintain and safeguard" allowed of little enterprise. As Law 52
was clarified by SHAEF for those who had to administer it, its aim was "to
maintain the status quo with property, in order to facilitate the application
of affirmative measures by Military Government and to prevent fraudulent
transfers or attempts to conceal ownership."

These rules and interpretations must be seen in the context of a conquered Germany in which looting and lawlessness in a nation swarming with
displaced persons could be, and were, widespread. Simply pickling the assets
in aspic would have met this definition; putting them to work could even
have risked jeopardizing their value. But throughout the British stewardship
of the works at Wolfsburg, Law 52 was and remained their touchstone.

WITHIN THE BRITISH CONTROL COMMISSION of Germany
(CCG), the responsibility for asset administration devolved upon the
Property Control Branch of its Finance Division. Richard H. Parker in
Berlin was its director, the senior official in Germany; economist Leslie
Barber, responsible for Wolfsburg, had the task of formulating policy for
the disposition of the VW entities. The Finance Division delegated
accountants to Wolfsburg as well. The first was Alasdair McInnes, who
had proposed making the plant into an industrial park. He was followed
by the ambitious F. T. Neal, a fluent German-speaker who became deeply
involved in the works' affairs.

Extraordinary problems and responsibilities under Law 52 were in
store for Property Control at Wolfsburg, particularly because the factory
was producing cars under the direction of the CCG's Industry Division.
"The utilisation of the factory by the British involved special responsibilities in the works," said a high-level Property Control summary of the
plant's history:

The Board of Control and the resident officers gave much attention to the need to maintain and operate the Works in such a way as to gain credit for the British Occupying Authorities. This task involved much work on the problems of finding suitable Germans for responsible positions, denazification, the institution of a good Works Council, the just and equitable administration of the farms and housing estates.

The challenge was all the greater as a result of the status of the factory, which under the Level of Industry Plan for Germany was superfluous to requirements. It won this honor simply because it failed to commence production before the war began and was thus by definition redundant in a postwar Germany that was restrained by its conquerors to a moderate production capacity.

Thus the works was regarded as a virtual certainty for dismantling. "The CCG's Senior Resident Officer at the works told the local German officials in early January 1946 that the long term future of the works was uncertain and that in his opinion the existing facilities for production would not be retained as they exceeded the requirements of Germany's peace-time economy."

Of course this was distressing news for the inhabitants of the town of Wolfsburg, which existed solely to house the VW workers and their families. This concern was highlighted in a July 1947 Property Control position paper:

> The continued utilisation of the factory, the township, farms and forests presents a major social problem, for it must be remembered that the factory with its 8,000 employees and its town of some 17,000 people is a pocket of self-sufficient industry in the midst of a mainly agricultural area. On the soundness of the long-term policy will depend the proper employment and housing of 17,000 people for whom in the present state of German housing and industry it is impossible to provide alternative location.

Moreover the huge powerplant at the works, the second largest in Lower Saxony, not only heated and provided electricity to the factory and town but also delivered daily up to twenty megawatts of electricity to the grid in the British zone. This was equivalent to about two-thirds of the requirement of a major city like Hannover. Against this background, argued Property Control, "As the property is on the list of reparations only as a factory surplus to the German economy, if the ceiling of that economy is raised there can be no logical reason for dismantling and distributing the productive machinery."

Strictly from a technical perspective some of the main options for the disposition of the plant were set out by the British Ford engineers who visited the plant, in their report on the Wolfsburg facility. They put the position as follows:

> The three most obvious possibilities of the plant's future are:
>
> (a) To operate the factory on its present site.
>
> (b) To remove the plant and equipment en bloc to a reparation site.
>
> (c) To close the plant down and disperse the machinery in lots or units as reparations.

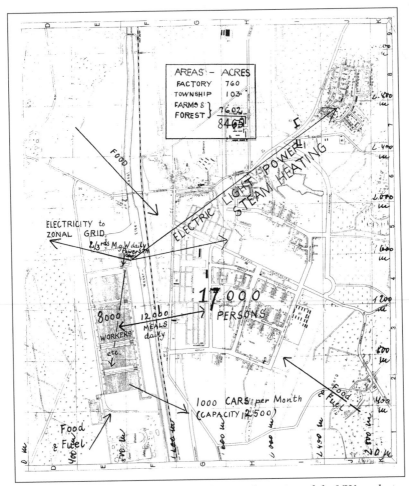

AREAS – ACRES
FACTORY   760
TOWNSHIP   103
FARMS & FOREST 7602
8465

Counting heavily against the possible transplantation of the VW works to Britain or elsewhere was the role that the factory played in the economy of its immediate area. This sketch was prepared in mid-1947 to indicate the numerous ways in which the factory was interlinked with the local infrastructure and economy.

(a) and (b) are dependent on many factors beyond the scope of this mission, but if action to adopt one or the other is likely to be considered, and at a period when military and inter-zone control has ceased to exist — much thought is necessary in the case of (a) as to the continued availability of sub-contracted parts, or alternative means of supplies; and in the case of (b) — to the availability of major spare parts for the more complicated machines.

So far as (c) is concerned, the team makes no recommendation that any of the machinery be acquired for use in England. No advantage would accrue — not already available from our machine tool resources.

Any piecemeal dispersal of equipment would, of course, have brought production to a halt. An elaborate charade once had to be staged at Wolfsburg to keep a French team from discovering and removing a butt welder for the steel sheets for the car's roof that was then essential for Type 11 production. Requests from Larry Hartnett for heavy presses and from Billy Rootes for a nonexistent Keller die-making machine were successfully rebuffed. But if someone with adequate credentials sought either to run or remove the entire factory, little could have been done to resist.

A further consideration that was not stressed unduly by those assessing the resources of the works was the actual condition of the machine tools in the plant. To be sure they were relatively young, having been installed in 1939–40, only six to seven years earlier. In July 1946, however, Ivan Hirst wrote, "All machine tools that remain are serviceable, but in poor condition from war time use, and movement to and from dispersal sites." We can imagine as well that little was done to make them look especially appetizing to visitors who were on the prowl for useful machinery.

The Allies did, however, obtain machinery from Germany under the war reparations procedures. One source estimated that 10 percent of the total machine park in the British, French, and American zones was dismantled for the benefit of those Allies. Australia's Newcastle Steelworks, for example, received German equipment that ranged from electric motors to large hydraulic presses.

The French too were not shy about asserting their rights. They commandeered virtually all private cars in their zone. The French initially occupied the territory close to Stuttgart; when Mercedes-Benz regained the keys to its factory nearby at Sindelfingen it found the plant utterly bereft of equipment.

While the Americans annexed few if any production operations, they were successful in claiming the lion's share of the research and development facilities in the western zones. This included the V-2 rocket know-how of Wernher von Braun's team and BMW's astonishing Herbitus test cell, which allowed aircraft jet and piston engines to be dynamometer-tested under simulated high-altitude conditions.

Reparations were treated differently in the zones of Germany and Austria controlled by the Soviets, whose homeland the Germans had so deeply and damagingly invaded. Russia was quick to liberate the Opel Kadett production facilities. It was quick as well to lay claim to many machine tools in BMW's Munich plant, having also gained control of the main BMW car production facility in their own zone of Germany. This led to the bizarre sight in Munich's Milbertshofen suburb of the last machines for Russia being loaded on rail flat cars for the trip east while brand-new ones were arriving from the west, paid for by Marshall Plan aid.

In Austria the plants of Steyr Daimler Puch, at Steyr, Graz, and Wiener-Neustadt, had the misfortune to be in the Soviet occupation zone. Of the total of eighteen thousand machine tools held by the Steyr factories, used to make a wide range of engines and vehicles, only five thousand did not depart with the Russians.

A similar fate befell the East German factories of the Auto Union group, especially those of car and motorcycle maker DKW at Zschopau. They were stripped and their tools transported east, where credible replicas of the successful two-stroke DKW RT125 motorcycle were produced for many years in Poland as well as Russia. The circumstances of the machines' abduction were poignantly described by Dr. Kurt Richter, who witnessed the cynical and practiced Russian techniques:

> The organization of the dismantling was conducted according to a quite primitive formula that was as effective in Zschopau as it was later in the wised-up Zwickau factories: The Russian finance officers started by giving the factory a substantial production program. In accord with that the layout of the machines was established, organized according to the necessary and available machine tools. That gave the wary Russians an error-free checklist [for dismantling]. Packed amateurishly without weather protection, the machines arrived at Brest-Litowsk by the thousand, the accompanying railway personnel told me.

In the turbulence of the weeks just after war's end when zonal frontiers were fluctuating the British enjoyed some reparations success. Drawings of the DKW RT125, introduced in 1939 as the latest creation of the German firm that built the world's best-selling two-wheelers, were whisked out by truck to Britain, where they were taken up by Birmingham's BSA. There draughtsmen created a BSA Bantam model in the mirror image of the DKW, putting the kick-starter and shift pedal on the right where they suited British tastes.

The new BSA was launched in 1948 and "went on to become the best-selling motorcycle in Britain in the 1950s and 1960s (perhaps the nearest equivalent to the Beetle in motorcycles)." By 1971 BSA built more than half a million Bantams in 125, 150, and 175 cc engine sizes. They might have sold even more if they'd bothered with development: "Indeed for many years BSA waited for DKW to uprate the little bike and then simply copied the changes."

Helped by their connections with the Bristol Aeroplane Company, the former stamping ground of Sir Roy Fedden, the Aldington brothers, makers of Frazer-Nash cars and prewar importers of BMWs to Britain, succeeded in getting through to Munich twice in 1945. On their second trip they arrived in a four-engined transport that was able to airlift six experimental BMW engines and numerous drawings back to Britain. With the aid of engineers from Munich, these helped Bristol design and produce its own BMW-derived passengers cars as early as 1946.

Nor was the United Kingdom completely outflanked in the battle to obtain general-purpose machine tools from Germany. As early as February 1947 Britain had collected 299 machines with a residual value of £460,000. Ultimately, estimates thought "probably on the low side" were that Britain obtained some 24 million pounds in value of machines and equipment of all kinds from Germany after the war — not all of Britain's industries were as shy of the reparations opportunity as were its major carmakers.

THE STRUGGLE TO LAY CLAIM to the assets of a vanquished Germany took a distinctive twist with Volkswagen. The VW factory had a unique status in occupied Germany, Charles Radclyffe reminded his colleagues in December 1946: "In general where a works are activated by Mil Gov the assets belong to private individuals or companies. Therefore, [in such cases] the responsibility of German custodians and/or managements is primarily to United Nations or Neutral nationals or to special category German nationals. In the Volkswagenwerk, there is a direct relationship with Mil Gov and therefore with the ultimate decision of the Occupying Powers on the disposition of NSDAP property and the claims of persecuted persons or societies such as trade unions."

Property Control's Leslie Barber explained the peculiar status of VW in an internal memo in September 1947, his last major contribution to the debate before taking up new responsibilities in Geneva: "The policy of the CCG to hand back industry to the control of the originally owning Germans is not possible in the case of the Volkswagenwerk Complex," he wrote, "as the Works were built by the DAF for the whole of Germany and financed from compulsory levies in lieu of Trade Union and other voluntary contributions confiscated by the DAF. There is therefore *no* German to whom the property can be handed back. It remains the responsibility of Property Control Branch under Law 52 until Quadripartite disposition is decided."

Dr. Robert Ley's DAF, the pseudo-union German Workers Front, had indeed built and equipped the VW works. Its legal entities still held the plant's capital: RM 145 million by the D AF Property Administration and RM 5 million by a D AF Trust Company — a total capitalization of RM 150 million. The DAF ownership was an added annoyance for the custodians of the works, Charles Radclyffe explained: "The problem at the works has been aggravated by the popular view of the workers that the factory was DAF property and therefore fair game for all kinds of thefts and damage." They thought of it as their factory with which they could do as they liked.

Leslie Barber's use of the term "Quadripartite" was a dutiful albeit hollow nod to the no-longer-functioning four-power occupation of Germany, the Russians long ago having ceased any form of constructive cooperation with the other wartime Allies. Having lost any chance of gobbling up the Beetle's factory, however, the Soviets had ceased calling for its dismantling. They did so by acknowledging that the plant had originally been intended as a social experiment — in the communist context an entirely commendable initiative.

A special situation called for a special solution. The VW works was one of the largest properties in the anomalous position of belonging to the DAF, but was not the only such property. Accordingly on 29 April 1947 the CCG issued its Directive 50 setting out a policy for the DAF-owned properties. Relevant sections were these:

ARTICLE II

1. Title to property not subject to disposal or use under Article VIII having belonged to a trade union, cooperative, political party or any other democratic organisation before it became the property of any organisation referred to in Article I hereof, shall be retransferred to such organisation provided that it is authorised and its activities are approved by the appropriate Zone Commander.

2. Where retransfer of title to property cannot be made because no existing organisation is completely identical with the organisation which was the former owner of the property, title to such property shall be transferred to a new organisation or organisations whose aims are found by the Zone Commander to be similar to those of the former organisation.

ARTICLE VIII

1. The Zone Commander shall destroy property subject to being destroyed as war potential, designate for reparation property subject to reparations, use for the purposes of occupation property subject to such use and restitute property of victims of Nazi persecutions.

This allowed of several interpretations. One was that the VW works was being used for purposes of occupation, namely to produce the vehicles needed by the Allied authorities in the western zones, not to mention the German economy, and thus was not subject to disposal while this need remained. Another interpretation, clearly, was that there was not, and could not be, a successor organization that was similar in any way to Robert Ley's Nazi-era DAF. This being so, said Property Control, it was obliged "to conserve all the assets of the Volkswagenwerk Complex against claims arising from trades unions, cooperative societies and other [organizations mentioned in the Control Council] directive intended to dispose of all claims against the DAF organisation of the NSDAP."

Although Directive 50 was crafted to deal with the disposition of DAF property, which the VW works assuredly was, here again this extraordinary factory received special dispensation. It was "specifically excluded from the list of DAF properties to be transferred under Directive 50: its future was to be announced through a separate Military Government ordinance. The question of who the final owner of the company would be once the British control was lifted was, of course, an issue every bit as controversial as the dispute over the ownership of land in the town."

Another matter had to be resolved before any action could be taken over the disposition of the VW factory. The land for the works and its worker city had been acquired at one and the same time; did the city have a separate political existence? Sketchy evidence suggested that the original intention had been to spin off the town as an independent legal entity, but this had not been achieved before Germany's collapse.

Against repeated efforts by the town to gain its independence the British Property Control officers were obliged to defend the unitary nature of the works and town, unpopular though this made them in the area. When the local authorities tried to have the occupied VW works appointed the legal successor to its DAF-era counterpart, so that it could bestow largesse on Wolfsburg, Property Control responded: "Where is that to come from? All the properties in Wolfsburg are bankrupt, at least the organisations which financed them, a legacy of Nazi mismanagement."

THE EXCLUSION OF THE VW WORKS from the strict provisions of Directive 50 was a consequence as well of the Mil Gov's deliberations on a claim to possession of the plant from Germany's trade unions: "There had always been a populist mystique attached to the Volkswagenwerk, and this was reinforced in the immediate post-war period by the tacit understanding that the works would remain 'Eigentum des Deutschen Volkes' [property of the German people]. Although this clearly implied some form of state ownership, the trade unions also laid claim to the works."

They did, but their claim was anticipated by Property Control in an exchange of communications between Messrs. Parker and Goff in May 1948. Could the unions be regarded as the plant's owners because they were the legitimate successors of the DAF? "It seems quite clear from the evidence," wrote Parker from Minden, "that though the DAF was the medium the real owner of the Volkswagenwerke was the Reich which used it as a method of diffusing the people's car to the people of Germany whether the purchaser belonged to any labour organization or not. It is even more clear that at no time did it ever belong to any Trade Union or Co-operative Society."

If that were the case, wrote Parker, he was inclined "to rule that the Volkswagen Werke is not subject to Directive 50 but should be disposed of when other Reich property is disposed of." He got no argument from Goff in Hannover. In a three-page review of the history and the financing of the VW works Goff said that "it can quite reasonably be supposed that the cost of building the Volkswagenwerke was financed from subscriptions from German workers and NOT from any dispossessed Trade Union property. I therefore consider that as the Volkswagenwerk Organisation did not exist at the time of the dissolution of the Trades Unions the latter can have no legal claim to the Company."

Thus Property Control was of a single mind when in July 1948 in Hannover it received a letter from Hermann Beermann of the Lower Saxony trade union association. Beermann set out the facts as he and his colleagues saw them:

In view of the fact that the Volkswagen works in Wolfsburg are a property of considerable value and originate from contributions made by German workers, we request that a Managing Council be established to work with the Custodian. This Council should consist of representatives from the Lower Saxony Ministries of Economics and Finance and also of representatives of the German Trade Unions in the same way as in the case of the Council of the Reichswerke AG.

The Volkswagen works originate from DAF property which in its turn represents property dispossessed from the Trade Unions and as Trade Unionists we have very special interests and also an obligation to interest ourselves in the management of these works.

We, therefore, request you to examine the matter and are at your disposal to discuss the problem at any time.

The Industrial Relations Branch of the CCG easily divined the thrust of this attack by the union association. "On the face of it," it parried in a letter to Property Control, "the proposal of the Niedersachsen Trade Unions looks like an attempt to anticipate a decision as to the ultimate disposal of the Volkswagen Works."

Calling the union's arguments "at least debateable," Industrial Relations said that the issue of the plant's ultimate ownership had to be clearly separated from the establishment of a council as requested by Herr Beermann. Well prepared as it was, Property Control was able to shrug off this trade-union challenge to its authority.

THAT THE UNIONS WERE SEEKING to stake a claim to the VW works was hardly astonishing. So was almost everyone else on both the German and Allied sides. Here, after all, was a huge factory with a virtual monopoly on the production of the most craved commodity in Germany. If fingers had not been ultrasticky it would have been more surprising.

Property Control recapped some of the events of the first half of 1947 when the CCG, following a general policy in Germany at that time, sought to relax its supervision of activities at the VW works and devolve more authority on the German management. The ability of the German staff members to behave in an ethical and efficient manner was conditioned, it found, by the following factors among others:

Natural psychological tendency of Germans appointed to positions of authority to use such authority for their own ends e.g. the appointment of nominees to positions useful to the German management, pressure exerted on farm managers and others to supply food and services for their personal use etc.

Their failure, either wilfully or by neglect, to take action in obviously dishonest transactions of departmental managers.

The endeavours of German management to obtain control of German Works Police, an essential element in the cleaning up of the works, leads one to suspect that the Germans do not want to stop the persistent and extremely serious thieving and the nefarious activities of departmental managers.

Black Market dealing is used by industrial undertakings both for personal benefits and for the arrangement of earlier delivery of materials.

An example of the latter was the allocation by the German managers of fifty Beetles to the plant's subcontractors to gain their cooperation. As for black market dealing, said Property Control, "a German employee was found in possession of 1,200 English cigarettes and 5 lbs. coffee (i.e. 7,800 RM plus 2,750 RM equalling 10,550 RM) in consideration of services rendered and spare parts supplied."

Although this was not at all the way that the British wished to see business being done in the zone under their occupation control, these reports may well have been given exceptional emphasis by Property Control to justify a return to closer British oversight of the works. Certainly the British acted quickly to deal with any arrogation of assets whenever it was detected.

Nor could it be maintained that all the British officials who held responsibilities at Wolfsburg were purer than the driven snow. In these postwar years some felt that after leaving Germany they would face an uncertain future in the austere Britain of Messrs. Attlee and Cripps. A few vested their hopes in the VW works, either angling for a permanent position in the company's management or seeking a beneficial role in the final disposition of the factory. Such men saw those hopes dashed.

ANOTHER ISSUE THAT NEEDED TO BE SETTLED before the VW works could have an independent existence was that of its rights to the designs of the cars it was producing. VW's relationship to the Porsche companies was defined by a contract signed on 16 September 1943 between the Volkswagenwerk GmbH and the Porsche KG. This committed VW to use the services of Porsche and in turn gave VW exclusive rights to those services in the engineering of cars and light trucks with retail prices of less than four thousand marks.

According to the 1943 agreement Porsche would be paid a royalty of one mark per car produced for the use of his patents. As well, VW committed to the yearly use of a minimum of 2,500 engineer-days and 30,000 workshop hours from the Porsches. Generous though this was, DAF leader Robert Ley sought in 1944 to ameliorate the terms to almost outlandish levels "to thank Professor Porsche in any way at all for his achievements hitherto and thereby to bind him even more closely to the works, also to link him financially to the factory."

Although these efforts by Ley to sweeten the deal with Porsche failed to reach the stage of a signed contract, they "delineated an exceptionally favorable financial arrangement which in any case secured the survival of the Porsche KG."

> The negotiations showed that as a result of the intervention of Ley the position of the Porsche KG with respect to the Volkswagenwerk GmbH had been substantially strengthened, which helped to secure its existence in the postwar period. In fact after the end of the war the Porsche KG, which had been

Among the issues that had to be resolved before the British could decide the disposition of the VW works was its relationship to the Porsches, father and son, seen at the Nürburgring in August 1950. Ferry, right, reached new agreements with the works in 1948 and 1949 that were of considerable later value to the Porsche company.

transplanted to Carinthia, seamlessly continued its engineering activities, even though there was no clarity at all about the future of the Volkswagen factory.

Although under British control the engineering capabilities of the Porsche rump group in a former sawmill in Gmünd in Austria's state of Carinthia were not actually being drawn upon — there was no new product development as such for the moment — the terms of the contract called for payments from VW to Porsche that were mounting by the month. It also defined the terms under which Porsche's design patents could be used by the VW works.

Late in 1947 these conjoined issues were raised and reviewed at a meeting which was also attended by members of the Research Branch. The meeting, as Ivan Hirst reported to the eighteenth convening of the Board of Control on 7 November, "showed that the patent question was a most complex one."

Soon thereafter the position was clarified by Ferry Porsche during his first postwar visit to Wolfsburg. Ferry had been released by the French in July 1946 to return to the Porsche holdings in Austria, but he had not immediately regained his freedom to travel more widely through the zonal boundaries of Austria and Germany. Nevertheless he "felt it a duty toward my father and my brother-in-law to make contact with the Volkswagen factory in Wolfsburg and at the same time to start all possible preparations to return to our own factory in Stuttgart. It was obvious that we were not going to get any financial assistance in Austria.

Therefore a new contract between Volkswagenwerk and Porsche was the most desirable expedient."

In mid-December of 1947 F. T. Neal reported to the Control Board that "Information regarding the early contracts between Porsche KG as the designers of the Volkswagen, Reichsverband der Deutschen Automobilindustrie, the DAF and Volkswagenwerk GmbH was obtained" from "Porsche Junior," as he was called. Porsche also told the surprised custodians of the VW works that the Volkswagen company possessed the rights as well to the Volkspflug or people's tractor designs.

Although both parties considered an early resolution of the rights and payments situation desirable, not until the following October did the Board of Control learn that "negotiations had taken place between representatives of the company and the Porsche interests in regard to the liabilities devolving from the contract made by the Volkswagenwerk GmbH and Porsche K. G. Stuttgart and Prof. Dr. Porsche in October [sic] 1943."

The negotiations referred to were held at considerable length in September 1948 at Bavaria's Bad Reichenhall, near Salzburg on the German side of the border with Austria and not far from the rubble of Hitler's Eagle's Nest at Berchtesgaden. Heinz Nordhoff led the VW side of the discussions in which, recalled Ferry Porsche, "everything went off all right."

The Porsche people gave up their former complete monopoly on VW development work in favor of a specific definition of their engineering responsibilities. This, said the VW works' German custodian Hermann Knott, was a "liberation of the works from its hitherto very comprehensively uncontrollable payment obligations toward Porsche," which included "more or less uncontrollable expense reimbursements." Of special importance and ultimate value to Ferry's sister Louise Piëch, who had been living in Austria since 1943, was the granting of a condition that the Porsche side had imposed: the allocation to them of the Volkswagen sales rights for Austria.

Porsche agreed not to engineer competitive car models in the displacement range of 1.0 to 1.3 liters. It would receive a royalty of a percentage of the retail price of each Volkswagen, replacing the previous arrangement of one mark per car. This, said custodian Knott, "was a burden the works could easily bear." "There was no legal obligation to pay any royalty or anything at all, for that matter," said Heinz Nordhoff later. "The original contract had been with the Nazi Labor Front, not with Volkswagenwerk. But the Volkswagen was Porsche's design and we were building it. It was the right thing to do."

Signed on 17 September 1948, the Reichenhall accord still had to survive the scrutiny of Mil Gov's Legal Division. Here the agreement smote the buffers — thanks in part to a derailment engineered by the Porsche men themselves. Through intermediaries Rudolf Hruska and Karl Abarth they had been contracted to design sports and racing cars for Cisitalia in Italy. But to do this, Ferry argued to the British occupation authorities in Austria's Klagenfurt, he and his men would need the same freedom of action and movement as was granted to any Austrian enterprise.

"The matter was taken up at the Allied headquarters in Vienna," wrote Ferry, "where it was determined that the Porsche company was really half Austrian by virtue of the origin of its founders." Since 1938 the Porsche engineering company had been a Kommanditgesellschaft (K.G.) or limited partnership, so the nationality of its partners could play a role in such a determination. "From there it was also decided that the half operating in Austria was, in fact, Austrian and not German," Ferry added. An internal Porsche contract of 20 February 1947 confirmed this. "This enabled us to go ahead without further controls — at least, on the Gmünd end of the enterprise."

With this ruling, the occupation authorities could scarcely execute a sharp about-face and say that Porsche's Austrian company, signatory in Reichenhall, was identical with the Stuttgart firm that had signed the 1943 contract with the VW works. Nor did they in June 1949:

> Property Control Branch advised the factory that the Legal Division had decided that Porsche Konstruktion GmbH, Gmünd, Kärnten, Austria were not the legal successors to Dr. F. Porsche K.G. Stuttgart and therefore the provisional contract dated 17 Sep 48 could not be approved by Mil. Gov. It was now suggested that the Company should prepare a contract between Porsche Konstruktion Gmünd, Porsche K.G. Stuttgart and Volkswagenwerk GmbH. When this had been prepared it would be submitted to Property Control Branch Land Niedersachsen for approval before signature.

A supplementary contract was duly executed in August 1949, involving Ferdinand and Ferry Porsche personally in the agreement, but its implementation had to await the ultimate disposition of the VW works because the British occupation authorities were not partners to the Reichenhall compact. Thus, at last, a new agreement between the Volkswagen factory and the Porsche interests was in place. But it had to await activation until the final decision had been made on the disposition of the works at Wolfsburg.

DURING THEIR CONTROLLING YEARS in Wolfsburg the British understandably concentrated on making the model that the works was already tooled to produce, the classic Beetle Type 11. This was the vehicle most needed by the occupation authorities and most desired by Germans and the export markets. But even in the absence of the skills of the Porsche office some development did take place, in fact ultimately leading to the introduction of a brand-new model.

One of the boldest new-product ideas was also one of the first, put forward in the early days of the postwar period by the irrepressible Michael McEvoy. "Why not make a sports VW?" he said to Ivan Hirst. "Just turn the

One of the first adventures in new product development by the VW works was the creation by its small experimental shop of a two-seater roadster, authorized by Ivan Hirst after an inspiration by Michael McEvoy.

engine around, put it ahead of the rear wheels, and make up a tubular frame." Some German car enthusiasts were doing just that, as indeed was Ferry Porsche in Gmünd with a prototype that first ran in the spring of 1948. But Hirst realized that he'd do better to concentrate on Beetle-building.

Still, McEvoy's suggestion gave Hirst an idea. Earlier, the plant's little experimental department, supervised by Rudolf Ringel, had built a cabriolet version of the standard Beetle. Now Hirst suggested to Ringel that he make a two-seater convertible. This used a modified hood panel as its trunk lid, suitably louvered to admit cooling air. Equipped with a more lively twin-carburetor engine, the unique convertible became a great favorite of Charles Radclyffe.

This one-off car served as a prototype for a two-seater cabriolet VW model to be produced by Josef Hebmüller and Son at Wülfrath in the Ruhr district. On commission from Heinz Nordhoff, Hebmüller completed three prototypes by the end of 1948. The handsome new VW model, launched at the Geneva Salon in March 1949, was another new asset of the factory still under British control. Although Nordhoff had asked for 2,000, problems at Hebmüller meant that only some 750 were made.

In parallel Osnabrück's Wilhelm Karmann was asked to design and build a four-seater cabriolet version of the Beetle. This too was completed in prototype form in 1948. The formal launch of Karmann's open car was on 1 July 1949; production began the same month. From then until the model

Former Porsche workshop chief Rudolf Ringel modified a front hood to serve as the rear deck of the two-seater convertible Beetle. The one-off car became a particular favorite of Charles Radclyffe.

Under the rear deck of the "Radclyffe" Roadster was a VW engine equipped with twin carburetors. The resourceful Rudolf Ringel had access to some of Porsche's development bits and pieces.

was phased out in January 1980 Karmann built 331,847 cabriolets, creating one of the most charismatic of all the Beetle variants.

These open versions were created with the help of outsiders. But could VW engineer a new model of its own? It had done so on a modest scale for the transport of components inside the factory when a fleet of forklift trucks loaned to Wolfsburg by the British army had suddenly to be returned. Ivan Hirst suggested making a replacement from VW drivetrain and chassis parts. These were joined together by a trussed tubular steel frame that supported a flat platform. The driver sat at the extreme rear of this very serviceable *Plattenwagen* (flattened car).

That ubiquitous Dutchman, Ben Pon, spotted a Plattenwagen during one of his works visits. He was struck by its resemblance to a pedal-powered delivery vehicle that was popular in Holland, with its operator seated at the rear, pedaling the single rear wheel, and a platform at the front sup-

Based on the concept created at Wolfsburg, coachbuilder Josef Hebmüller created a production version of the two-seater Roadster. This new VW model was launched at the 1949 Geneva Salon.

Like the Hebmüller roadster, the four-seater cabriolet designed and built by Wilhelm Karmann was commissioned, designed, and launched while the VW works was still under British stewardship. It was made for VW by Karmann until 1980.

ported by two steered wheels. Could Wolfsburg supply him with something like that?

Pon had another idea too. In his looseleaf notebook, opposite his notes on a visit to Minden on 23 April 1947 to meet with Charles Radclyffe, he sketched an alternative design. It was a fully enclosed van, shaped like an American loaf of bread, in which the driver sat right at the front. The engine was under a hutch at the rear; bold horizontal strokes of the Pon pencil showed that the rest of the body was free to carry cargo.

These ideas, Ivan Hirst told Pon, had to wait for an increase in VW's engineering capacity, which Hirst was working on. To supplement the little drawing office led by Josef Kales, Hirst was looking for engineering talent. An outstanding candidate was suggested by Michael McEvoy: Rudolf

A cutaway shows how well the front and rear suspension, including the hub reduction gears, of the wartime Kübelwagen served the Type 2 Transporter, the development of which commenced while the works was still under British authority.

Uhlenhaut, who at the time was assisting at the vehicle repair facility the REME had established at Hanomag in Hannover.

Uhlenhaut, who had joined Daimler-Benz in 1931, had led the testing program for the Mercedes-Benz 170V before being named to head the company's new racing department in 1936. Fluent in English, Uhlenhaut had led the successful Mercedes-Benz racing effort of 1937 to 1939. In that role he had worked closely with McEvoy and Pomeroy on their experimental adaptation of Zoller supercharging to his racing cars.

Rudy Uhlenhaut was by any measure an extremely competent and creative development engineer. He spent two days at Wolfsburg with Hirst and the German on-site team, sizing up the opportunity. He would have been welcome there. But the engineer declined the offer. "I'm a Mercedes man," he told Hirst, "and the company will come back."

Hirst interviewed another man, Alfred Häsner, an engineer who had been at Phänomen, a maker of light air-cooled vehicles. After a lengthy discussion Hirst concluded that the engineer was capable but only interested in designing air-cooled engines; Volkswagen needed rather more. In 1948, however, with Heinz Nordhoff managing the works, Häsner was engaged after all. His first major task was to realize Ben Pon's concept of a big box on wheels, the light transport vehicle that Germany desperately needed.

In 1949 a first prototype was ready. Its breadloaf-shaped body was mounted on the normal VW platform frame. To get the lower gearing a van needed, it used the reduction-gear rear hubs that had originally been developed for the Kübelwagen; the height of the front suspension was adjusted accordingly.

Initial attempts to build a van on the Beetle chassis failed when the weight of the body proved too much for the platform. The creation of a unique frame was necessary to make the Transporter into the great success it ultimately became.

"They took it out at night for testing," Ivan Hirst recalled, "and when they came back to the works in the morning it was six inches lower. The weight of the body and the load broke the back of the hat-section at the center of the platform frame." Heavy revisions were needed. Broken as well was Häsner's spirit, whose career at Wolfsburg was terminated after a year by this debacle.

The van's Beetle platform was replaced by a bespoke frame. Its two main longitudinal members were topped by five crossmembers under the load floor. These extended out to box-section side sills to which the van's body sides were welded, forming a robust yet light monocoque structure. In this form the Type 2 Transporter, as it was known, entered production at Wolfsburg in March 1950. Though this was after the plant's future was resolved, the initial preparations had been made during the final months of Mil Gov control of Volkswagen.

A FINAL ISSUE CONSTRAINING the disposition of the works was its role as a major overhaul and repair center for the Royal Electrical and Mechanical Engineers on behalf of the British vehicle fleet. Its first task under the Allied occupation, this repair work continued. A mid-1947 review characterized this activity as follows:

> Part of the shop area of the factory was taken over by 2 R.E.M.E. Auxiliary Workshops for the undermentioned repair work. The workshop occupies 16%

of the total shop area used at present and employs 8% of the labour force employed at the works.

4th line overhauls Volkswagen
    monthly capacity   250
Engine overhauls monthly capacity   800
Major assemblies monthly capacity   400
Engine Overhauls
    All British Army Vehicles
    monthly capacity   450

This was no negligible enterprise within the Wolfsburg walls. The works received the Class 5 hard cases among the Beetles needing repair, the ones whose over-enthusiastic drivers, reveling in the agile handling of these little cars, had spun, rolled, or crashed their charges. Unrepairable cars were simply stripped, their useable parts cannibalized to keep others going. Wrote a VW historian:

> The department overhauling cars and assemblies for the British continued for some time, but from the organizational standpoint it became part of the service department. Later, when the British fleet was beginning to show its age, the overhaul operation was shut down. The British then exchanged older cars for new ones and the factory sold off the "trade-ins" to dealers for overhaul and resale to the public. This provided a shot in the arm for these dealers as secondhand cars were in short supply. These ex-British cars were known as "CCG-Wagen."

THUS THE VW WORKS' REPAIR SERVICES to the occupiers were being phased out. The plant had a small development capacity of its own and an agreement with Porsche waiting in the wings. It had resolved its issues with the town of Wolfsburg, for the time being at least, and had fended off a budding grab for power on the part of the trade unions. It was no longer scheduled for dismantling as war reparations, according to the revised 1948 list of companies qualifying for that distinction. The chance of interesting a major motor company in its management or ownership *in situ* was remote. What, then, was to become of the Beetle builder?

Through most of 1947 the solution favored by Property Control was to establish a trustee corporation to hold the plant's assets and guide its policies. First adumbrated at midyear, the trusteeship concept was articulated further by Richard Parker in an internal memo of 27 October :

> It is submitted that eventually the Volkswagenwerk group of companies and their properties should be restituted in some form to the German people (some 300,000 families have paid 268 million RM) but that every step should be taken to ensure that such a large industrial unit should not pass into such pure State control as might prove a dangerous weapon in the hands of a State Government and could be used ultimately against the interests of the victorious powers.
>
> It is therefore submitted that the long term policy should be the creation of a trustee company, say, comparable to the London Passenger Transport Board, above the Land Government and above particular social interests such as Trades Unions. The Trustee Company would provide a democratic body working for

the German people and showing that the Volkswagenwerk group can demonstrate a democratic efficiency rather than being a showplace of NSDAP discriminatory politics.

The sudden appearance of the London Transport Board in a discussion of the future of Volkswagen may occasion surprise. The board was the creation of arch-administrator Herbert Morrison when he took the chair of the London County Council in 1932. At that time he created the Transport Board as a trusteeship that took control of all the capital's coach, tram, bus, and underground services. Now Morrison held the chair of several of Labour's key postwar committees, including the Lord President's Committee, the Ministerial Committee on Economic Planning, and the Cabinet Socialisation of Industries Committee. With its links to one of Labour's senior politicos, it was a reference that could hardly have failed to appeal to officials in London.

The concerns expressed by Richard Parker over the threat of an uncontrolled or mis-controlled VW works were real. "The Works in full production would command a control over passenger vehicle output for domestic requirements and export," Parker had written in July. "The output could mean that the German motor industry might attain European influence that would be dangerous if the undertaking were not controlled by a trustee corporation not directly connected with the central government and so beyond the manipulation of any one interest."

That was the negative aspect of the plant's potential as seen by its British custodians. There could be a positive aspect as well, Parker wrote in mid-1947:

> The Volkswagenwerk Complex was intended as a showpiece for Nazi organisation and Nazi political policy, but became in fact a by-word for corruption including land purchase at inflated prices, overpayment of certain Hitler favourites like the designer of the car and cynical party discrimination in the grading of staff. Now it is possible for the British to create out of the Volkswagenwerk a real example of democratically controlled industry by forming a trustee undertaking on behalf of the German people.

This was not idle palaver; the trusteeship concept was in full accord with the way the Mil Gov members on the ground in Germany saw their responsibilities. "We were 'trustees'," said Ivan Hirst, "who felt that in some form or another VW should remain German. The ethos was that we were there to control and disarm Germany and to plant the seeds of a new government that would be more stable than Weimar. Then Marshall Aid began, and it became clear that we had to build up Germany as a bulwark against communism."

In this line of defense there was one loose cannon: Heinz Nordhoff. Nordhoff had made independent attempts to interest the Ford Motor Company in Volkswagen — and in Heinz Nordhoff. The VW plant's new chief seemed reluctant to accept any future for the factory other than one he personally engineered. He was not yet the Nordhoff of towering legend; but he was already the Nordhoff of overweening pride and total self-confidence.

Auto importer Max Hoffman, seen in New York during an early meeting with Ferry Porsche, left, met Heinz Nordhoff in that city in April 1949 to discuss the future of the VW factory. Hoffman balked at Nordhoff's suggestion that he make an offer to the British for a controlling share of the factory.

The engineer's pride had taken a knock when he applied for a visa to visit America to investigate the American market for his Beetles. His wartime role as a *Wehrwirschaftsführer*, a leader of the defense economy, that had blocked his future at General Motors was also a barrier to entry to the United States. Not until the spring of 1949 was Nordhoff granted a visa to attend an exhibition of German goods at New York's Museum of Science and Industry. Held between 9 April and the twenty-fourth, the "Germany 49 — Industry Show " included a Volkswagen, the first to be officially exhibited in the New World.

During his New York stay Nordhoff met with the best-known importer of foreign cars in the eastern United States, Max Hoffman. After his negotiations with Rosengart on behalf of the Erfiag design of his friend Josef Ganz, Hoffman had embarked for America with the aim of importing the cars he knew so well in Europe. He had arrived in New York in June 1941 only to have the American declaration of war postpone his execution of this plan, but in early 1947 the Hoffman Motor Car Company finally opened a showroom at Park Avenue and 59th Street in the heart of Manhattan.

Extremely knowledgeable about Europe's cars and the men who made them, Max Hoffman was an admirer of the engineering skills of Ferdinand Porsche. Already familiar with the Volkswagen, he had been approached by Ben Pon during a selling trip to the States in January 1949. Now in April he and Nordhoff discussed the car and the future of the plant.

"Nordhoff said that the future of the factory was still uncertain," Hoffman later recalled. "He said that if I were interested I could probably get control of it for something like two million dollars. I had the money; I could have done it. But I was worried about the situation in Europe. The East German border was too close to the plant. The Communists were not far away. I told him I wasn't interested."

After his discussions with Ford officials, Heinz Nordhoff was well aware that Charles Radclyffe, at least, was concerned about Volkswagen's ability to survive without some independent links with the motor industry, some partners who could help it endure through the difficult postwar years. In his contact with Hoffman, Nordhoff certainly had this requirement in mind. He may well have seen Max Hoffman as a compatible spirit with the where-withal to negotiate credibly with the British for a controlling share in the works. Still new to Volkswagen, Nordhoff would have viewed Hoffman's participation as a way of securing his own position in the company. With the end of the four-year reservation nearing, such a solution would have been neither improbable nor impossible.

In early 1949, speculation about the future of the VW works was rife, as reported in *The Autocar:*

> The Volkswagen factory, by far one of the best confidence tricks which paper-hanger Hitler put over on his faithful followers, forms a continuous source of discussion in the German motor industry. While it is at the moment under British management, the centre of interest in any discussion lies in who will eventually own it.
>
> The works provide a tidy slice towards the occupation costs, equipment and buildings being of considerable value; under present economic conditions the cost would make it impossible for an independent German concern to contemplate even offering the bare valuation price. So should the Volkswagen works ever change hands it is most likely to go to one of the two German motor firms which are controlled by American interests.

As many had forecast, the VW plant's product was already causing disquiet in Europe's auto markets. Holland, Belgium, and Switzerland were the leading export markets for the Beetle. Pierre D'Ieteren's desire to become the Belgian VW importer was fulfilled on 16 March 1948, when D'Ieteren Frères signed a contract with the Volkswagenwerk. His first ten cars were collected by company drivers in August of that year and delivered to eager customers. Under D'Ieteren's aegis the assembly of VWs in Belgium, sought by Col. John Dufour in 1946, would begin in 1954. It has never ceased.

"In January, 1948," wrote the British SMMT's R. Gresham Cooke to the *Times,* "Germany sold three cars in Switzerland, but in October it sold 295, and ousted this country from its premier position so far as small cars are concerned." By mid-November 1948 more than one thousand Beetles had been shipped to AMAG, the Swiss importer. "Knowing the pre-war record of German subsidised exports," continued Cooke, "it is not surprising that manufacturers here feel concerned that some of their best European markets are being unfairly attacked by our former enemy now operating under British and American approval."

Switzerland has always been regarded as Europe's most neutral car market because it has no indigenous producer and thus is equally open to imports from all nations. The quick acceptance of the Beetle by Swiss buyers was thus an early wake-up call to automakers in Britain and indeed in other lands.

The leading Swiss motoring publication, *Automobil Revue,* was respected throughout Europe for its thoroughness and impartiality. Its editors took special care over their test, published in June 1949, of a new Volkswagen. They remarked that this was their first trial of a postwar car built by an industry that had much lost ground to make up. They selected a brand-new car from the Swiss importer's stock and ran it in carefully before testing; their test Beetle had been manufactured around January 1949.

Automobil Revue found the VW to be "one of the few economy cars that offer the space, performance, and riding comfort that is required by those motorists who, rightly enough, would like to motorize themselves and their friends with the minimum financial outlay. Volkswagen sought to reach this goal not by shrinking an ordinary car but rather by striving to keep the interior and cargo room of a medium-sized car, as much as possible, and then to diminish the need for space for the mechanical elements so that smaller outer dimensions, lower weight, and reduced production costs resulted."

These were perspicacious comments by the authoritative biweekly, contrasting the VW with the many "shrunken ordinary cars" that then populated the ranks of Europe's small autos. The VW, instead, had been developed as a functional small car from first principles by experts, the magazine noted: "The Volkswagen perhaps differed most strongly from almost all other passenger cars in the manner of its creation, in that from the beginning of its development neither sales director nor works proprietor were on hand; we can probably attribute to this the car's very sober, Spartan, and at the same time purposeful design."

The editors likened the VW's combination of steering, cornering, roadholding, and even braking to those of "much more pretentious cars." The VW rolled little in turns and its ride quality, hard at low speeds, smoothed out at faster rates of travel. They found it offered exceptional security and traction in snow, thanks to its heavily loaded drive wheels.

Absolute performance was not impressive, said the Swiss, because the engine's output was deliberately reined in to reduce its rate of wear. Even so, they found, "the Volkswagen can maintain average speeds that categorize it as a quite quick vehicle." This required active use of the gearbox, they reported, which in turn needed a good ability to double-clutch on downshifts with the nonsynchronized transmission.

Practical details of the car were well thought through and laid out, said *Automobil Revue*. The built-in heating/demisting was "not exactly to American-style climate control" but still useful in spite of a smell of oil from the engine compartment. Over 1,865 miles the test car was reliable apart from a hoarse horn, a lamp bulb failure, and a clutch adjustment. Good fuel economy gave a driving range of 280 to 310 miles, "exemplary for a small car."

The Swiss auto experts concluded their test as follows: "During the test period the Volkswagen proved itself to be a reliable and economical vehicle with a capability for high average speeds. Doubtless it does not offer all the comforts of newer, more modern, and more expensive cars, but rather meets

In mid-1949 VW introduced its Export model, offering for the first time a selection of colors, improved interior trim, and chrome on the exterior. Exports to other European countries were already well under way.

the needs of many heads of families, businessmen, and drivers with sporting inclinations for a completely usable car at a relatively low price and very low maintenance costs."

It would be hard to improve on this as a capsule summary of the characteristics and merits of the Volkswagen as it faced its new life in still provisional form in the year 1949. While informing its readers about the technicalities of the VW, *Automobil Revue* concentrated on disclosing the benefits that the car's unorthodox design offered to its owner and driver. Its positive assessment was not, it seemed, one that was ready to be grasped by an orthodox European motor industry that was already experiencing strong and profitable demand for its warmed-over prewar models.

If the voice of the customer was sought, it too could be found in the *Automobil Revue* report. The magazine surveyed 360 Swiss VW owners, all of whose cars were produced in 1948 or earlier — hence to a very early and unrefined standard. It considered such a survey to be especially needed because there was so much controversy over the qualities, or lack of them, of the Volkswagen.

There were complaints, of course. Engine noise was noted and the paint quality was criticized. Repairs were judged "too many" by 15.1 percent of respondents. But performance was judged "good" by 97.3 percent and general driving behavior "good" by 96.2 percent. Overall 9 percent called the VW " very good" and 76 percent called it "good". Twelve percent were "satisfied". Only 2 percent of the owners said that they were in any respect "dissatisfied." This was a stunning and unambiguous vote of confidence in the Porsche design.

These comments referred to what became known as the Standard Type 11 VW when the new Export version was launched at mid-1949 with better interior trim, chrome exterior touches, and a choice — for the first time — of colors. A Standard model was tested by German's *Motor Rundschau* for an August 1949 issue and called "one of Europe's most advanced cars — a really mature family car."

Roll in corners was "only slight" and cornering was "secure with a full load, even on wet, slippery roads." When lighter loads were being carried under slippery conditions, *Motor Rundschau* suggested putting luggage in the front compartment to add weight on the front wheels. "For air cooling the engine is not too loud," said the magazine; "nevertheless better sound insulation between the engine and the passenger compartment would be desirable." This, as well as the synchronized gear-shifting requested by the editors, would be taken care of in due course.

BY THE END OF AUGUST 1949 the total exports of Beetles added up to 9,801 units. Their sales abroad had been encouraged by the decision of the Joint Export-Import Agency in the British-American "Bizonia" to keep to pre-currency-reform wholesale prices for export contracts that had been written before the introduction of the Deutschmark in June 1948. Ben Pon in Holland was the import leader with 3,674 Beetles, followed by Belgium (2,790), Switzerland (2,625) and Sweden, Denmark, and Luxembourg in the low triple figures.

Here, then, was an auto company that in the words of Ivan Hirst "was a going concern." Added Hirst, "It had a first-class management, staff and labour force, industrial relations were good, the factory had been rebuilt and was all set for higher production, the VW itself had been developed into a thoroughly serviceable and saleable car, a sales and service organisation had been set up, exports had started, and there was money in the bank."

Without the affection and indeed enthusiasm for the car shown by the British Mil Gov and their resourcefulness and determination in support of the German staff, there might well have been no Volkswagen works in 1949, let alone one in such good shape. "Had this handful of British officers not engaged themselves so daringly for the factory and its workers," wrote one VW historian, "there could never have been a VW today. Inevitably, the factory would have decayed or been dismantled. Despite their dedication, hard work, and self-sacrifice, the German Volkswagen executives there at the time would have been powerless to save the plant in those years, had they stood alone. Fortunately they did not."

THE BRITISH MIL GOV HAD ONE MORE task to perform. At the sunset of their stewardship they had to settle the ownership of Volkswagen. The trusteeship idea had not found enough friends in Whitehall, with or with-

By 1949 the press shop, miraculously spared much of the wartime destruction, was busily stamping out the panels needed for a gradually growing output of VW Beetles. Better materials were available and quality was improving.

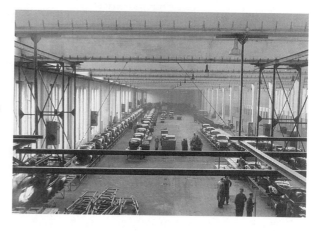

In the big halls underneath the north-facing skylights the painting and trimming of Beetle bodies was beginning to take on the pattern that the creators of the car and factory had envisioned in the 1930s. The people's car was to be a reality after all.

out its resemblance to the London Transport Board. Property Control had favored it to keep the works out of the direct control of German's central government, an entity which all too recently had been inclined to use its powers unwisely. As a fallback position Property Control preferred lodging the works with the state government of Lower Saxony, which at least would be presumed to manage it for the benefit of the business and the region.

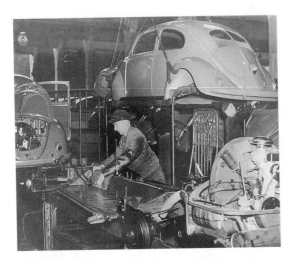

Although significantly improved from earlier conditions at Wolfsburg, the Beetle body drop was still a relatively primitive proposition in October 1948. Nevertheless, the works was becoming more organized and its products were gaining in respect in the few markets in which they were available.

Gazing into the gnashers of this gift horse, Lower Saxony found it wanting. In July 1949 its president cautioned that allocating former DAF property among the various German states could result in some states inheriting liabilities and others assets in an unjust and disproportionate manner. In the case of Volkswagen he was clearly more worried about the liabilities than the assets.

It's unlikely that Lower Saxony's *Ministerpräsident* Kopf had reservations about the business's balance sheet. It could only have improved since the summary drawn up at the end of August 1948, which showed assets valued at DM 85 million and liabilities booked at DM 41 million, leaving a net worth of DM 44 million. The land and buildings were valued at DM 43 million, the stocks on hand at DM 30 million, and there was cash of DM 3 million in the bank. This didn't look too bad.

In June 1949, however, the chickens hatched by Robert Ley and Bodo Lafferentz came home to roost. A newly formed Union of Volkswagen Savers launched legal proceedings against the Volkswagenwerk GmbH to resolve the question of the cars they were supposed to receive for their RM 282 million invested. This comprised a liability of unknown yet potentially huge dimensions for the works, as did a debt from the DAF years of RM 110 million still owing to the plant's suppliers in wartime. Lower Saxony's leadership was well aware of these outstanding and controversial obligations.

These events placed time pressure on the Mil Gov to make a decision about VW's future, as did an exogenous factor: the creation of a new West German federal government, set to take power in the latter part of September 1949. In the elections on 13 August a turnout of more than 70 percent gave power to the Christian Democrats and their leader Konrad Adenauer. In Lower Saxony, in contrast, the rival Social Democrats led the state's coali-

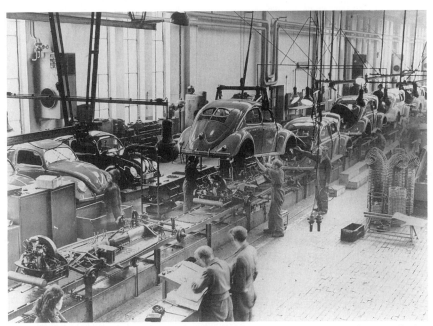

Steady progress at the factory had created a more efficient marriage between body and chassis by 1949. Workers and managers at Wolfsburg could see the potential for the future. But who, after the British, would have responsibility for the huge factory?

tion government. The disposition of the Wolfsburg works was shaping to make some politicians unhappy — just what the British wanted to avoid.

THUS IN THE SUMMER OF 1949 the bandwagon was rolling toward some sort of handover of VW to some sort of German government entity. Was this handover always seen as being total? Was there no prospect of a retention of some rights to the factory by the nation that had helped it survive? Finance man Alasdair McInnes, who had proposed that the works be transformed into an industrial estate to keep it from emasculating the exports of Britain's motor industry, took a contrarian view here as well.

"What we should have done, perhaps, was to have taken fifty percent of the Volkswagenwerk shares," McInnes told *Safer Motoring* in the 1960s. Asked whether anything could have prevented this, he replied, "I don't think so, although that sort of action would be going into the realm of politics, which I would not know anything about." The Whitehall records give no inkling that any such initiative was considered, beneficial though it might have been to the British economy. Rather they support McInnes's view "that primarily it was the British code of justice that prompted us to hand the factory back to the Germans."

Federal economics minister Ludwig Erhard, right, and another official look on as Charles Radclyffe, on behalf of the British occupation authorities, signs the document confirming the handover of the VW works to the state of Lower Saxony under the direction of the Bonn government. The signing took place on 13 October 1949.

The view of Property Control that Lower Saxony should have a prominent role in the handover still prevailed. But on behalf of the Industry Division Charles Radclyffe defended the value of an involvement by the national government, which was better placed to ensure that the plant was run for the benefit, and with the support, of West Germany as a whole. Both viewpoints were represented in the text of Ordinance 202, issued on 6 September 1949 under the authority of Gen. Sir Brian Hubert Robertson, GCB, GBE, KCMG, KCVO, DSO, MC, Britain's military governor and commander-in-chief in Germany. Sir Brian stayed on in Germany as the U.K. high commissioner to 1950.

The thirty-ninth and last meeting of the British Board of Control of the Volkswagenwerk GmbH was convened at the works at eleven o'clock on Friday, 30 September. Thirteen days later celebratory cigars were at the ready when representatives of both government bodies joined Charles R. Radclyffe CBE DSO and Heinrich Nordhoff on Thursday, 13 October to sign the documents marking the handover. Ludwig Erhard, economics minister in the new federal government, was prominent at the signing, prompting fears among Social Democrats that an early privatization of the people's car factory was under contemplation by the liberally minded Erhard. Thereafter the handover was made public; *The Motor* carried the news in its 19 October issue.

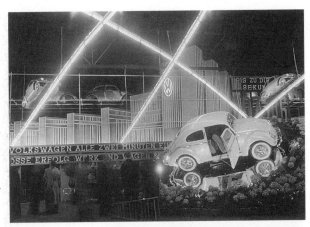

Inside the Frankfurt Show in 1951 Volkswagen erected a spectacular display that used, as its dramatic signature, the distinctive design of its Wolfsburg factory. Out of an old legend a new one was being created.

The half-millionth Volkswagen was produced on 3 July 1953. The mood was appropriately celebratory.

Fireworks over the factory on 3 July 1953 hailed the production of half a million Beetles. The workforce got a bonus totalling DM 2.5 million.

Wolfsburg was in a festive mood in 1955 when the production of the millionth Volkswagen was celebrated. It was standing room only in the factory halls for the great occasion.

Under Ordinance 202 Lower Saxony was "responsible for the control of the Volkswagenwerk, but on behalf of and under the direction of the Federal Government until such time as the responsible German authorities issue other directions." Commented Ian Turner, "The ordinance was a masterpiece of equivocation: it transferred the company to two different government authorities, yet without making any clear and definite decision on the question of ownership. German lawyers puzzled at length over the exact identities of the 'responsible German authorities' referred to in the text."

"In part deliberately," wrote Steven Tolliday, "in part through clumsiness, the British had botched the issue of control. In seeking to avoid concentrated control they had come close to negating control altogether." This annoyed and frustrated many and delighted one: the factory's director general, Heinz Nordhoff, a complex and controversial man who relished his independence of action.

At the October signing Heinz Nordhoff was able to inform those in attendance that VW production was already running at a 65.5 percent share of the new Export model with a better finish and hydraulic brakes, priced at DM 5,450, against 34.5 percent for the Standard model (DM 4,800). The plant's planned output for 1950 of sixty thousand units, he announced, had already been sold.

Not even Nordhoff would have foreseen that in less than six years, on 6 August 1955 to be precise, his plant would produce the *one millionth* Volkswagen. Or that as soon as 1961 it would realize the ambitious dreams of its Nazi-era creators by building more than one million Volkswagens in a single year. And these were but a few bare facts from the remarkable consequences that were destined to flow from the huge factory on the north bank of the Mittelland Canal.

11

Epilogue for a Battle

The car needed no more evocative name than Concept 1. It spoke for itself across the generations who saw and heard of its launch at the Detroit Auto Show in January 1994. And four years later its production-car counterpart was first unveiled, also in Detroit, in the very heart of the industry that its predecessor — the Type 1 Volkswagen Beetle — had once confused, bemused and abused. The Beetle was back — an icon for new generations as well as old.

"The Beetle is the core of the VW soul," said the Volkswagen board member with North American responsibility. "If we put it back in people's minds, they'll think of our other products more." Here was a new car that not only reinforced the company's VW trademark but also is the very personification of the Volkswagen brand. Its production at the VW plant in Puebla, Mexico, from 1998 is fitting: it is being built alongside the original Beetle, still being produced in robustly rude defiance of those who considered it already out of date in 1947 — more than fifty years ago.

The memorable character and appeal of the Beetle can be attributed to the hardheaded obstinacy and, indeed, insight of one man: Heinz Nordhoff. He rejected the multibrand and multimodel policy of his alma mater, General Motors, and opted instead for the single-model style of car building that had served Ford and its customers and workers so well through their Model T years. "I went out on a limb," Nordhoff said. "I took the chance of breaking away from the beaten path, and of doing something unusual but highly constructive for transport-hungry Europe, and not Europe alone."

NORDHOFF'S CHOSEN COURSE OF ACTION was anything but obvious. Many saw the Type 60, with its separate fenders, split rear window, and prominent body moldings, as a design of the 1930s rather than the 1950s.

The paramount role that the Beetle occupies in the history of Volkswagen was emphasized by the rapturous reception given to the new Beetle, launched in the United States in 1998 and in Europe in 1999. It captured much of the charisma of the original car.

The slab-sided pontoon-fendered look was in; Cadillac had already introduced tailfins. Many objections to the Beetle's adoption by countries and companies centered on its "dated" appearance, which was seen as sure to limit its market appeal. The French intended to restyle it to make it more attractive for their market. Ford would have put through a restyling, if only to get away from the VW's reputation as the hated "Hitler Car."

Heinz Nordhoff received endless counsel and "help" from his friends in the industry: "I had the dubious benefit of a great many well-intentioned advisers. Not only should I not foolishly break my own neck on this hopeless undertaking, I should change name, design, everything about the car, in no time. Perhaps I was too busy to listen, and in any case I myself knew exactly what to do. I was determined that, of all things, Volkswagen should have the best service in the world. So I brushed away all the temptations to change model and design."

In taking the remarkable decision to keep the appearance of the VW Beetle unchanged while constantly improving it under the skin, Heinz Nordhoff chose a profoundly radical action that went against all precedents and the experience of his previous employer, General Motors. It was a quite astonishing decision.

The oval rear window for the Beetle — seen here crowded nose to tail through the body and trim shop — was introduced on 10 March 1953. In the following year demand would increase further with the establishment of VW's own importer-distributors in the United States.

From the man who had once ridiculed the expensive "airplane engine" proposed for the Volkswagen by Ferdinand Porsche, this was a turnabout for the books. He would make the car as Porsche had designed it. Nordhoff could not and did not continue to object to the car's engineering sophistication, now that the DAF had built the plant and paid for the tooling to make it. "In any sound design there are almost unlimited possibilities," he said, "and this certainly was a sound one. I see no sense in starting anew every few years with the same teething troubles, making obsolete almost all the past.

"Offering people an honest value, a product of highest quality with low original cost and incomparable re-sale value," continued the engineer, "appealed more to me than being driven around by a bunch of hysterical stylists trying to sell people something they really do not want to have. So I have decided to stick to the policy that had served us so well," Heinz Nordhoff said a decade after he had been given command at Wolfsburg:

> Based on Professor Porsche's original design, the Volkswagen of [1958] looks almost exactly like the prototype model that was produced more than 20 years ago, but every single part of this car has been refined and improved over the years — these will continue to be our "model changes." This policy has required, of course, a great deal in the way of determination and courage, on the part of

myself and the members of our organization. But it has led us to success, and there is no greater justification than success, as every engineer will agree.

By 1958 the improvements in the Beetle included hydraulic brakes (1950, first on the Export model), synchronized gear-shifting in 1952, an oval rear window in 1953 to replace the two-piece style, then a thirty-horse-power engine in 1954 and tubeless tires in 1956. Coming improvements were a front anti-roll bar in 1959, improved heating and a fuel gauge in 1962, and substantial suspension improvements in 1965 and 1966 — by which time horsepower was boosted to forty-four.

Big changes for 1967 included the availability of an automatic transmission and dual-circuit braking. Power soared to fifty horses for 1970, doubling the original output, and in 1972 a new instrument panel complemented a panoramic windscreen. Fuel injection and a catalytic converter for the American market arrived in 1974. The Karmann-built cabriolet version, launched in 1949, continued in production two years longer than the Beetle sedan in Germany. The Emden plant built the last German *Käfer* on 19 January 1978, a humble 1200 model with matt black trim.

We know why the British-overseen plant couldn't put the robust and versatile Kübelwagen back into production in 1945–'46: the body dies were in limbo in the Russian-held sector of Berlin. But couldn't something similar have been built soon thereafter? This was a question posed to Heinz Nordhoff in the late 1960s:

> Nordhoff replied that the largest block of Volkswagen stock, 20 percent, was owned by the state of Lower Saxony, and that the Saxons' pacifism was unbounded, for years having been pressed to the sword of their warrior neighbors to the east, the Prussians. The Saxons (and the Erhard government in Bonn, which owned another 20 percent) didn't want any military, para-military, pseudo-military, crypto-military nothing, i.e. NO JEEPS.

By 1969 these reservations had moderated enough to allow this gap in the range to be filled by the Type 181, built in Mexico and ultimately launched in the United States as the Thing. As handsome as the latter was ugly, the Karmann-Ghia coupe and cabriolet versions of the Beetle broadened its appeal. Built by Karmann in Osnabrück, these variants did not sully the purity of the fine-honed production operations at Wolfsburg. They remained dedicated for decades solely to the Beetle.

Nordhoff's model monomania produced a surprising statistic in 1997 when Volkswagen celebrated fifty years of exports, dating from its first shipment to Ben Pon in Holland in October 1947. Until the end of 1996, said Wolfsburg, the company had exported more than 32 million vehicles to almost two hundred nations and territories. The export champion was still the Beetle, with some 10 million exported. The Golf ranked second with 8.2 million exported and the Beetle-derived Transporter third with a worthy 3.9 million exports.

THUS WAS WRITTEN ACROSS THE GLOBE an unparalleled record of success in car production and sales. This was remote indeed from the prospect faced by the factory soon after its completion. In his massive history of the Volkswagenwerk and its workforce Professor Dr. Hans Mommsen reported that an internal assessment at the end of 1939 forecast a loss of RM 1,080 per car even at an annual production rate of a quarter-million cars per shift. He took stock as follows of the outlook at that time for the works and its product:

> After a run-in period the continuous financing of the production would have had to collapse, because it functioned with prices which were significantly below the origination costs. But even at the originally established price [of RM 990] the Volkswagen could not have been managed, with respect to its service and running costs, by the general public. Only a decisive improvement in real income would have been able to change that. In this respect the DAF chased a socio-economic utopia which would necessarily have led to a fiasco, which was avoided as a result of the changeover of production in the Second World War.

It is not the purpose of this work to speculate on the way the VW works would have developed if the war had either been brief or had not broken out at all. Nevertheless it is noteworthy that the KdF savers were much more middle-class, as a group, than working-class. In other words, most of those who had first ordered Beetles could in fact afford to keep and run them.

This had several implications. One was that the other German carmakers had been entirely right to fear this initiative. Instead of establishing a new stratum below them, the Volkswagen struck straight at the heart of the market for cars from Opel, Hanomag, Adler, and DKW. Part of the Auto Union group, DKW thought that it had strategized its way around the KdF-Wagen by developing a new model in the late 1930s, the F.9. Learned a study team from the British Intelligence Objectives Sub-Committee,

> The [DKW] F.9 car was developed solely to meet competition offered by the Volkswagen. The Volkswagen (subsidised) was cheaper than their F.8 model, and had more room and was faster. They reckoned that in producing the F.9 which had a much better appearance than the Volkswagen and was about 15 k.p.h. faster, they would hold the market somewhere between the Volkswagen and the higher priced cars.

Unfortunately for this prognosis, many potential DKW buyers saw no reason to overlook the availability of a roomy and cheap-to-run car that was slightly slower but sensationally less expensive to acquire. Owning and driving one also exhibited solidarity with the Third Reich. The KdF-Wagen's impact on its domestic rivals would have been severe.

The resourceful managers of the Fallersleben factory would most certainly have adapted the business to the actual market situation. Further factory expansions would have been rolled out less quickly and the product would have been upgraded with features and options that allowed its price, for luxury versions, to come more in line with its cost. Export markets, where prices could be higher, would also have been more aggressively developed. In short, a fiasco rating high on the Mommsen Scale would have been warded off.

AS A CONSEQUENCE OF THE VW'S postwar success the factory was expanded — but not in the manner envisioned by the GEZUVOR planners. They had foreseen a doubling and then a tripling of the productive modules of the original factory to increase the production volumes accordingly. The plant grew to the north, as planned, but by accretion instead of by great leaps.

Where the tool shop had been, to the west, a new press shop was built — directly under the gaze of the directors in their new (1959) thirteen-story administration tower. A new tool shop with an apprentice training facility was built north of the artificial harbor. North of the original buildings completely new body assembly, paint, and final assembly halls were built, allowing the dedication of the original buildings to machining and subassemblies. A research and development facility was added as well.

By the mid-1970s the Wolfsburg workforce had risen to 45,000 and the population of the town had swollen beyond 100,000, the size envisioned when Peter Koller first planned it. It ultimately reached 130,000. Employment peaked at 66,000 in 1985; a decade later it was back at the 1970s level.

The plant's prosperity was a boon to its state as well. Engines and Transporters were produced at Hannover and transmissions at Kassel. Front suspension assemblies were made in Braunschweig. These three cities employed another 35,000 under the blue and white Volkswagen banner in the Beetle's heyday.

DURING THE 1950S THE GROWING SUCCESS and prosperity of the VW works was observed with special interest by a group that had every reason to follow its fortunes closely. The KdF-Wagen savers hadn't yet received their cars. They could only press their noses against the window, peering enviously at the shiny new Beetles going to many eager owners throughout the world — but not to them, to the men and women who had been the first to commit their support to this new enterprise with their hard-earned Reichsmarks.

To many the KdF's savings scheme was nothing less than a "swindle perpetrated by Hitler on the German workers." In *The Rise and Fall of the Third Reich*, William L. Shirer briefly described the project and said, "Tens of millions of marks were paid in by the German wage earners, not a pfennig of which was ever to be refunded."

By 1945, we recall, 336,668 savers had invested nearly 280 million Reichsmarks with the DAF to qualify as KdF-Wagen owners. Their savings went to the central finance offices of the DAF and were deposited in its bank, the BdA, in a special account at the Berlin branch. By the end of 1944 the sum on

Ultimately the VW works did expand along much the same lines envisioned by the prewar planners. It did so as an integrated factory, however, the many new buildings to the north (toward upper left) supplementing the production processes that were performed in the original works.

account there included not only the original deposits but also the accrued interest of some 32 million marks.

Thus, contrary to many assertions, the savings were used neither to build the plant nor to back Germany's military aspirations. "[Bodo] Lafferentz at no time considered using the savers' money for the construction of the plant," wrote Hans Mommsen, "and thus it remained untouched, as did the interest" — although technically the interest earnings could have been drawn upon for the plant's benefit.

This is not so say that Lafferentz had no opposition in his maintenance of this policy. Mommsen: "Even in the late years of the war Lafferentz held rigidly to this course and shrugged off the repeated urgings of Anton Piëch to use the money for the long-planned expansion of the factory and for the reduction of the loans extended for war production, and to concede a comparable interest to the savers."

Lafferentz was dogged in defending the DAF's allegiance to those who saved and to the savings concept, as he was able to testify after the war. Against all attacks he had been resolute that the DAF would keep its promises and would deliver cars to the faithful savers even if they "cost two thousand marks and more" to produce.

Commendable though the DAF official's actions were at the time, displaying unshakeable loyalty to the savers and their rights and aspirations, in retrospect Bodo Lafferentz might have done better on their behalf to permit some of their money to be gainfully employed. In the collapse of Germany the Russians took Berlin and, with it, the BDA branch there and the savers' 310 million marks. The e xhausted Soviet economy was the sole beneficiary.

Thanks to the intransigence of Bodo Lafferentz, the VW works could maintain with right and resolution that it had never held or had access to the funds of the savers and thus was not legally obliged to make good the promises of the collapsed and disgraced Nazi regime. This cut little ice with the savers, however. The implicit threat that they represented was a sword of Damocles over the VW works in the early postwar years that curtailed interest in it by some of the parties who could have acquired or run the factory.

The sword shivered threateningly on 7 October 1948 when the Charitable Society for Former Volkswagen Savers was formally registered at the town hall of Niedermarsberg in Saxony by Karl Stolz. By 1949 the society had its first thousand members and by 1951 three thousand, paying in fifty pfennigs monthly to support a court action against VW. Their plea was not that the VW works should honor the former commitment outright but rather that it should be "helpful," in cash or in kind, toward the acquisition of a VW by former savers.

From the first judgment of the court of Hildesheim, in the VW plant's district, on 19 January 1950 until the fi nal German Supreme Court finding of 18 October 1961 Germany's legal world battled over the rights of the KdF-Wagen savers. Volkswagen argued, rightly enough, that the savers were no different than others who, losing their investments in the bankrupt institutions of the Third Reich, had no legal recourse. The savers argued, rightly enough, that "Volkswagenwerk GmbH" appeared at the bottom of the front page of each savings book and that the works, not the DAF, issued the delivery order number. Only with the factory's permission could a saver withdraw from the scheme, they pointed out.

The savers' aim of gaining a "helpful" resolution was ultimately achieved. Under the court ruling Volkswagen would give a saver with completed books of stamps either six hundred marks credit against a new VW or one hundred marks in cash. This was considered generous, keeping in mind that in 1948 each new Deutschmark had been equivalent to ten of the old Reichsmarks. Claims against the plan were made by three out of five of the original savers; they were evenly divided between those who took the cash and those who used their discount to buy a new Volkswagen.

WHILE THE COURTS WERE ADJUDICATING the rights of the Volkswagen savers, the financial world was taking a renewed interest in the ultimate fate of the company that made the popular Beetles. Successful and profitable though it was, the Volkswagenwerk GmbH was still technically ownerless. *The Observer* noted the state of play in September 1956:

> Nominal owner is still the non-existent Nazi Labour Front. A sort of loose, undefined trusteeship has passed from British "Mil. Gov." to the West German Government; civil servants from the Ministry of Finance see that the books are in order. For the rest, Ministers have been inconclusively discussing from time to time what to do with the works: Herr Erhard has wanted to turn them into an ordinary private company, Herr Schäffer to nationalise them.

The former spoke for Germany's national government and the latter for the state of Lower Saxony; both had an interest in the fate of the factory under the loose guidance given by British Mil Gov at the 1949 handover of the trusteeship.

In the spring of 1955 Ford's head of international operations, Arthur J. Wieland, perceptively summed up the Volkswagen situation for Henry Ford II and Ernest Breech:

> There are constant rumors that Volkswagen will be sold to private interests. I personally believe this is inevitable as I cannot see how Germany can continue to nationalize only one company in the automobile industry. It seems to me that inevitably they may decide to either nationalize the entire automobile industry, which is out of the question in Germany at present, or get the government out of Volkswagen ownership and management.
>
> My personal guess is that the Volkswagen factory, when it is denationalized, will be offered to the public as a stock company. I cannot believe that the German government would seriously consider selling Volkswagen to foreign interests inasmuch as General Motors and Ford are already substantial contenders in this field.

Speculation over the prospects of the plant intensified at the end of 1955 when the company, which was not obliged to publish its finances routinely, released information on its 1951–54 results. "The figures were large enough to make the rest of Europe's car makers gasp," reported the *New York Times*. "With sales last year at 1,064,000,000 marks (about $252,000,000) the little rear-engined 'beetle' is threatening to run away from the panting opposition." Gross profits for 1954 were DM 382 million, equal to $90 million, but expenses, investments, and allocations to reserves reduced the reported net profit to only DM 4,257,000.

Investments were impressive: DM 201 million over the four years. But the size of VW's reserves was the big surprise. Called by the *Times* "a cool 148,300,000 marks (about $34,720,000)," its cash reserves were a war chest, the company said, to be drawn upon only in the event of a court ruling in favor of the savers. The battle with the savers was another reason given by Volkswagen for keeping its accounts under cover until 1955. "But now that a financial statement has been published," added the paper, "officials believe it was the first step toward disposing of the works."

Ferry Porsche, left, and Karl Rabe were quick to put on their thinking caps, after establishing their new contractual relationship with Volkswagen, to design new and improved versions of the car. Heinz Nordhoff ruled against their introduction, however.

The other shoe didn't drop until 1960. Chancellor Konrad Adenauer intervened to resolve differences between the nation and the state and by 9 May the necessary legislation had been passed to transform the Volkswagenwerk, at midyear, from a GmbH to a company of shareholders, an *Aktiengesellschaft* or AG, capitalized at 600 million Deutschmarks. Lower Saxony held 20 percent of the shares and the federal government 20 percent.

Sale of the balance of the shares, 60 percent of the total, to the public began on 16 January 1961. "The shares were subdivided into maximum lots of five per person with a sliding scale 'social discount' of up to 25% available for lower income purchasers." Oversubscribed by 84 percent, the 3,600,000 issued shares speedily soared to 1,100 percent of their face value. Renamed simply Volkswagen AG in 1985, the company initially had some 1.5 million public shareholders.

With the Federal Republic placing its shares on the market during that decade, Lower Saxony remained VW's largest shareholder and a strong voice on the company's supervisory board. Its power was reinforced by a special "VW law" that set 20 percent as the largest permissible shareholding and barred shareholders from allowing others to vote their shares as proxies. As well, "Shareholders could not resell their stock without the consent of the company, thus effectively blocking any domestic or foreign takeover." In 1996 these and other constraints on the rights of shareholders in Germany were coming under attack. This final mopping-up in the battle over the VW works' ownership was still to be completed.

At the public offering of the VW shares in 1961 some billion marks flowed in from stockbrokers. As we well know, no one was in a position to receive it in this ownerless company. This gap was filled by the establishment on 19 May 1961 of the Stiftung Volkswagenwerk, a charitable foundation chartered to support science, the humanities, and technology in research and university teaching. The Volkswagen Foundation was also awarded annual sums equivalent to the dividends payable to the shares held by the Lower Saxony and Bonn governments. When the federal government sold its VW shares the foundation received those proceeds as well.

Independently operated from offices in Hannover, the Volkswagen Foundation is run (like its Ford counterpart) without reference to the eponymous auto company. In 1997 it held assets of DM 3,300 million and in 1996 its grant allocations totaled DM 181 million. Since 1962 it has made more than 23,700 appropriations for research adding up to awards of DM 4,600 million, chiefly to German institutions but also to foreign ones with German scientific and academic links.

ANOTHER ORGANIZATION THAT BENEFITED from the largesse of the successful VW works was that run by Ferry Porsche. Present at the creation, Ferdinand's capable and experienced son, as diplomatic as his father was forthright, was a symbol of the survival of the Beetle, the car whose success built the foundation of the postwar Porsche firm.

After the 1949 handover of the VW works the agreement reached the previous year in Reichenhall with Porsche came into effect, which allowed its loose ends to be clarified. A redrafting of Reichenhall which took effect on 9 December 1949 foresaw "a close working relationship" between Porsche and VW. This took the form of a monthly payment to Porsche of 40,000 marks for development work, an amount which sextupled by 1952 and later doubled further to 480,000 marks monthly, equal to 120,000 dollars.

The period during which the VW works was obliged to pay license fees to Porsche for the use of its original designs in the Beetle was set to conclude at the end of 1956. The relevant fee was 1 percent of the gross sales price of the VW's standard version — around five Deutchmarks per car. With VW sales booming in the early 1950s, a cap of 150,000 units was placed on this formula in 1952; henceforth sales in excess of that level rewarded Porsche with the Third Reich royalty of one mark per car.

The Beetle's creator had been held prisoner, with Anton Piëch, by the French at Dijon until August 1947. His son Ferry picked them up there and drove them back to the family holding at Zell am See in Austria. Much was new along the roads they traversed but one change was obvious above all: Volkswagens were visible, a new picture on Europe's roadways. Ferdinand Porsche was not only surprised but moved to see so many Beetles scuttling about.

Through the rest of the 1940s the Porsches were occupied with creating a car of their own design and manufacture and transplanting their business back to Stuttgart. Not until late in 1950 did Ferdinand Porsche, just turned seventy-five years of age, have the opportunity to travel to Wolfsburg. Unhappily, reports of this historic visit differ irreconcilably. Here are six examples:

Recorded his nephew and secretary, Ghislaine Kaes, "In October 1950 I drove with Professor Porsche in his [Porsche] 356 to Wolfsburg. Porsche and Nordhoff met each other. Both of us were given special works passes granting access even to locked experimental departments."

"At the end of September 1950," wrote VW historian Walter Henry Nelson, "Ferry drove [his father] to the Volkswagenwerk in Wolfsburg, where he spent a day talking with Heinz Nordhoff and technicians about the future development of the car . . . Ferry remembers that his father was very much moved. 'He had to pull himself together not to start crying,' Ferry says."

Reported Ferry himself, "In November 1950 we went to Wolfsburg to visit Nordhoff and Volkswagen. This was the first time that my father had seen the phenomenal success of the Volkswagenwerk since the war. He looked over the whole factory and was particularly happy with what he saw, since it was part of his own life's work."

Arthur Railton also placed the visit in November 1950 and quoted Heinz Nordhoff as saying, "It was a sentimental visit. He had come to see his brainchild, but he was a sick man and he knew it. We stayed in my office as he didn't feel well enough to visit the production halls. He seemed to have given up on life."

Dr. Michael Thiriar pinpoints the date as 18 November 1950 and has Ferry accompanying the elderly professor: "When he gazed at the thousands of VW Beetles that circulated around the enormous buildings, he became aware of the incredible success of his work. Overcome by emotion, he could not finish visiting all the workshops that had been decorated to celebrate his arrival."

K. B. Hopfinger has both Ferry Porsche and Ghislaine Kaes accompanying Porsche to Wolfsburg in 1949: "The initial meeting between Porsche and Dr. Nordhoff, the new general manager of the Volkswagen concern, did not last long. Porsche was impatient to see the 'workshop,' as he always used to call any plant he was associated with. Not many minutes later an old man wearing a dark overcoat and trilby hat stood amongst the machines and assembly lines."

The frustrating discrepancies among these reports cannot be blithely reconciled. Porsche certainly visited Wolfsburg and met Nordhoff, probably in November of 1950. He was not in the best of health and probably did not physically tour the plant. There can be little doubt that he was well respected at the works that he had helped create by the men and women whose dedication to the Volkswagen was inspired by his personal courage and conviction.

And it is entirely believable that he said to Nordhoff of the factory and the car, as he was later quoted, "Only since you proved it do I know that I was right."

The nineteenth of November 1950 could have been the night after they returned from their trip to Wolfsburg, as Ferry Porsche said and Dr. Thiriar implies. Ferry said that during that night his father was felled by a stroke that left him partially paralyzed. The son would always believe that the harsh treatment given his aged father by the French authorities contributed to his declining health. Too weak to shake off pneumonia, the senior Porsche died in hospital in Stuttgart on the morning of 30 January 1951.

LAST IN LINE FOR LARGESSE at the privatization of the VW works were the British. What might the consequences have been if, as Alasdair McInnes suggested, the British government had reserved the right to a tranche of shares in the VW works, in just recognition of its services in helping revive the moribund factory and restore it to commercial viability? A link between Britain and Germany might have been forged that could have had positive political as well as economic consequences. A link did remain, one that was personal rather than financial: former Major Ivan Hirst, among the first on the scene at the VW works in 1945, later retired in his native Yorkshire.

Hirst had rejected, as we recall, a position with Ford in Britain. He stood by as a loyal backstop during the Nordhoff regime while the plant was still under Mil Gov control, gradually concentrating more on after-sales service and investigating vehicle defects. In August 1949, shortly before the hand-over to the Germans, Hirst left VW to become a Mil Gov regional industry director. He continued to serve British interests in Germany to 1955, when the auto industry beckoned again.

Having successfully exploited Henry Ford, Sir John Black of Standard, and the British government, persuasive Irishman Harry Ferguson was then launching his British campaign to weave a web of four-wheel-drive rights and patents for passenger cars. Racing driver Tony Rolt, managing the Ferguson project, invited Hirst to join the team in charge of sales and service for the car that they were planning to produce — "a plum of a job," Hirst recalled. While arranging to join Ferguson Ivan Hirst stopped in Paris to visit carburetor maker Solex and also the Organization for Economic Cooperation and Development, the club of the world's developed nations. There too he was offered a position, which he accepted on the spot. "The appeal of international work was perhaps stronger than that of the motor industry," he reflected later. Hirst ultimately retired from the OECD.

Ivan Hirst became and remained the personification of the links between Britain and the VW works. Thoughtful, knowledgeable, and personable, one of the authentic heroes of the British occupation era at Wolfsburg, he was its welcome and friendly face at later gatherings and celebrations of historic milestones in the development of the factory and its products. And when in 1997 Volkswagen decided it was about time that it reconstituted the scattered archives of its remarkable history, one of the first visits its emissaries made was to the home and hearth of Ivan Hirst.

Although offered a Beetle by the works in 1949 as a token of appreciation for his efforts, Hirst declined such a gift as inappropriate for a civil servant. He settled for a scale model instead — a model that later became so valuable it had to be kept in a bank vault. In the meantime, Hirst's fellow Britons began developing a taste for these unusual cars.

Many VWs were brought back to the British Isles by returning servicemen who were eager to prosletyze on their behalf. This enthusiasm was catered for by A. John Coleman-Baber, who serviced and sold these cars, including rebuilt CCG Wagen, from his Colborne Garage in Ripley, Surrey. Colborne's official VW spare-parts service was provided under the auspices of none other than Michael McEvoy, who had traveled to Wolfsburg with Coleman-Baber to secure the concession.

A British franchise to sell factory-fresh right-hand-drive Beetles was awarded to Irishman Stephen O'Flaherty, who opened the doors of VW Motors Ltd. on 1 January 1953. He received a sample brace of Beetles in 1952 and in 1953 sold 945. Sales swelled to 3,260 in 1954 and the VW soon became the best-selling imported car, reaching five-digit sales in 1960 with 13,098 units.

VW Motors became part of the Thomas Tilling group of companies in 1957 and changed its name to Volkswagen Motors in 1965. From 1970 through 1973 sales were at the 30,000 level, reaching an all-time high in 1972 of 33,525 Beetles sold in Britain. Sales dropped off with the launch of the Golf and Polo; the last year of official Beetle imports was 1978, with 540 sold. In all, Britain welcomed 341,788 Type 1 VW models to its shores.

MIRRORING THE CONTROVERSY IN BRITAIN over Hitler's people's car and its factory before, during, and after the war, attitudes toward the VW in the United Kingdom contrasted vividly. John Bullock of Rootes wrote, "It was, perhaps, fortunate for the British motor industry that war started before Volkswagens began to make further inroads into car sales in Britain and other export markets." Although the inroads made in Britain after the war were not massive, they were significant, while the VW's incursions into the export market denied substantial sales to Britain's car producers. They would count Beetles, not sheep, while they tossed and turned.

Motor Sport magazine was strongly pro-Beetle. Its editor William Boddy embraced the car's peculiar combination of vices and virtues and came up with a positive net assessment, based more on long-term ownership than on a brief trial that could leave a tester more puzzled than convinced.

One road test, however, provided a fascinating and revealing British coda to the battle for the Beetle. *The Motor* tested a 1956 Volkswagen De Luxe Saloon. Although not credited, the test was obviously written by Laurence Pomeroy, Jr., the magazine's technical editor, who had experienced the preproduction KdF-Wagen personally in February 1939. The engineer had been close to the issues surrounding the VW throughout its inception. Pomeroy knew the players in Britain's industry and reckoned on his ability to inform and influence them, both personally and through the pages of *The Motor*.

"Few cars have aroused more controversy than the VW," Pomeroy dictated to his secretary; "none have inspired more words, spoken and written, to explain how a car intended to sop up surplus spending power in a totalitarian state by providing low-cost personal transport to party members has become one of the most widely sold cars throughout the world."

In his introduction to the road test Pomeroy reprised the battle that had raged a decade earlier over the future of the VW and its factory, a battle in which he was a war correspondent observing at close hand:

> What are the characteristics in design and performance of the car which make many of the million and more buyers almost passionate in the defence of their choice, and, almost equally important, why do a number of professional engineers and journalists take the view that the car is crude in design, mediocre in performance and difficult, or even dangerous, to drive?

The erudite Pomeroy reminded his readers that a car is normally the product of a rich array of compromises among conflicting requirements imposed by various managers whose demands are often in direct conflict. "By this method," he explained, "it is hoped that every potential buyer will be attracted in some degree by at least one feature and that none will be positively repelled by any." He pointed out that the characteristics of the VW "show that it is a product of quite different circumstances."

Recalling the career and activity of Ferdinand Porsche, Laurence Pomeroy gave his readers the impression that the designer and his team simply sat down one day to design the KdF-Wagen, which ignored the numerous predecessor projects and prototypes worked out by the Porsche office. But he well encapsulated the essence of the assignment:

> They were encouraged to pursue limited aims by knowing that their product would have no sales competition, and although the resultant dominant strength in some respects and the manifest weakness in others have been smoothed out by post-war production and selling in a competitive world, this dualism remains a prime characteristic of the car.

Lacking in acceleration but unburstable when cruising at its top speed, noisy but immune to heat or cold, roomy for passengers but not for luggage, gripping well on slippery roads but tending to wag its tail, the VW was indeed a car of extremes. The Swiss *Automobil Revue* had noted the same contrasts in its June 1949 test.

The Volkswagen was so free of softening or debilitating compromises that, as Pomeroy said, "if one did not know that Ferdinand Porsche had been personally responsible for it, one would have to invent some similar figure." The buck obviously stopped with Porsche. One might not like everything that the designer had done, but in Pomeroy's view one had to respect it.

On a visit to Wolfsburg in the early 1950s a British labor union leader was informed by a German labor leader at the VW factory that his country's carmakers had not only turned down the VW but had done so "with contempt. They said it was pre-war and not what the public wanted."

The rejection still rankled years later. "The people of the world are not looking for fancy cars," the Germans told the union official. "They are looking for a means of transport that will stand up and not fold up on the *Autobahn* like some of your cars." Here was an echo of Maurice Olley's assessment of the wartime Beetle and its prospects in the global auto markets of the postwar world — markets that begged for more Beetles. It was a view shared as well by many in Britain's CCG and engineers such as Roy Fedden who were able to look beyond the raw, underdeveloped Type 11 of the mid-1940s.

Little solace for Britain's motor moguls was supplied by a report from W. J. Castle of the British High Commission in Bonn about a conversation during a dinner party at his home with Professor Öftering of the Federal Finance Ministry in the autumn of 1953. Öftering at the time represented the Bonn government on the Volkswagen supervisory board and thus was considered to be a valid source. Reported Castle,

> [Öftering] was very cock-a-hoop about the future prospects of selling Volkswagens abroad. He said that they were convinced that they had an absolute world-beater in the Volkswagen; their present production plans were to work up to a 1,000 cars a day and they were only being held up in attaining this figure by difficulties over a cellulosing plant. It was the most advanced design in the world and they were confident that they would not have to make any major changes in design for a very considerable period. This gave them a considerable advantage over their competitors as they had no retooling costs to write off and no experimental charges. As regards prices, he said they had a very big margin in hand and if they wanted to they could cut the price to such an extent that they could corner the world market. He was particularly confident that the Volkswagen would completely oust the British light car in Switzerland where they had already captured 52% of the market.

In forwarding Castle's note to the Board of Trade, Roger Jackling, also of the Bonn High Commission, reminded them that it only reinforced points that he himself had already made. "There are two points about the Volkswagen," Jackling wrote: "(a) It can be driven at its maximum speed, in excess of 60 miles per hour, all day long, without showing any signs of distress. (b) It is economical and gives very little trouble. I have reported from the Hague in the past that unless and until we produce a small car competitive in price, which has these two features, the Volkswagen will continue to outsell us."

Continued Jackling "Their guidance, so far as their export market is concerned, is to sell at more than the Austin A.30, but less than the Austin A.40. I should judge that the new small Ford should give them a run for their money, and I should be interested to know what plans Dagenham have for getting into the German market. The new Standard, judging from its specification, will certainly not be an effective competitor. The Continental motorist likes to be able to drive hard without worrying about repair bills. This is the quality which sells the Volkswagen."

In a letter following up on these advisories Castle could not resist another zinger or two. "I believe," he wrote, responding to a suggestion from Whitehall that the German executive was delivering disinformation, that Öftering "was quite serious and that our own producers are being very optimistic if they are relying on the possibility that the Volkswagenwerke will, in fact, have to retool and change designs and so become less competitive in world markets. I may say that I personally had a trial run in the new Standard 8 the other day, and I do not think that it will stand any comparison with the new Volkswagen under Continental road conditions."

The worst fears of Britain's motor makers were on the brink of being realized. They had fought in vain to curtail exports from the plant when it was British-controlled; now those exports were controlled only by the price that the VW works elected to set for its products, according to Professor Öftering. They had failed to cripple the plant by picking and choosing among its tools and machines. Yet they had lacked the courage to seek total control of the VW works to exploit it for their own purposes.

COULD THE BEETLE HAVE PROSPERED as a car built in and for Britain in a shadow factory, say, equipped with machine tools and presses supplied as reparations from Wolfsburg? Produced by a British workforce in a plant run by British managers? One who doubted this was designer/racer/journalist Gordon Wilkins, who like Pomeroy had followed the car's career since 1939 and had contributed to the design of a counterpart in postwar Britain, the Fedden car.

"I think it would have been totally unsuited to the British market," said Wilkins, "as indeed it turned out to be." To be sure, the Beetle did not take the British market by storm; there it fell short of the icon status that it was awarded in America. Nevertheless as the best-selling import for many years it was welcomed in Britain for its many assets in spite of its many liabilities.

Gordon Wilkins knew that Ferdinand and Ferry Porsche, Karl Rabe, and others of their engineering team could not have been thinking of Britain as a potential market for their Type 60 design. Here was an odd-looking car whose appearance was alien to British tastes; a medium-sized car by U.K. standards, yet with a puny and noisy air-cooled engine; a car built to cruise at its top speed on long motorways, of which Greater Germany had 1,310 miles by 1942, while Britain would not open its first motorway until 1959; a car that needed little service in a nation of devoted tinkerers, polishers, and tuners. And here was an imported car penalized by a tariff adding one-third to its price that had been engineered and tooled to sell very cheaply.

Nevertheless, as developed and quality-assured under Nordhoff's direction, the VW became just the export world-beater that Britain so desperately needed in its straitened postwar circumstances. Britain could have annexed the plant as war reparations, had its claim won out over other interested nations. Or its carmakers could have evolved and produced a successful version of the Beetle that would win friends and sales around the world; whether Britain *would* have done so is a matter of speculation.

In retrospect the best and perhaps the only way for Britain to have obtained physical possession of the Volkswagen works would have been to have acted as decisively and indeed ruthlessly as the Russians did in grabbing Opel's production tools for the Kadett. Russia took quick advantage of the initial posture of the Americans, which had favored reducing Germany to a bucolic state that could never again wage war, and of GM's uncertainty about regaining responsibility for its German factories. Coincidentally, the Russian action also deprived Germany of the only car that would have been a strong direct rival for the Volkswagen in the postwar domestic market.

The VW works was a different proposition than the Opel Kadett production line. Its sprawling size and dispersed machinery posed daunting challenges. It was anything but obviously portable. And once it regained a coherent form it was already producing the vehicles that the British CCG and its own and other armed forces urgently needed in Germany. Unlike Russia, Britain already had a domestic motor industry; the need for the huge added capacity that the VW plant represented was robustly disputed by the British motormakers — especially if it were to be government-owned. And only the government itself would have been capable of the decisive action that could have wrested the works from Wolfsburg as a British prize of war.

EVEN WITHOUT THE PRESENCE of the factory itself, the concept of the Volkswagen did have an impact in Britain, specifically in the Fedden and Kendall projects. Another project took shape after the handover of the plant to Germany, tracing its roots to a most unlikely source: the very same Humber Motors that had been so disdainful of the potential of the Beetle lurking under the corrugated sheet metal of the cacophonous Kübelwagen.

In the fuel-rationed 1940s one of Humber's senior development engineers, Craig Miller, built a prototype of a small car nicknamed Little Jim. Among its features was a rear-mounted air-cooled flat-twin engine. Like Porsche, the experienced Miller had clearly concluded that, at the time, putting a flat-opposed air-cooled engine in the rear represented the low-cost solution for small-car design.

In 1955 none other than Bernard "B. B." Winter startled young Humber engineers Mike Parkes and Tim Fry by giving the green light to their plan to develop a small two-seater car to be built by the Rootes Group. Like Miller, but unaware of his project, they started out with an air-cooled flat-twin engine (built by Villiers) mounted at the rear of their Slug prototype.

One of Roy Fedden's key team members, Peter Ware, succeeded B. B. Winter and supervised the work of Parkes and Fry at Rootes on their rear-engined car that showed that even at conservative Humber some radical ideas could prevail. The two creators were well matched, Ware recalled: "Tim Fry was a very good engineer, and Mike Parkes a bit of a madman."

Judged to be too small, the Slug grew into a four-seater which became the Apex project. It was given a water-cooled in-line four-cylinder engine still mounted in the rear in the "outboard" location. Apex in turn evolved into the Hillman Imp, a two-door four-seat car to fill a gap at the bottom of the Rootes range. Contemptuous though the Rootes brothers had been of the VW on numerous occasions, they were not above building a rear-engined car of their own if the circumstances warranted it.

Like the Beetle, the Imp was given a dedicated factory built from scratch; it was sited at Linwood in Scotland. But both the factory and the car were hastened to premature completion. "The Rootes family were desperately short of money, after a strike," Peter Ware said, "so they rushed it into production. We missed out a year of development." Launched in 1963, the Imp won friends for its design and performance but not for its poor reliability.

IN THE MEANTIME another engineering team was at work on a new rear-engined small car: a successor to the Type 60 Volkswagen was being designed by Porsche. The first such studies were made in 1949 when Ferry and his engineers were still in Austria's Gmünd. Under Type 402 they limned proposals for a new VW with smooth, flowing lines like those of their own Porsche 356 and with an integral body/frame construction. Responding to market trends that indicated a shift of demand to smaller cars, the Type 402 proposed shorter wheelbases as well.

After Porsche moved to Stuttgart, it signed an agreement on 21 September 1951 with VW to launch Project 522. This would create the car that Wolfsburg would build when demand flagged for the aging Project 60 Beetle. Ferry Porsche:

The rear-engined Hillman Imp, designed and built against all odds by the conservative Rootes organization, was launched in 1963 in an underdeveloped condition from a new and untried Scottish factory — not a good combination.

The four-cylinder water-cooled power unit of the Hillman Imp was overhung behind the rear wheels. Its all-aluminum construction kept the little car from being disastrously tail-heavy.

Our first aim was to modernize it and we succeeded fairly well. We used the same engine and transmission as before, but with a unitized body and chassis and a redesigned front [suspension] using McPherson struts. The use of the shock absorber as [a suspension] arm allowed us to provide more luggage space up front. The prototype of this new Volkswagen was ready in December 1952.

Demand never did flag, of course, so the Type 522 was never required. Nor were the many other advanced studies that Porsche conducted for Volkswagen under its agreement, including the 534 of 1952, a Porsche-like coupe with a one-liter engine, or the 555 of 1953, a roomier four-seater. Both were completed as running cars. "All these drawings and modifications were set aside," wrote Ferry Porsche, "since the Beetle business continued to prosper year after year,

Judging that the European auto market was favoring smaller cars, the Porsche engineers produced an attractive alternative VW design on a shorter wheelbase in their Project 402 of 1949. The trademark split rear window was retained.

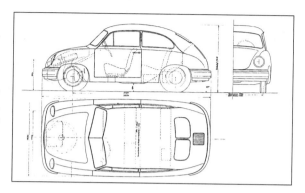

In an alternative design prepared in 1949 under Project 402, the Porsche engineers suggested wraparound front and rear window glass as well as full-width bodywork for an improved Volkswagen. Although chunkily good-looking, it would have been a car of less character.

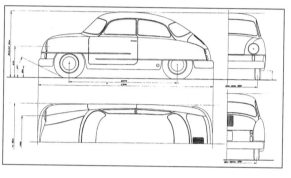

The studies carried out in 1949 by Porsche under Project 402 for Volkswagen included the preliminary planning of an integral body/frame structure for the new car. Traditional VW running gear would have been retained, however.

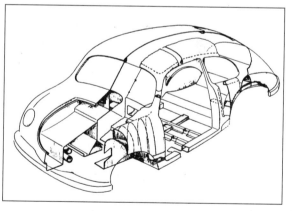

without the need for major modifications. Wisely, the company took the position that no drastic change was needed."

In parallel with its work on the Type 522, Porsche was designing a new car for, of all people, the Studebaker company of conservative South Bend, Indiana. Studebaker's president Harold Vance had vetoed the idea of becoming the U.S. importer of Volkswagens. But Vance's verdict didn't exclude the production by Studebaker of a car conceived by the Beetle's designers. With that end in view a Porsche delegation met with Studebaker officials in Indiana in May 1952 to discuss the creation for them of "a Volkswagen for America." For their South Bend show-and-tell they brought along a standard Porsche 356 and a unique prototype: their Type 530, a Porsche with its wheelbase stretched to make it roomy enough for four.

Any thought of Porsche designing a VW-like car for Studebaker soon went by the boards as the talks progressed. The Midwesterners, with constrained resources, preferred a larger car that would use some of their existing components and be easily produced on their assembly lines. That his design for Studebaker would be larger than expected was good news for Ferry Porsche: it would take his company even farther away from a possible contractual conflict with Volkswagen.

Under an agreement signed on 16 May 1952, the Porsche office would design a car with more power, less weight, and advantages in manufacturability over the 1952 Studebaker Champion. It was to have three forward speeds, six cylinders, and a maximum speed of at least eighty-five miles per hour. It would use brakes, wheels, steering gear, overdrive transmission, steering wheel, and door handles supplied by the South Bend parts bins.

To meet these parameters Karl Rabe's team designed the Type 542. Conventionally laid out in the style of an American four-door sedan, the 542 had one radical component: a six-cylinder engine in vee format with a 120-degree angle between its triple-cylinder banks — a novel idea. With the same 3,054 cc displacement the engine was built in both air- and water-cooled form at Studebaker's request. Both developed around one hundred horsepower.

After shakedown drives in Europe the Type 542 and its spare engines were delivered to Studebaker late in 1954. Although appraised positively in many respects, the car's advances could not be exploited by a company so weak that it was on the brink of absorption by Packard to form the Studebaker-Packard Corporation. And if the not-invented-here factor weighed against its adoption, this was only normal to Ferry Porsche after his years in the industry: "Never in my experience has an engineer given a positive assessment of a design that originates on the outside."

Even as he was handing the Type 542's keys to Studebaker, Ferry Porsche was aware that the car he had built was not quite what his client needed. While Porsche had been designing, Studebaker had been surveying the American public to find out what kind of small economy car they would most like to buy. Some three-quarters of their respondents favored a light, simple, rear-engined, air-cooled car — exactly the kind of American Volkswagen that had brought Porsche and Studebaker together in the first place.

Forewarned about these survey findings, for his South Bend trip Porsche tucked into his briefcase a red-covered prospectus for a smaller car, the Type 633. It showed and described a two-door notchback sedan with a Porsche-like hood and an air-cooled flat-four engine mounted VW-fashion behind

Porsche designed and built two types of 120-degree V-6 engines for the Studebaker project. One was liquid-cooled and the other, shown here, was cooled by air. The ambitious project was completed in 1954.

Photographed in Germany before its dispatch to South Bend, Indiana, this was Porsche's Type 522 designed for Studebaker. Fees received for the project, brokered by Max Hoffman, contributed to the expansion of Porsche's car production.

the rear wheels. Using the same cylinder-bore size as the Type 542, its engine displaced two liters. Vee-inclined overhead valves in hemispherical combustion chambers would help it produce eighty-three horsepower.

Four forward speeds, all-independent suspension, torsion-bar springs, and thirteen-inch wheels — the Type 633 was an admirably practical compact car concept measuring fourteen feet in length. The proposed styling was fresh and contemporary; Raymond Loewy's industrial design studio, then under contract to Studebaker, would have had the last word on its appearance.

According to Studebaker's survey the Type 633 was the car that America was waiting for but, Ferry Porsche recalled, "We were told that they lacked the financial means to do it. They said that they were just not in a position to throw away what they had done so far and start over again." Instead, Americans would have to buy a similar but somewhat smaller economy car: the Volkswagen.

THE LINK BETWEEN PORSCHE AND STUDEBAKER had been forged by none other than Max Hoffman, the entrepreneurial Austrian who had brought Josef Ganz and Rosengart together before the war and who had been approached by Heinz Nordhoff in 1949 to consider investing in the VW works. Hoffman, who knew much more than most in America about the background of the Volkswagen and the men who had designed it, was intensely interested in the Beetle's potential. He didn't want the company, but he did want the cars.

The sales possibilities of the VW, created and flaunted as a national showpiece by a recent arch-enemy country, were otherwise unrecognized in America. Said one executive then active with an importing firm: "It was my firm opinion that the Volkswagen would not sell in the United States." Added a former importer: "In 1951–52 if somebody offered me Volkswagen I also would have laughed." But Hoffman was undeterred. Indeed, when it seemed that he might not be able to get Beetles directly, Hoffman tried to arrange shipments through Ben Pon in Holland.

Finally the stubborn Hoffman was approved as America's East Coast VW importer. On Monday, 10 July 1950, twenty sample Volkswagens marked for the Hoffman Motor Car Company were unloaded at a Brooklyn pier. One week later his showroom floor on New York's Park Avenue was cleared for a five o'clock cocktail party "on the occasion of the American première of the famous 'Volkswagen' Popular-Priced West German car," as the official invitation read. To the assembled press Max Hoffman announced that he intended "soon" to import one thousand cars a month and ultimately to reach a rate of three thousand Beetles monthly.

The well-connected Russell Birdwell public relations agency issued a news release in support which commenced: "West Germany today entered the American low-priced automobile field with the introduction of their Volkswagen. Twenty cars in four models were demonstrated in a private showing before going on exhibition to the American public at the First U.S. International Trade Fair in Chicago, August 7th to 20th." Prices were $1,280 for the Standard car, $1,480 for the Export model, $1,550 for the latter with a sliding canvas roof, and $1,997 for the Karmann-built Cabriolet.

Birdwell's skills helped give an all-American gloss to cars which only a few years before were transporting the Wehrmacht's finest into battle against Yankee troops. "This startling little 'people's' car," rhapsodized *Speed Age*, "was skyrocketed to fame during the war by such writers as Ernie

Porsche tried hard to interest Studebaker in the design and production of a smaller car, its Project 633. This was an attractive, medium-sized automobile with agreeable overtones of Porsche style.

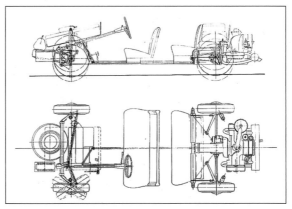

Showing a notchback body style, the Porsche sketches suggested that the Type 633 could have been just the car that Studebaker determined the American public was looking for. However this, and the Type 542 itself, represented steps too far for beleaguered Studebaker.

Porsche's chassis layout for the Type 633 showed an axial-flow blower to cool the two-liter engine, luggage room at both front and rear, and a column-mounted shift lever that allowed three-abreast front seating.

Pyle and Bill Mauldin, who drove Volkswagens in their activity. They popularized the cars by calling them 'the German Jeep'."

Max Hoffman, an excellent driver with racing successes to his name on two wheels and four, put his personal prestige on the line for the VW. Said his distributor in Washington, "He took me for a test drive up Fifth Avenue in the Volkswagen, and scared me to death, he drove it so fast. He told me it was the best car in Europe for the money. I gave him an order that afternoon."

Hoffman was skilled at selling cars to his distributors but the American public was slow to grasp the concept of the Volkswagen. "It had to be driven to be understood," wrote Arthur Railton, who became public relations chief for Volkswagen of America. "It was not a passenger's car." Hoffman sold a meager 157 cars in 1950 and 390 in 1951. Through 1953, his last year with VW, imports fell short of a thousand a year — a far cry from a thousand a month, let alone three thousand. "I tried, and I tried hard," Hoffman recalled, "but I just could not do it."

In 1954 VW began setting up its own North American distributors — and the rest, as they say, is history. From 1954 to 1958 the company's point man in eastern America was Will W. Van de Kamp, a hard-driving perfectionist who deployed his fractured English and sheer determination to convince dealers that they could become millionaires selling these peculiar cars — if they would do it his way. They did, and they did. The summer of 1960 saw America receiving her half-millionth Volkswagen. By the late 1960s VW was selling more than half a million cars a year in the United States.

IN THE WAKE OF THE BEETLES the Type 2 Transporters came to America as well. The appearance of these boxy Volkswagens on the streets of Phoenix, Arizona, had a poignant significance for a retiree living there, William Bushnell Stout. Here was a vehicle designed in precise accord with all the ideas for advanced automobiles put forward by the "imagineer," who lived until 1956 — not long enough to see another such vehicle, the Chevrolet Corvair Greenbrier.

The Type 2 VW had not only Stout's favored flat-opposed air-cooled rear engine and integral body-frame, but also a body design that followed his 1943 recommendation: "The body will not be streamlined in the old sense of the term. Rather it will be smoothly contoured to give the greatest possible amount of interior room. It is not at all impossible that it will more nearly resemble the well-designed bus than the airplane." Could the name Microbus have been any more appropriate for the Type 2's passenger-carrying version?

So exuberant were the American prospects in 1955, the year the millionth Beetle was built, that the VW works spent four million dollars to acquire a former Studebaker assembly plant in New Brunswick, New Jersey. Redundant after Studebaker's merger with Packard, the plant offered 430,000 square feet of space — a bit more than half the size of the original Wolfsburg body and assembly building — and large enough to make 85,000 Studebakers a year. The banner headline in the *New York Times* read, "Volkswagen, the People's Car in Germany, Will Try to Become the Same Thing Here."

Visiting the four-year-old plant in October 1955, Heinz Nordhoff said VW was aiming at American sales of a 250,000 cars a year within five years, an order of magnitude increase from the 35,000 then being sold. A scant

GM's designers took full advantage of the flat floor made possible by rear engine mounting to give the Corvair strikingly low and clean lines. If proof were needed that a rear-mounted engine could contribute to advanced vehicle design, the Corvair provided it.

three months later, however, Nordhoff executed one of his rare reversals of policy. VW would not build Beetles in New Jersey after all, he said, saying that its studies had shown doubtful profitability for the purchasing of parts and assembly of vehicles in America.

It would not take Volkswagen long to conclude that this decision had been premature and that the assembly of its cars in the huge American market would offer advantages. Not until 1978, however, a decade after Heinz Nordhoff's death at the age of sixty-nine, would VW open an assembly plant in Pennsylvania, a converted Chrysler facility. This served the company until its American sales were swamped by the surging Japanese newcomers.

IN THE 1950S THE AMERICAN AUTOMAKERS were still speculating about the future of the government-held Volkswagen company — as were others who had an interest in its fate. In 1951 Ford's Arthur Wieland had not hesitated to recommend to his top management that the acquisition of the VW works would be "a much sounder alternative" to trying to build up Ford's German company as a viable European competitor. Although West Germany and Lower Saxony were still holding Volkswagen in trust, they had not resolved its ownership status.

"To compete price-wise," Wieland wrote about the Cologne Fordwerke in February 1951, "we would have to become as highly integrated as VW, which would entail an expenditure of $10–20m. After the investment of millions of dollars . . . we would be competing with an operation that would not be bound by any profit incentive. Taxes, depreciation, amortization, even operating deficit, could be covered up in the government budgets."

Hard-driving and capable engineer Edward N. Cole was behind the creation of Chevrolet's Corvair, introduced as a 1960 model with its twin-carburetor flat-six air-cooled engine mounted in the rear. Insiders called it the Chevy-VW.

The subject came up again in 1955 when VW began revealing a few facts about its finances. "There were rumors in January," Arthur Wieland reported to Ernest Breech, "that Ford was making a deal with Volkswagen for participation and also that General Motors was interested. We of course had nothing to do with the rumor regarding Ford and it is obvious that General Motors with their tremendous investment in Opel would have no interest in buying out Volkswagen."

Wieland was right: General Motors instead was building a Volkswagen of its own, a car similar in concept but sized to meet the needs of the American continent. This was introduced in 1959 as the Chevrolet Corvair, a 1960 model, a radical rear-engined air-cooled car that embodied many of the advanced technical features that engineers from Ledwinka and Porsche to Fedden and Stout had been advocating for the rational automobile. Although the code name for the Corvair was Holden, GM's Australian marque, General Motors insiders nicknamed it the Chevy-VW.

The driving force behind the creation of the Corvair was Edward N. Cole, a brilliant engineer and executive who in his youth had driven the rear-engined Burney that had come to Detroit for evaluation in 1932. Wide-ranging in his interests, Cole followed Bill Stout's work and in 1946 was driving a rear-engined Pontiac coupe built by Cadillac, where he was employed.

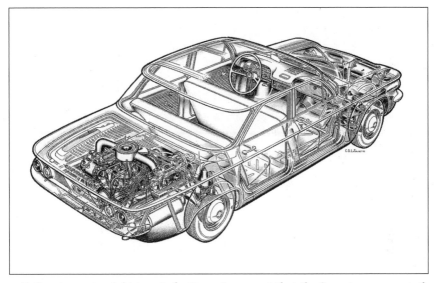

Failure to meet weight targets for its engine meant that the Corvair was more tail-heavy than the design intended, which in turn contributed to wayward handling that challenged some drivers if tire pressures were not closely monitored. Improved suspensions gave later models much better handling.

Air-cooled flat-six engines also figured in Cole's pantheon of technologies. One powered his personal Beech Bonanza light plane and another drove the M-42 tank whose engineering he led from 1950. Ed Cole would also have been familiar with the Jack & Heintz range of flat air-cooled engines, made in Cleveland, Ohio, where GM's tank plant was located. These engines, which Ford had considered for a rear-engined prototype, were made with each half of the unit a single aluminium casting — a method that Cole would try but abandon as infeasible in volume production for the Corvair.

Moving from Cadillac to GM's Chevrolet Division as its chief engineer in 1952, Cole lost little time in gathering an engineering team to create a rear-engined small car. Building something so radically different, he convinced GM's top brass, would keep the small car from cannibalizing the sales of the company's profitable larger models. Neither would it be a direct competitor for the sale of used cars. It would attract a completely different buyer cadre, the people who were buying those pesky "furrin cars." With this argument — and with the Corvair's design — Cole shrewdly neutralized the objections that had stalled previous small-car projects at Ford and Chrysler as well as GM.

By 1957 Ed Cole had a running "Holden 25" prototype and by early 1958 he had the green light from General Motors to build his smaller car, by far the most radical contemplated by a major American automaker since the war. A recession, together with the success of the American Motors Rambler in

In 1959 a prototype Corvair-based Greenbrier van took center stage between a VW Transporter (right) and a Ford Thames van. The sophisticated Greenbrier became a well-appreciated member of the Chevrolet product family.

1958 and the Studebaker Lark in 1959, encouraged GM in its introduction of the Corvair into a new class called "compact" cars. A new plant to produce it was built at Willow Run in Michigan.

The Corvair became one of the most controversial cars ever made. Heavier than forecast, its "outboard" engine tipped its weight distribution to 61.5 percent rearward — beyond the 60-percent boundary observed by Josef Ganz and Ferdinand Porsche. This made the first Corvairs handle in a tail-happy manner that was greatly moderated by better suspensions in later models. The early cars, however, gave safety campaigner Ralph Nader enough grist for a chapter in *Unsafe at Any Speed* that put the Corvair through the mill.

Although plagued by class-action lawsuits, Chevrolet's Corvair was produced and sold successfully throughout the decade of the 1960s. Total Corvair output was a highly respectable 1,786,243 units, 7 percent being the Greenbrier minivans. So covetable were the latter that when the Willow Run production lines were shutting down several top GM executives sent emissaries to comb dealerships to secure fresh Greenbriers for their families. With new smaller 1971 models Detroit's giants took more direct aim at the persistent Beetle: Chevrolet with its Vega and Ford with its Pinto. Both proved, in different ways, to be flawed.

THE BEETLE'S APPEAL IN AMERICA DIMINISHED after its sales reached a peak in 1968 (567,975 units sold), but not quickly enough to suit the men who ran the U.S. motor industry. In 1961 Ford had tried to stamp out the cheeky bug with its Cardinal small-car project, a front-driven V-4–powered car, but lacked the nerve to produce it in America as had been intended. Made in Germany as the Taunus 12M from 1962, it was too pricey to pose much of a challenge to the Volkswagen.

The Wolfsburg factory that Ford had strategized to co-opt after the war was proving every bit as formidable as its assessors had forecast in 1948. In

1969 Henry Ford II told *Fortune*, "I keep thinking that the Volkswagen will turn out to be another Model T — that one of these days it will go down the drain. I keep saying that, but it doesn't seem to happen."

Although Ford was not one for looking back — "Never complain, never explain" was his motto — he thus acknowledged the peculiar but enduring appeal of the car and company he had once come close to making a member of the Ford family. Nor was he the only car industry executive to imply consideration of what might have been. By the early 1950s Sir William Rootes was well aware that the VW he had so shortly shrifted was rapidly becoming a tough competitor not only in Germany but also in the world auto market.

At the British Motor Show, Billy Rootes and his entourage were negotiating a stairway between floors at Olympia when they encountered a distinctive balding figure wearing a clipped moustache and a patch over his left eye. "I remember you," said Rootes to Richard Berryman, halting his escorts. "Weren't you with the VW in Germany?" To the assenting Berryman he added, "I wish I had listened to you a bit more the last time we met." In this Rootes was unusual; few others admitted their oversight so openly. There were no medals for the losers of the Battle for the Beetle.

Endnotes

CHAPTER 1

1. "In former . . . the time." Blaine Taylor, "Adolf Hitler: the dictator and his automobiles," *Automotive News*, Centennial Celebration Issue, 30 October 1985, p. 257.

2. "would be discovered . . . Cars were an obsession . . . tram or bus again" and bright-red Benz: Hanfstaengl, pp. 44, 95. These personal reminiscences by a member of Hitler's then small circle conflict with and, I believe, outweigh later assertions that Hitler's first car in 1923 was a Mercedes, bought as a result of his friendship with Jakob Werlin, the Daimler-Benz representative in Munich.

3. Kempka and gasoline: Taylor, "Adolph Hitler," p. 260.

4. Motorization as a major Nazi goal: At the 1933 Berlin Auto Show Hitler remarked to Franz Josef Popp, the head of BMW, that he had read an article by Popp in 1924 that dealt with the motorization of Germany. Popp, Hitler reminded him, had specified a car costing $1,000. The price, Hitler said to Popp, should be RM 1,000 instead, then equivalent to about $420. (Mommsen and Grieger, quoting Horst Mönnich). Jakob Werlin was also an influence in favor of the promotion of motorization.

   Some say that Hitler declared his interest in developing Germany's transport network in *Mein Kampf*, written in and after Landsberg Prison with the help of Rudolf Hess. I have searched for such a reference in vain, although Hitler certainly made clear in that turgid volume his conviction that his countrymen needed more *Lebensraum*, which could be considered to imply that improved transport would be needed as well.

5. "he set out . . . motorsport": Matthias Bickenbach and Michael Stolzke, "Schrott — Bilder aus der Geschwindigkeitsfabrik," http://www.textur.com/schrott/schrott3b.htm, 1997.

6. "outstanding designer" and Porsche's lawsuit against Daimler-Benz: Mommsen and Grieger, pp. 58, 72.

7. Porsche not contracting again with a single producer: He did have a brief alliance with Steyr in Austria, whom he joined at the beginning of 1929, but this company was small-time for him after Daimler-Benz. Porsche needed a bigger challenge — and he certainly found it.

8. "My father . . . he couldn't!": Ludvigsen, Porsche, p. 15.

9. "As the creator . . . 'German Automobile Exhibition' ": Mommsen and Grieger, p. 78.

10. Hitler loyal to Mercedes and Hess's help with the appointment: Etzold, Rother, and Erdmann, 1873–1945, p. 339.

11. Appointment on Wednesday, 1 March 1933: In conducting the research for this book I found numerous references to this meeting but no clear consensus on its date, which ranged in vari-

ous sources from 1 March to 10 May. Many said it was in April, including Porsche's nephew and secretary Ghislaine Kaes, who however was not present. The date of 1 March is given by Cancellieri and De Agostini, p. 20. I find it convincing in the context of "the beginning of March" mentioned by von Oertzen and also in relation to other meetings held at that time. A preliminary meeting for contract drafting was held at Zwickau on 7 March and a contract with Porsche to design the racing cars was signed on 17 March; such a contract would never have been agreed to by the conservative Auto-Union management in the absence of an assurance of government backing for the venture. That the exact date has been so elusive can be attributed to the fact that Porsche had been asked by Auto-Union to keep his meeting with Hitler — important as the first substantive meeting between the two — entirely secret at the time.

12. Meeting on the preceding Monday: Kirchberg, Grand-Prix-Report AUTO UNION, p. 12.

13. "To this meeting . . . with Hitler": Etzold, Rother, and Erdmann, p. 339.

14. "Under his arm . . . he would be" and painting of Hitler: Stuck, p. 96.

15. "Hitler supported . . . liking Porsche": Etzold, Rother, and Erdmann, p. 339.

16. Frosty relations between Daimler-Benz and Porsche: Mommsen and Grieger, p. 75.

17. Werlin meeting and torsion-bar patents: Hopfinger, pp. 76–77. Porsche did not invent torsion-bar springing which, as its name implies, uses a long steel bar or bundle as a road spring, anchored at one end to the chassis and twisted by a lever at its other end by the movement of the wheel's suspension. In 1878 in Norway a patent for a torsion-bar suspension for wagons was obtained by Anton Lövstad. In 1923 and 1924 both Marlborough-Thomas and Thomas racing cars were given torsion-bar front suspension by J. G. Parry-Thomas, who had patented such a concept in 1919.

Porsche's accomplishment was the practical realization of torsion-bar springing through the mastery of stress calculation for durability and the provision and patenting of suitable suspension linkages. Porsche used torsion-bar springs for the Auto-Union racing car and in a chassis he designed for Mathis in France in 1933. He undertook a similar project for Röhr in Germany in the same year. Thus he was well up on torsion-bar technology when he built the NSU small-car prototypes and, of course, the first VW prototypes.

That torsion bars were not a Porsche monopoly was illustrated by their use by Citroën on its new front-drive model in 1934, by M.G. for its all-independent suspension R-Type racing car of the same year, and later in the 1930s by BMW for rear suspensions.

18. "The time in which . . . betwen the axles." and "that the engine-gearbox . . . shorter boxer engine.": Müller, p. 21.

19. "outboard motor": Josef Ganz, Motor-Kritik, Issue 1, 1934, p. 9.

20. "The first test drives . . . reasonably useable one.": Müller, pp. 21–22.

21. Possible marketplace competition between the Mercedes-Benz 130 and Porsche's NSU: The Type 130 Mercedes-Benz was a resounding sales flop for Daimler, which made only 4,298 from 1933 to 1936. This contrasted sharply with the company's ambition, which had been to build and sell 1,000 Type 130s a month. "Unit sales stayed within modest limits," admitted engineer Josef Müller. "Customers strongly disliked the tendency to oversteer and the tiny boot. Not to mention the nasty word fishtail that even came from our own ranks," referring to the car's tendency to slide its rear end (Müller, pp. 22–23) .

A successor, the 160, was introduced in 1936 and only 992 were produced. The Type 170 was a larger car with similar architecture. Between 1935 and 1939 its sales amounted to 1,507 units. In its reporting on the 1939 Berlin Auto Show the ATZ speculated that the early appearance on the roads of the similarly shaped Beetle would help the sales of the M-B Type 170 because "people will no longer view the owner of a Mercedes '170' with rear engine as a vulgar outsider." (ATZ, Issue 4, 1939, p. 86.)

22. Porsche-Werlin-Hitler meeting at Hotel Kaiserhof Berlin: Based on Jakob Werlin's recollections on file at Daimler-Benz, Mommsen and Grieger place this meeting as late as March 1934. In so doing, however, they state that Hitler then added a military dimension that was entirely lacking in the document that Porsche prepared for January 1934. This is erroneous. In fact the document prepared by Porsche after the meeting responded directly to the require-

ments set out by Hitler and thus, in the author's opinion, could only have been written after he was briefed by the Führer. Consequently I place the meeting in the autumn of 1933.

23. "You see, . . . for some time" and Hitler's technical suggestions: Hopfinger, pp. 70–71.

24. "At any price . . . below 1,000 Marks!": Hopfinger, p. 71. As we have seen, this was not the first time that Hitler had mentioned this figure. But it was the first time he had mentioned it to Porsche.

25. Discussion in last week of September: Hopfinger, p. 73.

26. Porsche's "Exposé": Etzold, *Der Käfer II*, pp. 32–38 in a facsimile of the original.

27. Selling price of RM 1,550: At such a price, the author surmises, if criticized Porsche could have said that he had misunderstood the assignment, that he thought the factory cost was to be RM 1,000 and he had simply added to that the various commercial discounts, profits, and distribution costs to arrive at the figure of RM 1,550.

28. Produce as rationally as Buick: Railton, p. 21.

29. "Germany has . . . by the millions.": Railton, p. 18. Sources disagree as to whether Hitler used the word "Volkswagen" in this speech; Hopfinger says he did not.

30. Three-wheeled configuration: In the 1932–33 period Porsche's design office laid out a three-wheeled vehicle chassis for Zündapp as its Project 24.

31. "furthering . . . the German people": Mönnich, p. 169.

32. "out-Ford Ford": Mommsen and Grieger, p. 66.

33. "In the event . . . German Volkswagen": Etzold, p. 34.

34. Meeting with Minister Brandenburg: Hopfinger, p. 75.

35. "You will shortly . . . Automobile Manufacturers": Hopfinger, p. 77.

36. RDA board decision: The sequence of events given is the conclusion of the author based on statements in Mommsen and Grieger and in a Porsche memo of 13 December 1935, published in Etzold (pp. 68–69), which in turn was based on extracts from an RDA report of 24 July 1935.

37. "The ministry . . . those meetings.": Hopfinger, p. 78.

38. "then increased . . . one million marks.": Railton, p. 20.

39. Building and testing of V1 and V2 prototypes: It would be inappropriate here to do more than sketch the high points of the technical evolution of the VW Beetle. Later chapters will touch on many engineering aspects of the car in the contexts of the evaluations of the VW made by various authorities.

   The reader interested in more detailed information is commended to Jonathan Wood, *The VW Beetle — a collector's guide*, Motor Racing Publications, Croydon, 1983, 1987, and 1989; Terry Shuler with Griffith Borgeson and Jerry Sloniger, *The Origin and Evolution of the VW Beetle*, Princeton Publishing, Princeton, 1985; and Hans-Rüdiger Etzold, et al, *Der Käfer II — eine Dokumentation*, Motorbuch Verlag, Stuttgart, 1992, among others.

40. "A number of . . . further development.": Railton, p. 26.

41. "The RDA . . . tell them.": Railton, p. 30.

42. "Free of any . . . not crudely.": Ing. G. Vogelsang, "Über die technische Entwicklung des Volkswagens," ATZ, January 1961, p. 2.

43. "Porsche and . . . engineering history.": Dr. Heinz Nordhoff, "The Volkswagen — its past and its future," Society of Automotive Engineers, New York, 13 November 1958, a talk given on the occasion of the presentation of the Elmer Sperry Award. In the 1930s Nordhoff was an executive at GM's Adam Opel AG in Germany.

44. "It was . . . no Volkswagen.": Railton, p. 27.

45. "were . . . had misgivings.": Porsche and Bentley, p. 213.

46. Opel's Volkswagen: Hopfinger, p. 85.

47. "This is . . . thousand marks.": Railton, p. 21. The executive was Heinrich "Heinz" Nordhoff.

48. "Ley was . . . its destruction" and "He was . . . to be somebody.": Smelser, p. 3.

49. "is that today . . . new super-union.": Roberts, p. 219.

50. "While total . . . billion marks.": Smelser, p. 165.
51. Suppliers gouging other car producers and idea of restricting VW buyers to DAF members: Mommsen and Grieger, pp. 120–121.
52. "that twenty-five to thirty percent . . . through its many branches.": Mönnich, p. 171.
53. "flight from management responsibility": Mommsen and Grieger, p. 124.
54. Schirz links to Werlin: Mommsen and Grieger, p. 125.
55. Goebbels comment and Hitler's relief: Mommsen and Grieger pp. 126–127.
56. Kaiserhof Hotel dinner: von Seher-Thoss, p. 331.
57. Announcement attracted little notice: Mommsen and Grieger, p. 127.
58. Acquisition of land: Parkinson, p. 15.
59. Acquisition of land: Parkinson, p. 15.
60. Naming of Stadt des KdF-Wagens: Mommsen and Grieger, p. 187.
61. Presentation of KdF-Wagen model: Mommsen and Grieger, p. 127. Hitler did not actually take personal delivery. It remained in the hands of Porsche, who donated it in September 1938, after it had served its purpose, to the great collection of Munich's Deutsches Museum. It can still be seen there in one of the museum's halls dedicated to the automobile.
62. "What has been . . . on this car!" and "This car . . . KdF-Wagen!": Smelser, p. 172.
63. Choice of car name: Mommsen and Grieger, pp. 184–186. They inform us that the canny works authorities took the precaution of reserving some other names as well: Volksautomobil, Deutsches Volksauto, and Deutsches Volksautomobil.
64. Ley's Cologne remarks of 1 August 1938: Otto D. Tolischus, "Five Marks a Week to Buy Reich Autos," New York Times, 2 August 1938.
65. KdF-Wagen board game: The author saw this game at the exhibition Käfer: der Erfolgswagen [sic] at the Lokschuppen Rosenheim. The exhibition, showing the origins and evolution of the Beetle, was originated by Hamburg's Museum für Kunst und Gewerbe. It showed as well a very similar game produced after the war on the Volkswagen theme — this time omitting the need to save stamps to acquire a car.
66. Analysis of VW savers: Mommsen and Grieger, pp. 197–201.
67. Daimler-Benz opening its workshops to KdF-Wagen owners: Mommsen and Grieger, p. 335, n. 47.
68. "resembled . . . ant heap.": Porsche and Bentley, p. 115.
69. "The four huge . . . factory below.": Railton, p. 53.

CHAPTER 2

1. Anton Piëch: In the 1990s the Volkswagen company was headed by his son, Ferdinand Piëch.
2. 6 September 1939 meeting: Mommsen and Grieger, p. 363.
3. "At most . . . Hitler's father.": Porsche and Bentley, p. 141.
4. KdF-Stadt March 1940 meeting: Mommsen and Grieger, p. 366.
5. Porsche and Udet on Mercedes-Benz airplane engines: Ludvigsen, Mercedes-Benz, pp. 198–200.
6. Junkers grab for VW factory: Mommsen and Grieger, pp. 340–341.
7. "comprehensively available": Mommsen and Grieger, p. 368.
8. Ju 88 refurbishment: Mommsen and Grieger, pp. 378–379.
9. V-1 workforce of 1,453: Mommsen and Grieger, p. 687.
10. The V-1 flying bomb: It is not our mission here to describe the sorry story of the lives lost to, and damage caused by, this deplorable yet at the same time undeniably innovative weapon in Britain and on the Continent. For further reading on this subject I recommend the following: Bob Ogley, Doodlebugs and Rockets — the Battle of the Flying Bombs, Froglets, Brasted Chart, Westerham, 1992; Wilhelm Hellmold, Die V1 — Eine Dokumentation, Bechtle, Esslingen, 1988, 1991; Peter G. Cooksley, Flying Bomb, Robert Hale, London, 1979; and Dieter Hölsken,

V-Missiles of the Third Reich — the V-1 and V-2, Monogram, Sturbridge, 1994. "The flying bomb was a unique, brilliantly conceived, indiscriminate and short-lived weapon that was launched by the Germans in a last-ditch orgy of terror, designed to turn the tide of war" (Ogley, p. 2).

11. Production of 19,500 V-1s: Mommsen and Grieger, p. 709. Another source (Engelmann, p. 41) refers to the production of 23,748 core fuselages under Fallersleben's direction in 1944.

12. Disabled British Lancaster bomber: This bomber has been variously identified as an American B-17 and a British Wellington or Lancaster. It has also been described as crashing into the press shop. Photos of the destroyed area clearly show the damage it did to Hall 1, the tool and die workshop. When former RAF Wing Commander Richard Berryman OBE arrived at the works, he said later, "Identifiable remains of the Lancaster were to be seen all over the place" ("The Berryman Story," *Safer Motoring*, 1965–66). I prefer this direct testimony.

13. "one plant . . . priority targets." and "the damage . . . safer quarters": Hinsley, p. 538.

14. Six weeks to shift production: Engelmann, p. 44. The Nordhausen site was under the complete control of Heinrich Himmler's SS, which sought to exploit the war to build for itself a peacetime industrial empire. It had no compunctions about using captive labor under the worst conditions imaginable. At first the prisoner workforce was housed in the fetid and unsanitary factory tunnels themselves; later they were moved outside to the nearby Dora camp where they fared little better.

Under SS supervision, a workforce of captives needed six weeks to shift VW's key V-1 production operation to Nordhausen. There it was installed in a set of tunnels near the South Portal. The V-1 found itself being produced near its rival, the Army's rocket-powered V-2, Mercedes-Benz airplane engines, and other critical war materiel.

15. Appeal from Porsche to Himmler and role of Degenkolb: Mommsen and Grieger, p. 704.

16. Percentage of V-1 production: Engelmann, p. 41.

17. 1944 VW works turnover and slow Central Works payments: Mommsen and Grieger, p. 709.

18. Porsche Type 300 jet engine: Hellmold, pp. 196–198.

19. "presented very . . . war budget.": Porsche and Bentley, pp. 168–169. In this autobiography Ferry Porsche described his company's work on a special engine for the V-1 but made no mention of the dominant role of the Volkswagen works in the manufacture of this crude civilian-killing "vengeance" weapon.

20. Numbers and allocations of wartime Type 60s: von Pidoll, p. 156. Dr. von Pidoll's book is recommended for the detailed accounting it provides of the facts and figures of the earliest Volkswagens.

21. Gift of Volkswagen to Messerschmitt: Mommsen and Grieger, p. 619, n. 52.

22. "In 1936 . . . the industry.": Kirchberg, p. 126.

23. "If the industry . . . in any case.": Kirchberg, p. 126.

24. "As a result . . . of their own.": Mayer-Stein, p. 26.

25. December 1937 tests and "as much as . . . existing vehicle.": Mommsen and Grieger, p. 328.

26. "Even if Dietrich . . . and Porsche.": Mommsen and Grieger, pp. 330–332.

27. "Every little . . . performance evaluation.": Porsche and Bentley, p. 129.

28. Porsche project numbers: Ludvigsen Library, copy of Porsche project list to Type 522 provided by Ghislaine Kaes.

29. "military elements": Wiersch, p. 4.

30. Ley tour of Poland: von Seher-Thoss, p. 311.

31. "You had to . . . military purposes.": Porsche and Bentley, p. 131.

32. Army's Type 82 acceptance: Wiersch, p. 10.

33. Ambi-Budd coachwork: According to Parkinson, the body of the Type 60 Beetle made use of American Budd Corporation steel-pressing techniques under a licensing agreement: "Part of this agreement was that Budd reserved the right to make the bodies for the first Volkswagen derivative. They had expected this to be a cabriolet but instead it was the Kübelwagen and so

the bodies for this vehicle were made by the Berlin works of Ambi-Budd. When Volkswagen began to build the Kübelwagen, Germany and America were not at war and Budd insisted upon producing the bodies as agreed" (p. 43).

34. Type 87 designation: Many references show the 4x4 version of the Type 82 as the Type 86. Nevertheless the Porsche type number listing shows Type 87 as VW-Allradantrieb Basis Typ 82, which is clear enough. As well a Porsche specification sheet for the Type 87 clearly shows a vehicle derived from the Type 82. Type 86 refers to VW-Allradantrieb, or the 4x4 version of the standard Type 60.

35. "The two . . . country roads." and "The Wünsdorf . . . off-road gears": Wiersch, pp. 10, 13, 17.

36. First Kübelwagen orders: Mommsen and Grieger, pp. 389–390.

37. "Weeks went by . . . to manufacture . . . ": Porsche and Bentley, p. 133.

38. ""involved mostly . . . Harz mountains." and "I was ordered . . . Jeep order": Railton, p. 61.

39. "Mr. Churchill . . . ends victoriously.": Mayer-Stein, p. 82.

40. "severe defects . . . steering, etc.": Frank, p. 28.

41. "All special . . . four-wheel drive).": Frank, p. 15.

42. "If they . . . of treatment!": Porsche and Bentley, p. 137.

43. Hitler gives VW a monopoly: Mommsen and Grieger, p. 504.

44. "For military . . . damaged chassis.": Mayer-Stein, p. 24, quoting Henry Picker and Heinrich Hoffmann, *Hitler's Tischgespräche.*

45. Army order for Type 128: Four days later the contract was expanded, as usual, to cover making three prototypes instead of one. Wiersch, p. 27.

46. Army requirements for amphibian version: Mayer-Stein, p. 47.

47. Front wheels to serve as rudders: Mayer-Stein, p. 47. We are not so innocent as to imagine that the vehicle's specifications were established independently by the HWA without prior consultation with Porsche.

48. Type 128 testing and "During this . . . off-road tests.": Wiersch, pp. 33–34.

49. "The Führer . . . the Schwimmwagen.": Mayer-Stein, Porsche memo reproduced on p. 50.

50. "demonstrated . . . half a ton.": Wiersch, p. 34. Due attention and respect must be given to'the extensive and intensive testing of new vehicle designs conducted by the HWA, in spite of the urgent requirements of war. This was consistent with the German tradition of thorough engineering and to the concept that it was best to go into the field with proven equipment. This was not always the case, but Germany maintained a higher standard in this respect than most of her enemies.

51. Replacement for motorcycles with sidecars: The idea of designing a motorcycle powered by the KdF engine was explored but not pursued. Professor Porsche argued successfully that a motorcycle with sidecar would never be a well-integrated vehicle.

52. Motorcycle problems in difficult terrain: Of course, the motorcycle makers did their best to rise to the challenge. The first step was to add a drive to the sidecar's wheel. Tests of whether a differential was needed were inconclusive. Zündapp came up with the idea of a special spur-gear differential that allocated the drive torque in proportion to the center of gravity loading across the vehicle's track. This was found to work very well; the ratio settled on was 2.2:1, motorcycle to sidecar. Blower-cooled engines were also being studied near the end of the war.

53. "In the light . . . of the day.": Schreier, p. 26.

54. Type 166: Virtually all sources identify the final Schwimmwagen as Porsche's Type 166 so that term is used here. However, an original list of Porsche type numbers in the Ludvigsen Library allocates Type 166 differently (VW-Krad-Wagen) and allocates Type 188 to a Schwimmwagen with four-wheel drive.

55. "We began . . . for testing" and "I was asked . . . to be pleased.": Porsche and Bentley, p. 141.

56. Himmler at presentation to Hitler: Mayer-Stein, p. 54–55.

57. Completion of first one hundred Type 166: Wiersch, p. 40.

58. Type 82E: Because the main production facilities at the factory were for the Type 82, this

became the basis of the Type 51 VW built and sold after the war.

59. Role of Type 82E: Mayer-Stein, pp. 28–29.

60. Wartime improvements to the Beetle: Porsche and Bentley, p. 130.

61. Beier-type automatic transmission: Porsche Archive, Typ 89 — VW-Versuchsgetriebe System Beier, 1942.

62. Beier tested for 16,000 miles: Olley and Earl, p. 17.

63. Porsche staff numbers: Ludvigsen Library, Porsche document holdings.

64. Horten H IIIe: Dabrowski, pp. 5, 64.

65. Peugeot as supplier to VW works: Arthur R. Stella, "Activities of the Peugeot Organisation at Sochaux-Montbeliard," C.I.O.S., London, 18 December 1944, PRO FO 935/4.

66. Type 82 body dies to Fallersleben: Mommsen and Grieger, p. 885. Although authoritative, this testimony conflicts with postwar reports that the Kübel body dies remained in Berlin at Ambi-Budd, thus making it impossible to resume production of the Type 82 model.

67. Production in sub-story: Mommsen and Grieger, p. 636. The masterful company-sponsored survey of the life and times of the VW factory before, during, and after the war researched and written by Professor Hans Mommsen with Manfred Grieger is essential reading for anyone interested in the political background of Volkswagen and the nature of its management and workforce before and during the war.

   Mommsen and Grieger, with the support of Volkswagen, thoroughly researched and depicted the arrangements at the KdF-Werke for detaining foreign workers there during the war. In 1998 the Volkswagen AG set up a fund of DM 20 million from which surviving slave laborers would be compensated under the supervision of a former prime minister of Israel, Shimon Peres. VW estimated that between one thousand and two thousand forced laborers were still living.

68. "At first . . . trouble appeared.": Schreier, p. 26.

69. Reputation of military version of VW: Mommsen and Grieger, p. 649.

70. Rommel's African campaigns: Ferry Porsche later related how carefully he and his engineers had prepared five hundred special Kübels for Rommel to use in the Sahara. They had extra-large air filters, bigger cooling-air inlets, sealing to keep sand out of the ignition, and front-suspension changes to improve speed over the sand dunes. "Due to a fairly typical bureaucratic mix-up at the Military Supply Office," Porsche said, the special desert Beetles "were never sent to him. Instead, [Rommel] received a bunch of regular Kübelwagens, which nonetheless performed surprisingly well. The desert vehicles we had so lovingly prepared ended up in Russia!" (Porsche and Bentley, p. 137.)

71. "With its black . . . another.": Irving, p. 114.

72. "It was . . . a Kübelwagen.": Railton, p. 67.

73. "Hitler sat . . . deep in thought.": John Toland, *Adolf Hitler*, quoted by Railton, pp. 71–72.

74. Wartime VWs in North Africa: Bittorf, p. 68.

75. "Since the . . . troops retreated." Mayer-Stein, p. 78.

CHAPTER 3

1. "The historic . . . physical plant." and "the Americans . . . made easily" and "Mass production . . . the workpiece." and "the car buyer . . . own model": Dyckhoff, "Grundlagen," pp. 293–294.

2. "it would be . . . Detroit industry.": Porsche and Bentley, p. 92.

3. "What Herr Allmers . . . to see.": Hopfinger, p. 88.

4. "This trip certainly. . . the economy.": Porsche and Bentley, p. 92.

5. Help of Dyckhoff's brother: Mommsen and Grieger, p. 168.

6. "A conspicuous . . . to weight.": Otto Dyckhoff, "Der Werkzeugmaschinenbau und die deutsche Automobilindustrie," ATZ, 25 February 1941, Stuttgart, p. 75.

7. "Money is not a problem.": Railton, p. 34.

8. "As for . . . a question.": Porsche and Bentley, p. 104.

9. "Ford was . . . project.": Hopfinger, p. 106.

10. "Things are . . . the question." and "The design . . . the engineers.": Porsche and Bentley, pp. 101, 105.

11. "The author . . . Company.": Barclay, p. v.

12. Ford Dagenham as a model for VW Fallersleben: This conclusion conflicts with the many authoritative assertions that the VW plant is a replica of Ford's on the Rouge River. "The decisive example for the factory planning," wrote Mommsen and Grieger, "was the then-most-modern automobile factory in the world, the Ford River Rouge plant, whose ground plan [Fritz] Kuntze adjoined to his first sketches" (p. 251). Kuntze, the former powerplant engineer, would have done well to refer to the detailed flow of components within the Ford manufacturing buildings, but as an overall layout for a new factory the Rouge was egregiously unsuitable. Dagenham, not the Rouge, was then the world's most modern large automobile plant.

13. Kuntze August 1937 plan: Mommsen and Grieger, end papers.

14. Reversal of main plant buildings: I have not sought a rationale for this change, although one deserving consideration is an appreciation of the direction of the prevailing winds in the area.

15. Architects for the plant: Mommsen and Grieger, pp. 252–3.

16. "In the new . . . for labor.": "Zur Volkswagenfabrik," *Allgemeine Automobil-Zeitung*, 26 February 1938, p. 268.

17. Production hours and "For large-series . . . number" and "We are not . . . the machine.": Dyckhoff, "Grundlagen," pp. 295, 345.

18. Pillar spacing and roof height and thickness: Irving, p. 100.

19. "Seldom has . . . Volkswagen works.": Mommsen and Grieger, p. 250. The reader who wishes to be fully informed about all aspects of the construction of the VW works and the KdF-Stadt is urged to refer to this comprehensive history.

20. 1941 capital increase: von Seher-Thoss, p. 314.

21. 2,358 dwellings completed: Mommsen and Grieger, p. 277.

22. The machine-tool complement at the plant numbered 1,800 in all in 1939, including two hundred machines designed and built to order to help achieve high-volume production. Several hundred steel-shaping presses were also installed on site. When war production began in earnest in 1942, Porsche and Dyckhoff were able to order substantial numbers of new machine tools from Greater Germany's suppliers to meet their special needs. Multiple-spindle borers, roller grinders, automatic copy grinders, and vertical automatic machines were among those added to the inventory.

23. Peugeot equipment and materials: Loubet, p. 26. The numbers were substantial. Shipped out to Germany were 1,545 machine tools, 2,155 electric motors, 282 welders, and 586 other items of factory equipment such as furnaces, hoists, compressors, and measuring gauges. As well the trains rolled northeast from Montbeliard with 5,500 tons of sheet steel, 3,600 tons of machining steel, 720 tons of cast iron, 117 tons of non-ferrous metals, and 700 tons of tools and dies — materials Peugeot had been hoarding with the hope of soon resuming car production.

24. Disposition of tools from Peugeot: These tools were moved under the direction of the KdF works, but none of significance was delivered to the Fallersleben factory. The recovery of tools by Peugeot after the war was only from Eschershausen, according to Ivan Hirst.

25. A last-ditch effort was made to bring VW's share of the asphalt mine at Eschershausen up to a production standard. Ten stamping presses from Fallersleben were arriving and delivery was accepted of 144 of the 329 machines en route from Peugeot. Mommsen and Grieger (p. 847) say that somewhere to the south a twenty-two-car train carrying 45 machine tools from Montbeliard was thought to be on its way but in Germany's internal chaos its location could not be verified. Stamping presses from Citroën's Paris factory, needed to make V-1 and V-2 parts, got no farther than the border with Luxembourg by mid-1944 and were soon repatriated.

    The presses from Fallersleben were only a handful of the many machine tools that were outbound from the factory in the last year of the war. Before mid-1944 the additions to the VW plant's resources brought its machine-tool total to 2,776. The big American air raid on 20 June

1944 destroyed 225 and caused varying degrees of damage to 299 (Tolliday, pp. 286–287). The raid on 5 August demolished 8 presses and 60 more machine tools.

Further depleting the mid-1944 total was the dispersion to sites away from Fallersleben of 827 machine tools. Some 200 were uprooted and transported by rail to Longwy near the Belgium-Luxembourg border. There they were installed in caverns enlarged for the purpose by 3,500 prisoners from the concentration camp at Natzweiler — just in time to be captured by the invading Allies. Others went to the V-1 plant at Nordhausen and other defense production centers.

26. Ordering new machines: Mommsen and Grieger, p. 636.

27. "[Joe] Werner . . . production." : Railton, p. 69.

28. Dispersed production sites: Mommsen and Grieger, pp. 878–879.

29. U.S. Strategic Bombing Survey findings: I have not consulted these USSBS reports directly. The figure given for the number of machine tools is the one most quoted and is likely to be valid. Nevertheless Tolliday, using USSBS sources, says that "At the beginning of these raids the plant contained 2,776 machine tools . . ." (p. 286). The figure is a round 300 units higher, suggesting a typographical error.

30. "Captain Irving . . . due to him." and "dry retort": Segrave, pp. 190, 222.

31. "Due to . . . necessary tools.": Irving, p. 96.

32. Plant floor area: Minutes, 6th Board of Control meeting, 15 July 1946, PRO FO1039/797, Appendix A.

33. "a full size . . . steel parts." and "The roof . . . looks better." and "Without detracting . . . the writer." and "this proposition . . . world's markets.": Irving, pp. 72, 96–97.

34. "The [British] . . . industry elsewhere.": Bullock, p. 137.

35. "That a very . . . overseas markets.": Irving, p. 97.

36. "considerably damaged . . . machined there." and "disappointing . . . the Works." : A. C. Thursby, et al., Team G Report, S.M.M.T. Investigation of German Automotive Industry, Luton, 31 October 1945, pp. 38–39. SMMT Archive.

    Among this SMMT team's comments on the machinery and methods they found, the following are indicative:

    All three main bearing journals on the crankshaft were ground simultaneously on a Naxos-Union Grinding Machine.

    A two-spindle machine [is used] for chamfering the teeth on both sides of a small spur gear simultaneously. This machine was made by Gebrüder Schmaltz of Offenbach-on-Main.

    A considerable number of Krause fine borers were in use. The majority of these were of the multi-spindle type, an example being a four spindle machine for fine boring the big and small ends of two connecting rods simultaneously.

    The balance of the machining methods was of a high class standard. Good examples of this were to be seen on the con rod and cap production where surface broaching was employed wherever possible, and the use of a Vomag Plauen multi-spindle boring machine for machining eight cylinder blanks simultaneously.

    Reported the team to the Vauxhall senior managers, "The tour took 24 days during which 2,000 miles were covered in visiting 14 plants located in Western Germany, from Frankfort-on-Main south to the Austrian border, then north to the Ruhr and east to Brunswick."

37. "the machines . . . our tour.": J. Craig, et al., The German Motor-Cycle Industry, BIOS Trip No. 1281.

38. "the whole . . . necessary.": R. B. Douglas, Manufacturing Methods in the German Motorcycle Industry, BIOS Final Report No. 1318, H. M. Stationery Office, London, nd.

39. Plant's own 1946 machine tool census: Minutes, 6th Board of Control meeting, 15 July 1946.

40. "the factory . . . British concerns." : Bailey, p. 62. They gave a knowledgeable accounting of the characteristics of the key machine tools in the plant.

41. "Observers agree . . . gear-cutting.": Olley and Earl, p. 24.

42. "destruction was, in effect, total.": Tolliday, pp. 285–286.

43. "Closer examination . . . remained usable.": Mommsen and Grieger, p. 954. In making this judgment the authors relied on sources that included an August 1945 report to the British control authorities by Maj. Ivan Hirst, officer in charge at the plant.

44. "Every telephone . . . and burned." *Time* quoted by Nelson, p. 92.

45. Kuntze defending the power plant: Mommsen and Grieger, p. 950.

46. Bonderising plant destruction: The attentive reader will appreciate that this reference to the destruction of the bonderizing plant conflicts with the testimony of the many other reports which mention it as an asset of the factory. Because it was situated in the heavily bombed Hall 3, it may well have been damaged. In the recollection of Ivan Hirst, such a plant was in fact in operation during the British years of administration to rustproof the platform frames of the VWs that it produced, although not the complete bodies. Not until the autumn of 1949 was a complete new bonderizing plant for the Beetle bodies installed at Wolfsburg.

47. "The factory . . . to be done." and "Compared with . . . many years." and "Despite the . . . the U.S.A.": Bailey, pp. 11–12.

48. "An assembly line . . . a month.": *New York Times* quoted by Railton, p. 75.

49. Total wartime VW works turnover: Minutes, 6th Board of Control meeting, 15 July 1946.

50. "During the . . . for demolition.": "The Berryman Story," *Safer Motoring*, 1965–66, p. 281. Quotation attributed to Dick Berryman.

51. Mandated Krupp demolition: James E. Pool, *Who Financed Hitler*, Pocket Books, New York, 1997, p. 140. He quotes William Manchester's *The Arms of Krupp* (London: Michael Joseph, 1984) as his source.

52. "The [British] . . . for reparations.": Parkinson, pp. 37–38.

53. "the offending . . . this manner.": Turner, p. 199.

54. Rudolf Brörmann background: Mayer-Stein, p. 137.

55. "Beginning production . . . be procured." Turner, p. 71.

56. Stay of execution for the plant: Mayer-Stein, p. 137.

57. Plan for five hundred vehicles per month: Mommsen and Grieger, p. 952.

58. Reichsbank loan to the plant: Minutes, 3rd Board of Control meeting, 18 March 1946, PRO FO1039/797, p. 3.

59. "were still painted . . . to stop!": Parkinson, p. 34.

60. "Michael came . . . defective items.": Ivan Hirst to author, 26 March 1998.

61. "He was . . . some going.": John Dugdale, interview with the author, 25 October 1996.

62. "was fascinated . . . British Zone.": Parkinson, p. 37.

63. Hirst Brothers & Company Ltd. continues in business at this writing as part of the Time Products Group.

64. "before the war . . . suspension.": Parkinson, p. 37.

65. McEvoy recommendation of Hirst: Griffith Borgeson, "The Beetle's Debt to the Brits," *Automobile Quarterly*, vol. 28, no. 2, p. 177.

66. "He was . . . did excellently.": Ivan Hirst, interview with the author, 9 October 1997.

67. "Major Hirst . . . months to come.": Parkinson, pp. 42–43.

68. "His interest . . . its subsidiaries," and "He was . . . DAF Division." and "He was . . . Board of Control.": Ivan Hirst, interview with the author, 9 October 1997.

69. Thirty-nine Board of Control meetings: Minutes, 38th Board of Control meeting, 30 August 1949, PRO FO1046/194, setting the date of 30 September 1949 for what was certainly the last meeting of the board.

70. Personnel appointments: Parkinson, pp. 50–53.

71. Attracted by Ferdinand Porsche: Rolf Lohberg, "Wolfsburg," *auto + motor und sport*, no. 23, 1973, p. 134.

72. "So far as . . . of it left.": Report of the Working Party on the German Motor Vehicle Industry,

Economic and Industrial Planning Staff, 9 January 1945, p. 2. PRO FO1005/960.

73. BAOR occupation forces: Barnett, p. 42.

74. "(a) an intense . . . can accept.": Barnett, p. 50.

75. "He had . . . good idea.": Ivan Hirst, interview with the author, 9 October 1997.

76. "The big . . . being eliminated.": Ivan Hirst, in "Major Ivan Hirst Recalls," a chapter written for Terry Shuler, *Volkswagen — Then, Now and Forever*, Beeman Jorgensen, Indianapolis, 1996, p. 65. The Shuler book is a rich repository of original photos from the VW archives and other sources showing the origins and early years of the Beetle.

77. "It is alleged . . . policy grounds." and "Looking at . . . motor industry.": PRO AVIA 49/116.

78. "the British jeep": This was a reference to a vehicle being developed by the Nuffield Organisation. Sir Miles Thomas: "We were given the job near the end of the war of designing a substitute for the American Jeep. The specification of the 'Champ' demanded that it should do practically everything. Apart from a highly versatile road and cross-country performance, it had to be able to ford deep rivers, inhaling and exhausting air for the engine through snorkel tubes. It had to be able to charge wireless batteries, operate a powered take-off; indeed, as some wag had it, do everything except pick coconuts and wait at table" (Thomas, pp. 230–231).

79. "there has been no . . . available to the public.": PRO AVIA 49/116.

80. "there has been . . . something to say.": PRO AVIA 49/116.

81. "I am prepared . . . in due course." and "the orders proposed . . . can be avoided . . .": PRO AVIA 49/116.

82. Order for forty thousand cars: Minutes, 8th Board of Control meeting, 12 September 1946, PRO FO943/215, in which Major Hirst corrected the figure of four thousand given in the minutes of the previous meeting, saying that it should read "forty thousand."

83. "In July . . . bricks!": Tolliday, p. 299.

84. Dr. Feuereissen: von Seher-Thoss, p. 388.

85. "The vehicles produced . . . in every respect.": Director, Property Control to J. F. Cahan (attachment, Director, Property Control to Chief, Finance Division, 16 July 1947).

CHAPTER 4

1. "Besides satisfying . . . highly apprehensive.": Otto D. Tolischus, "Nazi Hopes Ride the 'Volksauto'," *New York Times Magazine*, New York, 16 October 1938, p. 21.

2. "the skill of . . . preliminary plans.": *The Motor*, 6 April 1937, p. 389.

3. "It is . . . of coachwork.": "Hitler's 'Volkswagen'," *The Motor*, 31 December 1935, p. 5.

4. "The disciplined . . . would be required.": "How Germany Plans to Produce Millions of Low-Priced Cars," *The Motor*, 6 April 1937, p. 389.

5. "The factory . . . lowest production costs.": *The Autocar*, 25 February 1938, p. 311.

6. "Germany is . . . great in itself.": "German 'People's' Car," *The Autocar*, 3 June 1938.

7. Extensive KdF-Wagen descriptions: Rolf L. Binder, "The Volkswagen," *The Automobile Engineer*, London, February 1939, pp. 47–50 and "The Berlin Show," *The Automobile Engineer*, London, April 1939, pp. 107–110.

8. "over a course . . . very low price.": E.J. Pratt, "The Volkswagen Tested," *The Autocar*, 24 February 1939, p. 320a.

9. "The feature . . . fast driving.": Gordon Wilkins, "Second Time Around," *Autocar*, 6 June 1981, p. 54.

10. "combines the skill . . . and his car.": "Monoposto," "Round the Ring in a volkswagen," *The Light Car*, 21 July 1939, pp. 11–12.

11. "Incidentally . . . screen wiper.": The Institution of Automobile Engineers, Proceedings, Session 1941–42, vol. XXXVI, London, 1942, p. 379.

12. "very concerned . . . three years." and "Production of . . . American plant.": Bullock, pp. 77–78.

13. "fixed at . . . crude." and "our manufacturers . . . engineering basis.": Laurence Pomeroy, Jr., "KdF Volkswagen — neither myth nor menace," *The Motor*, 28 February 1939, pp. 137–138.

14. "predictions on . . . real success.": Laurence Pomeroy, Jr., "Impossibilities of the Rear-Engined Car," *The Motor*, 25 October 1939, pp. 388–90.

15. "It is quite . . . post-war period.": Laurence Pomeroy, Jr., "The Truth Behind the KdF," *The Motor*, 12 March 1941, p. 120.

16. "By the end . . . in Europe." and "were farmers . . . extreme displeasure.": Wood, Wheels, pp. 86, 93.

17. "the engine . . . sweet and light": "The North-Lucas Light Car," *The Automobile Engineer*, April 1923, pp. 103–104.

18. "It is certainly . . . and ideals.": "A Light Car Without Chassis or Axles," *The Light Car and Cyclecar*, 15 December 1922, p. 92.

19. "Perhaps the . . . in operation." and "it certainly . . . persons interested.": [Miles Thomas], "A Storybook Car in Reality," *The Motor*, 12 December 1922, p. 982.

20. "As the engine . . . with mud.": "Experiences with a 'Radial'," *The Autocar*, 16 March 1923, p. 452.

21. "notably lethargic . . . uncouth appearance" and "As unorthodoxy . . . motor journals.": Anthony Bird, The Trojan Utility Car, Profile Publications, Leatherhead, 1967, pp. 3, 8.

22. "the fact . . . the road.": "The New Trojan Tested," *The Motor*, 24 June 1930, p. 973.

23. "Received . . . pyramids" and "In fact . . . understeer.": Frostick, pp. 7–8.

24. "an enormous 'lady bug'.": Carroll Binder, "England Sees a Radical Car," *Chicago Daily News*, 1930.

25. "Sitting in . . . sensation." and "the springing is . . . can be." and "Now that . . . accommodation.": "Burney Streamline Car," *The Motor*, 16 September 1930, pp. 277–281.

26. "The actual . . . turning it down.": John Price Williams, "A pioneer who was too far ahead of his time," *The Daily Telegraph*, 9 May 1998, pp. 10–11.

27. "it is understood . . . head resistance.": "Streamlining," *The Autocar*, 17 March 1933, p. 415.

28. "the soft . . . very light.": "12 h.p. Mercedes-Benz 130H," *The Autocar*, 16 November 1934. This type is correctly designated the 130, not 130H.

29. "was a vicious . . . gusty days.": Ronald Barker, "Were Those the Days?" *Autocar*, 12 April 1963, p. 620.

30. "a complete . . . his passengers.": "This Year, Next Year, Some Time —?," *The Autocar*, 15 February 1935, pp. 237–238.

31. "Two or three weeks . . . for air-cooling.": A. H. Roy Fedden, "Correspondence," *The Autocar*, 20 February 1942, pp. 137–138.

32. "That Tatra . . . public's taste.": W. M. W. Thomas, "Air-cooled Rear-engined Cars," *The Autocar*, 13 March 1942, pp. 182–184.

33. "a shy, reserved . . . at the rear.": Thomas, p. 221.

34. "have proved . . . 'a little wonder'.": "German People's Car is in War Service," *The Motor*, 24 September 1941, p. 133.

35. "Desert warfare . . . siege of Tobruk.": John Dugdale, interview with the author, 25 October 1996.

36. "has been achieved . . . corners and ribbed.": Capt. John D. Dugdale, R.A.S.C., M.T., " 'The People's Car' as a War Machine," *The Autocar*, 17 October 1941. pp. 820–823.

37. The Kübel decanted in the Midlands: The vehicle's attributes, including Afrika Korps stenciling on its doors, are such that it seems likely to have been one of the two that were seen and described in Africa by John Dugdale in September 1941. If so, why had it taken more than a year to reach Humber? To be sure, the British forces were being kept busy with other matters by Gen. Erwin Rommel; supply was a serious problem and sending vehicles back to Britain would have had a low priority. Other British agencies may well have wanted a look at this "little wonder" before it was handed to Humber for an official assessment.

Whether this had happened and why was moot to Captain Dugdale. With his unit, in the May–June period of 1942 he was "rolled up" by a German advance. He spent the rest of the war in German captivity.

38. "He was not . . . Winter regime.": Robson, p. 26.

39. "Looking at the general . . .British industry: Investigation, p. 10.

40. Publication in Automobile Engineer: "A German War Vehicle," *Automobile Engineer*, London, July 1944, pp. 259–269.

41. "The engine . . .après la guerre.": H. E. Ellis, "Motoring on the 'Far Shore'," *The Autocar*, 15 September 1944, pp. 309–311.

42. "The U.S. Army . . . for next year.": Laurence Pomeroy, Jr., "German Motor Show 1945," *The Motor*, 21 November 1945.

43. "perhaps a little . . . and road space.": Ivan Hirst to author, 5 March 1998.

44. "a liberal . . . Army law.": Davis, p. 208.

45. "The first VWs . . . circumstances.": Maj. Charles Bryce, "The Berryman Story," *Safer Motoring*, 1965–66, p. 278.

46. "collapsed" wheel bearing: Wrote Griffith Borgeson, "Front-wheel bearing problems derived from a manufacturing error. Due to worn chucks, the automatic lathe on which the brake drums were machined did its work out of round. This was resolved when the British manufacturer of the machine sent out new chucks free of charge" (Griffith Borgeson, "The Beetle's Debt to the Brits," *Automobile Quarterly*, vol. 28, no. 2, p. 184) .

47. The richness of the fuel/air mixture: A possible reason for the richness of the mixture was that to keep cost down the Solex 26VF1 carburetor was not fitted with an accelerator pump. Mixture richness would improve its performance in speed transitions. As Humber found, in the car the engine performed with excellent fuel economy.

48. "Although a number . . . technical faults.": Olley and Earl, p. 20.

49. "Let us design . . . handle it.": Bernard B. Winter, "Towards Better Cars," *The Motor*, 29 December 1943, pp. 381–382.

50. "The General arrived . . . the dies go.": Ivan Hirst, interview with the author, 9 October 1997.

51. "The car is . . . its present form." and "Karlos . . . separate frame" and "The intentions . . . minimum cost.": Bailey et al, pp. 62, 69–72.

52. "He was one . . . in 1946–47.": Griffith Borgeson, "The Beetle's Debt to the Brits," *Automobile Quarterly*, vol. 28, no. 2, p. 187.

53. "It would appear . . . the passengers.": Olley and Earl, p. 22.

54. Army intelligence report: Otis D. Treiber et al, Beier Infinitely Variable Speed Friction Drive Transmission, Joint Intelligence Objectives Agency, H. M. Stationery Office, 1945.

55. "This was given . . . of the press.": C. A. Dunphie to E. B. Bowyer, 27 September 1946, PRO SUPP14/397.

56. "an immediate outcry . . . civvy life." and "I have just completed . . . in this country.": Charles Fothergill, "£100 people's car comes well out of new, severe trial," *News Chronicle*, September 1946.

57. "It seems that . . . a Volkswagen!": Bryce, "The Berryman Story," *Safer Motoring*, p. 278.

58. "it has the . . . cornering capacity.": Gordon Wilkins, "Under My Easter Bonnet," *The Motor*, 8 May 1946, pp. 290–291.

59. "some hundreds of miles . . . creditably short time.": "The 1947 Volkswagen Saloon," *The Motor*, 7 May 1947.

60. "The car was . . . air to escape.": A. F. Carlisle, "A Private Owner's Viewpoint on the Volkswagen," *Motor Sport*, London, April 1949.

CHAPTER 5

1. "Thirty years ago . . . remain haunted?" and "are actually . . . intervals." and "this type . . . their elimination": P. M. Heldt, "Will Rear-Engine Design Come Back?" *Automotive Industries*, 25 April 1931, 2 May 1931 and 9 May 1931.

2. "At its June . . . to build.": Michael Lamm, "1925 Julian — The Beetle's granddaddy,"

Autoweek, 5 January 1998, p. 25. The Julian, unlike the North-Lucas, survived. Rescued and restored by Bill Harrah, it was preserved in the National Automobile Museum in Reno, Nevada.

3. "all except . . . run for fright.": Herbert Chase, "Hails Rear-Engine Streamlined Car and Increased Riding Comfort," *Automotive Industries*, 27 June 1931, p. 990.

4. "From an engineering . . . airplane design.": Herbert Chase, "Rear Engine-Mounting and Streamline Adapted to Small Cars," *Automotive Industries*, 20 February 1932, p. 256.

5. "Many objections . . . regular production.": F. B. von Barenyi, "Car Design Trends Call for New Deal in Chassis Construction," *Automotive Industries*, 28 April 1934, p. 520.

6. "never made . . . car behave.": John Tjaarda to author, attachment, 11 May 1960, Ludvigsen Library.

7. From the end of 1934 Mathis and Axel Wenner-Gren were in cahoots in a Paris-based company called the Société Mawen, its name a conflation of their surnames. Mawen's mission was the perfection of an exotic valveless rotating radial aircraft engine patented by an Austro-Hungarian inventor, Sklenar. Mawen, which would survive to 1938 in a fruitless struggle to solve the Sklenar's sealing problems, was one of the pair's ventures.

8. In 1933, in need of a new chassis, Mathis commissioned an all-independent-suspension design from a new engineering boutique in Stuttgart: the Porsche office. The project bore Porsche's Type 27 designation and featured an application of his torsion-bar springing in the Quadruflex chassis introduced with commendable celerity for numerous Mathis models at the 1933 Paris Salon and commercialized in 1934.

9. Jörgen Rasmussen was not exactly bereft after his dismissal. Among the several companies still in his family's hands was the Framo-Werke GmbH, a maker of motorcycle components and delivery vehicles. In 1933 and 1934, while Rasmussen was still an Auto-Union insider, Framo introduced first a front-driven three-wheeler, the Stromer, and then a minuscule four-wheeled car with its 300 cc single-cylinder two-stroke engine in the rear, the Framo Piccolo. Although priced at only 1,295 marks, the two-door Piccolo was too small and crude for an auto market that was already picking up steam, stoked by the Nazis' recovery schemes. Framo reverted to the production of delivery vehicles.

10. "After his . . . Chemnitz": Etzold, Rother, and Erdmann, Band 1, p. 333.

11. "were actually . . . car project.": John Tjaarda to M. W. R. Davis, 23 October 1959, Ludvigsen Library.

12. Tjaarda's strenuous objections: Tom Tjaarda, interview with the author, 26 November 1997.

13. "Dr. Porsche . . . them to him.": Mary Robertson Tjaarda to the author, 8 February 1968, Ludvigsen Library. Mary Tjaarda, the designer's third wife, was not with him at that time but could be expected to be well informed by her husband about those events. Tom Tjaarda, however, does not recall drawings being mentioned by his father. "Another interesting facet in the V.W. story," Mary Tjaarda added, "is the fact [that] S. Thompson Tjaarda — son — was with Ghia when the minor changes were made in the V.W. tail light assembly and rear window and Thompson created these changes. So the Tjaarda clan — father and son — have played a rather interesting part in the 'people's wagon'."

14. Lewis Airomobile: Michael Lamm, "1937 Airomobile — America's Almost VW," *Special-Interest Autos*, January–February 1971, pp. 15–18.

15. Airomobile engine: The same basic four-cylinder engine later powered the White Horse delivery vehicle made by the White Truck Company, mounted in the rear, and provided the foundation for the successful Franklin range of light airplane engines, manufactured by a restructured Doman-Marks company.

16. Josef Kales visit to Syracuse: Dan R. Post, "Split-Window Volks," *Special-Interest Autos*, November–December 1977, p. 54.

17. Aluminum cylinders on an iron crankcase: This was the opposite of the VW engine, which had cast-iron cylinders with aluminum heads on an aluminum (later magnesium) crankcase.

18. "objected strenuously . . . been improved.": Lamm, "1937 Airomobile," quoting the 1953 reminiscences of Carl Doman in *Air-Cooled News*, the magazine of the H. H. Franklin Club.

19. R Buckminster Fuller is justly immortalized by the name "Buckyballs" given by researchers to strong and versatile carbon molecules that are spherical with Fulleresque internal geodesic structures.

20. Rear-wheel steering of Dymaxion car: That rear-wheel steering as such need not be seen as disadvantageous was demonstrated in 1997 by Andy Green at the wheel of Richard Noble's Thrust SSC, the first car officially to exceed the speed of sound on land. But fine-tuning the car's tandem steering rear wheels was one of the Thrust team's toughest challenges.

21. Companies interested in Dymaxion car design: Pawley.

22. "His dark brown . . . astonishment.": Fred C. Kelly, "Not Afraid of New Ideas," *Today*, 28 July 1934, p. 10.

23. "This new car . . . automobile design." and "The engine . . . passenger room." and "a friendly . . . car manufacturers.": Thomas S. LaMarre, "Stout's Scarab," *Automobile Quarterly*, August 1991, pp. 7, 8, 10.

24. "The car was . . . kind of car." : Stout, p. 263.

25. "The rear-mounted . . . of passengers.": William B. Stout, "That Automobile of the Future," *New York Times Magazine*, 24 October 1943, p. 16.

26. "Future motor car engines . . . lower cost.": *New York Times*, 23 January 1938.

27. "Being the . . . for luggage,": William B. Stout, "Out of the Air — Tomorrow's Car," *Popular Mechanics*, January 1942, pp. 42–43.

28. "had drawbacks . . . rear-engine design.": Reginald M. Cleveland, "Rear Engine Discussed," *New York Times*, 7 March 1937.

29. "Hitler Making . . . a dictatorship).": Ralph W. Barnes, "Hitler Making Cheap Auto for Masses in Reich," *New York Herald Tribune*, 19 February 1937.

30. "maintained a reserved . . . danger of freezing.": W. F. Bradley, "Germany Dreams of a 'Popular' Car," *Automotive Industries*, 27 March 1937, p. 507.

31. "In a short time . . . own windshield.": "German Car for Masses," *New York Times*, 3 July 1938. Wrote VW Beetle expert Arthur Railton, "This may be the first time the word 'beetle' was used in print to describe the Volkswagen."

32. "pay-before-you-get-it": Ralph W. Barnes, "Nazis Attempt To Beat Ford on Cost and Output," *New York Herald Tribune*, 2 August 1938.

33. "Volksauto": Otto D. Tolischus, "Five Marks a Week To Buy Reich Autos," *New York Times*, 2 August 1938.

34. "The Nazi . . . cooperate.": Konrad F. Schreier, Jr., personal communication.

35. "the initials K.d.F . . . .unprecedented success.": "Volkswagen — $2 per week — F.O.B. 1940 in Germany," *Automotive Industries*, 24 September 1938, pp. 382–384.

36. Berlin Auto Show report: Edwin P. A. Heinze, "Berlin Motor Show," *Automotive Industries*, 25 March 1939.

37. "Hitler has . . . military movement:" Beasley, pp. 184–185. "Just a box body and a driver's seat" would not be an unfair characterization of some of the stripped-down designs that the Porsche office was studying then to try to reach Hitler's "impossible" target of a price of RM 995.

38. "streetwalkers, bums . . . was too light.": Beasley, pp. 162–163.

39. "Germany is handicapped . . . whole of Germany." W. F. Bradley, "Germany Dreams of a 'Popular' Car," *Automotive Industries*, 27 March 1937, pp. 507–508.

40. Copy of Allison V-12: Beasley, pp. 194–195.

41. "I have to report . . . German factory.": Ludvigsen, Opel, p. 55.

42. "a 'civilian chassis' . . . brought lightness." and "By utilizing . . . rough roads." and "indicating an . . . their job well." and "positive locking . . . gear differential.": *The German Volkswagen*, U.S. Army Ordnance School, OS 9-61, n.d., reproduced in Schreier, pp. 20–25.

43. "One point . . . mounted on Jeeps.": Konrad F. Schreier, Jr., private communication.

44. "The wide range . . . metallurgical practice." and "the unusual . . . weight of the vehicle.": Col. J. H. Frye, "Metallurgy of Foreign Automotive Materiel," *Society of Automotive Engineers*,

Detroit, 8–12 January 1945, pp. 1, 14. During the war the Porsche engineers experimented with iron castings for some drive line parts, such as the engine crankcase, but the added weight caused an unacceptably large deterioration of handling and performance.

45. "Practically all . . . single piece.": The German Volkswagen, U.S. Army Ordnance School, OS 9-61, n.d.

46. "One of the . . . cooling system.": Chester S. Ricker, "Aircooled Engines for Automotive Vehicles," SAE Journal (Transactions), July 1944, pp. 281–295.

47. April 1944 article based on BIOS study of the Type 82: Philip Ruskin, "Military Version of the German Volkswagen," Automotive and Aviation Industries, 15 April 1944, pp. 36–40.

48. "In general . . . seating accommodations.": TM-E 30-451, U.S. Army, 1 March 1945, p. VIII–1.

49. "Captured Volkswagens . . . very beginning.": The German Soldier, Director of Military Training, U.S. Army Service Forces, 1943, reproduced in Schreier, p. 19.

50. "It was inevitable . . . prior to WW II.": Konrad F. Schreier, Jr. to author, 30 June 1997.

51. "The torsion bar . . . salient features.": Lt. Col. G. B. Jarrett, Test of Volkswagen, Amphibious, German Model 1944 (FMCV 81), Ordnance Research and Development Center, Aberdeen, 1944, p. 6. Files of Australian War Memorial, Canberra, researched by Colin Gardner.

52. "On the surface . . . was designed." and "American vehicles . . . Volkswagen." and "There are important . . . a land vehicle." and "Efficient shaping . . . in manufacture." and "Road and water . . . and development." and "The general feeling . . . tendency to over-steer.": "German Amphibious Volkswagen Supplement," SAE War Engineering Board, August 1945, pp. 3–9.

53. "Thus it came about . . . barter or steal.": Menno Duerksen, "The Volkswagen Story," Cars & Parts, November 1975, p. 109.

54. VW order for "Graham" Howard: E. A. Seal, Chief, Trade and Industry Division, to _____, 16 September 1946, PRO FO1039/796.

55. "The Beetle belonged . . . tiny and austere car.": Konrad F. Schreier, Jr. to author, 30 June 1997.

56. "manufacturing plans . . . wood or light metal.": "Volkswagen Threat?," Automotive News, 12 May 1947.

57. "The Volkswagen plant . . . of its capacity.": German Motor Vehicles Industry Report, U.S. Strategic Bombing Survey, Munitions Division, BIOS Miscellaneous Report No. 69, p. 5.

58. "one of the most . . . be made available.": German Volkswagen Plant, Export Bulletin, Automobile Manufacturers Association, Detroit, Michigan, 30 August 1948.

59. "They sell for . . . 30,000 a month.": "Hitler's Car Dreams Come True," Detroit Free Press, 7 November 1948, section B, p. 3. The VW's designer is identified as "Dr. Otto Porsch."

60. "about two day's . . . the U.S. market.": The Detroit News Pictorial, 24 April 1948.

61. "What will the Allies . . . world once more?": "German Auto Plants?," Automotive News, 12 June 1944.

CHAPTER 6

1. French auto production: Laux, p. 198.

2. "I always had . . . for other purposes." and "No firm . . . conceived by nobody.": Emile Claveau, La Raison et l'Automobile, Paris, 21 December 1966.

3. "It should be able . . . electric welding." and "without any dramatics.": John Winding-Sorensen, "Claveau — Visionary with no future," Car, February 1973, pp. 60–62, quoting an address by Claveau to the SIA in December 1932.

4. "no car, unless . . . year or two.": Michael Worthington-Williams, "Two of a kind," The Automobile, August 1997, pp. 74–75, quoting from French Automobile and Allied Trades Exporter, October 1927.

5. "in 1926 . . . were concerned.": G. W., "12 Years Before the K.d.F.," The Motor, 10 March 1943, p. 94.

6. "Sponsored by . . . people's car.": Winding-Sorensen, "Claveau," pp. 61–62.

7. "moral cost . . . car's passengers." and "when long . . . did not exist": Emile Claveau to Cyril

Posthumus, 28 June 1969, p. 2, Ludvigsen Library.

8. The new generation of front-drive Claveaus appeared at the 1930 Paris Salon, with two-stroke engines behind their driven front wheels. Bodies were now slab-sided, fully enclosing the wheels, with a rounded nose reminiscent of France's Chenard-Walcker sports car designs, which were nicknamed "tanks" in honor of their shapes. Although still advanced, these concepts were more in line with current industry thinking, especially that of carmaker André Citroën.

   Claveau found in Citroën a rare industrialist capable of appreciating "the horizons that could be opened" by his designs. Over the objections of Citroën's engineering staff an agreement was signed between the two men on 2 November 1933 for the exploitation by Citroën of Claveau's designs. Scheduled for implementation in March 1934, the pact was rendered void by the financial collapse of Citroën's company, toppled by the costly launch of its own new front-wheel-drive car (Claveau to Cyril Posthumus, 18 July 1969, p. 3, Ludvigsen Library).

   By 1939 Claveau had almost completed the first prototype of a stunningly advanced envelope-bodied six-passenger sedan with a V-8 engine and aluminum alloy body/frame — the Audi A8 of its day. This was displayed at the first Paris Salons after the war. Claveau named it after the philosopher who had been his consistent inspiration: Descartes.

   Emile Claveau's final complete passenger-car prototype was the Claveau 56, shown at the 1955 Salon. Smooth-lined in a manner long familiar to Claveau but only then becoming widely accepted, this two-door car was DKW-powered — a return to the two-stroke engines the Frenchman had once advocated. It was the final act in a series of farsighted experiments that "cost a lot, horribly expensive for an individual — which I have always been — well in excess of one million dollars expended by me since 1923" (Claveau to the author, 17 January 1968, p. 2, Ludvigsen Library).

9. "He is a fascinating . . . accept real change.": Robert A. Lutz to the author, 23 December 1966, p. 1, Ludvigsen Library.

10. Proposals favoring various drive arrangements: Album de la Voiture SIA 2 Places, SIA, Paris, 1936, pp. 281–284.

11. Performance of the Dubonnet Dolphin: W. F. Bradley, "New Dubonnet . . . ," *Automotive Industries*, 11 April 1936, pp. 538–540.

12. "With associates, . . . were at war.": Karl Ludvigsen, "The Baron of Park Avenue," *Automobile Quarterly*, vol. 10, no. 2, p. 155. At that time he spelled his surname as "Hoffmann." After his arrival in America in 1941 he dropped the final 'n.'

13. "This is the first . . . never been done!": "La nouvelle KdF allemande," *La Pratique Automobile*, 1 July 1938, Paris, p. 16.

14. "Here we encounter . . . the three models.": Alfred Nauck, "Détails techniques sur la voiture KDF," *Englebert Magazine*, January–February 1939, p. 65.

15. "the great attraction . . . several years." and "The bodywork . . . actually of steel." and "If, as is hoped, . . . automobile market.": Henri Petit, "Le Salon de Berlin 1939," *Englebert Magazine*, March–April 1939, pp. 17, 19, 21.

16. "because its buyers . . . have to wait.": Charles Faroux, "Le Salon Automobile Allemand," *Englebert Magazine*, March–April 1939, p. 5.

17. Another who reacted was Pierre Boulanger of Citroën, "a long-time adherent of a simple and modest means of mobility for country use (he mentioned country doctors and midwives)," as described by Robert Braunschweig in a letter to the author.

   Boulanger asked his engineers to start work on a light, simple vehicle, an "umbrella on wheels" as he described it. With its air-cooled flat-twin engine of only 375 cc driving the front wheels, the resulting Citroën 2CV had much in common with many of the designs for the Voiture SIA competition. It was a full four-passenger car of unique conception, however, with its interconnected long-travel suspension and its engine cover corrugated like a sewer pipe for stiffness.

   Although a first prototype was ready at the beginning of the 1940s, the 2CV did not enter production until after the war. Citroën unveiled it at the 1948 Paris Salon where "it was greeted with deadly laughter by the media and public, except by *Automobil Revue*," wrote its then editor Braunschweig to the author. "We considered it an extremely useful vehicle. An automatic clutch and some improvements soon lifted its banning for Paris use, originally ordered by Bou-langer. They made a good nine million of this simple but practical and intellectually outstand-ing creation."

18. "Even though . . . doomed him to solitude.": Grégoire, *Best Wheel*, p. 112.

19. "Interested only . . . exist in France.": Rhodes, p. 160.

20. "a short and calm . . . in their columns!": Grégoire, *Best Wheel*, pp. 113–114.

21. What Renault learned in Berlin: Some accounts say that Renault called on Hitler in the Chan-cellery and "brought home with him a complete file on the new German car." No mention of such a visit is made by Renault's biographer, who rejects the idea that Renault admired Hitler. The availability of such a dossier on the Type 60 at the time of the 1938 Berlin Show is unlikely. Such stories are more likely to have been spread by Renault's many enemies. As Anthony Rhodes wrote, "He became further suspect among the communists and socialists by a visit to Berlin in 1938 to the automobile salon."

22. Prewar vehicle production: Loubet, p. 122.

23. "After the war . . . the Germans have.": Seidler, Challenge, p. 37.

24. "We'll build . . . Nothing else." and "The poverty in . . . not a Zèbre.": Picard, p. 105.

25. "Serre, who had . . . Berlin Motor Show.": Picard, p. 106. We can assume that this reporting was substantially the same as that cited above in the Belgian *Englebert Magazine*, in which the two experts' writings also appeared. And the fact that the engineers felt a need to have reference to it is further confirmation that Renault did not bring back a detailed dossier on the VW from Berlin.

26. Eighteen horsepower had been judged adequate for the 972-pound car; 19.2 were produced at 4,500 rpm on a blend of alcohol and gasoline in the first tests in February 1942. That was the only available fuel. Special stocks of gasoline had to be secreted at Renault dealerships at Grenoble and Marseilles to allow road trials of the first and second prototypes to be carried out through 1943 and 1944.

27. "Big, corpulent . . . controller of Renault.": Picard, p. 200.

28. "Louis Renault . . . his business conferences.": Rhodes, p. 177.

29. This was not news to the French carmakers. A Peugeot study mission to Detroit in 1937 had calculated that the cost of cars FOB the factory in France was 20 percent higher than in Amer-ica, based on a car weighing 2,425 pounds. The experts attributed three-quarters of this bur-den to more costly supplies and materials in France and the remaining one-quarter to less cost-efficient production rates, which were typically fifteen times higher in America than those in France.

Although realizing that it could not reach U.S.-style production volumes, Peugeot decided to make an effort. Wrote historian Jean-Louis Loubet, "There are five models in the 1935 Peu-geot catalogue, four in 1938 and only three in 1939 with only two types of engines. And in 1942 Jean-Pierre Peugeot continues the effort, demanding for the first time that one studies 'the production and cost price possibilities which a single model would provide.' Finally he falls in with the arguments of his technical director, Ernest Mattern, who has unceasingly argued the industrial advantages of monoculture for twenty years."

30. "Every manufacturer . . . peace-time variety.": Rhodes, pp. 159–160, quoting a Pons article in *Cahiers Politiques*, 1945.

31. "was not lacking . . . as they did.": Picard, p. 266.

32. The government asked Panhard to use the design of the Aluminium Français-Grégoire, an air-cooled front-drive flat-twin-engined small car that it had backed — although this plan was in some disarray because its designer, Jean-Albert Grégoire, had already received a commitment from Simca to produce his vehicle. This was resolved when Fiat, a Simca shareholder, discour-aged its French affiliate from making a rival car. Citroën, of course, had a new small car on its own stocks, the 2CV.

33. "After a few . . . reasonable price.": Picard, p. 280.

34. The uncertainties of planning a product range for postwar France were many. A market survey

conducted by Renault verified that there were many "purchasers with their purses wide open, as a result of the current scarcity of goods." Although the survey confirmed that a market awaited the 4CV, saying that "the best sale is on the small car," it warned as well that "there is quite an important place for the 11CV and a trough [in demand] on the 6–8CV." Renault had cars for all these segments; should it make them all or concentrate on a single model?

To most on the board it seemed that the safest course in such an uncertain world was for Renault to continue to offer a wide model range. Historian Jean-Louis Loubet: "Whether by habit, by respect of the former boss, by prudence, or sometimes even by ignorance, many wish to continue Louis Renault's range policy, to continue to offer various types of cars to satisfy different requirements. And the position would have been untenable if Pierre Lefaucheux had not had a decisive advantage on his side: the conviction that with market studies he possessed a tool which sufficed to be able to create a mass production and consumption in France."

To the directors who favored the broad-range approach Lefaucheux said, "This policy was good once. But it has had its time and now, if we want to achieve comparable [to the United States] production and prices, we must specialize. We must know how to abandon certain sectors" (Loubet, p. 310). Not forgetting the example of the Volkswagen that had intrigued Louis Renault, taking an even more robust position than the government's Paul-Marie Pons, the Renault chief felt he was right to advocate a focused approach.

35. "We'll build the 4CV," and "We'll put all . . . cars a day.": Seidler, *Romance*, p. 57.

36. Marcel Paul portfolio: Fernand Picard says that Paul became minister for industrial production in March 1946.

37. "We had . . . them to do." and use of 4x4 for forestry work: Ivan Hirst, interview with the author, 9 October 1997.

38. "had not been . . . reached there." Turner, p. 86.

39. Credit of 2,800 tons of steel: Minutes No. 15 and Supplementary, Branch Vehicle Industry, 25 February 1947, PRO FO1039/796 and Brig. S. G. Galpin, Volkswagen Production, Mechanical Engineering Branch, 26 July 1946, p. 4, PRO FO1039/796.

40. "The first consignment . . . were missing.": Richard Berryman, "The Berryman Story," *Safer Motoring*, 1965–66, p. 282.

41. "I think that . . . Trade Agreement.": R. H. King, Volkswagen to the French Zone, 2 May 1947, p. 1, PRO FO1039/796.

42. "As you know, . . . enough as it is.": R. H. King to Priorities and Allocations Branch, 26 June 1947, PRO FO1039/796.

43. "We soon discovered . . . reparations payment." and "pushed hard . . . for reparations.' ": Porsche and Bentley, p. 189.

44. "right to help. ..pillages suffered.": Loubet, pp. 26–27.

45. "wasted no time . . . this affair.": Porsche and Bentley, p. 190. The other half of the VW factory was to go to Britain.

46. "a typical French look.": Nelson, p. 105.

47. "It seems to me . . . against the project.": Porsche and Bentley, pp. 191–192.

48. Wartime relations with Jean-Pierre Peugeot and "No doubt . . . 'war criminal'.": Porsche and Bentley, pp. 193–194.

49. Porsche arrest and "not a glorious page in the annals of French justice." and Nauck and "like a Russian commissar." and sealing of court documents: Mommsen and Grieger, pp. 942–944.

50. "We can discuss . . . grandiose idea.": Porsche and Bentley, pp. 196–197.

51. "We don't want . . . him the worst!": Ivan Hirst, interview with author, 9 October 1997.

52. "Clearly there was . . . bringing over their families." Picard, p. 289.

53. "He tried to explain . . . the Renault factory.": Porsche and Bentley, p. 197.

54. "We consider that . . . to point out.": Picard, p. 289.

55. Road test comparison of VW and 4CV: Pete Molson, " '56 Volkswagen and Renault Road Test," *Motor Trend*, May 1956, p. 24.

56. "We were just . . . after the war.": Ivan Hirst, interview with author, 9 October 1997.

57. Renault transfer machines: Improving consistency of quality and reducing the number of operators required, Renault's transfer machines marked the next step beyond the production technology installed at Wolfsburg. They were the brainchild of a young engineer named Pierre Bézier. While a German prisoner of war, Bézier had continued his studies of such systems, according to author Edouard Seidler. To build the 4CV twenty-nine of his machines were set up in Renault's Hall U5, where they were seen by Hirst and Radclyffe. These transfer machines and other production systems developed into a separate business for Renault.

58. "I ran into Prince . . . involved a little . . .": Picard, p. 201.

59. "not only for . . . chosen for himself.": Müller, p. 22.

60. Renault 4CV and Dauphine: When the Japanese producers launched new automobiles after the war, most followed classical British design lines with licensed production of Hillman and Austin models. An exception was Hino Motors, which signed a pact in March 1953 to produce the rear-engined Renault 4CV under license. To enable Hino to build 4CVs with right-hand drive for the Japanese market, Renault shipped it the same kits of parts that were being assembled in Acton, west of London, for British buyers.

Although the agreement was initially for only four years, Hino kept building and selling the 4CV to 1961. In that year it introduced a new car, the 893 cc Contessa, which although Renault-inspired was Hino's own design, as the Japanese company had to prove to Renault lest it be billed for license fees. A sporty coupé styled by Giovanni Michelotti was added to the rear-engined Hino range in 1962.

Thus did Louis Renault's prewar infatuation with the Beetle, confirmed by his own engineers, lead to a range of rear-engined cars in Japan. Hino upgraded its Contessa range in 1964 with 1,251 cc engines, still "outboard" of the rear axle, and torsion-bar front suspension. Their Michelotti styling followed the trend set by Chevrolet's Corvair. In 1966 Hino became a satellite of Toyota, which took an eleven percent share in the smaller firm. Car production stopped in 1969 at Hino, which has since specialized in trucks.

61. "From 1934, . . . like Panhard.": Grégoire, 50 ans, p. 503.

62. "a miracle . . . commercial one.": Loubet, p. 129.

63. "was its robustness . . . over the others.": Picard, pp. 330–331.

CHAPTER 7

1. Übelacker and rear-engined Tatras: Margolius and Henry, p. 104.

2. "it will corner . . . small saloons." Gordon Wilkins, "Under My Easter Bonnet," *The Autocar*, 8 May 1946, p. 290.

3. "Have you already . . . our own fashion?": Tatra typescript about the career of Hans Ledwinka, in German, n.d., Ludvigsen Library, p. 3. Otto Dyckhoff was not only a competent and well-informed manufacturing engineer but also a man with a quip for every occasion. At the corner-stone-laying ceremony at Fallersleben he noticed an executive from Opel who had chosen a light-colored suit for the warm spring weather. "Since when," he gibed at the Opel man, "is it customary to wear a white suit to one's funeral?"

4. Fritz Todt's Tatra Type 87: Margolius and Henry, p. 114.

5. Type 87 drag coefficient: A contemporary measurement of a drag coefficient of 0.24 for the Tatra Type 87 (Cd, where 1.00 equals the aerodynamic drag of a flat plate) made contemporaneously on a one-fifth-scale model seemed too low to be true and indeed was. When an actual T87 (once Hans Ledwinka's personal car) was tested in the big Volkswagen wind tunnel in 1979 it was found to have a coefficient of drag of 0.36, still a stunningly low figure for the years in which it was built.

6. Tatra's patent priorities and the postwar resolution of license fees owed: Margolius and Henry, p. 93. On some occasions, at least, the Porsche team did keep patent infringements in mind. Ferry Porsche said that the decision to fit a cable braking system to the Type 60 avoided the payment of licensing fees to Lockheed. The Porsche office, of course, was eager to develop solutions of its own that would be patentable and licensable to other makers.

7. Misappropriation of VW works property: Mommsen and Grieger, pp. 927, 940. This was not an idle accusation, bearing in mind that Anton Piëch had liberated RM 10,500,000 and certain other assets from the works on his departure. However the Americans were able to convince the police from Gifhorn that they lacked jurisdiction in Allied-occupied Austria.

8. American suspicion of Czech interest in the Porsches: Mommsen and Grieger, p. 940. Fred W. Rauskolb of Wolfsburg is credited as the source of this research.

9. "was the low . . . available space.": Edward Eves, "Skoda 1000MB," *Autocar*, 6 November 1964, p. 984.

10. "I thought of . . . a great alliance.": Dymock, p. 50.

11. DKW-engined Philipin: Lindh, p. 21.

12. "It was a bold . . . a DKW substitute.": Dymock, pp. 46, 50.

13. Philipson rejection of VW sales for Sweden: Lindh, p. 30.

14. "The conflict between . . . but so does Britain.": Michael L. Hoffmann, "Volkswagen Puts British in Dilemma," *New York Times*, 9 July 1946.

15. "In order of . . . comparable world prices." and table, which is lightly edited for clarity: " 'Export' of Volkswagen," Lt. Col. R. S. Burn to _____, 4 September 1946 attaching memo of 29 August 1946, PRO FO1039/797.

16. Two cars for Swiss mission: Ivan Hirst recalls this provision as a means of getting two cars to meet a request from Liechtenstein. Allocations were made by Charles Carroll, who was a friend of Michael McEvoy.

17. "The car was . . . just propaganda.": Railton, p. 49.

18. "a Dutch Army . . . ill-fitting.": Ivan Hirst, interview with the author, 9 October 1997.

19. "not sure of . . . played with gusto." and first six export cars: Railton, pp. 92–93. According to Railton, Pon "was able to take only five of the six cars he ordered back to Holland. One of the cars failed to pass inspection at the end of the assembly line!"

20. "The Volkswagen car . . . Germany under license." and "the development . . . and bulk parts." and "The London end . . . for the climate.": J. L. B. Titchener to Sir Cecil Weir, 5 November 1947, PRO FO1046/193.

21. VW allocations to Belgian field units: Philippe Casseto to _____, 5 April 1998 based on research in the Belgian Centre de Documentation Historique de l'Armée.

22. "This car . . . mechanical efficiency.": Pierre D'Ieteren to Mr. Henly of Henlys Ltd., London, 16 October 1946, PRO SUPP14/397.

23. "a senior State . . . automobile industry." and "component parts . . . car in quantity.": M. Everard Taylor, report to Mr. Bennett on meeting on 21 March, 8 April 1946, PRO SUPP14/397.

24. Problems of Belgian motor industry: An inkling of the sad state of the postwar Belgian vehicle industry was given by the example of Minerva. Once a maker of luxury cars, Minerva had bowed out of that market in 1936 but continued its truck production. Minerva's Mortsel factory was in lamentable condition after the war, having been bombed by the Allies when it was rebuilding German aircraft engines, targeted by the V-1s when it was repairing Allied military vehicles, and left open to the winds, rain, and snow by the postwar occupiers who finally relinquished it as a repair site in early 1947.

Minerva's chief Mathieu van Roggen put his company back on its feet with a license to produce the new Land Rover. Adding 63 percent of the vehicle's value in Belgium, Minerva sold some thousands to the Belgian army from 1951 to 1954 — thus meeting the demand that Colonel Dufour had hoped to satisfy with the Volkswagen.

Seeking a proper motorcar of his own to produce, van Roggen came under the spell of an aborted project of Gianni Caproni in Italy. When Caproni's businesses were auctioned in 1950 all the tools, machines, and licenses needed to build the CEMSA-Caproni car with its flat-four engine were bought by Minerva. It intended a comeback with Antonio Fessia's ambitious front-drive design.

Finding the CEMSA-Caproni's engine too small, Minerva's engineers designed a completely new 1,501 cc unit to power their version of the car. Still a flat four made entirely in light alloy, it was now a side-valve engine with cooling by air instead of water. It was entirely lacking the sophisticated blower and ducting that Porsche had given the VW, Minerva's designers counting instead on a crude fan and the engine's placement at the front of the car to generate cooling breezes.

Completed in 1953, Minerva's version of the Fessia design was exhibited at the 1954 Brussels Show. Experiments were made with a two-liter version of the engine. But the faltering firm lacked the resources to commit to its manufacture. Not until the early 1960s would an improved version of the Fessia design reach production as the water-cooled Lancia Flavia.

25. "component parts . . . in quantity.": M. Everard Taylor to Mr. Bennett, 8 April 1947.

26. Activities of Van Luppen: Paul Frère to author, 11 November 1997.

27. "500 Volkswagens . . . together in Belgium.": "Export of Volkswagen to Belgium," E. Harle to Flint Cahan, JEIA, Minden, 9 May 1947, PRO FO1039/796.

28. "Such a car . . . worth worrying about.": M. Everard Taylor, report on 21 March meeting.

29. "I gather that . . . model is obsolete." and "we would view . . . necessary castings.": P. B. Hunt, Board of Trade, to E. J. Joint, British Embassy, Brussels, 17 April 1947, p. 1. PRO SUPP14/397.

30. "Radclyffe was skeptical. . . between their legs.": Ivan Hirst, interview with the author, 9 October 1997.

31. "complete manufacture . . . German drawings.": P. B. Hunt, Minutes, Board of Trade meeting, 4 December 1946, PRO BT211/92.

32. "We had to . . . a clue technically.": Berryman, "The Berryman Story," p. 281.

33. "From time to . . . get away fast." and "I think their . . . Russian troops.": Ibid., p. 280.

34. "In a week . . . more like it.": Karl Ludvigsen, "[BMW] Postwar Recovery," Automobile Quarterly, July 1997, pp. 40–42.

35. "The last life . . . industrial might.": Post, pp. 95–96.

36. "contrary to . . . and rewarding.": Turner, p. 739, referring to A. C. Sutton, Western Technology and Soviet Economic Development, vol. 3, Stanford, 1973, pp. 15–32 and passim.

37. "Opel has . . . cars in Leipzig.": Ludvigsen, Opel, p. 58.

38. "Reparations activity . . . remaining resources." and "The Russians one . . . sort of peninsula.": Post, pp. 96–97, 127.

39. "You can be . . . anything they want." and "Major Hirst, . . . Western imperialismus.": Ivan Hirst, interview with the author, 9 October 1997. Visitors to the plant did not always make their actual intentions known. Ben Pon disguised his real goals when he first visited after the war. And Hirst recalled a visit by an amiable American consul from Hamburg who seemed to make only a courtesy visit to Wolfsburg. Only when he read the draft of this book did Hirst discover that the consul had filed a detailed report on the status of the plant to Washington.

40. "Porsche went to . . . behind the Ural.": von Frankenberg, pp. 46–48.

41. "The vehicle had . . . good to drive." and "This type of VW . . . slam the door." and "I wouldn't have . . . go near it!": Long and Matthews, pp. 6–7.

42. "There is some evidence . . . batch of 1,785 cars.": Long and Matthews, p. 11. Confirmation of this is provided by Lees's report that the car is built on a Kübelwagen chassis, like all the first Beetles built after the war at Wolfsburg.

43. Australian interest in Adler and DKW: Loorham, Controller, Australian Reparations and Stores Team, Germany, Minutes of 31 January 1947, researched by Colin Gardner.

44. "instructed to prepare . . . special tools used.": Berryman, "The Berryman Story," p. 405.

45. Eleven-page report: R. H. Berryman, "Brief Statement on the Specification and Manufacture of the Volkswagen," Wolfsburg, 17 January 1947, Australian Archives MT105/8/1.

46. "A feature of the Volkswagen . . . received from the R.A.F.": J. T. O. Loorham, memo of 31 January 1947, Australian Archives, Melbourne.

47. "received instructions . . . about the production.": Berryman, "The Berryman Story," p. 405.

48. Berryman status for Antwerp trip: Lt. Col. D. C. Edwards, "Movement Order No. 44," H. Q. "T" Force, 19 February 1947.

49. "Apparently it was . . . the VW was it.": Berryman, "The Berryman Story," p. 405.

50. "The northern city . . . the main events.": Colin Gardner to the author, 25 January 1998.

51. "They sent four . . . three weeks there.": Ivan Hirst, interview with the author, 9 October 1997.

52. "A hand operated, electric . . . on the assembly chain.": J. W. Carter, memo from Wolfsburg of 22 March 1947, Australian Archives, Melbourne.

53. "important . . . Hartnett's programme.": Malet-Warden, FIAT Forward, "Signal 1875 basic," 12 Aug 1947. PRO FO1039/796.

54. Larry Hartnett and GM's Holden: Dennis Harrison, "1948–58 Holden, 'Australia's Own Car'," *Collectible Automobile*, October 1990, pp. 64–73.

55. "a large group . . . expand in Australia.": Rich, p. 137.

56. "The Australian Government . . . desirable in Australia.": Director Breen, Secondary Industries Division, to J. R. Cochrane, A.S.T.M., London, 2 May 1947, researched in the Australian Archives by Colin Gardner.

57. "my self-imposed . . . to interest me.": Hartnett, pp. 201–202.

58. "to meet a select . . . for Empire Defence.": Rich, p. 137.

59. "Dedman's cable said . . . beetle car in it.": Hartnett, pp. 202–203.

60. "I liked Hartnett . . . on the German side.": Ivan Hirst, interview with the author, 9 October 1997.

61. "Currency values . . . have public acceptance.": Hartnett, pp. 203–204.

62. "What did interest . . . a single spanner.": Long and Matthews, p. 11.

63. "I told them . . . to lose interest.": Ivan Hirst, interview with the author, 9 October 1997.

64. "Two German cars . . . Australian 'People's Car'.": Agenda, Cabinet Subcommittee (Secondary Industries), 4 September 1947, researched by Colin Gardner.

65. "One of these . . . inspect the car.": Agenda and minutes, Secondary Industries Commission, 4 February 1948, Australian Archives.

66. "I was particularly . . . had come off.": Berryman, "The Berrryman Story," p. 405.

67. "Some people may . . . as I had.": Hartnett, p. 204.

CHAPTER 8

1. "Some examples of . . . the least promising.": Platt, p. 151.

2. "such streamlining . . . utility value.": "GM Report A-12," 10 September 1935, p. 4, Ludvigsen Library.

3. "we started out . . . comfort and utility.": Leslie, p. 176.

4. "Both front and . . . assembly.": "GM Report A-12," p. 6.

5. "Prototypes were built . . . all our development.": Michael Lamm, "GM's X-Cars," *Special-Interest Autos*, November–December 1971, p. 17.

6. "The writer understands . . . tested the car.": P. M. Heldt, "Rear-Engined, Frameless Passenger Car," *Automotive Industries*, 22 April 1939, p. 522.

7. "handling the work . . . well worked out." and "'These procedures . . . fixed-mind conditions.'": Leslie, pp. 178–179.

8. "It is my impression . . . US at that time.": "On GM's X-Cars," Darl F. Caris to *Special-Interest Autos*, January–March 1972, p. 7.

9. "His report was . . . such poor judgement.": Platt, pp. 151–152.

10. Resumption of GM control of Opel: Ludvigsen, Opel, pp. 60–61.

11. Studebaker decision not to import VWs: Ironically, only a few years later under new management Studebaker would become the American importer of the cars of Mercedes-Benz and its sister company acquired in 1958, Auto-Union with its two-stroke DKWs. Revived in West Germany after the war, DKW was producing cars that directly rivaled the Volkswagen.

12. "I think everybody . . . was backing him.": Emil Zoerlein, Reminiscences of August 1952, Henry Ford Museum and Greenfield Village Research Center, pp. 64–65, 232.

13. "I don't know . . . people at work.": Lewis, p. 149.

14. "Of all the people . . . ways most definitely.": Zoerlein, Reminiscences, pp. 67–68, 228, 232.

15. "wearing the wide . . . star to the cloth.": Lewis, p. 149.

16. "Every year makes . . . maintains full independence.": Hitler, p. 583. The text that constitutes *Mein Kampf* was published originally in two volumes in 1925 and 1926 respectively. In the second edition, published as a single volume in 1930, the specific reference to Ford is replaced by "only very few" (n., p. 583).

17. "The citation accompanying . . . extended to Ford." and Ford as godfather, and "Ford officials admitted . . . by the company." Lewis, pp. 149–152. The "propaganda" reference is likely to have been to *Mein Kampf*.

18. Market's antagonism to Ford products: Lewis, p. 153. David Lewis wrote that a survey conducted in 1940 showed that four of five Americans were aware of Henry Ford's anti-Semitism.

19. Rear-engined Briggs-built prototype: With a 125-inch wheelbase, the rear-engined Briggs car hewed faithfully to Tjaarda's Sterkenburg principles. Its frame was integrated with the body structure with great artistry, approaching a bridgelike trussed design with boxed sills and pillars, liberally drilled out for lightness. At its core was a small tubular backbone, spread like a wishbone at the rear to accommodate the power unit in the style of Ledwinka's Tatras.

Contributing to the car's lightness at 2,500 pounds was its special aluminum-block V-8 engine. Following Ford design principles, the 2.7-liter eight weighed only 300 pounds and developed 80 horsepower at 4,700 rpm, sufficient to propel the highly aerodynamic prototype at 110 miles per hour. The Sterkenburg model was followed in placing the engine ahead of the rear axle. Also at the rear, fed by adjustable scoops in the body sides — later by fixed louvers — was a wide, low radiator.

Behind the rear wheels was a special automatic transmission that gave the Briggs the two-pedal control that Tjaarda had planned for his luxury Sterkenburg. Designed and built by the Eclipse Aviation Corporation, a division of Bendix, the transmission used special disc clutches, freewheels, and a control mechanism to provide upshifts when the driver backed off on the accelerator. A vacuum-operated overdrive raised the already high (for that era) top gear of 3.8:1 to an ultrahigh 2.8:1 for economical cruising.

Tjaarda and Briggs took no chances with the springing of the prototype, which used a transverse semi-elliptic leaf spring for each axle. Henry Ford would brook no other method, although he would have been startled by the car's all-independent suspension. At the front the spring was attached by shackles to stub axles which were free to slide up and down on vertical square-section guides. These guide pillars in turn were carried in ball joints that allowed the steering linkage to be fully sprung, unaffected in its geometry by wheel movement.

The running rear-engined Briggs car followed the body detailing of the wooden styling model, even to its twin rear-vision portholes inherited from the Sterkenburg. When the car was publicly revealed, in October of 1935, its rear windows had been opened out and the skin of its tail had sprouted a rash of cooling louvers. Cooling the engine was as much a challenge as heating the interior: Tjaarda said that the lack of any heating system chilled the interest of the Ford and Chrysler executives to whom it was hopefully demonstrated.

20. "Briggs thought . . . morning at Briggs." and "There was considerable . . . fingers in the water.": Eugene Gregorie, interview with the author, 11 August 1997.

21. "It was apparent . . . corrections in the design.": Sorensen and Williamson, pp. 74, 77.

22. "The assignments which . . . ever so slowly.": Albert O. Roberts, Reminiscences of January 1958, Henry Ford Museum and Greenfield Village Research Center, pp. 19–20.

23. "MOTOR MAY GO TO REAR": Herbert Chase, "Motor May Go to Rear," *New York Times*, 3 January 1937. Herbert Chase participated in and reported on an SAE meeting in 1931 in which rear-engined car concepts figured prominently.

24. "didn't go very far . . . thing out of it.": Terry Boyce, "Henry's Pushers," *Special-Interest Autos*, November–December 1971, p. 24.

25. "At that time . . . Ford's private ideas.": Zoerlein, Reminiscences, p. 93.

26. "In 1940 Mr. Ford . . . 51 miles per gallon.": Roberts, Reminiscences, pp. 23–24. In his oral history interview, conducted in August 1954, Mr. Roberts added, "Now that the engineering force has expanded to 6,300 men, we no longer have floor space for car testing."

27. "He had been talking . . . would come up.": Boyce, "Henry's Pushers," p. 24.

28. "We were always confronted . . . would come up.": Sheldrick's comment was equally relevant to a mainstream Ford program to develop a smaller postwar car, kicked off in 1944 and realized in the form of numerous prototypes. Their aim, to create a smaller Ford that could sell for significantly less than the company's standard-sized cars, proved frustratingly difficult to achieve. However, one of its prototypes was selected by Ford Société Anonyme Française as its postwar production model. It made its debut as the V-8–powered Ford Vedette in October 1948.

As part of a last-gasp effort in 1946 to make the American small-car project fly, wrote David Lewis, "Ford Research was instructed to develop plans for a 106-inch [wheelbase], 2,000-pound, five-passenger car with a Jack and Heintz rear-mounted, aircooled, in-line or opposed overhead-valve four to sell for $800."* The influence of the Volkswagen was too strong to be completely ignored by Ford.

Their price objective of $800 can be set against the retail price of the cheapest 1946 Ford, the Business Coupe, of $1,195. A two-door sedan ("Tudor" in the Ford terminology of the day) sold for $1,260 and a "Fordor" (of course) sedan for $1,325. Ford was trying to position a smaller postwar car at a decent price distance from its standard models, down in the three-figure price range for which its cars had sold through 1942.

According to a survey conducted early in 1947, such a car would have received a ready welcome. The public was asked by the Crowell-Collier publishing company: "If a leading automobile manufacturer were to bring out a new car, smaller (not a Bantam [American version of the British Austin]) or less luxurious than present models, that would sell for under a thousand dollars, would you buy it?" The answer was yes for 39 percent of those surveyed. One-third of those who were planning to buy a new car said that they would switch to one of these cheaper cars instead — chiefly to take advantage of the lower price.

General Motors too was aware of these sentiments. It was planning a new small car for the postwar market, the all-independent-suspension Chevrolet Cadet. The Cadet was engineered and steps toward its production in Cleveland, Ohio were taken. But by the end of 1946 both big companies deferred such plans indefinitely. It was hard enough for them to find enough steel to meet the strong demand for their existing models, let alone to tool and produce a completely new range as well. Not until 1959 (for the 1960 model year) did they enter the smaller-car market with the Ford Falcon and Chevrolet Corvair.

* David L. Lewis, "Ford's Postwar Light Car," *Special-Interest Autos*, October–November 1972, p. 26. Jack & Heintz Precision Industries Inc. of Cleveland, Ohio, had been wartime manufacturers of starters, inverters, and other accessories for wartime use. In 1946 J&H introduced a modular range of flat-opposed air-cooled engines for both aircraft and automotive use, featuring the Skinner split sleeve-valve system and light all-aluminum die-cast construction. The engine of interest to Ford measured 79.4 x 69.9 mm for 1,383 cc and developed 45 bhp at 6,500 rpm. The bare J&H engine weighed 150 pounds. No significant production ensued.

29. "In 1940 Boyer . . . on their own cars.": Lewis, p. 283.

30. "We designed a whole . . . welded by hand.": C. J Smith, Reminiscences, Ford Motor Company Archives, November 1951, pp. 29–30.

31. "occurred at a time . . . the nation's press.": Lewis, p. 284.

32. Rear-engined Ford dimensions: The 56-inch track is recorded on a drawing of the frame found by the author in the archives of the Henry Ford Museum and Greenfield Village Research Center, as is the estimated weight of the frame. The dimensions of the wheelbase and the frame tubes have been scaled from the drawing and may not be precisely accurate.

33. "The outbreak of . . . war was over.": Lewis, p. 285.

34. "Among his projects . . . diverted Mr. Ford too.": Sorensen and Williamson, pp. 297–298.

35. "telephoned the Ford . . . jet propulsion engine." and "The German propulsion . . . at the Rouge plant." and improved fuel nozzles: LaCroix, "Intermittent Jet Type Engine," unpub-

lished history of Ford in World War II, pp. 2–3, 14, researched in Henry Ford Museum archives by Tim O'Callaghan.

36. JB-2 flight testing and production volume: Werrell, p. 65.

37. Relations between Ford Cologne and VW works: On reading this passage Ivan Hirst noted, "I've no recollection but it's possible."

38. "everything was down . . . sides were shattered." and Niehl truck production: Wilkins and Hill, p. 344.

39. Thacker to Ford Belgium: The peripatetic and obviously able Charles Thacker later became managing director of Ford of Britain.

40. "Manchester mafia": Sir Terence Beckett, interview with the author, 20 October 1997.

41. "We spoke often . . . supply problems." Ivan Hirst, interview with the author, 7 October 1997.

42. "That was the . . . with the Russians.": Ivan Hirst, interview with the author, 7 October 1997. Release of the dies was eventually negotiated. On 2 June 1948 Ford Germany's Erhard Vitger cabled his colleagues in Dearborn: "for information all available dies for taunus now received from russian zone. these will be in repaired condition by end of july. truck dies with exception of hood grill running board and tank also received about 80% forwarded to various shops. repair to be finished by end of year."

43. Report on Ford plant status: John Portas, "Ford Works, Köln," 31 December 1946. PRO FO1039/808.

44. "during Lord Beaverbrook's . . . Factory in Cologne.": Sir Patrick Hennessy to Sir Cecil Weir, 17 December 1946. PRO FO1039/808.

45. "There is so much . . . and far between.": Sir Cecil M. Weir to Sir Patrick Hennessy, 21 December 1946. PRO FO1039/808.

46. "As regards the . . . a general talk.": W. L. Tregoning to Sir Patrick Hennessy, 10 January 1947. PRO FO1039/808.

47. "by two or even . . . Board Chairman.": Henry II Ford and Graeme Howard, *Report on European Trip*, 5 April 1948, p. 2.

48. "I turned it down . . . Cooper and Lonsdale." and "but I never packed up my kit,": Ivan Hirst, interviews with the author, 7 October 1997 and 10 February 1998.

49. "I was attracted to . . . the Surviving Two.": Hickerson, pp. 132–133.

50. "I advocated the . . . the American taxpayer.": David Burgess-Wise, *A Continent United — The Ford of Europe Story*, p. 48. Provided by David Lewis.

51. "Lincolnesque in . . . have found.": Nevins and Hill, p. 394.

52. "imposed a stranglehold on the place," and "was a warning . . . so to speak.": Ivan Hirst, interview with the author, 7 October 1997.

53. Movements of Wilhelm Vorwig: Etzold, Rother, and Erdmann, 1945–1968, pp. 27, 43.

54. "I never saw . . . when he first came.": Railton, p. 79.

55. Eduard Winter's assistance to Nordhoff: Winter did not go unrewarded for his services to Heinz Nordhoff in a time of considerable need. He was later given the Volkswagen distributorship for Berlin.

56. Nordhoff introduced to Hirst at Wolfsburg: Nordhoff came to the Hirst flat for a get-acquainted drink. There Marjorie Hirst's positive impression of the candidate was enhanced by a handsome tie he was wearing. "She played a part in choosing Nordhoff," Ivan Hirst said later (Ivan Hirst, interview with the author, 10 February 1998).

57. "This CCG Board . . . as soon as possible.": Col. C. R. Radclyffe to Heinrich Nordhoff, 7 November 1947. PRO FO1046/194. This letter and its terms are of particular interest because Heinz Nordhoff often bragged that he worked without a contract under the British at the VW works. The letter may not have been a contract in the German sense, lacking a specific term of employment and expiration, but from the British side it provided a clear definition of Nordhoff's responsibilities.

58. Meeting with Dr. Münch: F. T. Neal and Ivan Hirst, letter of 26 November 1947. PRO FO1046/194.

59. "when I assumed . . . an ugly duckling.": Gordon Wilkins, "Birthday Beetle," *Autocar*, London, 23 October 1985.

60. "This car had . . . a pedigreed dog.": Railton, p. 117.

61. "As a standard . . . and financial leaders." and "a fine asset . . . financially honest.": Henry Ford II and Graeme Howard, "Report on European Trip," 5 April 1948, pp. ix, 11–12. Henry Ford II held a less positive opinion of Dollfuss.

62. "Ironically when the . . . and went home.": Burgess-Wise, *Continent United*, ch. 1, p. 61. Hanns-Peter Rosellen says that the first inkling that Erhard Vitger, the Danish head of Ford Cologne, had of the impending trip was a news item in the German press on 2 February. In fact the itinerary for the trip did not firm up until 18 February, and left surprisingly little time for the visit to Cologne — only twenty-four hours, which were further curtailed by the need to drive instead of fly from Amsterdam.

63. "Well, it's a . . . No.": Rosellen, pp. 33–34. Rosellen says that Ford was accompanied by Ernest Breech, but in fact Breech was not along on this trip. It is the author's assumption that Graeme Howard was the third occupant.

64. "I was agreeably . . . rooms on wheels . . .": Burgess-Wise, *Continent United*, ch. 1, p. 66.

65. "Radclyffe felt that . . . for the factory.": Ivan Hirst, interview with the author, 7 October 1997.

66. "I hear unofficially . . . facilitate material supplies.": "Volkswagen Production — Suggested Acquisition by the Ford Company," W. L. Tregoning to Sir Eric Coates, 15 April 1948. PRO FO1046/193.

67. "No official proposal . . . on the American side.": "Volkswagen Factory," W. L. Tregoning to Denis W. G. L. Haviland, 30 April 1948. PRO FO1046/193.

68. "to study and recommend . . . in winning the peace.": Ford and Howard, "European Trip," pp. 16–17.

69. "the very epitome of luxury,": Railton, p. 109.

70. "Well, perhaps . . . American manufacturer.": Charles M. Barnard, "He Built the Boom in Beetles," *Small World*, Introductory Issue, p. 8.

71. "The acquisition of . . . Sir Stanford Cooper.": Ford and Howard, "European Trip," pp. 15–16.

72. "If you think it . . . leave that to you.": G. K. Howard to Heinrich Nordhoff, 7 June 1948, quoting Nordhoff's letter to him, p. 2.

73. "Howard discussed the . . . strongly to the idea.": Tolliday, p. 305.

74. "should have . . . entirely eliminated." and "Probably from a . . . a remote distance." and "Whether such a proposed . . . Ford Motor Company.": G. K. Howard to Heinrich Nordhoff, 7 June 1948, p. 2. Provided by David Lewis.

75. "General Clay, . . . European Recovery Program.": Ford and Howard, "European Trip," p. iv.

76. "it is a good vehicle . . . very paying business indeed.": J. Cahan to Sir Eric Coates, 21 April 1948, p. 1. PRO FO1046/193.

77. "Cahan had a word . . . the reform of the currency.": R. H. Parker to Leonard Tregoning, 29 April 1948, PRO FO1046/193.

78. "told him that . . . Ford in Washington.": R. H. Parker, Minutes of 12 May 1948. PRO FO1046/193.

79. "I cannot help thinking . . . presently Occupying Powers." and "His conduct seems . . . motoring industry.": R. H. Parker to G. P. Hampshire, 12 May 1948, p. 2. PRO FO1046/193.

80. "I would also like . . . itinerary will permit.": G. K. Howard to Heinrich Nordhoff, 26 July 1948. Provided by David Lewis. The record gives no indication that any of the senior principals on the Ford side — Ford, Breech, Howard, and Cooper — ever visited the VW works during these discussions, an omission that in retrospect seems surprising in view of the size of the commitment that it could have represented.

81. "The currency reform . . . choice at the time.": Railton, p. 111.

82. "for some twenty years . . . regard to the idea.": G. K. Howard to Heinrich Nordhoff, 7 June 1948, pp. 2–3. Provided by David Lewis.

83. "It was all but . . . any tangible result.": "SUBJECT: COLOGNE," E. R. Breech to Henry Ford

II, 24 October 1948, pp. 1–2. Provided by David Lewis. The Messrs. Bogdan and McKee referred to were members of the Ford International staff. By now the reader familiar with the Volkswagen literature will be wondering if this was the meeting where one of the Ford participants said, "I do not think that what we are being offered is worth a damn" or, in another version, "I don't think that what we are offered here is worth one red cent." Attributed by one source to a 1966 magazine article, the widely quoted and repeated comment was supposedly made to Henry Ford II about Volkswagen by Ernest Breech at a meeting in a German hotel room.

The reader will be aware by now that Ford and Breech never traveled to Germany together during this period. Breech flatly denied to his biographer that he made such a statement. One can picture the senior Ford lawyer, Bill Gossett, making a remark along these lines in this meeting as a negotiating ploy, a remark perhaps misunderstood or exaggerated by one of the non-native-English-speaking participants. Suffice it to say that the author was unable to find any foundation for this quotation.

84. Ford concern over closeness of Russian zone: Ivan Hirst, interview with the author, 9 October 1997.

85. "I think that they . . . opportunity missed by Ford.": Sir Terence Beckett, interview with the author, 20 October 1997.

86. Most-produced auto: VW's record-breaking production total was 15,007,034 Type 1 Volkswagens. Thus challenged, Ford revisited its own figures and announced that it had made 16.5 million Model Ts. No matter. On 15 May 1981 VW's factory in Puebla, Mexico produced the 20-millionth Beetle. When the VW's 50th anniversary was celebrated in 1988 the total produced was nudging 20.5 million.

87. "reminding [Ford] . . . automotive experience'.": Nelson, p. 95.

88. "Sir Henry Ford" and "written essays and books against the Jews.": Smelser, p. 294.

CHAPTER 9

1. "Even the most fervent . . . the world, would ensure?": A. C. Armstrong, "Reconstruction Plan . . . ," *The Motor*, 26 February 1941, pp. 76–78.

2. Warning by Lord Keynes: Barnett, p. 42.

3. The government was obliged . . . removed the dye).": Brendon, p. 250.

4. "there will be a . . . scale than elsewhere.": "Report of the Working Party on the German Motor Vehicle Industry," Economic and Industrial Planning Staff, 9 January 1945, p. 4. PRO FO1005/960.

5. "The motor car industry . . . to the home market.": Adeney, p. 192.

6. "Only two, cosmetics . . . their own home markets.": Barnett, pp. 30–31.

7. "We must provide . . . types and makes.": "Automobile Exports and Sir Stafford Cripps," *The Motor*, 28 November 1945.

8. "He was an individualist . . . people or organisations.": Bryant, p. 114, quoting D. N. Pritt, *The Autobiography*.

9. "No, no!" and "Tripe!": Wood, *Wheels of Misfortune*, p. 98.

10. "string of platitudes . . . Government control.": "Reality versus An ideology," *The Motor*, 21 November 1945, p. 301.

11. Export of British cars: One obstacle to the wider acceptance of the British auto abroad had been the U.K.'s annual car taxation system, which was based on a nominal horsepower rating developed by the Royal Automobile Club that took into account the engine's bore but not its stroke. This resulted in generations of engines with small bores and long strokes that were not unsuited to motoring in Britain, where speeds were low and shifting gears was unpopular, but lacking the high-speed durability demanded in export markets. Under the RAC rule the VW, built to meet the newer motoring exigencies with its cylinder bore (75 mm) larger than the piston's stroke (64 mm), would have been rated at a costly fourteen taxable horsepower.

After the war the motoring clubs and car companies ganged up on the new Labour government to lobby for a change in the system. They were helped, said Miles Thomas, by the fact that Chancellor of the Exchequer Hugh Dalton "had a good appreciation of mechanics." Thomas's Nuffield Organisation built wood models that helped Dalton appreciate the impact the RAC tax had on engine design. Succumbing, the chancellor agreed first to a tax on engine size and, in 1948, to a flat rate of annual tax. An important barrier to the possible acceptance of the Beetle in Britain had been lifted.

12. "certain appropriate . . . eventual acquisition.": " 'Auto-Austerity' in Parliament," *The Motor,* 28 November 1945, p. 322.

13. "In the case of . . . of the Motor Industry.": Lt. Col. H. Blake, for chairman, BIOS Group V, "Reparation Scheme," 21 November 1945. PRO SUPP14/397. Here was a specific early example of erroneous information being given to the British government as a result of the conclusion by some of the first survey parties that the sub-story was meant to be part of the plant's working area. The plant's area was in fact about half the 3.5 million square feet cited.

14. "bringing to the notice . . . claim for such plant.": A.S/S.S.11, "Reparations Claims from Germany," 24 November 1945. PRO SUPP14/397.

15. "with reservation . . . bid for the whole.": G. S. Knight, memo of 6 April 1946 and hand-written notes, PRO SUPP14/397.

16. "it is of course . . . available for running it." and ". . . if, as I suppose, . . . re-erecting it elsewhere." and "It is possible . . . able to do it.": G. S Knight to Metz, 24 April 1946, PRO AVIA49/116. The expression "too big a mouthful for our industry" has been represented elsewhere as a statement made by the SMMT on behalf of the British motor industry. There is every reason to believe that the author of this memo had been in contact with the SMMT about the VW factory issue; the memo may even make a contribution to an effort by the SMMT to achieve a breakup of the VW works. But the language in it is that of Mr. Knight of the U.K. Ministry of Supply.

17. "a meeting held . . . Vehicle Manufacturers.": W. Beard, "Motor Vehicle Plants from Germany," hand-written notes of 21 June 1946. PRO AVIA49/116

18. "The industry, which . . . for complete plants.": Beard, "Motor Vehicle Plants."

19. "It was recommended . . . up in this country.": C. P. Boas to A. M. Skeffington, 22 August 1946. PRO FO943/215.

20. "As soon as . . . tremendous obligations.": Thomas, p. 232.

21. "shadowing because . . . of the original.": Wood, *Wheels of Misfortune,* p. 73. The shadow scheme was the result of Lord Weir's guidance of the Air Ministry in his role as advisor to the Secretary for Air. Weir had much the same role in the First World War that Stafford Cripps did in the Second and was thus aware of the need to make adequate production preparations well before they would actually be required.

Requiring considerable diplomacy in its execution, the scheme required the aircraft engine makers to agree to license the production of their machines to the shadow factories, which would be built by the government and managed by the motor companies. The aim was to increase Britain's airplane engine capacity, but on a basis that would not leave the engine makers themselves with an excess capacity problem, either in the 1930s, if a war did not come, or after a possible war.

The scheme was launched with a meeting in April 1936 between the Air Ministry and representatives of Austin, Daimler, Rootes, Rover, Singer, Standard, and Wolseley. Wolseley dropped out after acrimonious and public disagreements between its chief, Lord Nuffield, and the government over engine purchasing policy; Singer wasn't up to the job. William Rootes eventually took a lead and rallied his fellow carmakers to the task. Each shadow plant operator was paid fifty thousand pounds a year as a management fee and seventy-five pounds for each engine produced.

22. Auto company shadow factories: Wood, *Wheels of Misfortune,* p. 74.

23. "very heavy demand . . . approved rental basis." and "If the German . . . the British jeep. ": G. W. Turner, attachment to memo of 12 July 1946. PRO AVIA49/116.

24. "was especially active . . . break up VW.": Tolliday, p. 293.

25. "Ferguson promised Cripps . . . himself at once." and "I need steel . . . on the production." and

"any public statement . . . reference to us.": Fraser, pp. 167–169.

26. Status of the Volkspflug: The Ford technical team that visited Wolfsburg in the early spring of 1946 quizzed Porsche engineer Josef Kales (whom they named as "Karlos" after the German pronunciation of his name) about the Volkspflug. They inspected a non-pristine example at the VW works. Among their comments was the following:

"The tractor is as light as possible, compatible with strength so that no excess weight be transported when it is not needed for adhesion purposes. When full draw bar pull is required of the vehicle the bonnet box structure is meant to be filled with stone to give the required weight.

"When asked for the reason for the light construction and the provision of space for the loading of rocks, Mr. Karlos replied that the lighter the vehicle, the less it cost and that while cast iron was expensive stone was extremely cheap. "

Not many BIOS reports brought the author as much of a smile as this on page 73 of BIOS Final Report No. 768.

27. "within a very . . . Leyland in 1960/61.": Robson, *Triumph*, p. 66.

28. "may well write . . . immortal 'Model T'.": *The Story of the Vanguard*, The Standard Motor Company Limited, Coventry, 1949, p. 3.

29. "accommodates four . . . reasonable comfort.": "Road Test, The Standard Vanguard," *The Motor*, 21 July 1948.

30. "the one-model policy . . . benefits of rationalization.": John Dugdale, "Launching of the Vanguard," *The Autocar*, 27 August 1948.

31. "Rootes came . . . the chassis.": Peter Ware, interview with the author, 1 November 1997.

32. "It's actually got . . . Never sell.": Gunston, p. 133.

33. "The 1930s were . . . to see all day'.": Wood, *Wheels of Misfortune*, p. 73.

34. "We had no love . . . each other.": Ivan Hirst, interview with the author, 9 October 1997.

35. "Mills had a vague . . . fool, young man.": Ivan Hirst, interview with the author, 9 October 1997.

36. "For a whole . . . the attractive skin.": Robson, *Rootes*, p. 26.

37. "We took a good . . . do it ourselves.": John Dugdale, interview with the author, 25 October 1996.

38. "Billy and the Rootes . . . similar British models.": Bullock, p. 78.

39. "I went over to . . . brought with me.": Berryman, "The Berryman Story," pp. 404–405.

40. "sufficient examples . . . British industry.": Turner, "British Occupation Policy."

41. VW suspension on Sunbeam-Talbot and "I tried to drive . . . do its job properly.": Garnier and Healey, p. 79. Donald Healey told his biographer that the suspension was "cannibalised . . . from a Volkswagen;" he does not identify the source. It is the author's conclusion that during the war, when Healey was making his front-suspension conversion, the logical source of the VW parts would have been the Type 82 that had been examined by Humber. He would have had to alter the stub axle carrier, which was the high-ground-clearance version to suit the Type 82.

42. "While Ben was busy . . . would be the best:": Browning and Needham, p. 6.

43. "for your information . . . relevant Trade Association.": Lt. Col. R. H. Bright to Derek Wood, 10 September 1946. PRO FO943/215.

44. "He had an unhappy . . . his painstaking care.": Gunston, p. 115.

45. Fedden's departure from Bristol: Among the points of friction with the Bristol board was Fedden's salary, which was said to make him Britain's highest-paid engineer. But he delivered value. Business historian Robert Schlaifer viewed Roy Fedden thusly: "There can be no question . . . that the one most important factor in Bristol's success was the immense personal drive of its Chief Engineer, Fedden, which stimulated the engineers of the company to give their best efforts, persuaded the management of the company to approve courses of action he believed technically advisable, and obtained from the government the funds needed to support the work."

In addition to his salary Fedden had another source of income that was one more burr under

Bristol's saddle. All the engine drawings were designated F-B for Fedden and his design draughtsman, "Bunny" Butler, whose diminutive size bore no relation to his talents, which Bristol colleague Alex Moulton considered "marvellous." Fedden had contrived to retain rights to his designs and was paid royalties on their use by Bristol as long as they made his engines — and they made a lot of them. "He must have had a tremendous royalty income," reflected aide Peter Ware in an interview with the author.

46. "His dream was . . . design and development." and "Fedden was anxious . . . of radical innovation.": Gunston, pp. 127, 134.

47. "American manufacturers . . . existing cars obsolete." and "much is to be . . . extreme road conditions." and "axes of link pivots . . . toe-in effect." and "A number of rear-engined . . . behind the rear axle.": Fedden car brochure, 1943, Alex Moulton Collection.

48. "We followed the . . . bewitched by it.": Alex Moulton, interview with the author, 17 September 1997. After making this comment Dr. Moulton laughed and said, "Perhaps in error!" In light of the fate of the Fedden project, a closer paralleling of at least the more practical aspects of the VW concept might have been prudent.

49. "The VW certainly did inspire Fedden.": Gordon Wilkins, interview with the author, 3 January 1997.

50. "The FEDDEN car . . . thoroughly competitive price.": Fedden car brochure, 1943, Alex Moulton Collection.

51. Characteristics of 1943 Fedden concept: The car's engine would have had three cylinders (80 x 100 mm adding up to 1,495 cc). If a triple was not optimally smooth in its power pulses, this was reason enough for including a hydraulic coupling in the drive line. A net power output of 62 horsepower at 5,000 rpm was forecast by Alex Moulton. With an estimated drag coefficient at a creditably low 0.375, the original Fedden concept would have been geared to reach a maximum speed of 95 mph.

52. "was quite a tower block,": Peter Ware, interview with author, 1 November 1997.

53. "the power plant . . . mass of machinery.": Peter Ware, "Resume of 1 EX Development and Road Test," Roy Fedden Ltd., 25 April 1947, p. 3.

54. "We had the . . . I had in mind.": Gordon Wilkins, interview with the author, 8 January 1998.

55. Cripps commissioning Fedden: Adeney, pp. 192–193.

56. "a serious attempt . . . modern American car.": Edward Eves, "Cars That Might Have Been — Fedden," Autocar, 27 March 1964, pp. 574–577.

57. "We must get this . . . catch me a crack.": Peter Ware, interview with the author, 1 November 1997.

58. "[Bevin] wants to do . . . would denounce them.": Plowden, p. 306, quoting from Hugh Dalton's diary.

59. Fedden car crash during handling test: Peter Ware commented to the author that the tests they were undertaking that led to this crash were early precursors of the Swedish "moose" or "elk" test that caused Mercedes-Benz so much grief with its A-Class and Smart cars in 1997. Unlike the latter, however, the Fedden crash injured one of the company's engineers.

60. "The main party . . . the whole thing.": Peter Ware, interview with the author, 1 November 1997.

61. "One of the knowledgeable . . . I wasn't sure!": Ivan Hirst, interview with the author, 9 October 1997. That the VW was not in fact of integral construction was a gift to many dune-buggy builders in years to come. To be sure, the attachment of the body to its platform frame added to the VW's overall stiffness. In 1941 the Porsche office first explored the development of a full integral body-frame VW in its project 160.

62. "Why waste time . . . won the war?": Gunston, p. 132.

63. Handsome four-door body: Frostick, p. 82.

64. "of an unconventional . . . on its merits.": "The Kendall 565 cc £100 Car," The Motor, 22 November 1944, p. 284.

65. "the suspension of the law of gravitation.": Young, pp. 20–21.

66. "There is just one . . . business in the past.": Jonathan Edwards, "Original lame duck?," *The Motor*, 27 December 1975, p. 47.

67. "Naturally the car . . . turning out cars.": Dudley Noble, "The £100 Car," *Picture Post*, 27 October 1945. This was kindly provided by John Reynolds, to whom I am indebted for other background facts and references about Denis Kendall and his project.

68. "to ask questions . . . producing the car.": "The Kendall '£100' Car," *The Motor*, 22 August 1945, p. 63.

69. "Poniatowski frowned . . . develop his vehicle." and "At the end of . . . his production tools." and "Grantham Productions . . . too much interest.": Grégoire, 50 ans, pp. 448–449.

70. "fell in love with it immediately.": Hartnett, p. 205.

71. 1945 election campaign in Grantham: Young, p. 21.

72. "I shall distribute . . . were suddenly withdrawn.": John Reynolds, unpublished manuscript, 28 August 1997.

73. "unlikely that special . . . least two years.": George Gibson to Hugh Dalton, 30 July 1946 and attachment. PRO FO943/215.

74. "Everyone seems interested . . . Industry ought to be.": Richard H. Parker to William Ritchie, 2 August 1946. PRO FO943/215.

75. "Porsche himself was given . . . qualifies for arrest." and "action . . . activities merit this." and "We are informed . . . the Porsche patents.": Control Office for Germany and Austria, "Volkswagenwerk GmbH and Porsche A.G.," 15 August 1946, PRO FO943/215.

76. "Frankly, this report . . . one to Supply.": D. A. Johnston to Derek Wood, 28 August 1946. PRO BT211/92.

77. "The Chancellor is . . . the Volkswagen factory.": Val Duncan to Derek Wood, 31 August 1946. PRO BT211/92.

78. "Among the surplus . . . tendered to H.M.G.": C. P. Boas to A. M. Skeffington, 22 August 1946.

79. "subtle and objectionable . . . against foreign competition.": Derek Wood to J. N. V. Duncan, 10 September 1946. PRO FO943/215.

80. "I've talked to Binny . . . more home model!": John Selwyn, note of 9 September 1946. PRO BT211/92. The author apologizes for not having tracked down the identity of "Binny."

81. "It is presumed . . . not at present know.": Lt. Col. R. H. Bright to Derek Wood, 3 September 1946. PRO BT211/92.

82. "It is suggested that . . . car in this country.": Maj. Gen. C. A. L. Dunphie, "Volkswagen GmbH," 5 September 1946. PRO AVIA49/116. He was later Sir Charles Dunphie, chairman of Vickers.

83. "one man who . . . from the chaff.": Thomas, pp. 231–232.

84. "is being retained . . . be allocated to us.": P. B. Hunt, Minutes, Board of Trade meeting, 4 December 1946, PRO BT211/92.

85. "We British at . . . and servicing organisations.": Ivan Hirst, "Divided Loyalties!" *Safer Motoring*, 1965–66, p. 524.

86. "very quickly realised . . . And that was that.": Alasdair McInnes, "VW a Threat to Britain — but My Protest Failed," *Safer Motoring*, 1965–66, pp. 30–31.

87. "It seems to me . . . America is waiting.": Lord Brabazon of Tara to the *Times*, 2 July 1947.

88. "The manufacturing costs . . . dismantled and lost.": Col. C. R. Radclyffe to Lord Brabazon of Tara, 15 July 1947. PRO SUPP14/397.

89. "came to me . . . motorcars in your ministry": Lord Brabazon of Tara to Sir Archibald Rowlands, 16 July 1947. PRO SUPP14/397.

90. "That, however, . . . of Germany to-day . . .": Sir Archibald Rowlands to Lord Brabazon of Tara, 28 July 1947. PRO SUPP14/397.

91. "to provide a means of regular . . . the latest German models.": "Report on Proceedings of the National Advisory Council of the United Kingdom Motor Manufacturing Industry" (summary prepared by the Economic Research Advice Section of the Division of Industrial Develop-

ment), n.d., p. 4, Australian Archives, Melbourne.

92. "the town of Wolfsburg . . . waste the accommodation.": M. A. Robb, letter and attachment "Volkswagen" of 13 June 1947. PRO SUPP14/397.

93. "I understand this is . . . in the United Kingdom.": E. J. J. Bailiss to Mr. Norman, 11 June 1947. PRO SUPP14/397.

94. "as an avowed nationaliser . . . pressing the idea forward.": Thomas, pp. 268–269.

CHAPTER 10

1. "Some people wanted . . . or a six-by-six.": Ivan Hirst, interview with the author, 9 October 1997.

2. "supreme authority . . . local government authority.": Turner, p. 20.

3. "to maintain the . . . to conceal ownership.": Turner, p. 636.

4. "The utilisation of . . . and housing estates.": Director, Property Control Branch, "The Volkswagen Complex in Control under Law 52," 17 July 1947. PRO FO1046/193.

5. "The CCG's Senior . . . peace-time economy.": Turner, p. 154.

6. "The continued utilisation . . . provide alternative accommodation." and "As the property is . . . the productive machinery.": Director, Property Control, "Volkswagen Complex under Law 52," p. 8.

7. "The three most obvious . . . machine tool resources.": D. Bailey, et al., *The German Automobile Industry, BIOS Final Report No. 768*, H. M. Stationery Office, London, 1947, p. 37.

8. "All machine tools . . . from dispersal sites.": Ivan Hirst, Attachment to Minutes, 6th Board of Control meeting, 15 July 1946. PRO FO1039/797.

9. Ten percent of Germany's machine park dismantled: Etzold, Rother, and Erdmann, vol. 2, p. 22.

10. "The organization of . . . personnel told me.": Etzold, Rother, and Erdmann, vol. 1, pp. 408–409.

11. "went on to become . . . Beetle in motorcycles.)": Tolliday, p. 294.

12. "Indeed for many . . . copied the changes.": Wilson, p. 14.

13. Value of machines and equipment obtained from Germany: Turner, pp. 738–739.

14. "In general where . . . as trade unions.": Minutes, 11th Board of Control meeting, 6 December 1946, p. 2. PRO FO1039/797.

15. "The policy of the . . . disposition is decided.": Attachment, Minutes, 6th Board of Control meeting, 15 July 1946. PRO FO1039/797.

16. "The problem at the . . . theft and damage.": Minutes, 11th Board of Control meeting, 6 December 1946, p. 2. PRO FO1039/797.

17. "article ii . . . of Nazi persecutions." and "to conserve all . . . of the NSDAP.": Property Control Branch, "The Volkswagenwerk Complex — Statement to the Board of Control," August 1947, p. 2. PRO FO944/196. The interpolated phrase is suggested by Ian Turner to fill an obvious gap in the text of the original document.

18. "specifically excluded from . . . land in the town." and "Where is that . . . Nazi mismanagement." and "There had always . . . claim to the works.": Turner, pp. 658–659.

19. "It seems quite . . . property is disposed of.": R. H. Parker to H. A. Goff, 7 May 1948. PRO FO1046/193.

20. "it can quite reasonably . . . claim to the Company.": H. A. Goff to R. H. Parker, 14 May 1948. PRO FO1046/193.

21. "In view of the . . . problem at any time.": Hermann Beermann to Property Control, 12 July 1948. PRO FO1046/193. The reference to the Reichswerke AG is understood to mean the former Hermann Goering steelworks in nearby Braunschweig.

22. "On the face . . . at least debateable": Industrial Relations Branch to Property Control, 25 August 1948. PRO FO1046/193.

23. "Natural psychological tendency . . . delivery of materials." and "a German employee . . . spare parts supplied.": Director, Property Control Branch, "The Volkswagenwerk Complex under Law 52," 17 July 1947, pp. 7–8.

24. "to thank Professor Porsche . . . of the Volkswagen factory.": Mommsen and Grieger, pp. 935, 937.

25. "showed that the . . . most complex one.": Minutes, 18th Board of Control meeting, 7 November 1947, p. 2. PRO FO944/196.

26. "felt it a duty . . . most desirable expedient.": Porsche and Bentley, p. 215.

27. "Information regarding . . . Porsche Junior,": Minutes, 19th Board of Control meeting, 16 December 1947, p. 4. PRO FO944/196.

28. "negotiations had taken . . . October [sic] 1943.": Minutes, 28th Board of Control meeting, 26 October 1948, PRO FO1046/194.

29. "everything went off all right.": Porsche and Bentley, p. 215.

30. "liberation of the works . . . works could easily bear.": Mommsen and Grieger, p. 939.

31. "There was no legal . . . right thing to do.": Railton, p. 122.

32. "The matter was taken up . . . end of the enterprise.": Porsche and Bentley, p. 207. Reference to Porsche contract of 20 February 1947: Mommsen and Grieger, p. 938.

33. "Property Control Branch . . . approval before signature.": Minutes, 36th Board of Control meeting, 24 June 1949. PRO FO1046/194.

34. British authorities not partners to the Reichenhall contract: Mommsen and Grieger, pp. 938–939.

35. "Why not make . . . a tubular frame.": Ivan Hirst, interview with the author, 7 October 1997.

36. Hebmüller and Karmann cabriolets: Wood, Beetle, pp. 99–111.

37. Ben Pon design sketch: An idea that made history, Volkswagen Public Relations, Wolfsburg, 1991, p. 20.

38. "I'm a Mercedes man . . . will come back.": Ivan Hirst, interviews with the author, 7 October and 22 November 1997. In Hirst's office Uhlenhaut met, personally for the first time, Dr. Feuereissen, then the VW commercial director but before the war the team manager of Auto-Union, fierce racing rivals of Mercedes-Benz. "They fell into each other's arms," Hirst recalled. Uhlenhaut went on to enjoy a distinguished career at Daimler-Benz, but suffered the disappointment of being denied a seat on the company's management board. We can safely surmise that his chances of a board-level appointment would have been much better at Volkswagen.

39. "They took it out . . . the platform frame.": Ivan Hirst, interview with the author, 22 November 1997.

40. "Part of the shop . . . monthly capacity 450.": Director, Property Control Branch, "The Volkswagenwerk Complex under Law 52," 17 July 1947, p. 3.

41. "The department overhauling . . . as 'CCG-Wagen'.": Parkinson, p. 121.

42. Revised 1948 list of companies scheduled for dismantlement as war reparations: Ivan Hirst to the author, 9 October 1997.

43. "It is submitted that . . . NSDAP discriminatory politics.": R. H. Parker, "Finance Division and Industry Division interests in DAF Property at Wolfsburg comprising VW Group of Companies and Associated Properties," 27 October 1947. PRO FO1046/193.

44. "The Works in full . . . of the German people.": Director, Property Control Branch, "The Volkswagenwerk Complex under Law 52," 17 July 1947, pp. 10–11.

45. "We were 'trustees', . . . bulwark against Communism.": Ivan Hirst, interview with the author, 7 October 1997.

46. "Nordhoff said that . . . I wasn't interested.": Max Hoffman, interview with the author. Railton has called this "obviously not true since Nordhoff did not own the company and could not sell it" (Railton, p. 124). However over an extensive series of interviews in both Germany and New York I found Hoffman to be a reliable witness of the events of his life in the motor industry. I have high confidence in the veracity of this recollection.

47. "The Volkswagen factory, . . . by American interests.": K. B. Hopfinger, "German Car Production — What Are They Doing?" The Autocar, 21 January 1949, p. 61.

48. "In January, 1948, . . . and American approval.": R. Gresham Cooke, "German Car Exports,"

Times, 10 January 1948, p. 5. Not one to miss an opportunity, the Swiss importer drove his cars to AMAG, then removed their tires and sold them back into Germany at the high prices they commanded on the black market. He then refitted his cars with new tires imported from Continental. "He made a bundle on that," Ivan Hirst recalled.

49. Road test comments of Automobil Revue: "Volkswagen Typ 11," *Automobil Revue*, no. 28, 22 June 1949.

50. Smell of oil from the engine compartment: This was the result of the still unsatisfactory supply situation, recorded Griffith Borgeson, who learned that the soft solder used initially to make the oil filters was not up to specification: "The soldered joints would crack in service so that the heater, which delivered warm air from the engine's air-cooling system, also delivered strong oil fumes to the car's interior" ("The Beetle's Debt to the Brits," *Automobile Quarterly*, vol. 28, no. 2, 1990, p. 184). This was later rectified easily enough.

51. "one of Europe's most . . . would be desirable.": Joachim Fischer, "Test: Volkswagen Type 11," *Motor Rundschau*, 10 August 1949, pp. 357–358.

52. Keeping to pre-currency-reform wholesale prices: Cooke, "German Car Exports."

53. "was a going concern . . . .money in the bank.": Ivan Hirst, "It's the Story of a Team," *Safer Motoring*, 1965–66, p. 525.

54. "Had this handful . . . Fortunately they did not.": Nelson, p. 104.

55. Disproportionate inheritance of assets and liabilities: Turner, p. 61.

56. "What we should . . . back to the Germans.": Alasdair McInnes, "VW a Threat to Britain," p. 31.

57. News carried by *The Motor*: "Volkswagen Trusteeship," The Motor, 19 October 1949, p. 398. Not long after the signing Radclyffe left Germany and returned to Britain. Within weeks thereafter, Ivan Hirst recalled, he died suddenly.

58. "The ordinance was . . . referred to in the text.": Turner, p. 663.

59. "In part deliberately, . . . negating control altogether.": Tolliday, p. 311.

CHAPTER 11

1. "The beetle is the . . . other products more.": Gabriella Stern, "VW's U.S. Comeback Rides on Restyled Beetle," *The Wall Street Journal*, 6 May 1997, quoting VW's Jens Neumann.

2. "I went out on . . . not Europe alone." and "I had the dubious . . . model and design." and "In any sound design . . . served us so well." and "Based on Professor Porsche's . . . engineer will agree.": Dr. H. Nordhoff, "The Volkswagen — its past and its future," *Society of Automotive Engineers*, New York, 13 November 1958, pp. 7–8.

3. Building the last German Beetle at Emden: Wood, Beetle, p. 97.

4. "Nordhoff replied that . . . nothing, i.e. NO JEEPS.": Steve Smith, "Volkswagen's 'Jeep' Is Alive and Well in Mexico. Literally.," *Motor Trend*, March 1973, p. 31.

5. "After a run-in period . . . the Second World War.": Mommsen and Grieger, p. 202.

6. "The [DKW] F.9 car . . . the higher priced cars.": H. B. Smith, and O. Poppe, *Investigation Concerning Research & Development for & Manufacture of D.K.W. Cars in Germany*, BIOS Final Report No. 909, H. M. Stationery Office, London, 1946, p. 2.

7. "a swindle perpetrated by . . . ever to be refunded.": Shirer, pp. 331–332.

8. "[Bodo] Lafferentz at . . . did the interest." and "Even in the late . . . interest to the savers." and "cost two thousand marks and more.": Mommsen and Grieger, pp. 198–200.

9. "Nominal owner is still . . . to nationalise them.": The Observer, London, 16 September 1956.

10. "There are constant rumors . . . contenders in this field.": A. J. Wieland to Ernest Breech, 11 April 1955. Ford Industrial Archives, Acc. AR-67-13.

11. "The figures were large . . . the panting opposition." and "a cool 148,300,000 marks . . . disposing of the works.": "Volkswagen Bares Its Finances; Cash Reserves at $34,720,000," *New York Times*, 24 December 1955.

12. "The shares were . . . lower income purchasers." and "Shareholders could not . . . or foreign takeover.": Tolliday, p. 343.

13. Payment arrangements between VW and Porsche: Mommsen and Grieger, p. 939.

14. "In October 1950 . . . locked experimental departments.": Etzold, p. 62.

15. "At the end of . . . start crying,' Ferry says.": Nelson, pp. 113–114.

16. "In November 1950 . . . his own life's work.": Porsche and Bentley, p. 230.

17. "It was a sentimental . . . given up on life.": Railton, p. 123.

18. "When he gazed at . . . celebrate his arrival.": Thiriar, p. 18.

19. "The initial meeting . . . machines and assembly lines.": Hopfinger, p. 157.

20. Securing the British spare-parts concession: Wood, Beetle, p. 128. Not without good reason, McEvoy felt himself the "forgotten man" among the Britons whose efforts at Fallersleben revived the VW works. Somehow, however, this was in keeping with his ebullient but mercurial character. McEvoy was always keen to move on to the next interesting challenge; others who stayed with the Volkswagen job emerged with greater credit.

21. "It was, perhaps, fortunate . . . other export markets.": Bullock, p. 78.

22. *The Motor* road test of the Volkswagen: "The VOLKSWAGEN de luxe Saloon," *The Motor*, 18 April 1956, Road Test no. 7/56, London. The author has made the assumption, on the grounds of both style and content, that Laurence Pomeroy, Jr. was its author.

23. "with contempt . . . like some of your cars.": Adeney, p. 209.

24. "[Öfting] was very . . . 52% of the market.": W. J. Castle, memo forwarded with letter by Roger Jackling of 20 November 1953. PRO SUPP14/397.

25. "There are two points . . . sells the Volkswagen.": Roger Jackling to _____, 20 November 1953. PRO SUPP14/397.

26. "I believe, . . . Continental road conditions.": W. J. Castle to _____, 30 November 1953. PRO SUPP14/397.

27. "I think it would . . . turned out to be.": Gordon Wilkins, interview with the author, 3 January 1997.

28. Work of Parkes and Fry on rear-engined cars at Rootes: Henshaw, pp. 5–41.

29. "Tim Fry was . . . bit of a madman." and "The Rootes family . . . year of development.": Peter Ware, interview with the author, 1 November 1997.

30. "Our first aim was . . . change was needed.": Porsche and Bentley, p. 222.

31. Porsche designs for Studebaker: The facts presented here emerged during the author's researches in the 1970s into the origins and fate of the Studebaker-Porsche project, which included an interview with Ferry Porsche.

32. "This startling little . . . 'the German Jeep'.": "Volkswagen . . . ," *Speed Age*, September 1950, p. 28. Ernie Pyle was a front-line war correspondent and Bill Mauldin a popular cartoonist of life in the trenches.

33. "He took me for . . . order that afternoon." and "It had to be . . . not a passenger's car.": Railton, pp. 126–127.

34. "The body . . . the airplane.": William B. Stout, "That Automobile of the Future," *New York Times Magazine*, 24 October 1943, p. 16.

35. "a much sounder . . . government budgets.": Tolliday, p. 332.

36. "There were rumors . . . buying out Volkswagen.": Wieland to Breech.

37. Chevy-VW nickname of Chevrolet Corvair: Karl Ludvigsen, "Remember the Corvair? Here's a Look at What We Lost," *Automobile Quarterly*, Summer 1970, p. 386.

38. "I keep thinking . . . doesn't seem to happen.": Railton, p. 118.

39. "I remember you, . . . last time we met.": Berryman, "The Berryman Story," p. 405.

Bibliography

The following published books were consulted while conducting the research for *Battle for the Beetle*. Not included here are the various intelligence reports referred to; these are described in the relevant notes and were, for the most part, published by H. M. Stationery Office. Similarly, magazine and newspaper articles referenced are described in the notes.

Documents, correspondence, and reports researched at the U.K. Public Record Office are appended with their file number as 'PRO.' Credit is also given in the notes where appropriate to other sources of documents. Interviews conducted by the author are so referenced.

Adeney, Martin. *The Motor Makers*. London: Collins, 1988.

Bailey, D. et al. *The German Automobile Industry. BIOS Final Report no. 768*. London: H. M. Stationers Office, n.d.

Barclay, Hartley. *Ford Production Methods*. New York: Harper & Brothers, 1936.

Barnett, Correlli. *The Lost Victory — British Dreams, British Realities, 1945–1950*. London: Pan, 1996.

Beasley, Norman. *Knudsen*. New York: Whittlesey House, 1947.

Bird, Anthony. *The Trojan Utility Car*. Leatherhead: Profile Publications, 1967.

Bittorf, Wilhelm. *Die Geschichte eines Autos*. Special ed. Limbach: Der Spiegel, 1954.

Brendon, Piers. *The Motoring Century — The Story of the Royal Automobile Club*. London: Bloomsbury, 1997.

British Intelligence Objectives Sub-Committee. *Investigation into the Design and Performance of the Volkswagen or German People's Car*. London: H. M. Stationery Office, 1947. Reissued in 1996 by the Stationery Office, Norwich, with an eleven-page introduction by Karl Ludvigsen.

Browning, Peter and Needham, Les. *Healeys and Austin-Healeys*. Henley-on-Thames: G T Foulis, 1970.

Bryant, Chris. *Stafford Cripps — The First Modern Chancellor*. London: Hodder & Stoughton, 1997.

Bullock, John. *The Rootes Brothers — Story of a Motoring Empire*. Sparkford: Patrick Stephens, 1993.

Cancellieri, Gianni and De Agostini, Cesare. *Le leggendarie Auto Union*. Bologna: Editrice Grafiche Zanini, 1979.

Dabrowski, Hans-Peter. *Flying Wings of the Horten Brothers*. Atglen: Schiffer, 1995.

Davis, S. C. H. "Sammy". *Memories of Men & Motor Cars*. 208. London: Seeley Service, 1965.

Dyckhoff, Otto. "Grundlagen für eine Grossproduktion und deren maschinelle Ausrüstung im Kraftzeugbau." *ATZ*, 10 June 1942.

Dymock, Eric. *Saab — Half a Century of Achievement*. Sutton Veny: Dove, 1997.

Engelmann, Joachim. *V1 — The Flying Bomb*. Atglen: Schiffer, 1992.

Etzold, Hans-Rüdiger, et al. *Der Käfer — eine Dokumentation II*. Stuttgart: Motorbuch Verlag, 1992.

Etzold, Hans-Rüdiger, Rother, Ewald, and Erdmann, Thomas. *Im Zeichen der vier Ringe 1873–1945*. Band 1. Ingolstadt: Edition quattro GmbH, 1992.

Frank, Reinhard. *Cars of the Wehrmacht*. Atglen: Schiffer, 1994.

Fraser, Colin. *Harry Ferguson — Inventor and Pioneer*. London: John Murray, 1972.

Frostick, Michael, *The Cars That Got Away*. London: Cassell, 1968.

Garnier, Peter, with Healey, Brian. *Donald Healey — My World of Cars*. Wellingborough: Patrick Stephens, 1989.

Grégoire, Jean-Albert. *50 ans d'automobile*. Paris: Flammarion, 1974.

———. *Best Wheel Forward*. London: Thames and Hudson, 1954.

Gunston, Bill. *By Jupiter — The Life of Sir Roy Fedden*. London: Royal Aeronautical Society, 1978.

Hanfstaengl, Ernst. *Hitler: the Missing Years*. New York: Arcade, 1994.

Hartnett, L.J. *Big Wheels and Little Wheels*. Melbourne: Lansdowne Press, 1964.

Hellmold, Wilhelm. *Die V1 — Eine Dokumentation*. Bechtle, 1988, 1991.

Henshaw, David and Peter. *Apex: The Inside Story of the Hillman Imp*. Minster Lovell: Bookmarque, 1988.

Hickerson, J. Mel. *Ernie Breech*. New York: Meredith, 1968.

Hinsley, F. H. et al. *British Intelligence in the Second World War, Volume Three, Part II*. London: H. M. Stationery Office, 1988.

Hitler, Adolf. *Mein Kampf*. London: Pimlico, 1992.

Hopfinger, K. B. *The Volkswagen Story*. Henley-on-Thames: G. T. Foulis, 1971.

Irving, Capt. J. S. et al. *Investigation of the Developments in the German Automobile Industry During the War Period*. BIOS Final Report No. 300. London: H. M. Stationery Office, 1945.

Irving, David. *The Trail of the Fox*. London: Futura, 1978.

Kirchberg, Peter. "Typisierung in der Deutschen Kraftfahrzeugindustrie and der Generalbevollmächtige für das Kraftfahrwesen," *Jb. f. Wirtschaftsgeschichte*, 1969/II.

———. *Grand-Prix-Report AUTO UNION 1934 bis 1939*. Stuttgart: Motorbuch Verlag, 1982.

Laux, James M. *In First Gear*. Montreal: McGill-Queen's University Press, 1976.

Leslie, Stuart W. *Boss Kettering*. New York: Columbia University Press, 1983.

Lewis, David L. *The Public Image of Henry Ford*. Detroit: Wayne State University Press, 1976.

Lindh, Björn-Eric. *The First 40 Years of Saab Cars*. Stockholm: Norden, 1987.

Long, Dave and Matthews, Phil. *Knowing Australian Volkswagens*. Punchbowl and Roselands: Bookworks, 1993.

Loubet, Jean-Louis. *Citroën, Peugeot, Renault et les autres*. Paris: Le Monde-Éditions, 1995.

Ludvigsen, Karl. *Porsche: Excellence Was Expected*. Princeton: Princeton Publishing, 1977.

———. *Mercedes-Benz: Quicksilver Century*. Isleworth: Transport Bookman, 1995.

———. *Opel: Wheels to the World*. Princeton: Princeton Publishing, 1975.

Margolius, Ivan and Henry, *John G. Tatra —The Legacy of Hans Ledwinka*. Harrow: SAF, 1990.

Mayer-Stein, Hans-Georg. *Volkswagens of the Wehrmacht*. Atglen: Schiffer, 1994.

Mommsen, Hans and Grieger, Manfred. *Das Volkswagenwerk und seine Arbeiter im Dritten Reich*. Düsseldorf: ECON Verlag, 1996.

Mönnich, Horst. *The BMW Story — a Company in its Time*. London: Sidgwick & Jackson, 1991.

Müller, Josef. *Die Freuden des Konstrukteurs*. Prien am Chiemsee: Eigenverlag, 1990.

Nelson, Walter Henry. *Small Wonder*. Cambridge, MA: Robert Bentley, 1970.

Nevins, Allan and Hill, Frank Ernest. *Ford: Decline and Rebirth, 1933–1962*. New York: Scribner's, 1962, 1963.

Olley, Maurice and Earl, Cameron. *The Motor Car Industry in Germany during the period 1939–1945*. London: H. M. Stationery Office, 1949.

Parkinson, Simon. *Volkswagen Beetle — the Rise from the Ashes of War*. Dorchester: Veloce, 1996.

Pawley, Martin. *Design Heroes: Buckminster Fuller*. London: Grafton. 1992.

Picard. Fernand. *L'Épopée de Renault*. Paris: Albin Michel, 1976.

Platt, Maurice. *An Addiction to Automobiles*. London: Frederick Warne, 1980.

Plowden, William. *The Motor Car and Politics*. London: Bodley Head, 1971.

Porsche, Dr. Ing. h.c. Ferry with Bentley, John. *We at Porsche*. Garden City: Doubleday, 1976.

Post, Dan R. *Volkswagen — Nine Lives Later*. Arcadia: Horizon House, 1966.

Railton, Arthur. "The Beetle". Pfäffikon: Eurotax, 1985.

Reader, W. J. *Architect of Air Power*. London: Collins, 1968.

Rhodes, Anthony. *Louis Renault — A Biography*. New York: Harcourt, Brace & World, 1970.

Rich, Joe. *Hartnett: Portrait of a Technological Brigand*. Sydney: Turton & Armstrong, 1996.

Roberts, Stephen H., *The House That Hitler Built*. New York: Harper & Brothers, 1938.

Robson, Graham, *Cars of the Rootes Group*. Croydon: Motor Racing Publications. 1990.

———. *The Story of Triumph Sports Cars*. Croydon: Motor Racing, 1972.

Rosellen, Hanns-Peter. Ford-Schritte. Frankfurt: Zyklam-Verlag, 1987.

Schlaifer, Robert. *Development of Aircraft Engines*. Boston: Harvard University, 1950.

Schreier, Konrad F., Jr. *VW Kübelwagen Military Portfolio*. Cobham: Brooklands Books, n.d.

Segrave, Sir Henry. *The Lure of Speed*. London: Hutchinson, 1928.

Seidler, Edouard. *The Romance of Renault*. Lausanne: Edita, 1973.

———. *The Renault Challenge*. Automobile Year, 1981.

Shirer, William L. *The Rise and Fall of the Third Reich*. London: Pan, 1964.

Shuler, Terry. *Volkswagen — Then, Now and Forever*. Indianapolis: Beeman Jorgensen, 1996.

Smelser, Ronald. *Robert Ley — Hitler's Labor Front Leader*. Oxford: Berg, 1988.

Sorensen, Charles E. with Williamson, Samuel T. *My Forty Years With Ford*. New York: W W Norton, 1956.

Stout, William Bushnell. *So Away I Went!* Indianapolis and New York: Bobbs-Merrill, 1951.

Stuck, Hans. *Tagebuch eines Rennfahrers*. Munich: Moderne Verlag, 1967.

Thiriar, Dr. Michael. *Porsche Speedster*. Indianapolis: Beeman Jorgensen, 1998.

Thomas, Sir Miles, *Out on a Wing*. London: Michael Joseph, 1964.

Tolliday, Steven. "Enterprise and State in the West German Wirtschaftswunder: Volkswagen and the Automobile Industry, 1939–1962," *Business History Review* 69 (Autumn 1995).

Turner, Ian David. "British Occupation Policy and its Effects on the Town of Wolfsburg and the Volkswagenwerk, 1945–1949." Doctoral thesis, University of Manchester, 1984.

van der Vat, Dan. *The Good Nazi*. London: Weidenfeld & Nicholson, 1997.

von Frankenberg, Richard. *Porsche — the Man and His Cars*. London: G.T. Foulis & Co., 1961.

von Pidoll, Dr. Ulrich. *VW Käfer: Ein Auto Schreibt Geschichte*. Hamburg: Nikol, 1994.

von Seher-Thoss, H. C. Graf. *Die deutsche Automobilindustrie*. Stuttgart: Deutsche Verlags-Anstalt, 1974.

Werrell, Kenneth P. *The Evolution of the Cruise Missile*. Alabama: Air University Press, Maxwell Air Force Base, 1985.

Wiersch, Dr. Bernd. *VW at War, Book 2*. West Chester: Schiffer, 1992.

Wilkins, Mira and Hill, Frank Ernest. *American Business Abroad — Ford on Six Continents*. Detroit: Wayne State University, 1964.

Wilson, Steve. *BSA Motor Cycles Since 1950*. Sparkford: Patrick Stephens, 1997.

Wood, Jonathan. *The VW Beetle*. Croydon: Motor Racing, 1983–89.

———. *Wheels of Misfortune*. London: Sidgwick & Jackson, 1988.

Young, Hugo, One of Us. London: Macmillan, 1989.

Index

Art Credits

British Motor Industry Heritage Trust: 130 (top, middle, bottom)

John Dugdale: 139, 140 (top, middle, bottom), 141 (left, right)

EMAP Archives: 103, 105 (left)

Edward Eves, Ludvigsen Library: 388 (top, bottom)

Henry Ford Museum: 261, 262, 263, 265 (top, bottom), 267, 268

Ford Werke AG: 279

Hulton Getty Picture Collection Limited: 318, 319, 320

Ludvigsen Library: 2, 3, 4, 5, 10, 13, 14, 17, 22, 23, 24, 42, 56, 61, 68, 83, 115, 125 (top), 126, 128 (top, bottom), 129 (bottom), 132 (top, bottom), 133, 134, 135, 146, 149, 158, 159, 161 (top, bottom), 165 (top, bottom), 166, 167, 168, 187, 190, 191, 192, 195, 196, 201, 208 (top, bottom), 212, 218, 222 (top, bottom), 223 (top, bottom), 225, 227 (top, bottom), 228, 229, 251, 254 (top, bottom), 256, 257, 258 (top, bottom), 274, 300, 301, 306, 315, 316, 351, 353, 358, 364, 371, 378, 391 (top, bottom), 393 (top, middle, bottom), 395, 396, 397, 398

Ludvigsen Library / Volkswagen: 370 (top)

Karl Ludvigsen, Ludvigsen Library: 9, 11, 157, 186 (top, bottom)

Rodolfo Mailander, Ludvigsen Library: 348, 367 (top)

Dr. Alex Moulton: 310, 311 (top, bottom), 313

National Library of Australia: 245

Tim O'Callaghan / Ford Archive: 266

Michael Pointer c/o John Reynolds: 321, 322, 323, 324

Porsche Archive: 389 (top, middle, bottom)

Public Record Office, Kew, UK: 340

Renarchive Service: 202, 203, 204, 206 (top, bottom), 207

Renault Presse: 200

SAE: 180, 181, 182

Konrad F. Schreier: 35

Stiftung Auto Museum Volkswagen: 15, 25, 31, 32 (top, bottom), 33, 38, 39, 43, 44, 46, 47, 48 (top, bottom), 49, 51, 52, 57, 59, 62, 63, 64, 65, 66, 69, 73, 84 (top, bottom), 85, 86, 88 (top, bottom), 89, 90 (top, bottom), 92, 97, 99, 105 (right), 106, 107, 110, 111, 113, 116, 119 (top, bottom), 121, 233, 275, 332, 352 (top, bottom), 354, 355, 361, 363 (top, bottom), 365, 366, 367 (middle left, middle right, bottom), 370 (bottom), 375

Acknowledgments

Blame for this book must be lodged with my library. Oh, and also with the Stationery Office. I see that I have a bit of explaining to do.

It all began when the Stationery Office (Britain's equivalent to the U.S. Government Printing Office) in England's storm-tossed Norfolk decided to re-release some of the Golden Oldies among its publications of the past. The first was Cameron Earl's insightful study of the prewar Mercedes-Benz and Auto-Union racing cars, conducted and published under the auspices of the British Intelligence Objectives Sub-Committee (BIOS). The second was a wartime report on the Volkswagen, also organized by the BIOS, with contributions from Humber, Ford, Singer, and A.C. Cars.

Thanks to a generous reference from Chris Nixon, I was asked by the Stationery Office to write an introduction to both reports to set their findings in perspective and to give the modern reader an inkling of their significance. Earle's racing-car report required me to delve into the background of its author, which proved astonishingly interesting and rewarding. The Volkswagen report required a different approach.

The core of this particular VW report was a technical assessment of the Kübelwagen, the wartime version of the VW Beetle. Conducted by Humber and completed in 1943 for the benefit of Allied engineers, this portion of the report ended with general observations which included the oft-quoted phrases "little or no special advantage has been obtained in production cost," "we do not consider that the design represents any special brilliance," and "it is suggested that it is not to be regarded as an example of first class modern design to be copied by the British industry."

These findings have since been widely quoted as exemplifying the myopia of the British establishment when confronted with the new and unusual. They have also been linked with a general perception that the motor indus-

453

try in Britain, and in other countries as well, rejected the Volkswagen car and its huge factory as being worse than worthless and thus not meriting attention when opportunities to possess and/or operate the VW works in whole or in part arose as a result of the war reparations policies that took effect after World War II. That was my impression, as well, when I began researching my introduction to the BIOS report on the VW.

My library began to change that impression. Reading Maurice Olley's omnibus report for the BIOS on the German vehicle industry, I found that this insightful and experienced engineer well understood the great global potential of the Volkswagen. I pulled down Larry Hartnett's autobiography and found how interested he and Australia had been in the Beetle and its factory.

Maurice Platt's autobiography mentioned that GM's William Swallow had urged General Motors to adopt the Beetle as a product well suited to third-world markets. To his biographer Ernest Breech related facts that conflicted with most perceptions of the way Ford had dealt with the Volkswagen opportunity. Suddenly the issues surrounding the postwar disposition of the Volkswagen works and its novel product looked much more complex and interesting than has hitherto been perceived and portrayed.

After completing the introduction for the Stationery Office in August 1996 I continued researching and writing. While doing so it dawned on me that if I were to describe the circumstances that led to the postwar disposition of the Volkswagenwerk I would need to help the reader understand the attitudes toward unusual and advanced automobiles with rear engines, air cooling, and independent suspension that prevailed in the countries and companies concerned. Those attitudes significantly conditioned government and industry perceptions of the car, its characteristics, its factory, and its marketplace potential.

By the same token, the battle for the Beetle also had its subsequent impact on many companies and motor industries. This was part of the story too, I concluded. This led me to follow the aftermath of Beetlemania and its effects on engineers, motor-industry leaders, and their products. Similarly, I felt a need to sketch the origins of the Volkswagen for the reader new to the story. This also gave me an opportunity to integrate into the saga much new information on key events and to attempt to resolve glaring inconsistencies in the Beetle's prehistory as we have known it.

At the heart of the story, the factory itself had to be described — how it was created and funded, what happened to its machinery and equipment, and what state it was in after Germany's collapse. Similarly, its remarkable wartime career had to be portrayed, with the usual disclaimer that the extensive review provided of the methods and actions of the Nazis is in no respect to be taken as implying approbation.

These imperatives motivated me to conduct research widely and in depth. So interesting was the material that this was never onerous. In fact I have had to draw an arbitrary line under the research to complete a text which I hope achieves my aim of portraying in some depth the very active postwar interest in the VW car and factory and the many factors that contributed to their repatriation from Nazi-era icons to bastions of the economic boom of the New Germany. I was also motivated to complete the book before the launch by Volkswagen of its handsome new Beetle was only a distant memory.

Highlights of the research have been the opportunities it presented to interview some of the principal actors in the VW drama. Past interviews with Ferry Porsche and Max Hoffman contributed insights, as have my general researches in the history of the German motor industry in the course of writing and translating books about Porsche, Opel, Mercedes-Benz, and BMW.

Relatively late in my research I arranged, through the kind intervention of Paul Buckett of Volkswagen UK, to meet Ivan Hirst. Before I did so I wanted to be reasonably sure that I had a grasp of the subject. Often interviewed, most knowledgeably by my friend Griff Borgeson, Ivan Hirst nevertheless had much of new interest to tell me.

I couldn't have found my way through the thicket of the CCG structure without Ivan Hirst's help. He was meticulous, balanced, and positive in his comments on my draft text. And I will be forever grateful and am indeed honored that he agreed to write the Foreword. I felt that former Major Ivan Hirst TD was the ideal man to put this book in perspective. Many thanks, Ivan. Thanks also to Maureen Lister who photographed me and Ivan together.

Gordon Wilkins, who attended the KdF-Wagen press launch in 1939, had much of value to contribute, especially concerning the postwar Fedden car project in which he was a prime mover. About Roy Fedden and his work I also spoke with Alex Moulton, who disclosed details of the unbuilt Fedden that still sparkles with elegant engineering and styling, and with Peter Ware, who also limned the aftermath including Hillman's rear-engined car adventure.

Sir Terence Beckett helped me understand the postwar mindset at Ford in Britain that influenced its attitude toward the Volkswagen. David Burgess-Wise, Guy Griffiths, Graham Robson, Harry Webster, and Jonathan Wood described relevant events in Britain. Kurt Sözen provided books on Auto Union that helped greatly and clarified DKW motorcycle issues. In Argentina, Federico Kirbus followed up the reference to Mayorga Hermanos, and from France Paul Frère responded to my query about events in his native Belgium.

With Jan Norbye and Jean-François Blattner I explored issues concering Emile Mathis and with Professor David Lewis aspects of the Ford story. David graciously provided exceptionally valuable material from his studies of the Henry Fords. Eugene "Bob" Gregorie responded to questions about Ford's rear-engined experimental cars and designs. At D'Ieteren Frères in Belgium,

Philippe Casse shared documents discovered during the researching of his company's half-century relationship with VW.

Professor Dr. Peter Kirchberg kindly sent a copy of his monograph on the von Schell rationalization program. Olaf von Fersen sent useful information and Robert Braunschweig responded with verve and clarity to my questions. Tim O'Callaghan sent gems from his research into Ford's aviation ventures. Michael Lamm clarified some important historical points for me and John Reynolds shared his research findings on the Kendall car adventure.

A special joy was an interview in New York with my old friend John Dugdale, who still has his photo albums and pencil sketches showing the Kübelwagens that he described in the African desert in 1942 for *The Autocar*. John was insightful about other aspects of the period, including the key role and character of lesser-sung hero Michael McEvoy. Kenneth Hurst kindly wrote with insights into McEvoy's work and character.

From California, military historian and former ordnance aide, Konrad F. Schreier, Jr., responded to my published request for information with invaluable personal comments on the U.S. military reaction to the Kübelwagen and a reference to a book he had compiled. His contribution was key to my grasp of the American military perspective. In Washington Gordon White did his best to extract useful material from the archives there.

In Australia I had the help of many, thanks to the network that is the Society of Automotive Historians, the Internet, and e-mail. Austin Gregory and Brian Hanrahan responded. So did Les Twiss, who provided useful information as well as a rare copy of *Knowing Australian Volkswagens*. A. John Parker sent a copy of an essential work on VWs down under by Long and Matthews. Bill Tully of the National Library of Australia sent helpful material. R. J. Copley of the Federal Chamber of Automotive Industries provided leads.

Phillip Schudmak kindly initiated researches in Australian archives; in Melbourne at the National Archives Warwick Hansted dealt with my relayed questions. There Bill Wellsted conducted archival research, while in Canberra Peter Makeham of the Department of Transport identified some files and David Swift clarified matters. Finally the knowledgeable and persistent Colin Gardner found very useful material at the Australian War Memorial and also at the National Archives in Melbourne.

Works by Ian Turner and Steven Tolliday provided valuable clues to the relevant files in Britain's Public Record Office in Kew. There the first-class staff and remarkable organization made researching as pleasurable as possible, a shining example of the civil service at its finest.

My work on BIOS reports for the Stationery Office led me to the repository of these documents, the Annex of the Imperial War Museum at Duxford. I am most grateful to Richard Bright for his keen, courteous, and knowledgeable guidance through the annals he tends. Paul Parker of the

Ludvigsen Library assisted me there and visited the War Museum's London base to obtain needed information. Paul also tracked down the invaluable interviews of Mil Gov personnel conducted by *Safer Motoring*, now *VW Motoring*. Many thanks to its editor, Neil Birkitt.

Other British archives consulted included that of the Royal Aeronautical Society; thank you, Messrs. Nayler and Riddle. Fortuitously the archives of the Society of Motor Manufacturers and Traders yielded a needed document, provided by Sharon Penfold. At Cambridge's Churchill College Carolyn Lye assisted with a relevant report from its Robinson collection. The National Motor Museum at Beaulieu responded reliably to requests for references from my colleagues.

Researches in Detroit hinged on the well-ordered archives of the Henry Ford Museum and Greenfield Village Research Center. Studies there were facilitated by a determined and knowledgeable staff, among whom were Mia Temple, Cathleen Latendresse, Charles Hanson, and Linda Skolarus. At the library of the American Automobile Manufacturers Association, the genial Dan Kirchner granted me a fruitful run of the files and bound volumes.

At the Detroit Public Library, Mark Patrick and Paul Scupholm welcomed me to the National Automotive History Collection. Now housed with the gracious sumptuousness that it deserves, this fine library yielded numerous nuggets. Detroit's Roy Nagel sent copies of BIOS reports in response to my plea for help in *Special-Interest Autos*. Howard Moon suggested research leads, as did Karla Waterhouse at Volkswagen of America. Many needed photos were provided by the Stiftung AutoMuseum Volkswagen with the invaluable help of Dr. Bernd Wiersch, Eckberth von Witzleben, and Renate Sänger.

Other archives responded by post to inquiries. From Chrysler's wartime files, now held by the Society of Automotive Engineers at Warrendale, Pennsylvania, Will Willems sent a much needed report. Darleen Flaherty at the Ford Industrial Archives found papers of value. Help came from Dr. Dale Prentiss at the Historical Office of the U.S. Army Tank-automotive and Armaments Command in Detroit. Stanislav Peschel of the Daimler-Benz Museum responded to a key query, as did Klaus Parr, historical archivist at Porsche.

Last but not least, the Ludvigsen Library in London held a remarkable amount of material that was of value, thanks in part to its acquisition of some of the archives of the late historian and friend of the author, Cyril Posthumus. Although predominantly automotive, its aerospace and military history sections proved of value in researching the British shadow factories and the V-1 flying bomb whose production at Fallersleben attracted the Allied bombers like the proverbial bees to honey.

My researches into the origins of the Beetle and the events affecting it and the factory in wartime were greatly facilitated by the timely publication of the VW-funded history of this period by Prof. Dr. Hans Mommsen and Dr.

Manfred Grieger. Fortunately their interests were not the same as mine, or this book would have been redundant. Mommsen and Grieger receive the citations they richly deserve. The many other works consulted are referenced as appropriate. Their publishers have granted specific permission for their use.

At my office Jean Branch and Inga Pone kept the voluminous correspondence moving and tracked down interviewees. Paola Arrighi and Zena Ally helped with the final arrangements for publication. When translations were required we were assisted by 1st Applied Translations. My colleagues at our motor-industry management consultancy tolerated my obsession with the Battle for the Beetle, as did my wife Annette. Thanks so much, Annette, for your help and encouragement.

Quite a few of the books in my library bear the imprint of publisher Robert Bentley. I came to know Robert Bentley and his Boston bookstore well during my years at Phillips Exeter and MIT; they fed my eager appetite for information on the doings of the world motor industry. Thus I am particularly pleased that the American edition of this book bears the Robert Bentley name. Many thanks to Michael Bentley, John Kittredge and Janet Barnes for their commitment, support, and editorial advice.

My references to these many willing hands in no way absolves me of responsibility for errors of fact and/or interpretation, for which there are many opportunities in a work covering important aspects of the evolution of the motor industry in the developed world over three decades. I will welcome any corrections or additions to the facts as set out in these pages.

My researches on this engrossing topic have answered many questions for me and have set aside many of the folk tales that have inevitably surrounded the birth and adolescence of a car as iconic in the twentieth century as the Volkswagen. I have found it worth my while to make the effort to understand the events of this dramatic period and I hope that you, patient reader, have felt the same.

— Karl Ludvigsen
Islington, London
November 1999

About the Author

Author Ludvigsen's understanding of the automobile world has been facilitated by his training and experience in mechanical engineering (Massachusetts Institute of Technology) and industrial design (Pratt Institute). He subsequently served in the motor industry at senior levels with General Motors, Fiat and Ford, a background that assisted his interpretation of the governmental and economic issues that influenced *Battle for the Beetle*. Active over the years in motor sports, Ludvigsen holds a current competition license.

Karl Ludvigsen has served as technical editor of *Auto Age* and *Sports Cars Illustrated* magazines, as east coast editor of *Motor Trend* and as editor of *Car and Driver*. He is the author, co-author or editor of several dozen books and reports about cars and the motor industry and the winner of numerous awards for his work as a writer and author. Books by Ludvigsen have received both the Montagu Trophy of the Guild of Motoring Writers and (twice) the Nicholas-Joseph Cugnot Award of the Society of Automotive Historians.

Ludvigsen has been a member of the Society of Automotive Engineers (SAE) since 1960. He is currently a member of the SAE's Vehicle Configuration and Historical Committees. He is chairman of London's Ludvigsen Associates, a motor industry management consulting firm, and managing director of Euromotor Reports, publishers of specialised automotive studies and reports.

Selected Automotive Books Available from Bentley Publishers

Volkswagen Model Documentation: Beetle to 412, Including Transporter
by Joachim Kuch

Volkswagen Beetle: Portrait of a Legend
by Edwin Baaske

Small Wonder: The Amazing Story of the Volkswagen
by Walter Henry Nelson

Volkswagen Sport Tuning for Street and Competition
by Per Schroeder

Audi: A History of Progress
by Audi AG

The Speed Merchants: A Journey through the World of Motor Racing: 1969–1972
by Michael Keyser

BMW 6 Series Enthusiast's Companion™
by Jeremy Walton

"Unbeatable" BMW: Eighty Years of Engineering and Motorsport Success
by Jeremy Walton

Glory Days: When Horsepower and Passion Ruled Detroit
by Jim Wangers with Paul Zazarine

Going Faster: Mastering the Art of Race Driving
by Carl Lopez

Think to Win: The New Approach to Fast Driving
by Don Alexander

Sports Car and Competition Driving
by Paul Frere

The Technique of Motor Racing
by Piero Taruffi

The Racing Driver
by Denis Jenkinson

Maximum Boost: Designing, Testing and Installing Turbocharger Systems
by Corky Bell

BMW Enthusiast's Companion
by BMW Car Club of America

Jeep Owner's Bible™
by Moses Ludel

Volkswagen New Beetle Service Manual: 1998–1999

EuroVan Official Factory Repair Manual: 1992–1999

Volkswagen Inspection/Maintenance (I/M) Emission Test Handbook: 1980–1997

Passat Official Factory Repair Manual: 1995–1997

Jetta, Golf, GTI, Cabrio Service Manual: 1993–1999

GTI, Jetta, Golf Service Manual: 1985–1992

Passat Service Manual: 1990–1993

Vanagon Official Factory Repair Manual: 1980–1991

Rabbit, Scirocco, Jetta Service Manual: 1980–1984 (Gasoline)

Rabbit, Jetta Service Manual: 1977–1984 (Diesel)

Super Beetle, Beetle and Karmann Ghia Official Service Manual Type 1: 1970–1979

Beetle and Karmann Ghia Official Service Manual Type 1: 1966–1969

Station Wagon/Bus Official Service Manual Type 2: 1968–1979

Fastback and Squareback Official Service Manual Type 3: 1968–1973

Volkswagen Transporter Workshop Manual: 1963–1967, Type 2

Volkswagen 1200 Workshop Manual: 1961–1965, Type 11, 14 and 15

Volkswagen Workshop Manual: 1952–1957, Types 11, 14 and 15

Robert Bentley has published service manuals and automotive books since 1950. Please write Bentley Publishers, at 1734 Massachusetts Avenue, Cambridge, MA 02138, visit our web site at www.rb.com, or call 1-800-423-4595 for a free catalog.